BUILDING A MAIL ORDER BUSINESS

Other books by William A. Cohen

The Entrepreneur and Small Business Problem Solver
(John Wiley & Sons, Inc.)
The Entrepreneur and Small Business Financial Problem Solver
(John Wiley & Sons, Inc.)
Developing a Winning Marketing Plan (John Wiley & Sons, Inc.)
Making It Big as a Consultant (AMACOM)
The Practice of Marketing Management (Macmillan Publishing Co.)
The Art of the Leader (Prentice-Hall)
The Entrepreneur and Small Business Marketing Problem Solver
(John Wiley & Sons, Inc.)
Making It! (Prentice-Hall) (with E. Joseph Cossman)
The Paranoid Corporation (AMACON) (with Dr. Nurit Cohen)
The Marketing Plan (John Wiley & Sons, Inc.)
Model Business Plans for Service Businesses (John Wiley & Sons, Inc.)
Model Business Plans for Product Businesses (John Wiley & Sons, Inc.)

BUILDING A MAIL ORDER BUSINESS

A Complete Manual for Success

Fourth Edition

William A. Cohen, PhD

JOHN WILEY & SONS, INC.

New York • Chichester • Brisbane • Toronto • Singapore

Copyright © 1996, 1991, 1985, 1982 by Dr. William A. Cohen
Published by John Wiley & Sons, Inc.

Library of Congress Cataloging in Publication Data:
Cohen, William A., 1937–
    Building a mail order business : a complete manual for success /
William A. Cohen. — 4th ed.
        p.   cm.
    Includes bibliographical references.
    ISBN 0-471-10946-0 (cloth : alk. paper)
    1. Mail-order business—Handbooks, manuals, etc.   I. Title.
HF5466.C56   1996
    658.8′72—dc20   95-23344

Printed in the United States of America

10 9 8 7 6 5 4 3 2 1

To my wife, Nurit,
who has participated
in every venture
and every adventure

Contents

Joe Sugarman's Foreword to the First Edition

Mail order is one of the truly exciting frontiers of the free enterprise system.

It is still possible to start a business on a shoestring from your basement or on your kitchen table. And it's still possible to build that business into a profitable company giving you independence and freedom—the goals that embody the American Dream.

I know firsthand that it can be done. I started in the basement of my home and built a sizable company, and I know others who have done the same. Mail order companies are generally started not by big corporations but primarily by entrepreneurs who have an idea or a dream and pursue it with vigor and determination.

But to pursue that dream, you've got to have knowledge—a road map showing where to go and how to get there. You need the basics and an overall perception of the factors involved in conducting a mail order business.

Bill Cohen's book gives you these basics in a straightforward and understandable way. He continually raises questions—the same questions you'd naturally raise as you read his book. And then he answers them very clearly.

Dr. Cohen has also done his homework well. He has studied all the current and past books on mail order, clipped many advertisements, and gleaned from this material the truly important details to make his book an outstanding primer for our industry.

Building a Mail Order Business gives you the "nuts and bolts" necessary to carry you through almost every aspect of mail order marketing from the very rudimentary basics to the same techniques used by the pros.

When I started JS&A in the basement of my home, I had a little head start. I had my own advertising business, and I was able to write my own advertisements. Despite the head start, I made many mistakes—many totally avoidable had I known much of the information in this book.

Even with this book the road to success will not be easy, but given the determination, a concept, and persistence, you can indeed succeed in the mail order business. Bill Cohen has just made it a little easier.

JOE SUGARMAN

Northbrook, Illinois

Preface

Some time ago I was in your shoes. I had picked up a book on mail order because I'd heard there was a lot of money to be made in that business and I wondered whether I could make it. The writer was kind of skimpy on details, but he seemed certain enough that it was easy to succeed, so I jumped in and immediately lost several hundred dollars. Discouraged, but far from down and out, I went to the library and took out every single book I could find on mail order and direct marketing. Some were packed with technical information, but they were very difficult for me, as a beginner, to understand. Others were intended more for the giant company already engaged in other operations, companies on the *Fortune 500* list, and senior managers; they talked about concepts that were a complete mystery to me, with my limited knowledge of mail order operations. Meanwhile, I tried again and lost more money. In fact, I fell victim to several mail order scams through which I sent off small sums of money against promises that such and such an individual would help me get established in one sort of mail order deal or another. The bottom line was that I lost money, even though I tried to learn as much as I could from the books that were available.

Eventually, and with considerable difficulty, I learned how to make money in the mail order business. I learned how the business should be started and what tricks could be used to start it in the most profitable manner and in the easiest way possible. I learned what the big companies were doing that was really necessary and how to actually beat the big companies in mail order by using my advantages, and how to develop mail order techniques and apply them to other business operations, such as job finding. Direct mail techniques that I perfected not only worked in marketing oneself for a new job, but they worked so well that a book I wrote on job finding using these techniques became a best seller. I heard from people all over the country who had used these techniques successfully. I began to apply mail order techniques to obtaining research for the university with which I became associated. One mailing gave us a response in excess of 30 percent, and in one short period I sold more in funded research through direct mail techniques than we were able to obtain over the previous three years through other methods. And, of course, I sold products successfully by mail myself.

Over the years, I have continued to learn about, teach, and practice mail order and to use direct marketing techniques to promote a wide variety of products and services. As a result, this book has been changed and expanded significantly since its first, second, third, and now its fourth edition. Still, its purpose hasn't changed.

There are other books on mail order and many that I can recommend because of the specialized nature of the various subjects and topics they discuss. This book is intended to be both basic and comprehensive. Therefore, I recommend that you read this book first. It will take you right from the start through every single concept you need to be successful. Further, not only is every concept thoroughly explained with examples, but you will find each chapter easy to follow since it is made up of many short subtopics. The subtopics are building blocks you can use to absorb the material at your own pace and then refer back to later as necessary. To assist you in referring back, there is a comprehensive subject index, which lists the mail order topics covered in the text.

The basic approach has not changed over the years. But this edition has been completely updated with new material, including more than 100 new illustrations and a complete reorganization of all chapters around "the 4 Ms of mail order or direct marketing": merchandising, media, message, and measurement. This unique way of presenting information about mail order has been found to be the best way for the reader to master the material and start using it as quickly as possible. Almost every chapter has been revised. There are new chapters on pricing, making money with 900 offers and the single chapter on copywriting has been expanded with new information and split into two separate chapters.

If you already have a mail order business, you may want to skip some of the basic chapters or some chapters with which you are already familiar and go right on to advanced techniques in other areas. If you don't already have a mail order business, I would recommend that you proceed from the first chapter to the last in the order in which they appear. Chapter 1, "Making Your Fortune in the Mail Order Industry," tells a great deal about the business, how much money there really is in it, and how some entrepreneurs made millions of dollars in it. In Chapter 2, I tell you how to get your own mail order business started at once. If you've always wanted to start your own mail order business, but never seemed to get around to it . . . read this chapter for all the details. In Chapter 3, I talk about avoiding legal problems in mail order and maintaining your professional ethics.

Some of the most successful mail order people are also those with the highest professional ethics. No matter how honest or ethical you are, you must know how to avoid legal problems in your profession. This chapter will explain how to do this.

In Chapter 4, I discuss mail order management and record keeping. Many firms with successful products or services, even some making good money, ultimately fail. Why? Because of an inability to keep correct and accurate records and to manage their businesses properly. There is no need for this to happen if you read Chapter 4.

Chapter 5 on fulfillment is crucial. Yet, it is left out of many books on mail order. In Chapter 6, I tell you exactly how to find profitable products or services to sell by mail. Some of these ideas are unique and have so much potential that you will probably want to read this chapter even if you already have your own product or service. You will learn of more sources of new products and services than you ever dreamed possible. And you will learn how to increase your chances of picking a product that will prove successful. Pricing is a way of increasing revenue without increasing cost. Yet to many, it is a complete mystery. As a result, they try to do it by simply adding an amount to cost. They sometimes lose money and fail with a product or service when they could have been successful. Chapter 7 explains all the details, including psychological factors in pricing that can significantly multiply your success. Chapter 8 discusses the critical importance of the mail order offer—what's special about it and how to develop it. Even if you have a great product or service, you can still lose money.

Chapter 9 is important for beginners, especially. It tells you how to make money with classified ads, one of the best ways to start out with a limited investment. But, eventually you'll want to go into other types of advertising, and this is explained in Chapter 10, "Making Money with Display Ads," Chapter 11, "Making Money with Direct Mail Ads," Chapter 12, "Maximizing Your Direct Mail Success with Lists," Chapter 13, "Making Money with TV and Radio Ads," Chapter 14, "Making Money with Your Telephone," Chapter 15, "Making Money with Your Own Mail Order Catalog," and Chapter 16, "Making Money with 900 Numbers." You will need the information in these chapters if you really want to hit it big.

Following the various mail order advertising media, in Chapters 17 and 18, you'll learn all about copywriting, including how to write your own copy or get others to write it for you. In Chapter 19, you will learn all about art and graphics and how to get all types of illustrations done as inexpensively as possible. In Chapter 20, printing is thoroughly discussed. Chapter 21 is one of the most important chapters in the book, for it is on mail order testing, and testing is the heart of mail order. Proper testing will enable you to build a mail order business. If you test right, it can almost guarantee mail order success. In Chapter 22, essential cost and profit calculations are explained. This is done in a way you can understand easily.

Finally, Chapter 23 tells you how to develop a marketing plan that works. With a marketing plan, you will know where you are heading before you invest a lot of money. Once you start, you will be able to avoid the daily "firefighting" or unexpected emergencies that cause so many mail order entrepreneurs to fail. Moreover, if you need capital to help you start your business, your marketing plan will help you get it.

Following these chapters I have included seven appendixes. Appendix A contains the Direct Marketing Association's Guidelines for Ethical Business Practices. Appendix B is a potpourri of mail order ideas and techniques, some of them little known and all of them having great potential. Appendix C is a list of mail order associations and direct marketing clubs. Appendix D is a list of mail order advertising agencies. In Appendix E, you'll find some sources of mailing lists, most of which will send you a free catalog. Appendix F is a list of magazines and newsletters on mail order. Appendix G is a business guide to the Federal Commission's Mail Order Rule.

This fourth edition has incorporated major changes from the actual practice of mail order from letters from my students and readers around the world. There are numerous new figures and illustrations, new examples, and revised appendixes. I have done everything I could think of to make this edition the most complete and up-to-date guide possible.

Let's start right in with Chapter 1. I'm eager for you to start and succeed in your own mail order business, and I'm eager to hear about your success. But success begins with the first step, which you are about to take.

WILLIAM A. COHEN

Pasadena, California

Acknowledgments

I would like to thank some of the many mail order entrepreneurs, business-people, scholars, students, and experts who have assisted me in preparing this book: Ed Burnett, Melvin Powers, Mark Varnes, Steve Popkin, Free-man Gosden, Jr., Henry R. "Pete" Hoke, Jr., Leonard Carlson, E. Joseph Cossman, Joe Sugarman, Paul Muchnick, Ron Ball, and the late Joe Karbo, who spoke before the first graduate academic course in mail order at his home.

Much credit and thanks also goes to my previous editors: Steve Kippur who was my editor for the first two editions and persuaded me to break new ground in writing the book, and Karl Weber, my editor for the third edition. Finally, many thanks to Ruth Mills, the editor for this edition, Nancy Land, my production supervisor, and editorial assistant Abra Nicolle Nowitz, who did terrific work in helping to improve the first draft of this edition.

Making Your Fortune in the Mail Order Industry

WHO'S DOING WHAT IN MAIL ORDER TODAY

As I write these words, I look at my own daily mail and I'm amazed at the wide variety of products and services being sold in the incredible mail order industry.

First, here's an offer for $10 worth of cheeses free, by mail, to entice me to join a cheese lovers' monthly club. Here is an industrial offer. Someone has sent me literature on a fantastic new cutter that cuts and fabricates all thermal plastics. Next I have an offer that includes a free sample of a keychain that can be imprinted with my company's name. The offer states that if I pay the standard price for several hundred, I will receive an equal number free. And here is a catalog of limited plate editions. These plates are ceramic and go for as much as $75 or more per copy. Next I see an intriguing envelope, which when opened proves to be a booklet describing a system for winning at blackjack. Another advertises steaks from Omaha, Nebraska. I open a bulky envelope to find a sample set of civil war cards. Each card has a picture of a famous general, battle, or event on one side and a full description on the other side. The offer entices me to receive additional cards on a regular basis. Now here's an interesting one—this individual researches patents and, noting that I have a patent for an invention, he has sent me a postcard stating that my patent has been cited during the issuing of a new patent. The card goes on to state that I will undoubtedly want to know whether my patent dominates later patents or any state of the art advances shown by the later patents. This company will send me a list of patent numbers at a cost of $15 each. Next I have a large envelope from American Airlines, which advertises all sorts of products, ranging from a Yashika SLR camera outfit to a computer to a vacuum cleaner. Here's a brochure describing a special science magazine for children. And right under it is a mailing from the American Management Association asking me to join the President's Association. Another thick brown envelope contains multicolor photographs of jackets, trousers, suits, shoes, and all sorts of wearing apparel. And a final package contains an offer to join a tape or CD club, the immediate attraction being an offer of six tapes or CD's for only 1¢ plus postage and handling. Truly, the variety of goods and services sold through the mail today is incredible.

This amazing group of products offered in my daily mail is indicative of the great size of the mail order market. The exact dollar figure for mail order sales has long been controversial. Some years ago, a *New York Times* article gave a figure of $140 billion a year. Recent figures in *Direct Marketing* magazine put the figure at over $200 billion. The precise figure is almost irrelevant. Remember, that's *billions* of dollars. Why, if you had only 1 percent of that market, you would have two billion dollars in sales. This huge volume has attracted major companies as well as individual entrepreneurs. In fact, today, over half the *Fortune* 500 companies in the United States have mail order divisions and sell products and services by mail. These include such firms as American Airlines, whose mailing I received today, Time-Life Books, Hewlett-Packard, American Express, Mobil Oil, and thousands of other major companies.

But if you think that the mail order business is only for the giants, against whom you cannot compete, you are wrong. There are thousands of entrepreneurs who either started small and grew big and who are right now making a fortune by mail, or who are well on their way to becoming rich and are knocking down incomes of $30,000, $40,000, or $50,000 or a $100,000 a year or more. We'll talk about some of them—Joe Sugarman, Joe Karbo, Richard Thalheimer of Sharper Image, and others—later. Further, in the coming chapters in this book I will tell you how you can meet, and beat, the competition of the giants as a small work-out-of-your-home mail order businessman or businesswoman.

MAIL ORDER . . . WHAT ARE WE TALKING ABOUT?

Before we get down to business, however, we need to get a couple of terms straight. Because the mail order, direct response marketing, or direct marketing industry is growing at such a rapid pace, new terms are continually being coined and the meanings of older terms are being changed. Therefore, even before proceeding we need to take a few minutes to develop a common language. The Direct Marketing Association (DMA), which is the largest and oldest trade association having to do with mail order, likes the term *direct marketing* to describe the activities of its members.

According to the *Fact Book on Direct Response Marketing* published by the DMA, direct marketing is "the total of activities by which products and services are offered to market segments in one or more media for informational purposes or to solicit a direct response from a present or prospective customer or contributor by mail, telephone, or other access."

Martin Baier, Henry R. Hoke, Jr., and Robert Stone, three well-known experts in the field, developed some concepts and definitions worthy of note that have been repeated in monthly issues of *Direct Marketing* magazine. They defined *mail order* as "a Method of Selling, which relies on direct response advertising alone, to effect a measurable response and/or transaction by mail, telephone, or other interactive medium," and *direct response advertising* as "that which effects a measurable response and/or transaction at any location."

In this book, the terms *mail order, direct response marketing,* and *direct marketing* will be used interchangeably. Important here is that while the term is *mail order,* common usage and technology have combined to make the term applicable not only to mail, but also to telephone, radio, television, and so on, and not only to order, but also to fulfillment of the product ordered.

One final word about a term that is sometimes used to mean *mail order* but does not. The term *direct mail* describes one medium of *direct-response advertising,* as *newspaper, magazine, radio,* or *television* each describes other media.

WHY THE MAIL ORDER BUSINESS IS GROWING AND WILL CONTINUE TO GROW

Even though the mail order business is measured in the billions of dollars a year in gross sales, it is still growing every year. It has even grown during recessions. By one estimate it grew 48 percent over a two-year period. This phenomenal growth is due to several factors. First is the growth in education in the United States. Mail order requires that your customer be able to read and understand the message you are trying to communicate to him or her. Unless the customer understands your message, he or she cannot buy. As the educational level of the United States has risen, mail order sales have also increased.

Along with the rise in education levels, there has been an increase in incomes. This means that individuals have more disposable income items that are essentially luxuries, not basic requirements of life. Most of those items I saw advertised in my own mail this morning—even food items, such as those special cheeses for cheese lovers or steaks—were marginal luxuries that require a higher-income buyer. As the income levels have increased in the United States, and in the world, so has your potential market for the purchase of mail order items.

Personal selling cost is another factor that has favored the growth of mail order. Personal selling costs have skyrocketed. The costs of many consumer items that could previously have been sold door to door and industrial products that could be sold through personal sales calls have gone up because of higher gasoline prices and higher incomes of salespeople, among other reasons. Each face-to-face call made by a salesperson costs much more today than it did 10 years ago, even in noninflation dollars. As a result, mail order has become extremely attractive, compared to personal selling, as a means of selling all sorts of products, both consumer and industrial. At the same time, various forms of mail order techniques have been used to assist personal selling, so that each expensive call can be made more easily and with a higher success rate.

Social changes have acted to influence mail order buying. Today, women hold down better than 40 percent of the jobs in the United States, a tremendous change from just a few years ago. And because women are working today, they no longer have the opportunities they once had for daily shopping. This change has extended by many times the products that people are willing to buy through the mail.

Technological and communications advances have also served to increase mail order growth. Such innovations and inventions as the computer, 800 toll-free telephone service, and 900 lines have made tremendous changes in the mail order industry. Through the use of the computer, costs of mail order selling can be greatly reduced. And as the computer has developed further, even small companies can use it profitably to lower their costs and thus increase their profits. In a similar fashion, 800 toll-free telephone lines have made it much easier for mail order customers to order, while 900 numbers amount to a whole new means of fulfillment. Ordering by mail is not a completely trouble-free task. A potential customer seeing your advertisement or receiving your direct mail piece must not only make the decision to buy, but must then sit down, write a letter, find a stamp, find an envelope, put together the entire package with the check, and mail it. Then he or she must wait a certain amount of time before receiving what was ordered. Through the use of an 800 line, a buyer can make a toll-free call. With a credit card (which, as we will see, has also increased mail order sales), he or she not only places the order much more easily but also shortens the period of waiting before receiving the order. Other technological advances that both lower costs for the mail order operator and make it easier for the potential mail order buyer to place the order are continually being made. Ordering or delivery of information by fax, is one of the newer innovations.

Consumer credit has also had a remarkable effect on mail order. Consumer credit, as exemplified by credit cards, not only makes it possible to order more easily by mail, but also provides a means for time payment on higher-priced items. Stop and think about this for a moment. Whereas once the mail order businessperson had to carry credit and perhaps act as a collection agency for the sale of a higher-priced item to a mail order customer, no the consumer has a credit system readily and immediately available.

Concern about the environment has helped the growth in mail order sales. Since energy, in the form of gas for the car, must be expended by a consumer almost every time he or she shops, it is much easier and less expensive simply to order many items through the mail.

Finally, as retailers and others note the effectiveness and efficiency of mail order technology, more and more have adopted this means of marketing. Today, you can buy almost anything through the mail. Choices and alternatives of products and services increase every year and play their part in boosting mail order sales. So my prediction is that mail order will continue to grow . . . and grow big.

WHY THE MAIL ORDER BUSINESS IS A
PERFECT PLACE TO MAKE YOUR FORTUNE

The mail order business is a perfect place to make your fortune as an entrepreneur. This is true not only if you have not yet entered business, but even if you have an ongoing, established business that has little to do with mail order. Here's why:

1. *Low Barrier to Entry.* If you want to enter the mail order business or employ mail order techniques to assist a business you already have in operation, there is little to prevent your entry. As a matter of fact, the U.S. Postal Service, which benefits from mail order sales, will assist you in every way possible. Unless you deal with certain restricted types of goods, there are no licenses to obtain other than a local business license, which we'll discuss fully in Chapter 2. There are no tests you must take to qualify. There are no educational requirements you must have completed to become a mail order practitioner. As a result, most people can enter the mail order business more easily and with less difficulty than they could enter any other business.

2. *Low Capital Requirement.* Although you cannot get into mail order without at least some money, this initial amount is really quite low compared to other businesses you might choose to enter. For example, it will require several hundred thousand dollars or more for you

to enter the restaurant business with a single restaurant, and yet you won't even know whether you have been successful for a year or longer. A machine shop will typically require a large capital investment, for various types of tools and machinery. A retail store requires not only an outlay for the store itself but also for inventory and sales personnel. However, a mail order business can be started with little capital equipment, no special offices or facilities, and no employees except yourself to begin with. In fact, as we will point out in a later chapter, you can start part-time and maintain a very low investment and overhead until the cash flow is right and you are successful enough for the business to become full-time. Or, if you wish, you may keep it a part-time business for as long as you desire and bring in thousands of extra dollars a year as a welcome addition to compensation coming from whatever else it is you are doing. Tyler Hicks, famous for his books on entrepreneurship, made a fortune through his mail order businesses while he held down an executive position in the publishing industry.

3. *Success or Failure. You'll Find Out Fast.* With most other businesses, unless you have misplanned for your capital requirements and go bankrupt very early on, you may not know for years if your business is really a viable moneymaker with great profit potential or if you will be forever "barely making it." A man in New York didn't realize for three years that the specialty restaurant he had started was wrong for the area in which he was located. An engineer worked for seven years on a robot lawnmower and finally succeeded in getting it into production, only to discover that a market did not exist for that item at that time. With a mail order business, regardless of the product or service sold, you can find out very quickly whether you have a winner or a loser. I will show you exactly how to do this in Chapter 21. Further, even if you have a number of losers, you can control your expenses so that once you hit a big winner, you will more than make up for your losses many times over. No other business will permit you to experiment in this way while you test and modify your products and concepts until eventually you achieve success.

For the established business, mail order also offers a number of distinct advantages.

First, you can target your specific market. For example, let's say you have developed a calculating device that is useful for everyone, but is especially useful for engineers. Through mail order techniques, you can either advertise in places such as engineering magazines, where those engineers are most likely to read your advertisement, or you can obtain specialized mailing lists and send direct mail pieces to reach your market directly. This is one of the reasons that Hewlett-Packard was so much more successful than its competition in introducing electronic hand held calculators. And did you know it was none other than mail order entrepreneur Joe Sugarman who beat even Sears, Roebuck to the market for the calculator through a direct mail campaign?

You can get to your market fast. If you have a retail business selling a certain item—let's say a special wrist radio—and if you advertise, your customers must come to you to purchase your item through your retail outlet. And without special advertising or promotion, you can sell the wrist radio only as word is passed from one person to another that you have it for sale. But in mail order, if you are successful with a certain item during a test, you can expand your promotion rapidly and nationally to get to the entire market. For example, the Hewlett-Packard people tested the sales potential of their electronic computers through the mail in a relatively small mailing to engineers, and when they found it successful, they expanded immediately and rapidly, getting to their entire market fast through a mailing to as many engineers as they could find. You can do the same thing.

You can time your promotion through the mail to coincide with other promotional activities. Let's say you are selling a special item at a trade show. A direct mail campaign promoting this item before the show can coincide with your trade show promotion, and both can work together to increase your sales dramatically.

You can test at a relatively low cost. Again, what does it cost to test other types of business or other types of product through other media? Sometimes, quite a lot. If you sell plants through a retail store, it will be a long time before you know whether the location and product are correct for the market you are trying to reach. Further, this "test" will cost not only the price of the inventory, but the price and rent of the store and other equipment. If you sell plants through mail order, through drop-ship arrangements, as we will discuss in Chapter 5, you may have no inventory cost whatsoever. The cost of your test will be limited to the cost of your mailing. If the mailing is successful, you have a winner and can expand immediately. If your product is a loser, you can drop it at once and your only cost is the cost of your test.

You can exploit winners fast, which goes along with getting to your market quickly. Let's say that your plant shop or your restaurant, as described above, is successful. How long will it take, then, to acquire another location or build another shop and open it up, even if you know that you have a winner with this type of operation? Not overnight, that's certain. But through the mail, you can exploit your winners the very next day after learning of your success.

For all the above reasons, the mail order business is a perfect place for you to make your fortune. One word of caution: You are not guaranteed success in mail order by these facts, nor is success in mail order easy in the sense that you do no work or need not apply yourself to achieve it. However, in no other business is it as easy to be successful, nor do you have better control over your future, the amount of success, and how quickly you can obtain it. Paul Muchnick, writing in a U.S. government Small Business Administration booklet on mail order, says this: "The success stories are countless of people who have not only made a good living selling products and services by mail, but have amassed fortunes—starting on a kitchen table, in a garage, or spare room."

WHY YOUR CUSTOMER WILL BUY BY MAIL

One basic principle in mail order selling is to always look at your market first and what it wants. Next, find a product or service to offer to the market. Most people try it the other way around and fail! So, in considering our market first, let's look and see why people buy by mail. Years ago, a man by the name of Joseph H. Rhoads categorized mail order buyers like this:

1. *Those Interested in Novelties.* These are buyers who want things that are different from their neighbors'. According to Rhoads, these people actually look over magazines for items of this sort that are different and that appeal to them. When they find products that are novel and relatively inexpensive, and that are not owned—or are thought not to be owned—by their neighbors, they purchase them.

2. *Those Pursuing a Hobby or Some Particular Interest.* These are people with special interests, such as gardening, stamp or coin collecting, financial investments, making money, and many other different hobbies or activities.

3. *Those Who Buy by Mail as a Matter of Convenience.* These are buyers or potential buyers who find it easier to buy by mail, especially if they live in a location somewhat removed from adequate shopping facilities. Very frequently, these people will send away for merchandise to benefit from a larger and wider selection of items than they can find at their local stores.

4. *Those Who Buy by Mail Purely for What They Consider to Be a Price Advantage.* These are individuals who are buyers because they look over mail order catalogs or see other advertisements and direct mail pieces, compare them with retail store selections, and order through the mail because they are certain that the cost in dealing by mail is a bargain, compared to the prices in their local stores.

Len Carlson, the founder of Sunset House and many other successful mail order ventures, developed a list of 29 reasons why people buy and a list of

13 reasons why people prefer to order by mail or by telephone. Here are Len's lists:

Why people buy

1. To be more comfortable.
2. To make work easier.
3. To safeguard self and family.
4. To protect family's future.
5. To be well liked and loved.
6. To add to life's pleasures.
7. To be in fashion.
8. To fulfill fantasies.
9. To own attractive things.
10. To collect valuable possessions.
11. To protect possessions.
12. To satisfy ego.
13. To accumulate money.
14. To preserve money already accumulated.
15. To save time.
16. To protect reputation.
17. To appease appetite.
18. To enjoy exotic tastes.
19. To live in a clean atmosphere.
20. To be strong and healthy.
21. To get rid of aches and pains.
22. To find new and uncommon things.
23. To be more beautiful.
24. To attract opposite sex.
25. To satisfy sexual desires.
26. To bring back "good old days."
27. To be "lucky."
28. To live longer.
29. To save money.

Why people prefer to order by mail/telephone

1. It's convenient.
2. It offers unusual items they can't find elsewhere.
3. Variety is bigger, with more complete selections.

4. Price is lower.
5. It saves time.
6. Product description is more complete.
7. It avoids contact with inept salespersons.
8. It saves gas, parking, security problems.
9. Liberal guarantee provides comfort.
10. "Surprise" element is fun.
11. It avoids embarrassment.
12. Additional credit is sometimes available.
13. Activity counteracts mailbox loneliness.

Researcher-writer Melodie Cingolani, writing in an issue of Bank of America's *Small Business Reporter* entitled *Mail Order Enterprises*, says that mail order buying retains appeal because many customers find it easy and pleasant, and because it has the advantage of convenience, selection, anonymity, economy, and fun.

Some years ago, *Better Homes and Gardens* did a special study on mail order buyers from its publication. One of the questions asked was, "Why do you purchase items by mail?" Respondents were invited to check one of five different reasons, and 63.3 percent indicated that they purchased items by mail because they couldn't find them elsewhere. Next highest was the 49.3 percent who said they purchased items by mail because of convenience. Price was third, with 25.2 percent. And finally, "Simply enjoy buying by mail" pulled in 12.1 percent. Only 4 percent checked "Other," and 0.5 percent did not respond to this question.

Similar results were reported by Jim Kobs, who is president of the direct marketing agency of Kobs & Brady and the author of the book *Profitable Direct Marketing*. Kobs analyzed the same question as in the earlier *Better Homes and Gardens* survey. He compared the responses with those of a second, more recent study done by a leading direct marketing catalog house, which limited its study to its own customer lists. The results were similar, but not identical: 49 percent said they shopped for convenience; 37 percent indicated they could not find the items elsewhere; 16 percent said they shopped for variety, 14 percent for price, 12 percent for service, 11 percent because of a desire for gifts or items for personal use, and 10 percent for quality. Ten percent in this survey indicated a variety of "other" reasons, including free gifts and utility items. If you have counted and are wondering why this total exceeds 100 percent, it is because this survey permitted multiple answers.

What do these studies suggest about products in mail order selling? Well, the fact that so many people buy by mail because they feel they cannot find these items elsewhere should be ample evidence that you should seek a product that is not easily found elsewhere by mail. Conversely, it is much more difficult to sell a staple item, such as bread, by mail unless there is something unique about it. Perhaps if it is homemade, if you can keep it fresh, and if it can be obtained nowhere else, it can be sold by mail. Or perhaps a bread that is self-warming as you open the package could be sold by mail. But the ordinary bread that can be found at your store, at almost every store, cannot be sold profitably by mail—that is, unless your price is so low as to attract attention, or you combine the bread with some other product to make it unique. The same is true for similar items.

Price is also clearly very important to the mail order buyer. However, it is a little-known fact that mail order selling is actually a very expensive way to sell. Therefore, one of your challenges as a mail order dealer is to find a way in which you can supply the item less expensively to your customer, or a way of making your customer at least perceive the item to be less expensive than what he or she can buy in a store.

All the reasons that mail order buyers do purchase by mail should be carefully considered by anyone who wants to enter the mail order business. They should be used as a guide to selecting a product and service and, further, to entering this market in a way that will maximize your chances for success. We'll explain exactly how to do this in some detail in the chapters to come.

SMALL-BUSINESS PERSONS WHO BECAME MILLIONAIRES THROUGH MAIL ORDER

As I noted earlier, mail order is not necessarily an easy way to success, nor does the mere fact that you enter mail order guarantee your success. It certainly does not guarantee that you will become a millionaire. Nevertheless, it is a fact that a number of small-business people who have entered the mail order business have gone on to become millionaires from very humble beginnings. I would like to mention a few of these individuals here, just to show you how it can be done and to show you that such success is possible for you, too. While certainly no one can say that you will be as successful as these individuals, certainly no one can say that you can't do better than they have, either.

Joe Cossman

Joe Cossman is the author of *How I Made One Million Dollars in Mail Order* and recently Joe and I wrote a book together called *Making It* (Prentice-Hall, 1995). Joe actually made more than $25 million selling mail order ant farms, toy soldiers, garden sprinklers, fly poison, potato spud guns, and even toy shrunken heads. In recent years he has been giving seminars around the country and helping others get started in their own businesses. Joe started after World War II, working after-hours from his $35-a-week job with a beat-up typewriter on his kitchen table. He tells an incredible story of his first success. After one year of writing letters all over the world, attempting to find customers for exports from the United States, he saw a large ad for soap. Writing his contacts abroad, he received a letter of credit for $180,000, which would be good when he delivered the soap at the ship and presented the bills of lading at the bank. At first he couldn't get leave from his job, and he had to go so far as to threaten to quit. Taking his life's savings of $300, he went to New York City and approached the soap company, only to discover that the soap company was nonexistent, and that the soap that was advertised did not exist. He went to the library and, using the *Thomas Register of Manufacturers*, called soap companies all over the country until he found one that made the soap that had been advertised. He then made arrangements to purchase the soap and persuaded a trucking company to drive from New York to Alabama to pick it up without payment up front. In the meantime, he had run up a telephone bill of $810. When he returned to New York with the soap, time was running out. The letter of credit was good for 30 days and if the bills of lading were not presented at the bank, the letter of credit would be worthless and he would be unable to collect the $180,000. In addition to his other debts, he also owed a great deal of money to the soap company for the 30,000 cases of soap. But even as the soap was being loaded onto the ship, Joe realized that, with less than an hour remaining until the letter of credit would expire, time had run out. Making a last desperate attempt to succeed, he barged into the office of the president of the steamship line and was able to convince the president to give him bills of lading and assume responsibility for the soap, even though it had not been loaded onto the ship. In fact, the president had his own limousine take Joe to the bank before it closed to present the bills of lading. Cossman made almost $30,000 on this first mail order project, and $30,000 was worth a great deal more just after World War II than it is today. This venture launched him on his multimillion-dollar mail order success trip, which is still going on.

Joe Cossman's story also illustrates some important principles about becoming successful in mail order. First, mail order is not necessarily a quick success. Although Joe made $30,000 with his first victory, it required a year's worldwide correspondence before the soap venture came together. Second, you need perseverance. The fact that Joe Cossman worked for a year says much for his perseverance by itself. The incredible difficulties that Cossman met and conquered to win the $30,000 says even more. Look at the steps Cossman had to follow to make this "easy money." First, he had to write numerous letters abroad attempting to locate a customer for products in general and, finally, for the soap product itself. Second, he had to get a leave of absence from his employer to make the trip to New York. Third, he had to meet the disappointment of finding the company that had advertised the soap to be nonexistent. Fourth, he had to spend the time and take the trouble and expense to locate a soap company that actually manufactured soap that could be exported. Fifth, he had to get the trucking firm to drive down and get the soap on credit. Sixth, he got back to New York and then realized only a desperate meeting with the president of the steamship line could save the deal, and then he made that last desperation attempt. Is it any wonder that Joe Cossman won and eventually became a multimillionaire? Joe says this: "I know of no business in the world that requires such a small investment to start, and yet holds promise of such tremendous financial gains as mail order."

Susan Powter

Susan Powter was a 260-pound depressed woman burdened with the psychological pain of being recently divorced and the economic pain of being a single parent. Desperately she tried diet after diet, and concluded that the entire diet and fitness industry worked against women by focusing on short term and temporary answers that not only set them up for failure, but fleeced them of their money and in some cases actually damaged their health.

After investigating the whole business of eating, dieting, and fitness on her own, she decided that what the so-called experts advocated was insane. She developed her own diet and exercise theories. With less effort than she had expended previously, she dropped 133 pounds . . . permanently.

Motivated to spread the word to other overweight women, she designed her own infomercial. Going against all advice and conventional wisdom, she wore her hair so short and cropped, that being blond, she appeared almost bald. Her call was "Stop the Insanity." Her message and passion were so clear, and her rapport with her target audience so unmistakable, that although she was a total unknown, she was able to raise the necessary money to launch her infomercial. Using direct response and mail order, this infomercial brought in millions of dollars.

Today, Susan Powter is a multimillionaire, has written two best sellers, produces tapes and seminars, and appears regularly on ABC-TV's "Home" show.

Tony Robbins

Tony Robbins was a bright young man who was determined to be successful. Impressed as a teenager by attending a seminar conduced by motivational speaker Jim Rohm, he started and participated in a number of business ventures. He had considerable success even before reaching the age of 21. This gave him the self-confidence to continue.

He read every book on success and the psychology of success he could lay his hands on. His reading of hundreds of these books gave him an outstanding education even though he didn't go to college. One day he happened on the new psychology of the mind called neuro-linguistic programming or NLP. He attended seminars conducted by John Grinder, one of the founders of NLP, and worked with him. Sensing his potential, Grinder suggested that Robbins stretch himself by doing something considered impossible. He suggested that Robbins learn firewalking. Robbins located a firewalking instructor and easily mastered the skill. Robbins realized that the potential for firewalking was not so much the act itself, as a vehicle for turning fear into power. He designed a seminar that utilized the firewalk in this fashion and promoted it around the country using direct mail and other direct marketing techniques. As his considerable gift for teaching and speaking increased, the number of attendees at his seminars grew, first to several hundred, then to a thousand or more.

As he became better known, a number of well-known people gave him testimonials, and Tony wrote his best selling book, *Unlimited Power*. In 1988, he created a set of audio tapes that he began to market through an infomercial with professional football great and businessman, Fran Tarkington. This informercial continues to sell in record numbers, making it one of the best selling infomercials of all time.

Meanwhile, Tony Robbins has expanded his seminars in number, length, and subject matter. His activities range from publication of a mail order catalogue combined with a newsletter to a tape periodical and numerous other products all promoted through direct marketing methods. He has also written a second best selling book.

Benjamin Suarez

Benjamin Suarez (also spelled Swarez) is the author of *Seven Steps to Freedom* and the genius behind numerous successful mail order campaigns, such as "How to Get What the U.S. Government Owes You," "The Secret of Having Good Luck," "Why People in Vermont Are Healthier, Less Overweight, Stay Younger Longer, Live Longer Than People of Any Other State in the Union," "The Machine That Peels Off Pounds While You Sit Back and Enjoy It," "Fountain of Youth Discovered by Little Known Civilization," "Famed Physicist Proves That Sitting in a Pyramid Causes Unexplainable Good Things to Happen," "The International Astrological Association," "Ohio Man Discovers the Secret of How to Escape the American Rat Race," and many others.

Benjamin Suarez started as a computer programmer and systems analyst with a major company. Assigned to a project for working with nuclear reactors and power generation equipment, he ran into trouble with his boss over his work innovations, so he decided that he would begin a part-time business and eventually become fully independent. His first project was a food delivery system. It failed. Then, he started a computerized poker system. It also failed. Next, he started two different projects—special financial tables published in book form, and a calculator. He attempted to market these in several ways, including mail order. After he invested in huge amounts of inventory and attempted to sell these products in the wrong way to the wrong list, these projects also failed. Finally, he started an astrology club, which he attempted to promote by direct mail. He got a 3 percent response. Although he only broke even, he still felt that he could make money. This he did by implementing an idea that he pioneered. Every flier he sent out was personalized by having the potential customer's name handwritten after the words "Memo to," and there was a real signature after the word "From." This innovation doubled Suarez's response to 6 percent, and the American Astrological Association was born. Comfortable with his cash flow, Suarez resigned his job with the major corporation and went into the mail order business full-time. Still, even with this success, he went through a lawsuit with partners, a suit to get his company name back, and many other tribulations until he really made it big—and paid himself a bonus of $80,000 in one month. Since that time Benjamin Suarez has gone on to earn hundreds of thousands of dollars a year and become a great mail order success.

Again, Ben Suarez's experiences underline the need for persistence and the fact that you must go to the market first and find out what your market wants, rather than try to sell something you want to sell.

Richard Thalheimer

Richard Thalheimer is the founder and president of the Sharper Image, a prestigious San Francisco mail order catalog house that has expanded into retail stores in major cities around the world. Graduating from college and yearning for the excitement of the Far West, he arrived in San Francisco. Unfortunately, although San Francisco was everything he had hoped it would be, try as he might he couldn't find a job. Desperate, Richard finally found work selling office supplies door to door. Somewhere he heard about the exciting possibilities of selling through the mail. He started a small company, the Ribbon House, to sell office supplies in this manner. Not only was his business successful, but in the hopes of learning a high-paying profession, he put himself through law school at night with his profits. The well-known Japanese firm, Seiko introduced the wristwatch chronograph. They priced it high, selling for several hundred dollars. Richard found another watch, which he could buy at a much lower cost and price it at ⅓ of Seiko's price. Using his mail order know-how, he placed a small ad and made $600 profit in one month.

Richard Thalheimer is a jogger, and he immediately thought he saw a potential market in joggers, especially since his small ad had been so successful. With some trepidation because of the higher risk, he placed a full-page ad in *Runner's World*. This ad resulted in 3,000 orders, each of which represented $30 in profits . . . an incredible $90,000 in profits from a single ad! Not bad for a mail order entrepreneur who was not yet 30 years old!

Unfortunately, there was just one small problem: Because of the demand, his source had run out of the product, so Thalheimer had lots of orders and nothing to fulfill them with. He immediately sat down and wrote the best letter he could to his customers, giving them a chance to cancel the deal, but stressing the advantages of waiting for the product. In this way, he stalled for six months. Finally, his father found an alternative source, and, three months later, the 3,000 watches arrived in Thalheimer's office. But when he opened the shipping container, he found that these watches were of lower quality. In almost every case, the watch face had separated from the rest of the watch.

As quickly as he could, he called around town and found a source of glue that was the correct type for reattaching the watch faces, and he laboriously reattached every one of the 3,000 orders. This project launched the Sharper Image, and the very first year, in addition to locating a source for high-quality chronograph watches, his new company hit $3 million in sales. Less than two years later he published his first catalog, and he soon reached $100 million in sales . . . and he never did get the opportunity to practice law. Today his annual sales are much higher. His catalog looks like a magazine. The cover of a recent "issue" is shown in Figure 1.1. According to the cover, the price is $2.00. That adds perceived value to it even though it may be given away.

Thalheimer's story illustrates the virtue of persistence and the willingness to take risks after a thorough analysis of the situation. Like other successful mail order entrepreneurs, Richard Thalheimer knows that his success comes from the value he provides to his customers, and as he told a recent gathering of mail order pros, "the success of the Sharper Image is due to our outstanding customer relations."

Len Carlson

Len Carlson founded Sunset House and was its president for 20 years. But he didn't start as president of a multimillion-dollar mail order company. Len worked in advertising and promotion at Topps Bubble Gum in New York City. One of the products he developed as a premium was a small rubber stamp that was made up with a child's name. This premium was advertised in comic books to help promote the bubble gum. Before the campaign was well under way, Len left the bubble gum business to live and work in California. A year after he had left Topps, he became curious about how the rubber stamp item had worked out. Much to his amazement, he discovered that the promotion had failed and that the company still had 75,000 rubber stamps in its warehouse.

Figure 1.1   Richard Thalheimer's Sharper Image Catalog.

But somehow, the idea of the personalized rubber stamp as a unique mail order item just wouldn't leave his mind. He approached a local manufacturer and was told, "Young man, we are the largest manufacturer of rubber stamps in the world, and my father was in the business before me—believe me, you can't sell rubber stamps through the mail. We know . . . we've tried." But Carlson couldn't be deterred. He worked out a deal with the manufacturer to supply rubber stamps that he would sell by mail. However, Len didn't call his device a rubber stamp; he promoted it as a personal name stamp and advertised it in *House and Garden* and *Sunset Magazine* for $1. When he checked his mailbox, he found it stuffed with envelopes containing dollar bills. Knowing he had to sell something to his customers after this first sale to really have a business, he studied every competitor's catalog he could get his hands on, and the very first year he was mailing his catalog to 50,000 names.

Carlson built Sunset House into one of America's largest specialty mail order companies. Since selling Sunset House in 1969, he has headed up several mail order operations, including Lenca, Inc., of Beverly Hills, a product development firm that has developed over 100 unusual items sold in the United States, Europe, and Asia; Perma Plaque Corporation, which offers a unique lamination process to preserve documents; New Silken/Sheer, which sells pantyhose by mail; and Better Life, Inc., a Japanese mail order joint venture that sells American health and beauty aids through mail order in Japan. Over the past 30 years, he has pioneered and merchandised almost 10,000 new and unique mail order products.

Lillian Vernon

Lillian Katz is a refugee from Nazi Germany who came to the United States in 1937 at the age of 10. In 1951, she set out to supplement her husband's $75 a week salary with a little extra money. With a baby on the way, she had to work at home. Mail order seemed the perfect way to earn a little money without leaving home. Lillian didn't have the cash to start, so she borrowed $2,000 from her father. She took part of that money and invested in an ad in *Seventeen* magazine. Her first products were monogrammed leather belts and purses. Much to her amazement, the ad generated $16,000 in sales. From this one ad (reproduced in Figure 1.2), she made more than her husband was making in a year! The name of her company, which came from the city and street where she lived at the time, was at first called Vernon Specialties Company. Then she added her own first name, and the company became Lillian Vernon, Inc. Today she has more than 4,000 items in inventory, and her multimillion dollar business is multinational. Her sons, David and Fred, are officers in the company, though she is still chief executive officer and even writes much of the copy for her catalog.

Charles Atlas

Charles Atlas was a poor immigrant boy from Calabria, Italy, whose real name was Angelo Siciliano. Beaten and humiliated by bullies, he resolved to strengthen himself so that no one would ever pick on him again. He

Figure 1.2 The ad that launched Lillian Vernon, Inc. It appeared in *Seventeen* magazine in 1951 and brought in $16,000 in orders.

began a series of experiments with body building, none of which were entirely satisfactory to him. One day while visiting the Prospect Park Zoo in Brooklyn, he saw a lion stretching in its cage. He was amazed at the muscles on the lion, which seemed to tense and bulge as the lion moved. Atlas realized that the lion must be exercising, and that in some natural way, the lion had developed a strong, muscular body.

From this visit to the zoo, Charles Atlas developed a whole series of exercises that he called Dynamic-Tension. In short order, he doubled his weight and became an artist's model and a famous strongman. Then one day he learned that physical culturist Bernarr MacFadden was sponsoring a contest for the "World's Most Beautiful Man." Atlas won. The following year, MacFadden sponsored a new contest for "America's Most Perfectly Developed Man." Atlas won that one, too. Now, feeling that he had something to sell and a message to impart, Atlas put together his own physical culture course and began selling his course through mail order. At first the business did well, but then sales fell off and the business was in trouble. Atlas consulted with his advertising agency and was assigned a new account executive who had just graduated from New York University, Charles Roman. Roman though he knew what was wrong with the ads. The business was failing, and the advertising agency didn't seem to care much about the account. But Roman did, and Atlas was convinced that Roman knew what he was talking about. Atlas offered Roman half the business as a working partner. In short order these two men were selling thousands of Charles Atlas courses every year, and when Charles Atlas died in 1972 they were selling more than 20,000 courses every year. Both the poor immigrant who'd had sand kicked in his face and his partner were millionaires several times over, and Charles Atlas was perhaps the best-known strongman in the world. His ad appears in Figure 1.3. They had trained literally hundreds of thousands of students to be strong . . . all by mail.

Joe Karbo

Like many mail order operators who are successful today, Joe Karbo never finished college; his college education was interrupted by World War II and service in the armed forces. That's not to say you can't be successful with a college education. A number of mail order entrepreneurs have PhDs! Joe started an advertising agency, and he and his wife ran one of the first all-night, 24-hour television stations in the United States. Joe would come on at midnight and, with talk shows, movies, and so forth, go through the night, until the daytime regulars began their cycle. Through the sale of advertising time, Joe was slowly but surely acquiring a fortune, earning $5,000 a week. Suddenly, the station from which Joe rented the time was acquired by a large corporation, and Joe was cut out of the business. He went from a net income of $5,000 a week to being $50,000 in debt. His attorney advised bankruptcy, but instead Joe called together his creditors, telling them that there was presently no money to pay them off, but that he fully intended to do so. If they did not believe him, they could take him to court. Since he had no money, this would not have helped them. Even if they sent him to jail, there was still no money to be had. However, Karbo promised his creditors that he would pay them every penny he owed them, and he did have a business idea he felt could make him successful and allow him to pay his creditors everything. Karbo asked only that the payments be made on a regular schedule and that his creditors not jeopardize the business each time he accumulated a little cash. Joe was able to persuade his creditors, and in a short period he had written and published a booklet called *The Power of Money Management,* for which he wrote an ad headlined "Get Out of Debt in 90 Minutes without Borrowing." He soon sold over 250,000 copies. Joe had many other mail order products, so that when he embarked on his "Lazy Man's Way to Riches" campaign, he had an income of several hundred thousand a year, a Rolls Royce, several homes, and other adornments of the very rich. For some time he'd had the

Figure 1.3 The Charles Atlas ad.

concept of a success booklet based on his own success story, a combination of what Joe called "Dyna Psych" and mail order marketing methods. One night he got up, unable to sleep. Within two hours wrote the ad that was to take him from an income of several hundred thousand dollars a year to multimillions. He then published his famous ad for his book, *The Lazy Man's Way to Riches,* and received $50,000 in orders and sales before he sat down to write the book itself. This is called "dry testing." The FDA no longer permits you to advertise unless you can deliver the product within 30 days of your receipt of the order or the date you promise in your advertisement. However, the idea of testing before you make a major investment in product is still valid. *The Lazy Man's Way to Riches* has been translated into many languages and sold in many countries around the world. It sold over 10 million copies. It wasn't Joe's only product. He sold a book on handicapping, a newsletter, a skin care product, and a device for seeing through doors, among many other successful products.

Joe's successful advertisement for *The Lazy Man's Way to Riches* was the first of many similar ads by advertisers who have sought to imitate him. His ads contained a number of innovations that have since been adopted by others. Among these are the use of large space advertisements in the classified sections of newspapers; the request for postdated checks, which are not to be cashed by the seller for a month while the merchandise is examined; and the use of an accountant's statement verifying what is said in the ad to add to credibility. We'll be talking about these concepts and others later on.

Joe's success again points out the importance of testing before making major investments. Like others before him, Joe Karbo tested to make sure that his market existed before he acquired the product in large inventory.

Melvin Powers

Melvin Powers, author of *How to Get Rich in Mail Order,* is president of the Wilshire Book Company and the dean of mail book publishing. But years ago he was a disappointed author who had written a book on hypnotism that no publisher would publish. He placed a small ad in *Popular Science* for $119. After nine days, only 12 orders had come in and Melvin wrote off the $119 and another $250 he had spent for printing the book. The twelfth day after the ad had appeared, Melvin's wife called him at work. 201 letters requesting his book had arrived in the mail. At $5 each, this was more money than Melvin made at his job in a month. Melvin started his operation in the garage, grew out of it, and moved into a small office rented from an advertising agency on Sunset Strip. Today, Melvin has a building of 15,000 square feet with additional storage space and carries 400 different book titles. He sells more than 100,000 books every month. He has sold millions of books by mail, including such well-known big sellers as *Psycho-Cybernetics, Magic of Thinking Big,* and *Think and Grow Rich.* He has also expanded into many other operations.

Melvin Powers was fortunate in making money from the start, but not all of his projects have been successful. Here's what he says about success in the mail order business: "Don't expect success with every mail order campaign. It just doesn't happen, not even to the experts. If you have given your best effort to a mail order idea and it doesn't work, put your energy into the next project."

Brainerd Mellinger

Brainerd Mellinger came from a mail order family. But his father once said that Brainerd would never learn to write copy, so perhaps partly to prove his father wrong, he too started out on a shoestring—less than $100 and a rented garage. Brainerd's ideas ran to import-export. During World War II, he had seen products he knew to be in demand in the United States firsthand. A little luck, timing, and genius gave him a big boost toward success. Recalling products he had seen in Europe, he hit on one of the greatest of import mail order success products. Further, he discovered he could have this product drop-shipped directly to a customer from Germany for less than a dollar. The product? A miniature version of the famous Black Forest cuckoo clock. The product was so successful that Brainerd tied up almost the entire production of these cuckoo clocks in Germany. Success at importing other products and selling them through the mail soon led Brainerd to the concept of training others through a mail order course for import and mail order selling, while he continued to do all three activities profitably himself. Furthermore, his concept had a new twist: He would locate dealers worldwide who would wholesale thousands of different products to his students. Brainerd's business grew tremendously and expanded into seminars, newsletters, and worldwide trips for his mail order students. Today, his company continues under his son's direction . . . another generation of mail order entrepreneurs.

Joe Sugarman

Joe Sugarman is the author of *Success Forces.* His book is well titled, for Joe's success is unique and motivating.

Joe Sugarman is another college dropout who started a little mail order business in the basement of his home. In a copy of *Business Week,* he read that a manufacturer was reducing the size and cost of electronic calculators so that they would fit in your pocket and cost $240. At the time, Joe was in the advertising business. He suggested that a client sell the $240 calculators, but the idea was rejected. Joe then went out and raised $12,000 from friends to sell the calculators through direct mail—that is, letters

Weird Story

I'm not asking you to believe me but please just read this incredible story.

By Joseph Sugarman

The red symbols are also used in the program

It takes a lot to shake me up. After all, I get to see the latest in space-age products years ahead of anybody else. But what I've seen and experienced over the last year has been quite incredible.

I was sitting in an office in New York City talking to Stuart, a very successful friend and businessman. I told Stuart that I had to make a very critical decision in my business and needed some advice.

MADE TWO CALLS

Stuart looked at me and said, "Joe, let me take you to two people who can help you." He picked up the phone, made two calls and set up appointments for me that evening.

As we drove to the appointments, Stuart briefed me on what to expect. "You're going to meet two different psychics—two ladies who will not only tell you what decisions will work out best but what to expect in the future."

Now I had heard about psychics being used by the police to find criminals or evidence and how some sensational newspapers always printed predictions made by psychics, but I never took them seriously.

I'm not into the occult or fortune-telling or any of the weird metaphysical garbage. And quite frankly, I'm skeptical by nature—I have to be with everybody trying to pitch their "revolutionary" products. But I was curious and decided to give it a shot.

START OF TRIP

That one evening with Stuart was the start of a mental trip that has taken me one year to travel—a trip that has led me to a few discoveries I want to share. Here's what happened.

The first psychic sat me down and told me about myself, my future and even described the situation surrounding my business deals—facts that nobody but I could know. She gave me advice and gave me a direction she saw me following. The second psychic (who did not know the first one) gave me pretty much the same advice.

Driving back to my hotel, I told my friend that the ladies seemed quite accurate and how impressed I was that they both came up with the same answers. "That's why I took you to two Joe. This way you get a second opinion."

As the months went by, sure enough most of their predictions came true. Not everything came true but enough did to cause me to go again to some top psychics in the Chicago area and in Los Angeles. I read many books on the subject. How do the psychics tap into the future? Do you control your own destiny? Can the skills be learned? Can a businessman use these skills in running his business? I came up with some interesting conclusions.

First, I learned that the subconscious is the key element in explaining psychic phenomenon. We all have, through our subconscious minds, the ability to tap into our intuition and get answers to problems that often lead us to the goals we want to achieve. A psychic is simply tapping into our subconscious and telling us what our own intuition could tell us if we would let it.

BEST DIRECTION

If we could follow our intuition, we could sense the best direction to take to achieve our goals. Decisions would come easier and would be made with greater confidence. With the proper insights we could make our own luck while easily achieving material and spiritual goals.

I also learned something else that came up in practically everything I studied. To communicate best with your subconscious and eventually develop your intuition you had to learn to relax totally.

Once in a relaxed state, you could program your subconscious to achieve practically any goal you want. You can become more creative, improve your health both mentally and physically and you can share these skills with others.

SKEPTICAL OR BRAINWASHED

Now I realize that this all may sound like I've flipped out or gone off the deep end. Remember, I said I was skeptical. What happened?

I discovered a cassette tape program produced in Australia called Access Track that encompassed the most valid concepts I had learned in my research. It also included a series of relaxation tapes that were quite effective and it gave tangible evidence that the program worked even during its initial use. I contacted the developers of the program in Australia and obtained the exclusive rights to the concept in the United States and Canada.

There are six cassettes and a workbook in the Access Track program. The workbook lets you evaluate your own personality and your level of self actualization so you can monitor your improvements in future months. The six cassettes give you first an explanation of the concept and the role of the subconscious. Then there are seven relaxation programs that help you tune into your subconscious and then achieve any goal—from improving your appearance to acquiring wealth or property.

NOT TYPICAL

The concept is not like the typical motivational cassettes. There is nothing about a "positive mental attitude" or a "think and get rich" theme. Yet the concept is so powerful that I contend you can achieve specific goals beyond your wildest imagination while tuning into your intuition just as a psychic does.

But we're all human. And for some of us this program might not work. So we give you a generous 45-day evaluation period to test and apply its principles. My hunches are correct that those of you who give it a chance and who follow the program and use its principles will achieve enormous personal satisfaction. If not, return Access Track and get all your money back.

SHOULD BE IN LIBRARY

I have found my research into psychic phenomenon to be an exciting experience. Access Track combines the basic principles of goal-setting with the most valid aspects of psychic phenomenon to provide a new approach to self enrichment and self-actualization. It does work, it certainly is avant-garde and should be in the library of every open-minded, success-oriented individual.

Order the Access Track cassette program at no obligation, today.

Access Track (5075F 4 00) **$69**

Figure 1.4   A page from Joe Sugarman's catalog.

direct to prospective customers. He was looking for a 2 percent return and needed only 2 percent to break even. No one was more dismayed than Joe when he failed to break even and lost most of his investors' money. However, he did some quick analysis and realized that 2 of the 10 lists he had mailed to were actually far above the breakeven point. It was the other 8 lists that were unprofitable. Joe reduced the price to $180 and remailed. His tactic was very successful. He has since changed his advertising from direct mail to large space ads in publications such as *The Wall Street Journal, Popular Science, Scientific American* and in "infomercials" on television. His company, JS&A, is the trendsetter in electronic gadgetry and other state-of-the-art technology. It is said that the giant firms of Sears, Montgomery Ward, Radio Shack, and others stock their goods according to what Joe sells.

I said that Joe Sugarman's success was big as well as fast, and this is true—Joe's annual sales exceed $50 million and he reached this level in only seven years. The product descriptions in his catalogs are unsurpassed, and as you can see from Figure 1.4, he writes them himself. You may have seen Joe on television selling his unique sunglasses.

SUMMARY

We've discussed the incredible size of this multimillion-dollar industry and how you can make your fortune in it, just as others have before you. The individuals I have discussed are all real-life people, but they are not the only ones who have gone on to become millionaires through mail order, nor are they necessarily even the largest. I could also have told you about Sears, Montgomery Ward, the Franklin Mint, Fingerhut Corporation, and hundreds of other large corporations, all of which started as small entrepreneurial companies headed by one individual who knew how to make the mail order concept of marketing work.

No one can promise you success or guarantee it in the mail order business, but if you read this book carefully and apply its principles, your chances of reaching success in mail order, making a significant contribution to your present income, or, if you will, becoming fabulously wealthy are greatly increased. Now, let's not waste any more time. Turn to the next section and we'll see how to get your mail order business started.

Part I

Starting and Growing Your Business

2

How to Start Your Mail Order Business

You may feel that starting your own business is something very difficult and mysterious and requires an attorney and an accountant watching over your shoulder every step of the way. Actually, many, if not most, small mail order businesses will require a minimum of help from either of these specialists, at least at the start. In fact, you can even incorporate your mail order business legally, without an attorney. In this chapter, we're going to discuss, step by step, exactly how to start your own mail order business. I'm going to cover the legal forms of businesses—the proprietorship, the partnership, and the corporation—and give you the advantages and disadvantages of each. I will explain exactly how to get a business license, how to obtain fictitious name registration if it is necessary, how to go about handling state sales tax, how to borrow money and sources of capital, and how to maintain a low overhead. By the end of the chapter, you will know exactly what you must do to start your own business and how to go about it with a minimum of fuss, problems, and expense.

WHICH FORM OF BUSINESS ORGANIZATION?

Let's look at the three legal forms of businesses first: the sole proprietorship, the partnership, and the corporation.

Sole Proprietorship

Of the three legal forms of ownership, the sole proprietorship is the simplest and easiest to start, and it is also the form which the majority of new businesses take.

Let's look at the advantages of the sole proprietorship. First, it's the easiest and quickest to initiate. Assuming your mail order business doesn't require a special license because of the product you sell (drugs and certain other types of product are controlled and regulated by the federal government), all you must do is visit your city or county clerk and obtain a business license. It takes just a few minutes and often costs less than $100. You can start to do business immediately. If you plan on doing business under your own name, there is no additional cost involved in setting up the business. You save on legal fees with a proprietorship because no special contracts must be drawn up or developed, as is the case with a corporation or a properly established partnership.

Another advantage is that you run the entire business as you wish. There is no board of directors or any other boss (except your customers) to direct you, supervise the decisions you make, or criticize your errors. Win, lose, or draw, you are the whole show, and what you say goes. You personally receive all the benefits and pay the costs of running and managing your new business.

It is also fairly easy to close down your operation and terminate your sole proprietorship. You liquidate your assets, pay your debts, and turn out the light, and that finishes the entire operation. Or, of course, you can sell your business. The point is, winding down the business is as easy to do as getting into it: It normally requires little, if any, legal assistance.

In terms of taxes, the government treats you and your sole proprietorship as one, and this can be very beneficial because you may or may not make money over the first few months of your mail order operation. If you end up losing money over the first year, you may deduct these losses on your tax return against any other income you may have earned during the year. This is especially valuable if you are running your new business part-time while holding a full-time position with another company.

However, a sole proprietorship is not advantageous in all situations. There are some disadvantages that you should consider before deciding definitely on this form of business organization. One major disadvantage is that you have unlimited personal liability in your business. Since you and your business are legally one and the same, all the liabilities that may occur to your enterprise are your own. If for some reason you are sued as a result of some actions of your business and you lose this lawsuit, you are personally responsible for payment. If the money available in your business does not cover that which you are required to pay, your personal assets—those items that you personally own outside of the business—can be taken to pay this debt. In the same way, if your business fails and it fails owing money to various creditors, those monies still owed to these creditors can be collected from your personal assets.

Certain circumstances may reduce the importance of these drawbacks in your situation. If you must borrow money for your business, the bank will usually require that you personally guarantee your loan anyway. In this way and for this purpose, the bank has succeeded in "piercing the corporate shield." Even if you are incorporated, the bank may be able to reach your personal assets through this guarantee. And if the type of product you are selling is not likely to lead to a lawsuit, the protective function of a corporation may not be important. For example, if you are handling products such as greeting cards, it is not very likely that anyone will sue you for product failure. If, on the other hand, you are selling a product such as protective body armor, a product I have handled, it would probably behoove you not to use a sole proprietorship organization since, by the very nature of your product, product failure can lead to a lawsuit. In fact, with any sort of product like this, some legal help will probably be needed.

As a sole proprietorship, you are essentially limited to your own skills and capabilities. This means that you must wear many hats and do many jobs by yourself. This could be a problem. What happens should you become ill and unable to work? Under such circumstances, you have a problem. Finally, if you need to borrow money for your business, you will find it more difficult to attract investors as a sole proprietor than if you were either a partnership or a corporation. This is because the individual, individuals, or institution that lends you money must rely on you and you alone to make good this debt. A partnership, where there are at least two of you, doubles the chances of the investors' receiving their money back. The bottom line is that an investor, recognizing the risk, will be less likely to lend money to an individual operating as a sole proprietorship.

The Partnership

I am against partnerships for a variety of reasons. In fact, almost every attorney I have talked to about forming a partnership has advised against it. Yet, strange though it may seem, most attorneys, when they band together to form a law firm, are organized as—you guessed it—a partnership. The partnership is somewhat controversial. Let's look at the advantages and disadvantages and we'll see why.

With a partnership, it is also fairly easy to start your business. Legally, a business license from your county clerk or city clerk is required, just as in the sole proprietorship. This business license generally costs no more than the license for a sole proprietorship. The difficulty comes in an examination of who does what in the partnership—but we'll get to that after we finish looking at the advantages.

Another advantage of the partnership is that the person with whom you are teamed is an excellent source of additional capital.

Although this can also be a disadvantage, a third advantage is that you can count on one or more of your partners to help you share in the decision making, the responsibilities, and the work. This advantage fits with the old saying that two heads are better than one. Having additional partners also makes it easy to take an annual vacation.

In the sole proprietorship, you had only your own resources to rely on. However, partners, having different experiences, skills, and strengths, add their own talent to the business, and if the partners' backgrounds are complementary, the chance of success is increased. For example, if your own background is in creating copy, one partner is an accountant, and another partner is skilled in marketing, the sum total is a definite asset to your business.

As with the sole proprietorship, there is a minimum of paperwork associated with the partnership, as opposed to the corporation. You must file Form 1065, *U.S. Partnership Return of Income,* each year for the IRS. But basically, the monies you receive from the partnership are treated as ordinary income, as are the monies that you receive from the sole proprietorship. And you can deduct losses in the partnership from another source of income when you complete your income tax form.

Along with these considerable advantages there are some decided disadvantages for the partnership. First, because you are not running your own show, there can be serious problems in decision making. Who has the final say? Who makes decisions about what? So serious is this aspect of a partnership that it has been described as having all the disadvantages of a marriage with none of the advantages. If you decide on a partnership, tasks and divisions of responsibility and decision making should be decided very early on. One individual should be designated as the chief executive officer so that continuous bickering and arguing about daily decisions do not cause you to become disorganized and unsuccessful. In fact, I would say that if you do decide to choose a partnership form of organization, your first step should be to decide who will be doing what.

Another serious disadvantage of a partnership is that you are liable for the actions and commitments of your partners. For example, if, while you are on vacation, your partner takes it into his head to use all the funds you have accumulated to purchase a new car, you are responsible for the debt incurred, even though you did not participate in this decision. The same applies, of course, to decisions concerning an addressing machine, word processor, mailings, hirings, firings, and so forth.

Just as with the sole proprietorship, you run the risk of incurring personal liability, and my comments regarding a potential lawsuit or obligation to creditors if your business should fail hold true for the partnership.

One additional aspect of the partnership organization that should be discussed here is that there may be both general and limited partners. Limited partners do not participate in the day-to-day operation of the business and are not held personally liable for business debts, except to the extent of their investments. If the business loses money, the limited partner can lose only to the amount of his or her investment. But of course, profits are also limited by the amount of his or her investment. A general partner is a full, participating partner and is personally liable beyond his or her investment. The general partner participates in the day-to-day operation of the business and usually receives compensation for his or her services. The general partner may own a greater share of the business at less investment in money because of his or her active participation and greater assumption of risks.

If you want to start and own a mail order business, you probably want to be a general partner, but to attract capital you may offer limited partnership.

All of these facts mean that this form of business organization is more complex. Therefore, some kind of written agreement or contract regarding the operation of the partnership should be drawn up with the assistance of an attorney. I wouldn't want to get into a partnership without an attorney's help.

The Corporation

The third major legal form of business ownership is the corporation. To set up a corporation, individuals must usually apply for a charter in the state in which they intend to conduct their business and in which the principal office is located. However, there are exceptions to this rule.

Corporate law is very complicated. Consequently, incorporation is usually accomplished by an attorney. The attorney's fee, which may be $1,000 or more, may be one reason that many new mail order entrepreneurs do not incorporate. But there are ways of incorporating by yourself. One good book on this subject is *How to Form Your Own Corporation without a Lawyer for under $50,* by Ted Nicholas. Because state laws differ regarding incorporation, many books describing how to incorporate in individual states have been written. These books may even contain tear-out forms for you to use. In California, there is *How to Form Your Own California Corporation,* by Anthony Mancuso, and others are also available.

Incorporation provides advantages for many companies in the mail order business. First, you generally avoid the problem of personal liability. With a corporation, your liability is limited to the amount of your investment. Your creditors cannot take your personal holdings or assets if the corporation fails or is sued for more funds than are available in corporation coffers. This fact alone is probably the major reason for many incorporations of small businesses. Remember, however, that, depending upon your product and whether it is necessary to borrow capital for your corporation against a personal guaranteed signature, this "advantage" may not be important to you.

Once, a significant advantage of incorporating was income taxes. A corporation paid taxes on a maximum 48 percent of its net profits, compared to 90 percent for personal income tax. The money you would normally pay in taxes would be used for company growth. At some time in the future, you would sell the much larger business and pay capital gains rather than income taxes. Because capital gains were lower, the net result was that if the business was really big when sold, like Geraldo Joffe's "Haverhills," you could really make a fortune. But tax laws have changed substantially and the maximum personal rate is now far less. Because you pay taxes on the corporation as well as personal income taxes, you are being double taxed. Today, you really need to talk to your accountant to see whether taxation is an advantage or disadvantage in you situation.

A major advantage of incorporating is that lenders—including banks, venture capitalists, and others—are generally much more willing to give you loans if you are a corporation that has been operating successfully than if you are an individual sole proprietorship, or even a partnership. In addition, as a corporation, you can sell stock to the public and raise money for further expansion or "cash in" without selling the whole business.

There are also advantages in the area of fringe benefits and perks such as pension plans, stock plans, insurance, company cars, although many of these can also be made available to the proprietorship or the partnership.

Now let's look at the disadvantages. One major disadvantage of the corporation is the immense amount of paperwork and other complications that are part and parcel of running a corporation. Maintenance of this paperwork takes time, effort, and money that you might otherwise spend in building your business.

As was explained earlier, if you lose money in your proprietorship or your partnership, these losses can be taken as deductions from other earned income on your income tax. However, if the corporation loses money, these losses cannot be taken against other earned income until you sell your stock or the business fails.

Corporations are very closely regulated by the state in which you have registered. This regulation not only requires the paperwork mentioned earlier but may also restrict your business activities. Furthermore, the corporation is required to have a board of directors and hold stockholders' meetings. You may be able to pick this board of directors so that you still run your company, but your control of your company and your ability to run your own show are certainly more complicated and difficult than with a sole proprietorship.

The Subchapter S Corporation

One interesting option is the S corporation. S corporations were created by Congress to give tax relief to small companies. Specifically, the purpose of the S corporation is to permit a small business corporation to have its income taxed to the shareholders as if the corporation were a partnership, if it so desires. The advantages of an S corporation are twofold: (1) It permits you to avoid the double tax feature of corporate income taxation; (2) it permits you as a shareholder to have the benefit of offsetting business losses incurred by the corporation against your income. Thus, you have the advantage of the protection of incorporation as well as the tax advantage of a partnership.

You should be aware that it may or may not be to your advantage to have an S corporation if your corporation enjoys substantial profits under the new tax laws, as corporate tax rates are higher than personal tax rates. Therefore, even if you forecast profitability, it makes sense to take a closer look and to work closely with your accountant and tax attorney before passing up the S corporation.

To qualify as an S corporation you must meet the following requirements: (1) You must have no more than 10 shareholders, all of whom are individuals or estates; (2) you must have no nonresident alien shareholders; (3) you must have only one class of outstanding stock; (4) all shareholders must consent to the election of an S corporation; and (5) a specified portion of the corporation's receipts must be derived from actual business activity rather than passive investments.

In an S corporation, no limit is placed on the size of the corporation's income and assets.

You should make the decision as to which legal form of business organization to adopt for your company after carefully considering your product and your own situation, and perhaps consulting with your attorney and accountant. In most situations you will find that the easiest route is that of the sole proprietorship because it is so easy to set up. In fact, unless you are reading this on a weekend, you can probably set up a sole proprietorship, complete with business license, this very day. This is not necessarily true with a partnership, and most definitely not true of a corporation.

IT'S EASY TO GET A BUSINESS LICENSE

What is a business license? It is simply a permit granted by a local governmental body, generally for a small fee, that allows you to carry on some business subject to local regulations. In some areas, the governing body, whether city or county, does not even require a business license. However, it may require special permits for businesses of a certain type. So your first step is to determine whether a business license is required for your area and your particular type of mail order business. To find out, simply contact the chamber of commerce, city hall, city licensing department, or whatever body is applicable for the area in which you live. If you live in an unincorporated area of a county, contact the county licensing department. They can also tell you whether a state license is required. In this case, you will be contacting the state licensing board or some similar department.

If a business license is required, you will have to contact the appropriate agency and fill out an application. In general, it is relatively simple to complete: The typical information required is your name, type of business—in this case, you would put mail order—a fictitious name if you have one, the business address, the mailing address, your telephone number, your personal residence address, when the business is starting, the type of organization of your business, the number of employees, and partners' names, if any.

Sometimes your new business will require zoning, fire, and police department notification, and clearance before your new business license will be issued. However, for a mail order business, it is usually necessary to state only that you will not maintain large amounts of inventory or have large package deliveries made to the residence if you are conducting the mail order business from your own home.

HOW TO GET FICTITIOUS NAME REGISTRATION

You may or may not need fictitious name registration when starting your new mail order business, depending on the law in your area of operation. Usually you must file a fictitious name registration statement if the business name you select is within the definition of "fictitious business name" used in your area. Generally, a fictitious business name is any name other than your own or those of partners with whom you may be associated. Therefore, if I use the name William A. Cohen and describe my operation as "mail order and direct mail," I would generally not need fictitious name registration. However, if I use the name William A. Cohen and Associates, or William A. Cohen and Sons, fictitious name registration would be required. Of course, any name other than your own—such as "the ABC Company" or "the Magic Peanut Company"—would definitely require fictitious name registration.

Obtaining fictitious name registration is also relatively easy and the fact that you must register it should not be considered an impediment to selecting a name that people will notice and associate with your business. To find out the law in your state, contact the appropriate agency listed in your telephone book under city, county, or state government and they will tell you what the requirements are. Usually they involve nothing more than completing a simple form asking for your fictitious business name and the business address, your own name and home address, and a description of the business you are in. This information must be published within 30 days after filing the statement, usually in a newspaper, and it usually must be published once a week for four consecutive weeks. Thirty days after the publication has been accomplished, an affidavit of publication is filed with the county clerk. This procedure is a lot easier than it sounds. Usually it can be done simply by contacting the newspaper and telling the newspaper that you want to publish fictitious name registration. The forms are frequently available right there on the spot, and the newspaper will take care of all the work for you by helping you to prepare the statement and filing it with the county clerk for you. The cost will vary, but it is usually minimal: The filing fee will probably be about $25, and the newspaper publication cost can range from $15 to $100. To minimize these publication costs, you should pick the newspaper with the smallest circulation possible within the area in which you are doing business, and of course, in accordance with any other legal requirements of the particular jurisdiction in which you are doing business.

Once you have filed, your statements must be refiled periodically, usually every five years. After you have filed the first time you may have several newspapers seeking your business to file in future times.

Another tip is to file for registration for more than one fictitious name, which is usually permitted, sometimes without additional cost. You can easily get more than one fictitious name at once if you write small and squeeze all the names you can or want to use on the fictitious business name statement form. Since this statement form is published exactly as you write it, the additional names you have managed to write on the form will also be given to you. These names can be used for a variety of different purposes.

Let's look at a few. For some types of promotions it may be advantageous to use some name other than your regular fictitious name. A very large and successful mail order company does exactly this when testing new products.

The advantage of doing this is that if the promotion fails, the failure will not be associated with the main name under which the company is doing business. Mail order consultants will sometimes use such fictitious names to test new products for their clients. In any case, you never know when you may wish to use another fictitious name for some special purpose (such as an in-house advertising agency as described later in this book). Some counties have started charging extra for additional names. For the few additional dollars, it's still worthwhile. I recommend that you get all the fictitious names you can all at once.

Some small businesspeople I know in mail order, although operating under fictitious names, have never filed for a fictitious name statement. Probably they will not be apprehended even though they may operate for years. I don't recommend this practice, but the truth is that penalties for failing to register are generally small, and most violators do not get caught. One very large mail order operator I know does considerable testing under various and assorted fictitious names, and, to quote him, he "forgets to file" fictitious name registrations for these one-time tests of new products. Although this has been his practice for the last 30 years, he has yet to be taken to task by the law. However, there is one major disadvantage of not registering: Some other mail order operator may beat you to the name you want!

Regardless of what name or names you decide to select for your business and then register as fictitious, the best possible name is one that best describes your product or services. An unusual or fancy name that does not describe your product or service can be confusing and may cause you to lose potential customers, or at the very least, may cause you to miss business that your name alone might otherwise attract. The Wilshire Book Company clearly must have something to do with books—publishing, retailing, or wholesaling them. In fact, they do all three and some business does come to them because the company name tells potential customers the kind of product and service they are involved with.

WHAT A SELLER'S PERMIT IS AND HOW TO OBTAIN ONE

A seller's permit, which can be obtained from your state board of equalization or similar organization, gives you the right to buy certain personal property that you intend to resell without having to pay sales tax or so-called use tax to your vendor for purchasing this property. Instead, you give the seller a resale certificate that indicates your seller's permit number. When you sell the property you collect the tax from the consumer and pay the tax collected to your state board of equalization. If you intend to sell any tangible personal property to which this tax can apply, you must obtain this seller's permit; otherwise, you will have to pay the tax to your vendor every time you buy property for your business—office supplies, inventory, or whatever. This applies whether you are a wholesaler or a retailer through our mail order business. The only exception is if you are in a service business, in which case you may be exempt from this requirement as services are usually not taxed.

To obtain a seller's permit, contact the sales and use tax department of your state, as listed in Figure 2.1. If a fee is required for a seller's permit, the appropriate office will inform you. Sometimes the board of equalization may require some security from you for the payment of future tax. If so, the amount is determined at the same time you make your application for the permit. This security deposit assures the state that if you fail to pay any sales tax due, the state can deduct the amount you owe from the security you have posted.

Because the required security can run as high as several thousand dollars, it is to your advantage not to post it for your seller's permit if at all possible. How much security is required, or whether any is required at all, depends on the information you provide the board on your application form. In some cases, if the security deposit is very high, an installment

ALABAMA
Department of Revenue
Sales and Use Taxes
Montgomery. Alabama 36130

ALASKA
Department of Revenue
Pouch S
Juneau, Alaska 99801

ARIZONA
Sales Tax Division
Phoenix, Arizona 85007

ARKANSAS
Sales and Use Tax Division
Department of Finance and
Administration
Little Rock, Arkansas 72201

CALIFORNIA
Department of Business Taxes
State Board of Equalization
P.O. Box 1799
Sacramento, California 95808

COLORADO
Department of Revenue
State Capitol Annex
Denver, Colorado 80203

CONNECTICUT
Sales, Use and Excise Tax Division
Hartford, Connecticut 06115

DELAWARE
State Division of Revenue
Wilmington, Delaware 19801

DISTRICT OF COLUMBIA
Department of Finance and Revenue
300 Indiana Avenue, N.W.
Washington, D.C. 20001

FLORIDA
Sales Tax Bureau
Department of Revenue
Tallahassee, Florida 32304

GEORGIA
Sales and Use Tax Unit
Department of Revenue
Atlanta, Georgia 30334

HAWAII
Department of Taxation
State Tax Office Building
425 Queen Street
Honolulu, Hawaii, 96813

IDAHO
Sales Tax Division
State Tax Commission
Boise, Idaho 83707

ILLINOIS
Department of Revenue
Springfield, Illinois 62706

INDIANA
Sales Tax Division
Department of Revenue
100 N. Senate Avenue
Indianapolis, Indiana 46204

IOWA
Division of Retail Sales and Use Tax
Department of Revenue
Lucas State Office Building
Des Moines, Iowa 50319

KANSAS
Sales and Compensating Tax Division
State Revenue Building
Department of Revenue
Topeka, Kansas 66612

KENTUCKY
Sales Tax Division
Department of Revenue
Frankfort, Kentucky 40601

LOUISIANA
Collector of Revenue
Baton Rouge, Louisiana 70821

MAINE
Sales Tax Division
Bureau of Taxation
Augusta, Maine 04330

MARYLAND
Retail Sales Tax Division
Treasury Department
301 W. Preston Street
Baltimore, Maryland 21201

MASSACHUSETTS
Sales and Use Taxes
Department of Corporations & Taxation
Boston, Massachusetts 02133

MICHIGAN
Sales and Use Taxes
Department of Treasury
Revenue Division
Treasury Building
Lansing, Michigan 48922

MINNESOTA
Sales and Use Tax Division
Department of Taxation
Centennial Office Building
St. Paul. Minnesota 55101

MISSISSIPPI
Sales and Use Tax Division
State Tax Commission
Jackson, Mississippi 39205

MISSOURI
Sales and Use Tax Bureau
P.O. Box 840
Jefferson City. Missouri 65102

(continued)

Figure 2.1 Sales and use tax departments.

NEBRASKA
  Sales and Use Tax Unit
  Department of Revenue
  Box 4818. State Capitol
  Lincoln, Nebraska 68509

NEVADA
  Nevada Tax Commission
  Carson City, Nevada 89701

NEW JERSEY
  Division of Taxation
  Department of the Treasury
  Trenton, New Jersey 08625

NEW MEXICO
  Revenue. Bureau of Revenue
  Santa Fe, New Mexico 87501

NEW YORK
  Sales Tax Bureau, State Tax Commission
  Department of Taxation and Finance
  Tax and Finance Building 9
  State Campus
  Albany, New York 12226

NORTH CAROLINA
  Sales and Use Tax Division
  Main Office—Revenue Building
  Raleigh. North Carolina 27611

NORTH DAKOTA
  Enforcement Director (Sales Tax)
  State Capitol Building
  Bismarck, North Dakota 58501

OHIO
  Sales and Excise Division
  Department of Taxation
  68 East Gay Street
  Columbus, Ohio 43151

OKLAHOMA
  Sales and Use Taxes
  Oklahoma Tax Commission
  2101 Lincoln Blvd.
  Oklahoma City, Oklahoma 73105

PENNSYLVANIA
  Bureau of Taxes for Education
  Department of Revenue
  Harrisburg, Pennsylvania 17128

RHODE ISLAND
  Department of Administration
  49 Westminster Street
  Providence. Rhode Island 02903

SOUTH CAROLINA
  Sales and Use Tax Division
  South Carolina Tax Commission
  Columbia, South Carolina 29201

SOUTH DAKOTA
  Sales and Use Tax Division
  Department of Revenue
  Pierre. South Dakota 57501

TENNESSEE
  Sales and Use Tax Division
  Department of Revenue
  War Memorial Building
  Nashville, Tennessee 37219

TEXAS
  Comptroller of Public Accounts
  Austin, Texas 78711

UTAH
  Auditing Division (Sales Tax)
  State Tax Commission
  201 State Office Building
  Salt Lake City, Utah 84114

VERMONT
  Department of Taxes
  State of Vermont
  P.O. Box 547
  Montpelier, Vermont 05602

VIRGINIA
  Sales and Use Tax Division
  Department of Taxation
  P.O. Box 6L
  Richmond, Virginia 23215

WASHINGTON
  Department of Revenue
  Olympia, Washington 98501

WEST VIRGINIA
  Sales and Use Taxes
  State Tax Department
  Charleston, West Virginia 25305

  Business and Occupation Tax
  State Tax Department
  Charleston, West Virginia 25305

WISCONSIN
  Income, Sales, and Excise Tax Division
  Department of Revenue
  P.O. Box 39
  Madison, Wisconsin 53702

WYOMING
  Sales and Use Tax Division
  State Tax Commission
  Cheyenne. Wyoming 82002

Figure 2.1   (Continued)

payment arrangement can be made. Small business consultant Wayde T. Gilliam, Jr. has made an extensive study of the security deposit and ways of minimizing it while receiving a seller's permit. In his book *How to Increase Your Standard of Living with a Small Business,* he lists seven facts on your application form that can reduce the security deposit required:

1. If you own a home.
2. If you have substantial equity in your home.
3. If your estimated monthly expenses are low.
4. If your estimated monthly sales are low.
5. If you are presently employed and this is a part-time business.
6. If you have no employees.
7. If you have only one place of business.

If you think the board of equalization in your state is setting too high a security deposit requirement, you should discuss it with the official and try to negotiate a more reasonable deposit. In my own first mail order business the board wanted me to deposit $2,000. We negotiated until eventually the requirement was no security deposit at all! So talking personally with the members of the board of equalization when you obtain your seller's permit is worthwhile.

HOW TO SELECT A BANK AND OPEN A BANK ACCOUNT

From the very start it is to your advantage to select a bank that will help you and your mail order business be successful. The best service for your needs is usually available at an independent bank with no branches, or a small chain of banks. In a small bank, your account may be very important, whereas in a large bank you may not even be noticed. Also, a small bank will assist you in becoming acquainted with as many of the employees in the bank as possible. In the course of your business, people who know you can be extremely helpful in assisting your operation and in acquiring business loans for expansion or just for operating capital.

A large bank is useful if your mail order business is involved in international trade. Let's see why. If the item you are going to sell is being imported from abroad or you are selling abroad through export, having a large bank can help you because most very large banks have international departments. They can assist you through the various mazes of payments, letters of credit, insurance, and so forth. One large international bank that we know actually assisted my friend Joe Cossman by having a member of its Hong Kong branch give free seminars in international trade to an international business group he was leading on a guided tour through the Orient. Such service would not be available with a small independent bank.

Regardless of what bank you decide to do business with, you should not move your account from bank to bank, if at all possible. Your bank reference can be very important for you in obtaining credit from suppliers, and in some cases can be very useful in acting as a reference to your customers as well, as we will discuss later in building credibility in your ads.

Your bank will not allow you to register a bank account in your fictitious name until you have already obtained fictitious name registration. To open the account, a small deposit of $100 or less is usually all that is required.

When you have your own bank, feel free to discuss various financial problems with your banker. This person can be of much help in running your mail order business, in finding an attorney or accountant, and in supplying various other services that will help you to succeed.

When you have your bank account, it's good to start building credit right away, rather than waiting until you actually need it. Most small mail order businesses will sometimes need capital to grow or to take advantage of opportunities that present themselves suddenly in the marketplace. One way of establishing credit is to take a small loan you don't need—for, say, $1,000 or less—and then pay back the amount borrowed with regular payments. In this way, you will have built a track record of paying off a bank loan, which can help later on when you need greater sums of money from your bank. Naturally, you should make certain that your payments are made exactly on time and when required.

Having your own business bank account is evidence of the fact that you are really in business for yourself, whether it is a part-time or full-time business.

BORROWING MONEY AND SOURCES OF CAPITAL FOR YOUR MAIL ORDER BUSINESS

The best source of capital for your new business is you—that is, money that you currently control. It is the easiest to make use of, and the quickest. Further, you need not surrender equity in your business or worry about paying it back.

The second best source for new capital is close friends or relatives. Why are close friends and relatives a good source of money? Because, except for your own money, it is usually the fastest, easiest, and cheapest way to raise cash that you need, and it also involves less paperwork and fewer legal problems. Larry O. started his new mail order business in Canada, selling a cosmetic product he had developed himself and patented. His sales suddenly boomed from a few dollars a month to $50,000 with one large wholesale order. He needed money immediately for raw materials, machinery to manufacture in large quantities, rental work space, and so forth. Larry raised $20,000 in less than two weeks, almost entirely from friends at his former place of employment, from which he had resigned upon receiving the $50,000 order. Larry's cosmetic business grew rapidly, and within two years he was able to cash in and sell out at a huge profit. One cautionary note, however: If you do borrow money from friends or relatives, be certain not to cut them in on your business. You are borrowing money, not making them partners. Close friends or relatives are very difficult to control in managing your business.

If you have money in a savings account, you can borrow against it. Usually the cost of this type of loan is low and the reason, of course, is that the savings institution in which you have the money can keep it as collateral until you repay what is borrowed. One additional advantage to this type of borrowing is that the money you have in the savings account continues to draw interest while you have the loan, even while it is held as collateral. So if your money is normally earning $3\frac{1}{2}$ percent interest and is costing you $7\frac{1}{2}$ percent, the real cost of the loan is only 4 percent.

A life insurance loan may also be possible. If your life insurance policy has cash value, you can generally obtain a loan of up to 95 percent of the accumulated value. An unusual aspect of a life insurance loan is that you don't actually have to repay the loan. You pay only the interest each year along with your premium. Of course, if you don't replace the money you borrowed, that amount is deducted from the face value of the policy paid to a beneficiary.

Getting a loan from a regular bank to start a new business is usually pretty difficult. However, if your credit is good, you can sometimes get a signature or personal loan for several thousand dollars almost immediately. Sometimes you can get more if you have dealt with a bank for some time and it feels that you are a good risk. Usually these are short-term loans that must be paid off within a three-year period. Such loans can be paid off in installments or the lump sum can be paid at a specified time.

Similarly, credit unions, which are really nonprofit banks, are an excellent source of loans for relatively small sums. Of course, you must already belong to the credit union to get a loan. Membership frequently depends upon place of employment or similar factors. The main advantage of dealing with a credit union over dealing with a bank is that the interest rates are usually several points lower than those of banks.

A finance company or loan company is also a source of money and can lend you from several thousand dollars up to much more, depending upon the individual state laws and how much collateral in real estate or other property you're able to put up and it is willing to accept. However, the most frequent loans from finance and loan companies are small—for a maximum of a couple of thousand dollars—and are granted providing you already have a credit rating. The advantage of dealing with a finance company is that the loan usually comes fairly fast—in a day if you already have a credit rating or several days if you haven't dealt with this particular loan or finance company before. However, the interest rates from finance and loan companies are fairly high, much higher than those of a bank or credit union.

Credit cards are a frequently overlooked source of credit. Depending upon the credit limit with every credit card you have—MasterCard, Visa, and so on—you can usually get at least $500 worth of credit. Here annual interest charges are much higher, but they are a ready source of credit in paying for many of your raw materials or products, whether you order face to face or by mail. The interest charges vary quite a bit, so check several.

Your suppliers are another frequently overlooked source of loans. If you order stationery and printing supplies and you do not have to pay until delivery, this is, in effect, a loan for that period. Further, if your supplier will grant you 30, 60, or 90 additional days to pay for the material you have purchased, this is a loan as well. Occasionally, suppliers give a discount for early payment, usually something like 2 percent for payment within 10 days. This discount should be weighed against your need for immediate funds. Never be afraid of asking for credit if you need this money for some valid business purpose.

For really large sums of money you should know about venture capital companies, the Small Business Administration, and small business investment corporations (SBICs) and business development corporations (BDCs). Small Business Administration loans are usually extremely limited, and even though you may be able to obtain a loan for several hundred thousand dollars, complete business plans will be required and a lead time of from nine months to a year or more is required. Similarly, a business plan is required with venture capital companies, SBICs, and BDCs.

Don't be afraid of business plans, however. The marketing plan I will show you how to prepare in Chapter 23 is really a business plan with very few changes. All of these types of firms with the potential for lending you money can be found either by contacting the Small Business Administration or by checking the *Wall Street Journal* or your local big-city paper in the business opportunities column of the classified section. SBICs, BDCs, and venture capital companies will want equity capital and controlling interest in your business. Further, the likelihood of their investing in your mail order company before your company has a track record is rather remote. Therefore, these sources should not be considered until you have already had a certain amount of success and you have demonstrated a clear potential for future growth. Finally, you must be willing to surrender a controlling interest in your company in exchange for the capital you need.

Another method of obtaining money to start your new business is a finder. The finder is a financial broker who locates sources of investment capital for you in exchange for receiving a percentage of that capital. For example, if you wanted to start a mail order business and required $20,000, you might engage a finder to help you find this money in exchange for 5 percent, or $1,000, when you receive the loan. Thus, if you are using a finder, you must be certain to allow additional money in the loan to pay the finder himself. Of course, the finder's fee is in addition to the interest rate you must pay to the individual who is lending you the money or investing in your company. Finders themselves can be located through your accountant, attorney, or bank, or sometimes through various business publications such as the *Wall Street Journal* and weekend editions of major newspapers in the *Financial* or *Loans Available* columns of the classified sections.

THE IMPORTANT PRINCIPLE OF MAINTAINING A LOW OVERHEAD IN YOUR NEW MAIL ORDER BUSINESS

It is absolutely critical to your success that you maintain a low overhead in your new mail order business. Overhead eats into all funds that you have available as your profits. Some years ago, a very successful manager in a large aerospace company quit to start his own mail order business, even though it would have been very easy to start the business part-time while he still had a large salary coming in from his regular work. To compound his mistake, he insisted upon renting a large office in a prestigious area and buying top-quality furniture and office equipment, even before he started. Because of the tremendous overhead with which this man saddled himself, his business was doomed to failure before he even started. He hadn't sold a single item when he went bankrupt.

Do not make this mistake. To maintain a low overhead from the beginning:

1. Do not give up your regular source of income, but start your mail order business part-time until it is off the ground and you are earning sufficient income to support yourself and your family.

2. Do not be afraid of working out of your home. Many mail order millionaires have started their businesses on the kitchen table or have used portions of their garage or a spare bedroom.

Mail order entrepreneur Benjamin Suarez says that fixed overhead breeds silently and rapidly to destroy your business because: (1) the entrepreneur or business owner wants to feed his or her ego by having fancy business accommodations and a lot of subordinates; (2) subordinates also want to feed their egos and make their jobs easier with fancy accommodations, extra help, and work-saving equipment; (3) government and institutions will encourage increases in fixed overhead and play upon the entrepreneur's ego because such increases feed the government more taxes and provide good business for the institutions; and (4) businesses that sell to businesses are constantly bombarding the entrepreneur or business owner with sales pitches for larger and fancier accommodations and equipment.

Richard H. Buskirk and Percy J. Vaughn, Jr., professors of business management say in their book *Managing New Enterprises:* "The management of overhead is one key to success in small business. In fact, it is the very reason that small business can frequently compete against bigger enterprises." So if you want to have a successful mail order business, keep your overhead low.

SHOULD YOU USE A BOX NUMBER OR A STREET ADDRESS FOR YOUR MAILING ADDRESS?

Many new mail order entrepreneurs worry about whether they should use a box number instead of their street address. When I started out, I had the same concern. I was afraid that if I used my home address, I would be bothered by would-be customers or even dissatisfied customers. On the other hand, some literature on mail order told me that I could not be successful if I used a box number because potential customers would think that I was a "fly-by-night" operator. Finally I decided to try a box anyway. No sooner had I rented the box than I tried to place my initial advertisement and discovered that California requires a street address to be listed in your advertisement, whether you use a post office box for mailing or not! My initial advertisement was in the *Los Angeles Times Magazine,* so I didn't have much choice. But this situation turned out to be a great mini-test because my out-of-state advertisements used the box address only. Here's what happened.

1. Some folks who had seen my ad came to my house to see the merchandise close up—and bought!
2. In my out-of-state ads, I didn't suffer one iota because of the postal box address.

After this experience, I used the following guidelines: If I advertised within the state, I used my home address; if I advertised out-of-state, I also used my home address, except in a classified ad, where each word means more dollars. With a classified ad I could save several words, which translated into several dollars, by using a box number.

If you still have concerns about using your home address, consider Joe Karbo's experience. Joe thought long and hard about whether to expose his family to any wrongdoing by putting his home address in his "Lazy Man's Way to Riches" ads. But in years of carrying a street address, he had no difficulties.

WHETHER YOU NEED TO CARRY
MASTERCARD OR VISA

Another question that has probably crossed your mind is whether to use credit cards, such as MasterCard or Visa, in your business. My suggestion is to do it. Here's why.

1. When you first start your business, your name is unknown. To use the old cliché, people don't know you or your business from Adam. But MasterCard or Visa? Everyone knows them, and the association with them is very good for your credibility.

2. If you sell-high-cost or so-called "big-ticket" items, you are going to have to provide some kind of time payment plan. Otherwise, you just aren't going to be able to get together enough customers. The sad fact is that if you provide this time payment plan yourself, even with a series of dunning and threatening letters, you will never collect from all your customers. What percentage will you be able to collect from? With luck, maybe 60 or 70 percent. To avoid this unpleasantness and get the money owed you from each and every customer, use the major credit cards.

3. It is a fact that, for most products in most situations, your returns will be better if you offer a credit card option. Part of the reason is the credibility factor noted above. But beyond that, it's just a little easier to order, with fewer immediate demands on your customer's financial treasure.

4. For some operations, a credit card is essential. A major example would be those late-night television advertisements for tapes, records, kitchenware, or whatever. When used in conjunction with a toll-free telephone number, which I discuss shortly, those advertisements can really pull.

Despite all these favorable reasons for using the major credit cards, there are some drawbacks. The first is that it's not free. It's going to cost you something. The percentage it will cost you for each order varies. If your monthly sales are smaller, you can expect to pay a higher percentage than if they are huge. I used to pay 4 percent when I was in business.

The second drawback is that, contrary to what you might think, neither Visa nor MasterCard is wildly enthusiastic about dealing with new mail order operators. Why? They have been burned in the past. People with little training and no preparation have gotten into the business. Unlike you, they didn't learn what it takes to succeed in mail order before they started. The result has been a lot of dissatisfied customers to whom the credit card people would rather not be responsible, even in an indirect way. As a result, you are going to have to be ready to present a pretty good story, business plan, personal background, and so on to convince the credit card people that you know what you are doing so that they let you join their system. Naturally, it helps if you were already in business and selling your product even before you decided to enter the mail order business. Also, be ready for some high-level negotiating. After being turned down by both major cards at the local level, I took my story to the corporate offices and succeeded with an argument that went something like this: "I'm sure your competitor is going to approve my application, so I'll be advertising with his card only. Now, my sales are forecast to be low the first year, but don't try to convince me to add your card when my sales reach $1,000,000." Usually the facts, some possibilities, and a good argument presented forcefully, but tactfully, will win the day. If you can't get either credit card for your business, don't despair. Numerous multimillion-dollar mail order businesses have been built without the use of credit cards, and many still don't use them.

If your application is approved, the use of these cards is simple. In your advertisement, you simply ask for the buyer's card number and expiration date in addition to his or her name and address. When you get this information, you can check whether the person's credit is good by use of a toll-free number. You then fill out a credit card form given to you by MasterCard or Visa. You can save these forms and send them in once a month, and you will be credited with the amount less the percentage owed, or you can take them to the bank and get your cash immediately.

SHOULD YOU USE A TOLL-FREE NUMBER?

Toll-free numbers are another way of increasing response. Why does response increase? Because they make it easier for your customer to order. Again, some operations, by their very nature, make the use of toll-free numbers a must—think about mail order commercials on late-night television shows again. However, the toll-free number is free to your *customer*, not to you. So before signing up, you should think about it a little. True, a toll-free number will probably help your credibility, but not as much as a credit card, and probably not enough to make it worthwhile for this reason alone. In general, toll-free numbers are useful when:

- You have a lot of business.
- You are selling a relatively high-ticket item.
- It is customary to provide a toll-free number for the product, industry, or method you are using to sell (CDs on TV).

You can increase sales sufficiently to pay for the increased cost. Many people have tried toll-free numbers for their mail order businesses and found that, for their situations, it wasn't worthwhile. Joe Karbo was one well known example.

There are two ways of getting a toll-free number. One is to rent the toll-free line from the telephone company yourself. This is the most expensive way, but it is worthwhile if your phone is going to be ringing all the time: It gives you the greatest control over the calls to ensure that your incoming orders are handled as you want them handled. If you decide to go this way, the telephone company will give you several options to choose from. Rates vary depending on your area and options, so check locally with your telephone company for the latest figures.

You may also want to investigate toll-free services that use your existing telephone line, eliminating the need for extra telephone lines. This is fairly economical. AT&T's toll-free number is (800) 222-0400. You can find other toll-free services in your local telephone book.

The alternative is to participate in a toll-free service offered by a firm that has rented a line from the telephone company. A typical ad response service may cost you 50¢–75¢ per minute. Usually it takes 4–5 minutes to take an order, and 2–3 minutes to respond to a request for a catalog or for information. If you are interested in this option, here are three companies that offer a toll-free service:

1. Call Center Services, 1-800-238-2255.
2. TCI Marketing, Inc., 1-800-999-4824.
3. West Telemarketing Corp., 1-800-542-1000.

SUMMARY

In this very important chapter, we discussed how to get your mail order business off the ground. First, we talked about the three basic legal forms of business: the sole proprietorship, the partnership, and the corporation. We concluded that you must pick the form that best fits your needs, your situation, and the products you intend to sell by mail. Next, we discussed how to get a business license so that you meet the basic legal requirements for your new business. Then we discussed fictitious name registration, when it is required and how to apply for it, and what a name means to your mail order business. Looking at the seller's permit, we learned how to apply for it and where to write in your particular state to obtain information about getting one. We also talked about what factors minimize the deposit required by your state board of equalization. Our next subject was banking, and we talked about getting your bank account and how to select a bank that will be most suitable to your operation. Then we discussed sources of money and capital for starting your mail order business. We talked about maintaining a low overhead so that you will maximize your opportunities for immediate success. This is most important. Finally, I gave you the alternatives in three relevant issues: box versus street addresses, credit cards versus none, and use or nonuse of toll-free numbers and your options if you use them.

Following the instructions outlined in this chapter, you will get your business off and running on the right foot for profitability. Do not short-change yourself by failing to apply these basics in your business. By following the principles discussed in this chapter you can become a mail order millionaire.

3

Important Legal and Ethical Issues

You can make a fortune in mail order, and you can do so honestly and without deceiving your customers. Believe me, it is not worth the legal headache or legal penalties should you, intentionally or unintentionally, break the law. But above and beyond the law, deception goes against all standards and ideals of those engaged in marketing by mail. The potential exists to make a fortune in mail order not because you can rip off the customer, but because you can satisfy his or her needs. Therefore, do not be tempted to rush through this chapter without reading it carefully, for not only are the penalties for breaking the law severe, but, as Joe Karbo once said: "It is you who must view yourself in the mirror on rising and before going to bed and be satisfied with what you see."

The Direct Marketing Association publishes a list of no less than 40 operating guidelines for ethical business practice for all direct response marketers, whether they are selling products or services or raising funds for nonprofit organizations. Perhaps the basic guideline is this one: "Direct response marketers should make their offers clear and honest. They should not misrepresent a product, service, publication, or program and should not use misleading, partially true, or exaggerated statements. All descriptions and promises should be in accordance with actual conditions, situations, and circumstances existing at the time the promotion is made. Direct response marketers should operate in accordance with the Better Business Bureau's basic principles contained in the Better Business Bureau's Code of Advertising and be cognizant of and adhere to the Postal Laws and Regulations and all other laws governing advertising in transactions of business by mail, telephone, and the print and broadcast media." Certainly this is a mouthful, but the essence is contained in the first sentence: Your offer should always be clear and honest. The complete list of

The Direct Marketing Association's Guidelines for Ethical Business Practices is contained in Appendix A.

The main agencies that must be dealt with regarding the laws of mail order and direct mail marketing are the U.S. Postal Service and the Federal Trade Commission. Either of these two government agencies can do you considerable harm if you go astray, and it is possible to stray from the regulations without ill intent. An advertisement that you place may be illegal if there is the smallest chance that your customer may be deceived by a statement or classification that is misleading. At one time I wished to sell information regarding job finding through the mail. I wanted to try something new. The idea was to place a short classified ad under the classification for various types of help wanted in the Sunday edition of the newspaper. My plan was a small test ad in the *Los Angeles Times,* and, if successful, I would expand into many different papers across the country. The first thing I discovered in attempting this was that it is illegal to advertise information on job finding in a column headed *Help Wanted.* The only legal way around this was to advertise "See Our Announcement under *Announcements*" and make the promotion for the information that I wished to sell in the *Announcements* column.

Whether your ad is legal or illegal may not be determined directly from the ad itself. Let's say you advertise a correspondence course for writers. In your ad, you say, "You can make $50,000 a year." The ad's legitimacy would depend upon whether writers of this category make $50,000 a year and whether graduates of your correspondence course make this much.

BEWARE OF DECEPTIVE PRICING

The Federal Trade Commission (FTC) has issued several guides and advisory opinions pertaining to how you may advertise pricing. These concern price comparisons with former prices, price comparisons with retail items, advertising prices that have been established or suggested by manufacturers or other nonretail distributors, bargain offers based on the purchase of other merchandise, and various other price comparisons.

Price Comparisons with Former Prices

If you offer an item at a bargain price, compared with its former price, the former price must actually have been offered to the public on a regular basis for a reasonably substantial period. If you establish a price that is obviously inflated and artificial for the specific purpose of offering the item later at a large reduction or as a "bargain," this former price is considered false by the FTC and is illegal. On the other hand, a former price is not necessarily fictitious merely because you made no sales at that price. For example, if you established a valid price for an item, advertised it at $12.95, but sold only a few, you could legally advertise a price reduction to, say, $9.95. The basic point here is that it is illegal to advertise a bargain price or reduction price if you never really intended to make any sales at the first price.

Retail Price Comparisons

If you advertise that you are selling at a price below that charged in your geographic area for a certain product, you must be reasonably certain that your price does not appreciably exceed the price at which substantial sales for the article are being made in that area. According to an advisory opinion by the FTC, there are two fundamental requirements for determining the validity of savings claims based upon the sale of the same or comparable merchandise. First you should be certain that the retail merchandise advertised is of essentially similar quality in all material respects to the product you are advertising. The second requirement is that you must be reasonably certain that the price advertised does not exceed the price at which such merchandise is being offered by representative retail outlets in the area. In other words, if you say yours is the lowest price, it should be the lowest price!

Advertising Prices That Have Been Established or Suggested by Manufacturers or Other Nonretail Distributors

Many a product has a suggested price set by the manufacturer that is totally disregarded when sold by a retailer. In fact, everyone in your area may sell the product at a much lower price. So when you are advertising by mail, if you suggest that your price is much lower than the manufacturer's or distributor's suggested retail price, you must be careful to offer a reduction from the price at which the product is generally sold in the area to which you are selling. If a number of retail establishments are selling this product at the list or suggested retail price, you are all right. However, according to the FTC, if they are already selling at a lower price, you cannot suggest in your advertising that your price is a bargain by comparing it solely to the manufacturer's list or suggested price.

Bargain Offers Based on the Purchase of Other Merchandise

As we will point out in a later chapter, there are many ways to make an offer, some of which will be much more interesting to your potential customer than others. Some offers are more profitable to make even though they are essentially the same as the less interesting offers. For example, two for $1 or one for $1 and one free are the same offer presented differently.

This is fine unless you advertise in such a manner that you increase the regular price of the first article to make up for the lower price of the second, or decrease the quantity or quality of the product or otherwise put such conditions on the offer that it is no longer the same. If you do any of these things, you may be deceiving the customer, and may therefore be liable for FTC action. Let's say that you are selling tape cassettes for $5 and you advertise, "Our regular tape cassettes 2 for $5." If you actually send your customers a cheaper tape cassette of lower quality than your standard cassette and don't tell them, this is deception.

Miscellaneous Price Comparisons

Other common deceptions in advertising prices upon which the FTC definitely frowns are advertising a retail price as a wholesale price when, in fact, it isn't or a factory price when you are not selling the items at the price actually sold by the manufacturer, or offering seconds or irregular merchandise at a reduced price without telling your customer that the merchandise is not in perfect condition. Do any of these things in pricing and you have violated the basic principle of mail order marketing, and you will be in lots of trouble with the FTC.

DELIVERY OF MAIL ORDER MERCHANDISE

One of the most important regulations affecting people engaged in mail order selling was passed by the FTC on February 2, 1976. It is called the Thirty Day Delay Delivery Rule. Basically, it says that if there is a reasonable basis on which to believe that the product you are selling will not be shipped within 30 days of receiving a properly completed order, your advertisement must include a clear and conspicuous notice of the time in which you expect to make shipment. If you make no statement, this rule requires that your shipment be made within 30 days.

Now, what happens if you cannot make the shipment within an unstated 30-day period or the period you've stated specifically in your advertisement? In that case, you must send a notice of revised shipment date to the buyer by first class mail before expiration of the original 30-day period. This statement must include a postage-paid reply form that notifies the buyer of the new shipping date and offers the option of agreeing to the delay or canceling the order and obtaining a refund. Your notice must also inform your buyer that, unless you receive a response rejecting the delay, the buyer will have consented to the delayed shipment. Finally, some states, such as New York, have delivery rules stricter than those of the FTC! So you should check state laws about this if there is any doubt.

There are other important aspects of this 30-day rule. Some years ago Joe Sugarman was fined heavily by the FTC for violating the 30-day rule when the computer that handled Joe's orders went out during a winter storm. Sugarman fought this tooth and nail, with blistering ads exposing the FTC's ability to destroy legitimate mail order businesses. In an article entitled "FTC: Change Your Mail Order Rule or Face Court Challenge" in *Direct Marketing,* Sugarman explained the reasons for his opposition and his proposals for a fair rule. He even testified before Congress on this matter. In the end, he still had to pay the fine. The point here is not that Sugarman was right or wrong in his attack on or defense against the FTC's contentions regarding the 30-day rule under extenuating circumstances. You must be aware of the rule and obey it to the best of your ability as it exists now. Figure 3.1 shows a typical letter used by Joe's company, JS&A, for a late shipment.

ENDORSEMENTS AND TESTIMONIALS IN ADVERTISING

The FTC has proposed several guidelines for use of endorsements and testimonials in advertising. This is most important because endorsements and testimonials lend a tremendous amount of credibility to whatever your proposition is. Some of these guidelines, quoted directly, are as follows:

1. Every endorsement must reflect the honest view of the endorser and may not use statements in endorsements that could not be supported if presented in the advertiser's words rather than the endorser's.
2. The advertiser may not distort the endorser's opinion or experience with the product by rewording the endorsement or by presenting it out of context. Further, the advertiser may continue to use the endorsement only as long as he or she has good reason to believe that the endorser continues to subscribe to the views presented.
3. Where the advertisement represents that the endorser uses a product, he or she must actually be a bona fide user of the product. Further, such endorsement may be used only as long as the advertiser has good reason to believe the endorser continues to be a bona fide user of the product.
4. Endorsements that reflect the experience of an individual consumer will be interpreted as representing the typical performance of the product under similar circumstances. If the represented performance is atypical, the advertisement must disclose what typically would be in the depicted circumstances.

(312) 564 7000 Telex 72 4498

One JS&A Plaza, Northbrook, Illinois 60062

We're late in sending you Mr. Sugarman's Success Forces book that you recently ordered.

Although we expect to ship the book to you within the next thirty days, we want you to know that you can always cancel your order if you wish.

If you prefer to cancel your order, simply call our toll-free number, (800) 323-6400, or return the Release of Order Form below to us in the self-addressed, postage-free envelope enclosed.

Again, our sincere apologies for being late, but be assured that we are concerned about your order and are doing everything we can to expedite its shipment.

Sincerely,

JS&A Group, Inc.

Mary Stank

P.S. If you placed the order using your credit card, the credit card will not be charged until such time that the book is shipped.

RELEASE OF ORDER

Please cancel my order for the Success Forces book and return my money.

Name   _____
          (signature)
Address   _____

City   _____   State   Zip _____

Date   _____

Figure 3.1   JS&A explaining delayed delivery.

5. Advertisements that represent endorsements of "actual consumers" must use actual consumers or disclose that the persons appearing in the advertisement are professional actors appearing for compensation.

6. Endorsements concerning the effectiveness of drug products shall not be made by laypersons.

7. When there is a connection between the endorser and the seller that might materially affect the weight or credibility of the endorsement, such connection must be fully disclosed.

These rules are frequently enforced by the FTC. Gordon Cooper, the former astronaut, was named in an FTC settlement involving ads for an automotive valve. The FTC said that Cooper represented himself as an automotive engineering expert when he endorsed the valve, when in fact he didn't have such experience, and that he failed to disclose the fact that he had a financial interest in the product's sales. Pat Boone was similarly charged by the FTC when he endorsed a product called Acne-Statin, and he had to pay $5,000 toward a $200,000 refund pool.

When people like Sugarman, Cooper, and Boone can get in trouble with the FTC, you know that folks like you and me must be careful.

Figure 3.2 shows an endorsement that former radio and television personality Art Linkletter made for the National Home Life Assurance Company. Note that Linkletter signed his endorsement letter as "Member of the Board of Directors with a financial interest in the Company." In this way, both he and the company avoided running afoul of the FTC.

Shortly after publication of the first edition of *Building a Mail Order Business* I received a call from a reader who had read this chapter and was concerned with what he had read. "You mean all those testimonials must be real?" he asked. "I thought people just made them up . . . and that's what I've been doing in advertising my product for the last six months." I assured him that testimonials must be "real," and I recommended that he cease his advertising at once. The government takes a very dim view of such fraudulent advertising. And the truth is, if your product or service has value it is not difficult to obtain actual and honest testimonials boosting your product, which you can legally use in your advertising. I will explain fully how to obtain these testimonials in Chapter 11.

DRY TESTING

Dry testing is extremely important in mail order because it allows the marketer to start promoting a product by mail before the product has been manufactured or stocked as inventory. This is a tremendous advantage because you, as a mail order seller, need not invest money in the product until

Figure 3.2 Art Linkletter's endorsement for National Home Life Assurance Company.

you are certain that the demand exists and that the size of the response of the solicitation is sufficient to be profitable. Dry testing is still legal in mail order. However, the FTC has issued an opinion—so far, it is an *advisory* opinion—in which it allows dry testing under strict guidelines to ensure that the potential customer is in no way misled about the terms of the offer. This opinion involved a promotion of a continuity book series by mail order and is the only opinion on the subject issued by the FTC known to the author at the time of this writing.

Specifically, the FTC stated that it did not object to the use of dry testing the continuity book series marketed by mail order as long as the following conditions were observed:

1. No representation expressed or implied could be made in promotional material that would mislead the public into believing that the books were or would definitely be published, or that by expressing

an interest in receiving a book, a prospective purchaser would necessarily receive them.

2. Clear and conspicuous disclosures would be made of the terms and conditions of the publications, distribution, and other material aspects of the continuity book series program, including the fact that the book series was only planned and might not actually be published.

3. If the decision were made not to publish the book series, notice was to be given to persons who subscribed within a reasonable time after the date of first mailing the solicitation for subscriptions. Four months or less was suggested as reasonable, "unless extenuating circumstances existed." If the decision to publish the book series were not made within that time, persons who expressed a desire to subscribe should be notified of this fact and should be given an opportunity to cancel their orders.

4. There were to be no substitutions of any other books for those that were ordered.

This opinion refers to a continuity book series only, and the FTC's position could be changed or modified at any time. Therefore, while dry testing is still legal and is in general a wise decision from an economic standpoint, the legal aspects of any dry testing should be investigated thoroughly with a lawyer before proceeding. Also, if you do dry test you should keep in mind the 30-day rule mentioned previously. You must have a reasonable basis for assuming you can meet the date you state in your advertisement or 30 days after the receipt of an order from your customer.

STATE TAXATION

Interstate Taxation

There are two types of state taxation with which you may be concerned—use tax and sales tax. Basically, use tax is paid when your place of business is located in the state whose tax you're paying. Sales tax is generally paid by the buyer on purchases made within the state levying the tax. The problem is that each of the 50 states has a different concept of what "place of business" means. As a result, the states are trying to impose some sort of taxation on direct marketers, whether or not the place of business is located in that state. This can lead to some real problems for the mail order operator who is dealing or selling goods by mail in a state that insists on controlling a direct marketer's business and taxing it, even though he or she may not be located in that state. Many larger mail order firms have fallen into line and are collecting these taxes for the various states. Various bills have been introduced into Congress that would prohibit the states from requiring smaller firms, or in some cases, all firms from having to do this. There have also been efforts to go the other way and make every mail order operator collect tax for all 50 states.

Meanwhile, the situation is confused. The *Direct Marketing Manual*, which is published by the Direct Marketing Association and covers a wide number of mail order and direct marketing issues including ethical, legal, and regulatory subjects, recommends the following:

> All states are now trying to impose jurisdictional nexus over direct mail marketers. If the states cannot prevent out-of-state sales, then they will protect local merchants and revenues by imposing the collection liability on direct mailers. Limiting your contact with a state to common carrier or the United States mail will help to relieve you of this obligation.

So, as of this writing there is no definitive answer to whether you must do this or not.

LOTTERIES AND GAMBLING

According to postal regulations, lotteries are synonymous with gambling and are forbidden through the mail. You should be especially aware of this in dealing in direct marketing as the use of a sweepstakes, which is a legal technique that will add greatly to your response to an offer with which it is linked, may be termed a lottery if not handled correctly. According to U.S. Postal Service regulations, a sweepstakes is legally considered a lottery if it contains the elements of prize, chance, and consideration. If any one of these elements is not present, a lottery does not exist. The usual and legal way of getting around this in promotional sweepstakes in mail order is to omit the element of consideration, making the sweepstakes technique legal. What do we mean by "consideration"? Consideration means that anyone may enter the sweepstakes, regardless of whether he or she orders the product, service, or item being promoted in conjunction with the sweepstakes. Therefore, there is no charge of any kind for entering the sweepstakes.

However, if you do intend to run a sweepstakes to promote a product or service, you should be aware that some states have laws concerning sweepstakes, which may range from outright prohibition to having to post a bond to guarantee that the prize does, in fact, exist. Therefore, if you intend to run a nationwide sweepstakes, you should definitely consult your attorney and a consultant specializing in sweepstakes promotions. You should also obtain a copy of the book, *Planning for Chance Promotionals*, by Frank T. Dierson, who is general counsel for the Promotion Marketing

Association of America. The book is published by the Promotion Marketing Association of America, Inc., 257 Park Avenue S., 11th Floor, New York, NY 10001.

PORNOGRAPHY

Pornography is a confused area at best, because very few people can agree on what's obscene and pornographic, and the definition has varied so much over the years that people have gone to jail for selling what is very common today. I do not recommend dealing in this area. It is a case, again, of having to look in the mirror every morning when you get up and every evening when you go to bed. However, if you do intend to deal in some fashion with a product or service that may, by even the most remote definition, be considered pornographic or obscene, my advice is to see a competent attorney before you do so.

CHAIN LETTERS

A chain letter is a variation on a theme that has existed for perhaps a hundred years or more, in which you are invited to make money in the same way as the promoter. Usually there is a list of names and you put your name at the bottom of the list. When your name reaches the top of the list, according to the promotion, you will be wealthy. One current variation is for you to sell a money-making plan that is sold to you as you join the chain and that, according to the promotional letter, makes the promotion legal. However, this is not true. Chain letters are always illegal, and if you are caught dealing in one, you will not only probably lose your money but also be liable for prosecution. A typical chain letter is shown in Figure 3.3. Remember, this scheme is illegal and definitely *not* recommended by the author or any other reputable consultant or writer in mail order. Also, the only person that makes money in these schemes is the person that starts them. Contrary to the claims, those that join up and add their names simply join a list of folks that lose their money. Don't do it!!!

DRUGS

Drugs fall into a special category because they are administered by the Food and Drug Administration (FDA). Be careful of new drugs that are not standard and accepted medical remedies. You cannot sell new drugs that fall into this category without special permission from the FDA. Naturally, this permission is not granted overnight or without extensive testing. Therefore, even if you have discovered a miracle drug that you

COULD YOU FIGHT INFLATION
IF YOU HAD ½ MILLION DOLLARS
(OR MORE) WITHIN 60-90 DAYS ?

Dear Inflation Fighter,

How many times have most of us said, "If only I had the money to buy that piece of property...that business..that gold...that stock...etc.,I would be financially independent by now."

To be financially independent is to be free; free to make the financial choices that really matter in our lives: "Shall I go into business or buy that investment or take that trip?" We no longer have to think in terms of "If only..."

Yet very few of us reach financial independence because either the opportunities never come along or, worse yet, when they do come along, we simply ignore them.

You can make $500,000 or more by following our simple marketing program. It's perfectly legal, affordable, practical, and, what really matters, IT WORKS!

The saying "He who hesitates is lost" has never been more applicable. Don't be so busy SEEKING an opportunity to let this one slip by!

The way it all works is as follows: You purchase a $5 report entitled "How to Fight Inflation," and then, in a very short period of time, you will be selling this report to thousands of others at $5 per copy. (The report you purchase can be duplicated for about 3¢ per copy!) Remember, only 5% (One out of twenty people) need to participate and you will reach your ½ million dollar goal.

Do not confuse this multi-level marketing program with the run-of-the-mill "Pie in the Sky" chain letter. We offer a product for every dollar that will be exchanged. This program conforms to all current postal regulations and is perfectly legal.

In fact, multi-level marketing has been around for a long time and has been used from time to time (quite successfully by the way) by major American companies. This marketing technique was examined by Dan Rather of "60 Minutes" and was found to be a tremendous success!

Figure 3.3 Chain letters.

personally know will cure what you claim it will, you cannot advertise it without permission from the FDA. Furthermore, you should expect to spend a great deal of money proving the truth of your claim.

USE OF FICTITIOUS NAMES

In the last chapter we discussed some of the aspects of obtaining proper fictitious name registration. As I said then, it is illegal to use words that imply you are something you are not. You cannot use words such as *university, institute,* and *bureau,* which suggest non-profit organizations of various types, if, in fact, you are not. Do not use words such as *laboratory* or *manufacturing company* if, in fact, you are not a laboratory or do no manufacturing. Remember that there are two different laws that come into play here. One is the law requiring a fictitious name registration for any name other than your own that you use for your business. The other law prohibits attempting to deceive the public by using a name that misrepresents the business functions in which you are actually engaged.

Then,

using your home or office typewriter, neatly retype the list of Advertisers below on plain white paper. Eliminate the person in the #1 position to whom you have just sent $5. Then, simply add YOUR NAME and ADDRESS to the bottom of the list in the #5 position. With scissors or razor blade, cut out your revised Advertisers' list and paste it into the Advertisers Section.

Now you are ready to take the letter to an offset printer (listed in the Yellow Pages); tell him to run off 200 copies (or more if you wish). Do not make any other changes of this letter as you may harm its "pulling power."

You then send out 200 (or more) copies of this revised letter to friends, relatives, smart business people in your local telephone directory or you can order names of opportunity seekers and small businesses from name brokers.

We recommend that if you purchase a name list that you use one of the following because of their up-to-date lists, quick service and low price. Ask for "opportunity seekers and small business buyers." Send cash or money orders (personal checks will delay your order two weeks). They have new names each week that really pull.

Or look in the yellow pages of your phone book under list brokers.

EXAMPLE: (FOR ONLY A 5% PARTICIPATION)

	You send 200 copies with your name in the #5 position - 5% respond =	10
Those	10 people send 200 copies with your name in the #4 position - 5% respond =	100
Those	100 people send 200 copies with your name in the #3 position - 5% respond =	1,000
Those	1,000 people send 200 copies with your name in the #2 position - 5% respond =	10,000
Those	10,000 people send 200 copies with your name in the #1 position - 5% respond =	100,000

At $5 Each and at Only a 5% Participation You Would Receive $500,000.

Your name simply moves up the list and multiplies as it reaches the #1 position. As you can see from the example . . . up to 100,000 people (or more) could be sending you $5 for your copies of the report or up to $500,000 in cash. Not at all shabby for a minimal investment.

Financial success is not reserved for just a few "smart" people. Take a look around your neighborhood; you'll see a lot of people who are less intelligent than you are. . . who don't work any harder than you do . . . but . . . for some reason, they are earning a lot more money. These people look for opportunity, and when the right one comes along, they act on it! Here's your opportunity to help assure your well being, and that of your family's. This offer will not be repeated; therefore, I urge that you take action, today!

Sincerely,

Your #5 Advertiser

ADVERTISERS

(b)

Figure 3.3   (Continued)

FRAUD

Fraud means taking money from your customer under false pretenses. Unfortunately, mail order rip-off artists have been doing this almost since mail order began. Julian L. Simon, in his excellent book, *How to Start and Operate a Mail Order Business,* has collected a number of old time mail order frauds from various sources. Here are a few from Julian's book:

1. An ad offering a steel engraving of George Washington for 50¢. The copy beneath the headline described the excellence of the

engraving, the beautiful, deep, rich color used, and the fact that the paper was deckled on all four edges. For 50¢ the buyer received a 2¢ postage stamp.

2. A patented potato bug killer for $1. The buyer was to receive sufficient equipment to kill all the potato bugs in a 10-acre field. For $1 the buyer received two slabs of wood, which were sent with instructions telling the purchaser exactly how to pick the bugs off the vines, lay them between the slabs, and press one slab firmly down on the other.

3. *"$3.95 for This Five-Piece Wicker Set"* was a headline for an illustration showing a handsome, sturdy table, settee, two straight-back wicker chairs, and a rocker. The copy included a guarantee that the set would be exactly like the illustration. When the set arrived, it *was* exactly like the illustration—not only in appearance, but also in size.

Modern frauds are just as vicious in taking an unsuspecting mail order buyer. One example is envelope stuffing with various variations. An advertisement reads, "Learn to stuff envelopes, work at home, make a thousand dollars a month. Free details." The potential customer receives a more detailed promotional asking for $15 to $35. For the money, one buyer received 200 brochures that promoted envelope-stuffing schemes, a chain-letter type of scheme. Sometimes the buyer receives a few pages encouraging him or her to enter the mail order business.

Another modern fraud is that of unclaimed merchandise. You receive a letter in which the writer claims to represent the Bureau of Unclaimed Merchandise. In this form letter you are told that, by filling out an enclosed card and remitting, say, $10, you will be shipped Parcel No. 740, which is awaiting claim. In return for your money you receive nothing.

One firm with which we are familiar sells phony job recommendations for any position you wish in a variety of dummy companies it has established across the United States and on Pacific islands. For a fixed sum you can obtain a letter of recommendation certifying that you performed outstanding work as an engineer, technician, technical writer, or whatever, and a statement indicating that the dummy company would be happy to hire you if you chose to return to their employ.

Another currently practiced deception that I believe is on the borderline of legality is catalogs or sales leaflets that are imprinted with your name and address. The promotional materials are described as ready to mail, and you are advised that you need not carry any inventory or stock of products as all items are stocked by the company selling you the catalogs. They offer to drop-ship direct to the customer for you and you keep somewhere between 40 and 50 percent of the revenue.

For many new mail order dealers this may appear to be a great way to get into the mail order business, primarily because catalogs are so expensive to develop on your own and because of the attraction of not having to carry any inventory. Sometimes these companies will even offer to sell you names of mail order buyers. I have myself received multiple, identical catalogs, all under different dealers' names. In fact, you can make little money with a deal like this unless you can mail these catalogs along with an item you are already successfully selling. What many of these companies are really selling to you is the printing, not the proposed service of catalog development and drop-shipping the merchandise. Although these schemes are undoubtedly a form of fraud, they have not yet been stopped by the authorities. But they have cost thousands of would-be mail order entrepreneurs money. I mention these here not only because you should avoid operating such a scheme yourself, but also so you can avoid investing your money in one.

E. J. Kahn, Jr., in his book *Fraud,* indicates that a list drawn up by the U.S. Postal Service included such fraud mail order schemes as "advanced fees, check kiting, unordered COD parcels, falsified contest entries, phony coupon redemption plans, credit card frauds, delinquent debtors schemes, fictitious classified directories, endless chain referral selling plans, alleged business opportunities, chain letters, missing heir swindles, false financial statements, numbers rackets and lucky charms, home improvement frauds, investments, supposed job opportunities, mortgage loan and debt consolidation schemes, phony manuscript and song publishing companies, matrimonial swindles, numismatic and philatelic swindles, real estate (improved and unimproved), shady correspondence schools and diploma mills, fake charity solicitations and dubious work-at-home schemes."

The penalties for wrongdoing can be severe and are mainly in the hands of the U.S. Postal Service or the Federal Trade Commission.

You may not know it, but the Postal Inspection Service Division of the U.S. Postal Service is the oldest law enforcement agency in the country. It is incredibly effective: On a yearly basis, 98 percent of the criminal cases it brings to trial result in conviction, compared with an average for the FBI of about 96 percent. Not bad, you might say! What can the Postal Service do? The Postal Service can arrest you, it can put you out of business, and it can apply stamps to your mail that read "Fraudulent," "Refused," and "Out of Business" and return them to your customer. If you weren't out of business before the stamps were applied, you certainly would be thereafter.

The Federal Trade Commission is not without teeth either. The FTC may give you a chance to state your case and appeal it, but after that it can order you to cease what it considers to be an illegal practice and can stick you with walloping fines.

Other government agencies such as the Food and Drug Administration can also have at you if you violate government regulations. They can also stop you, fine you, or send you to jail. Lest you think only the "feds" can do you in should you decide to take the wrong route in mail order, you should know that most states have state fraud commissions with various powers that sometimes exceed those of the federal agencies to punish you for your wrongdoing.

Also, some states have imposed their own rules which may be more restrictive than the federal government. It never hurts to check what is going on in your state.

In judging whether a contemplated mail order promotion is legal or illegal, consider the following:

1. Be honest with yourself. Are you trying to deceive or cheat a potential customer in some way? If you are, don't do it. When looking at yourself in the mirror, if you get a bad feeling, don't do it.
2. Consult the U.S. Postal Service and ask whether in that office's opinion the project you are thinking about will be illegal.
3. Consult the FTC and get an opinion as to whether a contemplated promotion is legal.
4. Consult the Better Business Bureau in your area and ask whether there have been complaints about similar operations.
5. Finally, you can and should consult an attorney in any questionable situation.

FIVE GUIDELINES TO AVOIDING LEGAL PROBLEMS

Here are five things you should do to minimize running afoul of mail order law.

1. If you're going to be late, give the buyer the choice of having his or her money refunded, and let him or her know about the delay as soon as you do.
2. Always give your customer maximum value for his or her money. While it is true that the price usually must be three to four times your cost for you to make any money selling through the mail, the value received should be perceived to be worth the price paid for any merchandise or service. Mail order expert Hubert K. Simon, author of *Out of the Rate Race and into the Chips,* recommends always giving your customers an additional and unexpected value when you fulfill their orders.
3. Do not try to cheat your customer. If you do, your business will not succeed in the long run, even if you escape fines or imprisonment.

4. Don't lie in advertising. The same result will occur as above, even if you aren't found guilty of some legal fault. Your credibility will suffer, and because mail order is a back-end business with much of your profits made with subsequent sales, your business will ultimately fail. Even if all your profits are up front in your first sale, if your advertising is untruthful, your project will fail because of returned products.

5. Finally, if you have any questions pertaining to legal issues, pay the money and consult an attorney. It will save you money in the long run.

As a consultant, I am frequently asked, "Why, if such and such is true and the FTC opposes it and the Postal Service can send you to jail, has such-and-such advertiser been using the same apparently fraudulent promotions for over a year?" I cannot honestly answer this question. I suppose some people have always gotten away with murder and will continue to do so. Some unscrupulous individuals always operate on the borderline of what is legal and what is not. They know from experience exactly what they can and cannot do. Maybe their firms are large enough to pay the legal fees or fines if they are perceived to have stepped over the line into illegality. You are not in this position. Further, you don't know that the individual's case has not been under study for some time and perhaps soon the individual will be arrested, tried, and fined or sent to jail. Therefore, even if you see a scheme that obviously violates the laws of the land but the individual is apparently getting away with it—*don't do it!*

The following books may be useful as references in deciding whether your anticipated promotion is legal and for other aspects of legalities of mail order and direct mail marketing.

The Law of Advertising, in two volumes, by George Rosden and Peter Rosden. Matthew Bender, 235 East 45th Street, New York, NY 10017.

Planning for Chance Promotions, by Frank T. Dierson. Promotion Marketing Association of America, Inc., 257 Park Avenue S., New York, NY 10001.

Postal Laws Transmittal Letter No. 24, December 12, 1974. Available from the Superintendent of Documents, U.S. Government Printing Office, Washington, DC 20042.

The Law and Direct Marketing. Publication Division of the Direct Mail Association, 6 East 43rd Street, New York, NY 10017.

Law for Advertising and Marketing, by Morton J. Simon. Norton, New York, NY 10017.

Mail Fraud, by the U.S. Chief Postal Inspector. U.S. Government Printing Office, Washington, DC 20042.

Do's and Don'ts in Advertising Copy, by the Council of Better Business Bureaus, 11507 17th Street NW, Washington, DC 20036.

A Primer on the Law of Deceptive Practices, by Earl W. Kintner. Macmillan, 866 Third Avenue, New York, NY 10022.

The Direct Marketer's Legal Advisor, by Robert J. Posch. McGraw-Hill, 1221 Avenue of the Americas, New York, NY 10020.

Direct Marketing and the Law, by Arthur Winston. John Wiley, 605 Third Avenue, New York, NY 10158-0012.

SUMMARY

In this chapter we have covered the legal problems you may encounter as a mail order operator and some basic ethics of the profession.

1. Never offer anything in an advertisement in which the promotion is not clear and honest.
2. Be careful of deceptive pricing.
3. Obey the 30-day rule for delivery of mail order merchandise.
4. Remember the rules of endorsements and testimonials, that they must be real, and how they should be used.
5. Dry testing is still legal with limitations but be aware of changes that might take place at any time.
6. Under certain circumstances you must pay state taxes.
7. Lotteries and gambling are the same. They are illegal. Sweepstakes are legal as a promotional technique when used properly.
8. In general, stay away from pornography and obscene literature.
9. Chain letters are always illegal.
10. Drugs are watched over by the Food and Drug Administration. Do not get involved in selling drugs without being aware of the FDA's regulations and without FDA approval.
11. Be careful of using fictitious names that are not representative of your actual business.
12. Beware of fraud. Don't be deceived yourself, and don't engage in deception under any circumstances.

Finally, we reviewed the penalties for wrongdoing, general guidelines as to what you should and should not do, and the fact that you should never assume that something is legal simply because some other mail order operator is doing it now.

4

Maintaining Your Management Records

Good management and accurate record keeping are an essential, but unglamorous, part of your mail order business. Why are management and record keeping essential? First, there's maintenance of a positive cash flow, which requires them over the long run. The basis of mail order is testing. But testing can be done accurately only if you keep good records. Throughout your business career you will be making various decisions based on what you must do to earn a profit. These decisions are also influenced by the records you keep. Finally, you will need to keep good records for tax purposes. Not only must you pay taxes, but to know what deductions you are eligible for and to take every deduction you can legally take, you must keep good records—and that is true even if you use an accountant.

In this chapter, we're going to discuss six essential records and how to keep them. In addition, you will be shown sample copies of each of the necessary forms to keep these records. The six types of records we're going to discuss are the daily inquiry/order sheet, advertising response sheet, customer card file, inventory status sheet, weekly expense record, and weekly expenses by category.

1. DAILY INQUIRY/ORDER SHEET

A daily inquiry/order sheet is shown in Figure 4.1. It is used as a running log to keep a record of people and customers who send inquiries to you if you are using the two-step method of selling, or inquire for other reasons, or have placed an order with you. This form can be used for a variety of purposes. It acts as a check to make sure that you fill every order placed

NAME	ADDRESS	AMOUNT	MEDIUM/KEY	INQUIRY REC/FILLED	ORDER REC/FILLED

Figure 4.1   Daily inquiry/order sheet.

and every inquiry that you receive. It also gives you a running account of how long it takes you to fill each order or answer each inquiry. It provides a check to make sure that, when your customers do order, the correct amount that is supposed to be enclosed is received and accounted for. And it can also be used to trace your orders and find out from what medium the customer order originated.

Now let's look at Figure 4.1. It's really quite simple and almost self-explanatory. In the first and second columns you put the customer's name and address at the time the order or inquiry arrives. The amount of money found in the envelope, if any, goes in the third column. The next column is for the medium key, used if the order or inquiry originates from a magazine, a direct mailing, or even a catalog. In the fifth column you write the date the inquiry was received and also the date that you sent literature in response to this inquiry, if applicable. Now, this is how the form is used for a two-step. For the final column, order received/filled, if it's a two-step, you wait until the order is received and go back and use the same line that you started earlier. The order received/filled column is also used if no inquiry was received, but the order was received direct. It takes just a few minutes to fill out the inquiry/order sheet every day, but these few minutes can be worth a lot of money to you as you do a profitability or media effectiveness analysis later on.

2. ADVERTISING RESPONSE SHEET

The advertising response sheet is shown in Figure 4.2. It allows you to analyze every single advertisement or promotion you do, including a classified ad, a display advertisement, television, radio, or even a direct mailing. It also acts as a sort of "how goes it" sheet, inasmuch as you can compare and project responses on a continuing basis, as well as profit or loss.

WHICH ADVERTISEMENT? _____   COST OF ADVERTISEMENT _____   PROFIT _____
MEDIUM _____   KEY _____
DATE ADVERTISEMENT APPEARED _____   DATE FIRST RESPONSE RECEIVED _____
(DATE OF MAILING FOR D.M.)

DAY	RESPONSE	CUMULATIVE RESPONSE	PROJECTED RESPONSE	PROJECTED RETURN (D.M.)	PROFIT (LOSS)
1					
2					
3					
4					
5					
6					
7					
8					
9					
10					
11					
12					
13					
14					
15					
16					
17					
18					
19					
20					
21					
22					
23					
24					
25					
26					
27					
28					
29					
30					
31					

Figure 4.2   Advertising response sheet.

71

The advertising response sheet starts with a description of the advertisement and the product the sheet is analyzing. It's a good idea to cut out a copy of the advertisement and put it on the opposite side of the sheet. Then there'll be no doubt as to which advertisement you're talking about. The medium is the magazine, radio station, television station, or list used to carry your promotion to your prospective customer. Below that is a statement that says, "Date advertisement appeared," or in parentheses, "Date of mailing for DM." "DM" stands for direct mail. In some cases you may not know the exact date that the magazine hit the street with your advertisement. In this case, you will have to use an approximate date. But you should know the exact date of a direct mailing and the date of radio or television appearances. The next column is headed Cost of Advertisement, and, of course, for a direct mailing you would list the cost of your mailing. Below that is a place for you to write the key that we discussed earlier to be used to identify this particular advertisement. Finally, below this is the date that the first response is received from the advertisement you're analyzing. In the far right is space for profit. This is the last figure that you write in at the end of the project, when you receive your final response. It's used later on so you can check the advertisement and compare it with others and its results.

In the lower portion of Figure 4.2, the first column is headed "Day" and is already filled in—Days 1 through 31. However, in actuality, you would continue to fill this out until the last response was received. The second column is Response. All you do here is go back to your daily inquiry sheet and look at the key. Match up the key for this particular advertisement and count the number of inquiries you received over the past week. Write this figure under Response. For the first day the cumulative response will be the same number as that in the Response column, but for the second day, you would add the responses you received in the second day to the cumulative response column, and so on. The next column is Projected Response. Here you use the projection methods given in Chapter 22, depending upon the type or medium of advertisement, to project the total response you'll receive. After you have been in the mail order business for awhile, you can develop your own formula for projecting response. For example, for a particular type of medium and a particular type of product, perhaps you've discovered that after day 1 you will receive 50 percent of your total responses. In that case, your total projected response, which goes in the Projected Response column, would be your response for the first seven days multiplied times two. So, if you receive 50 responses in seven days, your total projected response would be 100. The Projected Return column is next, and it is used only for direct mail. In this column, you list, depending upon what your cumulative response is to date, what the projected return is for the total project. You can use the formula that I give in Chapter 22 projecting response. However, as you become more experienced, you can work out your own formula for this as well, because your formula will differ, depending upon many factors, including your business, your customers, the business environment, and so forth. Let's say your response is 50 during the first seven days. If your formula indicates that first seven days' response for a direct mailing of this type would net 25 percent of the total, you would multiply the response you received during the first seven days by four, because 25 percent is one-fourth of the total: $50 \times 4 = 200$. You would then look at your total mailing to see what your projected return would be. If your total mailing in this case was 10,000, then 200 divided by 10,000 equals a 2 percent projected return. In the last column in Figure 4.2, you put your projected profit or loss, based on your responses so far. Let's take a look at that last example of a 2 percent projected return on our 10,000 mailing. According to the particular situation we might have and the profitability calculations shown in Chapter 22, let's say that 1 percent is breakeven and 2 percent is therefore profitable. List the amount of profit in dollars. On the other hand, let's say that our projected rate of return was only ½ percent and 1 percent was breakeven. Then there is a loss. Calculate this loss and write it in parentheses in the right-hand column.

You can see how valuable the advertising response sheet is in seeing the relative value of your different advertisements, and also in predicting success or failure fairly early on. You can also watch how the response situation changes on a continuing basis and later use this information to help in calculating what future projections would be for similar advertisements.

3. CUSTOMER CARD FILE

The customer card file is shown in Figure 4.3. It's a file card of convenient size, which you can buy at your local variety store. Each customer's file card contains the name and address of the customer, along with the date of first inquiry and the date of first order. Furthermore, as your customer places each order, you log the date, the items ordered, the prices, the total amount of the order, and in the remarks section on the card, anything else you think worth putting down. If the customer's check bounced, you definitely would want to log that. Or if the customer returned his or her merchandise, you would want to log that also. Why? If the customer's check bounced, you want to try to get paid for the product you shipped. On the other hand, if you don't get paid, you don't want to continue to ship merchandise to this customer against bad checks. If a customer returns merchandise once, okay, perhaps there's a reason. But if a customer returns your merchandise continually, then obviously the customer isn't someone you want to do business with. A review of the customer card file will inform you of either situation immediately as you log in the date and the

NAME _____   DATE OF FIRST INQUIRY _____

ADDRESS _____   DATE OF FIRST ORDER _____

CITY, STATE, ZIP _____

DATE	ITEMS ORDERED	PRICES	TOTAL ORDER	REMARKS

Figure 4.3   Customer file card.

item ordered. Now you may wonder why you list all the items ordered and the prices. As you continue with your business, certain products will be better to encourage customers to place a first order. Other products will be better to encourage larger orders over a period of time from your customer. Remembering that mail order is a back-order business, perhaps you wish to offer a special on these items to attract long-term customers for this very reason. Further, by a review of your customer card file from time to time, you will notice that after a certain period some customers no longer order at all. This is important information because you want to know what the life of your customer is, and if you're mailing catalogs, fliers, and so forth, you want to know when to stop so as not to waste money. After awhile you will be able to calculate an average life of your customer by reviewing your customer card files. Again, each customer card file takes but a minute or so to prepare, but can be very valuable to you for the future of your mail order business.

4. INVENTORY STATUS SHEET

The inventory status sheet is shown in Figure 4.4. With a valuable inventory, you will want to know what its status is at all times. You will also want to know when you need it, how much you need, from whom you ordered it, and so forth. All this information and more is contained on the inventory status sheet.

The first item is the inventory description—what exactly the product or material is that you have listed here. The inventory number is your own number that you've assigned to this particular product. The location is where you store this item, whether it is in your plant or someone else's. The lead time is how long it takes to get the item to the customer. Remember

INVENTORY DESCRIPTION_____	RATE OF USAGE_____
INVENTORY NUMBER_____	UNIT MEASURE_____
LOCATION_____	UNIT PRICE_____
LEAD TIME_____	REORDER QUANTITY_____

SOURCES	(NAME OF FIRM)	(ADDRESS)	(CONTACT)	(TEL #)
	(NAME OF FIRM)	(ADDRESS)	(CONTACT)	(TEL #)
	(NAME OF FIRM)	(ADDRESS)	(CONTACT)	(TEL #)
	(NAME OF FIRM)	(ADDRESS)	(CONTACT)	(TEL #)

				ON ORDER			PLANNED ALLOCATION
DATE	IN STOCK	ADD. NEEDED	P.O. #	QNTY.	DATE REC'D	QNTY. REC'D	(Project, Quantity, and Date Req'd)

Figure 4.4   Inventory status sheet.

that there is a certain amount of lead time associated with every product you order. The rate of usage in Figure 4.4 is an estimate and, of course, is approximate and may change. Unit measure is how the product is ordered—by boxes, pounds, ounces, or whatever. The unit price is also a changeable quantity and you should keep it updated. It is used to allow you to make estimates for planning. The reorder quantity is used if you have calculated an optimum number for reorder over a period of time, as discussed in the section on fulfillment.

The next item on the inventory status sheet is a list of sources, including the name of the firm, the address, and the contact—the name of the person you deal with and his or her telephone number. This allows you to get in touch with these people in a hurry.

The last part of the inventory status sheet starts out with Date, and refers to the date you placed an order. The next column is In Stock—how many of the items are in stock right now. Add. Needed means additional items needed. The next section is headed On Order, and under On Order are four different columns: P.O. Number, which refers to the purchase order; Quantity; Date Received; and Quantity Received. The purchase order number is the number you have used to order this material or product. The quantity is the quantity ordered. The date received is when you get an order. The quantity received is necessary because you won't always get everything you order at one time. Finally, the last column is headed Planned Allocation, and this means what you plan on doing with the inventory recorded under In Stock and Add. Needed. Probably it is for a project or promotional, so you record the quantity needed and the date by which you need it.

Use of the inventory status sheet will allow you to monitor the inventory you need and ensure that it arrives promptly so that you can fulfill the order, not get in trouble with the FTC, and maintain the good will of your customers.

5. WEEKLY RECORD OF EXPENSES

The weekly record of expenses is shown in Figure 4.5. It is a running record, and every week you should use a new form to keep track of what you buy. The first item is the date. The next, to whom you paid the amount. The third is the item or service you purchased, and the fourth, the check number. (Under the check number, if you pay in cash or by credit card or by some other means, you would note that information here. Otherwise, you note the number of the check you used.) Finally, the last column is the amount of the expense in dollars.

Sometimes, when you open your checking account, your bank will give you a form that will have this information on it. The problem is that it will be difficult to use the bank's form because it also involves the remaining amount you have available in the bank. This means you cannot use the form for this purpose unless you always pay by check and never by cash or through charge. Therefore, for most situations, you should not only keep a record in your checkbook of how much is remaining in your checking account, but make use of this weekly record of expenses.

6. WEEKLY EXPENDITURES BY CATEGORY

The weekly expenditures by category sheet, shown in Figure 4.6, is used in conjunction with the previous sheet. This sheet is most important for figuring out your income tax at the end of the year. Even if you do not do it yourself, but use an accountant, you will save much money and much grief by maintaining this simple log on a weekly basis. What you do is this. At the end of every week, you look at Figure 4.5 and record the expenditures you have made and put them under the appropriate columns, as listed in Figure 4.6. For example, advertising expenditures done during the week in several different newspapers would be totaled and placed under the first column. If you bought a fixed asset—let's say, a new typewriter—this would be logged on 4.5 along with the date, to whom you paid, the check number, and the amount. At the end of the week you would add this fixed asset with any other fixed assets you bought that week and list the total in

DATE	TO WHOM PAID	ITEM OR SERVICES PURCHASED	CHECK NUMBER	AMOUNT

Figure 4.5   Weekly record of expenses.

DEDUCTIBLE EXPENSES	TOTAL THIS WEEK	TOTAL PRIOR	TOTAL TO DATE
Advertising			
Bank charges			
Car and truck expenses			
Commissions			
Dues and publications			
Freight			
Insurance			
Interest of business indebtedness			
Inventory			
Laundry and cleaning			
Legal and professional services			
Office supplies			
Pension and profit-sharing plans			
Postage			
Rent on business property			
Repairs			
Supplies			
Taxes			
Telephone			
Travel and entertainment			
Utilities			
Wages			

NONDEDUCTIBLE EXPENSES			
Federal income tax			
Fixed assets			

Figure 4.6   Weekly expenditures by category.

the nondeductible expenses section of 4.6. The next column is Total Prior, and this means for all the previous weeks of that year. You add the Total Prior column with the Total This Week to result in the Total to Date. The Total to Date is also used on your income tax forms to get the correct amount for your deductions. Note that other spaces are left so that you can log other deductible or nondeductible expenses not listed on the form.

SUMMARY

In this short chapter, we've discussed the essential forms and how to use them to enable you to run a profitable and well-managed mail order business. These forms will also enable you to make accurate calculations and projections that will add greatly to your potential for profitability. This system can be used until you become big enough to have a completely or partially computerized operation.

5

Bringing Your Product to the Customer

FULFILLMENT: WHAT IT IS AND WHY IT'S IMPORTANT

Fulfillment means carrying out your part of the bargain with your customer. You've received money from your customer; now you must furnish the product or service in return. Fulfillment is important because without good fulfillment operations you will not have a satisfied customer. In mail order, a satisfied customer is crucial because a satisfied customer is a repeat customer, and repeat means back-end profits and a profitable mail order business.

Let me give you an example of how poor fulfillment can ruin an otherwise good mail order operation. Some time ago I received a unique catalog of special tools that I could not purchase at the hardware store. One of the offerings was a set of three dental picks, which have a number of different applications for a hobbyist. Because I had never dealt with this company before, I placed a single order for less than $10 for a set of the dental tools advertised in their catalog. A month went by and I heard nothing. But I did get my canceled check back. I sent a letter to the company with a copy of the original canceled check, asking what had happened to the merchandise I had ordered. Again I waited several weeks but heard and received nothing. Finally, I called the company on the telephone. The office manager answered and I explained the problem. While this individual was apologetic, she disclaimed responsibility, saying there were just too many orders coming in and if a mistake was made it was almost impossible to fix unless someone called by telephone—that complaint letters were routinely not answered. While the matter at hand was settled and I got my merchandise and money for the telephone call, I knew that if this company continued to maintain its fulfillment policy, it wouldn't have to worry about so many orders in the future because it would be out of business. As you might imagine, I never placed another order with this company—although their expensive and colorful catalog was sometimes mailed to my address, and I saw items I would be interested in buying.

Fulfillment is especially important because the more successful you become, the more important good fulfillment practice becomes to sustain your success. Sloppy fulfillment will soon terminate any initial success that you might have.

When you first get into the mail order business, fulfillment isn't too difficult because the relatively small number of orders you receive is easily handled. Also, there is an alternative to carrying a heavy product inventory. This is the drop-ship method by which another firm will agree to stock the product and send it directly to your customer for you. Once you receive the order and money, you merely send the percentage of the sales prices agreed upon beforehand to the company that has agreed to drop-ship, usually the manufacturer. This firm then fulfills the order to your customer. Of course, it is very expensive for a manufacturer to fill orders one by one and you can expect to pay much more than if you had ordered a quantity of the product for you to fulfill on your own. There are other drawbacks to the drop-ship method, some of which I've discussed previously. If you decide to do your fulfillment by drop-shipping, you should try to get an exclusive, so that only you have the right to sell this product by mail. Or you should use a drop-ship product to fill out your own line of products, because if you depend upon a single product or several over which you have no control because of drop-shipment, others will soon be able to copy your success. If they have greater financial resources, they will even be able to shut you completely out of the marketplace for a product you may have been the first to promote successfully.

Once you begin your own fulfillment, you must keep a watchful eye on your overhead. Do not hire additional people or rent buildings that do not contribute immediately to your mail order profits. As a matter of fact, I would look first at hiring individuals part-time rather than full-time, and use as many members of the family as you can to help you out. High school students represent a good source of part-time labor. Be sure you aren't violating any local laws if you do hire people part-time, however. Also, instead of large stocks of inventory in a separate rented building or warehouse facility, you should store as much inventory as you can in your home or garage and perhaps do your fulfillment operations on a workbench or on your kitchen table. Anything you can do to keep your expenses down at this early growth stage is good. Anything that costs money you need not spend is bad.

However, at some point in your mail order career, the money is going to start rolling in, and then you're going to have to get more sophisticated if you are going to maintain your success. You will have outgrown the garage and the kitchen table, and part-time labor will no longer fill the bill. Now you should look at each step of fulfillment and ensure that you are doing it in the most efficient manner possible, at the same time taking care that each time you fulfill an order you have a satisfied customer on the other end of the line.

THE FULFILLMENT STEPS

Here are the fulfillment steps necessary to maintain your hard-won success.

1. Estimating required inventory before mailing.
2. Adjusting your required inventory after initial response.
3. Ordering.
4. Receiving.
5. Warehousing.
6. Mail opening, reading, and sorting.
7. Responding.
8. Location controlling.
9. Inventory withdrawing.
10. Packing.
11. Metering and shipping.

Estimating Required Inventory before Mailing

To estimate your inventory before mailing, you must know how many units will be sold in the first part of your campaign. If you have sold a similar product in the past, you can develop an estimate based on the relationship between the amount of your advertising and results achieved in the past. Let's assume that you have sold software for a computer, and now you are selling a newer version of that program. If you spent $10,000 in the first advertising campaign and sold 5,000 copies, you know that it cost $10,000 divided by 5,000, or $2, to sell each copy. If the initial stages of your new campaign call for $5,000 for advertising, you might estimate that you would sell 5,000 divided by $2, or 2,500 units, in the initial stage of this campaign.

This method works fine for those items on which you have previous results. However, if you are selling an item for the first time, you will have to use your best judgment to arrive at the number of units you should carry in initial inventory. Study the efforts of your competitors. Usually you can get some idea about demand from the amount of their advertising and whether their advertisements are repeated. If they are, chances are demand is great, and you can estimate toward the high side. On the other hand, if your competitors are not advertising in every medium available and not advertising every single month, chances are demand is not that great, and your initial estimate of sales should be just slightly above breakeven.

Adjusting Your Required Inventory after Initial Response

This is an important step because you now have some reasonably accurate data to go on. Use the forecasting methods outlined in Chapters 10, 11, 12, and 21 to estimate what the total response from a particular ad or direct mailing will be. You should continue to monitor your inventory as your campaign proceeds. Be very watchful for decreasing sales. One technique is to plot the trend line of sales from month to month, along with the amount of advertising you are doing every month. In this way, if total sales are increasing, but you are paying more and more to get each customer, you will know that demand is declining, even as your sales are still going up, and you can adjust your inventory requirements accordingly.

Ordering

Ordering has to do with when to buy and how much to buy at a single time. When considering when to place your order, you should consider the amount of time necessary to prepare the order—and the time it takes for whoever is going to fulfill your order to receive the order from you if you are not going to fulfill yourself. If the item is a manufactured item, you must also add the manufacturing time. Finally, don't forget the time it takes between the shipment of the manufactured product and receipt at your facilities. It is frequently a good idea to "pad" this ordering period to allow for an error either in your calculations or for delays in manufacturing or shipping.

Let's stop here and go back and look at an example. Let us say you're selling a product through a direct mail campaign. You have sold a similar product before and you know that you received a 3 percent return from your mailing of 10,000 direct mail packages. If this new mailing is also for 10,000, you can estimate that you will sell 300 units of the product. That's good information to have, but you would also like to know how these ordered units will be spaced out over the length of the campaign. You have sold a similar item in the past and you have fairly accurate records, so you can use this information as shown in Figure 5.1. If the product is a new one and you have no prior data with which to compare it, use Figure 5.2 to estimate orders. Please keep in mind that these figures

Weeks after receipt of first order	1	2	3	4	5	6	7	8	9	10	11	12	13	14	15	16	17	18	19	20
Cumulative % of total number of units sold (similar product)	1.3	7.6	28.0	56.3	69.0	77.7	83.3	86.7	89.7	92.7	94.3	95.3	96.3	97.0	97.7	98.3	98.7	99.0	99.3	99.7
Cumulative number of units to be sold after receipt of first order (new product)																				
Cumulative number of units sold after receipt of first order (actual)																				

Figure 5.1 Forecast of orders based on the results of a prior campaign selling a similar product.

Weeks after receipt of first order	1	2	3	4	5	6	7	8	9	10	11	12	13	14	15	16	17	18	19	20
Cumulative % of total number of units sold	50.	75.	85.	87.	88.	90.	92.	95.	96.	97.0	97.5	98	98.2	98.4	98.6	98.8	99.0	99.3	99.6	100
Cumulative number of units to be sold (forecast)																				
Cumulative number of units sold (actual)																				

Figure 5.2 Estimate of orders in a direct mail campaign for a new product.

are for estimates only, and that actual results may differ considerably from your estimate, depending upon the product, time of year, type of mailing, and various other factors. You will also have to estimate what the total response from your mailing will be. This will be a little trickier if you have no prior data to compare it with, and the best advice I can give you is to caution you to not be overly optimistic in your sales forecast. Try to use the closest product that you've sold or have heard about to come up with a reasonable figure.

Let's assume your total estimate is 300 in total orders to be received from the direct mail campaign in either case. You can use a "how goes it" check as the weeks of your campaign go by simply taking the total number of orders received at that particular time and dividing them by your estimated percentage. For example, using Figure 5.1, if in your seventh week you have received 255 orders, divide 255 by the cumulative percentage forecast, 83.3 percent. 225/83.3 percent gives us 306, which is slightly higher than the total forecast of 300. In a similar fashion, if you got 255 orders in the seventh week of your campaign with a new product, using Figure 5.2, you would divide by your estimated percentage of 92, which would result in a total orders-to-be-received forecast of 277 units, which is 23 units below the 300 you originally estimated. Naturally, as the campaign proceeds and the weeks go by, your forecast can be adjusted and will be more accurate relative to the final number. Once you have calculated the total number of units that will be sold, you subtract those that have been sold to date to arrive at the remaining number you need. In this way, you can check the original order that was placed to see whether you will need to order more units or whether you already have a sufficient number of units on hand.

We now return to the question of when to order. If, for the particular item in question, your order preparation time is one day, the manufacturing time is 19 days, delivery time is seven days, and you add a pad of 10 percent, you come out with a 30-day lead time, assuming that your supplier can begin manufacturing immediately upon receipt of the order. As the weeks progress and you use the charts in Figures 5.1 and 5.2 to compute the total demand for your product, you can tell whether you are going to be short, and if you are, make some decision about when to order, how much risk you are assuming if you do not have sufficient product to cover your orders, and whether you must write letters to your potential customers to give them the option of getting their money back under the FTC 30-day rule.

To help you decide how many units you should order, you have your forecast, which tells you on an ongoing basis whether your inventory is going to fall short. But that isn't the only consideration when you decide on how many units to order. Other factors you must consider are those that add cost to the merchandise because of the way you order. For example, every time you put an order together it costs money. If you make a telephone call to confirm the order, it costs money. The processing of the order costs money, and receiving, handling, and transportation of the merchandise also cost money. These costs are reduced when you order a larger quantity of the product at one time. Finally, you must consider availability of storage space, insurance on the inventory once you own it, and the fact that until it is sold, you have money invested in the product that is not bringing you a return on your investment.

There is a formula that will permit us to calculate the economic order of quantity as an optimum quantity to purchase:

$$O = \sqrt{\frac{2QC}{A}}$$

In this formula, O = the order size, Q = the annual quantity of the product in units, C = the cost of placing the order, and A = the annual cost of carrying a single unit of stock for one year.

Let's look at an example. Let us say that you sell 5,000 units of product every year. The average cost of placing a single order of product from your supplier is $50, and to carry a single unit of product in your warehouse, including insurance and other costs, costs $1 per year. In this case, the order quantity

$$O = \sqrt{\frac{(2 \times 5,000 \times \$50)/}{\$1}} = \sqrt{500,000}$$

which equals approximately 707 units as your optimum order quantity. If the demand in a certain project is for less than 707 units, you order the entire amount at once. On the other hand, if the demand is some multiple of 707 units, you may wish to place two orders to try to achieve that economical order quantity that we have calculated to be 707.

Receiving

Receiving pertains to the initial processing and handling of the goods you have purchased and will eventually sell to your customers. To minimize mix-ups and ensure that things go smoothly on the receiving end, you should require your vendor—who manufactures and supplies the goods you're going to sell—to mark each case with your purchase order number and the item number according to its catalog and the quantity enclosed in the package. You should also instruct your suppliers not to mix different orders or units in one package. With proper marking in packing, it is easier to log in the material that you receive and much easier to keep track of it as you take it, warehouse it, and put it into inventory. Until your goods are properly warehoused, you should stress security; make sure that the goods are well guarded and that you take an immediate count of all the material received.

Warehousing

Warehousing is putting the goods in storage until you retrieve them to fulfill customer orders. Many beginning mail order operators warehouse in their garages or homes. I know one mail order businessman who built a $100,000 business, drives an Alfa Romeo sports car, and still keeps his entire inventory in two rooms of his home. It is fairly easy to develop shelf and deck storage from wood or steel shelves or racks, which should be marked clearly with their contents. Here again, you are concerned with security, because this is valuable merchandise. At some point it should be protected with alarm systems and insured for its full value.

Mail Opening, Reading, and Sorting

The majority of your mail will contain orders, along with cash, checks, postal money orders, and letters to you. Your customers will expect to receive their orders as quickly as possible. You will also receive complaints, questions about merchandise that has been ordered and not yet received, and other mail that needs attention. If this mail comes in large quantities, you should make sure that the most important mail is attended to first. In most cases your customers' orders should get first priority, but you also want to make certain that other letters are handled expeditiously. Do not leave your customers dangling when they ask for information about an order. If the order is overdue, be sure to check *immediately* to ensure that the order has been sent out. Even Joe Cossman once slipped and failed at first to send an ant farm to his customer, Caroline Kennedy, who was ordering from the White House. You will also receive a considerable amount of business mail in which other people offer their services to you, and it should be separated from your customer mail.

Responding

Responding has to do with the result of your mail opening, reading, and sorting. It naturally falls into several classes, the major one, of course, being order fulfillment, which is the central act of the entire subject we've been discussing. It means simply that you send the product in return for the money received from your customer.

However, you may have to respond to a complaint or inquiry about a prior order, in which case you have several options, listed in increasing order of expense.

1. Form letters and using the customer's letter itself.
2. Computer letters.
3. Personal letters.
4. Telephone calls.

Form Letters and Using the Customer's Letter Itself.   A preprinted form letter is shown in Figure 5.3. All the usual replies are indicated on the single sheet and you simply check the reply applicable to answer the question asked by your customer. The advantages of this form of response

---

DEAR CUSTOMER:

Please excuse this form letter, but through its use we are able to expedite your order or answer your question. It also enables us to reduce our costs, and we pass these savings on to you.

The checked comment is applicable to your order or question.

_____ Shipment has been made and your order is on the way. Please allow two weeks for delivery.

_____ Your check was not signed. Please sign the check enclosed and return it to us so that we may ship your order.

_____ Your check was returned for insufficient funds. Please check with your bank and send us a new check so that we may ship your order.

_____ We did not receive your order. Please recheck your records to make sure the information you reported to us is correct.

_____ The item you ordered is temporarily out of stock. It will be shipped as soon as possible, or if you like, we will substitute another item or return your money.

_____ The item you ordered is no longer sold by us. A check for the amount of your order is enclosed.

_____ The amount of money you sent us for your order was insufficient to cover the entire cost. Please send us an additional $_____ so that we can fill your order as soon as possible.

_____ We do not stock the item you inquired about.

_____ The size or color of the items you orderes is no longer in stock. The following are still available: _____
_____

If you like, we will substitute one of these if you will circle the one that you would like. Alternatively, we will return your money. Please let us know your desires.

Sincerely,

Manager,
Customer Relations

Figure 5.3   A preprinted form letter for responding to customer inquiries.

are that it's quick, you do not have to stop to compose a different letter or answer to every different letter coming in from your customers, and it is extremely efficient. It has been estimated that as many as 80 to 90 percent of all communications from customers can be answered by a form letter with no difficulty. The major disadvantages here are the impersonality and the fact that some questions simply cannot be answered by form letters.

An alternative technique is to write on the customer's letter itself. You can make a photocopy of the customer's letter with your reply so you have something for your file. This can be done in handwriting, is very personalized, and you need not try to make your form letter answer a question or solve a problem for which it was not designed. The major disadvantage here is that if you hire someone to do this chore for you, you have less control over what is said to your customer than if you put a form letter together and simply have the individual check one of the approved answers you have already written.

Computer Letters.   The computer letter is somewhat more personal than the form letter, although the data are really prewritten, as with the form letter. The major advantage of the computer letter is, then, that you have a form letter that looks personalized.

Personal Letters.   Occasionally personal letters will be required. Personal letters cost money and if you must dictate them yourself, they cost a lot of money because they take your time as well as the time of someone to type the letter and send it to your customer. Sometimes it's unavoidable. For example, when the customer has a solid complaint because you have made a major error, that must be rectified. Occasionally this can be done simply by having the owner or president of the company send a letter to the individual who has been wronged. In this case, it is worth it because you want to keep your customer. And besides, your customer deserves it. However, don't make this action the norm. It is an expensive way to go.

Telephone Calls.   Telephone calls are perhaps the most expensive of all, though they are perhaps the most satisfying to a complaining customer. What can better calm an irate customer than a personal telephone call from the president of the mail order company? But some type of paperwork is usually necessary to follow it up anyway, so telephone calls should be reserved for extreme cases.

Location Controlling

Assuming that the response is order fulfillment, location control is the next step in the fulfillment process. It means that you must locate the merchandise to be sent to the customer. You have several alternatives here. If you don't have much of a product line, of course, there is no problem whatsoever. However, once your product line and inventory become extensive, a three-dimensional location system is generally called for. It identifies the location not only by aisle, but also by base position in that aisle and the tier height (see Figure 5.4). The box containing the merchandise itself (or, if it is a large item, the item itself) should be tagged with additional information confirming the contents. A computerized system, which maintains the exact location of your stock along with a running inventory of what is in stock and what is not, is also possible. We'll cover the computerized system shortly.

Inventory Withdrawing

Now that you've located the stock, the next step is withdrawal of the inventory. There are several different options here. One is called *gangpicking:* Similar items of inventory are located together and picked up at the

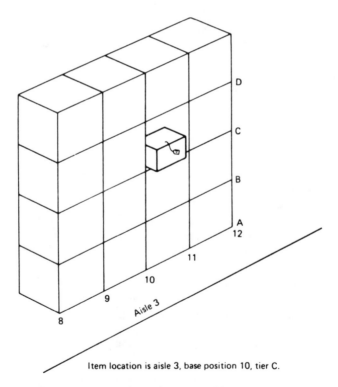

Item location is aisle 3, base position 10, tier C.

Figure 5.4   A three-dimensional location system.

same time. Another option is *individual order pick,* where one person fills a single order by going directly to the location and picking it up. Then there is the *sequel zone pick,* where several different individuals, each working a specific group of product numbers or zones, fill the order by forwarding it from zone to zone in a mobile container. There is also *order disassembly* and *reassembly,* where a computer disassembles the order into separate suborders and then reassembles the order at a given packing station. Finally, there is a system called *automatic pick,* used for high-volume fulfillment operations. At first you are probably going to use individual order pick, but as you grow, you should sit down and consider each of the options I mentioned against your situation and cost. You will be able to find individuals to help you with this decision in the classified sections of *Direct Marketing* and other mail order magazines.

Packing

Having withdrawn your inventory, you assemble the individual items ordered, put them together, box and wrap them, label them, and get the package ready for delivery to the carrier. Naturally this is an important step: If you fail to pack the items well and they are damaged, your customer will be rightfully indignant, even if you replace the order, because of the time delay involved. If your operation becomes fairly large, you can use a conveyor system to transport the order to the packing stations and then complete the packing prior to shipping. However, for most operations, a standard size packing table is perfectly adequate.

Metering and Shipping

The final step in the fulfillment process is metering and shipping, where you apply the postage and ship it out. At this stage you should have a scale to ensure accurate weights, and if a great deal of material is going out, get a postage meter from the U.S. Post Office. The meter is an economical, fast, and easy way to apply postage to your packages, but don't use one until your business is well established and you have sizable mailings every day.

More and more mail order companies are shipping by UPS (United Parcel Service), Fed Ex, or one of the U.S. Post Offices' new services. You should also consider the different classes of shipping, depending upon the weight and size of the mailing. For example, fourth class mail takes a long time to be delivered, but is the cheapest for many types of mail order merchandise. Accurate scales are very important, especially for large volume shipments. If you send out 10,000 packages, each with 2¢ more postage than necessary, you've wasted $200.

USING A FULFILLMENT COMPANY

Another option you have in fulfillment that we have not yet discussed is engaging a company that specializes in fulfillment to handle your entire fulfillment operation. These firms can handle as much as you desire—taking your inquiries, turning everything around, sending the orders out to your customers, and sending you the money. Or you can work out a deal where you handle the orders and instruct them where to send the orders. You can find such companies in the classified section of the professional direct marketing magazines, or check Appendix C and contact the direct marketing club in your area. They should be able to tell you what local fulfillment companies are doing business.

When you use a fulfillment company, you must give up some of the profit you would otherwise take for yourself. You also lose a certain amount of control of your business. However, again, you should find out what these services will cost and weigh that against what you are doing at the present time by yourself. Sometimes it's actually cheaper to go with a fulfillment company, especially when you consider that your time can be used in some other more creative way, which may be more important in making money for you. If your strengths are in writing copy, developing new ideas, finding new products, or other aspects of marketing, why waste time trying to do something at which you may not be as good?

SUMMARY

In this chapter we've discussed the entire fulfillment process—what it is and why it is very important in obtaining satisfied customers and repeat business. Fulfillment won't be a real problem for you until you start to grow. Also, you can avoid some fulfillment problems by drop-shipping. But at some point, fulfillment is going to be a major factor in whether your business grows or not. In this chapter you learned the 11 essential fulfillment steps—estimating required inventory before mailing, adjusting the required inventory after initial response, ordering, receiving, warehousing, mail opening, reading, sorting, and responding, location controlling, inventory withdrawing, packing, and metering and shipping.

We also looked into whether you should use the fulfillment services of another company. You will want to reread this chapter before you start to expand.

Part II

Mail Order Merchandising

6

Finding Profitable
Products to Sell by Mail

The basic principle of finding and then selling products successfully by mail is always to look at the market first and decide what the market wants before you zero in on a specific product to sell. This rule is altered only slightly if you already have an established product or service you are selling profitably through other means. In this case, you must evaluate your established product or service to see whether it can be sold profitably through the mail. In all cases, test before you sink huge sums of money into your product.

There are numerous examples of fortunes that have been made by following these principles. Joe Karbo recognized the need for a book to show people how to lead successful lives before he wrote it. But he wasn't the only one.

Robert Collier started working for $25 a week in his uncle's book publishing business. He built his own massive business. At one time, he did $1 million worth of orders in a single six-month period for a single book. How's that for a small businessman? Further, although Robert Collier died many years ago, some of his books are still in print and are still best-sellers. For example, I have *The Secret of the Ages* in its 27th edition. There may be even later ones. I know it's still going strong. I have also seen his book intended for mail order operators, *The Robert Collier Letter Book*, around. It is highly recommended. *The Secret of the Ages* was a great success and was originally entitled *The Book of Life*. For a long time Collier had the idea for a set of books on what he felt was simply "practical psychology." However, as with ideas that many of us have, he was never able to force himself to sit down and write the book. But sales letters were his bread and butter as a mail order operator and copywriter. So Collier wrote a dynamic sales letter describing *The Secret of the Ages before* he wrote the first page of the actual manuscript for the book. Still not ready to write the book, he did a test mailing of the sales letter to 10,000 individuals just to see what would happen. The return from this mailing was an incredible 9 percent. This was so exciting that Robert Collier got busy and wrote the entire book in a month. This was the book for which he received more than $1 million worth of orders within six months.

Robert Collier's success illustrates several important mail order principles. First, it is your market that is most important, not the product. You must make certain that you have a market before you stock up with a large inventory of products. Second, your successful product may be right under your nose—you may not have to look very far. Third, testing is important in mail order. If you have a loser, you must drop the product or service at once or change the offer or the advertising so that your product or service becomes profitable. If what you are selling is a winner, don't stop to congratulate yourself, but "roll out" and make your money as quickly as possible before the inevitable competition comes in to split your market. We'll talk about exactly how to do all of these things in a later chapter.

Joe Sugarman noted that there was a tremendous demand for high-technological electronic items and that this demand could be met readily through a mail order operation. And he was not alone. Drew Kaplan, founder of DAK, found a need for slightly different high-technological products, as did Richard Thalheimer. Brainerd Mellinger discovered an immense market, not only for items that he could import from foreign countries, but for assisting individuals who wanted to get into importing and exporting themselves.

In looking at the market first, concentrate on what your potential consumers are currently buying, as well as on economic conditions, the state of technology, culture, the political environment, the laws, and competition. Look at any factor you feel may affect your ability to sell the product. These factors are known as environmental variables, and each is crucial to your success in the mail order business.

Consider, for example, what your potential customers are currently buying. If there is no demand for a product that you want to sell, it is extremely difficult to try to build a demand, no matter how exciting your copy. You'll be far better off finding a product that already fills a demonstrated need in the marketplace and for which demand already exists, as proved by what your potential customers are already buying. In the same fashion, you cannot sell a product that is illegal, no matter what the demand.

Joe Cossman tells of a fabulous product he found on one of his trips to Thailand. Troubled by insect bites, the druggist gave him a product known as Tigerspaw, which instantly relieved the pain from his insect bites and stings. Thinking what a wonderful mail order product this would make in the states, Joe asked the FDA about Tigerspaw, only to discover that many people had tried to bring this product into the United States to sell. There was one problem: The main ingredient of Tigerspaw was morphine.

You can think of many products that might be successful in one culture but not in another, or in one political environment but not in another, or products such as the electronic devices sold by Joe Sugarman, which are very, very successful in a high-technology country such as the United States, but would not be in a country that gained widespread use of electricity only yesterday.

Consideration of competition is awfully important. This is as good a time as any to mention the copycat principle, which some mail order books advise as the only real way to mail order success.

According to the copycat principle, you simply copy someone else's success in mail order as closely as you can. That is, since mail order advertising is open to everyone, you simply observe what is successful by watching advertising in magazines or in your own mail. If a particular proposition is repeated over a long period of time, you know it is successful and you simply introduce an identical proposition or one that is as close to the original as possible without running afoul of copyright or other laws. This procedure is supposed to guarantee success.

I take issue with the copycat principle for selecting new products, depending upon how it is presented. I won't even go into ethics here—that is for every individual to decide on his or her own. But look at it this way: If you copy another mail order operator's product, medium, and so on almost exactly, what market are you going to go after? The identical market. This means that the market must be split between you and the original dealer. Now any market, no matter for what product, is only so large. Unfortunately, the mail order business is full of rip-off artists who constantly, and without much thinking, attempt to follow the copycat principle exactly. This means that in a very, very short time, unless the originator has total control over his or her product or service, numerous imitators will have jumped in and split the market to such an extent that there is little profit for anyone.

A second problem with following the copycat principle is that you may not know the whole story—that is, you are privy only to the advertising of your competition, not to his or her marketing plan. Because mail order is a "back-end" business, you don't know whether any profit is being made up front. Julian Simon, author of *How to Start and Operate a Mail Order Business*, tells a story of a copycat who copied another mail order success exactly and went broke at the end of the year. Eventually meeting with the originator, he said, "I can't understand it. I followed you exactly and I lost money on every single sale that I made." The eminently successful originator of the product smiled and said, "Of course; so do I, but I make great profits on those products I sell to the customer after the initial sale." That's what I mean about mail order being a "back-end" business.

A third problem with the copycat principle is that your competitor may already have established himself or herself in the marketplace so that an imitator can no longer break in. I think this is the reason that many imitators of Joe Karbo were unsuccessful with advertisements of books and manuals that attempted to imitate *The Lazy Man's Way to Riches*. Joe was so well established in the marketplace that any copier simply didn't have the stature or the financial resources to affect Joe's market significantly.

Consequently, I do not recommend your copying someone else's product. However, there is one way of using this principle successfully, and that is not to copy the product, medium, and so forth of the originator, but to give someone else's concept an entirely new twist. A good way of doing this successfully is illustrated by Melvin Powers, president of Wilshire Book Company. Noting that diet and weight control books were on the top of every list of best-sellers, and that a book called *How to Flatten Your Stomach* by Coach Jim Everroad had reached number one on the best-seller list with more than 200,000 copies sold, Powers created a tremendous spoof called *How to Flatten Your Tush*, by "Coach Marge Reardon," in less than a day. As Melvin described it in his book *How to Get Rich in Mail Order*, he sold 25,000 copies to major bookstore chains immediately and went back later and sold them another 25,000. He soon promoted a Miss Tush contest and got extensive national coverage through the press and on television. The *New York Times* called the book one of the year's funniest books and Melvin, continuing the spoof, printed across the outside cover, "Soon to Be a Major Motion Picture." He was amazed to receive letters from satisfied readers who wanted to know who was to produce the film. Powers' book was a fabulous success and an outstanding example of how to use the copycat principle properly by giving an old concept a new twist. He eventually sold more than 250,000 copies.

HOW TO SELL YOUR PRODUCT BY MAIL ORDER— AN IMPORTANT CONSIDERATION IN PRODUCT SELECTION

There are several different ways of selling your product through mail order, and the one you choose will affect your selection of new products. These methods are one-shot, inquiry and follow-up, repeat, and catalog. Let's look at each one individually.

One Shot

The one-shot product is probably every would-be mail order operator's dream. This is where you simply advertise a product in a display or classified advertisement or in a letter direct to your customer. Your customer sends you the money, you send the product, and that ends the deal. You make your profit immediately. While you obviously have your list of customers, you do not have a line of similar products to sell them. Examples of the one-shot were Joe Karbo's book *The Lazy Man's Way to Riches* or Joe Sugarman's early electronic devices. Each product is sold separately and individually. Usually the one-shot is defined by two characteristics: First, that you sell on a single, first advertisement, whether it is by letter or by display or by classified advertisement, and, second, that you have no other product to follow up and sell to your customer after selling your initial product. *One-shot* can refer to a product, the method of selling, or both. Sugarman has both follow-up products and a catalog today. Karbo also started a series of follow-up products.

While many people feel that the one-shot *is* mail order, the fact of the matter is that a one-shot operation has a number of significant disadvantages, and while it can clearly be successful (as evidenced by Karbo, Sugarman, and others), it is far easier to be successful in some sort of repeat business. Mail order is a back-end profit business because of the high cost of advertising to obtain your customer's name. In very simple terms, if you have a product that costs $2 and you sell it for $10, the cost of the product, plus the packaging, plus the postage, plus the advertising costs, is deducted from your profit. If the advertising, packaging, and postage cost a total of $8.50 (say, $7.50 for the advertising and $1 for the postage and packaging), the total cost to you for the first sale is $10.50. So for every single sale, you lose 50¢. On the second sale, or any additional sales you make of the same product from the same customer, the cost is still $2, but now your advertising is very close to zero. This is because you already have your customer's name. Your packaging and postage remain $1. So the total cost to you is $3. Because the sales price is $10, minus $3, your net profit is $7. In this simple example, as shown in Figure 6.1, we have eliminated factors such as overhead to illustrate the point.

Except for direct mail, another disadvantage of a one-shot is the relatively limited space you have to tell your story and make a sale. This is why selling direct from classified ads is so difficult. You just haven't got the words available to convince your potential customer to buy your product.

First Sale to Customer		All Back-End Sales to Customer	
Product cost	$ 2.00	Product cost	$2.00
Postage and packaging	1.00	Postage and packaging	1.00
Advertising cost	7.50	Advertising cost	.00
Total	$10.50	Total	$3.00
Profit	$10 − $10.50 = −50¢	Profit	$10.00 − $3 = $7
50¢ loss!		$7 profit on each sale!	

Figure 6.1 Mail order is a back-end profit business.

To summarize the one-shot, it is possible to be successful this way, but it is harder than if you sell a line of products to the same customer or if you use inquiry and follow-up.

Inquiry and Follow-Up

This is a method that can be used with either one-shot or repeat products. The basic difference between it and the basic one-shot method is the fact that, regardless of what you sell, your initial advertisement merely serves to bring in an inquiry for a more expensive follow-up to interested potential customers. The initial advertisement may be a space or classified advertisement, a postcard through direct mail, or a letter through direct mail. All have been used. Brainerd Mellinger is famous for very large full-page space advertisements that have a coupon at the bottom in which you write only to receive additional information about his proposition. Can you believe that these are advertisements that can cost $40,000 a page or more? That should make clear not only how expensive advertising is but also just how much profit there must be on the back-end of the mail order business. Otherwise, neither Brainerd Mellinger nor anyone else could afford to spend this kind of money just to acquire a potential customer's name.

Some years ago I used this same technique of inquiry and follow-up to sell $20,000 worth of research by mail. The first mailing was a direct mail letter to a number of senior aerospace executives. It outlined the general research I wanted to sell and provided a tear-out coupon to request the full proposal for the research. Those executives who responded with this coupon were mailed the expensive proposal, which contained all of the follow-up information and allowed me more space to sell the product.

Repeat Methods

Repeat methods of selling are the most profitable in mail order. After you sell an initial product to your customer, you continue to sell him the same or similar products. Examples of repeat methods are film developers who give you a special bargain or even free film so that you can continually buy developing services from them in the future, and book-of-the-month-type clubs where a special bargain brings you in the door and thereafter you are given the opportunity to buy books at reduced prices for as long as you retain your membership. Brainerd Mellinger's business also uses repeat methods. After selling a course on mail order import or export, the company sells products, seminars, newsletters, and other similar or related items. There are no disadvantages to repeat business except that when you sell your first product to your customer, you must have something else—a line of products, or a service, or something—ready to sell right away. In fact, with the very act of fulfillment of the initial item you sell, you can put in an advertisement for follow-up products or services. This, by the way, is known as a "bounce-back." Even if you sell by the one-shot method, having a repeat product to sell will greatly increase your profitability and chance for immediate success.

Catalog Sales

Catalog sales are a type of repeat business because the object is to persuade your customer to order again and again. It is very difficult for a beginner to make money with catalogs, although it has been done. Witness Gerardo Joffe with Haverhills, and Henniker's. However, putting together a catalog takes a huge initial investment and a great deal of talent in product selection, locating sources, controlling them, and so forth. This is usually not for the beginner. As we discussed in Chapter 3, some companies make a business of selling preprinted catalogs, which they will imprint with your own name. I strongly recommend against purchase of these catalogs. While, in theory, you save the cost of putting your own catalog together and the cost of inventory, these companies are ready to drop-ship the items to your customers and the markup on these products is so slight that you cannot make a profit from them, even if you find customers who are willing to buy from this type of catalog. Further, few customers will buy from a catalog they recognize as not coming from the original source. In fact, many of these potential customers may receive more than one identical catalog with different names on them just like I did. Save yourself some money—don't buy ready-made catalogs.

So many companies have made huge sales with catalogs—from Sears and Montgomery Ward to the Horchow Collection, Sunset House, Spiegel, and many, many others—that it is clear that mail order can be very profitable when practiced this way. However, you would be well advised to begin with a small product line and expand the size of your catalog slowly as you obtain experience and financial resources for investment. Roger Horchow, who created the Horchow Collection, says in his book *Elephants in Your Mail Box* that he planned on losing $1 million the first year with one of his first catalogs. He actually lost $2 million in both his first and second years.

These, then, are the basic methods you can use to sell a product through the mail. We will talk about more advanced methods in a later chapter. As you select your product for your first mail order venture, keep in mind this methodology of selling, as one or more of these methods will be your key to mail order success.

SELLING THROUGH THE MAIL

Many readers may already have a company in which they are selling products or services through means other than the mail and are wondering whether they can sell their established product through this channel of distribution. In considering whether you can do this, picture selling your product through the methods described above. Also consider the following factors.

1. Do you have competitors who are selling through the mail?
2. Do you have customers you know about who buy by mail right now?
3. Is your product lightweight and relatively easy to package for mail order selling?
4. Does your product have a high markup? Remember that, in general, if a product is to be profitable, you must be able to sell it at three to four times the mail cost to you. There are exceptions to this, which are mentioned elsewhere in this book, but this is the general rule.
5. Is your product easily obtainable in stores? Generally, if it is, there is no reason for an individual to buy it through the mail.
6. Can you communicate sales appeal for your product on paper? This is pretty important, because if you are going to sell by mail, that is exactly what you are going to have to do.

If the answer to every question except number five is yes, you have a good chance for success in selling your product through the mail.

THE RULES OF PRODUCT SELECTION

There are many rules of product selection. I have three general principles that I try to follow in selection of a new product, and I recommend these to clients, friends, and everyone else interested in mail order selling. Rule number one is to work with a product that you like to handle. Your main objective may be to make money; however, if you don't like the product or service, it'll be much more difficult for you to work with it. Conversely, if you really like your product, it really isn't work to sell it—it's fun. You'll work harder and have fun doing it. So find a product you like and your chances of success will increase.

Rule number two is to handle a product you know something about. Now obviously, if you are going to sell a large number of different products, you will eventually sell products at some time or other about which you know very little. However, at the beginning, you need everything possible going for you. Selecting products you know something about will be a real asset. Many people make mistakes in this area, including yours truly. When I first started dealing in mail order, I selected a jewelry product about which I knew absolutely nothing. I didn't make money—I lost it. I began to be successful in mail order when I selected products I knew something about. In my case, this was the selling of information about writing for publication. If you want to maximize your chances for success right up front, select a product or service about which you are knowledgeable.

The third rule, and perhaps the most important, is to handle a product you respect. I mentioned in the last chapter that it may be possible to skirt the line of legality and sell a product that is technically legal but ethically questionable. If you want to be truly happy and successful with your mail order business, handle a product that you and other people can respect.

Jim Kobs, author of *Profitable Direct Marketing,* developed a four-plus-one formula for product selection that he recommends for help in evaluating a new product. Here it is.

1. *Broad Appeal.* Kobs says always look for something that virtually every man, woman, or household can use and that has broad appeal to certain specific market segments that you can reach at low cost and high profit.

2. *Unusual Features.* Look for a product that has unusual features. This is good for mail orders, says Kobs, because little salesmanship is left at the retail level today. Therefore, a product selling by retail that has unusual features is usually not discoverable by the potential customer. As a direct marketer, you can highlight these unusual features and make a sale by emphasizing them.

3. *A Product That Is Not Readily Available in Stores.* This goes back to the reason and rationale for individuals' buying through the mail and has been mentioned previously. It is a fact that if you can't find it in stores or won't find it in stores at the price you are selling it for, or if it is not available in the way you are selling it as a complete package in stores, your chances of success are much better.

4. *Proper Price and Proper Margins.* According to Kobs, the starting point for any product or service being sold by mail is the right price. It is important to understand that the right price may not necessarily be the lowest price, as we will get into later in our full discussion on pricing.

Okay, those are Kobs' "four." What is his "plus"? It's what he calls the *dream element,* or the *story element.* The dream element is using your imagination to give the item a new twist that no one else has thought of before. The pet rock certainly falls into this category. The story element is the telling of an interesting or appealing story behind the product. Look at John Caples' ad, "They Laughed When I Sat Down at the Piano," shown in Figure 6.2. Is that an interesting story or not?

Bob Stone is the chairman of Stone and Adler, Inc., one of the country's leading mail order advertising agencies, and the author of one of the most successful books on direct marketing ever written, *Successful Direct*

"Can he really play?" a girl whispered. "Heavens, no!" Arthur exclaimed. "He never played a note in his life."

They Laughed When I Sat Down At the Piano But When I Started to Play!—

ARTHUR had just played "The Rosary." The room rang with applause. I decided that this would be a dramatic moment for me to make my debut. To the amazement of all my friends I strode confidently over to the piano and sat down.

"Jack is up to his old tricks," somebody chuckled. The crowd laughed. They were all certain that I couldn't play a single note.

"Can he really play?" I heard a girl whisper to Arthur. "Heavens, no!" Arthur exclaimed. "He never played a note in all his life . But just you watch him. This is going to be good."

I decided to make the most of the situation. With mock dignity I drew out a silk handkerchief and lightly dusted off the keys. Then I rose and gave the revolving piano stool a quarter of a turn, just as I had seen an imitator of Paderewski do in a vaudeville sketch.

"What do you think of his execution?" called a voice from the rear.

"We're in favor of it!" came back the answer, and the crowd rocked with laughter.

Then I Started to Play

Instantly a tense silence fell on the guests. The laughter died on their lips as if by magic. I played through the first bars of Liszt's immortal Liebestraume. I heard gasps of amazement. My friends sat breathless—spellbound.

I played on and as I played I forgot the people around me. I forgot the hour, the place, the breathless listeners. The little world I lived in seemed to fade—seemed to grow dim—unreal. Only the music was real. Only the music and the visions it brought me. Visions as beautiful and as changing as the wind-blown clouds and drifting moonlight, that long ago inspired the master composer. It seemed as if the master musician himself were speaking to me—speaking through the medium of music—not in words but in chords. Not in sentences but in exquisite melodies.

A Complete Triumph!

As the last notes of the Liebestraume died away, the room resounded with a sudden roar of applause. I found myself surrounded by excited faces. How my friends carried on! Men shook my hand—wildly congratulated me—pounded me on the back in their enthusiasm! Everybody was exclaiming with delight—plying me with rapid questions . . . "Jack! Why didn't you tell us you could play like that?"

"Where did you learn?"—"How long have you studied?"—"Who was your teacher?"

"I have never even seen my teacher," I replied. "And just a short while ago I couldn't play a note."

"Quit your kidding," laughed Arthur, himself an accomplished pianist. "You've been studying for years. I can tell."

"I have been studying only a short while," I insisted. "I decided to keep it a secret so that I could surprise all you folks."

Then I told them the whole story.

"Have you ever heard of the U. S. School of Music?" I asked. A few of my friends nodded. "That's a correspondence school, isn't it?" they exclaimed.

"Exactly," I replied. "They have a new simplified method that can teach you to play any instrument by note in just a few months."

How I Learned to Play Without a Teacher

And then I explained how for years I had longed to play the piano.

"It seems just a short while ago," I continued, "that I saw an interesting ad of the U. S. School of Music mentioning a new method of learning to play which only cost a few cents a day! The ad told how a woman had mastered the piano in her spare time at home—and without a teacher! Best of all, the wonderful new method she used required no laborious scales—no heartless exercises—no tiresome practising. It sounded so convincing that I filled out the coupon requesting the Free Demonstration Lesson.

"The free book arrived promptly and I started in that very night to study the Demonstration Lesson. I was amazed to see how easy it was to play this new way. Then I sent for the course.

"When the course arrived I found it was just as the ad said—as easy as A. B. C.! And as the lessons continued they got easier and easier. Before I knew it I was playing all the pieces I liked best. Nothing stopped me. I could play ballads or classical numbers or jazz, all with equal ease. And I never did have any special talent for music."

Play Any Instrument

You, too, can now teach yourself to be an accomplished musician—right at home—in half the usual time. You can't go wrong with this simple new method which has already shown almost half a million people how to play their favorite instruments by note. Forget that old-fashioned idea that you need special "talent." Just read the list of instruments in the panel, decide which one you want to play and the U. S. School will do the rest. And bear in mind no matter which instrument you choose, the cost in each case will be the same—just a few cents a day. No matter whether you are a mere beginner or already a good performer, you will be interested in learning about this new and wonderful method.

Send for Our Free Booklet and Demonstration Lesson

Thousands of successful students never dreamed they possessed musical ability until it was revealed to them by a remarkable "Musical Ability Test" which we send entirely without cost with our interesting free booklet.

If you are in earnest about wanting to play your favorite instrument—if you really want to gain happiness and increase your popularity—send at once for the free booklet and Demonstration Lesson. No cost—no obligation. Sign and send the convenient coupon now. Instruments supplied when needed, cash or credit. U. S. School of Music, 812 Brunswick Bldg., New York City.

U. S. School of Music,
812 Brunswick Bldg., New York City.

Please send me your free book, "Music Lessons in Your Own Home," with introduction by Dr. Frank Crane. Demonstration Lesson and particulars of your offer. I am interested in the following course:

....

Have you above instrument? ....

Name ....
(Please write plainly)

Address ....

City .... State ....

Pick Your Instrument

Piano	Harmony and
Organ	Composition
Violin	Sight Singing
Drums and	Ukulele
Traps	Guitar
Mandolin	Hawaiian
Clarinet	Steel Guitar
Flute	Harp
Saxophone	Cornet
'Cello	Piccolo
	Trombone
Voice and	Speech Culture
Automatic	Finger Control
	Piano Accordion
Banjo (5-String, Plectrum or Tenor)	

"They Laughed When I Sat Down at the Piano"

Figure 6.2   John Caple's famous ad. The emphasis here is on telling a good story.

Marketing Methods. He has developed a four-step method for evaluating new products. He recommends asking yourself the following to estimate potential marketability.

1. Does the product or service have a reason for being? Is there a perceived need or can it be created?
2. Does the product suit your prospect's taste, life-style, and the price he or she may be willing to pay?
3. Does the product have a perceived beauty, utility, or value for the individual prospect?
4. Will it appeal to the majority of your prospects?

Win Barnes, president of Kross, Inc., and former general manager of the mail order division of Shell Oil, a man who has selected literally thousands of mail order products of all types and sold over five and a half million items by mail, recommends that the mail order marketer ask 19 questions before making the decision to market the product by mail:

1. Is it available in retail stores?
2. Can everyone use the item or is it limited?
3. Has it a perceived value at least equal to offer?
4. Is it easy to use?
5. Does it solve a recognizable problem?
6. Will it photograph well?
7. Is it easy to describe?
8. Is it just another version of a readily available product?
9. Can installation be made by a novice?
10. Does it need to be put together upon arrival?
11. Is it unisex in nature?
12. Does it provide something of benefit for the buyer . . . savings, safety, security, fun, satisfaction, pleasure?
13. Is it needed immediately?
14. Are there choices that have to be made, that is, color, size?
15. Can it be offered at a competitive price with sufficient margin?
16. Is the time right for it?
17. Does it fit the media to be used in selling . . . telephone, mail, space, television, catalog?
18. Does a market have to be created for the product?
19. Is the supplier reliable?

THE MAIL ORDER PRODUCT EVALUATION FORM

The mail order product evaluation form is one that I developed over the years from a number of different sources. It is shown in Figure 6.3. I have formulated relative weightings I consider most important for overall mail order suitability. Under certain circumstances this relative weighting might change, and in this case, you must adapt the mail order product evaluation form to your own circumstances. Using it is simple. First, establish your own importance weightings so that the total equals 1.00. This should be based on your judgment for your particular situation. Then, multiply the relative weighting times from zero through four points. Use four points if the question gets a rating of *excellent* for your product. Three points indicates *very good*. Two points is for *good*. One point is for *fair*, and zero is for *poor*. Add up all the points after multiplying by the weighting. You should consider those products with the most points as candidates for your mail order product.

Here are 17 great sources of new mail order products:

1. Start with the concept of currently successful products, but be careful. Don't copy everything about your competitor's product. If you do, you will not win; you will lose because of the reasons I have stated earlier. However, if you change the basic concept, as Melvin Powers did with his book, *How to Flatten Your Tush,* you can find a successful product that can make you a fortune.

2. Attend inventor shows. Many inventors are not good marketers, and in fact, most inventions that are patented are never actually produced in quantity. At inventor shows you will see hundreds of new products that the inventors would like to license to you for a royalty or perhaps sell outright. To find out when an inventor show will be in your local area, contact your local chamber of commerce.

3. Consider foreign products. Foreign products not available in the United States can frequently be outstanding products for sale by mail. One additional factor that can help you is that every country would like to see the number of its exports increased. Therefore, one primary source of foreign products is the commercial attaché of foreign consulates and embassies. Find the telephone numbers in the telephone book of any large city and ask for the commercial attaché. One particular product I know about was available for licensing and hadn't yet been introduced in the United States; further, the government of this foreign country spent thousands of dollars assisting the entrepreneur in selling the item in the United States simply to better its trade position

MAIL ORDER PRODUCT EVALUATION FORM

Instructions: Give each evaluation item
4 points for an evaluation of excellent
3 points for an evaluation of very good
2 points for an evaluation of good
1 point for an evaluation of fair
0 point for an evaluation of poor

Multiply the evaluation points times the importance weighting. Only pick new products that have a high point total.

	Importance Weighting	Evaluation Points	Total
I. Marketability			
1. How large is the potential market?	.03	× _____	= _____
2. How important is the need that the product fills?	08	× _____	= _____
3. Can the customer buy the product easily in a store?	.03	× _____	= _____
II. Profitability			
1. What is the total and yearly profitability estimate?	.08	× _____	= _____
2. Can the item be sold at 3 to 4 times your cost?	.06	× _____	= _____
3. Does the product lend itself to repeat business?	.07	× _____	= _____
4. What is the ratio of total profit to total investment?	.03	× _____	= _____
III. Investment			
1. How much investment will the project require?	.05	× _____	= _____
2. How many units must be sold until the investment is recouped?	.04	× _____	= _____
IV. Legal Consideration			
1. Is the product strictly legal?	.15	× _____	= _____
2. Is the product completely safe?	.09	× _____	= _____
3. Can there be any legal repercussion through use or misuse of the product?	.08	× _____	= _____
V. Mailing			
1. Can the product be shipped and mailed easily?	.06	× _____	= _____
2. Is the product breakable?	.06	× _____	= _____
3. Can the product be shipped at low cost?	.07	× _____	= _____
	1.00	Grand total	_____

Figure 6.3 The mail order product evaluation form should help you decide which products to try to sell.

through exporting. If you do not live close to a large city where a foreign consulate or embassy is located, get a copy of *Business America,* published by the U.S. Department of Commerce. This magazine contains a license opportunity section in which many foreign-made products available for licensing in the United States are listed. To get a copy, contact the Department of Commerce's local field office, which you should also find in your telephone book. Other books are available that will be of help if you are looking for products to be imported. One is the *American Register of Exporters and Importers,* published by the American Register of Exporters and Importers Corporation, 38 Park Row, New York, New York 10038. Another is *Directory of New York Importers,* published by Commerce Industry Association Institute, Inc., 65 Liberty Street, New York, New York 10005. Finally, for almost every country there is at least one directory of importers and exporters, usually published annually. Frequently your local library will have one or more of these directories from each of the major countries of the world. These books are valuable for product selection because they list not only importers and exporters, but also product manufacturers.

4. Read the business opportunity section of your local newspaper, as well as such publications as the *Wall Street Journal.* Very frequently individuals who have a product to sell will advertise in one or more of these publications. You can contact them to negotiate the best deal possible for a product that may be very successful in mail order.

5. Call local manufacturers. Every manufacturer has created a product at one time or another that was not successful for his or her particular line of work. It could be very, very successful for a mail order product. This was one of Joe Cossman's secrets for finding successful mail order products. Joe would go to the Yellow Pages and look up plastic manufacturing companies and ask to speak with the president. The question to the president was always the same: "Do you have any tooling for discontinued products from your line?" This really has a twofold advantage because tooling for plastic products is generally very expensive. I know, from my experience as head of research and development for a plastics company. Very frequently we would sell tooling for which we had paid $40,000 or more for $300 or less, just to get it off the premises when the product had failed or been discontinued. Cossman used this technique to buy tooling for a few hundred dollars for such successful products as the potato spud gun. Cossman sold 1,585,000 spud guns, for which he had paid $600 for the tooling.

6. Repackage information from books printed by the U.S. government. Books published by the U.S. government generally are in the public domain and are copyright free (unless they contain copyrighted material from another source). This means that you can use the material and reprint it anyway you wish. It is a fact that several books on the best-seller list have been created by merely repackaging, retitling, and perhaps reorganizing material from U.S. government books that are already in print. You can do the same thing. If you live in a large city, there may be a U.S. government book store near you. If that's the case, you can see for yourself exactly what is available. You can obtain the latest catalog of books available from the government by writing the Superintendent of Documents, U.S. Government Printing Office, Washington, DC 20402, and asking for it.

7. Write or contact major corporations in the United States. Almost every large corporation that has a research and development division will, on occasion, develop products for which it has no use, by-products of the mainstream of its commercial interests. As a result, most major corporations have established special offices to market the licensing of their patents to individuals outside their companies. The titles of these special offices vary. However, you can usually get in touch with them by contacting a company or corporation that is large enough to have a research and development division and asking for the director of patent licensing. You should give this individual some general idea of the types of patent or product you would be interested in.

8. Consider distress merchandise. Many retailers have been in situations in which certain merchandise could not be sold. What do they do? They reduce the price greatly and attempt to sell it at bargain rates. This is distress merchandise. I do not recommend that you buy this merchandise for resale, because as soon as all of the products are sold, you will be out of a mail order product. Instead, if you see distress merchandise, which is identified as such because it has been greatly reduced in price by the retailer, and if you feel this might make an excellent mail order product, look at the item and see if it contains a patent number. If it does, you can locate the inventor by writing to the patent office and purchasing a copy of the patent. Or if you live close to a depository for patents, you can look at the patent at no cost at all. Every U.S. patent contains the name and address of the inventor. As I mentioned earlier, inventors are usually poor marketers, and the fact that this is distress merchandise indicates that if the inventor still controls the patent, he or she may well be interested in either an

outright sale of the patent or the licensing of the manufacture of the item to you. The address of the patent office is: U.S. Patent Office, Washington, DC 20231.

9.   Another source of mail order products is expired patents. In the United States, a patent is good for only 17 years. The only exception is an ornamental design patent, which is good for three and a half, seven, or 14 years. Remembering that many patents are never even put into production, expired patents, which are over 17 years old and are now in the public domain, are a ready source of new product ideas for mail order. In addition, you can look at the entire technology of any general product area by writing to the patent office and asking for a list of all patent numbers falling into your product area. The patent office will charge you a small amount for each patent number. Once you have the list of numbers, if you are close to a major library, check to see if it is a patent depository. This will be the case most frequently in large cities, such as Los Angeles and New York. If the library is a depository, every patent that has been granted is on microfilm there. All you need do is look up the number and you can get information about every patent in the product area you selected. Every patent is a source of ideas for you. You may approach the inventor about licensing the patent, or the idea itself may get you thinking about new ideas that don't violate the inventor's patent. If the patent has expired, you can do whatever you want with the invention.

10.   Overseas trade publications, such as *Made in Europe, Hong Kong Enterprise,* and others, are excellent sources for importing new products into the United States. Here is a list of typical foreign publications and their addresses. Write and ask for sample copies.

Hong Kong Enterprises, Hong Kong Trade Development Council, Convention Plaza, 36/F, Office Tower, 1 Harbour Road, Hong Kong.

Made in Europe, Hahnstrasse 70, Postfach 710601, D-6000 Frankfurt/Main, Germany. U.S. Distributor: Wilshire Book Company, 12015 Sherman Road, North Hollywood, CA 91605. Other foreign trade magazines can be found in your local library. Or contact any foreign embassy or consulate—my friend Melvin Powers tells me that many publish trade magazines. Sample copies can be obtained by requesting them from the commercial attaché at these consulates. They will contain many potential mail order products.

11.   Attend trade shows. Like inventor shows, trade shows will have hundreds of products, some of which will be outstanding for mail

order. To find out about trade shows, contact your local chamber of commerce.

12. Rework items from old magazines. If a product was a great mail order seller 10, 15, 20, or more years ago, it may well make a great mail order seller today. When Joe Cossman sold more than a million potato spud guns this product was in its fiftieth year and had had frequent resurrections. You can find old magazines containing mail order products at your local library. Also, old catalogs—such as Sears and Montgomery Ward—are currently being reprinted to contain items that may even now be of interest to the mail order market. Get these old magazines and catalogs, read them, and use your imagination.

13. Personalize items. People like to see items with their names on them, and this device has been used again to sell products of all sorts, from card cases to briefcases to wallets to address labels and paperweights. Do some research. If you can figure out a new twist or way to personalize an item, you have a good possibility for a winner.

14. Write a book or a correspondence course. Many of the successful mail order entrepreneurs I mentioned in Chapter 1 succeeded because of their ability to write and sell information. Information meets many of the outstanding criteria of a mail order product, including low cost, light weight, and relative indestructibility in the mail, and, as we'll see shortly in discussing controlling your product, printed products you write yourself are relatively easy to control at low cost. Look in the classified section of any magazine containing many mail order products, such as *Popular Mechanics* or *House and Garden,* and you will find individuals either advertising directly or using the two-step inquiry and follow-up method of selling information, books, booklets, and correspondence courses through the mail.

15. Go to the library and look at manufacturers' directories, such as *Thomas' Register of Manufacturers.* You will find not only names and addresses, but also products and the individual to contact about obtaining them. Every page is a potential source of a new mail order product.

16. Sell instructional tape cassettes. Learning by listening to a tape at home or even in a car while driving to work is very popular today. If you have special knowledge of anything, you may be able to tape it on a cassette and sell the information in this way for $5.95 to $9.95 or more per tape. You can obtain duplicate tapes for $1 or so depending on the quantity, so the markup is quite good. Video tapes are almost as inexpensive, and they sell for much more.

17. Get a copy of *The Wholesale by Mail Catalog* by the Print Project and published by St. Martin's Press. This book lists over 350 companies selling all sorts of products wholesale by mail. The discounts offered are 30 to 90 percent off retail for single items, but you should be able to negotiate much larger discounts, in quantity buys for resale. Some may also offer a drop-ship arrangement whereby they will ship each item individually directly to your customer. Your profits will be much less if you use drop-shipping, but you can fill out your product line in this way, and of course it has the definite advantage that you need carry no inventory of that particular product.

WHY YOU MUST CONTROL YOUR PRODUCT AND HOW TO DO IT

Controlling the product is of utmost importance in any mail order sales, and you should consider it right from the start. What do I mean by controlling your product? I mean that no one else can sell your product except you. This is so important because when you advertise in mail order, your competitor not only sees your proposition, but can determine that you are successful, if you continue to advertise. Your competitor knows that you must be successful or you would not be spending the money for advertising. This is one of the dilemmas of the beginner in mail order. If one is successful, every copycat competitor in the world will jump in to rip off the product by selling the same one. Because many will have much greater financial resources than you, they will be able to undersell you and take your market away from you if you do not control your product. How can you control the product? There are six basic methods: a patent, a copyright, an exclusive, a secret formula, a proprietary methodology, and a trademark.

The Patent

A patent is a grant issued by the government that gives you, as the inventor, the right to exclude all others from making, using, or selling your invention within the United States, its territories, and possessions. It is important here to understand that we are talking about the United States only. Each country has its own patent laws and there is no such thing currently as an international patent. If you wanted patent protection all over the world, it would cost you thousands and thousands of dollars to obtain. Therefore, you should get a patent only in those countries in which they feel the item might be made, used, or sold.

The patent law is for your protection if you invent or discover a new and useful process or improvement. My patent for body armor is shown in Figure 6.4.

Many misunderstand the type of protection provided by a patent in the United States. First, the U.S. government does not protect your patent. This is why the patent is frequently referred to as "a license to sue." If someone violates your patent, it is up to you to sue them to obtain redress. This you do with your own money. Further, the mere fact that you have a patent does not guarantee that your patent cannot be invalidated by the court when you do sue. Thus, if the individual who is violating your patent is able to show prior usage, your patent can be invalidated even though you have the initial patent on a device. You will receive nothing in return, despite the fact that you may have spent thousands of dollars on patenting the items and on court costs.

There are two further disadvantages you need to consider. The first is that a new patent may be granted which copies your concept without copying your idea and violating your patent. For example, an individual who had a patent on a slide fastener or zipper for putting two sections of a suit together would not be violated by Velcro tape or a button, either of which performs the identical function. Another disadvantage has to do with the cost. Usually, a patent in the United States costs several thousand dollars. It is worth the money only if you have something totally unique, which is difficult to design around and which has not seen prior usage. How the patent is written—the claims it makes and so forth—can determine whether you will be able to protect your patent successfully. That is why a lawyer can be critical.

However, it is possible to patent something yourself legally. If you want to know more about this, read *Patent It Yourself,* by David Pressman, published by Nolo Press, 950 Parker Street, Berkeley, CA 94710. Pressman is an electrical engineer and has had more than 18 years of experience as a patent examiner for the U.S. Patent and Trademark Office, as a corporate patent attorney, and currently as a patent attorney in private practice.

The Copyright

The copyright is the right of an author to control the reproduction of an intellectual creation, and it protects your original and creative works from unauthorized reproduction by others. In effect, you get a complete monopoly over whatever you have copyrighted. Your copyright work may not be printed, published, dramatized, translated, adapted, broadcasted, or reproduced in any other way without your consent.

The copyright has important advantages over a patent. It costs only $20, is extremely easy to register, and does not require an attorney. For

United States Patent [19]

Cohen

[11] **3,803,639**

[45] **Apr. 16, 1974**

[54] **BODY ARMOUR JACKET**

[76] Inventor: **William A. Cohen,** 1556 N. Sierra Madre Villa, Pasadena, Calif. 91107

[22] Filed: **July 11, 1973**

[21] Appl. No.: 378,207

[30]   **Foreign Application Priority Data**
         Oct. 4, 1972   Israel............................ 40502

[52] **U.S. Cl.** 2/2.5
[51] **Int. Cl.** F41b 1/02
[58] **Field of Search** 2/2.5

[56]   **References Cited**
            UNITED STATES PATENTS

2,640,987	6/1903	Ehlers..............................	2/2.5
2,743,446	5/1956	Persico et al.	2/2.5
2,748,391	6/1956	Lewis et al.	2/2.5
2,954,563	10/1960	DeGrazio..........................	2/2.5
3,130,414	4/1964	Bailey et al.	2/2.5

3,392,406   7/1968   Pernini et al. 2/2.5

Primary Examiner—Alfred R. Guest
Attorney, Agent, or Firm—Benjamin J. Barish

[57]   **ABSTRACT**

A body armour jacket, which may be easily donned and doffed and may be conveniently opened for purposes of comfort or ventilation, includes a front body assembly and a back body assembly, the front body assembly comprising a right armour section, a left armour section, and a center armour flap. The ends of the right and left armour sections are in abutting relationship and are fastened together by a fastener. The center armour flap is hinged to one of the sections along a line spaced from its abutting end and is fastenable by another fastener to the other section along a line spaced from its abutting end, such that the center armour flap, when closed, bridges the abutting ends of both sections.

7 Claims, 4 Drawing Figures

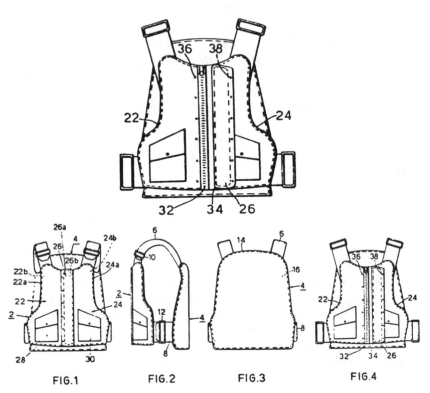

Figure 6.4   A U.S. patent for body armor.

3,803,639

BODY ARMOUR JACKET

BACKGROUND OF THE INVENTION

The present invention relates to body armour jackets such as are used by soldiers and policemen to provide body protection against small arms fire, shrapnel, and the like.

A number of body armour jackets have been designed. In one type, the front assembly of the jacket includes a fabric carrier and a one-piece armour insert. Such a jacket, however, is not openable from the front and therefore is inconvenient to don and doff, sometimes uncomfortable to wear, and difficult to ventilate. Another known form of body armour jacket is made of flexible armour, such as ballistic nylon, and includes a front closure arrangement by overlapping the armour on the inside. Such an arrangement, however, would not be satisfactory with rigid armour, as distinguished from flexible armour, since rigid armour would produce undue discomfort in the chest and abdominal regions because of the armour rigidity.

Insofar as I am aware, a rigid armour body jacket having a front closure has not yet been devised. An object of the present invention is to provide such a body armour jacket.

SUMMARY OF THE INVENTION

According to the invention, there is provided a body armour jacket including a front body assembly and a back body assembly joined thereto, characterized in that the front body assembly comprises a right armour section, a left armour section, and a center armour flap.

The ends of the right and left armour sections are in abutting relationship and are fastened together by a first openable and closable fastener. The center armour flap is hinged to one of said sections along a line spaced from its abutting end and is fastenable by a second openable and closable fastener to the other of said sections along a line spaced from its abutting end, such that the center armour flap, when closed, bridges the abutting ends of both said armour sections.

According to another feature of the invention, the right and left armour sections and said center armour flap each comprises a fabric carrier and a rigid armour plate insert.

In the preferred embodiment of the invention described below, the center armour flap is hinged to one of these sections by stitching. Also, the first mentioned fastener is a slide-fastener, and the second-mentioned fastener comprises a series of snap-fasteners.

According to a further features, the front body assembly is joined to the back body assembly by adjustable shoulder and waist straps.

Such a body armour jacket, since it is provided with a front closure, may be easily donned and doffed, and may be conveniently opened when desired for purposes of comfort or ventilation.

Further features and advantages of the invention will be apparent from the description below.

BRIEF DESCRIPTION OF THE DRAWINGS

The invention is herein described, by way of example only, with reference to the accompanying drawings, wherein:

FIG. 1 is a front elevational view of a body armour jacket constructed in accordance with the invention;

FIG. 2 is a side elevational view of the body armour jacket of FIG. 1;

FIG. 3 is a rear elevational view of the body armour jacket of FIG. 1; and

FIG. 4 is a front elevational view corresponding to FIG. 1 but illustrating the center armour flap in its open position to permit opening and closing the front closure fastener.

DESCRIPTION OF THE PREFERRED EMBODIMENT

The body armour jacket illustrated in the drawings comprises a front assembly, generally designated 2, and a back assembly, generally designated 4, both joined together by adjustable shoulder straps 6 and adjustable waist straps 8. The straps are made adjustable by the provision of buckles 10 in the shoulder straps, and buckles 12 in the waist straps.

The back assembly, as shown in FIG. 3, comprises a single fabric carrier 14 and a single rigid armour plate insert 16 disposed within the fabric carrier. The shoulder straps 6 and waist straps 8 are fixed, as by stitching, to the fabric carrier 14.

Front assembly 2, is made of three parts, namely a right armour section 22, a left armour section 24, and a center armour flap 26. Each of the foregoing is also made of a fabric carrier (22a, 24a, 26a), and a rigid armour plate insert (22b, 24b, 26b) carried within its respective fabric carrier. If desired, the fabric carriers of the right and left sections may also be formed with pockets as shown at 28 and 30, respectively.

As shown particularly in FIG. 4 (wherein the center armour flap 26 is pivoted open), the ends of the right and left sections 2 and 4 are disposed in abutting relationship and are fastened together by an openable and closable slide-fastener 32, e.g., a zip-fastener. The center armour flap 26 is hingedly mounted, as by stitching, to the left armour section 24 along line 34, which line is spaced from the abutting end of that section. In addition, the center flap is fastenable to the right armour section by a line of snap fasteners, the female snaps 36 of which are located along a line on the fabric carrier 24a of the right section 24 spaced inwardly from its abutting end, and the male snaps 38 of which are located along a line on the fabric carrier 26a of the center armour flap 26 spaced slightly from the corresponding end of the flap.

The arrangement is such that when the center armour flap 26 is closed (FIG. 1), its rigid armour insert 26b completely bridges the abutting ends of the right and left armour inserts 22b, 24b of the sections. The armour insert 26b of the center flap thus provides armour portection for the region occupied by the front closure 32.

It will thus be seen that the body armour jacket illustrated may be opened from the front merely by detaching snaps 36, 38, thereby permitting the center armour flap to be pivoted open; and then opening the center slide-fastener 32 to open the jacket. To close the jacket, slide-fastener 32 is closed, and then fasteners 38 are snapped into fasteners 36 to close the center armour flap 26.

The armour inserts may be rigid reinforced fiberglass or ceramic. The invention could also be used with soft armour inserts, such as nylon.

It will thus be seen that the body armour jacket illustrated is provided with a front closure system which

Figure 6.4   (Continued)

3,803,639

3 | 4

permits the jacket to be conveniently donned, doffed and opened for purposes of comfort or ventilation.

Many modifications, variations, and other applications of the illustrated embodiment will be apparent.

What is claimed is:

1. A body armour jacket including a front body assembly and a back body assembly joined thereto, characterized in that the front body assembly comprises a right armour section, a left armour section, and a center armour flap, the end of the right and left armour sections being in abutting relationship and being fastened together by a first openable and closable fastener, the centre armour flap being hinged to one of said sections along a line spaced from its abutting end and being fastenable by a second openable and closable fastener to the other of said sections along a line spaced from its abutting end such that the center armour flap, when closed, bridges the abutting ends of both said armour sections.

2. A jacket according to claim 1, wherein said right and left armour sections and said center armour flap each comprises a fabric carrier and a rigid armour plate insert.

3. A jacket according to claim 1, wherein said center armour flap is hinged to said one section by stitching.

4. A jacket according to claim 1, wherein said first fastener is a slide-fastener.

5. A jacket according to claim 1, wherein said second fastener comprises a line of snap-fasteners.

6. A jacket according to claim 1, wherein said front body assembly is joined to the back body assembly by adjustable shoulder and waist straps.

7. A jacket according to claim 1, wherein said back body assembly comprises a fabric carrier and a rigid armour plate insert.

* * * * *

Figure 6.4   (Continued)

additional forms write to the Register of Copyrights, Copyright Office, the Library of Congress, Washington, DC 20559.

Another advantage is that unlike the patent, there is an international convention of copyrights. With the indicia ©, the date, and your name, you are protected in every country that is a member of the convention.

On March 1, 1989, the United States joined the Berne Union for international copyright protection. The Copyright Office furnished the following information about the results of this action:

Beginning March 1, 1989, copyright in the works of U.S. authors will be protected automatically in all member nations of the Berne Union. (As of September 1988, there were a total of 79 member nations in the Berne Union.)

Since members of the Berne Union agree to a certain minimum level of copyright protection, each Berne Union country will provide at least that guaranteed level for U.S. authors.

Members of the Berne Union agree to treat nationals of other member countries like their own nationals for purposes of copyright. Therefore, U.S. authors will often receive higher levels of protection than the guaranteed minimum.

Overall, piracy of U.S. works abroad can be fought more effectively.

Beginning March 1, 1989, works of foreign authors who are nationals of a Berne Union country and works first published in a Berne Union country are automatically protected in the United States.

In order to fulfill its Berne Convention obligations, the United States made certain changes in its copyright law by passing the Berne Convention Implementation Act of 1988. These changes are not retroactive and are effective only after March 1, 1989.

Mandatory Notice of Copyright is Abolished

Mandatory notice of copyright has been abolished for works published for the first time on or after March 1, 1989. Failure to place a notice of copyright on copies or phonorecords of such works can no longer result in the loss of copyright.

Voluntary use of notice is encouraged.   Placing a notice of copyright on published works is still strongly recommended. One of the benefits is that an infringer will not be able to claim that he or she "innocently infringed" a work. (A successful innocent infringement claim may result in a reduction in damages for infringement that the copyright owner would otherwise receive.)

A sample notice of copyright is: © 1989 John Brown.

The notice requirement for works incorporating a predominant portion of U.S. government work has been eliminated as of March 1, 1989. For these works to receive the evidentiary benefit of voluntary notice, in addition to the notice, a statement is required on the copies identifying what is copyrighted.

A sample is: © 1989 Jane Brown. Copyright claimed in Chapters 7–10, exclusive of U.S. government maps.

Notice Unchanged for Works Published
Before March 1, 1989

The Berne Convention Implementation Act is not retroactive. Thus, the notice requirements that were in place before March 1, 1989, govern all works first published during that period (regardless of national origin).

- Works first published between January 1, 1978, and February 28, 1989: If a work was first published without notice during this period, it is still necessary to register the work before or within five years after publication and add the notice to copies distributed in the United States after discovery of the omission.
- Works first published before January 1, 1978: If a work was first published without the required notice before 1978, copyright was lost immediately (except for works seeking "ad interim" protection). Once copyright is lost, it can never be restored in the United States, except by special legislation.

Mandatory Deposit

Copyright owners must deposit in the Copyright Office two complete copies or phonorecords of the best edition of all works subject to copyright that are publicly distributed in the United States, whether or not the work contains a notice of copyright. In general, this deposit requirement may be satisfied by registration.

Registration as a Prerequisite to Suit

Before a copyright infringement suit is brought for a work of U.S. origin, it must be submitted to the Copyright Office for registration.

When is the United States the country of origin of a work? The United States is the country of origin if:

- Publication first occurred in the United States.
- Publication occurred simultaneously in the United States and a non-Berne Union country. "Simultaneous publication" means within the first 30 days of publication.
- Publication occurred simultaneously in the United States and other Berne Union country that provides the same term as or a longer term of protection than the United States.
- The work is unpublished and all of the authors are nationals of the United States. (U.S. domiciliaries and habitual residents are treated the same as nationals.) In the case of an unpublished audiovisual work, all the authors are legal entities with headquarters in the United States.
- The work is a pictorial, graphic, or sculptural work that is incorporated in a permanent structure located in the United States.
- The work is first published in a non-Berne country and all of the authors are U.S. nationals. In the case of a published audiovisual work, all the authors are legal entities with headquarters in the United States.

Although Berne Convention works whose origin is **not** the United States are exempt from the requirement to register before suit can be brought, a person seeking the exemption bears the burden of proving to the court that the work is not subject to the registration requirement.

Benefits of Registration

Berne Convention works whose country of origin is not the United States need not be registered with the Copyright Office in order to bring an infringement suit. However, registration is still strongly recommended.

Presumption of copyright validity. The copyright owner who registers before or within five years of first publication receives the benefit of a legal presumption in court, called prima facie evidentiary weight. This means that the court will presume:

- that the facts stated in the copyright certificate of registration are true; and
- that the copyright is valid.

Statutory damages and attorney's fees. Another benefit of timely registration is that the copyright owner of works registered for copyright protection within three months of publication, or before infringement, is eligible for an award of attorney's fees and statutory damages. These damages are now double the amounts previously provided. A copyright owner may elect to receive either actual damages or statutory damages. Where statutory damages are elected, the court determines the amount of the award, within a certain range. The Berne Convention Implementation Act doubles statutory damages to:

- A range between $500 and $20,000 for ordinary infringement;
- A maximum of $100,000 for willful infringement; and
- A minimum of $200 for innocent infringement.

Under current laws, a copyright protects for the life of the author plus 50 years, as compared with the patent, which runs out in 17 years and cannot be renewed. Items that can be copyrighted include books, periodicals, speeches prepared for oral delivery, dramatic composition, usable compositions, maps, works of art, models or designs, reproductions of works of art, drawings, plastic works of scientific or technical character, photographs, prints and pictorial illustrations, commercial prints and labels, photoplays, motion pictures, nondramatic films, music for mechanical instruments, and sound recordings.

One of my copyrights for a book is shown in Figure 6.5.

The Exclusive

The exclusive is another way of controlling the item or product you are going to sell by mail. An exclusive usually means obtaining an agreement from the manufacturer, located either in the United States or abroad, that you alone can sell his or her product in a certain area or through a certain means such as mail order. Many times foreign exporters of manufacturers

CERTIFICATE OF COPYRIGHT REGISTRATION

This certificate, issued under the seal of the Copyright Office in accordance with the provisions of section 410(a) of title 17, United States Code, attests that copyright registration has been made for the work identified below. The information in this certificate has been made a part of the Copyright Office records.

(signature)

REGISTER OF COPYRIGHTS
United States of America

OFFICIAL SEAL

FORM TX
UNITED STATES COPYRIGHT OFFICE

REGISTRATION NUMBER

TXu   451 787

TX   TXU
EFFECTIVE DATE OF REGISTRATION

DEC 28 1990
Month   Day   Year

DO NOT WRITE ABOVE THIS LINE. IF YOU NEED MORE SPACE, USE A SEPARATE CONTINUATION SHEET.

1 TITLE OF THIS WORK ▼

SELLING BY MAIL ORDER

PREVIOUS OR ALTERNATIVE TITLES ▼

PUBLICATION AS A CONTRIBUTION   If this work was published as a contribution to a periodical, serial, or collection, give information about the collective work in which the contribution appeared.   **Title of Collective Work ▼**

If published in a periodical or serial give: Volume ▼   Number ▼   Issue Date ▼   On Pages ▼

2 NAME OF AUTHOR ▼

a   William A. COHEN

DATES OF BIRTH AND DEATH
Year Born ▼   Year Died ▼
1937

Was this contribution to the work a "work made for hire"?   ☐ Yes   ☒ No

AUTHOR'S NATIONALITY OR DOMICILE   Name of Country
OR { Citizen of ▶ USA
{ Domiciled in ▶

WAS THIS AUTHOR'S CONTRIBUTION TO THE WORK
Anonymous?   ☐ Yes   ☒ No
Pseudonymous?   ☐ Yes   ☒ No

NOTE
Under the law

NATURE OF AUTHORSHIP   Briefly describe nature of the material created by this author in which copyright is claimed. ▼
ENTIRE TEXT

NAME OF AUTHOR ▼
b

DATES OF BIRTH AND DEATH
Year Born ▼   Year Died ▼

Was this contribution to the work a "work made for hire"?   ☐ Yes   ☐ No

AUTHOR'S NATIONALITY OR DOMICILE   Name of Country
OR { Citizen of ▶
{ Domiciled in ▶

WAS THIS AUTHOR'S CONTRIBUTION TO THE WORK
Anonymous?   ☐ Yes   ☐ No
Pseudonymous?   ☐ Yes   ☐ No

NATURE OF AUTHORSHIP   Briefly describe nature of the material created by this author in which copyright is claimed. ▼

NAME OF AUTHOR ▼
c

DATES OF BIRTH AND DEATH
Year Born ▼   Year Died ▼

Was this contribution to the work a "work made for hire"?   ☐ Yes   ☐ No

AUTHOR'S NATIONALITY OR DOMICILE   Name of Country
OR { Citizen of ▶
{ Domiciled in ▶

WAS THIS AUTHOR'S CONTRIBUTION TO THE WORK
Anonymous?   ☐ Yes   ☐ No
Pseudonymous?   ☐ Yes   ☐ No

NATURE OF AUTHORSHIP   Briefly describe nature of the material created by this author in which copyright is claimed. ▼

3 YEAR IN WHICH CREATION OF THIS WORK WAS COMPLETED   This information must be given in all cases.
1990   ◀ Year

DATE AND NATION OF FIRST PUBLICATION OF THIS PARTICULAR WORK
Complete this information ONLY if this work has been published.
Month ▶   Day ▶   Year ▶   ◀ Nation

4 COPYRIGHT CLAIMANT(S) Name and address must be given even if the claimant is the same as the author given in space 2 ▼

DR. WILLIAM A. COHEN
1556 N. SIERRA MADRE VILLA
PASADENA, CA 91107

APPLICATION RECEIVED
DEC 28 1990
ONE DEPOSIT RECEIVED
DEC 28 1990
TWO DEPOSITS RECEIVED
REMITTANCE NUMBER AND DATE

(DO NOT WRITE HERE / OFFICE USE ONLY)

TRANSFER If the claimant(s) named here in space 4 are different from the author(s) named in space 2, give a brief statement of how the claimant(s) obtained ownership of the copyright. ▼

MORE ON BACK ▶   • Complete all applicable spaces (numbers 5-11) on the reverse side of this page.
• See detailed instructions.   • Sign the form at line 10.

DO NOT WRITE HERE
Page 1 of ___ pages

Figure 6.5   A copyright.

located in other countries will grant you an exclusive if they are convinced that you can sell large quantities of their product. You can convince them by a track record of success with prior products, your professional conduct and professional stationery in correspondence with the manufacturer, and your statement that to market this item in large quantities, you must have an exclusive for this product.

Secret Formula

Although formulas can be patented because of the nature of the patent law, it is sometimes difficult to patent a formula and still have it protected. But as long as you can keep the formula secret, you can control the product. This can be much longer than 17 years. An example is Coca-Cola, for which the exact formula for manufacturing is over 100 years old and has never been patented. It is said that the formula is known only to the chairman of the board and the president of the company at any one time, and that these two individuals never fly on the same airplane.

Sometimes it is definitely in your interests *not* to patent an item, but rather to keep it as a secret formula. One example is the special paper used to correct typewritten mistakes, sold in stationery stores. This is going out of use now due to computers, but once it was a big seller. The typist simply typed over the mistake with the special paper and that "whited-out" the mistake. Had this product formula been kept a secret and not patented, the inventor would have made a lot of money. However, the patent office refused to grant a patent unless the exact percentage of chemical impregnation in the paper was provided, even though a correction would occur or the material could be used for correcting typewriting over a large range of impregnation. As a result, the inventor selected the optimum formula and patented it. His competitors purchased his formula for 50¢ from the patent office, and by a slight modification, they were able to go around the patent without violating it. The result was that instead of one brand of correction paper on the market, there were half a dozen or more. Keeping the formula secret might have saved this inventor's control over the product. A secret formula can be an effective way of protecting and controlling your mail order product when a patent is ineffective.

Proprietary Methodology

Proprietary methodology is similar to the secret formula and has to do with how you put something together. Again, this may be patentable. But before patenting it, you should consider whether your patent would be easy to design around. If so, you should consider keeping this methodology proprietary, rather than using the patent office to attempt to control and protect your process.

Trademark

A trademark is a word, name, symbol, design, or combination of these that identifies a product with the owner of the trademark.

A trademark is somewhat different in that it should be registered only if you contemplate long-term use, and it is important to protect it from copying. Unlike a patent, the trademark must be used in commerce for some time prior to your registering it, and evidence of this use must be filed with the trademark application. Like patents, trademarks are filed with the U.S. Patent Office and a search is necessary to make certain that the mark you are submitting does not conflict with other trademarks that someone else may be using. In general, if you are going to file for a trademark, consult a patent attorney.

A trademark does not protect your product per se, but only the name. If you have a product whose name is important to you and it cannot be protected by copyright, this method of protecting and controlling it may be essential for you.

PRODUCTS THAT MADE THEIR PROMOTERS A MILLION

Joe Cossman lists the following products as having made a fortune for their creators: the fountain pen, zipper, roller skates, disposable diapers, chip soap, frozen food, dancing lessons, prepared dog food, bandages, the cash register, cellophane, the kiddie car, gelatin capsules, sanitary napkins, schools by mail, Dixie cups, Good Humors, book clubs, home hair wave, bottle caps, deodorant, snap fasteners, Scotch tape, the teddy bear, chewing gum, shorthand systems, the pink hairpin, the paperclip, the rubber heel, ready-made bows, tea bags, corn plasters, vacuum cleaners, and alarm clocks. Remember, any one of these could have made you a fortune. There are still unlimited product ideas out there which can do the same for you.

ITEMS THAT CONTINUE TO SELL BIG

Standard Rate and Data Service, which publishes a number of important directories we will talk about in a later chapter, has developed sales statistics on mail order items, which Benjamin Suarez analyzed to determine the current best-selling products in mail order. Here was one year's annual sales in dollars.

1. Books, 21.4 million.
2. Wearing apparel, 9.9 million.

3. Hobby and craft items, 8.9 million.
4. Housewares, 8.1 million.
5. Agriculture, 7.4 million.
6. Automobiles, 6.4 million.
7. Cosmetics, 5.9 million.
8. Health and comfort items, 5.8 million.
9. Foods, 5.5 million.
10. Entertainment, 4.2 million.
11. Sports and outdoor equipment, 3.7 million.
12. Greeting cards and stationery, 2.7 million.
13. Devices and gadgets, 2.2 million.
14. Collectors' items, 1.5 million.
15. Child-care and nursery items, 1.1 million.

In another survey, *Better Homes and Gardens* asked its readers about items they had bought or inquired about. The percentage breakdowns for these different classifications of mail order products were as follows: collectibles, 14 percent; books, 37.9 percent; clothing, 57.6 percent; food items, 14.3 percent; fund-raising contributions, 3.5 percent; garden/nursery, 25.7 percent; gift merchandise, 38.1 percent; health foods, 3.7 percent; home study courses, 1.6 percent; insurance, 2.3 percent; photofinishing, 10.0 percent; records, tapes, and cassettes, 18.0 percent; self-improvement, 1.4 percent; none of the above, 8.4 percent; and no answer, .9 percent.

The Maxwell Stroge Company, a major consulting and research company for the mail order industry, picks the top 10 mail order product categories and publishes them in their *Mail Order Industry Annual Report.* Here is one year's results.

1.	Insurance	$4,000,000,000
2.	General merchandise/home furnishings/ housewares/gifts	$2,700,000,000
3.	Magazine subscriptions	$1,900,000,000
4.	Books	$1,388,000,000
5.	Ready-to-wear	$1,340,000,000
6.	Collectibles	$ 920,000,000
7.	Sporting goods	$ 780,000,000
8.	Crafts	$ 550,000,000
9.	Foods	$ 500,000,000
10.	Records and tapes	$ 478,000,000

Don't pay too much attention to these surveys—they change from year to year. What you should notice is that there is plenty of room for you to make a fortune with almost any kind of product. As a beginner, follow these guidelines to maximize your chances of success right from the start:

1. Control your product. If you do not, someone else will steal your justly deserved success from you.
2. Stay away from things that can commonly be bought at the store.
3. Don't start with a fad item. You don't know where the product is in its life cycle. You can lose as much money as you can make.
4. Stay away from low-quality goods. Your goods don't need to be the top of the line. However, if they are really cheap, you are going to get lots of returns and start with a bad reputation.
5. Unless you are thoroughly familiar with the business, stay away from products closely regulated by the government, such as drugs.
6. Again, unless you are already in the business, do not get involved initially with perishable goods, such as foods.

Finally, to quote Joe Karbo, "The best product is between your ears." By this, Joe means that it is not the product or service itself that will sell to your market and become a profitable mail order product, but rather your own ingenuity, imagination, and perception of the product and how you communicate this to your potential customers.

SUMMARY

In this chapter we have learned that the basic principle of success for product selection is to look at the marketplace first, and then decide what the market wants before selecting a product. Next we considered the different methods of selling in mail order and how selection of our product depended on what methods we decided to choose. Then, we looked at general rules of product selection and I gave you 17 sources of mail order products. We next turned to the methods of controlling your product—patent, copyright, exclusive, a secret formula, proprietary methodology, or a trademark. And finally, we talked about which products are selling best and which have made and continue to make fortunes for their promoters.

7

Pricing Your Mail Order Product or Service

Pricing is a major revenue-making decision for anyone that wants to be in the mail order business. Price too low or too high, and you won't make any money. Pricing is one of the few ways to generate income without generating costs.

HOW TO ESTABLISH A FAIR PRICE

If you are new to business, you may think: Why all the fuss? All you need to do is add a fair profit to your cost. Unfortunately, if you follow that simple formula, you have a guaranteed recipe for failure. The first thing you'll realize is that there is no such thing as a "fair profit" or a "fair price" . . . with one exception—if you have a monopoly on something vital that everyone wants.

Let's say you discovered a guaranteed cure for some fatal disease. Anyone who has that disease will pay you any price you set. That means you would be in a position to take advantage of your customers and take an unfair profit. That would not only be unethical, it would be bad business. With your next product, when you don't have a monopoly, potential customers will go out of their way not to do business with you. You must always deal with your customers fairly, or they will not be your customers very long.

However, a monopoly is an exception. In most cases, adding what you think is a "fair" profit will just get you into trouble. Let's say that you invent a "whatits" and that each "whatits" costs you $1 to make. What would a "fair profit" be? 10, 20, 30, 50, 100 percent? The sad truth is

125

that if you add 100 percent for profit and sell your "whatits" for $2, you will lose money. You must consider all of your costs. Consider your advertising costs; they are significant. Because of these costs, unless you can get at least a three or four to one markup on your in-the-mail cost, you will probably lose money. In fact, a good friend of mine who has made millions in the mail order business says that you must price your product for a minimum of a five to one markup. That's 500 percent. In other words, if your "whatits" costs $1 to make, you must price it at $5 or more.

However, even that isn't the whole story. Other important factors also come into play. For example, many people won't buy a product priced too low, regardless of how little it cost you, or how fair the price according to your calculations. They feel that if you are pricing it so low, it must be of inferior quality, or that something else must be wrong with it.

If you stand on a street corner with a basket full of $1 bills and try to give them to passersby, you will find a good many people will be suspicious and won't take one. You may even get arrested. That's because a good many people will think there must be some kind of catch or that you are crazy. Ultimately, you may be able to persuade them, or they may take a $1 bill because they see others doing so.

In mail order, this phenomenon can be deadly to the acceptance of your offer, because you get no feedback to counter or objections to overcome. Nor will a prospect see others purchasing the product at your fair price and be persuaded because of their purchases. You need to be honest and ethical in everything you do in the mail order business. However, do not think that there is one fair profit or fair price, because there is not.

THERE ARE MANY "FAIR PRICES" FOR A PRODUCT OR SERVICE

When teaching, I use an exercise to show students that there are many different prices that both buyer and seller consider fair. "Buyers" and "sellers" each receive confidential instructions regarding the purchase of a large computer system for a business, or sometimes an old 1947 Packard. The product I use makes no difference at all.

If the exercise is with computers, the *sellers* are told that the system they must sell is now obsolete. If it can't be sold within one day, they must give it away for salvage and receive nothing.

The *buyers* are told that their entire business was built around this type of computer system. If they can't buy an immediate replacement within one day from the seller, they must buy a similar system elsewhere for $50,000.

Neither buyers nor sellers know the others' situation. With no more information than this, students are given 20 minutes to "negotiate the best price." Both must sign a bill of sale before the deal is complete. If they can't agree on a price in 20 minutes, there is no sale. Sellers know that if there is no sale, they must salvage the computer and get nothing. Buyers know they must then pay $50,000 somewhere else. So, the buyer and seller almost always come to an agreement, and have motivation to do so.

Amazingly, for exactly the same product, sales prices in a single class may vary from a few dollars all the way to almost the full $50,000. In all cases, both buyer and seller consider the price "fair," whatever price they agree to. That is, until they learn the full story about the other side's situation.

The point here is not that you should rip-off your customers, but that there can be many "fair" prices for a product or service and these prices do not depend solely on your cost. Always remember, if you don't deliver value for the money, soon you won't have any customers.

WHAT IF NO ONE WILL BUY YOUR PRODUCT AT A 300 PERCENT OR BETTER MARKUP?

If you can't get the markup I have suggested, it means that your product or service is not a good one for mail order, and you shouldn't try to sell it by mail. Find another product or service, or try to sell that product through some other means where the required markup is lower. For example, store retailers may sell at a much lower markup, roughly 100 percent. In comparison, successful mail order products have this, or even a higher markup, with two exceptions.

Remember Joe Karbo's offer of the *Lazy Man's Way to Riches?* Joe tells you right in the first part of his advertisement that he's going to charge you $10 for something that only cost him 50 cents. If you have your calculator handy, you can see that is a whopping 2,000 percent markup. That's typical for books and tapes, both audio and video, and for computer software, too. In quantity, a taped audio will probably cost you a dollar or less to produce. It may sell for $10 or more. Similarly, a video tape costing you $2 each is successfully priced to sell by mail from $20–$50 dollars each. However, other products can also have high percentage markups.

Some years ago, there were many advertisements for cubic zirconium, the imitation diamond which actually cuts glass. They were priced at $15 and up. One of my students imported these stones for resale. The cost? Forty eight cents each!

What are the two exceptions? Well, one is if you are selling many products through a catalog. You can then amortize your advertising costs over many products. The second exception is if you intend to lose money by selling a "loss leader." This means you lose money on the first deal in order to get a new customer to respond. You make your loss up by selling other products to him or her in the future.

DON'T THINK YOU CAN ALWAYS LOWER PRICES TO SELL MORE

Economists teach an interesting theory regarding the demand for products and services. It's called the downward sloping demand curve. It says that if we reduce the price, the market will demand more of a product or service. That's why the curve slopes down. However, in truth, the curve doesn't always slope down. As we saw earlier, if you have an exclusive on some life-saving medicine, market demand won't change regardless of the price you charge and the "curve" will be a horizontal line.

Let's say your product is an expensive piece of jewelry. You will probably find that as you raise the price, you will sell more, not less. This will continue to a certain point, and then as you keep raising the price, the market will start demanding less again. Why is this? Price and image go hand in hand. As you raise the price for an expensive piece of jewelry, you are also enhancing its image. Remember what I said earlier about pricing too low? People may think your product is of low quality. With a high price, the reverse is true. However, if you raise the price too high, buyers will start looking around for jewelry of the same perceived high quality at a more competitive price.

As you can see, you must be very careful about the price you set. Set it too low, and many people won't buy your product or use your service, even if it's a bargain. Set it too high and they won't buy it either.

HOW TO PRICE NEW PRODUCTS OR SERVICES

If you're introducing a new product or service, there are three basic tactics you can follow. They are price skimming (pricing high), penetration pricing (pricing low), and meet-the-competition pricing (pricing in the middle). I'll discuss this further in Chapter 23. For now, what I want you to know is that any of these alternatives can work well for you. It all depends on your situation and what you are trying to do. If you have a product that is brand new to the market, you should think about skimming. That is, charging on the high side. If the product you want to introduce is already in the market, your approach should be either to go low to get prospects to buy your product over others in that market, or to charge a similar price, but to offer additional benefits that your competitors do not offer.

BUNDLING FOR PROFIT

One technique that you can use with any of these tactics is called *bundling*. You bundle customer benefits together to increase value. The

Ginsu™ knives advertised on TV were a good example of bundling. What the Ginsu™ people did was to bundle many different knife options together and sell them as one package. So, you not only got a set of steak knives, but a bread knife, a meat knife, and even an upholstery knife. Interestingly, their bundling was so successful, that the $19.95 price of their set was probably more than the individual knives might sell for if bought separately. This is frequently the case when you bundle several products together into one set.

Big companies like automobile manufacturers frequently use the same tactic. They make all kinds of options standard: tinted windows, bucket seats, padded dash, and so on. Yet, the manufacturers' costs for these added values are much less than one would expect. At retail, tinted windows might cost the purchaser an additional $200 or more. But the typical cost to the manufacturer is less than $20. The objective of bundling is to add value to the product or service without raising your costs substantially.

PUT PSYCHOLOGY IN YOUR PRICING

You can use psychology in your pricing to good advantage. Odd/even pricing is one example. People tend to read $13.99 or $16.98 as $13.00 and $16.00 rather than $14.00 or $17.00. So, for many products, whether you charge $16.00 or $16.98, your prospects will perceive either as $16.00. You can see that it is good psychology to ask for the odd price, since it means almost an extra dollar in profit.

This probably won't work with prestige products, however. If you sell anything in which you are trying to give the product some sort of image value, setting an odd price may cause your product not to appear as prestigious. That's true whether your product is a book, jewelry, or a Rolls-Royce limousine.

The absolute versus a relative price difference can also be important from a psychological standpoint. At the $1 to $2 range, a 10 percent difference in price may be perceived as significant. It may make a considerable difference in sales. However, if the product is currently priced at $30 or $40, a 10 percent reduction may not be seen as meaningful. This is because $3 or $4 is such a small amount compared with $30 or $40. This factor is especially important if you are trying to price below your competition.

DISCOUNTS AND HIGH MARKDOWNS

A high markdown, such as for a special sale, also has a psychological component. It will encourage prospects to purchase your product if there was perceived value for the product at the pre-markdown price. In other words, if your product was priced attractively and people bought it to begin with, they will buy more of it if you drop your price significantly.

However, although a high markdown increases sales in the short run, it may make it extremely difficult to return to the original price in the future. So, you shouldn't do it unless you are getting out of that particular product line, or you have a definite plan as to how you are going to be able to raise your price again.

This doesn't mean that you should never give discounts. There are certain situations where the buyer will expect a discount. You could even lose business if you don't offer a discount in some circumstances.

A small company I know, proposed a new type of pilot's kneeboard to hold the pilot's maps in flight. It was cheaper and safer than what was formerly used. After extensive testing, the U.S. government ordered the item. However, the company that had proposed and invented the product didn't get the contract. This company lost millions of dollars in sales because it refused to lower the price of the item when it was ordered in quantity. As a result, the government felt it was getting cheated and went elsewhere.

Earlier we noted price bundling as a potential tactic for meet-the-competition pricing. But bundling may also be considered a special form of discount pricing. Some examples are: travel packages that include (in one price) travel, lodging, meals, and car rental; credit card memberships that include a magazine subscription and life insurance; and health club memberships that include exercise classes, showers, massages, and use of the exercise equipment.

Mail order expert Joe Cossman made millions in the mail order business, and he is a genius at discounting as well. He introduced the type of garden sprinkler made of a flexible plastic hose with little holes in it. Unlike other sprinklers, it was flexible so you could lay it out in the exact pattern of watering you wanted. It was lightweight, wouldn't rust, and since there was nothing mechanical to fail, it was more reliable than rotating sprinklers. It was relatively cheap to make and didn't require very expensive tooling. It cost only forty cents each to manufacture.

He set the initial price at $4.95 and did a direct mail campaign to supermarkets. That was a skimming strategy. The first season, the sprinkler was very successful. Everybody that had a lawn or garden wanted one and there was virtually no competition.

However, because tooling was so cheap to make, practically anyone could make them once they found a different way to do it. Cossman knew that his competition would introduce a similar item the second spring season. In fact, he had five competitors the second year and they were going to sell their product for $3.95.

Cossman knew that $4.95 was a good price for consumers. It was more expensive than rotating sprinklers, but it offered so much more that

Cossman got a lot of feedback that he should have charged more. He knew it was perceived as a good value by his customers. To keep his market, experts said he would need to reduce his price below the competitor's price of $3.95. However, with additional marketing costs and a lower retail price, he would make a lot less money. Also, reducing the price brought it closer to the price of rotating sprinklers. It might lose its image value.

Cossman decided to keep his retail price at $4.95, but give the supermarkets a big discount. Previously, supermarkets bought the sprinklers from him at $3.00 each. So, they made $1.95 for each sprinkler sold. His competitors charged the supermarket $2.40 for each sprinkler. At a selling price of $3.95, the supermarket made $1.55 for each unit sold. Cossman reduced his wholesale price to $2.25. This meant the supermarket made $2.70 for each unit sold, since he held the selling price at $4.95. It only cost him fifteen cents more than his competitors to offer this discount, and the supermarkets ordered a lot more product. As a result, he not only held onto his market, he actually made more money the second year than the first.

YOUR CUSTOMER MUST PERCEIVE A RELATIONSHIP BETWEEN PRICE AND VALUE

Your customer has a right to expect value for his money. There are important relationships between price and value. You can charge more for a product or service that is seen as offering more value. In one instance, a researcher by the name of Elliot B. Ross compared prices for a four-ounce serving of different brands of ice cream against *Consumer Reports* rating of quality. He found that there was a direct relationship between what the consumer was willing to pay and the ice cream's rating of quality according to *Consumer Reports*.

However, it works both ways. Most people judge quality by price. So if the product or service is priced high, the perception of its quality tends to be high also. This is especially important when other cues as to quality aren't available. How many times have you paid more because you wanted to make certain you got a quality product? This has to do with the important influence of image on price, which I mentioned earlier.

IMAGE WILL ALWAYS INFLUENCE PURCHASE OF YOUR PRODUCT OR SERVICE

The image of your product or service in the mind of your customer has a great influence on the amount you can charge. The actual cost to the manufacturer of "name" brand perfumes priced at $100 an ounce or more may be just pennies. Frequently, the bottle costs more than the perfume! Nowadays, some mail order dealers are capitalizing on this by selling the identical scent of expensive perfumes at a few dollars a bottle.

FINE-TUNING YOUR PRICE

Once you apply the basics of pricing and develop a price, you must fine-tune it for maximum sales and profits. This is done by testing as explained in Chapter 22.

SUMMARY

You can see that there is a lot more to pricing than just adding up your costs and tacking on a profit. Selling price is calculated by considering the markup you need to make a profit, the situation you face as you introduce your product into the marketplace, image, and the various psychological factors we have discussed. It is your customer that ultimately decides the price he or she wants to pay for your product or service, or whether any price will be paid at all. You can help your customer do this and make big profits for yourself by applying the concepts and techniques discussed in this chapter to your unique circumstances.

8

Developing a
Unique Offer

The mail order offer is certainly one of the most critical factors you must consider in selling by mail. It has been said that success in direct mail and mail order operations for any given project is due one-third to your creative package, which includes copy and graphics.

Smith-Hemmings-Gosden, now a division of one of the world's largest advertising agencies, used to say that no less than 40 percent of success in any effort is due to the offer. Regardless of the exact percentage, it is clear that with a poor offer you will fail. In fact, differences in response for a given promotion have been as much as 25, 50, or 100 percent, or even more, depending only upon the offer for the same product.

What are we talking about when we speak of the offer? The offer is the proposition you present to the customer. Let's consider an item we are offering, called a widget. Ordinarily each widget costs $1, but we are trying to build up our customer list and so we're offering a special. We're going to give two widgets for $1. How can we best present this to our potential customers?

Well, one way is simply to state that we will offer two widgets for the price of one, or two for $1. But there are other ways. We could say we are going to offer our widget for $1, which is the standard price, and those who purchase within a certain time will get an additional widget free. Or we could say we are going to offer one widget for 99¢ and the buyer can purchase a second widget for 1¢. Or we could offer two widgets free, but require our prospect to send us $1 for postage and handling.

Look at these different offers again and you will see that they are identical. All result in the customer's receiving two widgets for $1, but the differences are in the presentation of the identical price. This is what we are

133

talking about when we speak of the offer, and this is what can make such a tremendous difference in whether or not a project is successful.

Bob Stone relates three ways in which the same offer was stated in an actual mailing. The first was "*half-price.*" The second was "*buy one, get one free.*" The third was "*50% off.*" Each statement conveyed exactly the same offer, but they did not elicit identical responses. The second offer pulled 40 percent better than either the first or third. Clearly, customers felt that "*buy one, get one free*" was the most attractive of the three. But this wouldn't necessarily be true with all products, prices, or customers.

How do you decide which offer is best? There is only one way, and I stress it throughout this book: Test. You must always test to find out which offer is actually better than another. However, certain psychological principles come into play here, and there are reasons that consumers tend to perceive certain offers to be better than others. It only makes sense to consider the needs and desires of our customers when we structure and decide on the components of the offer before we invest our money to advertise it to our potential customers or even test it.

Dr. Abraham Maslow of Brandeis University developed a theory of human motivation that is directly applicable to mail order. Maslow's theory, which has been substantiated by much research, is that people are motivated by their needs. He classified these needs into various levels of importance: Level one includes our physiological needs, those for food, rest, oxygen, and so forth. Level two includes our safety or security needs such as protection against danger, threat, and deprivation. Level three is our social needs. This includes the need for belonging, association, acceptance, and giving and receiving love and friendship. Level four concerns our ego needs. This includes the need for self-confidence, independence, achievement, knowledge, status, recognition, appreciation, and respect for others. Level five is our self-fulfillment needs. This includes the need to realize one's own potential, to experience development, and to be creative. Maslow identified two additional needs which he did not associate with a particular level: knowing and understanding, and aesthetic needs.

Two important points about Maslow's hierarchy of needs are most important for our purposes. The first is that once a need is satisfied, it no longer motivates the individual's behavior; the second is that if a need is frustrated at any level, it is of particular importance. For example, if an individual's safety or security needs are totally satisfied in a totally safe environment, it would be ridiculous to structure an offer to appeal to these needs. You are not going to be able to sell a burglar alarm to someone who lives in an area in which there are no burglaries or in which they are otherwise fully protected.

Two basic offers have withstood the test of time, and you must offer them to your potential customer for a successful mail order appeal. These are the money-back guarantee and the free trial. Both appeal mainly to the security needs of your prospects.

The money-back guarantee is one of the oldest offers known to mail order. It appeals to your potential customers' safety and security needs in that they must send their money to an unknown source for a product they may have never seen before. This may be perceived as a considerable risk. Therefore, you must give them the strongest guarantee you can possibly make. The objective is to give them confidence that if, for any reason, they are dissatisfied with the product or service you offer, they can get their money back easily and with no problems. Some media in which you may want to advertise will insist that you offer a money-back guarantee for any product or service that you advertise. The publication itself may state that all advertisers have agreed to a money-back guarantee. Never mind whether this is said by the medium you are advertising in. You should restate this guarantee in the strongest terms you possibly can in your own ad: "Iron-Clad Guarantee," "No-Questions-Asked Guarantee," and so forth.

The second basic offer, essential in mail order, is the free trial. The free trial allows your customer to use the product for a specified period and then return it without question, even though it is used, and receive his or her money back if dissatisfied. Traditionally, this period has been from 10 days to two weeks, and both of these free trial periods are still used successfully by many mail order operators. However, many innovations to increase the response of potential mail order buyers have taken place. These have included the 31-day free trial period, combined with the money-back guarantee. Joe Karbo's advertising that he would hold a check in escrow for 31 days before cashing it to allow for the free trial period is one of these innovations. Several advertisers, including Melvin Powers and Joe Sugarman, have offered no less than a money-back guarantee for a one-year period. Response will definitely increase with such a guarantee. But will it increase sufficiently to make up for the increased returns sure to occur with such a long trial period for the merchandise? That you must test to find out.

You may wonder whether offering a free trial period won't allow someone to copy your merchandise, if it is printed, a tape, or computer program or to use it and then return it for a refund. Of course, such things are possible—and there are people in this world who will take advantage of you. However, generally, for a satisfactory product or service, your returns will not exceed 15 percent, even including those customers who are rip-off artists. The 15 percent is sort of a working figure that many mail order operators use to decide whether there is something wrong with their product or service. If the return is less than 15 percent, everything is all right; if it's more than 15 percent, something is wrong. Joe Karbo's book *The Lazy Man's Way to Riches,* had a return of about 7 percent. That's a pretty good rate!

Tabulate your returns carefully and then use these tabulations as a guide to whether there is something wrong with your offer, product, or advertising. If you are getting more than 15 percent returns, you should consider changing your product, dropping it, or looking at your advertising appeal to see if it is in some way overstating the case and raising the expectations of your potential customers to such a degree that they are disappointed when they receive the product.

In any case, remember that these two basic offers—the money-back guarantee and the free trial period—are essential to success in direct mail operations.

Ray W. Jutkins of Rockingham-Jutkins Marketing states that the offer must be outstanding and must make the individual want to buy through a promise or an offer that he or she cannot refuse. He lists nine basic appeals the offer can make. Note how well these basic appeals fit in with Maslow's hierarchy of needs. Make an offer to make the purchaser feel: (1) more important; (2) happier; (3) more comfortable; (4) more prosperous; (5) that his or her work is easier; (6) a greater sense of security; (7) more attractive or able to have a better life; or (8) some distinction. Finally, (9) convince the purchaser that you're offering a bargain.

DEVELOPING THE COMPONENTS OF YOUR OFFER AND STRUCTURING THEM

There are two parts to the offer. The first is the components, which include the price, product and packaging. The second is the *structure,* which means how the components are put together. In considering both the components and structure of your offer, you should consider the effect the offer will have on your objective for this project. Bob Stone says that only one question is the key in the design of any offer: "How will this offer help to accomplish my objective?" Therefore, before deciding how to structure or develop the components of your offer, decide what your primary objective for that offer is. Consider the following alternatives: (1) Is your objective to make an immediate profit on this offer? In other words, you're going to disregard back-end profits? (2) Is your objective to make back-end profits? In that case, repeat business is critical. (3) Are you breaking in or penetrating into a new market? Then, you probably want to get the maximum number of new customers for your product or service as quickly as possible.

Jim Kobs, author of *Profitable Direct Marketing,* actually came up with 99 different offers. He says: "When you sit down to make a list of direct response offers and their variations, it's amazing how many you can come up with." Let's look at some of the most important types of offers and some examples of how companies engaged in mail order are using them profitably. We'll use Kobs' classification system of the different types.

Remember as we look at these examples that there is nothing stopping you from developing your own variation of the offer that may be even more profitable.

Basic Offers

Basic offers are used to overcome the reluctance of a potential customer to order a product sight unseen by mail and they also include different payment options.

Right Price.   The price is, of course, one of the critical components of the offer. "Right" might be higher or lower than what your competition is charging. Basically, you must consider what your market will pay as well as what the competition may be charging for similar products or products that do the same thing. But at the same time, you must make certain that you have charged a high enough price that the offer is profitable. Remember that the general rule in mail order is that you must sell your product for at least three to four times your in-the-mail cost of the product. Also, you should know that price has an image value. Thus, a higher priced product is usually assumed to be better than one that is priced lower.

Free Trial.   This is the offer we discussed earlier. Remember that it is not an option—it is a must. You must offer a free trial period to your customers under almost all circumstances in mail order to be successful. To decide what time to offer for a trial period, you should look at your competition as guidelines. Later, when you are an experienced mail order operator you may become innovative like Joe Karbo, Melvin Powers, or Joe Sugarman.

Money-Back Guarantee.   This was also discussed earlier, but is so important that it is worth repeating. And for success in mail order, you must make this offer for most products. If a customer is dissatisfied, he or she can return the product to you for a full refund. To a certain degree, inertia is on your side, because it is some trouble to send a product back. Tabulate your returns and use the 15 percent rule. As long as your product has less than 15 percent returns, your product or service is probably all right, and your advertising claims are probably being met.

Cash with Order.   This is normal, perhaps the basic, payment alternative. Your customer sends the money with the order for your product. "Cash" here can also mean a check or money order.

Bill Me Later.   This is another payment option and is considered the basic one if a free trial offer is used in lieu of the money-back guarantee. This will sometimes occur in selling books by mail. The bill is enclosed with the merchandise or sent a few days after the merchandise is delivered. Response, as you might expect, is usually much greater than if you required cash with the order. However, it is a fact that in some cases, you will not receive the payment or the returned merchandise. This is a cost of doing business, and as long as this "cost" does not stop you from being profitable, it should not stop you from making the offer.

Installment Terms.   This is where you offer a payment option in which your customer pays over a period of time, rather than all in one lump sum. Some sort of installment plan is generally needed when a "big-ticket" or high-priced item is sold. It will increase response, although, again, in many cases you will not receive full payment. Even with collection agencies, most mail order firms that sell through this offer ultimately collect payment from only 60 to 70 percent of the customers who order.

Charge Card Privileges.   Charge cards offer advantages similar to installment plans as there is a built-in installment plan with the charge card. The advantages here are that you don't have to assume the risk of nonpayment. However, when using charge cards, you will be charged a certain percentage—4 percent or more—by the credit card company.

C.O.D.   C.O.D. stands for *cash on delivery* and is a service offered by the U.S. Postal Service. The mail carrier collects your money when your product is delivered to the customer. Sounds too good to be true? Well, there are some problems. First, this service is expensive. And, not infrequently, your potential customer's interest in your product has cooled by the time the mail carrier appears with the item in hand. Then you must pay not only for the item to be delivered to the potential customer, but also for its return to you. If you do decide to use C.O.D., it is usually better to ask for a certain percentage of the money with the order, so that the customer has already made a commitment toward purchasing the item, and it is harder for him or her to refuse payment when the postman comes. Also, ship as soon as possible after the order is received so there is less time for your customer's interest to wane.

Free Gift Offers

Free gift offers are used to encourage the potential customer to do something else that you want him or her to do—usually buy another product. However, there are some important cautionary notes here. A gift should have something to do with the product or service that you want the prospective customer to buy. Otherwise, the folks that order your free gift may not be the same kind of folks who are interested in buying your product in the future. There is also a decision to be made as to which item is to be sold and which is to be the free gift. This is another decision that you must make in structuring your offer.

Free Gift for an Inquiry. In this case, you will offer the free gift merely for requesting more information about the product or service you are selling. This will increase your response for inquiries at the same time. However, it will also increase the cost of the response, because many of the respondents will be merely curious and will not be as interested in buying your product as those who might inquire without the offer of a free gift. The same rule applies regarding the connection between your free gift and what you are selling. Notice the Mellinger Company's advertisement in Figure 8.1 and how the free sample import is tied in with his product. This and similar advertisements have brought in millions of dollars.

Free Gift for a Trial Order. This is where you offer a free gift if the potential customer will merely place the order for what you are trying to sell on a trial basis. For example, I once sold three books called *The Writer's Guide to Publication and Profit.* With the order, the respondent got a free book on punctuation. Further, he or she was to keep this whether or not the other books were returned. Figure 8.2 is certainly an unusual free offer. You buy a Vermont cob-smoked turkey breast, and get a half-pound of bacon and 10 ounces of cheddar to go with it—free!

Other Free Gifts

This classification includes a number of different free gifts for different markets. There is an important principle at work here regarding all free gifts, and that is that as you offer more free gifts and more valuable free gifts, you will increase the quantity of your responses. However, the quality of the responses will not be so great, since many curiosity seekers will respond. On the other hand, if you offer a relatively inexpensive free gift, the quantity of your responses will be less than that if you offered more, but their quality will be greater. In other words, even though not as many responded to your free offer, these respondents will order more. It is part of your job to pick the offer that works best for you.

Free Information. This is where you offer additional information for merely responding to your offer. When selling my writer's book, I once advertised in classified ads, "Write for profit. Complete details free." This was free information offered to get inquiries that I could then use to present my full-paying proposition.

Free Catalog. A free catalog is useful for a number of different businesses and as a way of selling your mail order products. I'll be talking

Figure 8.1 The Mellinger Company's advertisement of a free gift for an inquiry.

Figure 8.2   An example of a free gift with trial order.

about catalogs in detail in Chapter 15. Figure 8.3 shows a full-page advertisement for a free catalog.

Free Booklet.   A free booklet can be of great assistance in selling either your product or service, even though the book may or may not mention the product or service explicitly. Figure 8.4 shows Quill Corporation's offer for a free booklet on "How to Write Effective Business Reports." The booklet doesn't mention Quill Corporation's office supply products directly. But note that the free booklet is of interest to people who would also be interested in office supplies.

Figure 8.3   A full-page advertisement for a free catalog.

Figure 8.4 Quill Corporation offers a free booklet for an inquiry.

Free Fact Kit.   A fact kit can contain a number of different items, all of which may help to sell your product or service. It may include reprints of articles, free booklets such as I described above, samples, and so forth. Free fact kits enable your prospective customer to visualize exactly what you are selling, and they may contain a number of different types of sales approach, all of which can add up to a sale. Of course, a fact kit costs you something to put together, so as always, you should watch not only the number of responses but also profitability.

Free Film Offer.   This is used by many companies processing film through the mail. The customer gets a new roll of film when one is sent in for processing, or sometimes an initial roll is offered free in return for a promise to send the film in for processing after the pictures have been taken.

Free House Organ Subscription.   Newsletters are booming throughout the country, and many of them contain helpful information for customers and prospective customers. An offer might be for a year's free subscription or for a free sample issue, or you might offer the subscription free as long as your customer continues to buy from you.

Free Talent Test.   Many home correspondence courses have used this offer. A test of writing or drawing ability, for example, has been used for years. However, the FTC has tightened up on these talent tests: They must measure real ability, rather than be only an opener to sell the product or service. But you are not prohibited from making the offer, as long as the test measures what it is supposed to.

Discount Offers

Discount offers appeal to the bargain instinct of your prospective buyers. But you must be careful that your discounting doesn't affect the image you want to project of the product. We discussed the effect of discounting and price on image in Chapter 7.

Cash Discount.   This is where you offer a price discount or a discount certificate for the product. This offer is an alternative to one of the free gift offers we discussed earlier. Figure 8.5 offers a discount on a new subscription.

Short-Term Introductory Offer.   This is where you offer a discount, but only for a short period. You have probably received a mailing like this from an insurance company, stating that your insurance is only 25¢. Sometimes subscriptions are offered for a short trial period at a reduced price in

Figure 8.5   An example of a discount offer.

same fashion. The key here is whether you can convert enough short-term buyers into long-term buyers. If you can't, this offer will do nothing but cost you a great deal of money.

Refund Certificate.   This is a rebate or delay type of discount. An order for a catalog for $1 may include a discount certificate for the same amount, or you may offer the rebate after the customer tries the product. The Mellinger Company sometimes uses a discount certificate in the form of a "check" to induce individuals to "buy now."

Introductory Offer Discount.   This is a discount offer to only new customers, to get them to place an initial order. The problem with the introductory offer discount is that you may upset your old customers. Further, some old customers will also place the order for the introductory offer. You must be very careful about testing here and watch your results to make certain this offer is profitable. Figure 8.6 shows an introductory offer discount by History Book Club.

Trade Discount.   This is a discount offered to members of certain types of institutions or businesses merely because of their membership. For example, the Direct Marketing Association offers a special membership discount to college or university professors.

Early-Bird Discount.   This is a discount that attempts to get potential customers to order before the normal buying season or period. It is frequently used to sell books; a so-called prepublication price is offered before the book is actually published. It has also been used for Christmas cards, gifts, pre-school buying, and in many similar situations.

STORIES OF GUTS AND GLORY.
Any 3 for $1 Each
Plus a 4th at the low Members' Price.
NO RISK, NO COMMITMENT.

(First price is publisher's list./**Boldface** is Members' Price.)

Save on the best recent history titles.

No matter what area of history you enjoy reading about most, you'll find that History Book Club offers some of the finest selections being published today. And no book club we know offers greater savings–as much as 25% off publishers' list prices. You can save even more by taking advantage of our Introductory Offer. Select any three books on this page for $1 each when you take a fourth book at the low Members' Price, plus shipping and handling. Thereafter, you're not obligated to order any more books. You may cancel your membership at any time by notifying History Book Club. You may cancel your membership if you elect not to buy at least one book in any six-month period.

How the Club works. You'll be able to choose from 150 to 200 books featured each month. History Book Club always offers its members well-made, long-lasting editions.

You'll receive our *Review* and a dated Reply Form up to 17 times a year (about every 3 weeks). If you want the "Editors' Choice," do nothing–the book will come automatically. If you want another book, or no books at all, return the Reply Form by the date specified. A shipping and handling charge is added to each shipment.

Your HBC guarantee: If you receive an unwanted "Editors' Choice" because you had less than 10 days to decide, simply return it and pay nothing.

History Book Club®, Camp Hill, PA 17012-0001. Please enroll me in History Book Club according to the no-risk, no-commitment terms outlined in the accompanying ad. Send me the four books whose numbers I have listed below. Bill me $1 each for 3 choices, and the fourth at the low Members' Price, plus shipping and handling. Guarantee of Satisfaction: You may examine your introductory books for 10 days, free. If you are not satisfied, for any reason whatsoever, simply return the books and you will be under no further obligation.

3 choices at $1 each: 4-13

| — | — | — |

4th choice at the low Members' Price: —

H337-1-0

Name _____
(Please print clearly)

Address _____ Apt. #

City _____ State ____ Zip ____ #053

To help us serve you, please tell us what you like to read.	STRONGLY DISLIKE	SOMEWHAT DISLIKE	NO OPINION	SOMEWHAT LIKE	STRONGLY LIKE
A. Civil War	1	2	3	4	5
B. Ancient History	1	2	3	4	5
C. Military History	1	2	3	4	5
D. American History	1	2	3	4	5
E. British History	1	2	3	4	5
F. Russia, Asia, the Middle East	1	2	3	4	5
G. European History	1	2	3	4	5
H. Current Affairs	1	2	3	4	5
I. Social/Intellectual History	1	2	3	4	5

© 1994 History Book Club, Inc. All orders subject to approval. Prices and offer may differ in Canada.

Figure 8.6   An introductory discount offer.

Quantity Discount.   "Buy more and you get a discount" is not unique to mail order, but it is used frequently to sell magazine subscriptions and many other types of products and services.

Sliding Scale Discount.   In the sliding scale discount, the discount itself is variable—2, 5, or 10 percent—and may be linked to the amount of the order. Or the discount can be tied to when the payment is made—that is, a 2 percent discount if payment is made before 10 days, full amount thereafter.

Selected Discounts.   These are discounts made on certain selected products, usually in catalogs. Discounts are given on certain products to push their sale harder or to give the appearance of a general sale, or sometimes simply to close out on merchandise that hasn't sold.

Sale Offers

A sale and a discount may be the same thing described in a different way. This group of offers is classified this way because the sale itself, rather than a discount, is emphasized in the offer.

Seasonal Sale.   This may be a post- or pre-Christmas sale, a back-to-school sale, a summer vacation sale, and so forth. It is usually related to a certain time or season and is generally repeated every year at the same time.

Reason Why Sale.   In this type of sale, a reason must be given for the sale's occurring. It could be a fire, clearance, going out of business, inventory reduction, or some other reason. But in every case, you give a reason for the sale's taking place. This makes the sale more credible in the prospective customer's mind.

Price Increase Notice.   This type of sale is being held because at the future date indicated in the offer, the price will be increased. Therefore the customer gets a last chance to order at the old price and has an incentive to order right away. Notice how this is done effectively in Figure 8.7.

Random Drawing Sale.   This type of sale is used when there is a limited amount of merchandise—that is, you are using the sale only to bring names in. Because you will probably have more orders than products to fill the orders, only a certain number of your customers can buy at the price advertised. Therefore, a random drawing is used to pick those customers who will receive the product at the sale price advertised. Of course, you must let your customers know, in your advertising literature and offer, that

The Mellinger Co. *Exporters – Importers*

LOS ANGELES BANK
BANK OF AMERICA

MEMBER
FOREIGN TRADE ASSN. OF SO. CALIFORNIA

TELEPHONE (213) 884-4400 • CABLE: OVRHAUL
6100 VARIEL AVENUE • WOODLAND HILLS, CALIFORNIA, U.S.A. 91367

LAST CHANCE TO GET MY PLAN AT OLD LOW PRICE!

Dear Ambitious Friend...

Regretfully...I have found it absolutely necessary to raise the price of my Mellinger Mail Order World Trade/Home Business Plan!

BUT WITH ONE BIG DIFFERENCE!

Because you wrote <u>before</u> price went up...I am offering you...for a short time only...the opportunity to enjoy all benefits of the Mellinger Plan <u>at old original low price</u>. I have authorized the enclosed order form for your personal use only...this offer is not transferable to anyone else!

Price simply had to go up. Costs for everything here at International Traders Headquarters have gone through the roof. Salaries of our staff, our foreign travel expenses, supplies, all have gone up and up, just as your own daily personal expenses have moved up with the times. New applicants for my Mellinger Plan now pay new higher price. This is why my special offer to you covers only a very limited time.

EXTRA! Did you catch the extra benefit as you looked over the enclosed order form. You're right! New I.T. Members joining at the new price will enjoy a TWO YEAR membership in International Traders. <u>But even though you will be ordering at the old low price, you will still receive a full TWO YEAR I.T. Membership.</u> That's just like finding an extra $10!

This is the perfect time to get started. I.T. Members I talk with at my Mellinger Seminars around the country tell me their home businesses are booming... thanks to exciting new import products discovered on my recent foreign travel. Even more exciting Imports are coming! With my help and the Mellinger Plan to guide you...opportunities for profit are far better today than when I started my own business in a rented garage and less than $100 to work with!

<u>Save while you still can</u>! This must be your last opportunity to save on the Mellinger Plan and start your big profit future as an International Trader. Check payment Plan 1 or Plan 2 on the enclosed special Inspection Request—and mail it to me today! Either payment plan entitles you to my positive home inspection money-back guarantee! Mail your order to me today.

Sincerely,

Brainerd L. Mellinger
President

P.S. Profits on imports are often <u>five times cost</u>! The money you save will buy enough imports to more than pay for entire Plan. Order today!

BLM:jk

Figure 8.7   A price increase notice. The idea is to convince the reader that the price will never be lower.

you have limited merchandise. Meanwhile, you get the names of all those customers who respond, whether they were those fortunate enough to be picked by the random drawing or not. Of course, you return the money of those whose orders you could not fill.

Sample Offers

Sample offer is good when you believe that simply getting your product in the hands of the customer will result in future sales. It is clearly not good for a marginal product in which you think the customer will not be fully satisfied, and here again, you will lose a lot of samples to the ever-present curiosity seekers.

Free Sample.   A free sample is an outstanding method if your product really can sell itself once the customer uses it. You have to be careful here that this criterion is met and also that the project will ultimately be profitable even though you are giving away free samples.

Nominal-Charge Sample.   Through charging a small sum of money, you share the cost of the sample with your customer. This small price also helps to qualify and weed out those who would order anything that is free but nothing that they must pay for. The main disadvantage is that you will have a much lower response than if you charged nothing.

Time Limit Offers

As I said before, in mail order, the idea is always to get your potential customer to act at once and not to delay, for it has been shown and proved time after time that people who delay are far less likely to order. Therefore, a time limit helps to hype the order and get the individual to order at once.

Limited Time Offer.   In this instance, you make your offer good only for a certain time. Here you have a choice: You can say that the offer is good for two weeks or you can indicate a specific cut-off date, such as the first of June. The theoretical advantage in use of a time period rather than a date is that because you won't know exactly when the letter will arrive, you won't compromise your offer if it arrives a little late. Also this will allow you to use the same advertising piece over a greater period of time. However, the fact is that research has shown that people respond much better to a specific date than to a time period. Figure 8.8 makes it clear that the offer is guaranteed only to a certain date.

Prepublication Offer.   This is really a type of early-bird discount, as mentioned earlier, and it allows individuals to order something, usually a

Figure 8.8   A limited time offer.

book, at a prepublication price lower than the price that will be charged later.

Charter Membership or Subscription Offer.   *Charter* implies that you are offering something new. This type of offer is used for new clubs, magazines, and other types of associations. It usually includes a special introductory price or some other incentive, such as a special charter member's certificate, which appeals both to people who like to be innovators and to those who like to be joiners.

Limited Edition Offer.   The offer implies that there will be only so much of the product available and no more. It therefore appeals very much to people who collect things and it is used to help sell books, plates, coins, works of art, and many other types of collectibles. Figure 8.9 is a limited edition offer.

Guarantee Offers

The money-back guarantee is a requirement in mail order because it helps the customer overcome his or her considerable reluctance to order an unknown product from an unknown firm. The more strongly you can word your guarantee and the more generous you can make it, the greater will be your response for any particular offer.

Extended Guarantee.   I mentioned earlier that the period of the money-back guarantee had been lengthened to include a year or so. I have also seen offers for products such as knives in which the money-back guarantee for breakage has been increased to a lifetime. Such a guarantee has a tremendous effect on overcoming the resistance of a potential customer to order. The reality is that few of the types of products used with

Figure 8.9 A limited edition offer.

this guarantee are ever returned after a year or so—it's difficult for most people to retain even the seller's address that long!

Double-Your-Money-Back Guarantee. This type of offer really intends to demonstrate your confidence in a product. However, it has two disadvantages. One is that you could lose your credibility if an individual believes that you are not as likely to return double the money as you would be simply to return just the money invested. Second, unless your product is really good, you can really lose your shirt by paying double money back for a product with which your customer didn't really fall in love at first sight.

Guaranteed Buy-Back Agreement. This is a type of extended guarantee, but it is very effective with certain types of collectibles that mail order buyers—and especially investors—may purchase. Basically, what you do is offer to buy the item back for the purchase price up to a certain specified period, or indefinitely. This proposition does a lot to convince the potential buyer of your belief in the present and future worth of the item.

Build-Up the Sale Offers

These are offers that increase the size of the average order, certainly a goal any mail order operator can and should subscribe to.

Multiproduct Offers. This is where you offer two or more products or services in the same advertisement. You must be careful in offering more than one product that you do not confuse the customer. Remember that confusion leads to delay, which could cost you the sale. There is something of a paradox here, for clearly, one very successful multiproduct or multiservice medium is none other than the catalog. However, it is a fact that if you have offered two or more products in the same advertisement, your total response may be lower than if you have offered only one product. It is okay to offer the customer different colors, sizes, and styles, or, where the opportunity exists, to trade up for a more expensive version of the same product. A good example is a watch in which the stainless steel version is priced at $39.95, while a gold version is offered in smaller print for $49.95. However, if you confuse the customer with a number of different watches you risk losing the sale rather than increasing your chances of making a sale. So, as a general rule, save multiproduct offers for the catalog.

Piggyback Offers. This is really a multiproduct offer, but the ad or offer features one main item, and then, tucked away somewhere in the corner or at the bottom of the advertisement, complementary products are offered.

The Deluxe Offer.   This is where you give the opportunity for the customer to trade up after you have already sold him or her. A deluxe version of a book with a much better binding and with letters in gold sells for a higher price than the standard version.

Good, Better, Best Offer.   This is a variation of the deluxe offer, except that instead of one or two choices, you offer three. That's where the "good, better, best" comes from. One book seller we know of offered a standard edition, a deluxe edition, and then a grand edition. I needn't add that the price went up with the description of the edition being offered.

Add-On Offer.   This is where you attempt to get the prospective customer to buy something else after you have sold him or her the main item. For example, you might sell a knife for $9.95 and then, for $2.50, offer a sheath to go with it.

Bounce-Back Offer.   This is where you simply add on to the original sale by promoting another product when you fulfill the original product order. This is really a tremendously profitable situation, and I don't know why every mail order operator doesn't take advantage of it. You not only save the money of obtaining the customer's name, but you even save the postage. Besides, what better time to sell to your customer than when he or she is delighted by receiving the first product ordered!

Increase and Extension Offers.   This is another type of offer that builds on the original sales made to your customers. Again, the object here is to sell them while they're hot from their first purchase. With the magazine subscription, an extended subscription may be offered with some sort of reduced price. Or perhaps additional accessories might be offered to the buyer of the knife and sheath, such as a matching belt, a pocketknife, and so forth.

Sweepstakes Offers

Sweepstakes offers have really come into their own over the past 10 years, even though they are now closely controlled by the federal government and many states. Recall from Chapter 3 that you must have a contest in which all prizes are awarded, and the respondent must be able to participate in the sweepstakes whether he or she places an order with you or not. However, when you consider that responses increase as much as 400 percent when sweepstakes are used over when they are not, it clearly makes sense to use a sweepstakes type of offer in conjunction with some types of mail order promotions.

Lucky Number Sweepstakes.   This is where the winning numbers are preselected even before they are mailed to your prospective customers. In this case, your copy emphasizes this fact to your prospective customer: "You May Already Have Won," or "You May Already Be A Winner." Figure 8.10 shows a preselected sweepstakes offer.

Involvement Sweepstakes.   Involvement means that the potential customer becomes involved in some way in entering the sweepstakes. He or she must play a game, match a number against an eligible number list, or perform some other task to determine the prize. Involvement of the potential customer has been shown to be clearly effective in increasing responses not only to the sweepstakes but also to any other type of promotion that can be linked to potential customer involvement. Figure 8.11 is from another type of sweepstakes.

Talent Contests.   This isn't really a sweepstakes in the strictest sense of the word, but it requires the prospective customer to do something involving talent—write a story, draw a picture—and the winner is offered a free scholarship or some other type of prize.

Figure 8.10   A personalized sweepstakes form.

Club and Continuity Offers

These are the offers of the book clubs, CD clubs, and others that sell repeat products over a period of time. They were developed back in 1920 by Maxwell Sackheim and Harry Scherman, when they founded the Book-of-the-Month Club.

Positive Option.   This is where you are in a certain type of club and are notified every month of the monthly selection. However, to order you must take some positive action and thereby request the order.

Negative Option.   This is generally much more effective than positive option. You are notified in advance of the new selection, but under the terms you agreed to when you joined the club, this selection is shipped to you unless you return a card or something else that rejects the offer by a certain date. This works better because you have human inertia going for you. Figure 8.12 is an example of a negative option book club.

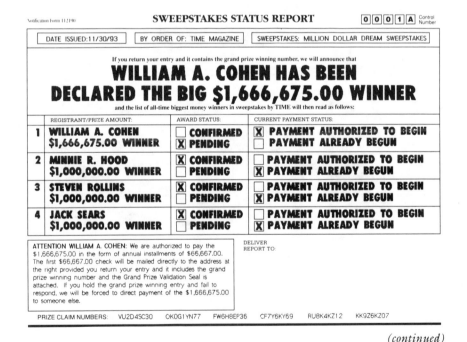

(continued)

Figure 8.11   A sweepstakes that requires involvement.

Issuance of this report confirms that if you return the grand prize winning entry, we will declare that

WILLIAM A. COHEN NOW RANKS FIRST AMONG OUR ALL-TIME BIGGEST MONEY WINNERS!

Dear William A. Cohen:

Until now, the three $1,000,000.00 winners on the above list have shared a very special distinction: Minnie R. Hood of Pennsylvania, Steve Rollins of California, and Jack Sears of Illinois have been the biggest winners EVER in a sweepstakes presented by TIME. But now, that's all going to change! Because the name **WILLIAM A. COHEN** of Pasadena, California could appear in the NUMBER ONE SPOT on our list. We are pleased to announce that we stand ready to award you the $1,666,675.00, making you and you alone one of the newest winners in the sweepstakes presented by TIME if you return the grand prize winning number.

So this is no time to hesitate, William A. Cohen. On the contrary, we urge you to attach the Grand Prize Validation Seal to your entry and mail it at once! Because if you fail to return an entry, there is simply no way you can be awarded the $1,666,675.00 prize. But if you return your entry and it includes the grand prize winning number,

IMPORTANT:
Affix appropriate
seals to entry below

WE WILL BE AUTHORIZED TO BEGIN PAYMENT OF THE $1,666,675.00 DIRECTLY TO WILLIAM A. COHEN!

It's true, William A. Cohen. We are authorized to begin payment of the $1,666,675.00. In fact, our three previous winners are now receiving payment of their $1,000,000.00 prizes in the form of annual installments of $40,000.00. But because the $1,666,675.00 prize is our biggest prize ever, we have increased the size of the annual payments to $66,667.00! More importantly, the $66,667.00 annual payments are unconditionally guaranteed to continue for twenty-five years -- until the entire $1,666,675.00 is paid in full!

And with a guaranteed annual income of $66,667.00 for twenty-five years to look forward to, William Cohen's address would have to change from 1556 Sierra Madre VII A. to EASY STREET! Because while everyone else's nose is to the grindstone, you'd be smelling the roses -- and spending all your time doing the things you've always wanted to do! But remember, you MUST return your entry with the Grand Prize Validation Seal attached and it must contain the winning number. Otherwise, someone else's name may go in the number one spot on our winners' list. And you will have to kiss this chance for a life of leisure goodbye forever. And make sure you return it immediately, because

WILLIAM A. COHEN IS ALSO ELIGIBLE FOR THE $100,000.00 BONUS PRIZE!

Be sure to also attach the Bonus Prize Validation Seal to your entry, and then, mail it today! If you act quickly and return your entry before the deadline below, you'll qualify for the $100,000.00 Bonus Prize. But time is of the essence. And

over, please

Figure 8.11   (Continued)

How Popular Science
Book Club Works

Just mail the postpaid card to get your $24.50 4-VOLUME CARPENTERS AND BUILDERS LIBRARY. Send no money now. We'll bill you later for only $3.95 plus delivery and handling.

Then, about every four weeks (15 times a year), you'll receive a Club bulletin describing the coming main selection and alternate books also available, all at Club discounts. If you want the main selection only, do nothing. It will be sent automatically. If you don't want the main selection, or want alternate books, or no books, please make sure to indicate your wishes on the Instruction Form and return it to us by the date shown. Club mailings are carefully scheduled to assure you of at least 10 days in which to do this. But in the unlikely event that you don't have 10 days, and you receive an unwanted selection, you may return it at our expense.

After receiving your joining shipment, your only obligation is to buy two more regular selections or alternates in the next year. After that, membership may be cancelled at any time, by either you or the Club.

Club books are comparable in every way — paper, printing, binding, jacket — to original publishers' editions, yet you may save up to 50% and sometimes more on hundreds of special books offered each year in the club. To become eligible for these bargains, mail the card today!

Figure 8.12 How the Popular Science Book Club works. The negative option is described in the second paragraph.

Specialized Offers

This group of offers includes those that can't be grouped easily into the other categories.

Yes/No Offers. Your potential customer is asked to indicate in some special way whether he or she is ordering or not ordering. Obviously, a "no" order is not much value to you. However, it has been found that forcing an immediate decision actually increases the number of "yes" responses over what you would otherwise have ended up with. Figure 8.13 is a yes/no offer. Another twist is the "maybe" involvement offer in Figure 8.14.

The Super-Dramatic Offer. This is an offer that contains some sort of dramatic appeal. For example, one old mail order offer selling revolvers advised potential customers to "hammer the hammer." The hammer containing the firing pin was to be struck with a carpenter's hammer to prove that the gun would not fire without pulling the trigger. Another ad I recall for a hunting knife invited the would-be buyer to try to break the blade.

Figure 8.13   A yes/no involvement offer.

Figure 8.14   A maybe involvement offer.

Trade-In Offer.   This is where you get your prospective customer to return something for which you give a discount. Several years ago a credit card firm offered a discount on its prestige credit card by encouraging the prospective customer to cut up and send in old credit cards from competing firms. This accomplished two things at once: It sold the customer the new credit card service at a discount and eliminated the competition at the same time.

Third-Party-Referral Offer.   A third party is used to recommend your product or service. It is important here that the third party have credentials that are respected by your prospective customers or this offer will not be very effective. Also, remember the applicable laws on testimonials covered in Chapter 3. An example of this is shown in the advertisement for my book *The Art of the Leader* in Figure 8.15. Actually, I thought this advertisement could have been a lot better. Not only Admiral Zumwalt, but also presidents of major corporations, Barry Goldwater, and Mary Kay of Mary Kay cosmetics recommended the book. Unfortunately, the publisher didn't consult me when they wrote the ad!

Member-Get-a-Member Offer.   You make this offer to a member or customer who is currently buying from you. You offer him or her something free if he or she gets another member to join. This is an offer frequently used by book clubs. Members who sign another member up receive free books in return.

Reduced Down Payment.   This is for big-ticket items in which some sort of installment plan must be used for purchase. If the initial purchase is not made and a customer does not respond to your offer, you offer a reduced down payment. There are many ways of doing this. One is the "damaged merchandise" offer. If you're selling an item such as a course of

"Dr. Cohen's book makes a significant contribution to the art of leadership ... "

— Admiral Elmo R. Zumwalt, Jr. USN Ret.

To order call 1-800-753-7500 24 hours a day
or mail the coupon below for a FREE examination copy!

THE ART OF THE LEADER
by William A. Cohen, Ph.D.

General George S. Patton once remarked that leadership is "the art of getting your subordinates to do the impossible."

Throughout history, there have been great leaders who inspired others to overcome seemingly insurmountable odds, and who by dint of their courage, steadfastness, vision, and integrity were able to lead their people to ultimate triumph — whether in combat, in sports, in business, or any other area of human endeavor.

Though leadership is a rare and highly valued quality, Dr. William A. Cohen, a West Point graduate with an MBA from the University of Chicago, believes that anyone — regardless of his or her formal position — can become a leader by following the practical techniques he sets forth in this book. Armed with these techniques, you will be able to get others to perform far beyond even their own expectations, and lead them to the accomplishment of virtually any task, objective, or project you set your sights on.

Using scores of real-life case examples, *The Art of the Leader* demonstrates how you can:

- *Win over the minds of other people and get them to believe in you and your cause.*

- *Inspire a strong sense of common purpose among your team players and infuse them with an unquenchable desire to excel.*

- *Attract the favorable attention of people in top management and convince them that you deserve their full trust and support.*

In any organization, just one person can make the difference between success or failure. By becoming a leader, you can be that person. You don't need to be a manager or an executive to be a leader. You don't need to wait to be promoted. If you apply the techniques set forth in this book, you can become a leader immediately.

"Destined to be a best seller, and possibly a management classic."
— Library Review

ABOUT THE AUTHOR

WILLIAM A. COHEN is a graduate of West Point with an MBA from the University of Chicago, and an MA and Ph.D. in Management from the Claremont Graduate School of the University of Southern California. He is also a graduate of the Industrial College of the Armed Forces at National Defense University in Washington, DC. Currently a full colonel in the U.S. Air Force Reserve, and Chairman of the Marketing Department at California State University, Los Angeles, Dr. Cohen has led numerous organizations both in and out of the military. In addition, he is the author of 18 previous business books, which have been translated into seven languages.

Call 1-800-753-7500 24 hours a day with your VISA or MasterCard.
For fastest service be sure to specify Priority Code S8111-W1(5)

100% satisfaction guaranteed, or your money back.

Or for a FREE 15-day examinaiton, mail this coupon to
Prentice Hall Book Distribution Center
Route 59 at Brookhill Drive
West Nyack, NY 10995

☐ Yes! Please send me **The Art of the Leader** for a FREE 15-day examination. After 15 days, I will pay your invoice for $19.95 plus local sales tax, postage and handling, or I will return the book and pay nothing.

Name _____

Firm _____

Address _____

City _____ State _____ Zip _____

Dept 4   04665-6   S8111-W1(5)

Figure 8.15   An advertisement for *The Art of the Leader.*

instruction, you can offer a reduced down payment for "slightly damaged merchandise," such as a slightly torn book cover. The damage is "very minor and even hard to locate" but still "cannot be sold as new."

The Nominal Reimbursement Offer. This is where you offer some nominal reimbursement in return for some services rendered by the respondent. A research survey fits this criterion. You must have the highest percentage of response to ensure the accuracy and completeness of the survey. A few years ago, I received a survey with a brand new, crisp $1 bill attached to the letter that asked me to respond. You may think that the average person would keep the dollar bill and still not respond, but the fact of the matter is that the dollar not only acts as an inducement, but it works on the guilt feelings of the respondents. I responded to the survey.

Established Value Offer. If you are offering a special deal, such as an item at a reduced price or a free gift, you can show the value of this offer to your potential customers by offering to send an extra one of your products to them for a friend or a member of their family at the regular going retail price. This does two things for you. First, it helps to establish the value of your free or reduced price offer. Second, you will pick up a few additional sales.

SUMMARY

In this chapter, we have discussed the importance of the offer and why it is so critical to promoting your product or service successfully. To maximize your response, your offer should be constructed in such a way as to motivate your potential customer to order. Remember Abraham Maslow's hierarchy of needs: physiological, safety and security, social, ego, and fulfillment needs.

Structure your offer in accordance with the objective you are seeking to attain—whether it is to break even or make a profit up front, to get repeat business, or to obtain a maximum number of new customers through penetration of a new market.

Finally, consider our discussion of proven direct response offers. Select those offers that are applicable to the business proposition to your customer and use them to increase response—or create your own variations.

Do not forget that it is essential to do two things if at all possible: Offer the strongest money-back guarantee that you possibly can and allow a free trial of your product or service.

Part III

Mail Order Media

Making Money with Classified Ads

Classified ads are found in thousands of newspapers and magazines. They represent a great medium for the beginner as well as the experienced professional in mail order. But a classified ad cannot be used for all products or in every situation, and in this chapter we are going to examine both when to use a classified ad and when not to, along with the advantages and disadvantages of using them. I am also going to tell you how to use a classified ad for maximum effectiveness, as well as how to construct a classified ad, how to write one, how to pick the right medium to place it in, how to classify the ad, how to minimize your costs and maximize your profits through a sound strategy of pyramiding, and how to make additional money through the inquiries received in your classified ads. I am going to give you 10 proven ways to increase your classified ad results dynamically. Finally, I am going to share with you the full details of a classified ad strategy I have used myself. To understand when and when not to use classified advertising in your business, it is necessary to look at the advantages and disadvantages of using a classified ad. Let's look at the advantages first.

ADVANTAGES

Low Cost

The cost of classified advertising is extremely low when compared with that of direct mail, space advertising, or electronic media. A classified advertisement in *Entrepreneur,* a magazine read by what are known as "opportunity seekers," currently costs about $5 a word, as opposed to up to several thousand dollars for a display advertisement in the same magazine. This cost difference between classified and display or space advertising is typical for all other magazines used by mail order dealers. In fact, classified advertising today is perhaps the only method of mail order advertising in which an advertiser can advertise his or her product or service for less than $100.

Highest Profitability

Classified advertising usually offers a mail order dealer the highest profitability potential of any form of mail order advertising. This does not mean you can make more money with classifieds. It does mean for every dollar invested, a classified will bring you a greater return on your investment compared with dollars invested in display advertising, direct mail, or other media. Ron Playle, who used classified advertising almost exclusively in the sale of several self-published booklets, including one entitled *Thirty Thousand Dollars Worth of Classified Results,* says "Dollar for dollar, they will produce more inquiries and sales than any other method." If this is true, you may wonder why you should not use classified advertising exclusively. The answer, which I will explain in detail in this chapter, has to do with the limitation of the size of your market if you use only classified. But for profitability, classified is the unchallenged winner!

A Good Way to Start Your Business

Classified advertising, because it does offer such a high profitability potential at low investment, is a good place to start your business in mail order. Melvin Powers says that classified is "one of the lowest and least expensive ways of getting started." Eric Weinstein, who built a million-dollar mail order business in less than eight months at the age of 23, says this about classified ads: "You don't have to be a brilliant copywriter and you are not risking thousands of dollars every time you advertise."

You may wonder whether any large companies started in this way. *Popular Mechanics,* a magazine that has a great many classified mail order ads, published a small booklet called *Profits from Classified Advertising,* which mentioned an ad that appeared way back in 1913 in *Popular Mechanics* under the heading of *Agents.* It read as follows: "We are the largest manufacturers of Twisted Wire Brushes in America, highest grade goods, best service, highest profit. Write for our new catalog. You are sure to win." Who placed this small classified advertisement in 1913? None other than the Fuller Brush Company, which went on to sell millions of dollars worth of brushes. Of course, by then they were using door-to-door salespeople. But the company started with this small classified advertisement.

No Need for Layout or Artwork

With display or space advertisement and in direct mail, professionally prepared artwork and layout are essential. This means additional cost and additional delay in planning and getting ready for your promotional campaign. The allocation of these resources and the delay are unnecessary in classified. You can easily write the ad yourself, and a professional artist or other specialist is not required to prepare the ad for you.

A Good Medium for Test

Because of classified advertising's low costs, it is a very good medium in which to test a new product or service, either directly or through use of the two-step inquiry and follow-up method. You can do your test for just a few dollars and, if profitable, not only expand the number of magazines in which you place your classified ad, but also expand into display, direct, or other more expensive mail order advertising media for additional profits.

Building Up Your Inquiry List

Lists of potential customers are critical for a mail order business. Your house list, which consists of those people who have responded to your ads, is very important for your company, both for your use as a list of individuals interested in the type of product or service you have to offer, and also, as we will talk about later, for you to rent to others and make significant profits from this rental. Classified advertising offers a good, quick way to build up your list of names of house customers.

Useful Adjunct to Display Advertising

Even those firms that have already "arrived" and are doing millions and millions of dollars worth of business in mail order still advertise in classified. Why is this? Well, one reason is that it is a useful adjunct to a display ad. Classified attracts people who are looking for a specific item under a specific classification, as opposed to a display ad, which attracts the casual passers-by. As a result, a classified advertisement, placed precisely under a certain heading, will draw people who are sometimes missed by your display ad. Many advertisers use a classified advertisement to refer to their larger display ad: "Look for our display ad on page 20." For just a few dollars more, your display advertisement is made much more effective.

Hot Prospects

Because your customers must actually be looking for your type of ad, not just stumble across it as is the case for a display or a space advertisement, or be targeted as in a direct mail campaign, the inquiries you receive from a classified advertisement are frequently of higher quality. These are people who are actually interested in the product or service you are advertising. You can believe that people who read the classified section under the heading *Hypnotism* are actually interested in that subject.

Lower Drop-Off

As you advertise in any medium month after month, there is a drop-off as your ad is seen by more of the readers of that particular magazine. However, with classified ads, the drop-off is lower, and the reason relates to the fact that a much smaller percentage of total readership sees your ad in any one month than is the case with a display advertisement.

DISADVANTAGES

Though you can make good money with classified advertising, there are disadvantages to using it, and recognizing these disadvantages before you start your campaign can save you money.

Not Every Product Can Be Sold

You cannot sell every type of product that can be sold by mail through a classified advertisement. Classified advertising does not give you very much space to describe your product, so your potential customer must already be familiar with the sort of product it is before he or she sees the ad. This is the main reason that if any product is sold directly from classified advertising, it usually consists of information.

You cannot sell expensive items directly through classified advertisements. Many beginners make this mistake. They hear of the huge profit potential in classified advertisements and so they attempt to sell a relatively high-priced item in just a few words through a classified ad. A little reflection will indicate just how impossible this is. One of the most successful ads ever written was Joe Karbo's advertisement for his book, *The Lazy Man's Way to Riches.* Yet it took somewhere between one-third and a full page and thousands of words to tell Joe Karbo's story and to sell this $10 book. The same was true for Mark O. Haroldsen's $10 book *How to Wake Up the Financial Genius Within You* and other books selling for similar amounts. Now, if it takes Joe Karbo or Mark O. Haroldsen a third of a page or more to tell his story and sell a $10 item, and these two ads are among the most successful ads ever written for this type of mail order product, how can you possibly sell your product, costing $10 or so, in just a few words? The answer is, you can't. In fact, you will probably be unsuccessful in selling a product directly from any classified advertisement.

Therefore, I recommend that you use the two-step method, which I've discussed earlier and which I will talk about a little later in this chapter.

Limit to Low Volume

I mentioned this earlier when I talked about the profitability of classified advertising. Yes, you get more bang for the buck, more return on your invested dollar than any other means of mail order advertising. The problem is, you just cannot reach your entire potential market by using classified. Ron Playle, a successful classified advertiser who advertised a single product intensively for five years, was able to locate only 35 magazines that could carry his product, even though he spent $30,000 in advertising. We will talk a little more about Ron Playle's experience in a moment. I just want you to realize that here was a successful advertiser who spent sufficient money and was making good profit, but 35 magazines were all he could find to carry his ad profitably.

Limited Space to Tell Your Story and Sell

One thing that you should always remember when you're talking about mail order is that it is selling, just as if it were face to face or through any other means. To sell, you must be able to communicate your story so that your prospective customer wants to buy. Usually a classified advertisement is not sufficient for this purpose.

THE PROFESSIONAL AND CORRECT WAY TO USE CLASSIFIED ADVERTISING

In the old days, one might have been able to sell a product directly through a classified ad and, though the dollars received were few, the ad was profitable because the breakeven point was so low. For example, once upon a time you could reach one million potential buyers with a classified ad for only $1 a word. So for $20 you got a 20-word ad. If your product sold for $1 and cost only a few cents, your breakeven was very low, considering the number of potential customers who looked at your ad. Even if you made a profit of only a few dollars on each ad, multiply this times the number of ads in different magazines and the 12 months of the year, and with a number of different products, you had a pretty profitable little business. The problem today is that costs have gone up tremendously. To reach enough prospective buyers today will cost you considerably more. That means your breakeven is much, much higher. Furthermore, other costs, such as printing, make your product costs higher. To add insult to injury, postage costs have increased many times since the good old days when selling a product direct from classified was frequently possible. The 1¢ stamp for first class is ancient history. Yet, that's all it cost at the time that classifieds were so inexpensive. If you have a heavy product to send, costs are significant. Well, you say, why can't you simply increase the price of the product? Instead of selling the product for $1, we will sell the product for $5 or $10. Good thought. But we are back to the other problem again: You haven't got sufficient space to tell your story to sell a $10 product in classified. The fact is that there is an upper limit to what people will pay for a product advertised in a classified ad. It has been estimated to be a maximum of $5. Until such time as our money becomes even less valuable because of inflation, I would consider $5 the extreme upper limit if you are going to attempt to sell direct from a classified advertisement.

However, you can make reasonably good money with a classified ad by using the two-step method of operation, where you get inquiries from your classified ad and then mail a sales package to each inquiry. Do inquiries from a two-step classified advertisement lead to sales? Cahners Publishing Co. did a study designed to determine the actions taken by inquirers after they received the requested information. Three separate surveys were conducted and a combined total of 9,200 inquiries were analyzed. Based on replies they received from their survey, Cahners determined that more than 12 percent of the inquirers either bought the product or saw that it was bought if the respondent was an industrial customer. This method has been used by all the experts, and I used it myself in selling my booklet, *The Writer's Guide to Publication and Profit.*

Ron Playle used this method, as described in his booklet, *Thirty Thousand Dollars Worth of Classified Ad Results,* which unfortunately is no longer in print. Ron ran a single classified advertisement and spent approximately $30,000 for his ads over a five year period. Of course, they were profitable or he would not have continued to advertise. Ron's ad read, "Never won anything? Anyone can win sweepstakes contests. Free details. Services, Box 644, Des Moines, Iowa 50303." Those individuals responding to Ron's classified ad were sent a package that contained a sales letter, a circular with a coupon, and a self-addressed reply envelope. What was the product? It was a booklet called *Anyone Can Win Sweepstakes.* Ron sold it profitably through the two-step method, first at $3 and later at $3.95. The little booklet was only 22 pages long and cost Ron only a few cents. Ron Playle draws this conclusion from his experience: "This is not a get-rich-quick scheme, but you can make a nice profit if you are prepared to work hard and can learn as you earn."

THE TELEPHONE TWO-STEP

One of the newest types of classified two-steps is the telephone two-step. It has come about because of the availability of telephone answering machines. What you do is this. Instead of giving a mailing address in your classified, you state your telephone number. Now, that telephone number must be dedicated to your advertisement and nothing else. When your prospect calls the number, your answer message gives him your full sales presentation and instructions how to order your product or service.

One advantage is that you won't need to pay for printing, postage, and so on, for your sales package. Your prospect even pays for the telephone call. You will usually increase the number of inquiries significantly if you employ this method in conjunction with a toll-free 800 number. Of course, then you will be paying for the calls. Take a look at your competition. If your competition is using toll-free 800 numbers, you may not have a choice unless what you offer is clearly superior and this can be made obvious in your advertisement. Another advantage is that your classified advertising costs will be lower. Remember, with classified advertising, you pay by the word. A telephone number counts as one word, as opposed to a street address, or post office box number that must include city, state, and zip code. Finally, done right, the human voice can be more persuasive than print and you can convert a higher percentage of your inquiries to sales. Naturally, as with other aspects of mail order advertising, the key is to test one method against the other and to see which is more profitable for you.

THE FOUR ESSENTIAL ELEMENTS OF A CLASSIFIED AD

In any classified ad, there are four elements that are essential for success: the attention-getter, the promise, the call to action, and the key plus address. The attention-getter is a one- to two-word headline written to grab the attention of the reader looking through the classified advertising section. Some good attention-getters are "Free," "Write for Profit," "Play Piano Instantly," "Big Money." The promise may be combined with the attention-getter. For example, "$1,000 per Week Is Possible" is a promise, but it may also be what draws the attention of your prospective customer. Or how about "Lose 10 Pounds in One Week." This too is both a promise and an attention-getter. If you can combine both elements, you will save money in your ad, as combining these elements will result in fewer words.

The call to action is what you use to tell the reader what you want him or her to do. "Send $2" is a call to action if you are selling direct from the classified ad. Or the simple words "Write" or "Free details" followed by your address are calls to action.

The last element in any classified ad is the key plus the address. The key is necessary so that you can tell from what magazine the response came and also from which issue. We'll talk more about keying in just a moment. First I want to show you how to write a classified advertisement.

HOW TO WRITE YOUR CLASSIFIED ADVERTISEMENT

The first step in writing your classified advertisement is to look at your competitors and see how they are advertising similar products or services. As a starting point, I would recommend going to the library and looking at their selection of magazines. Look for magazines that are likely to advertise the type of product or service you want to advertise. Once you locate your competitors' advertising in certain magazines, make copies of these ads and also make note of the magazines that they are advertising in. In general the more classified advertisements, the better the mail order medium. The more classified advertisements for your product, the better for the product or service you have to offer because your ad will have more readers—don't concern yourself about the competitors just yet. If your library has collections of magazines going back several years, try to find ads that have been repeated over many months, or a year, or even over several years. If the ad wording has changed little in this time, this is a fairly successful ad. This suits your purposes for two reasons:

1. It tells you that there is a viable market for the product or service you intend to offer.
2. It gives you some guidelines as to what is selling or bringing in the inquiries by the way the copy is written.

In Figure 9.1, I have shown a number of classified advertisements, containing various headings under which your product might fall. You can refer to these as a starting point and look for competition ads under these headings. However, it is a starting point only, and no substitute for your own thorough examination of many different magazines.

The second step in preparing your classified advertisement is to write a letter to your potential customer as if you had no word limitation. Tell your potential customer your proposal and what you want him or her to do at this point—either purchase the product outright or send for additional information. Let's look at the classified advertisement for the *Writer's Guide to Publication and Profit* as an example. Figure 9.2 is the entire story of the *Writer's Guide to Publication and Profit,* the story I want to put in the classified advertisement to secure an inquiry from my potential customer.

The next step is to write the headline for your classified. Remember that the headline must be brief and dramatic. It must also capture the reader's attention. In this case, you already have a person who is looking through the classified section under the very heading you chose for your advertisement.

AUTOMOTIVE/ETC.

SPRING CARLISLE '90 collector car flea market and corral. April 19-22. Carlisle Pennsylvania Fairgrounds. Spring's biggest car event! 8000 spaces filled with cars, parts & memorabilia for sale. Info: Carlisle Productions/ The Flea Marketeers. 1000 Bryn Mawr Rd., Carlisle, PA 17013, Phone (717) 243-7855.

BOOKS & MAGAZINES

TUGS ON MY SLEEVE. Poems. Unique gift for seniors. Read aloud at senior's gatherings. $15. Hundreds sold. Hamilton, 148 S. 90th Pl., Mesa, AZ 85208.

SOCIAL SECURITY GUIDE. Simplified, easy to read book of everything you need to know about Social Security and Medicare. Easy to understand. $7.95 plus $1 to: Exceeding Expectations, 1859 N. Pine Island Rd., Dept. 106AA, Plantation, FL 33322. Satisfaction Guaranteed.

BUSINESS OPPORTUNITIES

$20 PER HOUR/PART TIME! Call (800) 826-7039* EXT K-715. Sell Mason Shoes in your spare time. We'll help you turn Saturday mornings into big money. No risk · No investment. It's easy! Call today, or write: Mason Shoes, Dept. K-715, Chippewa Falls, WI 54774.

LET THE GOVERNMENT FINANCE your small business. Grants/loans to $500,000. Free recorded message: (707) 448-0270 (KD5).

COLLECTIBLES

EISENHOWER CENTENNIAL. Bronze medallion of Eisenhower Historic coin from Abilene, KS. Send $7.95 plus $1.50 handling: Medallion, 302 Summit, Abilene, KS 67410.

WANTED: OLD FIRECRACKER packs, labels, boxes, catalogs. Anything 4th of July. American Museum, P.O Box 2010AL, Saratoga, CA 95070.

DO-IT-YOURSELF

"GETTING STARTED WITH PVC PIPE FURNITURE." Casual, Box 208-A, Tewksbury, MA 01876.

FINANCIAL

DEBTS? BILLS? BAD CREDIT? No problem. We'll help now. Applications accepted $500-$50,000. Not a loan company. Free applications. TCAC, Dept. AL, 400 Century Park South #117, Birmingham, AL 35226, or call (205) 979-1400.

FLAGS

DISPLAY, PROTECT YOUR FLAG! Write: Flagcase Company, One Ten Grant, Suite 10-B1, Minneapolis, MN 55403.

EDUCATION & INSTRUCTION

PARALEGAL-GRADED CURRICULUM. Approved home study. Most affordable and comprehensive. 100 years of legal training. Free catalog (800) 826-9228. Blackstone School of Law, P.O. Box 790906, Dept. AL, Dallas, TX 75379.

BECOME A PARALEGAL. Work with attorneys. Lawyer-instructed home study. America's finest program. Free catalog. (800) 223-4542. Dept. LE142.

EMBLEMS

CUSTOM-EMBROIDERED EMBLEMS, pins, caps. Free catalog. Stadri, 61AL Jane, NYC, NY 10014. (212) 929-2293.

HEALTH & HEALTH CARE PRODUCTS

GOOD NEWS TO BACK PAIN SUFFERERS. Watch TV lying down. Free brochure. Taico, P.O. Box 7289, Dallas, TX 75209.

INDIAN ITEMS

WHOLESALE. Lancepoints and arrowheads. List/ sample. $1. Westco, 10251 Combie-6US, Auburn, CA 95603.

INVENTIONS

PATENTS. W. Scott Ramsey, 5253 Even Star Place, Columbia, MD 21044.

FIREARMS PATENT FOR SALE. P.O Box 1175, Ft. Myers, FL 33902.

MONEYMAKING OPPORTUNITIES

FREE REPORT on new homework opportunities. Enclose stamped envelope. Home-Data, 496A-L Hudson, New York, NY 10014.

PROFITABLE HOBBY making wishing wells. 36" 56" 72" high. Instructions and photo. $5. Trojan Horse, 712 N. Main, Paris, IL 61944.

NEW! TALKING BALLOONS. Make megabucks. BTW Enterprises, P.O. Box 49049L, Philadelphia, PA 19141-0549.

AD SPECIALTY BUSINESS! Set your own hours selling advertising calendars and gifts to businesses. No investment. Many make $20,000-up part-time. Newton Mfg. Co., Dept. JAL4, Newton, IA 50208. (515) 792-4338.

EARN MONEY MONTHLY working at home! Send $1 SASE to: WBD Enterprises, 4027-C Rucker, Suite 910, Dept. L, Everett, WA 98201.

$2,000 MONTHLY POSSIBLE for men and women willing to do assembly and clerical work in their home. Apply: Charlin-Stone Corporation, Personnel Dept., P.O. Box 925, Clarksville, TN 37041.

REAL ESTATE

REPOSSESSED VA & HUD HOMES available from government from $1 without credit check. Your repair. Also tax-delinquent foreclosures. Call (805) 682-7555, Ext. H-1514 for repo list your area.

RECIPES/FOODS

GALLON KALUHA at 1/5 cost. $2 for recipe. McLaughlin, 12434 111th Dr., Youngtown, AZ 85363. (602) 974-9016.

ENJOY BARBECUE AGAIN. Low fat recipe. $2. Bednar, 1372 S.W. Knollwood Dr., Palm City, FL 34990.

DISABLED VETERANS offering mother's recipes. Twelve for $5. SASE. Walter, Rt. 1, Box 60, Ashland, MO 65010.

STAMPS

1,000 STAMPS, $2.95. Guaranteed worth over $30 at standard catalog prices! Money back if not delighted. Approvals. Kenmore, 0M-081, Milford, NH 03055.

TRAVEL/RECREATION

FARMHOUSE VACATION. Puerta Rico. $400 wk. (413) 525-1314.

VIDEOS

SEE YOUR FAMILY ON TV. Relive favorite memories. Hear music bring scenes alive. Videotapes made from pictures, movie film, slides. Memories, 4070 Alto St., Oceanside, CA 92056.

WANTED

JUKEBOXES (612) 866-6183.

WANTED: FAMOUS PERSON'S AUTOGRAPHS! Northern Company, Dept. AL, 448 Henry, Detroit, MI 48201. (313) 961-7572.

AUTOMOBILE LITERATURE WANTED. 1900-1975. I buy automobile sales brochures, manuals, etc. Walter Miller, 6710 Brooklawn, Syracuse, NY 13211. (315) 432-8282.

WINE & BEER MAKING

WINEMAKERS, BEERMAKERS. Free catalog. Fast service. Large selection. Kraus, Box 7850-LM, Independence, MO 64053.

HOME BEERMAKING! Free 32-page catalog includes everything imaginable for quality brewing. William's, Box 2195-AL, San Leandro, CA 94577.

Figure 9.1 Classified advertisements for various products and services.

Tells exactly how to write and sell articles to magazines.

Is not an academic course; no time wasted on theory.

Shows how to organize and write ideas for maximum impact.

Details how to sell articles step by step.

Is complete in every respect.

Lists and describes more than 200 ideas for subjects.

Tells how to find subjects.

Shows how to change an outline into an article.

Shows how to illustrate article at little or not cost.

Comprises four volumes of material.

Tells how to get free copies of sample magazines.

Is sold only through mail order.

Includes a money-back guarantee.

Tells how to obtain free instructions about writing for certain magazines.

Tells how to sell your article to more than one magazine.

Tells how to get an editor to buy your article before you write it.

Tells how to sell your rejects.

Tells how to avoid legal problems.

Figure 9.2 The complete story of the *Writer's Guide to Publication and Profit*.

However, there may be hundreds of other advertisements for the same or similar products under this single heading, so your advertisement must stand out if it is going to be read. In the case of the classified for the *Writer's Guide to Publication and Profit*, I considered several different headlines: "Write Profitably Now," "Get Published Immediately," "Write for Big Money," "Huge Profits in Writing," "Dollars through Writing," and "Profitable Writing." I finally settled on "How to Write for Profit."

Now trim your letter until it looks like a telegram. Take out every word that is unnecessary to accomplish your objective. But be careful here; tests have shown that the longer your ad is, the more sales or inquiries your classified ad will bring in. On the other hand, since every word costs money, you cannot measure profitability simply by the number of inquiries or sales. You must measure it by the profits. You must weigh the increased number of returns or respondents against the increased cost of the ad. Usually, you can drop indefinite and definite articles or any word automatically understood by your prospective customer. The results of an initial trimming are shown in Figure 9.3.

In refining your classified ads, you should be sure to use simple words that are easily understood and be specific in what you say. What do I mean by "simple words"? Use *doctor*, not *physician*. Use *lawyer*, not *attorney*. Use *arrest*, not *apprehend*. Use a short word like *grouping*, not a long, complicated word such as *apportionment*, which means the same thing. By specific, I mean exact figures or exact things. Instead of "big profit," it's much better to say "make $500 profit." It's better to say "learn in 30 days" than "learn quickly."

You should now check to make certain that you have a phrase that calls the prospective customer to action, and you should also check to make sure you have your address and a key in your advertisement. As I mentioned before, it is essential to key your advertisement so that you know what the "pull," or response rate, is from each magazine and each issue. It is necessary to know and separate these figures so that you can forecast your response from any given magazine within 30 days after receiving the first response. In this way, you will know whether to continue this advertisement or to stop and reconsider. Even a successful classified ad may not be profitable in every magazine you test or in certain months of the year. One way to key your advertisement is with the words *department, suite, room,* or *drawer*, followed by the key. For example, you may have numbers 1 through 24 represent 24 different magazines in which you are advertising—

HOW TO WRITE FOR PROFIT. You can get complete details free by writing to Global Associates, P.O. Box 575, Dept. 1-A, Sierra, California 91079.

Figure 9.3 A classified ad in the initial training stages. There are 24 words to be paid for.

1, *Mechanix Illustrated;* 2, *Popular Mechanics;* 3, *Popular Science,* and so forth. You can then use letters to represent the months of the year—A for January, B for February, C for March, and so forth. In any case, your system should identify both the magazine and the month of advertising. Now there is one problem with using *drawer* or *room* or *suite* or *department.* Many experienced mail order buyers recognize this as a key and to save a couple of seconds they simply do not put this part of the address in their response, defeating the entire purpose of a key. One way of getting around this problem is with use of your initials. By using different initials in front of my name—A. A. Cohen, B. A. Cohen, C. A. Cohen, and so forth—I can represent different magazines and their months of publication. Some people do this by spelling their names in different ways, such as Cohen, Cohn, or Kohn. Another possible way of keying that works fairly well if you have a post office box number is to add two letters to the box number after a hyphen. If your post office box number is 575, you can add a dash and then add a letter and number combination such as A1 or B2. The letter would stand for the magazine, the number for the month of publication, so that a mailing address of Box 575-A1 might indicate the January issue of *Popular Mechanics.* You should probably check with your postmaster on this to ensure that the mail will be delivered even though it has additional figures after the hyphen, but usually there will be no problem. One method I hit upon and I eventually used in my advertisement for the *Writer's Guide to Publication and Profit* was shortening my company's name, Global Associates, to one word, Global, and then adding figures after this word to form my key. The advertisement read, "Global-1A" or "Global-2C." In this way, I accomplished two things. First, I saved one word since I did not have to use *department, suite, room,* or some other word to designate my key. Also, because this word was combined with the company name, respondents did not omit it when responding to the ad. All of these methods of keying your ad work. Pick the one that works best for you. You can see the final results of all this work in Figure 9.4.

HOW TO PICK THE MAGAZINES TO ADVERTISE IN

When you are first picking magazines to advertise in, you should know all the magazines that are potential carriers for your advertisement. The *Standard Rate and Data Service* (SRDS) has published several volumes, including some that deal with lists, other media such as television and radio, and

---

WRITE FOR PROFIT. Free details. Global-1A, Box 575, Sierra, California 91079.

Figure 9.4 The classified ad in final form. The same information is given as in Figure 9.3, but you pay for only 11 words.

two that have to do with magazine advertising. The first of these covers business publications and the second, consumer and form publications. Go through the SRDS and list all those magazines that might be potential vehicles for your classified advertisement. Write to these publishers and ask for a sample copy of their magazine and a rate card. This information will be useful later for display advertisement.

Always look at your competition and advertise where they do. Now, this does not say that you do not have to be innovative, but only that until you are successful enough to afford to assume more risk, it is wise to go where the tried, true, and proven advertisers go and not to strike off on your own. Joe Karbo was the first to learn how to advertise with a mail order ad in the classified section of the newspaper, even though his was not a classified ad. What Joe did was to put a display ad in the classified section. Joe not only developed this technique—he made millions with it. However, before he did this, he had plenty of previous experience in mail order and was already making several hundred thousand dollars a year. Mark O. Haroldsen once took a full-page ad in *Time*. *Time* is not known as an especially good medium for either his type of product or their type of mail order ad. The ad failed, and Mark did not advertise in *Time* again. (How do I know the ad failed without talking to Mark? It was never repeated!) Haroldsen could afford to drop $45,000 for such a test ad. Most beginners cannot, and so it's far better to use the fact that other people are advertising with similar ads in the same medium, rather than to try new territory before you have some experience under your belt.

Newspapers usually don't work for the average classified ad for a mail order product, though there are some exceptions, such as *The Wall Street Journal*. But the average home town newspaper is simply not a good mail order medium for the average product, although I guess every mail order person has tried the newspaper at least once with some idea or another, as I have done myself.

Several years ago while on jury duty, I discovered that the greater part of a day in the life of a prospective juror is spent in waiting. I had about 30 days of waiting to be selected as a member of a jury, and only about 10 days of actually working as a juror. Most prospective jurors spend their waiting hours reading, talking, playing checkers, watching television, or whiling away the time in some other way. The year before, I had written my first book, *The Executive's Guide to Finding a Superior Job*, and it had been very well received by top managers seeking a career change. I decided to sit down and write down some of my job-finding ideas in an explicit and concise form for anyone looking for a new job. I thought that perhaps I could find some way to sell these ideas by mail. At the end of my jury duty, I had completed about 5,000 words of closely typed material that I thought I could market through a classified ad for about $2. Because in quantity, the printed material cost only a few cents, I had sufficient markup so that I really didn't need to sell many copies to break even. My idea was to advertise in the weekend classified section of major newspapers. I decided to run my test ad in the *Los Angeles Times* and, if successful, expand to classified ads in Sunday newspapers throughout the country. One of the first things I discovered is that you cannot place an advertisement under the column headed *Employment Opportunities* unless you have an actual employment opportunity, so I was forced to put a separate ad under *Employment Opportunities* saying "See our ad under *Announcements*" and then run the actual ad under the *Announcements* heading in the classified ad section. At any rate, the Sunday issue of the *Los Angeles Times* came out, and my breakeven was computed at something like 20 respondents. Because breakeven was so low, I was pretty certain that the project would be successful and I was all set to expand the operation throughout the country and make a fortune all at once. I had already consulted SRDS and I was ready to roll out as soon as those dollars started rolling in. Well, the *Los Angeles Times* has a Sunday circulation of 1.2 million. I don't know how many actually read my ad, but I do know how many ordered. At the fantastic price of $2 with a full money-back guarantee, I got exactly one buyer!

Joe Karbo maintained that any medium can be used for mail order once you learn how. Unfortunately, not many mail order operators have found how to use the classified sections of newspapers yet.

After finding a magazine in which classified mail order advertisements appear and in which the competition is advertising, the third thing to look for is volume. We want to reach the largest number of readers for a particular advertisement right at the start. This does not mean we don't advertise in magazines that have a lower volume of readers, but that we go to those with higher circulations first. Why does it make a difference? First, you must test your ad before you can make really big profits with it. But who says you can't make money with a test ad? You have a better chance of doing so if you reach a bigger market. Secondly, because you are going to have people trying to copy you if you are successful, it's better that you get to more people first, which you can do by advertising in larger circulation magazines first.

HOW TO CLASSIFY YOUR AD IN THE CLASSIFIED SECTION

Once we locate the initial magazines for our tests, we are faced with an array of different classification headings—*Salesmen Wanted, Distributors Wanted, Advertising Specialty Salesmen Wanted, Agents Wanted, Money-Making Opportunities, Business Opportunities*—the headings go on and on. Under which of these classifications do we advertise, as in many cases, we will find several headings under which our ad could fit? The standard rule—look for the competition—holds. If a competitor is advertising the same or a similar product successfully, chances are that the ad's heading is where our ad belongs as well. But what if we have an item so new or so different that the competition isn't there yet? In that case, look for as similar an item as you can possibly find. If you had wanted to sell electronic calculators to engineers back in the days when these calculator were just introduced, you would have selected a heading under which slide rules could be found. Why? Because a slide rule was the existing product that performed the same function as electronic calculators.

Now, what if there are no similar items? In that case, look for those classified headings that would be of interest to a group of people who would also be interested in your item. The same people who are interested in purchasing government surplus may also be interested in bargains and close-outs.

Finally, if there is no heading, do not be afraid to ask for one. If you look at almost any classified columns in magazines, you will find some headings with only a single advertisement underneath. Very frequently, it is a case of the advertiser's not finding a heading for his or her product. The advertiser simply asked the magazine to provide a separate heading. This has an additional advantage: With only one ad under a certain heading, the chance of your ad being read is much greater, so never be afraid to ask for one. You may not get one, but it's always worthwhile to ask.

In many cases, and because your product or service will fit under more than one classified heading, you can advertise under more than one heading. You may want to do this at the outset to determine which heading is more successful. Or, after you have determined that your test is successful with a single ad under one heading, you may advertise under two different headings. Now, if you do advertise under more than one heading, do not expect to double your number of responses. But who cares? As long as your response rate is profitable for each heading, you will increase your total profits.

HOW TO INSERT YOUR AD
IN A MAGAZINE

Inserting a classified advertisement is very easy to do. No artwork or graphics are required, so you simply type the ad as you would like it to appear and state under what classification you want it to run. If you are a first-time advertiser, you must usually include a check or money order for the full amount of the ad. Be careful of the closing date of the magazine, which is the final date on which the magazine will accept advertising for the specific issue in which you wish to advertise. It is not unusual for the closing date to be six weeks prior to the date on the cover of the magazine. If you want a weekly magazine with a quicker response, you may consider the *National Enquirer* or *Grit* whose lead times are usually less.

Many magazines will require a sample of what you are selling or are going to send in response to an inquiry you receive from your ad. By policing itself, the industry attempts to keep unethical or dishonest mail order dealers from advertising in their magazines.

SAVING MONEY WITH YOUR CLASSIFIED ADS

There are several ways to save money when you place your classified ads. In many publications, it is possible to save 2 percent on your advertising by paying within a specific period, usually 10 days. This discount will be indicated on the rate card you receive from the magazine upon request.

Another way you can save money when you place a classified ad is by having your own in-house advertising agency. Advertising agencies make money by getting a 15 percent discount for any ads they place with a publication. So if you have your own advertising agency (see Chapter 10), you can save 15 percent. Most publications say they do not give discounts to in-house agencies. But most publications *will* give you a discount if the fact that you are an in-house agency isn't made so obvious that they must reject it so as not to displease their regular advertising agency customers.

Another way to save money in your classified ad campaign is called "till forbid." Many magazines will offer you a discount if you give them a till forbid order, which means they will continue to run your ad until you tell them to stop. This saves money in several ways. First, there is the discount, usually for three insertions or more of the same ad. You also save labor and postage in writing every month to request the ad be repeated. However, you should be cautious about use of till forbid. Many advertisements will not make money every month in every magazine. Also, you want to make certain your ad is going to make money before you run a "till forbid." So don't run "till forbid" until your testing is complete. But once it is, all you need to do is inform the magazine of your key so it can automatically be changed with each new issue.

THE STRATEGY FOR PYRAMIDING YOUR PROFITS IN CLASSIFIED ADVERTISING

To pyramid your money in classified advertising, you start with one test and one magazine. If the test is successful, then and only then do you proceed. You continue to advertise in that magazine and start testing in another magazine of the same category, as defined by SRDS. Let's look at some types. There are shelter magazines, such as *Better Homes and Gardens,* and *Good Housekeeping.* There are opportunity magazines, such as *New Business Opportunities, Entrepreneur,* and *Income Opportunities.* There are the hunting and fishing magazines, such as *Field and Stream, Hunting and Fishing,* and *Outdoor Life.* Every magazine can be grouped in this fashion. Well, after you have tested successfully in two magazines in a group, you know that your classified ad will probably work in all the other magazines in the same group. So after testing several magazines in one group, move on to another group and start testing in one magazine in that group. If you are successful, continue to advertise in the magazine. If you are unsuccessful, stop, take note, and move on to something else. In this way you can expand from group to group, repeating the process in every group and making increasing profits as you find more groups that are profitable for your classified ad.

In doing this testing, you will discover that some months are better for your ad than others. This is especially true with seasonal products. A Christmas item naturally sells best in the Christmas season, and some summer products, such as suntan oil and beach towels, would not sell at all during the winter. Many surveys have been done to show when advertising works best. They are useful as a starting point for testing if you do not have a seasonal product. You will find such a rating of months in Chapter 10. January is usually considered the best month for the average mail order product. (January will be the month in which your ad actually appears, *not* the month printed on the magazine cover, which may precede the actual month in which the magazine appears by several weeks or a month.) Remember that any listing such as the one in Chapter 10 is an average only, and you must work with your particular product to discover which months are best for you. You may find that in some very good months it pays to increase your advertising, whereas in particularly bad months, it pays not to advertise at all.

Being able to forecast future returns based on early returns from your ad will help you pyramid your profits quickly. It has been found that 50 percent of the responses you will ever receive from a classified ad in a monthly magazine will occur about a month after you receive the very first order inquiry. So it's easy to forecast returns accurately. As soon as you get an inquiry or order, write down this particular date, using the records systems I will show you later on in the book. One months after this date, you will have received 50 percent of the responses you will ever receive. Multiply this number by two and you will have accounted for 100 percent of your responses. The forecast is different with a weekly magazine or newspaper. You will receive 50 percent of the orders or inquiries you will ever receive about two weeks after receipt of the first order or inquiry. You can make your decision much more rapidly with this technique than if you waited until all your orders were received, which, for a monthly magazine, would be about a year. You can't afford to wait this long to make decisions in mail order because your competition will always jump in if your advertisement is successful. It's up to you to do what you can to capture as much of the market as you possibly can before that happens. Using your forecasting figure, you can make a decision as to the ad's profitability and whether to proceed or stop running it in that magazine.

THE SECRET OF MAKING MUCH MORE MONEY WITH YOUR CLASSIFIED ADVERTISEMENTS

There is one important way in which you can make a lot more money with your classified advertisements, and that is to rent the names you receive from the response to your ads. Those names are very important in mail order, because people who respond have qualified themselves as mail order buyers. If they will buy your product by mail, they will buy other mail order dealers' products, so their names are valuable. In fact, some mail order businesses make as much as 25 percent of their annual sales simply from renting the names of respondents. Now, here's how it works in classified. Let's say that in your first year of operations, you receive 10,000 names. A typical rental fee may be $70 per thousand, so 10 times $70 is $700. However, we are not through. It is a fact that some companies rent their names as many as 24 times a year or more, so you could make several thousand dollars just from renting your 10,000 names. Do not overlook this additional source of income.

THE MOST CREATIVE CLASSIFIED AD I EVER READ

Figure 9.5 is the most creative ad I ever read. The ad was given to me by one of my students. By the time I received the ad, the toll-free number had been disconnected, so I have no idea what the offer was—great ad though!

TELEMARKETING
STUPID BOB
Hi, my name is Stupid Bob, I earn $1,000 per week talking on the phone. If you are half as stupid as I am you can make $500 per week part time. Call Stupid Bob at 1-800-748-6970.

Figure 9.5

SUMMARY

Here are ten proven ways to increase your results from classified advertising.

1. Get your prospect's attention. This is the first and most important job your classified ad must do, from the very first word.

2. Because you are paying for classifieds by the *word*, you can make your advertisement look longer by avoiding abbreviations that don't save you words. For example, do not use "CA" for California. Spell it out. Similarly, do not abbreviate your city. Your ad will look bigger without adding one penny to its cost.

3. Do use abbreviations that save you money: "$1" compared to "one dollar" saves you an additional word. Each word saved is money in your pocket.

4. Once you have a successful ad in a magazine, try to run an identical ad simultaneously under a different classified heading. In this way you can overcome the limitation of the number of magazines in which you will be able to advertise.

5. If you can use a street address rather than a box number, do so. A street address lends credibility to your company and to your advertisement. Omit the word "street," "avenue" or "blvd.," if you can, to save money.

6. Form your key with a one-word company name. "Global-1A" instead of "Global Associates, Department 1A" saves several words and a lot of money.

7. Test before you leap. Start with one ad and one magazine. The chances of your competition's reacting to one ad are just about nil. Your competition is like you: It is going to look for repeated ads in many magazines as a sign of success, and only then attempt to get into your market. Don't assume success before you have proven it by testing. You can have more failures than successes and still make a million dollars by exploiting your winners and dropping your losers right away.

8. The two-step inquiry and follow-up is much preferred in classified over attempting to sell a product directly from your classified ad. If you do sell direct, it is better to use even dollar figures such as $2 or $3 rather than $1.98 or $2.99, because most people will send cash rather than checks for these small amounts, and the 98¢ or 99¢ is hard to mail in an envelope.

9. Always be aware of what your competitors are doing. Consider the magazines in which they advertise as a place to start. Look at the classifications your competition is using as starting places for you.

Follow your competition when you are a newcomer and you will save a lot of money and have a much better chance of succeeding.

10. Be as brief as possible in your classified ad, but make certain that you have included the words necessary to obtain the inquiry or the sale.

Many companies have started with classified ads and gone on to other media. Other companies are successful using only classified ads. Still other companies use classified ads as an adjunct to their business. So don't neglect use of the classified ad in your mail order business: The ad may be small, but its size belies its ability to contribute significantly to your business.

10

Making Money with Display Ads

To many people, display advertising is synonymous with mail order. And no wonder, when display ads can run as long as 40 years, as did the ad in Figure 10.1, "Do You Make These Mistakes in English?" This ad, which was written by Maxwell Sackheim, continuously outpulled ads written by many of the country's top mail order copywriters from the time it was written in 1915 until the mid-1950s. How many orders for Sherwin Cody's course in English do you think this ad brought in during this 40-year period? It had to be in the millions! Figure 6.2 shows another great mail order ad that ran for years: "They Laughed When I Sat Down at the Piano . . . but When I Started to Play!" This ad for the U.S. School of Music was written by ad genius John Caples. Not every display ad can bring in millions of orders as these two ads did, but you don't need millions of orders from one display ad to make a good living from mail order, which is what you are going to learn to do this chapter.

WHAT IS A DISPLAY AD?

A display ad is space in a medium such as a magazine or newspaper in which advertising is placed. For this reason, *display* and *space* are two words that are frequently used interchangeably in mail order. Both mean the something. Figure 10.1 shows a full-display ad. However, a display ad can range from a single inch in height by one column in width to an entire page. Why do people use display ads when they are far more expensive than classified advertising? Well, as I mentioned earlier, for many people, display advertising *is* mail order. A full-page display ad is placed to offer a product that can be ordered immediately by a potential buyer through use

Do You Make These Mistakes in English?

Sherwin Cody's remarkable invention has enabled more than 100,000 people to correct their mistakes in English. Only 15 minutes a day required to improve your speech and writing.

MANY persons use such expressions as "Leave them lay there" and "Mary was invited as well as myself." Still others say "between you and I" instead of "between you and me." It is astonishing how often "who" is used for "whom" and how frequently we hear such glaring mispronunciations as "for MID able," "ave NOO," and "KEW pon." Few know whether to spell certain words with one or two "c's" or "m's" or "r's" or with "ie" or "ei," and when to use commas in order to make their meaning absolutely clear. Most persons use only common words—colorless, flat, ordinary. Their speech and their letters are lifeless, monotonous, humdrum.

Why Most People Make Mistakes

What is the reason so many of us are deficient in the use of English and find our careers stunted in consequence? Why is it some cannot spell correctly and others cannot punctuate? Why do so many find themselves at a loss for words to express their meaning adequately? The reason for the deficiency is clear. Sherwin Cody discovered it in scientific tests which he gave thousands of times. *Most persons do not write or speak good English simply because they never formed the habit of doing so.*

What Cody Did at Gary

The formation of any habit comes only from constant practice. Shakespeare, you may be sure, never studied rules. No one who writes and speaks correctly thinks of rules when he is doing so.

Here is our mother-tongue, a language that has built up our civilization, and without which we should all still be muttering savages! Yet our schools, by wrong methods, have made it a study to be avoided —the hardest of tasks instead of the most fascinating of games! For years it has been a crying disgrace.

In that point lies the real difference between Sherwin Cody and the schools! Here is an illustration: Some years ago Mr. Cody was invited by the author of the famous Gary System of Education to teach

SHERWIN CODY

English to all upper-grade pupils in Gary, Indiana. By means of unique practice exercises Mr. Cody secured more improvement in these pupils in five weeks than previously had been obtained by similar pupils in two years under old methods. There was no guesswork about these results. They were proved by scientific comparisons. Amazing as this improvement was, more interesting still was the fact that the children were "wild" about the study. It was like playing a game!

The basic principle of Mr. Cody's new method is habit-forming. Anyone can learn to write and speak correctly by constantly using the correct forms. But how is one to know in each case what is correct? Mr. Cody solves this problem in a simple, unique, sensible way.

100% Self-Correcting Device

Suppose he himself were standing forever at your elbow. Every time you mispronounced or misspelled a word, every time you violated correct grammatical usage, every time you used the wrong word to express what you meant, suppose you could hear him whisper: "That is wrong, it should be thus and so." In a short time you would habitually use the correct form and the right words in speaking and writing.

If you continued to make the same mistakes over and over again, each time patiently he would tell you what was right. He would, as it were, be an everlasting mentor beside you—a mentor who would not laugh at you, but who would, on the contrary, support and help you. The 100% Self-Correcting Device does exactly this thing. It is Mr. Cody's silent voice behind you, ready to speak out whenever you commit an error. It finds your mistakes and concentrates on them. You do not need to study anything you already know. There are no rules to memorize.

Only 15 Minutes a Day

Nor is there very much to learn. In Mr. Cody's years of experimenting he brought to light some highly astonishing facts about English.

For instance, statistics show that a list of sixty-nine words (with their repetitions) *make up more than half of all our speech and letter-writing.* Obviously, if one could learn to spell, use, and pronounce these words correctly, one would go far toward eliminating incorrect spelling and pronunciation.

Similarly, Mr. Cody proved that there were no more than one dozen fundamental principles of punctuation. If we mastered these principles, there would be no bugbear of punctuation to handicap us in our writing.

Finally he discovered that twenty-five typical errors in grammar constitute nine-tenths of our everyday mistakes. When one has learned to avoid these twenty-five pitfalls, how readily one can obtain the facility of speech which denotes the person of breeding and education!

When the study of English is made so simple, it becomes clear that progress can be made in a very short time. *No more than fifteen minutes a day is required.* Fifteen minutes, not of study, but of fascinating practice! Mr. Cody's students do their work in any spare moment they can snatch. They do it riding to work or at home. They take fifteen minutes from the time usually spent in profitless reading or amusement. The results really are phenomenal.

Sherwin Cody has placed an excellent command of the English language within the grasp of everyone. Those who take advantage of his method gain something so priceless that it cannot be measured in terms of money. They gain a mark of breeding that cannot be erased as long as they live. They gain a facility in speech that marks them as educated people in whatever society they find themselves. They gain the self-confidence and self-respect which this ability inspires. As for material reward, certainly the importance of good English in the race for success cannot be over-estimated. Surely, no one can advance far without it.

FREE — Book on English

It is impossible in this brief review, to give more than a suggestion of the range of subjects covered by Mr. Cody's new method and of what his practice exercises consist. But those who are interested can find a detailed description in a fascinating little book called "How You Can Master Good English in 15 Minutes a Day." This is published by the Sherwin Cody School of English in Rochester. It can be had by anyone, free upon request. There is no obligation involved in writing for it. The book is more than a prospectus. Unquestionably, it tells one of the most interesting stories about education in English ever written.

If you are interested in learning more in detail of what Sherwin Cody can do for you, send for the book "How You Can Master Good English in 15 Minutes a Day."

Merely mail the coupon, a letter or postal card for it now. No agent will call. SHERWIN CODY SCHOOL OF ENGLISH, 8811 B. & O. Building, Rochester 4, N. Y.

Figure 10.1 Maxwell Sackheim's successful display ad for an instruction book.

of a coupon. The potential buyer sends in money and receives your product in return. But notice that neither of the two ads in Figures 10.1 and 10.2 attempts to sell the product directly from the advertisement itself; rather, they invite the potential customer to request additional information. Both are attempts to sell through the two-step method. The same technique is used in the Mellinger advertisement in Figure 8.1.

Okay, to many people, display advertising *is* mail order. But why use it if classified advertising is far more profitable in that the per order cost of advertising with classified is a lot less than that of display advertising? Here are the reasons:

1. It is a good way to build a volume business that cannot be built with classified ads.
2. For many products and services, you can reach more readers or potential customers cheaper than you can through a direct mail campaign.
3. It is a good way of getting the names of many potential customers fast.

Let's look at each of these reasons in detail. If you are going to make big money in mail order, you must have a volume business, and you cannot build volume business through classified advertisements. This means there is a limit to the total profits you can make with a classified ad campaign because not enough people look at classified advertising. Further, there is a limit to the number of magazines and newspapers that carry classified advertisements. No such limits exist with display ads. So even though it may cost more per inquiry or order received, a display ad produces potential profits far greater than a classified ad, and it is only through display advertising that you can build a volume business.

Display advertising is also cheaper than direct mail for many types of products you may want to sell. Why is it cheaper? Well, let's look first at reaching 1,000 potential customers who are interested in an entrepreneurial type product through a direct mail campaign. What is this product? It could be a computer program for developing a marketing plan, a newsletter on new products, or something similar. First, you must rent the names, which will cost you $50 to $100 per thousand. Next, you have your mailing package, which includes a sales letter, a brochure, a self-addressed envelope, a guarantee, and other essential items that will be explained in Chapter 11. Let's say that this costs us another 50¢ per unit, or $500 per thousand. Next, we have postage. The total cost to reach potential customers interested in this entrepreneurial type of product will be close to $900 per thousand.

Now, if we can find a magazine read by individuals interested in entrepreneurial products, we can reach a much larger readership at a much

Figure 10.2 An advertisement to mail order and direct marketing dealers.

lower cost. Is there such a magazine? Of course, there are many, and we can find such a list in one of the Standard Rate and Data Service publications. Let's say a full-page advertisement appearing one time in a magazine costs approximately $5,000. From SRDS we also learn that it reaches approximately 200,000 potential customers. What's our cost per thousand potential customers here? Only about $25. That's quite a difference in the cost of reaching our potential customer through a display advertisement compared to direct mail in this case! This does not mean that display ads are always better than direct mail. I'll explain why not later in the book.

The third main reason we may want to use display advertisements to build our business is to get as many customer names as we can, fast. Now, this goes along with the fact that mail order is a back-end business and that we can made additional revenue by renting the names we receive. The more names we get, the more revenue we can get through these two methods. But there is another reason for getting customer's names as rapidly as we can: our competition. If our product or service is successful, as proven by the fact that we continue to advertise it, we will have imitators. They will attempt to jump into the same market with a similar product and similar ad. Of course, we will protect ourselves if possible through the protection techniques discussed in an earlier chapter. However, perfect protection is usually impossible. Therefore, our strategy must be to capture a major share of the market as rapidly as we can by selling our product and getting a list of customers' names before our competition does. This we can do very effectively through display ads. Look again at the Charles Atlas ad in Figure 1.3. The entire ad offers a free book. The only thing that Atlas gets is the name of a potential student!

WHAT YOU NEED TO KNOW TO MAKE IT WITH DISPLAY ADS

Here are 13 questions you must understand and be able to answer to make money using display advertisements:

1. How do you create an effective display ad?
2. Where do you advertise?
3. When and how do you advertise?
4. How frequently do you advertise?
5. What size should your advertisements be, and should they be black and white or in color?
6. Where in the magazine should your advertisement appear?
7. How do you place your advertisements?
8. How do you buy display advertising at less than the standard rates?

9.   How can you get free advertisements for your products?
10. What results should you expect from display advertising, and how quickly should you expect them?
11. How do you do media planning strategy, and pyramid your profits?
12. Should you use an advertising agency, and how do you find one?
13. What can you do to multiply your display advertising success?

HOW TO CREATE AN EFFECTIVE DISPLAY AD

Before considering whether to create an effective display ad on your own, perhaps you should consider the alternative—having someone else create it for you. Most advertising agencies will make a commission of 15 percent on the cost of your ad, so if the cost of the display advertisement is $2,500, the agency will get a $375 commission. This commission comes out of the total cost of the advertisement and is not an additional cost to you, so it may sound like an immediate good deal. However, there are some factors about using a mail order advertising agency that you should be aware of, not the least of which is the fact that many advertising agencies will not want to deal with you until you are a fairly large advertiser.

Are there other alternatives you could choose? Certainly. There are many free-lance copywriters and artists around. For a fee, they can create the entire advertisement for you. Here are several sources of copywriters and creative designers:

1.   *Your Telephone Book.* Look in the *Yellow Pages* under *Writers, Copywriters, Advertising Agencies, Artists,* or *Creative Designers.* Contact these experts and explain your needs to them. Show them examples of the type of advertisement you want and let them go to work. Remember that the copywriter is the one who writes the words and the creative graphic designer does the artwork. Sometimes you can get this done under one roof and sometimes not. Check with whomever you are speaking with to find out if they do both. Remember that these are two different specialities and it would be rare to find a single individual capable of doing both, although you may find both specialists working in one firm.
2.   *Your Local College or University.* Call the department of journalism, art, or advertising.
3.   *Mail Order Magazines and Newsletters.* These are the professional magazines and newsletters of the mail order industry. You will find all types of specialists advertising their services. For example, Figure 10.2 is a recent advertisement. Not only does it offer professional

services for the mail order operator, but the ad itself is a good example to emulate. See Appendix F.

If you decide to create your own advertisements, be aware that a learning process is involved, and while you may be fortunate enough to create great advertisements right from the start, the chances are that you will not. The best advice I can give you is to glance through magazines and pick out advertisements for similar products that have been running for a reasonably long period. Copy not the ad, but the concept. Try to create an ad that follows the same winning principles as the successful ads you see and admire.

In creating a full-page display ad, there is a one-third, one-third, and one-third rule. As with any rule, it is frequently violated. However, as a basis for starting, it should be considered. This rule says that one-third of your display ad should be devoted to headlines, one-third to graphics, and one-third to copy. Look at the display ads in Figures 10.1, 6.2, and 8.1, and you will see how this rule is applied.

There are many effective display advertisements without any illustrations at all. Karbo's ad was an excellent example. If you do decide to use an illustration, make it serve some definite purpose. In the Mellinger ad in Figure 8.1, the purpose is not only to show a picture of Brainerd Mellinger, which says that this man does exist and that his business is import/export and mail order, but also to show some of the many thousands of products he mentions in the advertisement. John Caples's ad in Figure 6.2 shows a line drawing of the incident described in the headline. The purpose here is to reinforce the benefit implied in the headline and throughout the copy. Do you recognize this benefit? It is the triumph of the writer who played the piano successfully after his friends had laughed because they thought he could not play. Maxwell Sackheim's ad in Figure 10.1 shows the author of the course, Sherwin Cody. A picture of this type is almost always used for credibility purposes. It shows the reader that this is a real person who actually exists, not a figment of someone's imagination.

When constructing or deciding upon the illustration for your display advertisement, you should keep two questions uppermost in your mind: (1) Why am I putting this illustration in the ad? and (2) What purpose will this illustration serve? Putting an illustration in your ad just to have one there is counterproductive. It wastes space that could be used for hard-selling copy. What if Joe Karbo had used several square inches of his ad to show a picture of his book? Do you think this illustration would help the reader to make his mind up to purchase the product more than the copy that Karbo carries in his advertisement? The only way to find out is to test. Karbo did. He also tested with a picture of himself. Neither did as well. Karbo thought his picture didn't help because he had a beard. He thought it easier to drop the picture than shave.

If you aren't showing a picture for credibility, the purpose of the illustration should be to show the benefit of the product, which is usually done best by showing the product in use. In the case of Karbo's book, the benefit is success, a difficult concept to portray visually in a display advertisement usually carried in the classified section of the Sunday newspaper.

HOW TO APPLY THIS CONCEPT TO OTHER PRODUCTS

Let's say you are selling a pair of earrings. The picture of the earrings themselves may or may not elicit interest. But what if you showed a picture of a woman wearing such earrings, with several women and men admiring them? This shows satisfaction of the need—the benefit of the product. Always stress and show the benefit of a product by showing the buyer receiving the benefit.

SHOULD YOUR ILLUSTRATION BE A PHOTOGRAPH OR A LINE DRAWING?

Many people say photography is always superior. Others argue for illustrations, and still other mail order dealers use a combination of both. Gerardo Joffe, author of *How You Too Can Make at Least One Million Dollars (but Probably Much More) in the Mail Order Business* and the founder of Haverhills and Henniken's mail order houses, says that photography is probably suitable in many cases and that you should probably stick with it until you find a really good illustrator or artist. Joffe also feels that products such as clothing and food are probably better shown by photography. However, according to Joffe, for gadgets, equipment, and many other inanimate products, a good draftsman can often do things a camera cannot quite bring out. The draftsman can subtly emphasize points, bring out highlights, show attractive features, and suppress distracting details that cannot be readily accomplished with photography except by extensive and fairly expensive retouching. Do a little experimenting with both until you are satisfied with the results. Once you are successful, it's probably better to stick with your final choice to establish your own image.

HOW YOUR AD WILL BE REPRODUCED

There are three basic methods of printing, and depending on the type of printing used by the medium in which you are going to place your display advertisement, different materials must be furnished. These three types are offset, rotogravure, and letterpress.

Offset

Today most magazines and newspapers are printed by offset. The printing is done with a flat plate that has been treated to make the ink adhere to portions of the plate that will be printed, while no ink will adhere to those portions of the plate not intended to be printed. The process gets its name because the ink from this plate is transferred to another cylinder that offsets it to the paper. As an advertiser, you must furnish "camera-ready artwork" to the magazine or newspaper. Camera-ready artwork is a paste-up of the artwork and copy display you want or a good, photographic positive copy of it. This positive copy is also called a reproduction proof. Your artist can prepare either for you.

Rotogravure

Rotogravure is used for Sunday supplements and similar publications. The areas to be printed are pressed and ink is deposited in these depressions. Again, all you need to furnish is camera-ready artwork or a reproduction proof. The publication itself will make its own plate from the material you send.

Letterpress

In a letterpress process, the printing is done with regular metal plates. Many magazines that strive for expert and fine reproductions use the letterpress process. Here your cost is going to be higher because camera-ready copy is not enough. You must supply the plates to the publication yourself, or you will have to pay to have a special plate made for you.

WHERE TO ADVERTISE

To decide where to advertise, the first step, as with other aspects of mail order, is to go where your competition goes. Therefore, if you know your competition is advertising heavily in certain magazines, they are as good a place as any to start. However, at some point, you must learn to use the publications from SRDS, Standard Rate and Data Service, Inc., 5201 Old Orchard Road, Skokie, Illinois 60077. SRDS produces a series of subscription publications throughout the year that are extremely useful to everyone in the mail order industry. For display advertising, the particular SRDS publications include *Community Publication Rates and Data,* which comes out semiannually, *Consumer Magazine and Farm Publication Rates and Data, Newspaper Rates and Data,* and *Business Publications Rates and Data,* which come out monthly.

To use SRDS, turn first to the classification groupings section of the publication. In *Consumer Magazine and Farm Publication Rates and Data* you will find approximately 50 different classifications. In a recent issue these were *Airline Inflight; Almanacs and Directories; Art and Antiques; Automotive; Aviation; Babies; Boating and Yachting; Brides and Bridal; Business and Finance; Campers, Recreational Vehicles, Mobile Homes, and Trailers; Camping and Outdoor Recreation, Children's; College and Alumni; Comics and Comic Technique; Crafts, Games, Hobbies, and Models; Dancing; Dogs and Pets; Dressmaking and Needlework; Editorial and Classified Advertising; Education and Teacher; Entertainment Guides and Programs; Entertainment and Performing Arts; Epicurean; Fishing and Hunting; Fraternal, Professional Groups, Service Clubs, Veteran's Organizations, and Associations; Gardening; Gay Publications; General Editorial; General Editorial/Contemporary; General Merchandise Catalogs; Health; History; Home Service and Home; Horses, Riding, and Breeding; Humanities and Contemporary Topics; Labor-Trade Union; Lifestyle Service; Literary, Book Reviews, and Writing Techniques; Mechanics and Science; Media/Personalities; Men's; Metropolitan; Military and Naval; Motorcycle; Music; Mystery, Adventure, and Science Fiction; Nature and Ecology; News Weeklies; News Biweeklies, Semimonthlies; Newspaper-Distributed Magazine; Photography; Physical Sciences; Political and Social Topics; Religious and Denominational; Romance; Science; Senior Citizens; Sex; Snowmobiling; Society; Sports; Travel; TV and Radio/Communications and Electronics; Women's; Women's Fashions, Beauty, and Grooming;* and *Youth.* That's quite a collection. How do you pick the right classification?

Begin by selecting those classifications of publications whose readers are most likely to be interested in your product or service. For example, under the *Youth* classification the following magazines are listed: *Boys' Life, Campus Life, The 18 Almanac, Exploring, Junior Scholastic, Laufer Youth Publications, Scholastic Magazine Groups, 16 Magazine, Teen Beat, For Seniors Only, National 4-H News, New York News For Kids, Scholastic Newstime, School Guide, Vica,* and *Young Miss.*

Now look up the number assigned to this classification under the general classification listings. (See Figure 10.3.) For *Youth,* the proper classification number is 50. In the general classification section, you will see all of the magazines listed, including extensive information on each magazine, as in Figure 10.4. This information includes the local representatives and branch offices with addresses, the commission and cast discount, the general rate policy, the black/white rates, the combination rates, discounts, color rates, covers, inserts, bleed, special position rates, classified and reading notices, split run and special issue rates and data, geographical and/or demographic additions, contract and copy regulations, mechanical requirements, issue and closing dates, special services, circulation, distribution, print order, and other pertinent information. In short, you will

Classification Groupings - U.S. Consumer Magazines

Figure 10.3 SRDS classification groupings of consumer magazines.

find everything you need to know to advertise in every major magazine you might be interested in.

The next step is to write to every magazine that is a potential publication for your promotion and ask for a sample copy and a rate card. The rate card should have information identical to that contained in the section describing that magazine in SRDS. However, because it is coming from the publisher, it may have additional details and may be slightly more current, even though *Consumer Magazine and Farm Publication Rates and Data* is published monthly. A typical rate card is shown in Figure 10.5.

Figure 10.3 (Continued)

WHEN SHOULD YOU ADVERTISE AND HOW FREQUENTLY?

The month in which you advertise your product or service can have a great impact on your results. For general guidelines, you will find the following to be true:

1. Some products can be advertised all year. Some can be advertised and sold only during certain seasons.
2. Major events can affect the results of your promotion. Ordinarily, November is a good month for your products, but it may not be

Figure 10.3   (Continued)

good depending upon what product you are selling in an election year, as an election is a major event. Similarly, a war, the death of an important person, or other major events will affect your results in a mail order promotion.

3. Whatever your product, some months are better than others. You can only find out what months these are for your product by testing. As a starting point, here is a list of months from best to worst, as compiled from various sources: January, February, October, November, March, September, August, April, December, July, May, and June.

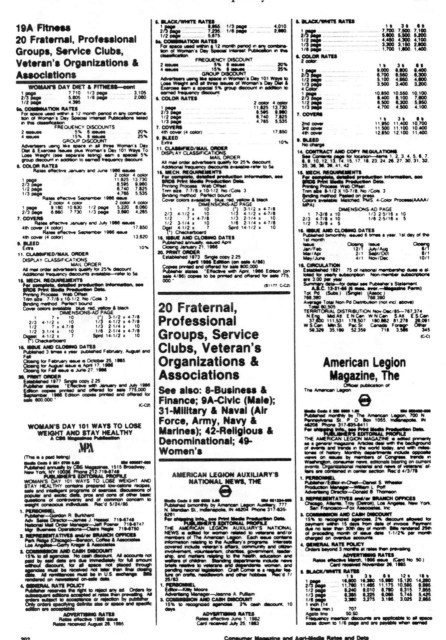

Figure 10.4   SRDS information listing for advertising in consumer magazines.

Figure 10.5   A typical rate card.

If you start your testing in a "good" month, recognize that your results may be much better than had you tested in an average or poor mail order month. In the same way, if your test ad appears in a "bad" month for a general mail order product and the results you achieve are only marginal, you should recognize that you may achieve much better results in other months.

When first starting off with your new product or service, start with the logical months, considering your product and the season of the year. If you are successful, depending upon the strength of your response, you can consider additional months of the year for your advertising. For example, if the strength of your response from your selection was extremely strong, you can consider advertising this product quite frequently. The Mellinger Company runs ads for import/export and mail order courses continuously and has for years. If the strength of your response is only moderately strong but still profitable, you should advertise less frequently—perhaps every other month or even once a quarter, or only during certain months. Finally, if you are profitable but the response is weak during a good mail order month, you may be able to advertise this particular product or service only infrequently during the year. Again, the only way to discover when to advertise is through testing.

Jerry Buchanan, who has made a fortune selling his *Writer's Utopia Formula Report* and the *Towers Club Newsletter,* has found that he can safely shut down his operation two months out of the year and not publish his newsletter at all. He uses this time for vacation. Jerry has also discovered that certain months don't pay for him to advertise at all, despite the fact that both his newsletter and report are fabulously successful. Lesson: You can be very successful and take a two-month vacation to boot without year-round advertising.

WHAT SIZE SHOULD YOUR AD BE?

There is a basic trade-off between the space you need to tell your story and the cost of the ad space. In other words, a large ad in which you can tell your entire story will cost more money than a small ad in which you don't have as much space to say everything that will convince a prospective customer to buy.

There are also standard sizes for magazines and newspapers, and when considering the construction of your ad you must also consider what size is available. For a typical magazine, the standard page is 7 by 10 inches. Each page is divided into three columns. Each column on the page is 140 lines deep or 14 lines per inch. Of this area, a full page is always available. You can also obtain two-thirds of a page, which is two columns wide; one-third of a page, which is one column wide; or a third of a page that is one-third of the page square. You can also obtain one-sixth of a page, which is half a column wide; and one-twelfth of a page, which is one-quarter of a column wide.

Sometimes you can buy magazine space by the number of lines you need. Consult the SRDS publications or the rate card of the magazine in question.

There are also standard sizes for newspapers: Most have advertising columns $1\frac{7}{8}$ inches wide. But these sizes vary, and you can choose depending upon the column width. There are other standards for the Sunday supplement, *TV Guide,* and so forth.

Here are the facts you must consider in your decision about the size of your ad. First, consider cost per order per inquiry: Given a certain size, how much money does each inquiry cost you? You must test to find this figure. Take the total number of inquiries or orders you generate from your ad and divide by the cost of the advertisement.

The second consideration is speed in establishing yourself in the marketplace. Remember that everything you do in mail order is seen by everyone else, including all your competitors. One successful strategy for beating the competition is getting established in the marketplace before your competition can do so. A large ad helps in doing this by appearing before a large number of people in a relatively short time.

The third aspect to consider is the size of the market reached. A classified advertisement is seen by only a small portion of the readership of any particular publication. To reach a larger market, you need a larger ad. Therefore, in many cases, even though the cost per inquiry or order may be much higher with a large advertisement, it still makes sense to pay the higher price to reach a much larger market.

The fourth factor to consider is the nature of the product or service you are selling. Some types of product demand a very large advertisement—one with which the public is unfamiliar, for example. You need more time and space to describe and sell this product as you must describe and sell not only its unique features but also the advantages of the product as a generic type. Another example might be an intangible or informational kind of product, such as those sold by Karbo, Haroldsen, Suarez, and Buchanan. Finally, you will need more space to sell a more expensive, or "big-ticket," product than a cheaper one.

There are some other guidelines to help you decide whether your product requires a large or small ad. Let's be honest: Sometimes the size of your ad, although not optimal, will be dictated by your budget. If you have determined that you cannot sell your product or service effectively through a small advertisement, you should consider borrowing money (see Chapter 2). The old saying that you can't squeeze blood out of a stone holds here. Your product may be the type that can be totally successful through a large advertisement but cannot be successful at all in a smaller one. If you are in this situation, borrow the money you need for a proper campaign or wait until you have the money to do the job right. Once again, look at your successful competition for similar products or services. If your competition sells with a large ad and it is successful, chances are you will have to do the same. If your competition is successful, this means it has already been in business for some time and has probably tested smaller ads as well and found that the larger ad is the one best suited for this particular product or service. Conversely, if your successful competition is using smaller ads, this means the exact opposite. Finally, consider the strategy and tactics you have decided upon to introduce your product. Are you selling direct from the ad or through a two-step method? Sometimes the inquiry and follow-up can be done with a smaller ad. Sometimes it is still more effective to use a larger ad, and many do so successfully.

Cahners Publishing Company did two studies that are important to your ad size decision. One study analyzed how the readership was influenced by ad size as the size of the ad increased. Cahners sorted 2,353 advertisements by size classification and response. An average response was calculated and assigned an index number, an arbitrary number used for the convenience of the researcher. This index number for the average response was 100. Against this number, ads had index scores as follows: a quarter-page ad had an index score of 55, a little over half the average; a half-page ad had an index score of 91; and a full-page ad had an index score of 124. Note here that doubling the ad size did not result in doubling the index score. Cahners concluded that as the size of the ad increased, reader influence, as measured by response, increased, but not in direct proportion.

In a second study, Cahners measured the average number of inquiries generated by advertisement size. In this survey, Cahners analyzed 500,000 inquiries generated by several industrial magazines, as shown in Figure 10.6. As ad size increased, more inquiries were generated. However, again, the increase in the average number of inquiries was not in direct proportion to the size, indicating that cost per inquiry is probably less for smaller ads than for larger ones.

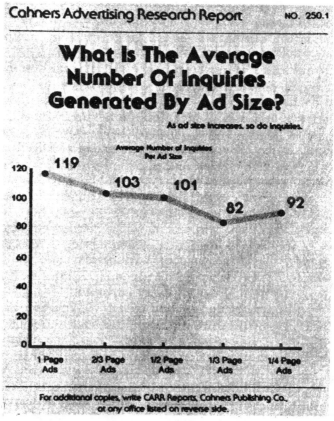

Figure 10.6 Results of a survey comparing ad size and number of inquiries. The larger the ad, the more inquiries.

SHOULD YOU USE COLOR OR BLACK AND WHITE FOR YOUR ADVERTISEMENT?

Color costs more money than black and white. To make up this additional cost, you will generally need a 20 percent greater response. Does color bring in a 20 percent greater response? The answer is "yes" when it is appropriate, and that depends upon your product. Bob Stone reports an increase of 30 to 60 percent in response to color ads for appropriate products. What is meant by appropriate products? If your product is the kind that must be seen to be appreciated, where the colors are vivid and make an impact on the potential buyer, color is worth considering. But if color does not have this anticipated effect on your potential buyer, it should not be used, or its use should be delayed until you have a successful black and white test completed.

WHERE IN EACH PUBLICATION SHOULD YOU ADVERTISE?

You may be surprised to learn that, depending upon the location in the magazine or newspaper, the identical ad will result in different numbers of responses.

There are two major rules to follow regarding ad positioning. The first is that the better visibility your advertisement has, the better results you will get. The second general rule is that the front of the magazine produces better results than the back. A major exception to this rule is the back cover, which produces excellent results.

There are other general rules. The upper part of the magazine appears to do better than the lower part. The outside of a page does better than the inside of a page. It is usually better to be near editorial matter—that is, appearing close to the regular copy of the magazine, rather than away from it. Finally, it is usually a little better to be in front of the editorial matter than after it. If you think about it, you'll see that all of these results are due to visibility.

How important can positioning be? Let's look at an example. Let's assume that the standard cost of advertising in a magazine is $10,000 for a full-page ad. Now, most magazines recognize the fact that some positions are much better than others. So, we'll say that we want to advertise on the back cover. A full-page ad on the back cover will cost 50 percent more, or $15,000. Which position is more profitable for us? Well, if our $10,000 ad appears at one of the less favored positions in the magazine, it may bring in only half the response of the back cover. Therefore, let's assume that our normal response is 1.5 times the cost of the ad in sales—that is, our $10,000 ad cost will bring us $15,000 in sales for our product. If we subtract the $10,000 ad cost and, let's say, $500 for the cost of the product, that leaves a $4,500 profit. Now, let's look at the back cover. This ad will cost us $15,000. Because our response is twice that of the other location, this ad would bring in $30,000. From this, we subtract the $15,000 cost of the advertisement and $1,000 cost of product, leaving $14,000 in profit. That's a big difference in profits. The location of the ad is very important.

How can you control the location of the ad? You can pay a premium, as in our example. However, sometimes locations are not recognized by the publication as being better or worse. If special rates aren't mentioned for particular locations in the SRDS publication or on the rate card, good positions are not recognized by the magazine, and you can ask for a favorable location. Sometimes the magazine will grant it. However, if you are a new advertiser with a small budget, you will probably have little luck with your request until you are a bigger advertiser, spending more money. But if your ad appears in a poor location and fails to do well, ask the publication if it will rerun it in a better location at no extra charge. Sometimes it will, because it recognizes that the mail order advertiser must make money with his or her ad or not advertise at all. A magazine won't always do this for you, and how much advertising you are currently doing there will probably affect its decision, but it never hurts to ask.

HOW TO PLACE YOUR AD

If you are placing your own advertisement without going through an agency, all you have to do is follow the instructions in the SRDS publication or on the rate card. For example, Figure 10.4 is an extract from the SRDS. It includes instructions for advertising in *The American Legion Magazine*. One of the important items to remember is the issue and closing dates for your advertisement. In item 16 of Figure 10.4, *Issue and Closing Dates*, it is stated that the magazine is published monthly and issued the first day of the publication month. This paragraph also states a firm order closing date for black and white and two-color forms: the tenth of the second month preceding month of issue. So if the month of issue is December, you must submit your order and advertisement by October 10. Paragraph 16 further states that the firm order closing for four-color forms is the fifth of the second month preceding the month of issue. These lead times vary from one magazine to another. The month of your ad appearance can be very important, so make certain that you read this section of the SRDS or the rate card very closely.

Your letter to the publication should state that you intend to advertise and include the details regarding the size, color, special locations of your ad, and so forth, and should include whatever copy is required. Some magazines will require that you submit a sample of your product or the sales package with which you will respond to inquiries. Be certain to include this material if it is requested. Otherwise, the magazine may not run your ad.

HOW TO BUY DISPLAY ADVERTISING AT MUCH LESS THAN THE STANDARD RATE

The pros in the business buy advertising at a lot less than the price paid by most beginners. These differences are significant and can spell the difference between profitability and failure with your advertisement, so please don't skip this section.

Here are 12 methods of saving money with space advertising, each of which can save you hundreds, or even thousands, of dollars:

1. Mail order discounts.
2. PI (per inquiries) deals.
3. Frequency discounts.
4. Standby rates.
5. Help if necessary.
6. Remnants in regional editions.
7. Barter.
8. Bulk buyers.
9. Seasonal discounts.
10. Spread discounts.
11. Your own advertising agency.
12. Cost discounts.

Mail Order Discounts

Magazines know that, as a mail order advertiser, you must make money directly from your ad or you will not advertise again. Further, unlike an institutional advertiser, you will know immediately exactly how well your ad did and whether it is making money for you. So many magazines give special discounts, up to 40 percent, to mail order advertisers. That means that a $100 ad will cost you only $60. That is certainly nothing to sneeze at and can easily spell the difference between a failure and a very profitable promotion.

PI Deals

A PI deal is one in which you agree to pay the publication only for those inquiries or sales that the ad attracts. In return for this agreement, the magazine runs your advertisement at no charge to you. Sometimes the mail is sent directly to you. At other times the publication will insist that the mail be sent to it. Of course, the ad must be keyed and, if the mail is sent to you, you must keep accurate records and send the money owed to the publication at fixed periods agreed to between you and the magazine. If the orders go to the publication, it will send you the names of those who order so that you can send the product to the customer. It will also send you the money owed for each product. For a PI deal, most magazines will require something like 50 percent of the price of the product you are selling in return for running your advertisement with no money up front.

Sometimes it's difficult to locate PI deals, and you should talk to the salesperson representing the magazine. Few magazines would like their other advertisers to know that PI deals are accepted, so don't expect to see them advertised on the rate card and don't expect every magazine to offer them.

Melvin Powers, the dean of mail order book publishers, says, "I have several PI deals that are resulting in thousands of orders every week for my books."

Frequency Discounts

Most magazines will offer a discount for frequency. For example, if you advertise every month, you can expect to get a substantial discount. If you advertise six times, four times, or three times a year, you can also expect a discount. The one cautionary note about frequency discounts is that you should not arrange to advertise in a medium at a fixed frequency until you do the proper testing. If your ad is not working, advertising frequency is no bargain, no matter what the discount.

Standby Rates

A magazine or newspaper is committed to publication on a regular basis. At certain times, all the available advertising space may not be sold out at the last minute. The magazine, therefore, has a choice: sell this advertising space at a greatly reduced amount or put in editorial content, which does not generate additional profits. To get the standby rate, you must first let magazines know that you are interested in this type of deal. Of course, these magazines must be able to get hold of you quickly by telephone. Usually the standby rate is available only after you have advertised in a magazine for some time. Then the people at the magazine know you and trust you. This is important because the magazine is offering to run your ad based on a telephone conversation with no money from you in advance. But asking for the standby rate is well worth it. You may pay as little as 40 or 50 percent of the normal cost of the advertising. That's quite a bargain and can mean big profits for you.

Help if Necessary

You cannot always get "help if necessary," but again, many magazines will give you help when they recognize that they are dealing with a mail order advertiser. What this means is that, although you agree to pay for the ad in advance, if the advertisement runs and is not profitable, the publication agrees to run the ad again and repeat it if necessary until you at least break even. You may not make any additional money with a "help if necessary" arrangement, but you sure can prevent yourself from losing a lot. And, as in every business situation, avoidance of losing your valuable financial resources can be as important as reaching your profit goals immediately. Why? Because retaining your financial clout means you can change your ad, offer, or product to win out eventually.

Remnants for Regional Editions

Today, many national magazines will allow you to buy space only in certain regions, rather than providing space for advertising nationally. This situation reduces your advertising cost and is ideal for testing, especially when you want to test one copy in one region and one copy in another, or only to advertise in certain regions that may be profitable to you. The result for many regions, however, is remnant space—space left over much as in the standby situation we talked about before. Again, you find out about this by asking the salespeople or publishers whether they have regional remnant space available and having them contact you. Typical discounts for remnant space are as much as 50 percent.

Barter

If you have something to trade, a publisher may allow you to trade for something he or she wants and run your ad for nothing or at a reduced cost. This occurs where the publisher has interests other than publishing the magazine and can make money from the product or service you are offering. Or, if you are a publisher yourself, sometimes you can trade or barter advertising space with other publications. Barter has an advantage in addition to getting advertisements at a greatly reduced or net cost: It builds up sales of the product you are bartering. Although you may agree to barter at wholesale, usually you make money on it anyway as your production costs are lower than the wholesale costs you charge.

Bulk Buyers

Bulk buyers buy huge amounts of space from a magazine at reduced cost. The bulk buyer fulfills the contract by either running the advertisement for his or her own products or services or selling off unused space to other advertisers. The price you pay with a bulk buyer will vary greatly and is negotiable. You may be able to get as much as a 50 percent discount from what you would normally pay.

You may have a problem locating bulk buyers. There are not a whole lot of them. One way is to keep your eyes open in professional magazines of the mail order industry mentioned earlier in this chapter. Look in the classified section. Another way is to have a mail order consultant locate a bulk buyer for you. Consultants can also be found in these magazines.

Seasonal Discounts

Some magazines whose advertising decreases in certain seasons will offer a discount to a mail order advertiser who will advertise then. Again, if this information is not on the rate card, ask for it and see whether the magazine offers a seasonal discount. The one thing you must be careful of here is that your product is profitable to advertise during this magazine's off season. As we talked about earlier, profitability will vary by season, depending on the product you are selling. However, it may be that your product fits perfectly into the season for which you can get a discount. If so, it's your lucky day and you can save a lot of money this way.

Spread Discounts

If you are a really big advertiser and advertise on two or more pages in one issue of a particular magazine, you may be able to get a spread discount. Here again, this may not be on the rate card so you should ask about it. A spread discount can run as high as 50 percent of the total cost of your advertisement.

Your Own Advertising Agency

Advertising agencies get an automatic 15 percent discount from any medium in which they place your ad. As a result, many mail order dealers have established their own in-house advertising agencies. They then place their own ads with the magazines through their in-house agencies and get automatic 15 percent discounts. Most magazines say that they will not deal with in-house agencies and will not accept advertisements from them at the 15 percent discount. But the fact is, most will. They say this only to protect the advertising agencies who are their regular customers. However, you should not make it obvious that you are an in-house agency when you place your ad. This means:

1. Your in-house advertising agency should have a name different from your company's.

2. You should have special stationery printed with the in-house advertising agency's name.
3. You should not volunteer the fact that you are an in-house agency.
   Merely indicate that you are placing the ad for the company indicated and give other instructions in accordance with the rate card
   or SRDS publication.

Cash Discounts

Many people dealing in mail order advertising overlook the fact that most
media will give a 2 percent discount for payment of cash within 10 days.
However, if you do not take this discount, very few magazines will automatically return your money. So look for this information in the rate card
or in the SRDS publication and, if you do pay for the ad with cash or
check within 10 days of billing or follow whatever other instructions are
required, take the discount offered. If you are a big advertiser, 2 percent
can amount to a significant amount of money.

HOW TO GET FREE "ADVERTISING"

Every magazine is constantly looking for new ideas, new news, and new information to tell its readers, so whenever you have a new product or service, magazines will be happy to publicize this for you at no charge if it
thinks its readers will be interested. This free "advertising" has the advantage, in addition to not costing anything, of appearing to be a recommendation by a very credible, impartial source—the editor or writer of the
magazine in which this material appears. You should understand that not
every new idea or product will be run by every magazine you approach.
Therefore, you must conduct a mini-direct mail campaign to locate magazines that will be interested. Your campaign package should consist of
three basic elements:

1. A cover letter.
2. Suggested editorial material about your new product or service.
   This is called a publicity release.
3. Either the new product itself or a four-by-five-inch glossy photograph of the product. Sending the product itself does not necessarily enhance your chances of getting this free advertising, so send a
   photograph except for those products a photograph of which would
   not in any way add to a reader's or editor's understanding of what
   the product is. For example, if you are selling a book or booklet, the
   product itself may do better than the photograph.

Figure 10.7 is a letter to the editor for free promotion for a body armor product I sold several years ago. Follow this general format when asking for free promotion in a letter. Do not mention that you may become a paid advertiser later. If you are sending money to the magazine for a paid display advertisement, do not send it with the letter to the editor requesting free editorial mention.

Figure 10.8 shows a typical publicity release that might accompany a letter such as the one shown in Figure 10.7. Figure 10.9 shows a photograph of the product. While you can have publicity information as listed in Figure 10.8 reproduced in quantity, the letter to the editor works better if individually typed. Photographs can also be reproduced in quantity cheaply, although usually not by your standard photographer. For example, four-by-five-inch glossies in quantities of 100 can be obtained for as little as 50¢ a copy by a photo duplicating service. Check your Yellow Pages. Here is one photo duplication service that deals through the mail,

---

Mr. A.B. Jones
Editor
World Military Gazette
101 New State Drive
New York NY   10065

Dear Mr. Jones:

I am writing to you because my company, Global Associates, has just developed a new product which will have a tremendous effect on casualty reduction in military operations. This new product is a personal protective body armor which is half the weight of current models but gives slightly more than double the level of protection.

This amazing armor is called "KPC Composite," and it is soft and flexible although it has five times the tensile strength of steel. A special patented carrier has been developed for the KPC Composite material. The whole unit is called "The Commando MK III Armor Jacket."

I know that your readers will be interested in knowing not only of the existence of this life-saving garment, but also that individual soldiers can order their own Commando MK III Armor Jackets directly from Global Associates at $300 per unit, insurance and postage costs included. I have enclosed a publicity release along with a photograph for your use if desired.

Sincerely,

President
GLOBAL ASSOCIATES

Figure 10.7 A letter to a magazine editor to try to obtain coverage—in other words, free advertising.

PUBLICITY RELEASE

New Body Armor Announced

Global Associates, a body armor company, announced the development of a new personal protective body armor today. The new armor, known as KPC Composite, is half the weight of current body armor, but offers twice the level of protection. The armor also has the unusual properties of being soft and flexible although it displays five times the tensile strength of steel.

The armor has defeated projectiles travelling as fast as 2000 feet per second. It has also been tested against and has stopped various small-arm ammunition, including .38 caliber, .45 caliber, .22 magnum, 9mm, .41 magnum, and .44 magnum.

A special patented carrier has been designed for the armor and designated the Commando MK III Armor Jacket. This garment itself has many unusual features. It is worn like a jacket, with a closure in the front. This permits increased ventilation during use and allows the armor to be donned or doffed without removing the helmet or other headgear.

In addition, a special lockstrap suspension system has been developed. Although the straps cannot be pulled apart, under emergency conditions the armor can be completely jettisoned in less than three seconds. For normal armor closure, a protected slide fastener is provided.

The entire ensemble comes in three sizes—small, medium, and large. It weighs just 4½ pounds.

Interested buyers can purchase the Commando MK III Armor Jacket by sending $300 to Global Associates, P.O. Box 1975, Sierra, California 91076.

Figure 10.8   Publicity release to accompany the letter shown in Figure 10.7.

which I have used and found satisfactory: Duplicate Photo Laboratories, Inc., P.O. Box 2670, 1522 North Highland Avenue, Hollywood, California 90028.

RESULTS TO EXPECT AND HOW QUICKLY TO EXPECT THEM

An advertisement itself may be profitable and yet you can still lose money because of overhead. Also, because mail order is a back-end profit business, you must also consider this factor when you talk about the profitability of an ad. So see the chapter on mail order profit calculations. As a rough rule, a space advertisement should bring a return on your investment of at least 30 percent to be profitable. Let's say that the advertisement cost is $8,000; 30 percent of $8,000 is $2,400. Because you want a return on your investment of $2,400, you must add this to your investment, making a total of $10,400.

Figure 10.9 Photograph of the product, included in the publicity packet sent to a magazine editor.

From this figure we can calculate how many responses are needed. If the price of your product is $10 and the product cost plus the fulfillment cost (that is, postage, package, etc.) is $1, your gross profit is $9 for each unit you sell. Take the $10,400 and divide this by $9: we must sell about 1,156 units for the ad to give us a 30 percent return on our advertising investment. If we sell this many, the ad is profitable and worth repeating. If you want to know the total sales required, just multiply 1,156 times the sale price of $10: $11,560.

Now we must deal with another problem. The results from your advertisement will come in over a year or more. How can we estimate these returns quickly so we can decide whether to increase our advertising?

Responses to advertisements seem to come after about the same length of time, regardless of which monthly magazine you are advertising in. One week after your first response, you will probably receive 5 percent of the responses you will ever receive. After two weeks for a monthly magazine, you will probably receive 20 percent of your total returns. After one month, you will probably receive 50 percent, and after one year, you will probably receive very close to 100 percent. (I must tell you that on several

occasions I have received responses more than four years after the advertisement appeared in a particular issue of a particular magazine, but these
are unusual cases.) Therefore, by simply multiplying the number of responses you have received after one month by two, you will know the total
number of responses you can expect from this particular ad. In the case of
the example we used earlier, where 1,156 responses were required, if after
one month we received 600 responses, we would multiply times two, giving 1,200 responses. Because 1,200 is greater than 1,156, it would be
worth repeating this advertisement. If, however, only 500 responses were
received, 500 times two is 1,000, which is less than 1,156, so we probably
would not repeat the ad without making some changes.

The response period for weekly magazines and newspapers is not identical to that of monthly magazines, so you must adjust the formula somewhat.
With weekly magazines, in general, 50 percent of your total responses will
be received two weeks after the first response; and with newspapers, 90 percent of the total responses will be received by the end of the second week.
Take these calculations into consideration when you decide whether to repeat the ad.

Once you start your advertising, keep your own records because some
differences may occur, depending upon the type of weekly magazine or
newspaper and your product. Sometimes conditions such as improved mail
delivery may change these patterns.

MEDIA PLANNING STRATEGY AND PYRAMIDING

Before you submit your first advertisement, you should anticipate ahead of
time that if you are successful you will want to expand your advertising
rapidly. This procedure is called media planning strategy and it is especially
important if you have a limited budget. You must develop your media plan-
ing strategy and pyramid your advertising rapidly because if you are successful, you will invariably have imitators who will attempt to copy your
product, your service, and your advertisements, and even the magazines
you advertise in. Therefore, the trade-off is the money you must risk versus the competition that will attempt to split your market. The general
principle to follow is to pick the various categories or groupings discussed
earlier in this chapter in which the readers may be interested in what you
have to sell and advertise first in one of these. If successful, expand your
advertisement into another category, at the same time repeating your ad in
the successful magazine as well as an additional magazine in the same category. Now, you are advertising simultaneously in two categories. If the
second magazine of the first category you advertised in is successful, you
can then assume that the entire category of magazines will be successful
for that ad and for that product. You should then advertise in as many of

the magazines in that first category as possible, considering your budget. Now look at the second category. Was it successful? If so, repeat that ad and run it in a second magazine in that category, and meanwhile expand into a third category with one advertisement. Once you really have a winner, you can roll out and begin to take some increased risks. But the important principle here is to walk before you run. Do not assume that because a magazine in one category is successful, all magazines in that category will be successful until you have tested at least two of them.

SHOULD YOU USE AN ADVERTISING AGENCY?

Many beginners feel that they must have an advertising agency to be successful; others feel equally strongly that they should never use an agency. Either approach may be correct, depending on the situation. It is very difficult to get an advertising agency to work with you at the beginning because they usually work on commission. If you are doing a very small amount of advertising, and this is usually true of the beginner, the agency can't make enough money from you to make a business relationship worthwhile. On the other hand, if you do not use an advertising agency, you will have to do much of the legwork yourself, including finding and engaging the necessary freelance copywriters and creative people. One major advantage of using an agency is that you can get professional and expert help all at one stop. If you decide to use an agency, you can contact one through your Yellow Pages. But be absolutely certain that they have mail order experience, and do not be bashful about asking for samples from mail order experience they have had. Ask for some client references in the mail order field, then contact them to find out their experiences with this particular agency. Many agencies like to think that they have had mail order experience, although, in fact, they've really been concerned mainly with non-direct response ads. You will find a list of advertising agencies that deal primarily in mail order or direct mail in Appendix D of this book.

I believe that if you can do without an advertising agency at the beginning, it's a good way to learn a lot of the things that you should know when dealing with them. Once you have started to make big money, it makes more sense economically to contact an advertising agency to perform as many professional services as you would like. And as you have done a lot of work yourself previously, you can approach their recommendations on a much more professional basis.

From Ron Ball, manager of marketing services for Pentel of America, Ltd., and reader of the first edition of *Building a Mail Order Business,* comes the following story, which illustrates well how to put it all together to develop a successful space advertising campaign.

How to Take a Product That Won't Fly and Make It Soar like an Eagle

In May of 1981, Pentel, manufacturers and marketeers of some of the most innovative writing instruments in the world, proudly introduced its unique, laser cut, Ceramicron pen to the marketplace. It never took off the ground.

Why? Several reasons. First, Pentel relies heavily on the wholesale trade to move products to the retail level. This means the product benefits have to be communicated to the Pentel sales force, to the wholesale buyer, to the wholesaler sales rep, to the retail buyer, retail sales clerk, and finally the consumer. Too many variables to effectively communicate what the product is and does.

Second, the marketing department felt this was a specialized pen for people who need very fine writing. It's not a general writing instrument. It required a rifle shot instead of a shotgun blast. Third, it was a totally new type of pen, utilizing new technology which had to be communicated.

Enter direct marketing. For the previous two years, I had pushed the idea of direct marketing specific products. Persistence paid off because the Pentel Ceramicron pen was a product Pentel had put a lot of research and development in. The CEO said it had to move.

So I went to work and quickly put together a direct marketing subsidiary called Omnex to test the idea. Pentel wanted to market the pen through a company with a different name because they were concerned they'd get complaints from wholesalers and retailers about selling directly to consumers. The results later proved the ads we ran did the reverse—they created greater product awareness and increased the wholesaler and retail business. People who buy by mail order purchased their pen through Omnex. Customers who buy retail walked into stores with the ad in their hand.

I had been studying direct marketing for five years and felt confident I had the variety of skills necessary to make the program work.

As I mentioned to you when we met, Dr. Cohen, your book, "Building a Mail Order Business," has been an important educational tool for me. I've got about 15 good books at home on mail order and direct marketing. Your book is the best and the first book I'd recommend anyone to buy.

Even though I have never written a direct marketing space ad before in my life, I literally put together everything from A to Z concerning concept, copy, and management. Within five weeks we went from nothing to a company with an ad in the *Wall Street Journal.*

Don Malucky, our art director, was my partner in preparing the visual elements of the ad, literature, and packaging. [The actual ad is shown in Figure 10.10.]

I came up with the name Omnex because I wanted a short, easy-to-remember, high-tech-sounding name. And, it took me about a week to come up with a name no other company was using.

I set up the banking and credit cards. We use the National Communications Center in Shingle Springs, California for our toll-free service and Motivational Packaging and Fulfillment in Commerce, California for our cashiering and fulfillment. [The results were as shown in Figures 10.11, 10.12, and 10.13.]

Figure 10.10 Omnex ad in the *Wall Street Journal*.

Publication	Type	Date	Orders Pulled	Ranking
Wall Street Journal Eastern Edition	daily	2/2/83	378	4
Wall Street Journal Midwest Edition	daily	2/2/83	418	5
Wall Street Journal Western Edition	daily	2/2/83	268	6
Wall Street Journal Southwest Edition	daily	2/2/83	136	8
American Medical News	weekly	2/4/83	557	1
Journal of Accountancy	monthly	2/83	378	3
Wall Street Journal Midwest Edition	daily	5/6/83	385	7
American Medical News	weekly	5/6/83	317	2

Figure 10.11   Omnex media testing.

Offer	Ceramicron Pen Offer	Bounce-Back	Total
Sales revenues (As of January 31, 1983)	$72,313	$12,691	$85,004
Unit sales	4837 ea.	1414 ea.	6255 ea.
New profit	$ 9,987	$ 5,885	$15,872
Total investment	—	—	$29,192
Return on investment (ROI)	34%	20%	54%

Figure 10.12   Omnex sales results.

	Number of Orders	Percentage
By toll-free number and credit cards	2000	41
By mail and credit card	709	15
By mail and check	2128	44
W Customer who bought pen and bounce-back offer	1418	29
Returns from customers	15	.3

Figure 10.13   How people bought.

What I Think the Omnex Program Proves—

1. A company can take a good product, lagging in sales through regular channels of distribution, and turn it into a sales winner using direct marketing techniques to effectively communicate product benefits.
2. A company can use direct marketing ads to generate a self-perpetuating advertising budget and increase the retail awareness of the product.
3. A person who is a self-starter, persistent, has attention to detail, entrepreneurial skills, and a willingness to study everything he or she can find about direct marketing can build a mail order business.

To me, the most exciting thing about this program was being able to blend all my creative and management skills together and put everything into action in a short period of time and on a tight budget and see it all work. I'm an entrepreneur at heart. And I've always been fortunate enough to work in companies where I have tremendous freedom and total responsibility.

I've done a lot of things in my career. For three years, I produced radio special programs and interviewed over 150 recording artists. Everybody from Paul Anka to Stevie Wonder. I also spent three years at Vivitar Corporation writing everything from ads to booklets on all kinds of photography. At Pentel, I've been able to use all my marketing communication skills. But nothing I've done feels as great as the first order that somebody sent in at Omnex. There is nothing that compares to it. Self-esteem fireworks go off.

SUMMARY

In this chapter, you have learned important facts and techniques for running profitable display ads. In review, keep in mind these important points.

You will use display ads because you can build a bigger volume business in this way, reach more readers less expensively than by other methods such as direct mail, and get many names for the back-end part of your business.

You can create an effective space ad by yourself or through the help of an agency. If you create a display ad on your own, you locate the copywriters and creative people yourself . . . or you write the copy yourself.

You will advertise in those magazines that are better for advertising your particular product or service.

Some months and some seasons are better for advertising than others. The frequency of advertising depends on the product and the success you had with your initial ad.

The appearance of your ad is important. How large the ad is can determine success, as can proper use of color and black and white.

Different responses can be expected depending upon whether your ad appears on the back cover, near editorial matter, away from editorial matter, in the upper part of the magazine, on the outside, and so forth. Usually the key is visibility.

When placing your ad, allow sufficient lead time, as indicated on the rate card.

Twelve different ways were given in which you might greatly reduce the cost of your display advertising from standard rates. These were use of mail order discounts, PI deals, frequency discounts, standby rates, help if necessary, remnant space in regional editions, barter, bulk buyers, seasonal discounts, spread discounts, use of your own in-house advertising agency, and cash discounts.

You can get free promotion in magazines, and this can greatly increase sales of your product.

To know how to expand, you must first know the results you can expect from a display advertisement and how quickly to expect them. Basically, for a monthly magazine, 50 percent of your total returns will arrive after one month. To predict the returns you will get, multiply that number by two.

Finally, we discussed the advertising agency, how to find one, and whether you need one.

Display advertisements can cause your business to skyrocket in profits. Don't neglect them!

11

Making Money with Direct Mail Ads

Direct mail involves sending your sales material directly to your prospective customer, without the preliminary step of gathering names through some type of advertisement, as in the two-step method for classified or display. It is made possible by the rental of lists of names from others or by special mailings to your own house list of customers. For the professional mail order dealer, direct mail is an important and powerful strategy. It has major advantages over other strategies of mail order selling.

THE IMPORTANT ADVANTAGES OF DIRECT MAIL

Direct mail has five important advantages over other mail order processes:

1. Selectivity.
2. Personalized approach.
3. Speed in getting to the market.
4. Concealment of test information.
5. More sales copy possible.

Let's look at each of these in turn. Direct mail means selectivity. It is the rifle approach as compared to the shotgun. With this rifle, you can aim very precisely at your target market through the rental of the name list you use. Are you interested in selling to women executives? List manager Ed Burnett offers breakdowns in the category of women executives by age, income, and job functions; whether divorced, single, widowed, or married; special classifications of women executives such as Catholics, Jews, women's college graduates, executives of major corporations, women golfers and country club members, high school graduates, investors, lawyers, and so on. You do not reach this degree of precise market segmentation accuracy when advertising through classified ads or with display advertisements in magazines or newspapers. Because of this accuracy, many mail order firms do virtually all of their business by direct mail. Paul McDonald, president of Procurement Associates, Inc., which gives seminars around the world, promotes to its potential attendees entirely through direct mail. McDonald has reached more than 20,000 seminar attendees this way, and his business exceeds $2 million a year.

Personalized contact is possible through the use of direct mail. When you deal with direct mail, you are dealing with a one-on-one situation— you are speaking directly to your potential customer. Furthermore, your letter can be personalized through use of the computer in a way that is absolutely impossible for other mail order methods. For example, look at the cover of the catalog in Figure 11.1. Would you believe that every one of the millions of recipients in this catalog received it with his or her own name and address, just as the one shown? This personalization greatly increases your chances of success.

One of the most successful techniques in my book *The Executive's Guide to Finding a Superior Job*, is a direct mail campaign to individuals who may be interested in hiring you, and this letter goes out with the potential employer's name and title on each and every letter. This direct mail strategy yields phenomenal results in getting interviews and job offers. Yet space advertising that promotes an individual seeking a job is usually unsuccessful. It is this personalized feature of direct mail that helps to make it a winner. And it works equally well whether you are selling a product, a service, or yourself.

The lead time with many magazines for placing an advertisement can be six weeks or more; and then after that, you must wait a full year before you receive most of the responses you will ultimately receive. Not so with direct mail. You can mail whenever you are ready. With direct mail, you will receive half your response only one week after the first inquiry! This means you will know at once whether your proposition is profitable or not. If it is, you can expand your promotion immediately with little lead time. Furthermore, you will receive all your responses six months after receiving the first inquiry and you will have 95 percent after only two months. If mail order has the potential of being a fast way to riches, the direct mail method has the potential of being super fast.

Maintaining confidentiality of your operations to the maximum extent possible is very important in mail order because it is easy for potential competitors to see what you are doing. With display advertising or even classified, it's impossible to conceal success. Your success can be spotted easily by your repeated advertising. Direct mail is also open to your competitors

Figure 11.1 Lure of big winnings.

because many names on a list will be individuals who are interested or engaged in mail order operations. However, it is much harder for your competition to track what you are doing as it is unlikely that any one competitor will see more than a small portion of your mailings to different lists. Because you're being able to keep much of your advertising confidential except to the individuals who receive the ads, it is also easier to test various prices with little chance of confusing or irritating your potential customers. Although not a major problem, it is true that if you take a full-page display ad that indicates one price, it is difficult to show the same display ad in another magazine at another price without creating some confusion and question in the minds of your prospective customers. With direct mail, you can test many different prices with a reduced chance that the same potential customer will see many of your different prices being tested.

Advertising in media such as magazines and newspapers allows you to use sales copy from a few words in a classified ad up to many hundreds of words in a full-page display ad. However, this cannot compare at all with direct mail, in which you can tailor the advertising copy to achieve maximum profitability. You are not limited to one full page. In fact, your letter to a customer may be from four to six pages, and letters are usually not the only element of the direct mail package. Consequently, you have a much greater chance of making the sale than if less copy was necessitated by limitations of space and cost in a magazine.

Like any other business or any other method of dealing in direct response, it is *not* a guaranteed success, and in some cases other mail order strategies will be more profitable. Your product may not be suited to a direct mail campaign and your ads may work better with space advertising or classified. Also, direct mail is relatively expensive as far as reaching total numbers of potential customers is concerned. As was pointed out in Chapter 10, costs per potential customer reached by space advertising are a lot less than those required by direct mail if you consider the numbers of readers as representing potential customers. So don't assume that any direct mail campaign will automatically be successful.

WHEN TO USE DIRECT MAIL

You should use direct mail when you have a clearly defined product with a clearly defined market segment to which it appeals. When Ed McLean developed a very successful campaign for selling Mercedes-Benz cars with diesel engines by direct mail, his specialized product was introduced to a clearly defined market segment, consisting of individuals who not only were interested in expensive foreign cars, but who had the income to purchase them. Correct use of direct mail was extremely successful and won for Ed McLean the Golden Mailbox Award of the Direct Marketing Association. AMACOM, a division of the American Management Association, sold more than 20,000 copies of my book *The Executive's Guide to Finding a Superior Job* through direct mail because it was a specialized product offered to a clearly defined market segment of executives who were members of the American Management Association or who had previously bought similar products from this organization. Chase Revel in Los Angeles started a simple eight-page information newsletter on new businesses. He started with direct mail and built it into a multimillion-dollar business including the magazine *Entrepreneur* and two large organizations, the International Entrepreneur's Association and the American Entrepreneur's Association. These organizations did a multimillion-dollar business annually selling booklets, business plans, the magazine *Entrepreneur*, seminars, and other information to individuals interested in small business. This was made possible because Chase Revel sold a clearly defined product to a clearly defined market segment.

Even if you meet the criteria of a clearly defined market segment and a specialized product that appeals to it, you must still test first to see whether your product and offer will work using this strategy. The principle is to test first, and then, if you have a winner, expand with more direct mailings fast. The term used is *roll-out*, and the implication is a much larger mailing mailed as soon as possible. Even such giants as Ben Suarez, author of *Seven Steps to Freedom*, and Joe Sugarman, with his multimillion-dollar electronics business operating mainly through space advertising, at first stumbled with products when using direct mail.

49 WAYS TO USE DIRECT MAIL

Richard S. Hodgson, in his encyclopedic *Direct Mail and Mail Order Handbook* lists 49 different ways to use direct mail. This list was assembled by the Direct Marketing Association when it was still known as the Direct Mail Advertising Association. But don't think that because the list is old the different ways are no longer used. On the contrary, each and every way listed is still bringing in millions of dollars every year.

If you already have a non-mail order business, direct mail can help:

1. Build morale of employees.
2. Secure data from employees.
3. Stimulate salespeople to greater efforts.
4. Pave the way for salespeople.
5. Secure inquiries for salespeople.

6. Teach salespeople how to sell.
7. Sell stockholders and others interested in your company.
8. Keep contact with customers between sales calls.
9. Further sell prospective customers after a demonstration or sales call.
10. Acknowledge orders or payments.
11. Welcome new customers.
12. Collect accounts.

If you want to build new business, direct mail can help:

13. Secure new dealers.
14. Secure direct orders.
15. Build weak territories.
16. Win back inactive customers.
17. Develop sales in areas not covered by salespeople.
18. Develop sales among specified groups.
19. Follow inquiries received from direct or other forms of advertising.
20. Drive home sales arguments.
21. Sell other items in line.
22. Get product prescribed or specified.
23. Sell new type of buyer.

Direct mail can assist present dealers by:

24. Bringing buyer to showroom.
25. Helping present dealers sell more.
26. Merchandising your plans.
27. Educating dealers on superiorities of your product or service.
28. Educating retail clerks in the selling of a product.
29. Securing information from dealers or dealers' clerks.
30. Referring inquiries from consumer advertising to local dealers.

Direct mail can assist in gaining customers by:

31. Creating a need or demand for a product.
32. Increasing consumption of a product among present users.
33. Bringing customers into a story to buy.
34. Opening new charge accounts.
35. Capitalizing on special events.

Some additional uses are:

36. Building good will.
37. Capitalizing on other advertising.
38. As a leader or hook in other forms of advertising.
39. Breaking down resistance to a product or service.
40. Stimulating interest in forthcoming events.
41. Distribution of samples.
42. Announcing a new product, new policy, or new addition.
43. Announcing a new address or change in telephone number.
44. Keeping a concern or product in mind.
45. Research for new ideas and suggestions.
46. Correcting present mailing lists.
47. Securing names for lists.
48. Protecting patents or special processes.
49. Raising funds.

Probably no business in the world can use all 49 ways of using direct mail, but in looking through this list you can see the wide variety of things you can do with it to help you build your business profitably.

THE FIVE SUCCESS STEPS IN DIRECT MAIL

There are five success steps for direct mail. If you follow these five steps, you will build a successful business through the use of this amazing tool:

1. Identify your market.
2. Prepare your package.
3. Pick your list.
4. Test.
5. Roll out if successful.

Let's look at each of these in turn.

Identify Your Market

Identifying your target market means identifying those people who probably have the greatest interest in buying your product or service. You may say that everyone in the United States is a potential candidate to buy the product you are offering. However, in reality, certain people have a much greater potential than others, and it is better to concentrate on that segment. So it is important to stop right here and think who exactly is going to buy what you are offering. Try to picture them in your mind. What are their interests? Where are they located? How much money are they earning? This process is called market segmentation and you can segment a market in a number of different ways by introducing different variables into your thinking and seeing which offers you the best opportunities for selling your product.

The major variables for market segmentation are geographic, demographic, psychographic, and behavioristic. Geographic variables have to do with location. Certain products, for example, can be offered only to those potential customers living in a climate such as Southern California or Florida. On the other hand, if you have a product that has to do with snow removal, this would not be the geographical area that would be interested. Demographics have to do with many factors, including age, sex, family size, family life cycle (that is, young; single; married; married, no children; retired; etc.), income, occupation, education, religion, race, and nationality. All of these demographic factors will affect the purchase of the product or service you are offering. Psychographic factors include breakdown by social class, life style, and personality of potential buyers. Finally, we have behavioristic variables, which include reason for the purchase, whether it is a regular or special occasion, benefit sought, whether the user is a first-time user, a nonuser, or an ex-user of the type of product, the rate of use, whether the potential customers are already informed about the types of product you are selling or are totally unaware that such a type of product exists, sensitivity to price, quality, service, and so forth.

You may think there is an awful lot of time to be spent in identifying the market segment to which you will sell your goods when "almost anyone would be interested." Believe me when I tell you that the time spent in identifying your market will pay dividends later on and will help to make your product successful and profitable, whereas if you jump in and try to sell to everyone, your campaign may well fail.

Prepare Your Package

Having identified the target market you are after, you must prepare your mail package, considering all of the above factors. Typically, a direct mail package will include an outside envelope, sales letter, guarantee, order form, self-addressed and stamped envelope, publisher's letter, and testimonials.

The outside envelope is critical for the direct mail package and you have some major decisions to make here. Unless the recipient opens your direct mail package, he or she will never see the offer that is inside. There are different approaches to this problem. One is to use an envelope with nothing

Figure 11.2 The lure of a great deal.

on it but the customer's address. The theory is that the individual will open it out of curiosity; he or she does not know who is writing and whether it is important. Another solution is to offer a teaser on the outside of the envelope that will encourage your potential customer to open it. Figures 11.2 through 11.10 show different examples of outside envelopes

Figure 11.3 The lure of something free.

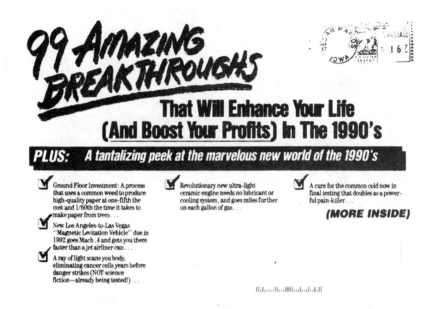

Figure 11.4 The curiosity factor—plus a promise of benefits inside.

used as teasers. Some mail order advertisers try to give their envelopes the appearance of an official letter—from the government or a lawyer or doctor—in hopes that the respondent will be sure to open it, believing it to be of some importance. I do not agree with this tactic at all, although I do believe that it serves its purpose of getting the respondent to open the letter. The problem here is one of credibility. If you take this approach, you

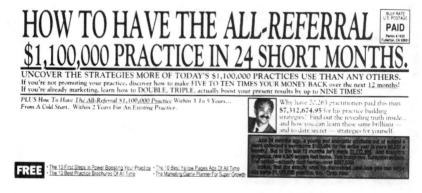

Figure 11.5 This envelope not only offers something free—it is almost a complete advertisement itself.

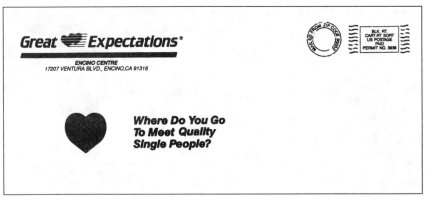

Figure 11.6 An appeal to a specific market segment—in this case singles.

are trying to fool your potential customer, and once he or she realizes that he or she has been fooled, your proposition will be much less credible. Of course, the same is also true with the teaser if it promises something that is not delivered inside. The bottom line is that you lose credibility, which will definitely hurt your response rate. You should also be careful of the use of the words *personal* and *confidential* on envelopes. Many industrial sales letters use them to attempt to circumvent the secretary, who is sometimes instructed to screen out all "unimportant mail." The problem here is that this is so overused that it is a dead giveaway for some sort of sales package. Furthermore, it also affects credibility if, in fact, there is no reason that the contents should be personal or confidential.

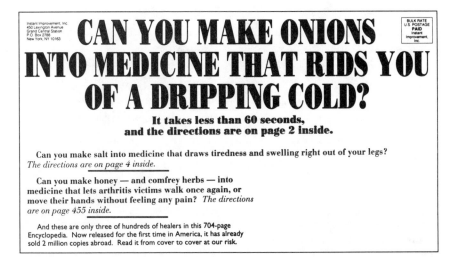

Figure 11.7 Here is a promise for a home remedy 60 second cold cure "inside."

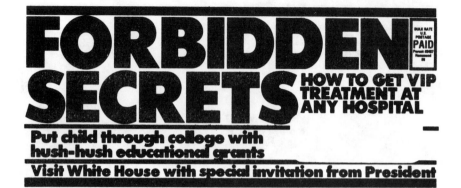

Figure 11.8   Few can resist something forbidden.

The Sales Letter.   The sales letter is an extremely important component of your overall direct mail package. As its name implies, its job is to sell your product or your service. One common myth is that the sales letter should be short. This is not necessarily true. For consumer sales letters, the sales letter should be four pages or more. In some cases, they are from 8 to 10 pages and are extremely successful. Sales letters selling industrial products should be somewhat shorter—one to three pages; but they must still sell and not just be a cover letter. I am going to tell you how to write copy for sales letters in a later chapter. For now, I want you to look at some really outstanding examples of sales letters. Look at the letters in Figures 11.11 and 11.12. Note how they get the reader's interest and attention immediately. Note

```
    H. R. Lynn
    P.O. Box 2299
    Gig Harbor, WA 98335


            Can you too turn back the hands of time??
            THIS STARTLING, AMAZING, YET TRUE STORY WILL HOLD YOU SPELLBOUND:

            The year: 1934.  A retired British Army Colonel is climbing in the remote
            Tibetan Himalayas.  Dusk is approaching.  Suddenly...he sees the ancient
            stone walls of a monastery.  He knocks on the heavy wooden door.  The man
            who answers looks 35, yet he is actually OVER 100 YEARS OLD!  But how...??
                                                               (Cont'd inside)
```

Figure 11.9   A story is started on the outside of this envelope, but finished only inside.

WOULD YOU PAY $100 FOR A NICE 3-BEDROOM HOUSE? DON'T LAUGH. YOU CAN GRAB BARGAINS THIS GREAT IN YOUR LOCAL AREA.

BULK RATE
U.S. POSTAGE
P A I D
PERMIT NO. 749
GLENDALE, CA

ZIP - 4 PRESORT

(Get ready to gasp when you see the super-buys inside!!)

Figure 11.10   This envelope asks a question.

also that both letters use a P.S. Why is that? Did the writer of the letter really forget something after spending so long writing it? Nonsense. The P.S. is always included in a good sales letter because a P.S. is always read. The sales letter is the centerpiece of your direct mail package. One offering, selling a $160,000 product, consisted of a seven-page sales letter and nothing else. It resulted in $600,000 in sales in one mailing. If done correctly, your sales letter can do similar things for you.

The Flier.   The flier is a brochure, separate from the sales letter, that contains additional information and frequently an illustration to capture the reader's attention and convince him or her to buy. The fliers done by large companies are frequently multicolored, printed on very thick paper, and extremely expensive. However, their high cost is justified because they bring in additional sales and help convince the buyer to purchase. An inexpensive flier is shown in Figure 11.13. It is not printed on glossy paper, but it serves the same purpose, and reinforces the sales presentation started by the sales letter.

Sometimes the envelope, sales letter, and brochure are combined into one, with additional components of the mailing packages stapled in. A very successful package of this type was the Harvey Brody direct mail piece, shown in Figure 11.14. It consists of a booklet explaining the program, inside of which was a self-addressed envelope, a letter, questions and answers, a list and description of bonuses, a page of testimonials, and an additional brochure highlighting the main points. The entire package was held together by a single staple.

The Guarantee.   The guarantee is important because it has an impact on your credibility. It must be stated in the strongest possible terms. To emphasize its importance, a separate guarantee is frequently included in direct

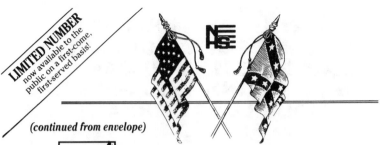

(continued from envelope)

*he enemy, now not 30 yards away. The effect was
surprising; many of the enemy's first line threw down
their arms and surrendered....Holding fast by our right,
and swinging forward our left, we made an extended
"right wheel," before which the enemy's second line broke and fell
back, fighting from tree to tree, many being captured, until we had
swept the valley and cleared the front of nearly our entire brigade."*

THE NATIONAL HISTORICAL SOCIETY

Proudly announces a special reprinting of the
nation's greatest Civil War information source...

THE OFFICIAL RECORDS OF THE CIVIL WAR

Dear Reader,

    The Civil War continues to be an endlessly fascinating and
compelling drama. One deeply embedded in America's conscience.

    As someone who has a serious interest in all aspects of
this epic conflict, you know how thoroughly it has been studied
and analyzed over the years and decades.

    But did you know that <u>our greatest Civil War information</u>
<u>source</u> -- the one most quoted, most sought after, just plain
unequalled in its depth of coverage -- is THE OFFICIAL
RECORDS OF THE CIVIL WAR.

    Why? Because this one-of-a-kind series reveals exactly
what happened and when -- hour-by-hour, day-by-day, battle-by-
battle, on land and on water -- <u>through the words of the</u>
<u>participants</u>.

        <u>Here is the authentic written record</u>
        <u>of The Civil War as it was being waged</u>.

    In one volume after another, on page after thrilling page,
you'll discover:

    THE REPORTS FROM THE BATTLEFIELDS...

"The balance of my force, with the exception of the reserve,
was promptly thrown forward, and drove the enemy foot by foot,
and from tree to tree, back to his encampment..." U.S. Grant,
Brigadier-General to Seth Williams, Assistant Adjutant-
General, Washington D.C.

(over, please)

Figure 11.11   A salesletter for The Official Records of the Civil War.

-2-

TROOP MOVEMENTS AND STRATEGIES...

"...my plan is to throw a considerable body of cavalry on
the railroad between Ironton and Saint Louis, with orders to
break up the road and burn the bridges..." W.J. Hardee,
Brigadier-General, to General Polk, Headquarters, Pocahontas,
July 29, 1861.

CONFIDENTIAL WAR CORRESPONDENCE...

"THE PRESIDENT OF THE UNITED STATES: Will the President read
my urgent dispatch to the Secretary of War?" J.C. Fremont,
Major-General, Commanding.

AFTER BATTLE THOUGHTS AND REFLECTIONS...

"...one of their 24-pounders struck us on the starboard
bulwarks, continuing obliquely through the spar deck, and in
its course taking off the head of one man and injuring two
others..." Commander Henry Walke, U.S. Gunboat Tyler, Mound
City, November 9, 1861.

AND MUCH, MUCH MORE!

No source can match the wealth of coverage
you'll find in THE OFFICIAL RECORDS.

Gathering together and organizing this series was a massive
undertaking. It took 21 years, 23 editors and nearly 3 million
dollars to complete.

All together there are 159 information-packed volumes.

For years it has been the most sought, indeed the most
treasured Civil War resource we have. Yet it has also been
almost impossible to obtain.

Why?

Because only 10,000 sets of THE OFFICIAL RECORDS were
originally printed...and soon after they were gone. Many were
quickly scooped up by government officials, others were grabbed
by fortunate historians. The few that survived would most likely
be found on the rare book market, selling at premium prices.

That's the bad news. Now here's the good news...

The National Historical Society has undertaken the noble
project of reprinting the entire series. All 159 volumes!

Now those with a serious interest in the Civil War can at
last possess the books that document it with unrivaled
authenticity.

But you must act quickly!

A limited number of sets will be printed. They will be sold
on a first-come, first-served basis.

I want you to see the first volume for yourself.
I'll send it to you for a free no-risk examination.

Return the enclosed reservation form today and I'll send you
the first volume to examine FREE for 15 full days. If it doesn't
meet your expectations, simply return it and owe nothing.

Figure 11.11   (Continued)

-3-

But if you do decide to keep it, you'll then have first-reservation privilege for the rest of the series! That means you'll receive future installments at the rate of five volumes per month -- all with the same 15 day free-examination guarantee, and all at the same low price. And you can cancel the series at any time by notifying us.

You will be surprised how low the cost of each volume is. Just $17.95, plus shipping and handling. Let me tell you what you'll be getting for this low price:

* The entire set has been reprinted on superior 45 lb. Glatfelter acid-free paper to ensure years of enjoyment.

* Working with collectors, we obtained the best available original copy of each volume, then applied the most up-to-date technology to enhance readability. The result: clean, dark, even type from cover to cover. In every volume.

* We improved the binding, enclosing each volume in reinforced buckram and impregnating the hard covers with pyroxylin to resist wear and tear.

* We're using special presses to ensure superior printing quality.

Simply put we have spared no expense to insure that these splendid volumes will stand the test of time -- and stand out proudly in your home library.

THE OFFICIAL RECORDS OF THE CIVIL WAR are ready right now...and you can examine your introductory volume risk-free for 15 days. To do so, just complete and return the enclosed postage-paid card.

As I mentioned before, a limited number of copies are available and orders will be filled as we receive them.

Reprinting this series for serious Civil War enthusiasts has been a satisfying -- but massive -- undertaking. For that reason, we cannot guarantee that we will be able to do it again.

Therefore, I encourage you to act promptly to lock in your first-reservation privilege.

Sincerely,

Jim Kushlan
Managing Editor

P.S. As a special "thank you" to series subscribers, we'll send you a great FREE GIFT -- William A. Frassanito's critically acclaimed ANTIETAM: The Photographic Legacy of America's Bloodiest Day. It's yours to keep when you purchase your introductory volume in THE OFFICIAL RECORDS OF THE CIVIL WAR.

Figure 11.11   (Continued)

Please understand this:

Dr. Vogel is not talking about relief or ordinary healing!

He is talking about

OUTRIGHT CURE

by purely natural means!

Here, Dear Friend, is what
92-year-old Dr. H.C.A. Vogel bluntly promises you,

"Has an immediate effect in strengthening weak heart muscles." Page 56.

"For an enlarged prostate, (see page 452) has proved most effective. Experience has shown that this plant remedy causes the enlargement to recede."

"If you take this bath once a week, you will be rid of your aches and pains." Page 10.

"An attack of influenza can be quickly overcome. . . What is more, you will not experience the lingering tiredness and other common after effects of flu." Page 55.

"When you have lost your voice, (see page 3) berries and (see same page) root are two of the best cures available."

"Even when other remedies have proved ineffective, this tincture will actually cause the wound to heal." Page 414.

"Swelling and Bruises – this double action ensures a rapid cure." Page 13.

"A successful remedy for angina pectoris, when heart cramps occur. These cramps are usually accompanied by stabbing pains in the region of the heart resulting in difficult breathing and a weak, irregular pulse. In this case, where immediate relief is necessary, take 5-10 drops every half hour." Page 384.

"With these treatments a bad sore throat can be cured fast." Page 78.

"Even bronchitis may be tackled with (see page 85), as it will help in every case."

"Cases of chronic bronchial catarrh can also be treated successfully with the syrup, even

(over, please)

(continued)

Figure 11.12   A salesletter for a book of natural cures.

if it has not responded to other medicines." Page 462.

"Plants rich in (see page 116) contribute largely to the prevention and cure of arteriosclerosis."

"If you follow this advice and repeat the treatment until the hay fever has completely cleared up, you will gradually get rid of this troublesome allergy and make your life more enjoyable even when the plant world bursts out in blossoms and flowers." Page 79.

Eczema. "Even the most difficult case will yield to this treatment." Page 176.

"Skin eruptions, including psoriasis, are generally curable if the patient perseveres with (see page 180)."

"Men who suddenly find themselves unable to pass water during the night will greatly benefit from (see page 10). This treatment will stimulate the flow of urine, bringing great relief, and the doctor will not have to be called out in the middle of the night to perform a catheterization."

A Fast Cure for Shingles. Page 184.

"This herbal antispasmodic against asthma. Often gives the most amazing positive results without any side effects at all." Page 98.

"In time it is possible to experience normal function of the sex organs." Page 438.

"People who always feel tired and weary are able to get rid of this tiredness by taking a teaspoon in the morning with their breakfast." Page 459.

"If everyone ate (see page 465), no one would suffer from poor digestion."

HOW TO MAKE ONIONS INTO MEDICINE THAT RIDS YOU OF A DRIPPING COLD:

If your eyes and nose are streaming, and your cough driving you crazy, and everything you're taking failing you, do this instead. Cut a half inch slice from an onion you just bought.
Put it in a glass of steaming hot water. Let the water cool. Then sip it throughout the day. The dripping will soon simply dry up.

(Onions are also fabulous as a stimulant for new hair growth. See page 313.)

"Intestinal putrefaction, which manifests itself by offensive smelling stools, can be gradually overcome by eating (see page 543)."

"If you know someone who frequently suffers from heavy nose bleeds, or who is a 'bleeder,' (see page 5) is the only natural remedy to stop it."

Rheumatism Cure. Page 653. "Feeling that the aches and pains are actually beginning to recede is a most welcome relief."

"Most important for arthritis is the juice of a (see page 263). It is not only its alkaline constituents which contribute to curing arthritis but possibly other, as yet unknown factors. Patients should take the juice daily."

"Many women prize (see page 495) juice as an ideal natural remedy that acts from within the body, not only keeping them slim but ensuring a good complexion."

"The curative effect of this syrup is so extraordinary that even doctors who have experimented with it are simply amazed." Page 462.

"Sinus Infections. Chop an (see page 76) finely, place it between two pieces of gauze and bind it on the neck before retiring, leaving it overnight. The two homeopathic remedies,(see same page), will help eliminate the pus and heal the sinuses. This treatment usually makes syringing superfluous."

"A diet consisting of (see page 116) can have almost miraculous results if adhered to consistently. By lowering the blood pressure in a natural way, it becomes unnecessary to take any radical medicines."

"Guarantees restful sleep." Page 653.

Figure 11.12   (Continued)

READ IT AT OUR RISK FOR AS LONG AS YOU WISH.

"There is a way to alleviate the pain and restore to normal any sprains and strained ligaments in the quickest possible time. Beat until stiff the whites of 3-5 eggs. Add. . ." Page 335. "This treatment will relieve the pain after only a short time, perhaps within a few days, and is therefore better than suffering pain and not being able to walk for even two to three months."

"Will cure the most stubborn gastric ulcers." Page 445.

"Hardening of the arteries will not incapacitate you, neither will coronary thrombosis, and you will have no need to fear a sudden end through a heart attack." Page 119.

"Successfully combats whooping cough and asthma." Page 457.

"In this way, even where heredity plays a part, varicose veins can be made to recede and can sometimes be completely removed, or at least regenerated to such an extent that they will not give you any further trouble." Page 135.

"Correct breathing, with (see page 152), can often stop a heart attack in its early stages, especially when the blood is then drawn away from the heart by bathing the arms as shown."

"You will notice that your bowels begin to function better. Regular movement will not fail to come." Page 581.

"This is a simple method of treatment of kidney stones, and will avert a ureter block-age with its serious consequences or even the need for an operation. The patient will re-cover astonishingly fast after the cure, whereas an operation can often have compli-cations, requiring a great deal of after-care." Page 168.

"When urination has become easy again, do not take it for granted that you are now rid of your problem." Page 174.

> **"All the following medicinal plants are easily collected free."**
> **Page 468.**
>
> "Found growing wild." Page 468.
>
> "Is sometimes found so plentifully along the sides of streams and brooks that it could actually be cut with a scythe." Page 349.
>
> "Since this has a medicinal effect, it should be grown in your garden, if you have one. It will then always be available." Page 414.
>
> "How many children might have had their waxen looks changed and their red cheeks restored, if only their parents had realized what wonderful medicinal value this despised plant has to offer! Much hard-earned money would not clink unnecessarily into the pharmacist's till." Page 368.
>
> "This simple weed can be found in the fields almost the whole year round. An infusion of it has to be taken only a few times, and the unpleasant symptoms will disappear, often never to return. At the same time, it strengthens the heart." Page 16.

"Even depression can be overcome by taking a (see page 584) for as little as an hour."

"It causes a flood of bile which carries the small and medium-sized stones with it. You should not be surprised if all the stones are eliminated from the gallbladder." Page 251.

"This simple treatment makes hoarseness disappear in no time at all." Page 3.

"Patients with rheumatoid arthritis who could hardly move around anymore became capable of taking up their normal work again. You will not only make possible a cure of the disease, but will also ensure that it is permanent." Page 271.

"For very stubborn cases of diarrhea, there is a simple plant that helps almost without exception." Page 7.

"It can considerably lengthen the lives of older people. It can help prevent a stroke, and if a person has already suffered a stroke, this simple plant can restore him to health better than some of the most expensive proprietary medicines." Page 349.

(over, please)

Figure 11.12   (Continued)

"Nasal polyps may restrict the proper intake of air through the nose. The only effective cure for them is (see page 72)."

"Has a wide range of applications as a pain-relieving drug. Excellent results have been reported in connection with its use for headaches, migraines, menstrual cramps, toothache, painful wounds and many other aches and pains." Page 352.

"One of the best medicines for pharyngitis. Five drops on a little sugar, taken every one or two hours, will almost certainly stop the symptoms in a short time." Page 394.

"Chronic skin eruptions that itch and burn, little blisters around the joints, the desire to sleep during the daytime and insomnia during the night can all be alleviated and cured." Page 396.

"Simply digests the parasites made of protein. It destroys them in a simple and harmless way. Even amoebas are destroyed." Page 446.

"With this diet it is possible to cure a stomach ulcer within a month. Gout will improve within two or three months and then slowly disappear. If you follow it consistently, you will find that even the most stubborn case of gout will eventually disappear." Page 498.

"Anyone suffering from impotence should not give up hope, but take (see page 522), which will certainly help, if not cure the problem completely."

"Once you establish the habit of breathing with (see page 580), you will no longer catch cold even in an unheated bedroom and will wake up refreshed for the day ahead. Also, if you snore, you will soon overcome this tendency."

"If the bronchial tubes have not degenerated beyond repair, it can sometimes even cure asthma." Page 581.

"A slim figure can be obtained. A 'spare tire' will disappear." Page 581.

READ IT AT OUR RISK FOR AS LONG AS YOU WISH.

Here's all you do —

Send in the no-risk, postage-paid order card today. Try this revolutionary new book for as long as you wish, at our risk. If you are not delighted beyond belief, simply return the book at any time and every cent of your purchase price will be refunded immediately, without question or quibble.

P.S. Even more home cures that you can use *right now*, on pages 6 and 12 of the flyers.

Sincerely,

Barbara and Eugene Schwartz
Instant Improvement, Inc.

Figure 11.12   (Continued)

MORE INSIGHTS. MORE ANALYSIS. MORE SOFTWARE. MORE PC EXCITEMENT.

Discover COMPUTE!'s PC magazine and disk by accepting our FREE software and magazine offer today!

SAMPLE COMPUTE!'s PC MAGAZINE AND DISK AT OUR EXPENSE, OUR RISK. If you currently use an IBM PC, Tandy or compatible at home, school or office, it's time you discovered the fabulous new programs and insightful editorials that appear in each issue of COMPUTE!'s PC magazine.

Simply detach the 5 FREE PROGRAMS stamp that appears on the addressing envelope. Affix it where indicated on the reply card and mail before the deadline date on the card.

We'll rush you 5 free programs on disk and a free copy of COMPUTE!'s PC for you to preview and enjoy. There is absolutely no cost, no obligation on your part. We're so certain that once you sample our fabulous magazine and programs — you'll want to become a subscriber and join the tens of thousands of other PC users who already receive COMPUTE!'s PC magazine with disk regularly. Remember, there are no "catches"...no gimmicks...no fine print. This is one "free offer" that *REALLY IS FREE!*

NEW INSIGHTS, NEW PROGRAMS AND A NEW DISK IN EVERY COMPUTE!'s PC ISSUE. You'll look forward to receiving future issues of COMPUTE!'s PC magazine. That's because each exciting new issue delivers page after page of informative features, reviews and columns, plus an all-new, program-packed disk — loaded with at least 5 never before published programs. Each new disk offers you valuable applications programs, educational programs, utilities, games and more.

EXTRA BONUS: THE BEST OF AMERICA'S BULLETIN BOARD PROGRAMS. Every COMPUTE!'s PC disk gives you *not only* original, new programs, but an extra bulletin board bonus as well. We review thousands of bulletin board files all across the nation to present you with the "best of the boards"— our choice of the country's outstanding bulletin board programs. *This alone* is worth much more than the modest subscription price.

SOURCE CODES MAKE PROGRAMMING A SNAP. If you're a programmer — or would like to be one — you'll appreciate the source code for selected programs included on every disk. You can examine valuable routines in a variety of languages, and even *customize our programs for your own use!*

REGULAR COLUMNS, REVIEWS AND NEW PRODUCT UPDATES, ALL TO HELP YOU GET THE MOST FROM YOUR PC. Our "PC News & Notes" section keeps you up-to-date with major events in the PC community..."The Ear" lets you in on the inside gossip and rumors... "Getting Down To Business" gives you tips for maximum PC efficiency..."Reviews" delivers honest, hard-hitting evaluation and insights on the most interesting hardware and software, new product releases, peripherals, expansion boards and more.

You'll learn how to add a 3.5" disk drive...how to organize your hard disk...how to build a PC clone...and more. Each important issue of COMPUTE!'s PC comes complete with a valuable Buyer's Guide...and a special column to help you get the most out of DOS. If it affects your PC, you'll hear about it in the pages of COMPUTE!'s PC.

START GETTING THE ABSOLUTE MOST FROM YOUR PC — WITH 5 FREE PROGRAMS AND A FREE ISSUE OF COMPUTE!'s PC. Prove to yourself that COMPUTE!'s PC will help you understand and enjoy your PC more than ever before by accepting a free copy and disk now. There's no hidden cost or obligation. But you must beat the deadline date that's printed on the reply card.

Take a moment now to detach the 5 FREE PROGRAMS stamp from the envelope, affix where indicated on the reply coupon and mail before the deadline date. That's all there is to it.

We'll rush you your free disk and magazine for you to preview. If you like what you see, subscribe — and receive 5 more issues of COMPUTE!'s PC (6 big issues and disks in all) — for a modest $39.95. You'll save $37.75 off the cover price — and guarantee that you don't miss a single issue or new program.

However, if you're not satisfied after previewing your free disk and magazine, simply write "cancel" across the invoice, keep the magazine and disk with our compliments and owe us nothing. You cannot lose. So be sure to beat the deadline date for your 5 free programs and free issue of COMPUTE!'s PC. Act immediately.

RETURN REPLY FORM BEFORE DEADLINE DATE

Figure 11.13   Another excellent flier.

Figure 11.14   Outside of Harvey Brody booklet and direct mail package.

Figure 11.15   Example of a money back guarantee.

mail packages. This guarantee, printed on a special paper, separated from the rest of the package, is frequently embossed with fancy artwork and contains big headlines that proclaim the guarantee is "ironclad." The potential customer cannot possibly miss it. It reinforces the idea that the potential buyer risks nothing by ordering by mail, and that whatever is purchased may be returned for a full refund. The guarantee helps to sell the item being sold. Figures 11.15, 11.16, and 11.17 show examples of the direct mail guarantee.

The Order Form.   You always want to make it as easy as possible for your potential customer to purchase from you, so an order form is frequently used. It serves several purposes:

1.   As with every other element of the direct mail package, it is a sales device and frequently restates the proposition in favorable terms so that it again reinforces the purchase idea in the customer.

Figure 11.16   Another guarantee. Buyer is encouraged to postdate check.

ONE-YEAR, FULL REFUND GUARANTEE

Our goal for the seminar is to *exceed* your expectations — and we believe we will. That's why we can offer the best guarantee in the industry.

Attend the seminar. If you don't think it's everything we promised, we'll send you a full refund. Just tell the registrar before you leave the seminar, or write us. Take up to one full year to decide (that way you can get all the information from the seminar and see if it works for you).

Won't people take unfair advantage of this guarantee? Some may, but the risk is all ours, not yours (which we think is a good way to treat our customers). We hope this revolutionary guarantee will convince you that we are worthy of your trust.

Figure 11.17 Career track guarantees the seminars it promotes through direct mail for a year.

2. It makes it easier for your customer to order because he or she does not have to write a separate letter to you.

3. It ensures that the customer does not forget to include his or her name and address, something that happens more frequently than you might think.

Many guarantees are combined with an order form as in Figure 11.18.

If you are selling on a time payment plan, the order form can also be constructed so it is, in effect, a contract for time payments. The most successful example I have seen of this is Mellinger's "inspection request" in Figure 11.19. It has been used for many years. What a beautiful way to

Figure 11.18 A guarantee and order form combined.

Inspection Request

ONLY $9 BRINGS YOU 20-SECTION PLAN, SUPPLEMENT, AND 11-PIECE VISUALIZER KIT

OR

SAVE $50.⁰⁰ BY PAYING CASH PRICE TO RECEIVE ALL MEMBERSHIP BENEFITS IMMEDIATELY.

Your money back if not satisfied.

POSITIVE MONEY-BACK Agreement

Order your Mellinger World Trade/Mail Order Plan with the understanding that you can examine it in your home for 7 days after it has been delivered. If within that time you decide for some reason—any reason—that you do not wish to keep The Plan, simply mail it back to us by insured parcel post and we will refund your inspection deposit in full.

THE MELLINGER CO.

SEE OTHER SIDE FOR PARTIAL LIST OF WHAT YOU RECEIVE.

Both payment plan and cash plan are covered by Positive Money-Back Agreement. You may examine The Plan for 7 days in your own home. If you keep The Plan after 7 days you agree to pay The Mellinger Co. 10 monthly payments of $26.60 each. **Amounts stated in U.S. dollars.**

Important for your records. The eleven digit number, above your name on the white label is your account number.   Enter it here _____

-------- TEAR OFF HERE AND KEEP OUR MONEY-BACK CERTIFICATE --------

THE MELLINGER CO.
6100 Variel Ave.
Woodland Hills, CA 91367-3779 U.S.A.

I want to examine the Mellinger World Trade/Mail Order Plan consisting of 20 Sections, the Supplement, and 11-piece Visualizer Kit. Ship to me by prepaid, insured parcel post with the understanding that I may mail it back by insured parcel post within 7 days after I receive it for a full refund of my inspection deposit if I am not satisfied.

BE SURE TO RETURN ENTIRE FORM BELOW THIS LINE

Please correct any address error above. Don't mark top number.

It is agreed that I am to have consultation service for one year. When paid in full, I am to receive my three-year International Traders Membership, FREE Sample Imports, 6 Trade Agreements, Drop Ship Directory, *Trade Opportunities* magazine for 3 years (published bi-monthly) packed with product information together with bulletins on Mail Order methods, and sample portfolio of business forms. I will follow The Plan carefully and restrict use of materials to myself. If I keep The Plan longer than seven days, I will pay as I have checked below.

☐ **PLAN NO. 1** – I enclose a $9. inspection deposit (add $6. for shipping, handling & insurance). If I keep The Plan, I will make 10 monthly payments of $26.60 each. CA residents will have 7 ¼% sales tax added to each monthly payment. L.A. county residents will have 8 ¼% added to each payment.

☐ **PLAN NO. 2** – I enclose $225. cash price inspection deposit (add $6. for shipping, handling & insurance). (I save $50.00.) CA residents add 7 ¼% sales tax. L.A. county residents add 8 ¼%. **Amounts stated in U.S. dollars.**

☐ **FREE BONUS BOOK** – I am ordering within 14 days! Send me the *How to Run Mail Order Advertising* book absolutely FREE…a $20. value.

On Plan No. 2 only, use your VISA, MasterCard, Discover Card, or American Express Card if you prefer. *(See back of this form.)*   VISA MasterCard DISCOVER

Send money order, cashier's check, or charge card authorization. Register currency. If under 18 have guarantor sign name, relationship, and address on margin. This Agreement is deemed to be entered into and performed in Woodland Hills, California. Accounts overdue 30 days subject to 1½% monthly service charge on overdue amount. If no PLAN NO. box is checked above, amount of remittance will indicate PLAN NO. desired.

Both plans are covered by Positive Money-Back Agreement.

Phone – Home: _____

Bus: _____

Check one: ☐ Mr. ☐ Mrs. ☐ Miss ☐ Ms.   (Please print in ink)

NAME IN FULL _____AGE_____

ADDRESS _____

CITY _____ STATE_____ ZIP _____

SIGNATURE_____ SIGN HERE

On both Plans be sure to add $6. for shipping, handling, and insurance so as not to delay shipping.

B.L. Mellinger III President/CEO   We'll show you how to make big money. — B.L. Mellinger III, President/CEO

Figure 11.19 The Mellinger Company's "Inspection Request," an effective order form.

ease the psychological trauma of having to obligate yourself for time payment for a high-cost item.

Self-Addressed Envelope.   Going back to the basic principle of making it as easy as possible for your prospective customer to order, a self-addressed envelope should always be included so that all that the prospective customer has to do is insert the order blank, enclose a check, put a stamp on it, seal it, and send it. One decision you have to make is whether to stamp this envelope or not. If you decide to have the envelope postage paid, you do not use regular postage stamps, as those who do not order will not use the envelope and that would waste your money. Instead, what you do is get a permit from the post office that gives you permission to have your printer print an envelope such as the one shown in Figure 11.20. Your printer knows how to do this for you—all he or she needs is the city and your permit number. The advantage of using an envelope like this is that, while you pay a premium for each envelope you receive, you pay none for envelopes that you send out that are not used. There is a disadvantage here that you should think about. In dealing in mail order you will run into a lot of nice people as customers. You will also run into some real nuts. Joe Karbo once received one of his self-addressed, stamped envelopes back with a sheet of lead inside. That lead cost Joe a couple of dollars in postage. I have received all sorts of strange things in stamped envelopes— from sheets of blank paper I had to pay for to things such as a sheet sent by a clearly unbalanced person who had written, over and over again in very tiny letters on both sides of the paper, in response to my sales package for the *Writer's Guide to Publication and Profit:* "I want to write for profit. I want to write for profit." You must pay the postmaster the required postage for whatever comes back with your name on it. Using a

Figure 11.20   A self-addressed, stamped envelope.

postage paid envelope will definitely increase your response. You must compute whether you are still profitable in paying not only for the legitimate responses, but also for those that come back with nothing inside, a blank sheet of paper, lead, or whatever.

Publisher's Letter. The publisher's letter is a more recent innovation. Its use began within the last 20 years and it has proved to be a very good idea indeed. The publisher's letter says something on the outside like, "Do not read this unless you intend not to order" (see Figure 11.21). When you open the letter, it used to start with a sentence that read something like, "Frankly, I'm puzzled." Current letters have a bit more variety as in Figure 11.22. The writer of the letter states that he or she doesn't understand why you would hesitate to order as this is such an unusually good offer. The letter then goes on to restate the offer. The publisher's letter is, of course, an additional expense to you. But, in many cases, it has proved to be worth its weight in gold: It brings in many more returns than a direct mail package without the publisher's letter.

Testimonials. As in a display advertisement, testimonials can be crucial in helping you to make sales because they affect the credibility of what you say. It's one thing for you to boost your own product in your sales letter, your flier, and on your order blank or guarantee. It's quite another thing when some previous buyer says something nice about your product or service. What the buyer says is much more believable than what you say. If you give the full name and address or the full name and at least the city

Please...
**READ THIS
IF YOU'VE DECIDED NOT
TO PARTICIPATE IN
THIS PRIVATE OFFER.**

Figure 11.21   Publisher's letter (outside).

Let Me Explain.

If you've decided to pass on this private offer, there are two reasons why perhaps you should reconsider:

First: The typefaces in the FontBank collection are premium quality, from the best designers in the business. They are guaranteed compatible with all your software, and install in just seconds. You get brilliant output quality at any size. The result is better looking documents.

Second: During this private offer, you can own the entire FontBank collection – 250 faces – for just $49.95! And for good measure, I'll include a copy of BorderBank – over 100 ready-to-use borders – FREE!

All in all, you've been selected to participate in quite an offer, wouldn't you say? A copy of each product is reserved in your name, just call us to claim yours.

C'mon, call us.

Why wouldn't you want to take advantage of such an outstanding type value?

Sincerely,

Carl Fiorentino

Carl Fiorentino
President, TigerDirect

Figure 11.22 Publisher's letter (inside).

and state, along with what is said about your product or service, this is the most credible form of testimonial. But to do so you must have the explicit permission, *in writing*, of the individual who has written to you with the testimonial. You cannot publish the testimonial simply because you received a letter congratulating you on your product. A considerable step down is merely a set of initials along with the city and state. Here, again, these must be real compliments for your product or service. The only difference is that if you use initials instead of the name, you need not have permission to publish and use the remarks. The problem is that initials just aren't as credible as real names. One way around this, used by Ben Suarez and mentioned in his book, *Seven Steps to Freedom*, is to use real testimonials but fictitious names. His argument is that he is obeying both the spirit and the letter of the law, even though the names used are made up. If you decide to go this route, you should definitely check with a lawyer before doing so. Remember the rules we discussed in the chapter on legal and illegal aspects of mail order. It is important that you obey them so as not to run afoul of the FTC.

Because testimonials are very useful for your mail order promotions, I am going to tell you here and now how to acquire them so that you may use them not only in your direct mail packages, but also in your advertising. First, you should understand that even if you have a great product, only a relatively few testimonials come without asking for them. Further, even those that do come unsolicited may not come as soon as you might wish. Therefore, it is far wiser to begin planning ahead to get testimonials before you advertise your product.

One good way of getting testimonials for a new product is to send samples to your present customer list along with a letter asking them to describe their impressions of the product and what good they have received from using it. Your cover letter should include a friendly note stating that you are sending this product to a select list of your own customers so that you may discover what their opinion of it is and that you are eager to hear from them. After your questions, always have a sentence that allows your customer to check "yes" or "no" as to whether you may use his or her statement as a part of your advertising campaign. And, of course, have your potential customer sign the response. Even though it may be expensive for you to get testimonials in this fashion, they will more than pay for your expense once you begin using them in your advertising.

Another way of getting testimonials is to include a product evaluation sheet in every unit you send out. It should also include a little note to the effect that you want to know what your customers think of your product and that you would like to use their information for improving it, as well as advertising it. Again, be certain to insert a sentence that indicates whether your customer will allow you to use his or her name. Usually I send a little gift to all those who respond. Figure 11.23 shows a product evaluation sheet you can use.

There are other sales devices you may consider putting inside your direct mail package, but the ones I have described are the major components and the ones that you should think about using first. Every component of the direct mail package costs money. If this component brings in enough additional sales, the component is worth adding. If a component does not bring in additional profits that more than make up for the cost, you should drop it after testing.

Pick Your List

To pick your list, it is again hard to compete with Standard Rate and Data Service. SRDS publishes a special two-volume *Direct Mail List Rates and Data,* consumer lists, and business lists. The editorial objective

---

TO OUR CUSTOMER...

We really appreciate your order. We would also like to know what you think about our product. Maybe it's perfect the way it is. Maybe some features should be kept the same, but others should be changed. In any case, we would like to know.

1. Overall I think this product is:
    a. excellent   b. good   c. fair   d. poor   e. very poor

2. The things I like best about the product are:

3. Features I think should be changed are:

4. Other comments I would like to make are:

Other potential buyers of our products would like to know what you think. May we quote you in our future advertising?
     a. yes   b. no

Signature _____   Date _____

Figure 11.23   An evaluation sheet for obtaining product testimonials.

of *Direct Mail List Rates and Data* is to compile, organize, classify, and arrange in sequential order all known available opportunities for using the mail for advertising. Because the listing is free, *Direct Mail List Rates and Data* probably contains most lists you may wish to use. Further, if you can't find the exact list you are seeking, SRDS will help you locate it. However, you should know that a subscription to *Direct Mail List Rates and Data* is not cheap. If you are interested, write Standard Rate and Data Service, Inc., 5201 Old Orchard Road, Skokie, Illinois 60077. We will be talking more on how to use *Direct Mail List Rates and Data* in the next chapter.

You can also get your lists through list brokers, list managers, and list compilers. List brokers, as you might have guessed from the name, put the user of a list and a seller of a list together. Actually, the term *seller* is inaccurate as rarely do you "purchase" a list, but rather rent it for one-time use.

A list manager is usually someone with a computer who is managing someone else's list. List managers may also act as list brokers, but they differ from list brokers in that they usually have exclusive authority to manage a specific list for rental purposes.

Finally, we have a list compiler, who actually compiles lists of various types. The compiled list is usually a demographic list or a list of people who have some factor in common. A compiler might compile a list of engineers by buying the membership list for various engineering organizations. Or a list compiler could compile a list of seminar attendees.

Bob Stone says that no one succeeds in direct marketing without working with competent list brokers and compilers . . . and we add list managers.

If you can go to SRDS yourself to pick lists, why do you, as a list renter and mail order dealer, need a list broker, manager, or compiler? The reason is for the expert consulting that you receive. At no extra charge whatsoever, these individuals will act as your own personal list consultants and advise you in your mailing, and in which lists to use. This costs you nothing because they get their money from the individual who owns the list. Their fees are typically 20 percent of the price of the rental fee. But you cannot save this money by dealing directly with the list owner. The price will be the same. The owner will simply pocket the 20 percent. If you are successful, you will reorder lists from the individual broker, compiler, or manager you have dealt with. Therefore, this individual wants you to be successful and will do everything to make it so.

You will find a list of brokers, managers, and compilers in Appendix E to this book. Most of them publish a directory or a list of their offerings in the form of a catalog. A page from the Ed Burnett Consultants, Inc., catalog is shown in Figure 11.24.

Testing Your List

I am going to tell you exactly how to test a list later in the book. But, for now, you should know that after picking your list, you want to test a certain percentage of the names on it. There are many rules for this. Basically, you need to obtain enough responses to have statistic validity, which lowers the risk of your investment—you don't invest big unless your test is successful. In practical terms, this usually means testing 10 percent of the list.

Because you will probably be testing more than one list simultaneously, just as we keyed our advertisements for space or classified ads, we must also key or code our advertisements when using direct mail. Because you may be testing other things, your code may have to be more extensive than the simple two-figure code we developed for advertising in magazines or newspapers. You can develop a code with the help of computers that will take care of all the variables in direct mail. For example, you may design a five-digit code as follows: The first digit would be whatever list you are using; the second would be the date of the mailing; the third, the year; the fourth, the particular package you used; and the fifth, the particular offer. Once you have established your code, it is essential that you ensure that

S.I.C. Selection 2361-2761ʙ

SIC CODE		NATIONAL QUANTITY
2361	Dress & Blouses - Children's	410
2363	Coat & Suit Mfrs.	120
2369	Outerwear Mfrs. - Children's, Nec	450
2371	Fur Goods Mfrs.	180
2381	Gloves - Dress & Work	170
2384	Robe & Dressing Gown Mfrs.	170
2385	Waterproof Garments	170
2386	Leather & Wool - Lined Cloth	150
2387	Belt Mfrs. - Apparel	300
2389	Apparel & Accessories, N.E.C.	470
2391	Curtain & Drapery Mfrs.	1,000
2392	Housefurnishings Mfrs., N.E.C.	1,180
2392A	Furniture Pads (Manufacturers)	90
2393	Bag Mfrs. - Textile	630
2394	Canvas & Related Products	3,170
2394A	Dock Covers	220
2394B	Sail Makers	300
2395	Pleating & Stitching	1,180
2395A	Needlework Mfg	180
2395B	Quilting Mfg.	590
2396	Trimming - Autos & Apparel	500
2397	Schiffli Machine Embroidery	140
FABRICATED TEXTILES		**7,000**
2399	Fabricated Textiles, N.E.C.	6,250
2399A	Sewing Contractors	2,710
2399B	Automobile Seatcovers	340
2399C	Emblems (Wholesale & Manuf)	940
2399D	Parachutes	90
2399E	Dusters & Dusting Cloths	60
2399F	Pennants (Wholesale & Manuf)	280
LUMBER		**45,110**
2411	Logging Camps & Contractors	5,250
2421	Saw & Planing Mills - General	5,820
2421A	Sawdust & Shavings	350
2421B	Lumber Mill Representatives	60
2426	Flooring - Hardwood Dimension	990
2429	Sawmills - Specialized, N.E.C.	210
2431	Millwork Plants	10,970
2434	Custom Cabinet Makers	19,330
2435	Veneer & Plywood - Hardwood	450
2436	Veneer & Plywood - Softwood	310
2439	Structural Wood, N.E.C.	790
2441	Box Mfrs. - Nailed Wood & Shook	1,120
2448	Wood Pallet & Skid Mfrs.	1,380
2449	Wood Containers, N.E.C.	350
2451	Mobile Home Mfrs.	860
2452	Wood Buildings - Prefabricated	700
2491	Wood Preserving Plants	710
2492	Particleboard Plants	90
2499	Wood Products Mfrs., N.E.C.	4,410
2499A	Wood Turning	360
2499B	Cork & Cork Products	150
2499C	Gavels (Wholesale & Manuf)	60
2499D	Mulches	380
2499F	Shoring	150
FURNITURE		**14,110**
2511	Furniture, Household - Wood	2,680
2512	Furniture, Household - Upholstered	1,430
2514	Furniture, Household - Metal	460
2515	Mattress & Bedspring Mfrs.	990
2517	Radio & Tv Cabinets - Wood	90
2519	Furniture, Household, N.E.C.	360
2521	Furniture, Office - Wood	650

SIC CODE		NATIONAL QUANTITY
2522	Furniture, Office - Metal	440
2531	Furniture, Public Buildings	840
2541	Partitions & Fixtures - Wood	1,550
2542	Partitions & Fixtures - Metal	860
2591	Blinds & Shades Mfrs.	740
2591A	Porch Shades	60
2599	Furniture & Fixtures, N.E.C.	7,110
PAPER		**16,420**
2611	Pulp Mills	230
2621	Paper Mills, Exc. Building Paper	1,700
2621A	Paper Mills - N.E.C.	260
2631	Paperboard Mills	340
2641	Paper Coating & Glazing Mfrs.	3,010
2642	Envelope Mfrs.	1,240
2643	Bag Mfrs., Exc. Textile Bags	2,340
2643A	Bags-Plastic	1,300
2645	Paper - Die-Cut & Board	590
2646	Pulp Goods - Pressed & Molded	750
2647	Paper Products - Sanitary	210
2648	Stationery Products Mfrs.	270
2649	Paper Products - Converted, N.E.C.	1,950
2649A	Tags (Wholesale & Manufactur)	580
2651	Boxes - Folding Paperboard	1,720
2652	Boxes - Set-Up Paperboard	330
2653	Boxes - Corrugated	4,450
2654	Food Containers - Sanitary	190
2655	Fiber Cans, Drums, Tubes, Etc.	390
2661	Paper Mills - Paper & Board	280
PRINTING & PUBLISHING		**117,060**
2711	Newspaper Publishing & Printing	18,010
2721	Periodical Publishing & Printing	7,900
2731	Books - Publishing & Printing	5,520
2732	Book Printers, Exc. Sic 2731	400
2741	Publishing Activities - Misc.	9,080
2741A	Maps (Printers)	1,170
2741B	Music Publishers	820
2741C	Post Cards	310
2741D	Posters (Printers)	1,490
2741E	Publishers Directory & Guide	1,370
2741F	Shoppers News	370
2741G	Art Publishers	80
2741H	Publishers Legislative Jud/Pub	40
2741I	Catalog Compilers	280
2741J	Construction Reports	310
2741K	Buyers' Information Services	100
2751	Commercial Printer(Tm)	69,540
2751A	Silk Screen Printers	10,820
2751B	Law Brief Printers	120
2751C	Decal Companies	1,920
2751D	Business Cards	350
2751E	Printers-Glass, Metal, Plastic	190
2751F	Printing Brokers	260
2751G	Quick/Instant Printers (Pip) Etc.	9,470
2752	Printing - Lithographic	17,140
2752A	Tickets & Coupons	550
2753	Engravers & Plate Printers	4,610
2753A	Engravers-Stationery	630
2753B	Engravers-Mechanical	510
2753C	Color Separations - Offset	590
2753D	Engravers - N.E.C.	2,360
2754	Commercial Printers - Gravure	430
2761	Business Forms - Manifold	4,220
2761A	Sales & Order Books	130
2761B	Paper - Adhesive - Pressure Sensitive	70

TOLL-FREE 1-800-223-7777 IN N.J. CALL 201-871-1100 **45**

Figure 11.24 A page from Ed Burnett's Consultants, Inc. catalog.

the individuals ordering your product or service respond with an order blank that contains this code. For this reason, many mail order dealers using direct mail ensure that the code goes not only on the outside of the envelope but also on the order blank. This has the additional advantage of ensuring that you receive the name and address of your customer and that it is written so that you can read it. You will probably be surprised as to just how many of your customers write illegibly. Finally, this method does not depend on your customer's writing in the code on the order blank for you as the code already appears. A variation is to use a type of pressure-sensitive label for the customer's name and address on the outside envelope that can be detached and put on the order blank. This saves the cost of an additional label.

Only one week after receiving your first response from your mailing you will have received 50 percent of your total number, so you can tell the total number after this short period by multiplying by two. You then make the calculation as to whether this particular list is profitable. If it is, you roll out your promotion to the remainder of the list, and at the same time, you start looking for new lists. You test them in the same fashion. In this way you can make huge profits in a short time, and you have also minimized your risks.

The list is not the only element you test in direct mail packages. However, you should never test frivolously.

Roll-Out

Roll-out is the last success step in dealing in direct mail. It is really the action step of the old saying, "Be sure you're right; then go ahead." In direct mail, you find out whether you are right during your testing. Once you have decided that you are right, you roll out and mail to the remainder of that list. Some cautionary words here:

1. Be certain that you draw names to give you a valid projectable test. Formerly the only way was an "Nth" name test. For this test your total number of names for your list are developed by taking every Nth name from this list. For example, if the total list is 100,000 and you are going to test 10,000, an Nth name test would mean that you received every tenth name on the list. In this way you can be sure that these names are not all bunched around one geographical location or certain alphabetical letters. Today there are better ways. You can do a random name selection. All lists are maintained by zip code. So, if you get a selection on a random basis you will also get a random geographical distribution. If you use more than one list, you'll need to do a "merge-purge" to eliminate duplication. You can also use the paired states method. This method is best if your test is small and you don't want to do a merge-purge. What you do is pair states that are close together. For one list you use New York, Ohio, Georgia, and Arizona. For the next you use New Jersey (paired with New York), Illinois (paired with Ohio), Georgia (paired with Louisiana), and Arizona (paired with California).

2. Be very careful that the names tested are no more recent than the other names on the list. We Americans are a very mobile people. Addresses and names change very rapidly, as much as 20 percent a year. You can see that if your test consists of this year's names and the remainder of the list is last year's, you are going to get very different results when you roll out after your test.

3. Be cautious in the use of very large lists. You must test sufficient statistical examples. Again, we will talk about this when we talk about lists and testing in coming chapters.

WHEN TO REMAIL

After your initial mailing, you may wonder when to remail, or when you can remail the same or a similar offer to the same list. Well, you have two situations here: One is where you have your own customer list, and the second is where you are using a rented list. For your own customer list, the rule is simple. You can mail as often as you have something to sell. Sunset House may mail out 12 or more catalogs a year to its customers. Publishers Central Bureau, which sells books, mails even more often. It's all up to you, and you should test to see how many mailings are most profitable. Ed Burnett says as a rule of thumb, response to remailings to the same list segment after a short interval can be expected to drop off from 33 to 50 percent. But the basic rule is that if you have something to sell, mail to your customers.

The rented list presents a somewhat different situation. If the list worked well for you with the product, it may work well again even though some of the individuals on the list have already ordered. But you should wait awhile, usually several months. And again, you should test to find out what happens in the case of your particular product in this particular situation.

WHAT THE COMPUTER HAS BROUGHT TO DIRECT MAIL

Massive use of the computer in direct mail has caused major changes and has made many of the old methods of addressing and keeping customer lists obsolete. In addition, through the computer we can do printing, individual addressing, management of your customer list, mailing to certain selected geographical zones or zip code zones, and so on. Further, the computer permits you to use one of the most powerful tools ever developed for use of your customer list—the Recency Frequency Monetary formula, which we will discuss in Chapter 12. The name refers to your customer list: How recently they have ordered, how frequently they have ordered, and how much money they have spent with each order. Close monitoring of these facts can maximize the profitability of mailing to any customer list.

11 MAJOR PITFALLS

Ed Burnett developed a list of 11 major pitfalls in direct mail and how to avoid them. Any direct marketer can profit from reading this list. So here it is exactly as Ed wrote it:

How to Avoid Pitfalls and Disasters in Direct (Mail) Response, by Ed Burnett

Probably the first thing to get straight is the title. *Response* (through any medium) is the "name of the game"—and direct mail is just one of the players.

With a typical in-person sales call now costing well over $175, the price tag on a direct mail piece—15¢ to 20¢ per unit—looks very attractive. But there is mail that works, and the mail that doesn't, and mail may not be the way to go.

So, Rule #1 is *determine your objective first*—then find out whether direct mail is the best, or only, or just one of the ways to reach the objective.

Rule #2 is *lean on the experts.* You can find out enough in a few phone calls to knowledgeable specialists to tell whether you are equipped to run a direct response operation without the help of a consultant or not. If a lot is involved, buy the best consultant you can locate. If the world doesn't rest on the result of a given test, you may wish, for cost considerations, to wing it for yourself. (But if it involves direct mail, at least *talk* to experts in the list business. They can improve by a significant multiplier, almost any result you can obtain by yourself.)

Pitfall #1

In direct mail you are in the *order margin business,* not the "markup" business. A book or booklet costing $1 and selling for $5 has a highly favorable markup—500 percent—but an order margin ($4/unit) that is a guarantee of disaster in the mails, where the cost in the mail may be $300/M.

Pitfall #2

Too high expectations. About twice a year a young administrative aide from some major management association comes to us to start his own seminar business. "You select the lists, and I will run the show—and if we hit 1 percent, we'll both make out like bandits." As gently as we know how, we point out that if seminars at $350 could achieve 1 percent (10 orders per 1,000—or $3,500 per 1,000 pieces in the mail—$10 for every dollar expended) everybody and his brother would be in the seminar business! It so happens the usual response to this type of offer is under 1/10th of 1 percent (less than 1 per 1,000 pieces mailed) and without non-profit status, profit is very hard to realize.

Pitfall #3

Gauging results on "A continuous series of *one* experiment." A great deal of mail, particularly mail sent by one business to another, consists of *one* offer couched in one grouping of words, wrapped in *one* package, and sent out at *one* time, to *one* list. What you know about such mail is what one offer did with one list. That's a pretty unsafe and unsatisfying way to go.

Pitfall #4

Buying the best copy, employing the best art department to lay out the piece, using the best graphics, worrying over the typography, selecting a top grade paper and a fine printer—and *then* sending your secretary or the mail clerk out to get the mailing list. *Response is affected more by list selection than by all other components of a mailing list put together.* It is therefore better to send a poor mailing to a good list, than a good mailing to a poor list. Lists are *markets.* You need to know markets to choose lists. And you need to know list marketers to help you choose lists intelligently.

Pitfall #5

The belief that direct response is "easy"—anybody can make a success of it. In truth, each form of direct response has its own unique problems, and relatively few (out of thousands) who start do a really good job of it. Some die due to the cost to buy customers . . . some die because they lack staying power . . . some die because they have not understood the iron rule of mathematics in this business . . . some die because they cannot handle the "back-end" (all the operations necessary once an order is received). This business, to paraphrase a well-known book, "never promises you a rose garden."

Pitfall #6

Very few direct response campaigns to cold prospects make a "profit" on an initial sale. Most mailers "buy" customers at a loss. This is true of magazines seeking subscribers, and fund raisers seeking donors—as well as establishments offering products or services for sale. If you are planning to use a mail request offer for *one* product—*one* sale—be very careful, or every dollar you spend will be lost.

Pitfall #7

Owners of lists of direct response customers rarely mail to them often enough. Customers *like* to receive mail from the firms they buy from. For every company concerned that it may be mailing to its customers too often, there are 99 where the list is not mailed often enough.

It is a hard lesson to learn—but your customers are not your exclusive property. Your mail order or mail-response individual can usually be found on a number of other mail-responsive lists . . . and they are asking him or her for help.

And a customer file is not truly homogeneous. It consists of current customers, old customers, former customers, dead customers . . . in effect cells of customers with distinctly different characteristics. You need to differentiate between them—and cultivate them differently.

Pitfall #8

In the building of a customer file in the business field, only the rare mailer is foresighted enough to recognize the need to code every customer by classification (S.I.C., or Standard Industrial Classification—the U.S. Government classification system)—and by size (number of employees, if possible, or net worth rating). Those that do can measure penetration by classification—and go where the sales are easier to make. Those that do not, are destined to repeat the same waste in prospecting over and over again—or experience the cost of finding out. Some time ago a penetration analysis by S.I.C. of computers in use which we did for a major publication, found some "raisins in the rice pudding of lists" at a ratio of 1 to 1, while others were at a ratio as high as 1 in 10,000.

Pitfall #9

In the building of a customer file in the consumer field, too few mailers really believe it is important to record the six keys of response—"**RFU$ISM**"—which stands for:

- Recency
- Frequency
- Dollars (US $)
- Item (or class)

- Source, and
- Method of payment (check, credit card, etc.).

A firm like Montgomery Ward or Sears or J.C. Penney will create up to 200 separate cells from "RFU$ISM"—each with its own distinct response rate to any given offer. Such segmentation is the art of direct response customer "massaging." Without it—it's like flying blind in a storm without instruments.

Pitfall #10

There are five acronyms which spell out the major problems most mailers encounter when it comes to computing a list of customers. They are:

KISS— *Keep it simple stupid!*—for never before has man had at his command a tool—the computer—that can make so many mistakes so fast!

GIGO— *Garbage in, garbage out.* You enter mish-mash, and that's exactly what the machine presents back.

DIDO— *Duplication in, duplication out.* Unless you can identify and tag duplicate records, your list is destined to suffer from a chronic case of "duplicatitus."

NINO— *Not in, not out*—undoubtedly the most important phrase in the computer lexicon. If you don't put it in in the first place, you cannot retrieve it. If you bury two or three separate kinds of business under one code, there is no way you can break out one of the segments later on. Remember NINO—and keep it sacred!

RAFO— *Research and find out.* If you leave something out and have to go back and "research and find out," the resulting cost can be horrendous. One year, this firm compiled a million-name business file, and in our wisdom decided to save a few thousand dollars and leave off coding for counties. We had Zip, didn't we? Then along came a good customer who said, flatly, that he would not rent or buy any part of the list unless and until it was county coded. It cost *12 times more* to RAFO and make good on the NINO, than it would if it had been done at the compiling stage!

Pitfall #11

"The usual response in direct mail is 2 percent." This is nothing but errant nonsense! Five major factors influence response. They are:

COPY	The words you use
PACKAGE	The "dress" or packaging your copy comes in
OFFER	The theme your copy and package attempt to convey
TIMING	The time of year in which your mail will be received
LIST	The market or market segment you are seeking to reach with your message

2 percent can be fabulous for one offer, and close to disaster on another. Offers can vary by 300 percent; lists by 1,000 percent . . . which underlines two answers to *every* direct response question:

1. "It depends."
2. "Test—and find out" . . . because for every mailer who tests too much, there are 999 who do not test enough.

SUMMARY

In this chapter we have discussed the great potential of direct mail for your business. Remember the following points:

1. There are important advantages in direct mail. These include selectivity and personalization, speed in getting to your market and concealing test information from your competitors, and being able to provide much more sales copy than you can in any other type of advertising.
2. Use direct mail when you have a clearly defined market segment to which you can appeal.
3. There is more than one way to use direct mail in your business. I gave you 49 different ways to use direct mail for profits.
4. There are five success steps of direct mail: Identify your market, prepare your package, pick your lists, test, and roll out.
5. When do you remail? Your customer list is used whenever you have something to sell. For a rented list, try remailing after several months.
6. A computer can do remarkable things for you today in direct mail. This tool is so powerful that, while you may have a computer yourself, you can also find competent direct mail computer services that can assist you in getting rid of duplicate names, doing a zip code or geographical analysis, or incorporating a Recency Frequency Monetary analysis of your customer list.

Maximizing Your Direct Mail Success with Lists

WHAT IS A LIST AND WHY IS IT CRITICAL FOR DIRECT MAIL?

A list for direct mail is no more than a collection of names and addresses that have something in common that is tied in with your product and greatly increases your chances of making a sale. Lists are critical to your success because of the marketing concept that, for successful marketing, the emphasis should be on your potential customer rather than on the product or service you want to sell. This implies that you want potential customers on your list—people who will want your product, who will have money to buy your product, and who will buy by mail. The bottom line is that the lists you select can be twice as important as your offer and five times as important as your direct mail package.

To give you some example of the importance of the list and its emphasis on the marketing aspects of the buyer, you need only consider the Yellow Pages or the telephone book as a list source. Now here is a list of thousands of names. Why won't the telephone book work for a product that you might sell by mail? First, only a small portion of people in the telephone book will actually want to buy your product. Secondly, only a small portion may have the money to buy your product. And finally, only a small portion of the listees in a telephone book actually buy by mail.

Here's another example that will help you to understand the considerable importance of the list. Let us say you are selling a baby product. You have two direct mail packages. One package contains great copy and tremendous graphics to advertise your baby product. But there is one problem: The only list available is one of garage mechanics. The other direct mail package isn't very good at all. It describes the baby product you are selling but the graphics and copy are both poor. However, when you mail this package, you are able to obtain a list of expectant mothers. In a situation like this, even though you have poor copy and poor graphics, this package will pull much better to the list of expectant mothers than the great copy and great graphics to the list of garage mechanics. Obviously, expectant mothers are far more likely to order a baby product than are garage mechanics.

TYPES OF LISTS

There are many ways to categorize different types of lists for use in direct mail—mail order response lists, in-house lists of mail order buyers versus lists of mail order buyers from other firms, compiled lists, and business versus consumer lists. Each has its proper time and place for use. Let's take a closer look.

Mail Order Response List

The mail order response list is a list of people who have responded to mail order ads. It can be broken down further into two other categories: Categorized inquiries and actual orders; and your own mail order buyer's list versus someone else's.

Inquiry lists are lists containing individuals who made an inquiry in response to a space, classified, or direct mail ad, or an ad in some other medium, but did not necessarily place an order. Inquiry lists can be useful in that they list individuals who have at least expressed an interest in the type of product or service that was advertised. On the other hand, buyer lists actually qualify the individual as a mail order buyer and specifically for the type of mail order purchase that was made: Be it a product, a seminar, a magazine subscription, or whatever, the customer actually sent in cold, hard cash. This is certainly a cut above a simple expression of interest. As you might expect, a list of individuals who actually order by mail is far more valuable than a list of people who only inquire about a product or service.

In-House Lists and Lists from Other Firms

We can also break down a mail order response list according to your own responses versus other dealers' responses. You might guess that your own customer list will be more valuable than some other dealer's customer list, because your own customers have already dealt with you and, assuming that you have been reliable and honest, they trust you. On the other hand, someone who has ordered a mail order product of a similar type from another company will trust that firm but may not trust your promotion quite so much. As a result, you will not get as many orders from such a list as you will from a mailing to your own customers.

There is another important factor about a mail order buyer list that I would like to emphasize here. Mail order purchase in itself is sometimes better than any other factor for determining whether a particular list will work for you. This is true because even today, with mail order growing at the very rapid rate it has over the last few years, not everyone buys by mail. In fact, the majority of people do not. Therefore, even great interest in a product or service in itself may not result in a sale. But mild interest *in a mail order buyer* may generate a sale. What I am saying here is that the deciding factor in a sale may be whether the individual on the list is a mail order buyer.

Let me give you an example. A company in Illinois was introducing a new miniature television set into the American market. Large television sets have not been sold sufficiently by mail to generate sizable lists for this single product. However, lists of purchasers of regular television sets from stores are available. A mailing to this list of television buyers from retail stores failed miserably. A similar mailing with the identical package to a list of mail order buyers of electronic goods succeeded. During testing, the company tried a list of non-mail order buyers who had bought special electronic goods similar to those of the mail order buyer's list. In other words, these individuals had bought special electronic goods but had not purchased them through the mail. This promotion also failed, illustrating the fact that it is frequently more important for an individual to be a mail order buyer than a non-mail order buyer of the identical or very similar product you are offering by mail.

Compiled List

Compiled lists come from previously printed sources. A list may be compiled from the telephone directory, a trade directory, the membership of an association, registration at a seminar, owners of automobiles, credit references, government reports, and so forth. A compiled list can also be compiled to order, but such a list will cost you much more than one that is already available.

List compiler and consultant Ed Burnett has found more than 40 different kinds of lists that are available from compilers. All but three of these are essentially developed by compilers. The three exceptions are contributors, mail respondents/business, and mail respondents/consumer. Here is Ed Burnett's complete tabulation of more than 40 different lists available from compilers:

Advertisers
Alumni
Business executives
Businesses
Canadian
Churches
"Clusters" around known groups
Homemakers
Contributors
Credit cards
Data qualified by field research or questionnaires
Editors
Education
Engineers
Ethnic
Financial
Foreign
Government
Influentials and opinion leaders
Institutional executives
Institutions (except churches and government)
Insurance
Investment and stock ownership
Libraries
Magazine subscribers and recipients
Mail respondents/business
Mail respondents/consumer
Membership
New businesses
Newly established households
Newly promoted executives
Occupant
Owners of products
Professionals
Retail
Scientists
Senior citizens
Stratified lists by demographic characteristics

Students—high school and college

Teenagers

Trade show registrants

Business Lists versus Consumer Lists

A consumer list contains the names of those who are the ultimate users of a product or service, while a business list contains the names of those who are in business and will somehow use the product or service in the resale of this product or another product or service to someone else. This distinction is crucial in all types of mail order and direct mail operations. For example, seminars are given to dispense needed information to businesses as well as consumers. The seminar operations, depending on whether they are given to a consumer or a businessperson, are entirely different. When a seminar is given to a business or employees of a business, it is held on a weekday, so that the employee is paid at normal salary while attending the seminar. Further, the pricing for a professional seminar to a business can be $250 per day per person or more. However, a seminar given to a consumer is entirely different. Let us say it is a seminar on how to start your own business to individuals who are not in business at that time. The seminar is on a weekend, because the attendee will not be compensated while attending the seminar. Furthermore, because the company is not paying for the seminar, $250 a day may be considered too high. Frequently the seminar is priced at under $100 per day. Because of the considerable differences in all types of products and services, SRDS publishes one volume for consumer lists and one for business lists. Many list compilers, managers, and brokers specialize in either one or the other.

HOW TO PICK A LIST THAT WILL BE SUCCESSFUL FOR YOU

I mentioned in the previous chapter that free consulting was available from list managers, compilers, and brokers because it is in their interest to help you succeed so that you will continue to do business with them. If this is true, why not always use these free consulting resources and not even attempt to pick a list yourself? There are several reasons why you must know how to pick your own list, even if you do use the services of one of these three experts in the direct mail business.

1. You know your business better than anyone else possibly can. Therefore, you can sometimes suggest and find lists that even an expert consultant, compiler, manager, or broker may not think of using.
2. You can help one of these experts. Your list expert will be doing the best possible job to help you. The more you know about list

selection, the better you can make suggestions to be followed up in trying to find outstanding lists for you.

3. As in any other type of business, there are experts who are good and experts who are not. There are experts who have been in the business for years, have had experience, and have proven themselves many times over. There are also experts who started yesterday on the off chance that they might be able to succeed at being a list compiler, broker, or manager. There are also fly-by-nighters who are totally dishonest. To protect yourself, you must know how to avoid being misled, which means knowing how to pick a list yourself so that you know whether what is being recommended makes sense.

SRDS AND *DIRECT MAIL LIST RATES AND DATA*

Congratulations! You are living in the age of SRDS. The publications I mentioned earlier are of immense help in the mail order business, but the volume of consumer lists and business lists, *Direct Mail List Rates and Data,* is superb. It has had a tremendous and positive effect on the industry. *Direct Mail List Rates and Data* is a catalog of mail list names that are readily available from thousands of different sources.

What *Direct Mail List Rates and Data* does is to invite every single list owner, manager, or broker to request listing questionnaires through which listing in *Direct Mail List Rates and Data* can be made. SRDS advertises and otherwise actively searches for individuals who are presumed to offer lists for rent. The bottom line is that SRDS leaves no stone unturned to get every single new list listed in its massive publications just as soon as it becomes available. Because listing is free, it is very likely that most lists available on the market are included in these two volumes. However, SRDS itself records nine reasons that mailing lists are withheld by the list owner and not submitted for publication. These reasons run the gamut, but generally boil down to the fact that some list owners do not want to rent, do not want to rent to everyone, or do not want to rent now. Every serious direct mailer should be familiar with SRDS. Even if you can't afford to subscribe, you should check with your local business library; many of these subscribe to these publications.

HOW TO USE *DIRECT MAIL LIST RATES AND DATA*
TO FIND AND SELECT POTENTIAL MAILING LISTS

The starting point for using *Direct Mail List Rates and Data* is the subject market classification index shown in Figure 12.1. All lists that pertain to a specific market are grouped together here and listed in alphabetical order. In some cases, several classifications contain similar items. When

Figure 12.1 Subject market classification from *Direct Mail List Rates and Data.*

this happens, the subject market classification index tells you what the other different classifications are. After each subject market listed, you will find a number. This number pertains to SRDS's own number and title classification system, shown in Figure 12.2. Note that the number system goes to 351 for business lists, from 502 to 612 for consumer lists, and finally from 700 to 718 for farm lists. Looking at the numbers in Figure 12.1, you can see that we are in the business list section. Let's look at an example. Assume that we want to look at the business list for the fur trade. Looking alphabetically, we'll see *Fur Trade, Fur Farming, Trapping,* and so on, Class 125, in Figure 12.1.

Figure 12.2   SRDS number and title classification system.

We now turn to the business section of *Direct Mail List Rates and Data* under the appropriate number, 125, shown in Figure 12.3. Under 125, the first list shown is *American Furriers,* which has the media code 3-125-2350-9.00. Note that each separate list described contains a series of numbered paragraphs. To the right of Figure 12.3, look at the list entitled *Furniture Design and Manufacturing Magazine Active Subscribers,* containing a total of 11 paragraphs. All listings in *Direct Mail List Rates and Data* are organized in exactly the same way to make it easier to use and to compare lists. For example, a description of the list is always contained in paragraph 2, and the rates are always contained in paragraph 4.

125—FUR TRADE, FUR FARMING, TRAPPING, ETC.

AMERICAN FURRIERS

Media Code 3 125 2360 9.00
Customized Mailing Lists, Inc., 158-23 Grand Central Parkway, Jamaica Estates, N. Y. 11432. Phone 212-969-8800.
For basic information on listing segments 1, 3, 5, 6, 7, 9, 10, 11 see Customized Mailing Lists, Inc. listing in Classification 45.
2. DESCRIPTION
Furriers.
ZIP Coded in numerical sequence 100%.
4. QUANTITY AND RENTAL RATES
Rec'd May, 1980.

	Total Number	Price per/M
Furriers & fur salons	1,790	35.00
Fur manufacturers	600	*60.00

Selections: state, title, addressing, 2.50/M extra; SCF, 5.00/M extra; key coding, 1.00/M extra.

FUR MANUFACTURERS

Media Code 3 125 4700 3.00
Ever Ready Mailers, Inc., 4021 Austin Blvd., Island Park, L. I, N. Y. 11558. Phone 516-432-0754.
For basic information on listing segments 1, 5, 6, 7, 9, 10, 11 see listing for Ever Ready Mailers, Inc. in Classification 46.
2. DESCRIPTION
Fur manufacturers.
ZIP Coded in numerical sequence 100%; by state 100%
4. QUANTITY AND RENTAL RATES
Rec'd May, 1980.

	Total Number	Price per/M
Total list	1,000	19.50

FUR TRADE

Media Code 3 125 4837 3.00
Member D M M A.
Market Data Retrieval, Inc., Ketchum Pl., Westport, Conn. 06460. Phones 203-226-8941; 212-582-5311.
For basic information on listing segments 1, 2, 3, 4, 5, 6, 7, 8, 9, 10, 11 see Market Data Retrieval, Inc. listing in Classification 46.
3. LIST SOURCE
Classified telephone directories and trade directories.
4. QUANTITY AND RENTAL RATES
Rec'd May, 1980.

SIC Code:	Total Number	Price per/M
2371—Fur goods mfrs.	507	35.00
5681—Furriers & fur shops	2,042	"

NATIONAL BUSINESS LISTS FUR TRADE, FUR FARMING, TRAPPING, ETC. LISTS

Media Code 3 125 4075 1.00
Member D M M A.
National Business Lists, Inc., 162 N. Franklin, Chicago, Ill. 60606. Phone 312-236-0350.
For basic information on listing segments 1, 2 & 3 (symbols preceding SIC's), 5, 6, 7, 8, 9, 10, 11, see listing for National Business Lists in Classification 46.
4. QUANTITY AND RENTAL RATES
Rec'd May, 1980.

SIC Code:	Total Number	Price per/M
x2371 Fur goods manufacturers	516	*45.00
†5681 Furriers & fur shops	1,651	45.00

(*) Price for total list.

ZELLER & LETICA FUR RETAILERS & MANUFACTURERS

Media Code 3 125 6600 5.00
Member D M M A.
Zeller & Letica, Inc., 15 East 26th St., New York, N. Y. 10010. Phone 212-685-7512. Toll free 800-221-4112.
For basic information on listing segments 1, 5, 6, 7, 9, 10, 11, see Zeller & Letica, Inc. listing in Mailing List Compilers Section.
4. QUANTITY AND RENTAL RATES
Rec'd May, 1980.

	Total Number	Price per/M
Fur retailers and fur mfrs.	2,300	35.00
Fur cleaning	850	*35.00

(*) Total list.
Minimum 75.00.

127—FURNITURE & UPHOLSTERY

(Also see Floor Coverings, Home Furnishings, Interior Design & Decorating)

AMERICAN FURNITURE INDUSTRY

Media Code 3 127 2175 6.00
Customized Mailing Lists, Inc., 158-23 Grand Central Parkway, Jamaica Estates, N. Y. 11432. Phone 212-969-8800.
For basic information on listing segments 1, 3, 5, 6, 7, 9, 10, 11 see Customized Mailing Lists, Inc. listing in Classification 45.
2. DESCRIPTION
Furniture Industry.
ZIP Coded in numerical sequence 100%.

---

4. QUANTITY AND RENTAL RATES
Rec'd May, 1980.

	Total Number	Price per/M
Manufacturing—all	10,000	30.00
Manufacturing—larger—presidents by name	6,200	"
Manufacturing—larger—executives	16,000	"
Wholesale	9,000	"
Upholster & slipcovers	20,900	"
Stores & showrooms	64,000	"
Antique stores	25,000	"
Repairing & cleaning	7,800	"

Selections: state, title addressing, 2.50/M extra; SCF, 5.00/M extra; key coding, 1.00/M extra.
Minimum 3,000.

FURNITURE

Media Code 3 127 4350 3.00
Addresses Unlimited, 14621 Titus St., Van Nuys, Calif. 91402. Phone 213-873-6114.
For basic information on listing segments 1, 3, 5, 6, 7, 9, 10, 11 see Addresses Unlimited listing in Classification 45.
2. DESCRIPTION
Retail furniture stores—U S A.
ZIP Coded in numerical sequence 100%.
4. QUANTITY AND RENTAL RATES
Rec'd November, 1978.

	Total Number	Price per/M
Total list	35,000	25.00
California only	2,500	"

FURNITURE DEALERS

Media Code 3 127 4825 4.00
American Business Lists, Inc., 5639 S. 86th Circle, P. O. Box 27347, Ralston, Neb. 68127. Phone 402-331-7169.
For basic information on listing segments 1, 3, 5, 6, 7, 8, 9, 10, 11 see American Business Lists, Inc. listing in Classification 45.
2. DESCRIPTION
List includes name, address, city, county name, ZIP Code, area code phone number and franchise information (if available).
ZIP Coded in numerical sequence 100%; numerically by state 100%; by state 100%; alpha-geo 100%; random 100%.
List is computerized.
Selections available: 3 digit ZIP Code-sectional centers, state.
4. QUANTITY AND RENTAL RATES
Rec'd May, 1980.

	Total Number	Price per/M
Total list	34,645	35.00

Renting
the list is just the first step.

Companies listed in the Suppliers and Services Directory will supply you with mailing services or equipment you'll need to process your mailing *quicker* and more efficiently. You'll find names of firms organized according to Business Classification:

I Creative & Consultant Services
II List Services
III Mail Advertising Services
IV Supplies
V Equipment

The Directory Section is *now* easier to use than ever! Take full advantage of its information!

DM—BMF—2x

FURNITURE DEALERS

Media Code 3 127 5300 7.00
Member D M M A.
Research Projects Corp., Executive Plaza, 50 Clinton St., Hempstead, N. Y. 11550. Phone 516-481-6410; 212-895-1048; toll free 800-645-2980.
For basic information on listing segments 1, 5, 6, 7, 9, 10, 11 see Research Projects Corp. listing in Classification 45.
2. DESCRIPTION
Furniture dealers.
4. QUANTITY AND RENTAL RATES
Rec'd May, 1980.

	Total Number	Price per/M
Stores—new	60,000	30.00
Second hand furniture	11,000	"

Furniture Design & Manufacturing Magazine Active Subscribers

Media Code 3 127 5425 2.00
Member D M M A.
Delta Communications Inc., 400 N. Michigan Ave., Chicago, Ill. 60611. Phone 312-222-2000.
1. PERSONNEL
Publisher S. L. (Sandy) Berliner.
Circulation Manager—Chuck Taylor.
Broker and/or Authorized Agent
All recognized brokers.
2. DESCRIPTION
Subscribers to Furniture Design & Manufacturing Magazine.
ZIP Coded in numerical sequence 100%.
List is computerized.
3. LIST SOURCE
Circulation.
Derived thru mail 98%.
4. QUANTITY AND RENTAL RATES
Rec'd May, 1980.

	Total Number	Price per/M
Total list	25,184	50.00

Minimum order 250.00.
5. COMMISSION, CREDIT POLICY
20% commission to recognized brokers.
6. METHOD OF ADDRESSING
4-up Cheshire labels.
Magnetic tape available (9 track, 1600 BPI).
7. DELIVERY SCHEDULE
15 days after receipt of order.
8. RESTRICTIONS
Advertisers must order from list owner direct.
Other mailers must order through broker.
Sample mailing piece must be submitted for approval.
9. TEST ARRANGEMENT
Minimum order 250.00.
10. LETTER SHOP SERVICES
Labels will be sent.
11. MAINTENANCE
Updated regularly with subscription mail returns and corrections.

FURNITURE MANUFACTURERS

Media Code 3 127 5500 2.00
Addresses Unlimited, 14621 Titus St., Van Nuys, Calif. 91402. Phone 213-873-6114.
For basic information on the following numbered listing segments 1, 3, 5, 6, 7, 9, 10, 11, see Addresses Unlimited listing in Classification 45.
2. DESCRIPTION
Furniture manufacturers.
4. QUANTITY AND RENTAL RATES
Rec'd November, 1978.

	Total Number	Price Per/M
Total list	4,500	30.00

FURNITURE MARKETPLACE

Media Code 3 127 6175 2.00
Ed Burnett Consultants, Inc., 2 Park Ave., New York, N. Y. 10016. Phone 212-679-0630. Toll free 800-223-7777.
For basic information on listing segments 1, 5, 6, 7, 9, 10 see Ed Burnett Consultants, Inc. listing in Mailing List Compilers section.
3. LIST SOURCE
Classified telephone directories, trade directories, credit reference directories.
4. QUANTITY AND RENTAL RATES
Rec'd May, 1980.

Pricing	Price per/M
Under 10,000	35.00
10,000 to 49,999	33.00
50,000 to 99,999	30.00
100,000 to 249,999	21.00
250,000 to 499,999	21.00
500,000 to 999,999	18.00
Over 1,000,000	15.00

Minimum order 4,000.

(This listing continued on next page)

Figure 12.3 A sample listing from *Direct Mail List Rates and Data*.

Analysis of
Direct Mail Listings

All listings in this catalog are organized in exactly the same way to make it easier for you to use SRDS and easier to compare list choices. For example, rates are always noted in paragraph #4 — QUANTITY AND RENTAL RATES. The eleven paragraph headings used throughout this catalog are outlined below:

MARKET CLASSIFICATION (product, industry, SIC, profession, service, demographics, consumer market, etc.)

TITLE OF LIST
Media Identification Code
Name of owner, membership identification (such as DMA), address, telephone, ZIP Code, TWX

1. PERSONNEL
Name of individuals in selling or service function
Branch office identification— brokers, authorized agents or list managers

2. DESCRIPTION
Description of characteristics:
Type & kind of pattern
Special features
Special selection capability
Response & characteristics
List arrangement
Average unit of sale
ZIP Coding sequence
Identification if list is computerized

2a. SELECTIONS AVAILABLE
5-digit ZIP   State
3-digit ZIP—   County
  Sectional   City
  Centers
             BUSINESS LIST
SIC or Type of   Size of Business
  Business   Other selections
Title only   Available
Name & Title
             CONSUMER LIST
Sex   Income
Age
Other selections available

3. LIST SOURCE
When, where and how developed or derived
Source of names
  For a published source
  For a response source
  For roster source

4. QUANTITY AND RENTAL RATES
Received by SRDS date
For total list and list parts:
  Total names
  Price per thousand
Combination rates — discounts
Special selection rates
Minimum order requirement

5. COMMISSION, CREDIT POLICY
Agency commission, broker's commission
Cash discount policy
Deposits, if any, with amounts and conditions
Credit conditions

6. METHOD OF ADDRESSING
Complete and detailed information concerning addressing methods, impression selections and rate differential, if any
Availability of lists on magnetic tape

7. DELIVERY SCHEDULE
Availability
Time lag or delay
Guarantees and/or special considerations

8. RESTRICITONS
Conditions of availability
Conditions regarding re-use or security

9. TEST ARRANGEMENT
Rates
Premiums
Minimum number requirement
Conditions

10. LETTER SHOP SERVICES
Services performed
Mailing instructions
Returned material

11. MAINTENANCE
Updating procedures
Guarantee, if any, on delivery
Refund conditions
Duplication considerations

Direct Mail - Master Index Section

Figure 12.4   Description of paragraphs from *Direct Mail List Rates and Data*.

A complete description of all 11 paragraphs is shown in Figure 12.4. Not all 11 paragraphs are contained under every listing in the book because a list renter may not provide certain information to SRDS. But clearly, much of the information listed is extremely important. Therefore, it is worthwhile to become familiar with Figure 12.4 so you can look for the essential information in which you may be interested right away. For example, it is worth knowing that in the description of the list, you will find not only the characteristics of the list, but the type and pattern of buying, special features, special selection capability, response characteristics, list arrangement, the average unit of sale, zip coding sequence, and whether the list is computerized. Of course, the name, address, and telephone number of the owner are always stated.

USING LIST CATALOGS

Catalogs are frequently available from list managers, owners, and compilers. In general, they offer information similar to that contained in *Direct Mail List Rates and Data*. The advantage they offer is that they bring a number of different lists of a similar type together. Also, they may provide more information about certain lists than is available in the SRDS publications. Finally, you can't beat the price: They are usually free. In general, you would use the catalog much as you did the *Direct Mail List Rates and Data,* except that usually you would write or call to request additional information about the list or perhaps a data card, as shown in Figures 12.5 and 12.6. Like the information obtained in *Direct Mail List Rates and Data,* the information on the data card will tell you what is available, how much it costs, what the delivery time is, and other important information.

However, a list catalog sometimes does not use the same classification system as do the SRDS books. Typical catalog publishers will probably arrange their lists alphabetically by class, perhaps separately for those that are mail response lists as opposed to compiled lists, and then very frequently by the Standard Industrial Classification (SIC) number.

HOW TO USE THE SIC NUMBER

SIC stands for Standard Industrial Classification, an index developed and sponsored by the Department of Commerce. This classification system provides a four-digit number to identify the function of every business, profession, or industry in the United States, as well as a specified product manufactured. In the SIC system, the first two numbers are used to define the 10 major fields of endeavor as follows: 01 to 09, agriculture, forestry, and fisheries; 10 to 14, mining; 15 to 17, contracting; 20 to 39, manufacturing; 40 to 47, transportation; 48 to 49, communication and utilities;

ZENITH MAILING LIST CO.

Data Card No. 1008

1347 DIVISADERO STREET　SUITE 409
SAN FRANCISCO, CALIFORNIA 94115
415-554-0532　FAX 415-554-0516

ZENITH MASTERFILE
DIRECT RESPONSE DATABASE

#111 HUMAN RESOURCES & MANAGEMENT RESPONDERS

Total File: 202,655
List Rental: $85/M

Average Order Size: $175
Updates: Quarterly

These professionals manage the human resource and personnel departments or functions of their organizations. They are active direct mail buyers of books, seminars, videos, employee programs, and subscriptions. Products and interests included are: TQM, recruitment and interviewing, executive education, management, career enhancement, teamwork, health & wellness programs, organizational development, communication and presentations, time management, legal issues and compliance, employee assistance, and safety.

Standard Selections (No Select Cost):

		Quantity
#270	Human Resources:	93,775
#271	Training & Development:	17,056
#272	Total Quality Management:	24,334

Also Available By Title(Add $3/M):

#273	President/CEO:	5,039
#274	Vice President, Human Resources:	7,602
#275	Director, Human Resources:	21,250
#276	Director, Training & Development:	2,472
#277	Manager, Human Resources:	29,308
#278	Personnel & HR Department Staff:	21,270
#279	Training & Development Staff:	14,584

Other Available Special Selections(Add $3/M):

#280	Management & Business:	52,997
#281	Health & Wellness Service Buyers:	14,884
#282	Compliance & Legal:	13,944
#283	Organization & Development:	5,103
#284	Employee Assistance Programs:	4,914
#285	Canada:	2,455

(turn page for more selections)

Each Zenith Direct Response Database combines the response files of several companies. These direct marketers offer books, newsletters, seminars, video programs, training, booklets and brochures, manuals, directories, software, and related services. Over a dozen different databases are available with hundreds of selections. Call List Manager Jerry Donohoe for information on our many other list opportunities.

Figure 12.5　Sample data card.

50 to 51, wholesaling; 52 to 59, retailing; 60 to 65, finance; 70 to 95, services. Each digit within the range of each of the 10 different classifications is used to define further a specialized kind of the endeavor noted. For example, the number 23 falls within the manufacturing classification, which is 20 to 39. The second two digits are used to show a specific line of activity of the company. Let's look at 2311 (2311 to 2399 happen to be reserved for apparel manufacturers and textile products made from fabrics and similar materials). The last two digits, 11, are reserved for suits, coats, and overcoats for boys and men. Thus, 2311 describes apparel manufacturers of suits, coats, and overcoats for men and boys. A complete SIC index can be obtained by writing the U.S. Government Printing Office, Washington, DC. An abbreviated SIC index is contained in Figure 12.7. The SIC code can be used to segment a larger list as well as to identify potential lists in the catalogs of those specialists in the mail order field who

Responsive Mailing Lists for Direct Marketers!

HEALTH CARE AND HEALTH EDUCATION
- [ ] Abbey Press CareNotes Buyers; 40,000; $90/M (131)
- [ ] Canadian Health Promoters; 7,000; $90/M (105)
- [ ] Career-Planning PTs and OTs; 20,000; $90/M (117)
- [ ] Chiropractic Practice Promotion; 14,500; $90/M (106)
- [ ] Counseling Aids for Facilitators; 15,000; $90/M (107)
- [ ] Drugs & Alcohol Education Resources; 30,500; $90/M (108)
- [ ] Employee Safety Resources; 20,000; $90/M (109)
- [ ] Health Care Administration; 49,500; $90/M (103)
- [ ] Health Promotion Resources; 50,000; $90/M (110)
- [ ] Physical Therapists; 30,000; $90/M (111)
- [ ] Physician Practice Promotion; 30,000; $90/M (112)
- [ ] Visual Health Patient Education Buyers; 24,500; $90/M (119)
- [ ] Wellness Reproductions Customers; 7,500; $90/M (114)

BUSINESS & MANAGEMENT PROFESSIONALS
- [ ] Book Marketing Update Newsletter; 7,000; $90/M (118)
- [ ] Corporate University Press; 20,000; $90/M (127)
- [ ] Creative Ways Writers & Entrepreneurs; 8,000; $90/M; (128)
- [ ] Human Resource Professionals; 95,000; $90/M (116)
- [ ] James L. Evers Bookbuyers; 20,000; $90/M (125)
- [ ] JSA Publications Bookstores; 9,500; $75/M (126)
- [ ] Organizing Solutions Professionals; 10,000; (123)
- [ ] Telegroup, Inc. Business Services; 110,000; $90/M (135)
- [ ] Volunteer Programs and Directors; 22,000; $90/M (115)

SPECIALTY CONSUMER LISTS
- [ ] Express Shipping Centers Customers; 250,000 (Qrtly.); $90/M (122)
- [ ] Passage Press Bookbuyers; 30,000; $90/M (120)
- [ ] The Family Travel Guides Catalogue; 20,000; $90/M (127)
- [ ] Unarius Academy of Science Books & Tapes; 30,000 $90/M (124)
- [ ] Vintage Drum Centers Buyers & Inquires; 9,000; $90/M (104)

Exclusive with HR Direct...
This database includes over 980,000 direct mail buyers, responders, and customers — licensed from the mailing lists of various publishers and direct marketers throughout the U.S.

Mailing List Owners:
Abbey Press
Book Marketing Update
Career News, Inc.
Carousel Press
Channel Publishing, Ltd.
Corporate University Press
Creative Ways
Express Shipping Centers, Inc.
Family Travel Guides
Interlaken Publishers, Inc.
James L. Evers Associates
JSA Publications, Inc.
Modern Sage
Morson Publishing, Inc.
Open Horizons Publishing Co.
Organizing Solutions, Inc.
Passage Press
SafetyLine
Stretching Charts, Inc.
Superior Medical Limited
Telegroup, Inc.
Unarius Academy of Science
Vanguard Resource Group, Inc.
Vintage Drum Center
Visual Health Information, Inc.
Wellness Reproductions, Inc.

Call for Datacards.

Contact:
David Hawthorne or Tom Glenn

BROKERS WELCOMED.
Spring 1994

HR DIRECT — Mailing Lists / Publishing / Direct Marketing

508 N. Second St.
Fairfield, IA 52556-2464
Tel: 515 472-7188
Fax: 515 472-5729

Figure 12.6   Sample data card.

handle lists. Ed Burnett provides fifth-digit SIC which adds 3,000 separate classification breakdowns to the approximately 900 published by the U.S. government.

HOW TO HANDLE LIST DUPLICATION

If you are going to become really successful, you will eventually use more than one list in your direct mail business at the same time. What do you do about duplicate names on various lists you're using? There is always the possibility of renting the same names on different compiled lists or even

01. Agricultural production
07. Agricultural services and hunting and trapping
08. Forestry
09. Fisheries
10. Metal mining
11. Anthracite mining
12. Bituminous coal and lignite mining
13. Crude petroleum and natural gas
14. Mining and quarrying of nonmetallic minerals, except fuels
15. Building construction—general contractors
16. Construction other than building construction—general contractors
17. Construction—special trade contractors
19. Ordnance and accessories
20. Food and kindred products
21. Tobacco manufactures
22. Textile mill products
23. Apparel and other finished products made from fabrics and similar material
24. Lumber and wood products, except furniture
25. Furniture and fixtures
26. Paper and allied products
27. Printing, publishing, and allied industries

28. Chemicals and allied products
29. Petroleum refining and related industries
30. Rubber and miscellaneous plastics products
31. Leather and leather products
32. Stone, clay and glass products
33. Primary metal industries
34. Fabricated metal products, except ordnance, machinery, and transportation equipment
35. Machinery, except electrical
36. Electrical machinery, equipment, and supplies
37. Transportation equipment
38. Professional, scientific, and controlling instruments; photographic and optical goods; watches and clocks
39. Miscellaneous manufacturing industries
40. Railroad transportation
41. Local and suburban transit and interurban passenger transportation
42. Motor freight transportation and warehousing
44. Water transportation
45. Transportation by air
46. Pipe line transportation
47. Transportation services
48. Communication

49. Electric, gas, and sanitary services
50. Wholesale trade
52. Retail trade—building materials, hardware, and farm equipment
53. Retail trade—general merchandise
54. Retail trade—food
55. Automotive dealers and gasoline service stations
56. Retail trade—apparel and accessories
57. Retail trade—furniture, home furnishings, and equipment
58. Retail trade—eating and drinking places
59. Retail trade—miscellaneous retail stores
60. Banking
61. Credit agencies other than banks
62. Security and commodity brokers, dealers, exchanges, and services
63. Insurance carries
64. Insurance agents, brokers, and service
65. Real estate
66. Combinations of real estate, insurance, loans, law offices
67. Holding and other investment companies

70. Hotels, rooming houses, camps, and other lodging places
72. Personal services
73. Miscellaneous business services
75. Automobile repair, automobile services, and garages
76. Miscellaneous repair services
78. Motion pictures
79. Amusement and recreation services, except motion pictures
80. Medical and other health services
81. Legal services
82. Educational services
84. Museums, art galleries, botanical and zoological gardens
86. Nonprofit membership organizations
88. Private households
89. Miscellaneous services
91. Federal government
92. State government
93. Local government
94. International government
99. Nonclassifiable establishments

Figure 12.7 An abbreviated SIC index.

different mail order lists, as one individual may be a member and register in more than one thing or may buy a mail order product from more than one company. One way of handling this problem is to do a "merge-purge." In other words, you take the lists you're going to mail and, using a computer, merge the names. Those that are duplicated are eliminated by the computer.

A second way of attacking the problem of potential duplication of names on different lists is spaced mailings. Don't mail to all your lists at the same time. Mail to one first and wait before mailing to another list. This means that even though duplicate mailings will be made, the individual will receive them at different times. In effect, this increases the chance for a sale since the first letter may not be opened, or the individual may not be ready to buy at the time the first mailing is received. Of course, you can have a third, fourth, or even more separate mailings this way. There is a disadvantage here: If you are going to test one list against another, you must mail at the same time because a spaced mailing will not give accurate results for your test.

Finally, there is one thing you can do about the problem of list duplication: Simply live with the fact that you will have duplication on your lists, and in your forecasting of results recognize that duplication may cause some reduction in results if the mailings are done simultaneously and the duplication is sufficiently large.

DEMOGRAPHICS AND PSYCHOGRAPHICS: WHAT THEY ARE AND HOW TO USE THEM TO YOUR ADVANTAGE

Demographics is measurable statistics of population and how it is actually distributed, including age, income, occupation, size of family, and so forth. Psychographics is a newer system of classification. It is measurable statistics of how members of a population behave.

To make maximum use of demographics, you must picture your customer in your own mind and make a list of different attributes you think your customer has: Is he or she of a certain ethnic background, certain age, or in a certain occupation; does he or she make a certain income, live at one residence for a certain period of time; have a certain educational level; in a household with or without children, and live in certain kinds of communities in certain states?

In the same way, if you are dealing with a business customer, you should sit down and work out a picture of what this customer looks like. You might, for example, list the SIC number, the number of employees, the business's sales volume or its net worth, and so forth.

This demographic picture of your customer is one way in which you enter the catalog or the *Direct Mail List Rates and Data* when you go to select a list. It is also your clue for finding likely lists in other locations.

Psychographics means how your potential customer thinks and therefore behaves. The mailings you receive addressed to "Resident" are based on psychographics. How so? Because they make the assumption that even if you have moved, another individual moving into your house will be interested in the same product or service you might have been. Research has shown this assumption to be accurate. It is for this reason that I recommend to my clients that in their mailings for business seminars they not use a particular individual's name, or if they do, that they do not request forwarding postage to locate that individual. Why? A vice-president of engineering who attends engineering seminars will be replaced by another vice-president of engineering, who will also be interested in attending engineering seminars. Please note that this does *not* mean that you should never address your mailings by name. Quite the contrary, in most cases, personalization will increase your results. But, as is evident by this example, there are exceptions.

Let us say that you have invented a new product to be used by someone interested in the outdoors, yet this product is so new that no list exists for selling it, or even a similar product, through the mail. In that case you must use psychographics. Someone who is interested in the outdoors is a potential buyer of your product. For example, a buyer of a book on camping, hunting, or fishing, or an individual who is buying hunting, fishing, or camping equipment, may be interested.

Here is another example. Let's say that you are selling classical records through the mail and have exhausted all possible sources and all lists currently available. What lists might you try next? According to psychographics, a list of someone whose purchasing behavior in general would indicate an interest in classical records. How about buyers of art?

You can probably think of a number of cases where people who hold one interest hold another. A purchaser of health foods may also be interested in exercise equipment, or vice versa. Someone who contributes to a museum may also contribute to a college or university. A member of a book club may also be interested in joining a record club.

A combination of demographics and psychographics can add greatly to profitability when you select your initial list and afterwards, when you have a successful product and really want to roll out to additional lists for giant profits.

USE OF GEOGRAPHICS

Sometimes a particular area is of great value to you for a particular product or service that you are selling. Yet, the basic list as described may not give the number of names available for any particular state or locality. Fortunately you can estimate this on your own if you know the total number of names on a particular list. Here's how you do it. A strong correlation exists between the geographic distribution of most lists and the geographic distribution of either total U.S. population, all U.S. manufacturing firms, or U.S. retail sales. Figure 12.8 is a chart showing the percentage distribution of population, manufacturing firms, and retail sales by states. For consumer lists, use the population distribution. For lists of manufacturers and wholesalers, use the manufacturing firm's distribution. For retailer service, financial institutions, and so on, use the retail sale's distribution. Look at the state you are interested in, multiply the percentage by the total number of names available on the list, divide this by 100, and you'll have a fairly good idea of the number of names available in this state. Research has shown that a state count is accurate to approximately plus or minus 10 percent. If you are looking for the number of names available on a list in a region, add up the percentages of each state and then multiply by the total quantity of the list before you divide by 100. Use of this technique can show you whether a particular list will be of any use to you, considering the geographic area in which you want to do a precise mailing.

One cautionary note, however: Certain industries—including mining, agriculture, communication services, and government—tend to be clustered in specific geographical areas. Do not use this technique for mailing in these industries.

HOW THE LIST YOU ORDER WILL BE FURNISHED TO YOU

Lists can be furnished to you in the following ways, and each has its own advantages, depending upon your business and the type of list you're mailing to.

1. **Gummed Perforated Labels**
   Gummed perforated labels need to be moistened, just as would a postage stamp. Each label is 3.44 by 1 inches and the print area is 30 characters. Usually you will be charged a small additional fee of something under $5 per thousand for receiving your names on gummed perforated labels.

2. **Pressure-Sensitive Labels**
   Pressure-sensitive labels peel off a waxed paper backing and then are stuck on. The dimensions are 3.2 by .92 inches. They are much easier to affix than gummed labels as they do not have to be moistened. They're ideal for small runs. However, the cost is slightly higher, approximately $8 to $10 per thousand over the cost of rental.

State	Population (%)	Manfacturing Firms (%)	Retail Sales (%)
Puerto Rico	.01	0.01	0.01
Virgin Islands	.01	0.01	0.01
Massachusetts	2.77	3.60	2.70
Rhode Island	0.47	0.81	0.45
New Hampshire	0.35	0.40	0.36
Maine	0.48	0.45	0.45
Vermont	0.22	0.22	0.22
Connecticut	1.49	1.86	1.59
New Jersey	3.54	4.63	3.57
New York	8.91	12.24	8.12
Pennsylvania	5.74	6.08	5.20
Delaware	0.27	0.16	0.32
Dist. of Col.	0.37	0.18	0.56
Maryland	1.93	1.17	1.95
Virginia	2.28	1.26	2.19
West Virginia	0.84	0.48	0.70
North Carolina	2.50	2.34	2.24
South Carolina	1.28	0.93	1.06
Georgia	2.27	1.19	2.20
Florida	3.40	3.01	4.47
Alabama	1.69	1.25	1.33
Tennessee	1.94	1.61	1.90
Mississippi	1.10	0.77	0.82
Kentucky	1.58	0.97	1.35
Ohio	5.23	5.19	5.14
Indiana	2.55	2.30	2.65
Michigan	4.38	4.61	4.47
Iowa	1.38	1.15	1.65
Wisconsin	2.15	2.38	2.14
Minnesota	1.86	1.84	1.84
South Dakota	0.32	0.21	0.31
North Dakota	0.30	0.16	0.31
Montana	0.34	0.26	0.35
Illinois	5.45	6.33	5.72
Missouri	2.31	2.11	2.41
Kansas	1.11	1.03	1.23
Nebraska	0.73	0.81	0.76
Louisana	1.80	1.11	1.42
Arkansas	0.95	0.80	0.84
Oklahoma	1.26	1.10	1.16
Texas	5.56	5.12	5.73
Colorado	1.10	0.98	1.29
Wyoming	0.10	0.12	0.15
Idaho	0.35	0.31	0.42
Utah	0.52	0.47	0.51
Arizona	0.88	0.64	0.99
New Mexico	0.50	0.28	0.51
Nevada	0.24	0.14	0.33
California	9.87	11.24	10.33
Hawaii	0.39	0.29	0.36
Oregon	1.04	1.30	1.17
Washington	1.68	1.50	1.76
Alaska	0.15	0.09	1.13

Figure 12.8   Percentage distribution of population, manufacturing firms, and retail sales by states.

3. **Cheshire Labels**

   Cheshire labels require a special Cheshire machine to be used to affix the labels. They come in columns of four across and 44 to a page and are neither gummed nor perforated. The size and number of characters are identical to those of gummed perforated labels. Usually Cheshire labels are furnished at no additional charge.

4. **Sheet Listing**

   Sheet listing is simply a list of names, but in addition to the standard name and address, you will usually receive other information such as SIC sales volume, number of employees, and so forth, if such information is available. A sheet listing rental may cost you an additional $15 to $20 per thousand names.

5. **Index Cards**

   Index cards are the standard three-by-five-inch cards. Each has the information as contained in the sheet listing above plus additional information as available. Index cards may also cost you an additional $15 to $20 per thousand names.

6. **Magnetic Tape**

   Magnetic tape is usually nine-track, 800 BPI, IBM mode, although other formats can be obtained. These can be rented for one-time use or purchased for unlimited use during the course of the year for compiled lists. Actually, use of the tape implies availability of your own computer. There is also an additional cost here, which can vary widely depending on the type of tape and length.

7. **Floppy Disks**

   As personal computers have become more and more powerful, lists have become increasingly available on floppy disks. For many small companies with access to a personal computer, this is the best option.

Regardless of the format in which you order your list, remember that you are renting names only for one-time use unless specified otherwise, such as names from a compiled source. You generally do not have the right to use these names repeatedly without permission of the list owner or those who control the list.

COST OF LISTS

List costs vary from less than $50 to more than $100 per thousand, depending upon the type of list. Obviously a compiled list that is easily obtained, such as those from a telephone book in a certain geographic area, is of least value. A highly specialized mail order list in a certain limited product area may cost you a great deal simply because the entire set of names is so limited and so difficult to obtain. There are usually no great bargains in this industry, and if you are paying much less for your names, it may mean that they are easily compiled or that they are old and have not been updated for some time and so are worthless. If you are paying more, you can expect the names to be more current and highly selective. Deal with a reputable list broker, compiler, or manager.

One final word on the process of renting lists: Be absolutely certain that you allow time for the delivery of the list prior to mailing. Delivery time will vary from list to list, because the individual from whom you are ordering may have to get the list from some other source. This and reproducing the list take time. Sometimes you must submit a sample of your direct mail package before the rental can be approved. Think in terms of ordering a list one month prior to your mailing date to be safe.

THE RFM FORMULA FOR SELECTING A LIST

Every professional today in the direct mail business uses the RFM formula to help select his or her list. What does RFM stand for? R stands for *recency,* which is how recently a mail order buyer has actually purchased. Someone who has purchased within the last month or so is a much hotter prospect for your proposition than someone who purchased a year or more ago. F stands for *frequency,* which refers to how many times the individual on the list has purchased. A mail order buyer may have purchased an item one time, been dissatisfied, and never ordered this type of product or through the mail again. However, someone who has ordered more than once has shown desire to purchase through the mail. Multiple buyers will always pull better than a one-time mail order buyers' list. M stands for *money,* which refers to how much in dollars the individual buyer purchased. It's no good trying to sell a $200 item to a list of buyers, mail order or not, who purchase only $5 to $10 items, and the opposite is also true.

You can use the RFM formula when mailing to your own in-house list and when deciding whether to keep mailing to someone on it. One way of doing this is to work out a special formula based on RFM. Assign points or weightings to each factor in the formula. Such a use of RFM is shown in Figure 12.9.

Another user assigns points this way. For recency: order in the current quarter, 10 points; order within the last six months, 5 points; order within the last year, 3 points; order before last year, 1 point. For frequency: multiply the number of points by 5. For money: use 10 percent of the average order maintained on a continuing basis.

Through the use of this formula, you can see who your hottest customers are or you can quickly analyze some other lists that may be available

	Months	Points
Recency		
Customer ordered _____ months ago.		
	3	25
	6	20
	12	15
	18	10
more than 18		0
Frequency		
Customer ordered on the average once every _____ months.		
	1	50
	2	45
	3	40
	4–6	30
	7–9	20
	10–12	15
more than 12		10
Money		
Size of average order was _____.	more than $300	25
	250–299	20
	200–249	17
	150–199	15
	100–149	14
	75–99	13
	50–74	12
	25–49	11
	10–25	10
less than $ 10.		5

The best customers are those with the highest point count.

Figure 12.9   An example of an RFM weighting formula.

for your product or service. Naturally, the points and weightings are up to you. The example shown in Figure 12.9 is only that. You should work out your own weightings and point system depending upon how important different factors are in your particular situation, product, or industry. Keep accurate records and you can develop a formula that will work for your company only. Best of all, because the point weightings are yours, unique to your products, industry, and company, no one can ever steal this formula from you because it will be of no use to anyone else.

A METHOD OF COMPILING A LIST
THAT IS EVEN BETTER THAN RFM

As good as RFM is, it has some limitations that can be improved upon by a more effective method. RFM only considers three characteristics of your buyers: How recently they have bought, how frequently, and how much money they've spent. Yet other variables may also be of importance in deciding on your best prospects. These may include categories of merchandise purchased, where the buyers' name originated (what magazine or what list), geographic location, type of promotion responded to, and so on. Also, RFM may not be as important as some of these other variables under all conditions.

Borrowing from statistical analytical methods, direct marketing experts have begun to adopt and use a research technique known as multiple regression analysis. With multiple regression analysis, you find the combination of different variables that best predicts response in your particular situation. You don't even need to know what these variables are in advance. What you do need to do is to keep your customer file so as to have available as much data as possible. Thus, in addition to name and address, you definitely want to keep information on RFM, what medium the customer responded to, what type of promotion, whether any type of credit was used, the category of product, and so on. Be careful not to overlook anything that you feel might in some way influence future response to a promotion. In the old days, keeping and accessing this data was quite difficult. But today, with the magic of personal computers, it can be very easy.

Paul Cohen (no relation), director of research at Garden Way Marketing Associates and an expert in this field, says that you can perform a valid analysis with as few as 300 buyers on your in-house list. If you own a personal computer, software is available for you to do your own multiple regression analysis. If not, contact a company that does computing for small business. They'll help you set up to get it done right.

The output of your multiple regression analysis should be a list of the best names on your list for any particular mailing, along with an average predicted response based on those variables that made a difference on similar mailings for you in the past. You can actually get a list of names ranked according to likelihood of purchase. Thus, if you need a 1 percent response to break even for a particular mailing, you can mail only to those names that on the average are predicted to give you a 1 percent response or better. If there are insufficient names in the category of a 1 percent response to make the project worthwhile, at least you'll know this before you invest your money and do the actual mailing.

Naturally, you should keep tabs on the results and monitor how closely the predicted response matches the response actually received . . . and you should repeat the regression analysis as environmental changes occur that would cause the multiple regression equation that you develop to deviate from reality in the marketplace.

HOW TO ORDER A LIST

Craig Huey, president of Infomat, Inc., a full-service agency, has prepared a special list-ordering checklist for his clients. With Craig's permission, this checklist has been reproduced in Figure 12.10 so that you can use it

1.	Clearance (mail date)	_____
2.	Clearance (sample)	_____
3.	Mail date protected?	_____
4.	Delivery date versus mail date	_____
5.	Mode of delivery (UPS blue)	_____
6.	85% net name available	_____
7.	Label format specified	_____
8.	All instructions written and sent to list broker	_____
9.	Split test?	_____
10.	Key coding?	_____
11.	Special selection? (hotline, etc.)	_____
12.	State select?	_____
13.	Nth select?	_____
14.	Omitting any previous orders?	_____
15.	Check acknowledgment from broker	_____

Figure 12.10   Infomat's list-ordering checklist.

too. "Clearance" refers to the fact that some owners of response lists want clearance approval authority before they will permit you to rent their in-house lists. This is so that your mailings will not compete directly with theirs. "Mail date protection" will ensure exclusive use of the list for the time of your mailing. It may or may not always be available as an option. "Mode of delivery" (such as UPS) refers to the method that you want the list delivered to you. "85% net name available" has to do with a merge-purge of two or more lists that you are renting. As noted earlier, a merge-purge saves you from duplicating your mailings because a prospect is on two or more lists. 85 percent net means that you pay only 85 percent of the rental fee of lists (plus a percentage of the computer running fee to do the merge-purge) even though you start with 100 percent of each list.

SUMMARY

In this chapter we've learned about how to maximize your success with direct mail through the correct use of mailing lists. We learned about the different types of mailing lists and which are best. We learned how to pick a list using *Direct Mail List Rates and Data* and independent list compilers, brokers, or managers. We also learned how to select a list using demographics and psychographics, and how to estimate current list geographical percentages in the areas in which we are interested. Finally, I showed you the RFM formula and the multiple regression analysis technique for using and judging others' lists as well as your own.

13

Making Money with TV and Radio Ads

Television and radio together are known as broadcast media, and they can be very effective in selling mail order products.

MAIL ORDER MARKETING THROUGH RADIO

Radio advertising has been around since 1922, and though it has declined somewhat with the introduction of television, it is still a tremendous medium for mail order sales. In fact, it was through the medium of radio mail order that Joe Cossman sold no less than 1,810,000 sets of 100 toy soldiers. Others have been similarly successful.

There are differences between space advertising and direct mail advertising in letters and buying advertising through time when using broadcast media. In space, we specify the magazine, the size of the ad, the date, and the position. If we are sending a direct mail package out, we develop the contents of this package and then decide when we will mail it. However, when we are buying time, no schedule is available in advance. In fact, program and spot positions are not known until the time of your purchase. This makes it a little bit more difficult for planning, although again, as with the other media we discussed in earlier chapters. SRDS has several publications available that can help us: *Spot Radio Rates and Data, Spot Television Rates and Data,* and *Network Rates and Data.* The last of these covers both radio and television.

The two broadcast media have something else in common. In both cases we can seek help from the stations in preparing our advertising. For example, stations can produce and provide programming service, write our ads, give us publicity and promotion, give us merchandising assistance and research guidance, and let us use their specialized broadcasting equipment for preparing our advertising.

THE ADVANTAGES OF RADIO ADVERTISING

Even today, there are reasons for using radio versus television advertising in many circumstances. Let's look at radio advertising first. Here are the advantages.

1. Relatively low cost per thousand listeners.
2. Outstanding segmentation of the market, geographically and demographically, much more than television.
3. Rapid change of schedule or copy.
4. Frequency of advertisement to our potential customers.
5. Quick response.
6. A wide range of stations.

Radio advertising costs much less than television to reach potential customers on a per-thousand basis. Further, because of this low cost, we can reach the listener with the same message far more frequently than we can through television. Also, because most radio copy is simply spoken or taped on a cassette, it is relatively easy to change and the schedule change can be made rapidly as well. Although stations may officially require two weeks' notice to cancel an ad, frequently they may let you do so instantly if your ad is not profitable. A quick response is possible because the lead time is far less than that of print media, such as magazines, and there is no mail time as in direct mail. Those who respond to a radio ad respond immediately. There is a wide range of stations throughout the country, which allows many, many possibilities for advertising your product. In fact, to advertise everywhere and take advantage of the full range of possibilities is more than the average mail order operator can afford. But perhaps the most important of the above advantages is the segmentation that radio permits. Current popular formats of radio programs may include talk, news, classical music, country and western music, popular music, rock music, and ethnic minority formats, sometimes even in a foreign language. This variety allows for incredibly precise segmentation of your market.

DISADVANTAGES OF USING RADIO

There are three basic disadvantages of using the radio medium. The first is called reach, which refers to the proportion of the total market you are able to get to with your message. Regardless of how much radio advertising you do, the maximum reach or amount of market that will hear your message is 60 percent, partly because not everyone listens to the radio for long periods.

The second disadvantage of using radio advertising it that, like television advertising, it is difficult to monitor. Even if you are a prime-time buyer, you yourself will find it difficult to sit down and watch the television or listen to the radio during the periods in which your ad is going to appear to ensure that it appears as advertised, with no mistakes and not cut short. Thus, if your sales begin to fall off for one reason or another or your inquiries begin to drop, you do not know whether it is a genuine drop that you must take immediate note of and act upon, or whether it was an error in the reading of your advertisement at a particular time.

The third basic disadvantage is time. You do not have the time to say everything you might wish as you have in most forms of print advertising. We'll talk more about this later.

HOW TO BUY RADIO ADVERTISING

The first step in the buying of radio advertising is to identify your market. Write out the demographics and geographics of your customer—where he or she lives, how old he or she is, whether he or she is male or female, what type of music, talk shows, or radio format he or she likes. Your next step in identifying this market is to compare your formulation with various surveys available in the industry. One such survey is done for both radio and television by the American Research Bureau and is called *Arbitron*. *Arbitron* collects information through panels of consumers. These detailed surveys cover who is watching or listening to what programs. Two surveys based on telephones have been started recently. One is called *Audits and Surveys Tract 7*, and the other, *The Burke Marketing Research.*

As with print media, name, address, telephone, and other information can be obtained from SRDS publications, in this case *Spot Radio Rates and Data* and *Network Rates and Data.*

Once you have matched your demographics and geographics with the station and program format, you must consider other variables.

The first radio variable to consider is network, spot, or program. We can pretty much eliminate program, which is where you sponsor an entire radio program and get your commercials during the program break. This is only for major advertisers. It's very expensive and is not generally for most direct response or mail order advertisers. Spot radio is radio at a particular time and by a particular station. Turn to the SRDS *Spot Radio Rates and Data* for detailed information. And finally, network is where you obtain national advertising through one of the major networks. Then the publication to look at is SRDS *Network Rates and Data.*

Having decided on the use of network or local spot advertisements, your next choice is station and program. Having matched up the demographics with one of the studies mentioned previously, you have a selection of these and you can start advertising on one or two stations. Because repetition is very important in this type of advertising, it is far better to advertise several times on one station than one time on several different stations. At this time you should also select the particular programs on which you would like your advertisements or commercials to appear.

As with print advertisements, the seasonality of your product is very important. You wouldn't want to try to sell a Christmas product during the summer or a swimming pool product in the middle of the winter. There is also an off-season for radio, which as I will point out later, can affect the cost. The radio off-season is January, February, and, to a certain extent, July and August. Although this is off-season for radio, it may not be off-season for mail order radio *ads.* So you may obtain a very good deal as a mail order advertiser during one of these periods.

The length of time of your commercial is another radio variable. You can buy a 10-second advertisement, which is almost totally useless for mail order. You can also buy a 30- or 60-second advertisement. For your purposes, a 60-second ad is probably the best. In fact, in many cases, a 30-second ad is priced at approximately 75 percent that of a 60-second ad.

Frequency is another important factor. As mentioned earlier, repetition is key in mail order advertising through this medium. One of the advantages of radio is the fact that you can hit your potential customers frequently with the same ad. How frequently depends upon your budget and what you are trying to achieve.

Finally, the last variable is spot time, meaning at what period during the broadcast day you want your ad to appear. The radio day is broken up basically into five periods. From 6:00 to 10:00 A.M. is called morning driving time, and from 3:00 to 7:00 P.M. is known as evening driving time. These are both expensive times for radio. There are also the periods from 10:00 A.M. to 3:00 P.M., 7:00 P.M. to midnight, and from midnight to 6:00 A.M. There are two principles to keep in mind when considering spot time. First, you'll pay more for the prime times. Second, for mail order-type advertising, sometimes a nonprime time is far better. Now it is a well known fact that during prime time you will have more listeners. However, for mail order advertising by radio or by television, there is no direct relationship in many cases between the number of orders received and the size of the audience. This is an important factor to keep in mind when selecting your spot time and also when considering your cost options.

COST OPTIONS IN RADIO

As with various types of print media, you are going to have various options available in which you can pay more or less for your radio advertisements. Your advertising options for radio advertisements are prime rate, TAP, or total audience plan, ROS, or run of station, off-season rates, and various rates depending upon spot time.

The prime rate is the top of the line. You pay the rate as per the rate card, but you get to specify when the ad goes on the air and your ad cannot be bumped.

In TAP, or total audience plan, spots are scheduled for each of the day parts. You don't have quite as much choice, but you are guaranteed that you have a spot in each day part specified.

ROS, or run of station, is a lot less money. But your ad runs at the station's choice. It's much like the remnant space in print advertising. Your ad will be run when the station is able to run it for lack of paid prime time or TAP time advertisers.

During the off-season, you pay less than you would during the rest of the year.

Spot time means that you pay according to the time spot in which your advertisement appears. For example, your ad, running in the late evening during the period from 7:00 P.M. to midnight, may cost only 50 percent as much as it would during the prime driving time.

PI, or per inquiry, is the same as described for print advertising earlier in the book. You pay nothing up front but work out a joint venture with the station so that you pay a certain amount for each order received. Again, per inquiry can be a terrific deal because you have no investment for your advertising and don't pay anything until your orders actually start to come in. But it's as difficult to locate stations for a PI deal as it is to locate magazines willing to do the same thing. Again, never be afraid to ask. If you are dealing through an agency or a media buyer and seek per inquiry-type advertising, be sure to ask about it.

HOW TO PREPARE A RADIO COMMERCIAL

In preparing a radio commercial, your first task is to list the objectives. Remember that, just as with a print ad, there are various tactics you can use to make the sale. For example, the basic objectives may be to sell directly from your radio advertisement; to use a two-step method where all you're seeking are inquiries to which you will send a further sales package through the mail; or to support a direct mail campaign by radio advertising.

If your objective is a support campaign, be certain and test first through your primary method of selling. By testing your primary method first (say, a display advertisement), you can see the change that the support advertising coming through radio either accomplishes or does not accomplish.

Once you have decided on your objectives, you have several alternatives regarding how your advertisement is presented to your potential customer. One is straight reading by the announcer or yourself or a professional actor on tape. Another is a dialogue, sort of a conversational situation between two or more individuals. You may have heard these witty dialogue situational advertisements on the radio selling everything from magazines to wine. Finally, the third option is that of a jingle, something sung. This may or may not be applicable to the direct mail proposition you envision.

You should definitely ask the advice of the representative of the radio station with which you intend to advertise when you begin to prepare your radio commercial. The radio station can help, as indicated earlier, with the various technical and research facilities at its disposal. In addition, radio representatives may be able to get you sample cassettes that have spot commercials for you to listen to and from which you can get ideas. These are obtained through your radio station or from the Radio Advertising Bureau. In addition to the cassettes, the station may provide you with results and how these commercials were used. It is permissible for you to copy the concept, but not the word-for-word presentation. In other words, you cannot simply substitute your name and your product for those in the cassette. But you can use the same idea, approach, or concept for your advertisement.

HOW TO PREPARE YOUR RADIO COMMERCIAL

First, I should say to you *do not prepare anything yourself.* The radio station can actually prepare the entire commercial for you. If you decide to go this route, find out exactly when it is being done so that you can be there while your commercial is being prepared. If changes are necessary you can make them immediately and do not have to waste money or time by going through the full cycle of having the commercial aired before you listen to it and are dissatisfied.

If you decide to prepare the commercial yourself, use the copywriting technique outlined in Chapter 17. However, you must limit yourself greatly in your copy. A 60-second radio advertisement contains only 150 to 170 words, far less than the full-page copy in a print advertisement. As some basis for comparison, a successful Joe Sugarman ad for JS&A Sales runs to over 2,000 words. You should also be certain that the address or phone number or wherever the response is to be sent and the order instructions are repeated several times. These instructions should be extremely simple. Remember that, in most cases, your potential customer is not sitting there with paper and pencil in hand waiting to hear your ad. Once your ad is written out, you should practice reading it yourself to see at what speed you must read to complete it within the required time. You will find that if you get much above 170 words, it will be impossible for you to articulate the words properly without sounding like a high-speed jet, so watch this point very carefully.

After you have the copy completed, type it out, double-spaced, in capital letters.

At the same time, if you decide that background music or a noise is needed in your ad, indicate when this noise is to occur. The way to do this is through elapsed time. In other words, if you want automobile noises to begin during a conversational situation in your advertisement, you could indicate that automobile noises occur at 10 seconds, a honking horn at 15, or whatever, depending on the situation. Whatever your noise or music description and its timing, it must be coordinated with your copy.

RUNNING YOUR RADIO ADVERTISING CAMPAIGN

As with print advertising or direct mail, you must walk before you run. You cannot assume a success merely because you are advertising or even because the product has been successful in the past with some other medium. Therefore, start with one or two stations and expand slowly. In every case you should compare your cost per order for different stations and different times and do testing as if it were print testing. Keep very close records of these costs per order. You may be able to use them later to negotiate a lower cost or better spot with the station, or if you can't get either to improve your response, drop the station entirely from your advertising.

TELEVISION ADVERTISING

There's been an incredible growth in television advertising for mail order operators in recent years. According to Bob Stone, during a four-year period, mail order television advertising increased no less than 469 percent. It's little wonder when we consider the fact that there are more than 75,000,000 homes with televisions in the United States, and that the average viewing period per day is six hours per person. Naturally, there are some distinctive reasons for this tremendous increase in mail order television advertising, and these have to do with the advantages of advertising in this medium. They are the following:

1. The fact that you can see as well as hear the advertisement.
2. The tremendous reach of television.
3. The quick response, which equals that of radio.
4. The fact that you can demonstrate the product in action.
5. The wide range of television stations across the United States.
6. The fact that television is relatively inexpensive for testing.
7. The synergism among audio, visual, and motion effects.
8. The capacity for repeats because of video recorders and taping by potential customers.

Let's look at these advantages. The fact that you can see as well as hear the advertisement is going to increase your response. The only question is: Will it increase it enough to justify the additional cost? Because television has passed radio as the major broadcast medium, there is a tremendous reach in this market. You can get to almost your entire potential customer market through the use of television, whereas the reach of radio at maximum is only 60 percent. As noted, television is no slower than radio in response, and it has the additional advantage that you can actually demonstrate your product in action, which is extremely important for such products as a special knife that has various kitchen household uses, a jogging board that allows you to count the number of steps you've taken in your exercise program, special frying pans and pots to which food cannot adhere, and so forth. Finally, as with radio, there's a wide range of stations throughout the United States.

Many people think television's cost is prohibitive. It *is* more expensive than radio, and if you are just starting out you may have difficulty using this medium. However, according to Jim Kobs, author of *Profitable Direct Marketing,* you can advertise your product or service through television, including creating the spot, producing the advertisement, getting the talent necessary, and buying the time, for less than $10,000.

If you advertise on cable television, you can advertise for a much lower cost. In fact, if you're interested in cable television, I recommend you contact Melvin Powers at (818) 765-8579, or write him at the Wilshire Book Company, 12015 Sherman Road, North Hollywood, CA 91605. He has not only done a lot of cable TV advertising himself, but has put together a marketing company to help others.

Synergism means that the sum total of parts is greater than each separate component. Here we're talking about the synergism among the audio, visual, and motion portions of the ad. When the sound (audio), sight (visual), and movement come together, they make for a tremendously effective method of communicating your message to your potential customer.

Finally, video recorders are becoming ever more popular, and though it is possible to eliminate the commercials when using a video recorder, many people do not. This means that, while in radio the life of the ad is only that short time it is actually being heard by the potential customer, television ads may "live" much longer through taping.

DISADVANTAGES OF TELEVISION ADVERTISING

The disadvantages of television advertising are similar to those in radio, except for cost:

1. *Cost.* Television, of course, costs more than radio and so may be difficult for a new mail order dealer to use.
2. *Time.* As with radio, the amount of copy is severely limited because of time. A full-page advertisement in print may be 2,000 words. A two-minute advertisement spot in television may be only a little more than 10 percent of that figure.
3. *No Life.* Except for those instances when the advertisement is recorded on a video recorder, the ad has no life.
4. *Little Control.* As with radio, you cannot view every single ad spot in the medium to ensure that it has come out exactly as you intended it to, or that no mistake was made in the advertisement.

THE USES OF TELEVISION ADVERTISING

The uses of television advertising are basically the same as those of radio: To sell directly from your ad; to use the two-step method—that is, to send additional information on receipt of an inquiry and to sell the potential customer through this material; to support a mail order campaign conducted primarily through some other means.

If you are considering use of television as support for another type of ad campaign, you should keep in mind that such a plan is workable only if you can saturate the identical market covered by television. If you have a direct mail campaign, the area and potential customers on which that campaign is focused must cover the same market being reached by television. It has been estimated that use of television to support a direct marketing or print advertising campaign in mail order may cost an additional 10 percent of your advertising budget. On the other hand, if the support campaign is successful, it can add 30 percent or more to your sales.

THE PARADOXES OF TELEVISION ADVERTISING

There are several paradoxes in television advertising, not the least of which is the fact that, as in radio, prime time may not be the best for your advertising. If you have watched the late, late show, you are more likely to see television mail order ads then than during prime time.

Another paradox of television advertising is the fact that low ratings may actually be good for you. How can this be? Well, for one thing, a program that has a low rating also has lower ad rates. In addition to that, certain types of programs that have low ratings have viewers that are much more responsive to mail order offers. Why is this so? There are perhaps several reasons. One is that during a prime time program, a viewer may be much less likely or willing to go for a pencil and paper because he or she might miss something important. On the other hand, an old movie is much less likely to cause the viewer to be afraid to leave the screen. Further, perhaps because of these factors, as mail order ads begin to gather around certain periods of time, the viewer is more likely to be thinking about responding to mail order ads. Certain periods of television viewing are becoming much like the classified ads in magazines. Individuals looking at television at these times may already be looking for a certain type of product or something to buy. What's more, they are thus more likely to purchase through mail order.

RATINGS AND WHAT THEY ACTUALLY MEAN

Ratings are actually a measurement of household viewing. One rating point is equal to 1 percent of the households in the market. If a particular program has a 10 rating, 10 percent of all households are thought to be viewing that program. Total advertising is calculated in gross rating points, or GRPs. GRPs are the total of the ratings attributed to each of the programs or time periods. Therefore, let's say that you have two different advertisements, one appearing on a program with a 20 rating and another appearing on a program with a 30 rating. Added together that's 50 percent, or 50 GRPs. You could also add up various combinations to achieve 100 GRPs, in which case you would reach the equivalent of 100 percent of the households in that market.

HOW THE TELEVISION DAY IS DIVIDED

Just as a radio day is divided into time periods, so is the television day. The television day is in four parts: Daytime, early fringe, prime time, and late fringe. Daytime is from sign-on in the morning until 4:00 P.M. Early fringe is from 4:00 to 8:00 P.M. on weekdays and all day on weekends. Prime time, the most expensive is from 8:00 to 11:00 P.M. And finally, late fringe is from 11:00 P.M. until sign-off in the early morning hours.

Television advertising costs vary greatly, but as noted earlier, more highly rated programs will cost much more for ad time. Prime-time advertising is far more expensive than that at other times. Yet, as I said before, neither prime time nor highly rated shows may be desirable for the mail order advertiser. Keep this in mind. It is a very important principle.

According to a publication of the Fact Book Direct Market Association, most buyers of television advertising deal directly with the station and can get from 15 to 45 percent off the regular rate for direct response advertising.

HOW TO BUY TELEVISION ADVERTISING

Television advertising must be purchased by first identifying the market you're going after. The breakdown isn't quite the same as in radio, but you can get information on viewers and what they are watching, just as with radio. Again, use the American Research Bureau's *Arbitron*. The Nielsen Company also provides research information, which usually includes the population being surveyed, the number of households owning television sets, program times and their names, and the number of households, men, women, children, and adults who are estimated to be watching each of the programs listed. And don't forget the SRDS booklets.

Because television is not so segmented by market as radio and does not have as many specialized stations dealing with special interest groups, you will not be able to advertise to as precise a segment of your market as you can in radio.

TELEVISION VARIABLES YOU MUST CONSIDER
FOR YOUR ADVERTISING

Just as certain important variables exist for radio advertising, others exist for television. These include network, spot, or cable television: the station or program; the length of time; the seasonality; and the spot you select.

Use of nationwide network or spot advertising is very similar to radio. However, cable television is growing greatly and represents yet another advertising opportunity for those potential customers who are watching current movies shown through the cable television network. Station program decisions can be made through the use of the research services already mentioned. The length of time is again a variable and an important one you must consider. Your options in time for television advertising are 30, 60, and 90 seconds, and two minutes, although all of these options may not be available with every single station. Thirty seconds is not very good for direct response advertising; 60 seconds is by far the most popular; 90 seconds is a compromise between 60 and the increased cost of a two-minute advertisement. One of the longer advertisements might be necessary for a product that needs a considerable amount of demonstration or is a big-ticket item. Again, seasonality plays its part, because television also has its off season: You can expect to pay higher costs during the period of October through April. There are certain special periods when television ads will cost much less—immediately after Christmas until about January 15, from January 16 through March 1, from July 1 through August 31, and then from September 1 until the new fall programming season starts. As noted earlier, the spot you select for your advertisement will cause the cost of the ad to vary. So, an advertisement that costs $1,000 at 6:00 A.M. may cost $10,000 during prime time.

COST PRICING OPTIONS FOR TELEVISION ADVERTISING

As with radio and the print media, you have various options regarding the price you pay for your ads.

1. In prime rate, you specify the exact time you want your spot to run. You cannot be bumped.
2. One level down from this is the TAP, or total audience plan. Here you schedule your spots to run in each of the day periods, but you can be rescheduled by the station if they find a fully paid advertiser.
3. Below this is the ROS, or run of station. A run of station plan is much less specific. You buy a certain number of spots per week and the station can run them whenever it gets a chance, whenever the time slot is open. This is the least expensive.
4. PI deals are also possible in television, but very difficult to obtain. PI in television works just as it does in radio or with print advertising.
5. The bonus to pay out is another option you may find with a local station. It is also very difficult to work out, but worthwhile if you

can. In this case, you negotiate the cost as well as a certain number of orders or inquiries. The station continues to run your ad until it fulfills its contract and you obtain the number of orders or the number of inquiries stipulated in your contract.

PREPARING A TELEVISION COMMERCIAL

As with the preparation of a radio commercial, your first step is to list your objectives and decide on the strategy or tactics you want to follow to bring in the order. Once you decide this, the next step is to prepare your copy.

Television copy should be short, simple, and direct, just as the radio copy. Remember that your time is very limited. In general, have a simple theme and message, and repeat your order instructions several times. Don't forget that you have another dimension with television. The viewer, your potential customer, can see as well as hear. So when you list the order information, have it *shown*, as well as having the announcer repeat the information.

One good way to prepare your television commercial is by use of a storyboard, as shown in Figure 13.1. As you write your dialogue, indicate the sound effects where required as you did with radio. You'll also draw a little sketch of what is being shown or what the viewer would see at that time.

Video 1. Sketch of Visual and number of seconds	Video 2. Second Sketch and seconds	Video 3. Third Sketch and seconds	Video 4. Fourth Sketch and seconds
Audio 1 (Copy 1)	Audio 2 (Copy 2)	Audio 3 (Copy 3)	Audio 4 (Copy 4)
Video 5. Fifth Sketch and seconds	Video 6. Sixth Sketch and seconds	Video 7. Seventh Sketch and seconds	Video 8. Eighth Sketch and seconds
Audio 5 (Copy 5)	Audio 6 (Copy 6)	Audio 7 (Copy 7)	Audio 8 (Copy 8)
Video 9. Ninth Sketch and seconds	Video 10. Tenth Sketch and seconds	Video 11. Eleventh Sketch and seconds	Video 12. Twelfth Sketch and seconds
Audio 9 (Copy 9)	Audio 10 (Copy 10)	Audio 11 (Copy 11)	Audio 12 (Copy 12)

Figure 13.1 A storyboard for a television commercial.

The basic options in preparation of your television advertisement are a film, a videotape, or slides. Again, the station can give you a lot of help in preparing your commercial.

THE RECALL TRAP

Alvin Eicoff helped pioneer television and radio direct-response advertising. So when a man like this speaks, it would be well to listen. Eicoff says it is a mistake to rely on recall scores as a measurement of an ad's success. Recall scores are a measurement of the ability of viewers to remember a particular ad. In mail order and direct marketing, the only true measurement of an ad's success is whether a prospect responded to it or not. But Eicoff says some of his clients have been overly concerned about the recall ability of ads he has developed for them.

Eicoff makes them an unusual proposition: "I will guarantee you the highest level of recall you've ever seen or I will pay for your entire campaign," he says. He says they are always enthusiastic until he explains how he will achieve this: "I will make a sixty-second commercial with an Indian pounding a tom-tom and repeating the name of the product every three beats. At he end of the sixty seconds people watching the commercial will have switched stations, thrown an ashtray at the TV, or called the station to protest this incredibly obnoxious commercial. But no one who sees the commercial will ever forget it."[1]

TACTICS TO FOLLOW IN TELEVISION ADVERTISING

If at all possible, try to use print advertising as a basis for your television advertising campaign. Finding out what works and what doesn't and who is ordering your product will be very helpful. Definitely start in a less expensive medium before you go into television.

Start your ad initially by running it a couple of times in one week on a very limited number of stations. As with radio, expand slowly only after proved success. Bob Stone suggests watching your television advertisement very closely, and when the responses begin to decline, stop advertising right then and there. Don't try to wrench every single possible order out of that particular advertisement. The reason, again, is the high cost. According to Stone, two series of advertisements a year is maximum for most offers.

Again, after advertising is completed, you should compare the results you obtain on a cost per order basis for the various stations and ads.

[1] Alvin Eicoff, *Or Your Money Back* (New York: Crown Publishers, 1982), p. 40.

Think again about whether to change your copy, whether your advertising costs must be lowered, or whether you should change your positioning during the day, time of advertising, and so forth. And again, this is good information to use in negotiating with the station for further advertising later. If you need a certain price to break even or to make money, because you are a mail order advertiser, you may be able to negotiate this lower cost of advertising and become profitable on an ad that otherwise might be marginal.

INFOMERCIALS

The use of infomercials has been increasing rapidly since the government deregulated TV advertising, allowing longer advertisements. In 1984, infomercials generated only a million dollars in sales. By 1994, infomercials generated a billion dollars in sales. What are infomercials? Infomercials are those thirty minute long advertisements you may have seen on Saturday, Sunday, or late at night that are intended to inform, entertain, and sell. The heroes of this form of mail order are entrepreneurs like Tony Robbins who sold $100 million in tapes one year, or Susan Powter who "stopped the insanity" and sold 80,000 of her weight reduction tapes in one month.

There is a lot of potential in infomercials for the mail order entrepreneur, but the risks are great and the investment not insignificant. For testing alone, you can expect to spend $25,000 to test in ten cities plus one national cable channel and that does not include your production and other costs. However, if you have a great idea, you may be able to find a company to joint venture the idea with you. Susan Powter went to five companies which said no before she finally found someone to work with.

If you are interested in exploring this high end of mail order, there is a National Infomercial Marketing Association (NIMA) at 1201 New York Avenue, NW Suite 1000, Washington, D.C. 20005. Contact them for additional information. Also, Infinnity Productions, Inc. has been giving seminars for beginners. You can contact them at 345 North Maple Drive, Suite 184, Beverly Hills, CA 90210 (310) 777-0100.

SUMMARY

In this chapter, we've covered broadcast media in some detail. Don't forget it as an important mail order tactic. And when you'd like to try some to these methods, refer back to this chapter. You'll be able to prepare your own commercials and run your own campaigns with minimum help and minimum cost, but with maximum effectiveness.

14

Making Money with Your Telephone

GIANT PROFITS THROUGH TELEPHONE
MAIL ORDER ADVERTISING

The advent of the WATS line, which stands for *wide area telephone service* and reaches nationwide, has been one of the main motivating forces in an explosion of telephone advertising over the last 20 years. In fact, telephone advertisers are currently making a little less than three billion calls a year to sell products and services over the telephone, which the customer then receives by mail.

There are decided advantages to telephone advertising, including:

1. Quick response, equal to that of television or radio.
2. The feedback that you can get from the potential customer while selling.
3. The usually higher response rate through telephone over direct mail, print advertising, or broadcast media.

Quick response is greater in telephone advertising and is, of course, an advantage over print advertising or direct mail. But the verbal feedback is possible with no other medium used for mail order. The telephone is very similar to a face-to-face selling situation, and the higher response rate can be termed truly incredible. One campaign, reported by Jim Kobs for an industrial product, produced 10.1 percent immediate orders, 46.2 percent future orders, and finally, 8.8 percent leads for salespeople. In other words, the success rate for the telephone calls exceeded 65 percent!

Murray Roman, who wrote *Telephone Marketing: How to Build Your Business by Telephone* and pioneered the use of taped messages by phone, once described a membership campaign that failed through direct mail but led to a preorder rate of better than 80 percent through the use of telephone mail order marketing.

BASIC USES OF TELEMARKETING

The three basic uses for telemarketing are order generation, either directly or through the two-step method; obtaining sales leads; and support for other campaigns being conducted by broadcast media or print media.

There are two basic tactics to be considered. One is delivery: Should the delivery of the telephone message be done totally live or partially live and partially by tape? Both totally live and live by tape delivery have proven extremely effective. The use of tape is particularly useful when a celebrity is involved, or someone who is of importance to the individual being telephoned. In this case, the individual making the telephone call can ask whether the recipient of the call could stand by for a message from, for example, a political figure asking for support during a campaign. Assuming the answer is yes, a short, taped message, asking, say, for a contribution of funds, is played. The live voice then comes back on to make the close and solicit the donation.

The second tactic is timing, which is very important when the telephone is used as a support medium. Is the telephone call made prior to the potential customer's receiving a direct mail package or being exposed to broadcast or print media, or should it be done after he or she has already received the package, or should it be done simultaneously? Each has its advantages and disadvantages. If you are calling before, you are prepping the individual to receive the other message through the other medium, and you depend then on the other medium to make the close. If you are calling afterward, you are trying to mop up those customers who have not already ordered and make the close through direct person-to-person contact by telephone. If you call simultaneously when the individual is to receive the direct mail package or be exposed to other media, you are looking for an overwhelming effect in which the combination will serve to get the individual to order.

COST OF A TELEPHONE MARKETING CAMPAIGN

The cost of a telephone marketing campaign is not low. According to the Direct Marketing Association, the estimated cost per 1,000 calls is from $750 to $5,000, several times the cost of a direct mail campaign. On the other hand, for items costing from $7 to $2,000, the response has been 3 percent to 40 percent. If you recall that a direct mail campaign response rate for breakeven is usually much lower, you can see just how successful telephone marketing can really be.

HOW TO BE SUCCESSFUL WITH TELEPHONE MAIL ORDER MARKETING

Success in telephone direct marketing rests on three major points: The ability to sell face to face (or in this case voice to voice), calls per time period, and ability to deal with rejection.

Because telephoning is a sales situation in which you're involved with person-to-person contact, the individual making the call must be a salesperson. One salesperson estimated that it is twice as difficult to sell by voice as it is face to face. On the other hand, you can reach 10 times as many people by telephone as you can through running around and seeing them on a face-to-face, person-to-person basis.

If the individual who's making the call talks too fast, he or she is apt to be distrusted and may not be understood. On the other hand, if he or she talks too slowly, it is annoying to the individual who is being sold and it also means that the salesperson will make fewer calls per time period.

I mentioned that a friend of mine has a seminar company and is extremely happy with a return on direct mailing of .25 percent. With that return he has built up a $2 million-a-year business, and he isn't despondent at all about the fact that 99.75 percent of the invitations he sends to people are rejected. On the other hand, the telephone, which has a much higher acceptance rate, will involve a personal rejection on a daily basis, day in and day out, and the ability of the individual who's making these calls to take this rejection will, to a large degree, determine your success.

SCRIPTING

Scripting your message ahead of time can greatly increase your response, or it can significantly decrease it. A script is simply your advertisement laid out in the exact form it will be spoken to your prospect. The idea behind scripting is to write the best copy you can and get it down in black and white. That way, you make the major impact you can. At the same time, individuals who are unfamiliar with your product can still sell it over the phone.

That's the theory. Now here's the problem. Reading a script frequently sounds forced and unnatural. "Good morning, Mr. _____." (Pause) "How are you feeling this morning?" Your prospect's sales resistance and irritation goes up and it's unlikely that a sale will be made.

Also, scripting is no substitute for training. You can have the greatest script in the world, and if it's spoken by someone who hasn't been trained properly, you're going to end up with a very poor response.

This doesn't mean that I don't believe in scripting. I do, but the person who is going to use your script must be trained to sound natural while using it.

If you're going to speak yourself, or those you employ have been well trained, you might consider an outline rather than a word for word script. That allows the telemarketer more flexibility and will sound more natural.

I am also against the standard openers used by 90 percent of the telemarketing salespeople. That's the one I gave you above. It's just too, too old and immediately sets up sales resistance in the prospect. A better way is to write a dialog just as if you were writing an ad. Skip ahead and look at the Karbo ad in Figure 17.3. Karbo might have sold his book by calling up by telephone. His script might have started off like this: "Mr. _____, most people are too busy earning a living to make any money . . ."

Finally, if you are selling by telephone, for goodness sake, be enthusiastic. If you're not enthusiastic about your product, no one else is going to be either. I heard a story somewhere which illustrates this very well. Imagine you are driving on the freeway and you suddenly spot stacks of yellow metal bricklike objects by the side of the road. You pull your vehicle to a screeching stop. Sure enough, it's the real thing . . . it's gold! You load as much of this gold as you can in your car, but it fills your trunk, the back seat, and the front seat. You barely have enough room to sit down, and still most of the gold is stacked outside. You rush to the phone to call a friend to bring a truck. Now the question. Do you ask him to bring a vehicle "if you have time?" I doubt it. You are probably excited and enthusiastic. And that's the way you or anyone else must be when selling by telling and following a script.

SHOULD YOU DO A DIRECT TELEPHONE CAMPAIGN YOURSELF?

It is possible for you to do a telephone mail order campaign yourself, but it is not easy. It depends on the consideration of a number of different things including:

1. *Your Own Training.* Are you the sales type and can you take rejection? If you have done a great deal of face-to-face selling and you have the time, it's possible for you to be your own direct caller and make a fortune through telephone calls combined with mail order.
2. *A WATS Line.* A WATS line costs money to rent. Can you afford to maintain one during the period of your campaign?

3. *Legal Requirements.* There are various legal requirements to be met in each state regarding calls made directly into a person's home or business and selling through the telephone. You must be aware of all of them because you will be responsible.

4. *Time.* Is making these direct calls yourself the best expenditure of your time? Or is it better for you to be planning, preparing copy, or just plain thinking? If you decide you want someone else to handle telephone marketing for you, you can locate a telephone marketing operation through your telephone book, through the classified advertising pages of *Direct Marketing, Target Marketing,* or other direct marketing magazines. Also check *Teleprofessional,* 209 West Fifth Street, Suite N, Waterloo, IA 50701-5420. You can also check with your local direct marketing organization listed in Appendix C.

SUMMARY

In this chapter, we have discussed telemarketing. The important points to remember are these:

1. The advantages and disadvantages of telemarketing, and when to use it.
2. What you have to do to run a successful telephone campaign.
3. Whether you should run a telephone campaign yourself or have someone else run it.

Do not overlook telemarketing. It can be used alone, or along with other media to multiply your success.

15

Making Money with Your Own Mail Order Catalog

CATALOGS ARE YOUR TICKET TO MAIL ORDER SUCCESS

Catalogs are certainly one way to reach success in mail order selling. They are advantageous in ways unmatched by other methods of mail order selling. Earlier in this book we discussed how repeat business will create big profits for you. The use of catalogs will result in that repeat business and will allow you to amortize the selling expense of all the items offered in one mailing. The importance of this amortization is easily seen in a comparison with a campaign in which you have only one product to offer. Each mailing containing your promotion costs a certain amount. It takes a certain fixed amount of money to stuff and mail the envelopes and do everything else associated with placing the promotional material advertising your product in the hands of your prospective customer. Now compare that with being able to offer 10, 20, 30, 50, 100, or more products to your customer simultaneously. The cost of this mailing may change very little, perhaps only by a few cents, depending upon the cost of the catalog itself. But instead of offering one product to your customer, you offer many. In addition, you have increased your chances of receiving higher dollar amounts from a single order.

There are many, many people who have succeeded in mail order through the use of catalogs, and three of them are worth noting here because two have written books specializing in this aspect of mail order. One is Roger Horchow, who once worked for Neiman-Marcus and wrote the book *Elephants in Your Mailbox,* published by Times Books. The second is Gerardo Joffe, who founded both Haverhills and Henniker's in San

Francisco and wrote *How You Too Can Make at Least $1 Million (but Probably Much More) in the Mail Order Business.* But certainly one of the greatest successes was Len Carlson, who, with a rubber stamp bearing a person's name and address, a product still sold, founded Sunset House, which grew to be perhaps the greatest of the specialty catalog houses.

WHAT CATALOGS DO FOR YOUR CUSTOMER

Clearly there must be some major advantage to catalog ordering or catalogs would not be so successful. Here are just a few.

Easier than Store Ordering

Ordering through a catalog is much easier than store ordering today. There is no hassle with salesclerks, waiting your turn in line, finding a parking place, and generally getting worn out through a full day's shopping downtown. With the increase in gasoline prices, it is also probably less expensive to order through a catalog than in a retail store.

Shopping at Leisure

Using you catalog, your potential customer can sit back, relax, and browse through the various types of merchandise you are offering. Further, your potential customer does this at ease for as long as he or she wants, being unhampered by store opening or closing hours, traffic, or the need to be somewhere else shortly.

Material All in One Place

Through the use of a catalog, especially a catalog dealing with a specialized type of merchandise, your potential customer sees all the different things he or she may be interested in gathered in one place. In many cases, it would be impossible to gather all the merchandise offered in a catalog under one roof in a normal retail store. But in a catalog, it is possible, and the millions of customers who purchase through catalogs realize this.

Hard-to-Get Material Available

In some cases, your potential customer realizes that the products seen in a catalog cannot be purchased anywhere else. For this reason, your catalog is eagerly awaited and orders frequently come in almost immediately after your customer receives your mailing. This is one of the primary reasons I buy from catalogs. In a catalog I found a rare book I had looked for for years after I had written numerous bookstores and others in an unsuccessful attempt to locate it. Last week I received a specialized catalog covering books on a certain topic. Not only was the book I was looking for advertised, but a new reprint of the book was offered at a much lower price than that of the original edition.

Thorough Product Description

Today, in the hustle and bustle of shopping in stores, few merchants or salespeople have the time—or seem to enjoy—explaining in detail the various products offered for sale. Many would prefer that you buy now and ask questions later. But in a catalog, the space is available to explain your product in some detail, and your potential customer appreciates it. Indeed, it is almost a paradox that though the customer cannot see or touch the product at the time of ordering, he or she frequently understands far more about it and what it can and cannot do than a person who goes to purchase a similar item in a store.

For all of the above reasons, catalog selling in mail order is growing at an astronomical rate. In fact, although there is a growth in retail selling that roughly follows the increase in population, catalog selling is growing at twice the rate of selling through retail stores.

THE INCREDIBLY WIDE SPECTRUM OF CATALOGS

Catalogs represent an extremely wide spectrum of products and items. A catalog can be a single sheet typed at a typewriter and reproduced by a cheap offset process, or it can be extremely expensive, glossy, and multicolored, intended for a customer market segment that drives Rolls Royces and jets around the world. We're going to look at some examples of different catalogs and the products they sell. Note the differences in layout, in how the catalogs are structured, in artwork, and in various other aspects that depend upon the intended market, the prices of the products, the cost of the catalog, and, of course, the types of product that are offered for sale. Figure 15.1 started as a simple black and white catalog for computer users, today it's multicolor. It's from MEI/Micro Center, 1100 Steelwood Road, Columbus, OH 43212.

Figure 15.2 is from one of the fabulous catalogs for high-technology electronics products put out by Joe Sugarman's JS&A, One JS&A Plaza, Northbrook, IL 60062. This catalog is printed on slick paper and is in black and white, as well as color. Each and every product offered in the catalog has a full page of technical information. To read it is an education by itself. Figure 15.3 is a page from Massachusetts Army & Navy Store,

Standard In Bulk Diskettes!

3.5" DS/DD Diskettes
(1 MB Unformatted)
For Duplicators • OEM's •
All Computer Users

GOLD SEAL™ QUALITY CERTIFIED

As Low As

28¢ each

SKU# 700302

3.5" DS/DD Quality Gold Seal Diskette Special Quantity Pricing

28¢ each for 1000 or more   **In Lots of 25**
29¢ each for 300 or more
32¢ each for 150 or more   **Lifetime Warranty**
33¢ each for 25 or more

Shipping: 60¢ per 25 diskettes
• Unformatted Capacity: 1MB DS/DD Diskettes • Sold in lots of 25 • 3.5" DS/HD Shipping - 60¢ per 25 Diskettes • 3.5" User Labels (SKU# 8707): add $1.50 per pack of 50 labels; contains yellow, green, blue, red, & gray - 10 of each color (Shipping: 10¢ per 50 labels)

★ **Save Even More...**
Order in master carton quantities of 500 diskettes and pay shipping charges of only $4.00 per carton

3.5" DS/HD Quality Gold Seal Diskette Special Quantity Pricing

34¢ each for 1000 or more   **In Lots of 25**
36¢ each for 300 or more
38¢ each for 150 or more   **Lifetime Warranty**
39¢ each for 25 or more

Shipping: 60¢ per 25 diskettes
• Unformatted Capacity: 2MB DS/HD Diskettes • Sold in lots of 25 • 3.5" DS/HD Shipping - 60¢ per 25 Diskettes • 3.5" User Labels (SKU# 8707): add $1.50 per pack of 50 labels; contains yellow, green, blue, red, & gray - 10 of each color (Shipping: 10¢ per 50 labels)

★ **Save Even More...**
Order in master carton quantities of 500 diskettes and pay shipping charges of only $4.00 per carton

3.5" DS/HD Diskettes
(2 MB Unformatted)
For Duplicators • OEM's •
All Computer Users

GOLD SEAL™ QUALITY CERTIFIED

As Low As

34¢ each

SKU# 691352

Duplicators: These diskettes are manufactured specifically for your business; offering you high grade, high yield performance at great prices!

End Users: This product is ideal for you as well because now you can buy the best quality disks at standard grade prices. Buy the best for less!

MEI Takes The Diskette Business Very Seriously!

• MEI has once again set a new higher standard in the bulk diskette business! Now you can buy "DUPLICATOR/HIGH GRADE" Diskettes for less than our competitors charge for "Standard Grade" Diskettes. MEI offers the highest quality grade available - product that software duplicators require. This means that the highest quality is now more affordable than ever!
• MEI is known in the diskette manufacturing industry as having the most stringent quality requirements. Here are just a few of the important things MEI does for you to ensure consistent high quality • We have our own factory qualification process • We buy only from a few select factories that meet all of our quality requirements • We have an incoming Quality Control department that ensures product shipped to us meets our requirements. We have a 100% Satisfaction Guarantee that covers every disk on every order.
• MEI is constantly striving to provide better products and value to you. Your data, time and money is simply too important for us not to take seriously.

We Don't Promise You Quality... We Guarantee It!!! 19
For complete ordering & shipping information, refer to page 13 & the insert flap between pages 26 & 27.

MEI/Micro Center™ Call Now!! **1-800-634-3478**

Figure 15.1   A page from MEI/Micro Center's catalog.

Boston, MA 02134, a catalog for military collectors. Figure 15.4 is a page from a catalog that contains literally hundreds of different pieces of cutlery from Atlanta Cutlery, 2143 Gees Mill Road, Box 839, Conyers, GA 30207. You can see from this catalog why someone who is interested in buying a knife would rather go here than to a retail store. Few retail

COLLECTOR'S CORNER

HELMET SET. Genuine U.S. Surplus. Any vet who's ever served in wartime conditions knows the benefit of wearing one of these. Plastic helmet liner fits inside steel pot, camouflage cotton cover completes the set. A real collector's item. Condition: very good/used. **MHB005 $20.00**

WWII HISTORIC HELMET SETS. Genuine U.S. Surplus. These were originally intended for issue to the U.S. Marine Corps personnel assigned to the newly commissioned battleship U.S.S. Wisconsin in 1943, yet never used. Each one includes rough, sand finished O.D. green steel pot with khaki chin strap, helmet liner with leather chin strap, HBT sweatband holder, leather sweatband, and HBT chin strap. Own a piece of history. **MEB155 $39.75**

A. BOSUN'S WHISTLE. This beautiful brass and copper whistle, still used by Her Majesty's boatswains, is only the beginning. You'll also receive an instruction booklet to help you quickly master the basic use of this instrument. Then you'll be free to master the 10 calls of the Royal Navy (we've included these instructions, too.) Whistle is 4¾" long. Chain included. **MEB032 $6.00**

B. BRASS SCOTLAND YARD WHISTLE. Genuine British Surplus. Steeped in the prestige and tradition of London's police organization, this instrument is crafted by England's famous Acme City. Nickel-plated brass 3¼" long, it is a wonderful collector's item for the detective buff. **MEB031 $5.50**

WWI 11-POCKET GRENADE VEST. Genuine U.S. Surplus. 11 identically sized pockets, (6 top, 5 bottom) designed to hold the grenades of the Great War. Each pocket features a chocolate brown snap button. Light brown colored canvas, typical of its time. Collectors: don't miss out on this one! Condition: new/unused. **MVB006 $12.00**

TO ORDER CALL TOLL-FREE
1-800-343-7749
(In Mass. call 617-783-1250.)
MASS FAX 617-254-6607

VISA **AMERICAN EXPRESS** **MasterCard**

W.W.II TELEPHONE. Genuine U.S. Surplus. Get back to basics with these EE-8 military field phones. They're the real thing and in guaranteed working condition. The only version issued from 1937 to 1957. Comes in their own original government carrying case with attached shoulder strap. Each phone operates on two D-cell batteries (not included) and a hand crank ringing mechanism. The only other requirements are connecting wire and at least one other phone! Telephones measure approximately 8"W × 10"H × 4"D, and weigh about 12 pounds. TM11-333 manual included. Condition: used in working order. **MEB850 Single $120.00** **MEB852 1 pair $225.00**

U.S. M-7 LEATHER 45 CAL. HOP HOLSTER. Genuine U.S. Surplus. Sturdy black saddle leather. Button-down. "U.S." imprint. For regular or pistol belt. Condition: new. Supply limited. **MEB008 $26.50**

A. U.S. NAVY STORAGE BOX. Genuine U.S. Surplus. 9½" × 4¼" steel box with a dozen divided spaces and interior bump protective top and bottom. Dividers remove to enlarge storage spaces. Condition: good/used. **MEB107 $5.00**
B. ARMED FORCES VIDEO BOX. Genuine U.S. Surplus. Video boxes will provide years of virtually indestructable service. Each case is shipped complete with foam inner padding for protection of contents, metal reinforced stress points, and carry handle. Can accommodate up to six videos. Will work equally well for a variety of other loads. Outside dimensions: 8½"h × 11"w × 9½"d. Condition: Used/excellent. **MEB849 $25.00**
BRITISH W.W.I. TOMMY HELMET. Genuine U.K. Surplus. (Shown left.) Vintage memorabilia from the Great War. Condition: excellent/used. **MHB004 $12.50**

Figure 15.3 From Mass Army & Navy Store's catalog of military collectibles and surplus.

merchants can profitably stock such a wide variety of products. Figure 15.5 shows a catalog published by the Worldwide Treasure Bureau, 2230 W. Sunnyside Ave., Suite 2, Box 5012, Visalia, CA 93278-5012. These products are rare artifacts. The figure shows rare coins. Did you think you had to buy stationery from your local printer? Figure 15.6 is one page from a multicolored catalog put out by The Writewell Co., 942 Transit Building, 5850 W. 80th St., P.O. Box 68186, Indianapolis, IN

Used by warriors from Persia to the Philippines for hundreds of years, these are the lightning fast, grimly effective, close quarter combat knives that emerged from centuries of use. They're made of hand forged, high carbon steel in India by the government contractor for military knives.

(A) Qama–with its long needle point on a 17½" long, double edge blade, the Qama is a deadly close combat design that dates back to the Roman Short Sword. Favored for quick, pierce and slash movements, the Qama was used with success by the Cossacks and Northern Persians. Considered to be the national weapon of Soviet Georgia. Buffalo horn handle scales. Overall length–22½".
#1-170......Reg. $42.00......$32.95

(B) Kindjal–*Stone's Glossary* calls the Kindjal "the inseparable companion of every man in the Caucasus...Decidedly dangerous in the hands of one who knows how to use it, more suitable for attack than for show, giving terrible, often mortal, wounds, at once knife, hatchet, cork screw, if necessary a paper cutter, accessory of the dance, the Kindjal is the offensive and defensive weapon *par excellence* of the Caucasus." The 16¼" long, 1½" wide, double edge blade has deep blood gutters on each side. Buffalo horn handle. Overall length–22".
#1-255......$29.95

(C) Khyber–known as the "Defender Of The Afghan Homeland" for centuries. Carried by the Pathan Freedom Fighters of the Khyber Pass area of Afghanistan. 18" long, 1⅛" wide blade has a ⅜" thick T-rib for exceptional strength. Genuine horn handle with iron bolster. Overall length–24½".
#1-127......Reg. $37.95......$29.95

(D) Choora–close combat knife designed when men wore armour of mail. The ⅜" wide T-shaped blade back provides excellent thrusting power. Carried by the Mujahadeen Freedom Fighters of Afghanistan. The 11¼" long blade is 1½" wide at the hilt. Polished horn grips. Overall length–16".
#1-153......Reg. $29.95......$23.95

(E) Jambiya–the hooking point perfectly suits the whirling style of knife fighting that Arab fighters perfected. Adopted everywhere the Moslems fought, the Jambiya became the most widely used fighting knife in the world. The 8¾" long blade has a ¼" thick, protruding mid-rib which reinforces the point. Buffalo horn handle with nickel silver medallions tooled with traditional Arab geometric decorations. Overall length–13".
#1-154......$49.95

(F) Philippine Kris–during the Philippine Insurrection, the fierce Moro warriors shocked the U.S. Army when the .38 S & W revolver failed to stop their charges. Their favored edged weapon was this Kris dagger. The 12¼" long blade has a curled integral crossguard, a steel bolster and a buffalo horn handle faithful to the original. Overall length–16½".
#3-253......$29.95

Figure 15.4   A page from Atlanta Cutlery's catalog of knives.

Worldwide Treasure Bureau Fixed-Price Offers (Prices valid until March 1, 1994)

A coin of the signer of the Magna Carta!

King John ruled England from 1199 to 1216 (during the time of Robin Hood!). Under the English custom of primogenitor (whereby the oldest son inherits the entire estate and the titles of his father), the younger son John was left with no land inheritance, giving him his first nickname of "Lackland."

However, during his reign, King John earned another even less desirable nickname: Softsword. This referred to his lack of control over his subjects and came about after he ran away from a fight for power which he had instigated with the King of France. He was looked upon with disdain and was the laughingstock of all England.

Rebellious subjects, led by Barons who had been heavily taxed without any representation in the government, captured London in 1215. King John could see that he was hopelessly defeated and was in a real jam. Rather than fighting on, he reluctantly agreed to sign the Magna Carta (Latin for "Great Charter"), drafted by his enemies. This was not just a peace treaty, but one of the most important documents in the history of basic human rights— guaranteeing all English subjects due process under the law. This was a big improvement over the way things had been under earlier kings, where many subjects were considered no more than the property of the Crown, disposable at the whim of any noble.

This treaty has since been hailed as the predecessor of the Declaration of Independence and the Bill of Rights. However, John considered his signing of this great document to have been a tremendous humiliation, and he immediately began fighting to have it overturned. He died a frustrated death the following year, but the concessions he granted live on in England and America today.

In the spirit of Robin Hood, Worldwide Treasure Bureau is now redistributing the wealth of King John in the form of 700-year-old Short Cross silver pennies minted during his reign. The obverse features a facing portrait bust of the king. The reverse has a cross in the style of the crusaders, of whom John's older brother Richard the Lionheart, was the most famous.

These coins were hand-struck ("hammered") and are in about Fine condition. This is an excellent opportunity to acquire an affordable coin from the king who signed the Great Charter which forever changed the course of western civilization. We have a small handful of pieces in stock at this price, and they will be sold on a first-come, first-served basis. On the obverse of the coin is a facing portrait bust of the king, and on the reverse is a cross.

Actual size

Short Cross Silver Penny of John I (1199-1216), the signer of the Magna Carta, in Fine condition
Item #F-120 . . . . **$375**

The Coins of Shah Jahan, Builder of the Taj Mahal

Mumtaz Mahal was Shah Jahan's favorite wife, constant companion, and valued political advisor as he built his powerful Mughal Empire. Also adored by the people, she gave alms to the poor, fed the hungry, and maintained lists of widows and orphans to see that care was constantly provided for them.

Tragedy struck in 1631, when Mumtaz died while giving birth to their 14th child. Shah Jahan was shattered. Building the Taj Mahal was his way of paying tribute to the woman he loved, and it took more than twenty years to complete. This graceful mausoleum is

considered by many to be the most beautiful building in existence.

The Taj Mahal was not only a physical tribute to his wife, but a spiritual one as well. The water that reflects the dome is a symbol of purity, while the dome itself represents heaven. Since paradise was seen as a mirror-image of this world, the reflection of the dome in the water was a reminder of these teachings to the people.

The Shah was planning to build an identical Taj Mahal, in black stone, next to the white one, with a reflecting pool between. This was to have been his own mausoleum, but he died before he could start this project, and was buried next to Mumtaz Mahal.

The coins we are offering are silver rupees minted under Shah Jahan from 1628 to 1658. They are fascinating in their design and in their history. Due to a special purchase, they have the added advantage of being quite inexpensive, and make terrific gifts.

Actual size

Silver Rupee of Shah Jahan, Builder of the Taj Mahal
Item #F-121 . . . . **$49 each**
Item #F-122 (3 or more) . . . **$44 each**

Framed Display, with a Silver Rupee of Shah Jahan, Builder of the Taj Mahal, parchment-printed history, and Certificate of Authenticity
Item #F-123 . . . . **$89.50 each**

12

Figure 15.5 Rare coins from the World of Treasure Bureau.

Writewell®
Bargain Box
Stationery

Large Quantity, Good Quality, and Low Price are features of this great value. Handsome gift box contains 100 sheets (size 5 3/4" x 7 3/4") that fit with one fold into 100 pointed flap envelopes. Both sheets and envelopes are printed with name and address, in rich blue ink, from a pleasing typeface, on 2 or 3 neatly centered lines. Paper is good quality vellum: medium weight (basis 24-lb.). Suits both airmail and regular letters. Perfect for pen or typewriter. Available in your choice of white or blue paper. Makes a marvelous gift.

L700-2WH   White;
    100 Sheets, 100 Env..$29.95
L700-2BL   Blue;
    100 Sheets, 100 Env....29.95
L700-NP   50 Non-Personalized
    Sheets.............5.95

> Order Toll Free
> TEL: 1-800-968-5850
> FAX: 1-800-329-1669

Writewell®
Memo Sheets in Desk Tray

Useful for Home or Office! Attractive acrylic Desk Tray with memo sheets, size 3 3/4" x 5 3/4", of good quality white paper. Each sheet is personalized, in rich blue ink, with one line in an elegant type.

L19-1   200 Memos $27.95
L19-2   400 Memos..41.95

NOTE: Attractive Acrylic Tray included . . . A $7.00 Value!

Palmetto
Self-Seal
Stationery

Our finest, heavy-weight envelopes are self-sealing and handsomely print lined in navy blue for maximum message privacy. Perfect for check mailing and general correspondence. Your name and address in navy ink on envelope flaps and the optionally available 6" x 7" lettersheets

L473-1   100 Envelopes,
    100 Sheets $31.95
L473-2   200 Envelopes
    200 Sheets........47.95
L473E-1   200 Envelopes
    Alone................35.95
L473E-2   400 Envelopes
    Alone................53.95
L473-NP   50 Plain Sheets ...9.95

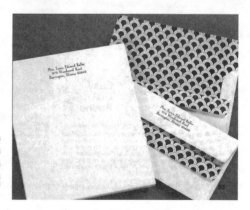

Figure 15.6   Stationery from the Writewell Company.

46268-0186. Figure 15.7 is a page from a catalog titled "Things You Never Knew Existed . . ." put out by Johnson Smith, 4514 19th St. Court East, P.O. Box 25500, Bradenton, FL 34206-5500. Is good health your concern? Take a look at Figure 15.8, which is a page from the L & H Vitamins, Inc. catalog of natural foods, vitamins, and health aids. This company is located at 37-10 Crescent Street, Long Island City, NY 11101. You can imagine how this catalog must supplement retail sales. Figure 15.9 is part of a very famous catalog from Edmund Scientific Co., 101 Gloucester Pike, Barrington, NJ 08007-1380. Edmund Scientific started with just a few pages some years ago and today lists more than 4,000 scientific products for hobbyists, schools, and industry in this catalog, which contains more than 112 pages. Do you make presentations or give seminars? Figure 15.10 is from the unique catalog put out by Damark, 7101 Winnetica Ave., P.O. Box 2990, Minneapolis, MN 55429-0908. Their catalog contains hundreds of liquidation and close-out products of every type. Do you like videos? Figure 15.11 shows a catalog put out by Video Yesteryear, Box C, Sandy Hook, CT 06482. Are you a sportsman? Take a look at Figure 15.12 from The Sportsman's Guide, 411 Farwell Ave. So., St. Paul, MN 55075-0239. This catalog features everything for the sportsman and every item is displayed in color. Figure 15.13 is from Tiger Software, One Datran Center, Suite 1500, 9100 S. Dadeland Blvd., Miami, FL 33156. This is a catalog of computers, computer programs, supplies, and accessories. Figure 15.14 is perhaps the most fabulous of all: Neiman-Marcus of Dallas, TX 75221-2960. The page shown is in full color and is, of course, printed on the highest quality glossy paper available. Some items sell for several hundreds of thousands of dollars. And you thought you couldn't sell high-priced items by mail! However, the items on this page are $25 or less. Do you remember Lilian Vernon and the simple ad shown in Chapter One? Well, Figure 15.15 shows a page from today's Lilian Vernon catalog from Virginia Beach, VA 23479-0002. You can even buy flowers through catalogs, as the Michigan Bulb Company, 1950 Waldorf, Grand Rapids, MI 49550 demonstrates in Figure 15.16. Or if you're hungry, consider almonds from the House of Almonds, P.O. Box 11125, Bakersfield, CA 93389 (Figure 15.17). If you need tools of any type, consult the catalog put out by Leichtung Workshops, 4944 Commerce Parkway, Cleveland, OH 44128, in Figure 15.18. In Figure 15.19 you'll find a page from DAK Industries Inc., 8200 Remmet Ave., Canoga Park, CA 91304. This catalog always contains interesting items. Figure 15.20 is from the Daughters of the US Army Gift Shop, West Point Museum, West Point, NY 10996. Yes, even West Point (my alma mater) does mail order! Finally, Figure 15.21 is a page from the catalog of one of my former students, Jeff Schmidt. His company, Schmidt-Cannon, imports hundreds of items from all over the

Figure 15.7 A page from "Things You Never Knew Existed . . ."

Figure 15.8   Items available from L & H Vitamins, Inc.

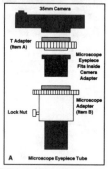

DIRECT PHOTOGRAPHY:
STILL CAMERA TO MICROSCOPE

A) 35MM CAMERA TO MICROSCOPE ADAPTERS
Diagram indicates the arrangement of your 35mm camera and two required adapters for taking pictures through your microscope.

Item A): See "T" adapter listing below for the stock number and price of the correct adapter for your specific camera brand.

Item B): Microscope adapter locks on the eyepiece tube. Microscope's eyepiece fits through the adapter and sits in normal position, utilizing the original optical system of the microscope. Black anodized all metal construction. Instructions included. 30mm I.D.
Microscope Adapter   H41,100 $39.95

B) INSTANT PHOTOGRAPH MICROSCOPE CAMERA
Produce instant Polaroid pictures with your microscope. Our special camera fits virtually all standard monocular, binocular and trinocular microscopes. Accepts all Polaroid film packs in the 100 and 600 series (color and black & white). Comes complete with universal instrument adapter, focusing tube, cable release and comprehensive instructions (16 pages). The quality is excellent because the camera utilizes the optical system of your microscope. Film and microscope not included. Yields 3¼" x 4¼" photograph. Excellent resolution.
Instant Microscope Camera   H31,825 $300.00

DIRECT VIDEO:
VIDEO CAMERA TO MICROSCOPE

A) Original Relay Lens System   B) New Relay Lens System

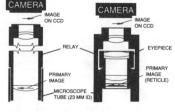

TYPICAL VIDEO-MICROSCOPY SET-UP

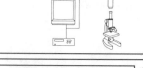

A) ORIGINAL RELAY LENS SYSTEM
Our original Relay Lens System was designed to replace your microscope eyepiece, it is approximately equivalent to a 10X eyepiece. The entire assembly fits into microscope eyepiece tubes designed to accept 23mm O.D. International Standard eyepieces. Works on any microscope with a tube length of 160mm to 170mm. The relay lens barrel has an external "C" thread at the opposite end to screw directly into your video camera.
Relay Lens System   H37,820 $225.00

B) IMPROVED ADJUSTABLE RELAY LENS SYSTEM
• **Utilizes Microscope Eyepiece**
• **Can Be Used With Reticle Eyepieces**
• **Assures Exact Power Specification**
• **Adjustable To Specific Camera Differences**

Our second generation relay lens incorporates several improvements to assure more exact adherence to magnification requirements and to allow for the small differential in mounting collar to image chip in different camera designs. The new system utilizes the eyepiece supplied with your microscope, it will accept only 23mm O.D. International Standard eyepieces.

We recommend a 10X eyepiece for which the system is maximized but it will work with other powers. The entire assembly then slips over your microscope's eyepiece tube and locks in place with a thumb screw. At the opposite end, the external "C" mount screws directly into your camera. A fine screw allows the internal lens system to be moved very slightly to adjust for your specific brand video camera and to calibrate a reticle, if in use.
Dimensions overall are 90mmL x 36mm Diameter. Reticle-type eyepieces are available through our Optical Catalog.
Adjustable Relay Lens System   H39,925 $225.00

A) SPECIFIC BRAND CAMERA TO "T" ADAPTER
One side has an external (male) screw(S) thread or bayonet (B) base to fit into your specific brand 35mm camera, the opposite side has an internal (female) "T" thread to accept our photo relay lens and other photo accessories.
Each: $19.95   *Specify Stock Number For Your Camera Type:

FITTING TYPE:			B = Bayonet S = Screw
Universal Thread Mount (S)	H42,832		
All SLR Minolta Models (B)	H42,834		
Leica (S)	H42,838		
Nikon (B)	H42,835	Konica (B)	H31,517
Canon (B)	H42,836	Olympus (B)	H42,837
Yashica (B)	H31,516	Pentax, All K&M, Ricoh, Vivitar, Chinon (B)	H42,833
Minolta Maxxum - for auto focus (B)	H37,819		

B) VIDEO "C" TO PHOTO "T" ADAPTER
External (male) "C" thread for video on one side, internal (female) "T" thread on opposite side to accept photo accessories.
Video To Photo Adapter   H38,114 $31.95 | 27 |

Figure 15.9   Some products sold through the Edmund Scientific catalog.

Figure 15.10 Closeout products from Damark.

SERIALS

Coming To A Video Recorder Near You!

Mystery Mountain

Ken Maynard and his Wonder Horse Tarzan
Who is "The Rattler" and why is he doing those terrible things to the Corwin Transportation Company. 12 Episode Mascot Serial. *1934, USA. 223 minutes.*
■ 706 ~~$69.95~~ $39.95

Buck Rogers (Planet Outlaws)

Buster Crabbe, Constance Moore
The famous serial made into a feature by deleting cliff-hangers, plot recapitulations, etc. and adding narration. *1939, USA. 70 minutes.*
■ 560 $29.95

Dick Tracy

Ralph Byrd, Kay Hughes, Smiley Burnette, Francis X. Bushman
Based on the comic strip by Chester Gould. It's Dick Tracy vs. the mysterious Spider Gang. 15 Episode Republic Serial. *1937, USA. 290 minutes.*
■ 552 ~~$69.95~~ $39.95

Holt of the Secret Service

Jack Holt, Evelyn Brent, Montague Shaw, Tristram Coffin
When a gang of brilliantly fiendish counterfeiters force a kidnaped treasury agent into making priceless engravings, super agent Jack Holt and his tough female partner attempt to discover the criminal mastermind's identity and stop his insidious activities. Constantly risking exposure and death, they daringly infiltrate the enemy's secret mountainside headquarters and his treacherous gambling ship. 13 Episode Columbia Serial. *1941, USA. 280 minutes.*
■ 175 ~~$69.95~~ $39.95

The Shadow of the Eagle

John Wayne, Yakima Canutt
Who is the mysterious "Eagle"? Five officers of a large corporation are sent a warning. "You shot down "The Eagle" and stole his invention. His shadow has returned, prepare to pay!" Echoes of another age live again! 12 Episode Mascot Serial. *1932, USA. 226 minutes.*
■ 789 ~~$69.95~~ $39.95

To order call 1-800-243-0987

The Adventures of Tarzan

Elmo Lincoln, Louise Lorraine
Tarzan has returned from civilization to his beloved jungle. Silent film with music score, correct projection speed. *1921, USA. 188 minutes.*
■ 466 ~~$69.95~~ $39.95

Tarzan the Fearless

Buster Crabbe, Jacqueline Wells
Tarzan tangles with a ferocious lion in hand-to-hand combat, and rescues a helpless young woman. *1933, USA. 86 minutes.*
■ 1231 $29.95

The New Adventures of Tarzan

Herman Brix, Ula Holt, and "Jiggs" as N'kima the monkey
Tarzan travels to the jungles of Guatemala in search of the "Green Goddess"- a native idol which also contains the formula for a powerful explosive. 12 episodes. *1935, USA. 266 minutes.*
■ 466 ~~$69.95~~ $39.95

Buy 3 get 1 FREE!

Movie Quiz: Which serial on this page—released over 50 years ago—has the villain flying an airplane that looks exactly like the Air Force's Stealth Bomber? (Dick Tracy)

Figure 15.11 A catalog selling old movies.

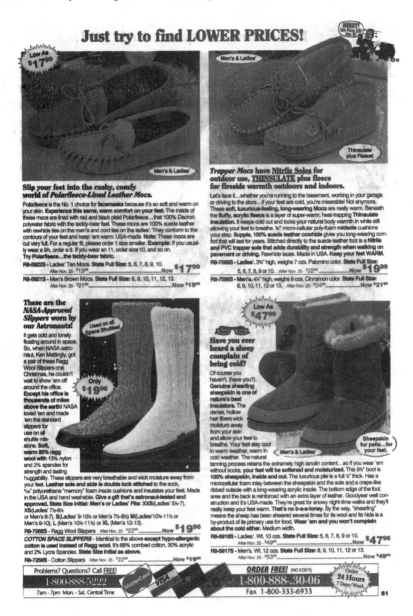

Figure 15.12 Footware from the Sportsman's Guide.

Figure 15.13 A catalog of computers and computer equipment from Tiger Software.

12A *Pigtails and Froglegs* is the progeny of our best-seller cookbook *Pure & Simple*. Barbara Bush, Joan Lunden, Elton John, Marlo Thomas, and celebrity chef Wolfgang Puck are among the Neiman Marcus InCircle® customers who have contributed to this collection of all-time favorite recipes for foods children like to eat, prepared by adults. Author royalties will benefit four national children's charities. The 256-page hardbound book is filled with lively illustrations by Chuck Jones (the creator of Road Runner, Pepé Le Pew, and Wile E. Coyote) and includes a special foreword by none other than Michael Jackson! Epicure and Children's World.

12A. *Pigtails and Froglegs*, 19.95

12B Glossy karung snakeskin on top, soft and expandable leather bottoms, golden metal framing. The 2¾"-diameter coin purses are available in green, metallic gold, red, purple, or (not shown) black. An NM® exclusive. From Small Leather Goods.

12B. Coin purse, 13.00.

12C A lush and colorful flower garden filled with cats decorates the sides of this block of approximately 850 3½"-square sheets of notepaper, 3¼" tall. There's a hole in the corner for a pen or pencil (not included). Imported from England. From Stationery.

12C. Flowers and cats notepaper block, 16.50.

12D,E Colorful pansies against a green and gold background grace porcelain desk accessories accented with gilt. The letter opener with gold-tone blade and the 9"-long tray are a set. The 6 x 4 x 1½" memo box includes 200 sheets of paper and a pencil. NM® exclusives. From Stationery.

12D. Tray and letter opener, 18.00.
12E. Memo box, 18.00.

Figure 15.14   Items from the Neiman Marcus catalog at $25 or less.

Easy Solution To Cleaning Mini-Blinds And Ceiling Fans! Custom-made vacuum cleaner attachments suck up dust instantly, end tedious work! Each slips onto vacuum nozzle or hose—we include a universal adaptor to fit all major brands. Durable, washable white plastic.

Mini-Blind Vacuum Attachment cleans 4 slats at once—unique "fingers" slide between them! Dustbuster Pro™ adaptor included. 6" long.
078762   Mini-Blind Attachment $9.98

Ceiling Fan Vacuum Attachment does both sides of blade at the same time with patented double-head—swivels for angled blades. 8¼" long.
078662   Ceiling Fan Attachment $9.98

Order Any 2 Attachments for $18.98

■■■ EXCLUSIVE! **Over-The-Washer Shelf** stores laundry essentials where they're handiest, keeps them off the machine and floor—ends clutter! White vinyl-coated steel is rustproof, has extra-strong grid to support super-size detergent and bleach containers. 25x11x11" high. Mounts to wall; easy to assemble, hardware included.
453062   Over-washer Shelf $14.98

■■■ EXCLUSIVE! **Easy Ironing Without A Board!** Big 27x47" insulated pad ends the need to lug out an ironing board, saves time and space—folds flat for easy storage and travel. Use on table or dresser for perfect pressing, great for touch-ups! Bright 100% cotton floral cover is sturdily bound and stitched, thickly insulated with 4 layers of polyfoam and felt to help prevent scorching. Stay-put ribbed plastic bottom. Machine wash. From Italy.
096062   Table-top Ironing Pad $19.98

Dry Twice As Much Laundry In Half The Space When You Buy 2! Stackable dryer saves time and space; keeps sweaters and knits shapely, no stretching, no hanger marks, dries them faster! Airy 2-ply nylon mesh and sturdy 27½"-square plastic frame—ideal for bulky knits! Fits in tub, stands on floor; non-slip feet remove to stack.
117762   Stackable Dryer $8.98   2 for $16.98

94

Figure 15.15   A page from a recent Lillian Vernon catalog.

Lilies Bring Elegance to Your Summer Garden

A. CALLA LILY $3.49 ea.

B. LILIES FOR NATURALIZING   10/$6.99

A *Pastel CALLA LILIES are popular for summer borders and patio containers.* Speckled foliage and graceful blooms thrive outdoors in shade or partial sun. For elegant indoor bouquets, Calla Lilies (Zantedeschia) last for 2 weeks! Bloom July and August on 15-20" stems. 12-14cm bulbs are imported from Holland.

Cat. No. X16	Pink	Only
Cat. No. X17	Yellow	$3.49
Cat. No. X18	White	each

CALLA LILY COLLECTION. SAVE $2.00. One each of the three Calla Lilies described above - 3 in all.
Cat. No. 881	1 Collection	$8.47

B *NATURALIZING LILIES are perfect for informal arrangements.* A carefree choice for sunny gardens and lightly shaded areas. Naturalizing Lilies return each year, producing bigger clumps and more flowers each season. Colorful blooms last all summer for an effect that's beautiful yet informal. 10-12cm. Hardiness zones 3-9, see map on page 25.
Cat. No. 331	10/$6.99

C. PINEAPPLE LILY   3/$3.99

"I especially like lilies for the partly shady areas of my yard. They really do add some sparkle."

MICHIGAN BULB'S FAMOUS DOUBLE GUARANTEE. You must be satisfied with your order on arrival or you may return any of the items within 15 days for a full refund. Items that do not grow and flourish will be replaced FREE! (3-year limit)

C *Star-shaped flowers grace PINEAPPLE LILY.* You'll love the unusual two foot-tall spikes of pale green, light pink and creamy white flowers. The small caps of foliage on this lily (Eucomis punctata) look like pineapples! Holland imported. 14cm bulbs.
Cat. No. 434	3/$3.99

D *Elegant HYBRID LILIES look fancy but are incredibly easy to grow!* Choose breathtaking CORINA LILIES, known for their bold red blooms. The delightful pink trumpets of CORSICA LILIES make them a special addition to any garden. Or choose DREAMLAND LILIES for a brilliant, sunny yellow accent. Don't miss the magic of Lilies! Plant them in sun or partial shade, in small clusters of three - or fill your entire garden bed for a spectacular color show. All three varieties grow up to 3' tall, are winter hardy and return each year. 12-14cm bulbs. Hardiness zones 3-9, see map on page 25. Be sure to order plenty of each!

No. X20	Dreamland (Yellow)	3/$4.49
No. X21	Corsica (Pink)	3/$4.49
No. X22	Corina (Red)	3/$4.49

HYBRID LILY COLLECTION. SAVE $2.00! Get three of each Lily variety described above for one low price. 9 bulbs in all!
Cat. No. X19	1 Collection	$11.47

D. HYBRID LILIES   3/$4.49

FREE PLANTING BOOKLET WITH ANY ORDER!

Figure 15.16   Lilies from the Michigan Bulb Company's catalog.

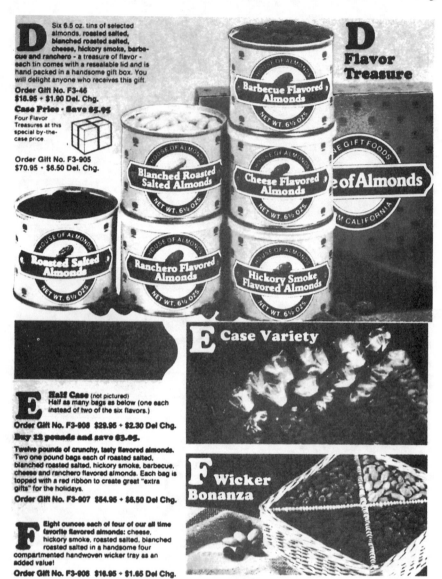

D Six 6.5 oz. tins of selected almonds, roasted salted, blanched roasted salted, cheese, hickory smoke, barbecue and ranchero - a treasure of flavor - each tin comes with a resealable lid and is hand packed in a handsome gift box. You will delight anyone who receives this gift.

Order Gift No. F3-46
$18.95 + $1.90 Del. Chg.

Case Price - Save $5.95
Four Flavor Treasures at this special by-the-case price

Order Gift No. F3-905
$70.95 + $6.50 Del. Chg.

D Flavor Treasure

E Case Variety

E **Half Case** (not pictured)
Half as many bags as below (one each instead of two of the six flavors.)

Order Gift No. F3-908 $29.95 + $2.30 Del Chg.

Buy 12 pounds and save $3.95.

Twelve pounds of crunchy, tasty flavored almonds. Two one pound bags each of roasted salted, blanched roasted salted, hickory smoke, barbecue, cheese and ranchero flavored almonds. Each bag is topped with a red ribbon to create great "extra gifts" for the holidays.

Order Gift No. F3-907 $54.95 + $6.50 Del Chg.

F Wicker Bonanza

F Eight ounces each of four of our all time favorite flavored almonds: cheese, hickory smoke, roasted salted, blanched roasted salted in a handsome four compartmented handwoven wicker tray as an added value!

Order Gift No. F3-908 $16.95 + $1.65 Del Chg.

Figure 15.17   From the House of Almonds.

Special Tools For Small Projects

Miniature Hand Drill *NEW!* With Bits

When you're working on miniatures, models and jewelry, or want pilot holes for small screws, you may need to bore very small holes. An electric drill can't do it without breaking the bit, but our well-designed hand drill with 6 bits will give you precise holes as tiny as .025" diameter (#72)!

The knurled handle gives you unerring, hands-on control to drill the hole exactly where you want it. 6 high-speed steel bits, sizes #62, 64, 66, 68, 70, 72, store in the aluminum handle. Quick-response brass collet. Pocket clip. 4½" long overall.

101196 - Hand Drill Kit $14.99

20-Pc. Miniature Drill Bit Set For Hand Drill Above. High-speed steel, in sizes #61 (.039") thru the "microscopic" #80 (.0135"). Metal case with index and individual bit compartments.
100255 - 20-Pc. Mini Bit Set $12.99

"Router Handbook"

Patrick Spielman
The definitive router book includes 600 photos that show you every step of your router's operation. Learn how to simplify every project with standard and unusual techniques. Dozens of projects, patterns. 8 x 10"; 224 pages. Softbound.
90498 - Router Handbook. ..$10.95

Get Your Order FASTER!
Ask for Federal Express®.
See page 46 for details.

11-Pc. Jeweler's Screwdriver Set

This is far and away the best set of jewelers screwdrivers I've ever seen. Not only is the steel better tempered but the set includes Nos. 00, 0 and 1 Phillips screwdrivers ... very rare tools. In addition to the .9, 1.2, 1.4, 1.8, 2.3 and 3.0 mm slotted screwdrivers, there is also a dandy little awl and a matching magnetic tool to pick up those tiny screws! Handsome storage case.
71019 - 11-Pc Jeweler's Set $9.99

Magnetic Push Brad Driver

No more whacked fingers, no more hammer-marred moldings or frames. Just slip your brad or finishing nail (up to 1½") head-first into the spring-loaded barrel. Permanent magnet holds it in place. Place the tube where you want the brad, then push it in, and the brad is set. Great for tight corners.

Use it on craft projects too, like model boats and planes, doll houses. Comfortable wood handle. Overall 6½" long.
100206 - Magnetic Push Brad Driver $9.99

Keep Both Hands Free For Electronic And Hobby Work

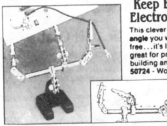

This clever little tool holds your work at any angle you want and leaves both your hands free...it's like having three extra hands! It's great for precision soldering, hobby kit building and electronic work.
50724 - Work Holder $9.99

NEW!

Work Holder With Magnifier. Same as above, and includes a 2x magnifying glass that attaches to it.
100883 - Work Holder W/Magnifier $14.99

38

Figure 15.18 Tools from Leichtung Workshops catalog.

Instantly slice your autobaked bread into toaster-perfect, sandwich-perfect and desert-perfect slices. It's easy with DAK's new bread slicer.

Perfect Slices

Finally! Now you can effortlessly slice your autobaked bread into perfect, even slices every time. Plus, discover my secret weapon for baking even higher-rising, better-tasting bread, cakes, muffins and more.

By Drew Kaplan

Nothing is perfect. Take for instance DAK's autobaked bread. It smells great as it bakes. Its preservative-free ingredients are good for my health. And, this fresh, homebaked bread tastes out of this world.

The only problem was that my wife and I (and many DAKonians who wrote me) had trouble evenly slicing this delicious domed-shaped loaf for toast and sandwiches. Well, enough was enough.

Finally, I've discovered an easy way for all of us to cut chef-perfect slices of deli-

cious autobaked bread without the mess.

**FAST, EVEN SLICES
FOR ANY MEAL**

Just place your autobaked bread into the custom-shaped cutting cradle.

Then, slide your bread-cutting knife through any of the nine knife-guide slots. Your knife will effortlessly and evenly slice through your bread with gourmet precision. It's as if an invisible chef is guiding your hand with every slice!

Each slot is spaced at ½" intervals for perfect ½"-thick slices. And of course, you can also cut precision 1", 1½" and 2" thick slices (or thicker). Just skip a slot or two.

You'll expertly slice your bread for breakfast toast, afternoon sandwiches or even elegant sweet bread desserts.

And oh, is it a joy to use when the Kaplan clan makes French toast, hot pocket

sandwiches with the DAK sandwich maker and even bread crumb croutons.

DREW'S SECRET WEAPON, TOO

It's a cordless flour sifter that I think (pardon the pun) is the greatest thing since sliced bread. Here's why.

Its unique gyration action will quickly and easily sift your flour to perfection. So your flour will measure perfectly.

And, with lighter, more aerated flour you'll bake moister cakes and tastier muffins and cookies and higher-rising bread (especially whole-wheat bread).

The Cordless Sifter uses one C battery (not included). And, both the DAK Bread Slicer and Cordless Sifter are backed by a standard limited warranty.

**ENJOY PERFECT SLICES AND MORE
RISK-FREE**

To order your DAK Bread Slicer for Precision ½" bread slices for toast, sandwiches, desserts and more PLUS the Cordless Flour Sifter for fluffier, higher-rising bread every time risk-free with your credit card call toll-free 1-800-325-0800 or send your check for just $29⁹⁰ ($6 P&H). Order No. 3406. ⬛

With unique cordless electric gyration, you'll expertly sift your baking flour for perfect measurements.

4 Minutes To Hot Meals

Now in just 4 minutes or less, you can create delicious, piping-hot, sealed gourmet sandwiches, tuna puffs, pot pies, low-fat vegetarian burritos and even fresh fruit pies, all with your favorite, preservative-free homemade breads.

By Drew Kaplan

Forget cold, soggy sandwiches. Forget greasy, fat-filled fast foods. And, forget not having time to make a hot, healthy meal.

Now you and your family can effortlessly enjoy wholesome, hot sealed 'pocket' sandwiches and snacks in minutes—without all the hard work of ordinary cooking.

It's easy with the DAK Gourmet Sandwich Maker. With it, you can create hundreds of different hot sandwiches, snacks and even entrees with the bread you bake in your DAK breadmaker.

DESIGNED EXCLUSIVELY FOR DAK

The DAK Gourmet Sandwich Maker is the only sandwich maker engineered specifically for your DAK breadmaker.

Its unique, non-stick, round cooking plates are designed for making hot, sealed sandwiches and snacks with the gourmet breads you bake in your breadmaker.

Plus, its dual cooking elements (with a full 800 watts of power) have 4 different heat settings. So you can customize the cooking temperature to match the type of meal you're making.

The result? Everything you make will be perfectly cooked—light and crispy on the

4 Heat Settings To Choose From

Unlike cheap sandwich makers that only have 1 fixed heat setting, DAK's Gourmet Sandwich Maker has 4 heat settings. So whether you're making hot, healthful vegetable pockets or sealed gourmet sandwiches, they'll be perfectly baked every time.

outside, tender and tasty on the inside.

HOT MEALS, FAST

It's easy. Simply choose your fillings (meats, cheeses, vegetables, fruits or just about anything). Put them between 2 buttered slices of your favorite homemade bread. (For low-fat sandwiches, you can use non-fat cooking spray or a drop of canola oil on the cooking plates.)

Then place it in the Sandwich Maker and close the lid. In 2 to 4 minutes flat you've got 2 hot, taste-tempting sealed sandwich pockets that are simple enough for snacks but fancy enough to serve at dinner parties.

Best of all, there's virtually no clean-up. Simply wipe off the removable non-stick cooking plates and you're ready to make your next hot, gourmet treat.

The DAK Gourmet Sandwich Maker is manufactured exclusively for DAK and backed by a standard limited DAK warranty.

**ENJOY HOT MEALS, FAST
RISK-FREE**

To order your DAK Gourmet Sandwich Maker with Specially Designed Non-Stick Round Cooking Plates, Dual Heating Elements and Multi-Setting Temperature Control for a 30-day risk-free trial, call toll-free 1-800-325-0800 or send your check for just $49⁹⁰ ($6 P&H). Order No. 5748. ⬛

Transform your fresh homemade bread into hot, delicious, fancy, sealed sandwiches and snacks.

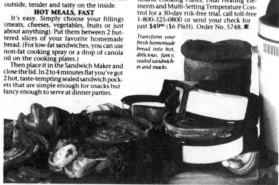

Figure 15.19   A page from DAK Industries Incorporated.

COLORFUL USMA PENNANTS

These brightly colored pennants are perfect to decorate your club room or take along to the game. Packed in a set of four, two 14" and two 25", so you can share them with a friend. Set of 4. #985 **$4.50**

FOOTBALL BANK

Miniature ceramic football is decorated with USMA crest and trimmed in gold. Cork base protects furniture. Makes an interesting and novel gift idea for football buffs. Measures 7 1/2" L x 4" H. #750 **$12.00**

CHILD'S SWEATSHIRT & SWEATPANTS

Our grown-up gray sweats are silk screened with black and gold USMA crest on shirt and USMA on pant leg and fashioned just for kids of a comfortable, washable cotton/poly blend.
Sizes: Toddler 3-4, 5-6. Youth 6-8, 10-12, 14-16.
#990 Sweatshirt **$14.00**   #995 Sweatpants **$14.00**

USMA SLEEPSHIRT

Sweet dreams are guaranteed with our generously cut Sleepshirt of comfortable, 100% cotton. One size fits all. Available in raspberry (shown), jade and black. Please specify color. Made in USA. #890 **$16.50**

ROLL-UP SLEEVE TEE SHIRT

The classic Tee gets a fresh, new look with our horizontal gray washed-out stripe. Short sleeve shirt is trimmed with contrasting tape at neck and roll-up sleeve cuff. Front sports USMA crest in black. Tee is made in the USA, of 100% machine washable cotton and comes trimmed in Jade #713 (shown), and Black #705 S,M,L,XL. **$14.50** each

CHILDREN'S ROLL-UP SLEEVE TEE & SHORTS

Just like the adults', the children's version of the Roll-up Sleeve Tee has contrasting tape at neck and sleeve on ash colored body. Contrasting trims include black or jade. Please specify color and size when ordering. 100% cotton, machine washable. Made in USA Children's sizes: 2,4,5-6,6-8,10-12,14-16 #868 **$12.50** Children's Pull-up Shorts with elastic waistband. Sizes: 2,4,5-6, Youth: S,M,L. #722 **$10.00**

Figure 15.20   From a mail order catalog of the West Point Museum.

E Photo Album
Keep 64 special memories in our
32-page photo album. Two regular
or jumbo prints quickly slip into each
4" x 6" plastic sleeve. The beautiful
floral cover is constructed of a durable
plastic laminate.
Item #41739
Case Pack: 72
Price: $1.79

F Plush Teddy Bear
Our snow-white bear with festive red
bow simply begs to be hugged. A full
7" tall, he is made of super soft plush
fabric and sits unsupported. Constructed to meet all child safety standards.
Item #60238
Case Pack: 48
Price: $2.29

G Round Serving Tray
These serving trays are an easy
and elegant way to present culinary
triumphs. Each chrome-plated tray
has fluted lip and etched design on
serving area. Round tray measures
12" in diameter.
Item #21963
Case Pack: 60
Price: $1.99

H Oval Serving Tray
Identical in decoration to our
round tray, the oval tray measures
13½" x 18".
Item #21962
Case Pack: 48
Price: $2.19

I Compact Umbrella
Our popular compact umbrellas
come in four high-fashion colors.
Each opens automatically with the
push of a button. Built-to-last in water-
repellent nylon over aluminum frame.
Includes cover in same fabric as
umbrella and a carrying strap on
easy grip handle. Teal, yellow, purple
and pink packed in each case.
Item #50659
Case Pack: 60
Price: $1.99

800-669-3733

Figure 15.21 From a catalog of premium items from Schmidt-Cannon,
International.

world, which he wholesales to companies in the United States. The address is 1208 John Reed Court, City of Industry, CA 91745.

Now let's look at how you can become a success in catalog selling.

MERCHANDISE SELECTION

As I told you earlier in this book, selection of your products for mail order is always very important. However, in the product selection for a catalog, there are other factors you must consider. For one thing, all of your products should have something in common. You should segment the products according to some common factor that appeals to your customers. If you look at the catalog examples mentioned earlier, you will see, in every case, that the catalog has some common theme running through it. Some of these examples are obvious. Arlene's knife catalog carries only knives and similar items. The Edmund Scientific catalog carries items that appeal to the curious lay person and to the professional. The International Entrepreneurs Association small business catalog appeals to people who are or wish to become entrepreneurs. In every case, the catalogs' common theme is the keynote of product selection for the catalog.

You must still look to your competition to see what's going on in the marketplace and to maximize your chances of success. To do this in the catalog business, you should get the catalog of every possible competitor. Certain items will be found in more than one catalog, an indication that the item is more successful and has a greater chance of success in your catalog as well.

Once you have decided on certain of these products because of their popularity, you must get the manufacturer's name and address. There are several ways you can approach this problem. First, you must ascertain whether the product is manufactured here or abroad, and if it is manufactured abroad, in what country. Usually the simplest and most direct method is simply to buy one of the products yourself and examine it to find out its source. If it's from the United States, start with a directory like the *Thomas Register of Manufacturers,* mentioned earlier. If it's a foreign product, you might consult some of the directories we talked about earlier such as *Hong Kong Enterprises, Made in Europe,* or others. Or, you could take the product directly to a commercial attaché at the consulate or embassy of the country from which the product originated. Once you locate the company that manufactured the product, you should write to ask for information as to the quantity discount. And here we deviate from the standard guideline of a 300 to 400 percent markup. You probably will not be able to get it. Also, if the product is already popular and carried by several different mail order firms, you will be unlikely to get the exclusive right to sell the product unless you can guarantee sales larger than those of all of your competitors combined. Therefore, look for a discount of about 50 percent from your selling price, larger for greater quantities. You can also find out about drop-shipping, which may be acceptable for your catalog sales where it cannot be if you have a single product or very limited product line. Clearly you will want to know about quantities on hand, how quickly your order can be filled, and how quickly larger repeat orders can be filled.

You cannot be successful by offering only products obtainable from other mail order houses or through other sources, so many of your products should be unique, and you should try to get exclusives on them. The basic idea here is this: If you have certain products that can be obtained only from your catalogs, the customers buying these products and wanting to buy other products that are available elsewhere will buy these other products from you because they are already buying from you.

GROWING INTO SUCCESS

Most successful catalog operations *grow* into success—sometimes slowly, sometimes more quickly, but it is always a growing process. It is unwise to try to be a giant catalog house right away. It is better to pattern your success after such successes as Len Carlson's or Joe Sugarman's. On the other hand, people like Roger Horchow have made it into the instant big-dollar catalog business. However, remember that Roger Horchow could afford to—*and did*—lose $2 million in his first year of operation. Gerardo Joffe recommends the rule of thumb that you should have at least 25,000 of your own customers before you attempt to publish a real, honest-to-goodness catalog. My opinion is that you can get into a catalog much earlier, depending upon your definition of a catalog and remembering that a catalog can also be a simple listing and description printed by offset of the various items in your product line.

COST CONTROL

You cannot have a profitable catalog if you continue to carry products that are not profitable to you. Therefore, you must keep constant track of which products are selling well and which are not. You eliminate those that are not selling and continue to experiment with new products. Just as with classified, space, or other types of advertising, you can figure out a breakeven for a particular product in your own catalog. Your costs would include the cost of preparing the art, the printing, mailing, paper, and so forth. If the product doesn't do better than break even, either drop the product or try to change the copy, graphics, or positioning to improve the results. There is no trick here. You simply track the results in your catalog and drop or change those that do not do well.

COPY AND GRAPHICS

As with other types of advertising and promotions that you use, copy and graphics are extremely important in catalogs; they count as much as product selection in any equation that yields success. Depending on how fancy a catalog you are going to produce and whether you are going to put the catalog together by yourself or have a company that is experienced in this type of work put it together for you, the price you pay will vary widely. However, there are many factors that enter in here that you must consider. For example, on one hand you may find that the stock, glossy photographs supplied by the manufacturer are totally unsuitable for a catalog operation. Why is this? For one thing, this photograph is taken of the product only; it may not illustrate the particular appeal that you decide to make clear to your customer. Also, you're displaying more than this one single product in your catalog, and all these different products must fit together to support your central theme. With the many different styles of photography, different viewpoints, and so forth that may be illustrated in the different photographs supplied by various manufacturers, you may end up with a hodgepodge of illustrations that will do anything but give your catalog the unified support of a single theme. On the other hand, for some products this differing photography will not disrupt your theme and not only can you use the manufacturer's photographs, but you can integrate them with your own and still be effective in selling.

For some types of catalog you can do your own work and not hurt sales. As a guideline, if you have no prior experience, look at what your competition is doing. If the competition isn't using an expensive catalog, you probably don't need one either. Note also that the copy for a catalog is usually much more limited than that for a space advertisement unless the item is relatively expensive and you intend to spend much more selling space on it. An example is JS&A's electronics catalog. The basic principles of copywriting still apply here. In fact, many very famous copywriters such as Maxwell Sackheim got their start in writing copy for catalogs such as Sears Roebuck.

COLOR VERSUS BLACK AND WHITE

Again, we have the trade-off between color and black and white. Generally color will sell better than black and white, but the big question is whether the additional costs bring in more profits. There is no universal answer to this question. In fact, for some items, color may have no effect on the number of items ordered. My advice here is to go slowly and consider your product carefully. Again, take a look at the competition. If none of your competition is using color, there is probably a good reason. The reverse is also true. So as a starting point, you may use the competition as a guide. Once you are established, you can begin to experiment. Full color is almost required for certain types of product, such as clothing, food, home furnishings, or jewelry. For other types of product, you can test after you start making money, are established, and can afford to experiment.

THE ORDER FORM, ONE OF THE MOST IMPORTANT PARTS OF THE CATALOG

The order form is one of the most important parts of your catalog. This is not to say that your potential customers cannot order without it, because they can. But it is convenient to order with an order form and it provides much important information. With this information you can track what is happening with your customers, your business, and your products. It is important that you design an order form that has all the information you need. Figure 15.22 is a checklist for order forms. If you follow this checklist, you can't go very far wrong.

1. Your name and address
2. A place for customer's name and address
3. A place for quantity
4. A place for your stock number
5. A place for full description of the items ordered
6. A place for unit price
7. A place for the number of units wanted
8. A place for the total price
9. A place for packing and shipping cost (you should help your customer to estimate this by geographic area, weight, or number of units ordered)
10. A place for insurance cost (you must help your customers estimate total cost here also)
11. Sales tax if applicable in your state
12. A place for Visa or Master Card information, including card number, interbank number, and expiration date, if applicable

Optional information depending on your circumstances
1. Your telephone number
2. A place for your customer's telephone number
3. A place where your customer can list the addresses of friends to receive a free copy of your catalog
4. Your catalog number (if you send out more than one catalog yearly)

Figure 15.22   A checklist to follow in preparing your order forms.

Your Name and Address. This is of first importance. Even though your address is contained elsewhere in the catalog (and most definitely should be, for when the order form is gone, that address won't be there any longer), you should always have a place on the order form where your name and address are clearly shown.

A Place for Your Customer's Name and Address. Include a space that clearly shows where your customer is to fill in his or her name and address. There are various alternatives to leaving a blank space. One is to leave a space that allows the customer to attach the label you have used to address the catalog. Special address labels are available for this purpose. Another is to use a computer to address the order form beforehand. In any case, it is a very important part of your form, for without this information, you cannot even fulfill the order.

A Place for Quantity. Very frequently your customer will want to order more than one of a particular product and, if so, you should be sure that the form allows him or her to do so. Also, the existence of such a place will encourage the customer to ask, "Do I want more than one?"

A Place for Your Stock Number. This is the number you have assigned to the goods in your catalog. It will help you to identify what your customer wants faster than if you ask only for a description.

Description. You should allow sufficient space for a full description of the item ordered, including size, color, and other details when appropriate, even though a number is listed. The number can be changed through the dropping of a single digit, but it is much more difficult to make a mistake in the description, so it provides a double check.

Unit Price. This is the price of one single item. If your customer is going to order more than one, he or she simply multiplies the number by the unit price.

Packing and Shipping Costs. You should make some provision for packing and shipping costs unless you intend to pay all the postage. Usually this is a varying amount that depends upon the weight of the package and the shipping distance. However, many mail order firms make it easier for their customers by simply figuring out an average, based on sales price. If the size and weight of your units do not differ greatly, this is a reasonably good solution to the problem.

Insurance Costs. If the item is lost in transit, either you or your customer must be responsible for the insurance. For big-ticket items, insurance is probably a must, and many companies require their customer to pay an additional amount to cover this cost. Again, you need to tell your customer how much to send, depending upon total value of the products ordered.

Sales Tax if Applicable. If your state has a sales tax and your customer is living within the state, you will be required to collect this tax. As explained earlier, you will be expected to pay it to your state at periodic intervals.

Charge Card. A charge card will increase your sales, both because of convenience and because it gives credibility and an easy method to pay for costly items.

Optional Items. Some items are just a good idea to include, but you must take your own circumstances into account when deciding. For example, many companies will ask for the page number of the item in addition to the catalog number and description to nail the material down and make certain that the item is, in fact, the item ordered. It also makes it easier for the person checking to find the item. In addition, if you are sending out many different catalogs, it may be a good idea to have your customer indicate which catalog it is. This also lessens the chances of confusion both in ordering and recording information about what your customer has ordered. If you have a toll-free number or a fax number by which your customer can order, by all means include it on the order blank. It makes ordering much easier and will boost the number of your sales. The order blank is a good place to reiterate the fact that you have a toll-free number. In fact, even if you don't have one, it's a good idea to list your telephone. You'll get some orders this way. It is an excellent idea to advise your customers that their friends can receive the same catalog if they will include their names and addresses, and then allow space for them to do so. This is a way of obtaining potential customers' names at no cost, and you should certainly take advantage of it.

The order form currently used by Edmund Scientific Company is shown in Figure 15.23. First, note that Edmund has printed the customer's name and address with a computer. In addition to a phone number for orders, there is also a fax number. A premium that is given free with every purchase of $40 or more is already on the form. Note that an envelope is attached to the form at the top. The back which you see in this view contains "4 convenient ways to order," a guarantee, and space for addresses of friends who might like to receive a free catalog. In Figure 15.24, the back of the form is illustrated. It includes a self-addressed envelope and general information, including information about telephone ordering, how to get faster service, how to get technical information, information on delivery and guaranteed delivery, a repeat of the guarantee, where and when to go for customer service, information prices, a warranty, how to get a gift certificate, mailing list information, information

Four Convenient Ways To Order

1 By Phone
1-800-547-8880
Eastern Time 8 a.m.-8 p.m.
Monday to Friday
9 a.m.-5 p.m. Saturday
Answering machine available to take your orders after hours and on Sundays. Please have your credit card information available.

2 By Mail
If you order by phone, ask about our weekly special values!

Telephone Specials
Fill out this convenient order form and mail. Or FAX: 1-609-573-6295.
Thank You.

3 Visit Our Factory Store
Visit us when in the Philadelphia area. See map on the back of order form for directions. Dial 1-609-573-6241 for retail store only.

4 FAX—1-609-573-6295

Send A Catalog To A Friend

Name
Co./School
Address
City   State   Zip
Apt. #

Name
Co./School
Address
City   State   Zip
Apt. #

Name
Co./School
Address
City   State   Zip
Apt. #

Name
Co./School
Address
City   State   Zip
Apt. #

YOU MUST BE PLEASED
The Edmund Guarantee: If for any reason you are not satisfied, simply return the item within 45 days for an immediate refund or credit.

MOISTEN TO SEAL   DETACH ALONG DOTTED LINE, FOLD FLAP, ENCLOSE ORDER FORM, ATTACH STAMP AND MAIL   MOISTEN TO SEAL

Edmund Scientific Co.
101 E. Gloucester Pike
Barrington, NJ 08007-1380, U.S.A.

Order By Phone
1-609-547-8880
FAX—1-609-573-6295

DATE
/ /

Eastern Time, 8AM to 8PM Mon.-Fri.
9AM to 5PM Sat.
Answer machine available after hours and
Sunday for credit card orders.

Product Number	Qty.	Item Description	Pg. No.	Price Each	Total
K 5 0 4 4	1	Edmund Scientific's Hand-Held Bi-Focal 2X-4X Magnifier		FREE with $40.00 or more purchase	

PAYMENT METHOD
☐ MasterCard ☐ Discover
☐ Visa ☐ Diners Club
☐ American Express ☐ Check
☐ Optima ☐ Money Order

Card Account Number

Expiration Date ___ / ___ / ___

Bank ID Number / Bank Name ___

Signature ___
(Required)

POSTAGE, PACKING & GUARANTEED DELIVERY
Shipping/Handling Chart for all orders shipped in the U.S., its territories, possessions.

Merch. Total	Shipping Charge
Up to $14.99	$ 3.75
$15.00 to $24.99	$ 4.65
$25.00 to $34.99	$ 5.75
$35.00 to $49.99	$ 7.00
$50.00 to $99.99	$ 9.00
$100.00 to $199.99	$10.75
$200.00 to $299.99	$12.50
$300.00 to $499.99	$13.75
$500.00 and Over	$16.75

Merchandise Total

N.J. Residents
Add 6% Sales Tax

Shipping & Handling

Express Service
Add $7.95 for Guaranteed Delivery within Four Working Days Within Continental U.S.A. Only

Total Amount
(Please no cash, stamps or C.O.D.'s)

THANK YOU FOR YOUR ORDER

Ordered By: Catalog #19C9

XXXXXXXXXXXXX 5-DIGIT 91107
19C9C237   068197
H COHEN
OR CURRENT RESIDENT

SHIP TO:
Name ___
Company ___
Address ___ Apt. # ___
City ___ State ___ Zip ___
Daytime Telephone Number (in case we have a question about your order.) (___) ___

MOVED?
ADDRESS CHANGE
Name ___
Company ___
Address ___ Apt. # ___
City ___ State ___ Zip ___

The Edmund Guarantee: If for any reason you are not satisfied, simply return the item within 45 days for an immediate refund or credit. **You Must Be Pleased**

Figure 15.23 Edmund Scientific's order form.

General Information

May We Take Your Order?

For Fast, Friendly Service Phone Us
1-609-547-8880
Eastern Time 8 a.m.–8 p.m. Saturday
Monday To Friday, 9 a.m.–5 p.m. Saturday
Answering machine available to take your orders after hours and on Sundays. Please have your credit card information available.
Send Us Your Order By Mail. Fill out this convenient order form and mail it today. Or FAX 1-609-573-6295. Thank You.
Visit Our Factory Store: Visit us when in the Philadelphia area. See map on the order form for directions. Dial 1-609-573-6241 for retail store only.

If You Need Faster Service
Express Service: Orders received before 2 pm eastern time for an extra $7.95, in addition to delivery charges, we will ship your order by express delivery. Guaranteed delivery within four working days. Only available in continental U.S. for credit card orders.

Need Help / Technical Information?
If you require additional information not stated in our catalog, call our technical experts for help.
1-609-573-6253   9 am to 5 pm, Eastern Time
1-609-573-6259   Monday–Friday

About Delivery Of Your Order
Most items are shipped from stock, assuring fast delivery to you. We use United Parcel Service whenever possible. If an item is temporarily out of stock, you will receive a prompt notice. The rest of your order will be shipped.

ES Guaranteed Delivery
While most carriers do automatically insure shipments to some value, there is considerable delay and red tape involved in processing your claim. Our guaranteed delivery provides full value coverage and hassle-free immediate service.

Our Guarantee and Service Follow-up
The Edmund Guarantee: If for any reason you are not satisfied, simply return the item within 45 days for an immediate refund or credit.

Customer Service: If you require delivery information or an order adjustment, call 1-609-573-6260
9 am to 5 pm, Eastern Time, Monday to Friday.
FAX 1-609-573-6295. TELEX 831-564 EDMUND BRTN
"Remember your satisfaction is guaranteed. Our staff is ready to help you."

Other Information To Help You
Warranty
Edmund warrants all the products in this catalog for 45 days, unconditionally. Edmund brand microscopes, magnifiers and telescopes have a 1 year warranty (see specific section for details). For other products, an additional manufacturer's warranty or material safety data sheets may be available. Write to: Warranty Information Department, Edmund Scientific, Company, Edscorp Building, Barrington, New Jersey 08007-1380, U.S.A. (No Phone Requests Please.)
If your unit is out of warranty but needs repairs, please write or call Customer Service 1-609-573-6260 for repair information.
Our Prices: All prices in this catalog are effective August 1, 1986. This catalog supersedes all previous catalogs. Prices F.O.B. Barrington, N.J.

Surprise Someone With A Gift Certificate
Give a choice of science gifts. We will send a certificate with your name and message plus a catalog. Available in any dollar amount from $20.00 up.

Mailing List Information
How To Receive A Catalog: You are assured of receiving our latest catalogs by making occasional purchases. Friends can receive a copy of our catalog by using the order blank on this envelope.
MAIL PREFERENCE SERVICE: As a service to our customers, we occasionally share our mailing lists with other high-quality mail-order companies so that you may learn about other products of interest. If you do not wish to receive such mailings, send an exact copy of your mailing label to:
Edmund Scientific Co.
101 E. Gloucester Pike
Barrington, New Jersey 08007-1380, U.S.A.
Attn: Mail Preference Supervisor

ES Publishes Two Giant Catalogs. . .FREE. . .

. . . to serve America's science community. Our 80-page Hobbyist Edition contains hundreds of general science items to serve your project needs. Our 172-page Industrial Educational Catalog features thousands of items, including optical components and scientific instruments. It is yours FREE, but by request only. (We prefer your office or school address if possible.)

EDMUND SCIENTIFIC COMPANY
Department #C900
Industrial Catalog #1987-C900
101 East Gloucester Pike
Barrington, New Jersey 08007-1380, U.S.A.

Visit Our Factory Store
It's a great place to buy all items in this catalog and much, much more.
Minutes from Exit 3 of the New Jersey Turnpike or from the "Route 30" East exit of Interstate 295. Call us for complete directions!
Dial 1-609-573-6241 for retail store only. No orders are taken at this number.

Store Hours:
Monday through Saturday
9 a.m.–5:30 p.m.
Sunday
Noon to 5:00 p.m.
Closed:
New Year's Day,
Easter Sunday,
Memorial Day,
Independence Day, Labor Day,
Thanksgiving and
Christmas.

BEFORE SEALING ENVELOPE, DID YOU REMEMBER TO:
1. Print your name and address.
2. Add correct shipping charges.
3. Fill in all information (item numbers and quantity).
4. Enclose your check, money order or credit card information.

Name _____

Company/School _____

Address _____ Apt. # _____

City _____

State _____ Zip _____

Place Stamp Here

Edmund Scientific Co.

Attn: Order Processing Department #19C9
101 E. Gloucester Pike
Barrington, NJ 08007-1380, U.S.A.

||..|.|.||..||..|..|..||.||.|.||....|.|.|

Figure 15.24   Reverse side of Edmund Scientific's order form.

on Edmund's two free catalogs, and information on visiting the Edmund Store, including a map. Not a bit of space is wasted.

HOW TO STIMULATE ADDITIONAL SALES WITH YOUR CATALOG

Just because a catalog is a catalog, many mail order operators overlook ways of stimulating additional sales though devices they may ordinarily use when selling a single product. Some of these items to stimulate your sales have already been discussed in earlier chapters. Others will be new here. Use this list as a checklist as you go through your catalog to make sure you have at least thought about doing these things to boost your sales from the catalog that you have put together.

1. *Money-Back Guarantee with a Free Trial Period.* Don't forget that, just as in other mail order selling, the strongest guarantee will boost your sales, and a free trial period of one sort or another is also good for products you sell from a catalog.

2. *Toll-Free Telephone Orders.* It's a definite plus if you can offer your customers the capability of ordering through a toll-free line. Here again, profitability is what counts. You will pay extra for the toll-free line, so you must make this trade-off of additional cost against the additional sales you will make.

3. *You Need Not Carry Every Credit Card.* However, accepting Visa and MasterCard, the most often used credit cards in the United States, will greatly increase your sales.

4. *Discounts Tied to the Size of the Order.* A discount tied to the size of the order will frequently get your customer to increase the order. Therefore, consider offering discounts for orders as they increase in magnitude.

5. *Free Gifts Tied to the Size of the Order.* People like to get something for nothing and if you offer free gifts, even though they may not be very expensive, it will have a positive impact on increasing the size of your customer's order on almost every order that you receive.

6. *Sweepstakes.* We talked about this in an earlier chapter. It can be particularly important with a catalog because of the seasonal nature of some of them, such as Christmas catalogs. If your customers don't order at once from such catalogs, they won't be ordering at all. Therefore, sweepstakes, or anything else that encourages your customers to send their orders in immediately will have a positive effect and will boost your catalog sales.

7. *A Fax Number.* Many people order by Fax today.

HOW FREQUENTLY SHOULD YOU MAIL
YOUR CATALOG TO YOUR CUSTOMERS?

There are two right answers to this important question. One is always to test to see what is most profitable for you, considering the fact that every time you send a catalog out you should get money back in sales. At the same time, there is a cost associated not only with mailing, but with the printing and producing of the catalog itself. However, there's another right answer: Keep mailing a catalog to your customer as long as he or she continues to purchase from you. Many people who are vitally interested in a particular subject will order the same day that your catalog comes in, throw that catalog out, and wait for the next catalog before ordering again. Not everyone will keep the catalog over a period of time. However, a useful concept to understand with catalog sales is that of the half-life of your catalog. The half-life concept refers to that period from the time you send the catalog to your customer until you get half the total orders you can expect from that specific catalog. In general, the half-life of a catalog is three or four months, but that is not a standardized figure and will vary significantly, depending upon type of merchandise, the type of catalog, your firm, your market segment, and environmental variables. So you must test to discover the half-life. Once you have half-life computed, you will know fairly easily about the success of a particular catalog and the products, and that knowledge will help you decide when to mail a new catalog to your customer.

THE INCREDIBLE OVERWRAP
AND WHAT IT WILL DO FOR YOU

The catalog overwrap is a relatively new idea. Basically, it is a four-page sheet stapled to the outside of the catalog. The overwrap is a great place to try new product ideas without making major changes in your catalog, remembering that changing the interior is going to run into money every time. The four-page overwrap can be changed for much less money. It's a good place to feature incentives to order, such as sweepstakes and free gifts. The overwrap is also an outstanding place for a letter to your customer. It has been discovered that a letter inside the catalog is the least read of any material in your catalog. But on the outside, your letter is read. You can be certain that you will reach your target audience. Now, you may not wish to include an overwrap at first, especially if your catalog itself is rather skimpy. But once your catalog begins to fill out substantially, think about using the overwrap. It's a great device.

HOW TO GET SAMPLE CATALOGS IN YOUR FIELD

Sample catalogs are a source of ideas as well as information on what your competition is doing. You can get sample catalogs by writing to various mail order companies. But how do you locate them? One way, of course, is to keep your eyes open while perusing magazines that are of interest to your customers. You will see your competition in these magazines and you can write for catalogs. Directories of catalogs are available too. Here are six such directories. They list thousands of mail order companies offering catalogs.

> *The Catalog of Catalogs III,* by Edward L. Palder. Woodbine House, 5615 Fishers Lane, Rockville, MD 20852.
>
> *The Great Book of Catalogs,* by Steve and Betsy Pinkerton. American Autocrafts, Inc., 135 Oak Terrace, Lake Bluff, IL 60044.
>
> *The Wholesale by Mail Catalog,* by Lowell Miller, executive producer, and Prudence McCullough, editor. St. Martin's Press, 175 Fifth Avenue, New York, NY 10010.
>
> *The Great Catalogue Guide,* Direct Marketing Association, 6 East 43rd Street, New York, NY 10017.
>
> *The National Directory of Catalogs,* Oxbridge Communications, Inc., 150 Fifth Ave., New York, NY 10114-0235.
>
> *The Directory of Mail Order Catalogs,* Grey House Publishing, Pocket Knife Square, Lakeville, CT 06039.

SUMMARY

In this chapter, we've discussed important points about selling through your own mail order catalog. First, we've considered the advantages of selling through catalogs both to you and to your customer. Then we've looked at a variety of different catalog samples in totally different businesses, offering totally different types of products. Finally, we've considered factors that lead to success in mail order catalog selling, including product selection, cost control, use of copy and graphics, making the decision between color and black and white, the great importance of the order form, use of various boosters to increase sales by catalog, and such decisions as how frequently you should mail your catalog and whether to use the catalog overwrap device. Finally, I've listed six sources where you can find sample catalogs to get ideas, check to see what your competition is doing, and compare products.

16

Making Money
with 900 Numbers

You may have been contacted through direct mail by a service bureau offering a free seminar and the prospect of making millions of dollars through 900 numbers in which the caller pays for the call and the phone company acts as your collection agent at a price per minute that you set for your service. You may have seen advertisements on television for various 900 or 976 numbers yourself, and wondered if it were worth looking in to. Is there big money to be made through these numbers in which customers call for information, advice, to express an opinion, or just to talk to someone?

THE HISTORY OF 900 NUMBERS

These numbers have become an important part of direct response and mail order businesses. 976 numbers came first. They are statewide, not national, billed at a flat rate per call, not by the minute. These numbers caught on fast, and they were extremely profitable. One 976 line in New York City gave sports scores. A 58-second message was updated every 15 minutes. That line brought in an incredible $250,000 to $350,000 a day in that one city alone. Soon, New York had a weather line, a lottery results line, an astrology line, and a horse racing line as well. With no competition, and charging just pennies per call, these lines still made big money.

Then, in the early 1980s, women were put on the line for what became known as "dial-a-porn." The first of these lines generated one to four million calls the first week. Others jumped in with Santa Claus, Easter Bunny, and cartoon lines and starting marketing to children. The bad publicity and market saturation combined to cause sales of 976 numbers to plummet in the period of 1983–1985.

Then, AT&T introduced the 900 number where one number could be used from around the country, greatly expanding the potential market. It was the 976 story all over again until 1988, when charges began being made per minute rather than per call. Now the numbers were interactive, and the longer the customer stayed on the line, the more money the company providing the service made. This interaction also caused the rise of the service bureau. This is because expensive computers and switching is needed. A service bureau has invested in the equipment and has racks of personal computers and telephone lines. A good service bureau will do much more for you, as I'll explain shortly. And the 900 line business? Well, it's currently estimated to earn $3–4 billion per year.

WHAT KIND OF SERVICE CAN YOU SELL WITH A 900 NUMBER?

What services can you provide using a 900 line? Well, as with all "products," even electronic ones, what you can provide is limited only by the law and your imagination. Dating lines have done well in the past. I've already noted lines giving late breaking sports scores, job lines, astrology information, and the more notorious "phone sex" 900 numbers. Prices charged are generally $2 per minute.

The potential for the right service is impressive. The biggest category in the business is entertainment. A few years ago, a 900 number was established promoting M.C. Hammer, the rap musician. It charged the caller $2 per minute. You could press "1" on your touch tone phone to join his fan club, another number to know about his social life, and yet another number to hear his latest song. Well, that M.C. Hammer 900 line grossed $8 million a year!

Another profitable line offered low cost legal information using a 900 number. In less than a year, they had over 900,000 members who had paid $9 just to make the initial call.

BEWARE OF "RIP-OFF" SERVICE BUREAUS

Unfortunately, the potential for this kind of money attracted a number of people out to rip-off entrepreneurs who wanted access to these 900 lines. To understand how the scam works, you need to understand that it is not economically feasible to operate without a "service bureau." The service bureau not only obtains the number from the phone company for you, but tracks everything, keeps your records, provides period accounting, and most importantly gives you good and ongoing marketing advice. A true service bureau makes its money from the profits your unique product generates.

Now, the scam service bureau. They offer free seminars. Many are conducted by some of the best motivational speakers you can find. Many of these speakers know little about the business. They either are brokers who get the lines from a service bureau and resell them to you, or salesmen who work on commission. They appeal to a sense of greed. They make a fortune, whether or not you make a cent in profits.

Here's how. Let's say they give only one seminar a day. I should add that some of these outfits manage to present as many as four seminars a day. They may have 100 attendees or more at each free seminar. As many as 50 percent of their attendees sign up for 900 lines. Typically, the "bureau" gets $500 up front before any other costs. If you can manage 200 seminars a year, that's 50 buyers × $500 × 200 seminars = $5 million!

As I said, many of these companies give even more than one seminar a day. Remember, they get this money even if you never use your lines, and this doesn't even count the percentage they take of the money you take in from your lines . . . whether your line is profitable for you or not. And usually, they are not profitable, because we haven't even talked about your advertising costs. As you know from what you've learned so far in this book, this is a major mail order expense, regardless of your other costs.

Many of these companies offer a so-called "turn key" operation. According to them, they've already tested these special lines, they've been running for years, and they are highly successful. Before you leap into this, reread what I said earlier about having your own unique product, and what will happen if you do not. You don't even control the quality of the product. And believe me, some are pretty bad. A friend who tried one of these "turn key" dating services on a limited scale not only got few responses, and lost money, he got some angry letters from people demanding their money back for their calls, as well.

What these dishonest companies don't tell you in their sales pitches is that making money with 900 numbers isn't that easy. Why not? Some of these companies point to individuals associated with their bureau who have made a lot of money in the business. They say, you can do the same thing just as easily.

The problem is, you can't. Most of these individuals made money during the years when the industry was relatively young and mostly unregulated. For many prospects, just calling in for any kind of 976 or 900 number service was exciting. Almost everyone made money with almost every product. Everybody hit it big! Now, the industry is mature. Prospects are far more sophisticated about using these services and it is no longer a technological fad. Furthermore, the industry is now closely regulated by the federal government. I'll tell you more about how you can get information about the government's rules shortly.

Today, reputable service bureaus will give you advice and consulting and help you to determine whether your potential 900 number products will be successful or not. These companies don't make their money by the money they charge you to sign up, but rather through the sale to you of call time. So, if they don't think you have at least a chance of being profitable, they won't want to deal with you. They'd rather spend time with someone who has a dynamite idea who will make them a lot of money.

HOW TO FIND OUT ALL ABOUT GOVERNMENT REGULATIONS

Just as there is a Federal Trade Commission (FTC) 30-Day Mail Order Rule, the FTC published a business guide for complying with their 900-Number Rule. To get the FTC's rules on television ads, radio ads, preambles (these are required introductory messages preceding your service), cost disclosures, print ads, billing errors, and advertising to children, contact your FTC regional office. You can find it located in the U.S. government section of the white pages in your telephone book, or you can call them in Washington at (202)326-3128. Ask for their free booklet entitled *Complying with the 900-Number Rule.* Among many important restrictions, you will discover that you cannot direct your services to children under 12 unless your service is a "bona fide educational service," and that you cannot direct your ads to those between the ages of 12 and 18 without a disclosure that individuals under 18 need a parent or guardian's permission to call.

HOW TO SET UP A 900-NUMBER LINE

You start first with your idea. This sounds like an over simplification, but it is not. I have talked to many who wanted to sell a service through a 900 number. The were led to believe that just about anything would work. Maybe once, when 900 numbers were new, but not any more. Reread Chapter 6 on finding new products. The same principles apply here. Not everything works, and some very well-known companies have lost a lot of money this way.

Revlon calculated a modest 1.8 percent response on a colorful insert included in 220 general circulation Sunday newspapers around the country. The actual response for their 900 number was less than one tenth of 1 percent from this expensive advertising. They lost a bundle, and Revlon's marketing vice president reportedly left the company over this loss. It can happen to you, so look before you leap.

PHONE COMPANIES, BROKERS, OR SERVICE BUREAUS?

Yes, you can deal with a phone company directly. If you do, current costs are $2,500 if you have never had a 900 number in your name previously, plus an additional $500 per month for leasing that channel. There are a few advantages to dealing directly with the phone company. One is, you'll have more control over the money. The phone company will send it to you directly. If we're talking about millions of dollars, that could be an advantage due to the interest accumulated during the additional delay.

Brokers work for service bureaus on a commission basis. I can't think of why you would want to deal with a broker instead of dealing with a service bureau directly, but there may be some reason. Maybe he is some sort of 900-number genius who always makes money for the service provider he represents and he gives free consulting (although I consider this highly unlikely).

In most cases, dealing with a reputable service business is best. First, the rates are more reasonable than if you were to deal with a telephone company directly. Instead of $2,500, the upfront money to get started is frequently only $500. Instead of $500 per month for leasing the channel, the going rate is about $125 per month.

PICKING THE RIGHT SERVICE BUREAU

As I mentioned previously, there are good, reputable service bureaus, and then there are those that simply make the bulk of their money from your $500 upfront money. How can you tell the difference? Here are some suggestions. First, get a copy of *Voice Processing Magazine*. It incorporates *Infotext*, the industry magazine. It is free to anyone in the business and you can get a copy by dialing (800)346-0085. A number of service bureaus advertise in it. Check with your local phone company. Most will provide you with a list of service bureaus. Check all prospective service bureaus with your local Better Business Bureau to see what experience they have had with them, if any. I recommend getting the full details on at least five service bureaus before signing up with anyone.

Since a reputable service bureau makes its money by generating time and your sales, they'll want to know your idea, and you'll want to know what the service bureau thinks of your idea. However, get someone at that bureau to sign and date a nondisclosure statement first. This means that whoever signs the form agrees not to disclose your idea to anyone else. It is not perfect protection, but it is better than no protection at all.

Ask for other service providers you can contact as a reference. And then, get the bureau's rates, but keep this in mind. With a telephone company, nothing is negotiable. With a service bureau, everything is negotiable.

NEGOTIATING WITH A SERVICE BUREAU

Service bureaus usually begin with talking about set up and installation fees. Keep in mind that there is really nothing to set up and nothing to install. However, there is an approval process with the phone company and the bureau must process this. This is the justification for the $500–$750 set up fee. Any justification for an installation fee is questionable.

Then there will be a per minute cost to you. The going rate for the per minute cost is 10 to 25 cents per minute. There is also a monthly minimum, usually $500. In your negotiations, the tradeoff is between cost per minute versus the guaranteed minimum you must pay.

Software is another potential negotiable cost. The average rate for software preparation is about $75 per hour. usually, existing software is used, but it takes two to four hours of work to customize it. Audio production is another cost to negotiate. This is usually about $40 per hour. The average audio production is about five hours per month. However, it may be possible to record you own audio directly over your phone into a computer, saving the entire amount. Then, there are a number of miscellaneous costs such as data reports. This may cost $100 per month.

Ask about other charges and costs. One is chargeback. These are amounts charged back to you for those cases where the telephone company doesn't collect the money for one reason or another. Usually, a percentage of your money will be held in reserve by the telephone company for chargeback. The service bureau will keep all your records for you and will send you your money and complete records of calls made periodically. This is pretty easy as the customer pays on his or her regular telephone bill, so the money goes to the service bureau, then to you.

Your contract is also negotiable. Most service bureaus ask for a three-month contract. However, from your viewpoint this is hardly favorable. Like most direct response advertising, you'll know in a few weeks whether you have a winner or a bomb. Also, you shouldn't have to pay anything until the phone company accepts your application. This will take about two weeks.

Lay your whole operation out on paper and work it out. You can get marketing and other advice from the service bureau you selected. Then, calculate the mathematics. Get advice from your service bureau on how much to charge and how long the call is likely to be. Once you know that you are going to charge $2 per minute and the average length of call is likely to be 5 minutes, you have some estimates to work with. Develop your marketing plan including your advertising strategies and tactics, the response you need to make money, and the costs. This will tell you whether or not it is worth it, and what your real potential for this project is.

SUMMARY

You can make money with 900 numbers. However, this is not a get-rich-quick scheme any more than mail order is in general. Treat the 900 number as you would any other mail order campaign. Keep careful records, do your homework, and apply the proven direct response techniques in this book. Don't hesitate to get advice from your service bureau about all aspects of marketing your specific service. A reputable service company makes their money through the minutes they sell through you, not through the upfront money you pay.

Part IV

The Mail Order
Message

17

The Truth about Copywriting

MUST YOU BE ABLE TO WRITE COPY?

A well-known expert in mail order spoke to my class at the university about copywriting, and was asked, "What if you can't write good copy yourself?" He answered, "If you can't write good copy, you don't belong in the business." I most emphatically disagree. The fact is that most large mail order businesses are run without the owner writing the copy. Certainly in most of the companies that are huge conglomerates, members of the *Fortune* 500 group, the manager of the mail order division does not write copy.

However, even if you decide that you are not qualified to write copy nor do you have the desire to do so, please don't skip this chapter. You must understand the basic principles to know what the copywriters working for you are doing, and whether what they propose in your advertisements has any chance of working. Let me give you a specific example here. At one point in my life, I was using a space advertisement in a magazine called *International Defense Review* to get leads for military body armor that would protect the soldier against various types of projectiles. At that time I'd written some copy, but not a great deal of mail order copy. Accordingly, I gave the idea and product to an agency and asked them to come up with a concept. After several weeks of activity, they presented me with an ad headlined, "What the Well-Dressed Soldier Wears." The body of the copy discussed various specifications of the body armor having to do with its size and the projectiles it would stop. Because I had taken the time to study the basic principles of copywriting, I knew this was wrong because the discussion centered not on benefits, but on a description of the product. I rejected this ad and wrote my own, which was highly successful, headed, "Body Armor Wins Battles." As you might imagine, the copy itself focused not on a mere description of what the body armor would do, but on how it benefited the wearer.

WHAT IS COPY AND CAN IT MAKE A DIFFERENCE?

Copy consists of the words used to communicate your message or offer to your prospective customers in a classified ad, a display ad, direct mail, or through some other medium. It can make an incredible difference in whether your proposition is successful or unsuccessful. World-famous copywriter John Caples, in his book *Tested Advertising Methods,* speaks of two ads in which the size was the same, the publications were identical, and both ads used identical photo illustrations; only the copy differed. One ad sold 19½ times as much product as the other. Stop now and think what this means. This is not only the difference between success and failure, but the difference between failure and making an immediate fortune. So the copy used in your ad is not just something you must consider somewhere along the way. It, by itself, can make you a mail order millionaire.

IS COPYWRITING POSSIBLE TO LEARN?

Copywriting can be learned by anyone who is reading this book and can write. It is simply a method of communicating with your customer. It is sales in writing.

Some years ago, Dr. George W. Crane, in his book, *Psychology Applied,* described how Professor S. N. Stevens of Northwestern University had a debate with some professional advertisers. Professor Stevens felt that he could identify which ads had been successful, based upon psychological principles. Eventually he challenged the professional advertisers to give him 10 advertisements whose results they already knew. His job would be to rank them in their order of merit, from best to worst, according to the response these advertisements had generated. Professor Stevens asked only the target market and the purpose of the advertiser in each advertisement. He then picked up his pencil and pad and ranked them in order of their actual pulling power. Out of 10 advertisements handed to him, he erred only in the last and two weakest samples submitted, which he transposed. He identified the first through the eighth correctly. This shows that while copywriting may be mysterious, there are known psychological principles that are used and that work.

HOW TO LEARN COPYWRITING

To learn copywriting, there are four steps that you must take. They are not always easy, but if you follow them faithfully you will be able to write good copy with confidence.

1. *Read Books on Copywriting.* I'm going to recommend three books right now because they are written by three great copywriters. The first is *Tested Advertising Methods,* by John Caples, published by Prentice-Hall, Englewood Cliffs, NJ 07632. The second is *My First Sixty Years in Advertising,* by Maxwell Sackheim, published by Prentice-Hall, Englewood Cliffs, NJ 07632. The third is *How to Write a Good Advertisement: A Short Course in Copywriting,* by Victor O. Schwab, published by The Wilshire Book Company, 12015 Sherman Road, North Hollywood, CA 91605.

2. *Collect and Read Successful Ads.* You will find them in magazines, through the mail, and so forth. You know the advertisement is successful if you see it repeated over a long period. I have a file of hundreds of advertisements and letters I have received. I read and reread all of them. In some cases I can tell you the copywriter simply by reading the copy. After a while, you will be able to do the same. More importantly, in many cases you will be able to pick up a magazine or a direct mail piece you have received and tell instantly whether the product has a chance for success, simply by reading the copy.

3. *Learn the Basic Principles.* We will discuss these principles in this chapter.

4. *Practice.* You can read books, you can read copy, and you can learn the principles and still not become a copywriter unless you practice writing copy frequently. One way to do this is to take an advertisement you feel to be a poor one and rewrite it, using the principles of good copywriting. Do at least one ad a week. Don't be satisfied with just rewriting the advertisement once. Try several different appeals and several different ways to reach your customers. Show your efforts to friends and ask them to pick which ad they would be most likely to respond to. (Retype the advertisement which appears in the magazine or in a letter so they cannot tell the difference.) When your ad is picked more often as the best ad, you will know that you are becoming an individual who can write good mail order copy.

HOW TO STRUCTURE THE COPY IN YOUR AD OR LETTER

There are many different formulas around for structuring copy. In fact, there are so many that some copywriters recommend that you not try any formula at all, but simply try "to communicate." My belief is that you should start out with a definite structure. Learn this structure and write your advertisements in this way initially. Once you know that you can write good mail order copy, you can experiment and try the more philosophical concept of communicating without reference to a formula.

The basic structure I recommend is as follows:

1. Get attention.
2. Develop interest.
3. Show the benefits and advantages of your product or service.
4. Build up and maintain credibility.
5. Deliver a call to action.

THE HEADLINE IS YOUR ATTENTION GETTER

The most important aspect of your ad and copy is the headline. Yet, many copywriters who will spend hours and hours slaving over the copy in the body of the ad will spend just a few minutes on the headline. David Ogilvy, chairman of Ogilvy Mather International, one of the world's best-known advertising agencies, says in his *Confessions of an Advertising Man,* "The headline is the most important element in most advertisements."

The weekly magazine *Advertising Age* once told how Maxwell Sackheim sold 500,000 copies of a book by changing the title slightly. The book was originally published as *Five Acres.* While it enjoyed reasonable sales, it was not a best seller and was about to go on the inactive list when Maxwell Sackheim got involved. Sackheim believes that the title of a book should be good enough to be used as the headline of an advertisement. So he changed the title from *Five Acres* to *Five Acres and Independence.* This small change caused sales to double and triple previous records, and within six years, 500,000 copies of the book were sold.

Want more proof about headlines? Book publisher E. Haldeman-Julius sold tens of millions of *Little Blue Books* through newspaper and magazine advertisements. These books were small paperbacks that sold for only 5¢ and 10¢ each. In the advertising, they were designated only by their titles, with no other description or copy. In his book, *The First Hundred Million,* Haldeman-Julius tells how he frequently changed titles of books about to be dropped from his line because they were not selling well. The right change brought a dramatic increase in sales. Dr. George W. Crane began using Haldeman-Julius' results in his lectures. The idea was for the subject to imagine himself or herself a publisher selling books to the general public. The subject was asked to pick which of a pair of book titles he or she would select to sell the greater number of volumes. Remember that *Little*

Blue Books were sold with no description whatsoever other than the title. This test was administered in conventions and society meetings to over 50,000 editors, physicians, dentists, lawyers, engineers, advertisers, salespeople, merchants, and teachers. Other individuals also gave the identical test to over 75,000 adults. Would you like to take this test? I have prepared a similar test from the results published in Haldeman-Julius' book, shown in Figure 17.1. Mark which one of the pair of titles you think would sell the most books. The answers are found in Figure 17.2, which shows both the old and new titles and the number of books sold with each. The more right answers, the better your understanding of headline writing.

Okay, you say, so titles of books can actually have a tremendous impact on selling them, and titles of books can also be used as the headlines for

---

The Tallow Ball_____
                or
A French Prostitute's Sacrifice_____

Privateersman_____
                or
The Battles of a Seaman_____

Fleece of Gold_____
                or
The Quest for a Blonde Mistress_____

Honey and Gall_____
                or
Studies in Mystic Materialism_____

A Book of Intellectual Rowdies_____
                or
Cupbearers of Wine and Hellebore_____

The Mystery of the Man in the Iron Mask_____
                or
The Mystery of the Iron Mask_____

The King Enjoys Himself_____
                or
The Lustful King Enjoys Himself_____

None Beneath the King Shall Enjoy This Woman_____
        `   or
None Beneath the King_____

Terse Truths About the Riddles of Life_____
                or
Apothegms_____

Pen, Pencil and Poison_____
                or
The Story of a Notorious Criminal_____

The Truth About Patent Medicine_____
                or
Patent Medicine and Public Health_____

Art of Controversy_____
                or
How to Argue Logically_____

Life of Barnum_____
                or
P.T. Barnum and His Circus_____

Casanova, History's Greatest Lover_____
                or
Casanova and His Loves_____

When You Were a Tadpole and I Was a Fish_____
                or
Poems of Evolution_____

An Introduction to Einstein_____
                or
Einstein's Theory of Relativity Explained_____

Markheim_____
                or
Markheim's Murder_____

Ten O'Clock_____
                or
What Art Should Mean to You_____

The Man Who Apes Nobility_____
                or
The Show-Off_____

The Love Sonnets of an Artist_____
                or
The Sonnets of a Portrait Painter_____

Figure 17.1 Which *Little Blue Book* title do you think sold best? (From Little Blue Book Company, by permission of E. Haldeman-Julius Publications.)

	Yearly Sales
The Tallow Ball	15,000
A French Prostitute's Sacrifice	54,700
Privateersman	less than 6000
The Battles of a Seaman	10,000
Fleece of Gold	6000
The Quest for a Blonde Mistress	50,000
Honey and Gall	almost 0
Studies in Mystic Materialism	15,000
A Book of Intellectual Rowdies	11,000
Cupbearers of Wine and Hellebore	almost 0
The Mystery of the Man in the Iron Mask	30,000
The Mystery of the Iron Mask	11,000
The King Enjoys Himself	8000
The Lustful King Enjoys Himself	38,000
None Beneath the King Shall Enjoy This Woman	34,000
None Beneath the King	6000
Terse Truths About the Riddles of Life	9000
Apothegms	2000
Pen, Pencil, and Poison	5000
The Story of a Notorious Criminal	15,800
The Truth About Patent Medicine	10,000
Patent Medicine and Public Health	3000
Art of Controversy	almost 0
How to Argue Logically	30,000
Life of Barnum	4000
P.T. Barnum and His Circus	8000
Casanova, History's Greatest Lover	28,000
Casanova and His Loves	8000
When You Were a Tadpole and I Was a Fish	7000
Poems of Evolution	2000
An Introduction to Einstein	15,000
Einstein's Theory of Relativity Explained	42,000
Markheim	almost 0
Markheim's Murder	7000
Ten O'Clock	2000
What Art Should Mean to You	9000
The Man Who Apes Nobility	almost 0
The Show-Off	10,000
The Love Sonnets of an Artist	6000
The Sonnets of a Portrait Painter	almost 0

Figure 17.2 These *Little Blue Book* titles sold best. (From Little Blue Book Company, by permission of E. Haldeman-Julius Publications.)

advertisements, and someone may buy a book based solely on the title. But will someone read copy in an advertisement based solely on a headline? Victor Schwab, in his book, *How to Write a Good Advertisement,* describes a story about Max Hart of Hart, Schaffner, and Marx, and his advertising manager, George L. Dyer. The story goes that they were arguing about long copy and Dyer said, "I'll bet you $10 I can write a newspaper page of solid type and you would read every word of it." Hart was ready to bet and said that he didn't have to read a line of copy to know that he would never read an entire page of solid type. But Dyer responded, "I'll only have to give you the headline. The headline would be, 'This Page Is All about Max Hart.'"

John Caples devotes more than one-fifth of his entire book to headlines, and he says, "This is not too much space to devote to this vital subject."

HOW TO WRITE HEADLINES

All good headlines have certain things in common. First, a good headline appeals to the reader's self-interest and stresses the most important benefit of the product or service. If the copywriter can arouse the curiosity of the reader or present startling news or suggest a quick and easy way that the reader might obtain a certain benefit in which he or she is interested, this will enhance the stopping power of the headline. That is what you as a copywriter are trying to do—stop the reader as he or she glances over the hundreds of advertisements in a magazine and get your copy read.

Look at this headline: "How to Wake Up the Financial Genius within You." This headline is from Mark O. Haroldsen's book, which sold several hundred thousand copies. Notice how this headline appeals to self-interest and states a very strong benefit. It also arouses the curiosity of the reader. How *do* you wake up the financial genius within you? The headline promises that, by reading the copy that follows, you will learn how.

Now look at this headline: "How to Form Your Own Corporation without a Lawyer for under $50." This is the ad Ted Nicholas used to sell more than 500,000 copies of his book. Again, self-interest is stressed. It is a news item. It arouses curiosity. And notice how the headline promises the benefit of a quick, easy, and inexpensive way of forming a corporation without even using a lawyer.

Or look at this headline: "Language Translator—Communicate in Any Language without Saying a Word or Learn a New Language with the World's First Computerized Language Translator." Again, this headline appeals to self-interest. It stresses the important benefit of communicating in any language without saying a word and the benefit of learning a new language by the use of what is being sold. This is one of Joe Sugarman's famous ads that has helped him to build a $50 million-dollar-a-year business starting from his garage.

The second thing that good headlines have in common is certain key words that are psychologically powerful in attracting potential customers and getting them to continue to read. David Ogilvy says that the most important of these key words are free and new, but there are other powerful words you can use to work in your appeal. Here is a list of some words psychologists have discovered to be powerful in stopping your readers and getting them to read your entire copy:

advice to	magic
amazing	miracle
announcing	new
at last	now
bargain	power
challenge	powerful
compare	quick
easy	remarkable
found	revolutionary
free	secret
how	sensational
how to	startling
hurry	success
important	suddenly
improvement	wanted
introducing	when
it's here	which
just arrived	who else
last chance	why

Another way to use key words in your headline is to find those words that are so startling and unusual that they stop the reader cold and urge him or her to read on: "Lazy man," "98-pound weakling," "quit work." All of these phrases are unusual enough that they stop the reader, which is the first thing you must do to get your potential customer to read further.

To write a winning headline implies winning out over others. Therefore, the key is to write more than one headline against each of several different appeals. These appeals should relate to Maslow's hierarchy of human needs, discussed earlier.

OTHER IMPORTANT ADVICE CONCERNING HEADLINES

Here are some other factors to consider when you write your headline.

1. *Be specific.* Being specific helps to lend credibility and makes your headline more believable. Don't just say, "Make a Lot of Money"; say, "Make One Million Dollars," or whatever the amount is. Or don't just say, "Do It Fast"; say "Do It in 30 Days or Less."

2. *Do not put negatives in your headline.* Salespeople have found that the positive sells better than the negative. Therefore, avoid the negative and accentuate the positive side in your headlines.

3. *Make certain there is a clear connection between your headline and the copy.* I have occasionally seen headlines that say something like, "Make 10 Million Dollars Today," and the copy goes on to say that what is promised in the headline is impossible and was used only to trick the reader into reading. I have never seen such copy work. No one likes to be tricked. Further, if you have tricked your customer once, he or she has every reason to believe you may do so again. Don't even hint to something like this. Make certain that what you say in the headline relates directly to what is said in the copy.

HEADLINES THAT MADE MILLIONS FOR THEIR ADVERTISERS

Let's look at some winning headlines. Victor O. Schwab, in his book, *How to Write a Good Advertisement,* lists 100 good headlines that were profitable for those who used them.

1. THE SECRET OF MAKING PEOPLE LIKE YOU
2. A LITTLE MISTAKE THAT COST A FARMER $3,000 A YEAR
3. ADVICE TO WIVES WHOSE HUSBANDS DON'T SAVE MONEY—BY A WIFE
4. THE CHILD WHO WON THE HEARTS OF ALL
5. ARE YOU EVER TONGUE-TIED AT A PARTY?
6. HOW A NEW DISCOVERY MADE A PLAIN GIRL BEAUTIFUL
7. HOW TO WIN FRIENDS AND INFLUENCE PEOPLE
8. THE LAST 2 HOURS ARE THE LONGEST—AND THOSE ARE THE 2 HOURS YOU SAVE
9. WHO ELSE WANTS A SCREEN STAR FIGURE?
10. DO YOU MAKE THESE MISTAKES IN ENGLISH?
11. WHY SOME FOODS "EXPLODE" IN YOUR STOMACH
12. HANDS THAT LOOK LOVELIER IN 24 HOURS—OR YOUR MONEY BACK
13. YOU CAN LAUGH AT MONEY WORRIES—IF YOU FOLLOW THIS SIMPLE PLAN
14. WHY SOME PEOPLE ALMOST ALWAYS MAKE MONEY IN THE STOCK MARKET

15. WHEN DOCTORS "FEEL ROTTEN" THIS IS WHAT THEY DO

16. IT SEEMS INCREDIBLE THAT YOU CAN OFFER THESE SIGNED ORIGINAL ETCHINGS—FOR ONLY $5 EACH!

17. FIVE FAMILIAR SKIN TROUBLES—WHICH DO YOU WANT TO OVERCOME?

18. WHICH OF THESE $2.50-TO-$5 BEST SELLERS DO YOU WANT—FOR ONLY $1 EACH?

19. WHO EVER HEARD OF A WOMAN LOSING WEIGHT— AND ENJOYING 3 DELICIOUS MEALS AT THE SAME TIME?

20. HOW I IMPROVED MY MEMORY IN ONE EVENING

21. DISCOVER THE FORTUNE THAT LIES HIDDEN IN YOUR SALARY

22. DOCTORS PROVE 2 OUT OF 3 WOMEN CAN HAVE MORE BEAUTIFUL SKIN IN 14 DAYS

23. HOW I MADE A FORTUNE WITH A "FOOL IDEA"

24. HOW OFTEN DO YOU HEAR YOURSELF SAYING: "NO, I HAVEN'T READ IT; I'VE BEEN MEANING TO!"

25. THOUSANDS HAVE THIS PRICELESS GIFT—BUT NEVER DISCOVER IT!

26. WHOSE FAULT WHEN CHILDREN DISOBEY?

27. HOW A "FOOL STUNT" MADE ME A STAR SALESMAN

28. HAVE YOU THESE SYMPTOMS OF NERVE EXHAUSTION?

29. GUARANTEED TO GO THROUGH ICE, MUD, OR SNOW—OR WE PAY THE TOW!

30. HAVE YOU A "WORRY" STOCK?

31. HOW A NEW KIND OF CLAY IMPROVED MY COMPLEXION IN 30 MINUTES

32. 161 NEW WAYS TO A MAN'S HEART—IN THIS FASCINATING BOOK FOR COOKS

33. PROFITS THAT LIE HIDDEN IN YOUR FARM

34. IS THE LIFE OF A CHILD WORTH $1 TO YOU?

35. EVERYWHERE WOMEN ARE RAVING ABOUT THIS AMAZING NEW SHAMPOO!

36. DO YOU DO ANY OF THESE TEN EMBARRASSING THINGS?

37. SIX TYPES OF INVESTORS—WHICH GROUP ARE YOU IN?

38. HOW TO TAKE OUT STAINS . . . USE [product name] AND FOLLOW THESE EASY DIRECTIONS

39. TODAY . . . ADD $10,000 TO YOUR ESTATE—FOR THE PRICE OF A NEW HAT

40. DOES YOUR CHILD EVER EMBARRASS YOU?

41. IS YOUR HOME PICTURE-POOR?

42. HOW TO GIVE YOUR CHILDREN EXTRA IRON—THESE 3 DELICIOUS WAYS

43. TO PEOPLE WHO WANT TO WRITE—BUT CAN'T GET STARTED

44. THIS ALMOST-MAGICAL LAMP LIGHTS HIGHWAY TURNS BEFORE YOU MAKE THEM

45. THE CRIMES WE COMMIT AGAINST OUR STOMACHS

46. THE MAN WITH THE "GRASSHOPPER MIND"

47. THEY LAUGHED WHEN I SAT DOWN AT THE PIANO— BUT WHEN I STARTED TO PLAY!—

48. THROW AWAY YOUR OARS!

49. HOW TO DO WONDERS WITH A LITTLE LAND!

50. WHO ELSE WANTS LIGHTER CAKE—IN HALF THE MIXING TIME?

51. LITTLE LEAKS THAT KEEP MEN POOR

52. PIERCED BY 301 NAILS . . . RETAINS FULL AIR PRESSURE

53. NO MORE BACK-BREAKING GARDEN CHORES FOR ME—YET OURS IS NOW THE SHOWPLACE OF THE NEIGHBORHOOD

54. OFTEN A BRIDESMAID, NEVER A BRIDE

55. HOW MUCH IS "WORKER TENSION" COSTING YOUR COMPANY?

56. TO MEN WHO WANT TO QUIT WORK SOMEDAY

57. HOW TO PLAN YOUR HOUSE TO SUIT YOURSELF

58. BUY NO DESK . . . UNTIL YOU'VE SEEN THIS SENSA-TION OF THE BUSINESS SHOW

59. CALL BACK THESE GREAT MOMENTS AT THE OPERA

60. "I LOST MY BULGES . . . AND SAVED MONEY TOO"

61. WHY [brand name] BULBS GIVE MORE LIGHT THIS YEAR

62. RIGHT AND WRONG FARMING METHODS—AND LIT-TLE POINTERS THAT WILL INCREASE YOUR PROFITS

63. NEW CAKE-IMPROVER GETS YOU COMPLIMENTS GALORE!

64. IMAGINE ME . . . HOLDING AN AUDIENCE SPELL-BOUND FOR 30 MINUTES!

65. THIS IS MARIE ANTOINETTE—RIDING TO HER DEATH

66. DID YOU EVER SEE A "TELEGRAM" FROM YOUR HEART?

67. NOW ANY AUTO REPAIR JOB CAN BE "DUCK SOUP" FOR YOU

68. NEW SHAMPOO LEAVES YOUR HAIR SMOOTHER—EASIER TO MANAGE

69. IT'S A SHAME FOR YOU NOT TO MAKE GOOD MONEY—WHEN THESE MEN DO IT SO EASILY

70. YOU NEVER SAW SUCH LETTERS AS HARRY AND I GOT ABOUT OUR PEARS

71. THOUSANDS NOW PLAY WHO NEVER THOUGHT THEY COULD

72. GREAT NEW DISCOVERY KILLS KITCHEN ODORS QUICK—MAKES INDOOR AIR "COUNTRY-FRESH"

73. MAKE THIS 1-MINUTE TEST—OF AN AMAZING NEW KIND OF SHAVING CREAM

74. ANNOUNCING . . . THE NEW EDITION OF THE ENCY-CLOPEDIA THAT MAKES IT FUN TO LEARN THINGS

75. AGAIN SHE ORDERS . . . "A CHICKEN SALAD, PLEASE"

76. FOR THE WOMAN WHO IS OLDER THAN SHE LOOKS

77. WHERE YOU CAN GO IN A GOOD USED CAR

78. CHECK THE KIND OF BODY YOU WANT

79. "YOU KILL THAT STORY—OR I'LL RUN YOU OUT OF THE STATE!"

80. HERE'S A QUICK WAY TO BREAK UP A COLD

81. THERE'S ANOTHER WOMAN WAITING FOR EVERY MAN—AND SHE'S TOO SMART TO HAVE "MORNING MOUTH"

82. THIS PEN "BURPS" BEFORE IT DRINKS—BUT NEVER AFTERWARDS!

83. IF YOU WERE GIVEN $200,000 TO SPEND—ISN'T THIS THE KIND OF [type of product, but not brand name] YOU WOULD BUILD?

84. "LAST FRIDAY . . . WAS I SCARED!—MY BOSS ALMOST FIRED ME!"

85. 67 REASONS WHY IT WOULD HAVE PAID YOU TO AN- SWER OUR AD A FEW MONTHS AGO

86. SUPPOSE THIS HAPPENED ON YOUR WEDDING DAY!

87. DON'T LET ATHLETE'S FOOT "LAY YOU UP"

88. ARE THEY BEING PROMOTED RIGHT OVER YOUR HEAD?

89. ARE WE A NATION OF LOW-BROWS?

90. A WONDERFUL TWO YEARS' TRIP AT FULL PAY—BUT ONLY MEN WITH IMAGINATION CAN TAKE IT

91. WHAT EVERYBODY OUGHT TO KNOW . . . ABOUT THIS STOCK AND BOND BUSINESS

92. MONEY-SAVING BARGAINS FROM AMERICA'S OLDEST DIAMOND DISCOUNT HOUSE

93. FORMER BARBER EARNS $8,000 IN 4 MONTHS AS A REAL ESTATE SPECIALIST

94. FREE BOOK—TELLS YOU 12 SECRETS OF BETTER LAWN CARE

95. GREATEST GOLD-MINE OF EASY "THINGS-TO-MAKE" EVER CRAMMED INTO ONE BIG BOOK

96. $80,000 IN PRIZES! HELP US FIND THE NAME FOR THESE NEW KITCHENS

97. NOW! OWN FLORIDA LAND THIS EASY WAY . . . $10 DOWN AND $10 A MONTH

98. TAKE ANY 3 OF THESE KITCHEN APPLIANCES—FOR ONLY $8.95 (VALUES UP TO $15.45)

99. SAVE 20¢ ON 2 CANS OF CRANBERRY SAUCE—LIM- ITED OFFER

100. ONE PLACE-SETTING FREE FOR EVERY THREE YOU BUY!

MORE OUTSTANDING HEADLINES

In the book, *Eighty Years of Best Sellers—1895 to 1975,* Alice Payne Hack- ett and James Henry Burke listed a compilation of both hardcover and paperback titles that sold in the millions. Here are some of the top selling headliners from the list compiled by Hackett and Burke.

Pocket Book of Baby and Child Care, by Dr. Benjamin Spock, sold ap- proximately 23 million copies; *How to Win Friends and Influence People,* by Dale Carnegie, sold 15 million; *Joy of Cooking,* by Irma S. Rombauer and Marian Rombauer Becker, sold 9 million; *Everything You Always Wanted to Know about Sex but Were Afraid to Ask,* by David Reuben, sold 8 million; *Thirty Days to a More Powerful Vocabulary,* by Wilfred J. Funk and Norman Lewis, sold 6.3 million; *Doctor's Quick Weight Loss Diet,* by Irving Stillman and S. S. Baker, sold 5.6 million; *The Power of Positive Thinking,* by Norman Vincent Peale, sold 5.2 million; *Let's Eat Right To Keep Fit,* by Adelle Davis, sold 4.4 million; *The Greatest Story Ever Told,* by Fulton Oursler, sold 3.9 million.

Note in the above list how the titles fit in with our general rules of selecting good headlines.

Here are some of the successful headlines used by mail order operators. Note how they too appeal to self-interest and stress important benefits to the potential customer at the same time that they arouse curiosity, sometimes give actual news information, and show a quick and easy way to reaching a benefit sought by a customer.

CAN YOU PASS THIS TEST? THE LAZY MAN'S WAY TO RICHES—MOST PEOPLE ARE TOO BUSY EARNING A LIVING TO MAKE ANY MONEY

OHIO MAN DISCOVERS THE SECRET OF HOW TO ESCAPE THE AMERICAN RAT RACE

USING A LAWYER MAY BE DANGEROUS TO YOUR WEALTH

THE SECRET OF HAVING GOOD LUCK

NEWEST DISCOVERY BY IAA MAY BE BIGGEST IN THE HISTORY OF ASTROLOGY

HOW YOUR HOROSCOPE CAN BRING YOU WEALTH, LOVE, SUCCESS, AND HAPPINESS

THE AMAZING DIET SECRET OF A DESPERATE HOUSEWIFE

ELECTRONIC INVENTION TURNS HOUSE WIRES INTO GIANT TV ANTENNA

NOW MEASURE DISTANCES QUICKLY AND ACCURATELY WITH RANGER

WITH NO PREVIOUS EXPERIENCE YOU CAN LEARN AT HOME IN SPARE TIME

LOSE TEN TO TWENTY POUNDS OR MORE

EXTRA INCOME EVERY WEEK

HOW TO BE YOUR OWN BOSS IN THE FABULOUS MAIL ORDER BUSINESS WITHOUT STOCKING, PACKING, OR SHIPPING

SEND FOR IT, IT'S FREE

HOW TO MASTER THE ART OF SELLING ANYTHING
HEWLETT-PACKARD PRESENTS THE WORLD'S FIRST POCKET
CALCULATOR THAT CHALLENGES A COMPUTER
FREE GIFT SAMPLE IMPORT
HOW TO GET RICH
AT 4½, SHE'S READING THIRD GRADE BOOKS
FREE MONEY
STEAL THESE BOOKS
FREE BOOK.

HOW TO GAIN INTEREST FOR YOUR ADVERTISEMENT OR YOUR DIRECT MAIL LETTER

Now that you've stopped your potential customer and gotten him or her to begin to read, you must gain interest immediately. There are four basic ways in which to do this: a story; a startling, shocking, or unusual statement; a quotation; or news.

A Story

Perhaps the most effective use of a story is shown in Figure 6.2, "They Laughed When I Sat Down at the Piano, but When I Started to Play . . . !" This ad, written by John Caples, ran for 40 years. Notice how it grabs your interest: "Arthur had just played *The Rosary*. The room rang with applause. I decided that this would be a dramatic moment for me to make my debut. To the amazement of my friends, I strode confidently over to the piano and sat down."

We've talked about Joe Karbo's ad, "The Lazy Man's Way to Riches," throughout this book. It too is a story. Look at the ad, in Figure 17.3. The title is, "The Lazy Man's Way to Riches," and the subtitle is "Most People Are Too Busy Earning a Living to Make Any Money." Then Joe gets into his story. "I used to work hard. The 18-hour days, the 7-day weeks, but I didn't start making big money until I did less, a lot less."

A Startling, Shocking, or Unusual Statement

Let's look first at Mark O. Haroldsen's ad, "How to Wake Up the Financial Genius within You." His lead-in read, "Millionaires are not 100 or even 10 times smarter than you, but it is a fact that millionaires are making 10 to 50 and even 100 times more than you." This ad sold 250,000 copies of Mark's book in one year. Another ad with copy using this technique is headlined, "New $20 Projector Turns Any Size TV Set into a Giant 7-foot

The Lazy Man's Way to Riches

'Most People Are Too Busy Earning a Living to Make Any Money'

I used to work hard. The 18-hour days The 7-day weeks.

But I didn't start making big money until I did less—a lot less.

For example, this ad took about 2 hours to write. With a little luck, it should earn me 50, maybe a hundred thousand dollars.

What's more, I'm going to ask you to send me 10 dollars for something that'll cost me no more than 50 cents. And I'll try to make it so irresistible that you'd be a darned fool not to do it.

After all, why should you care if I make $9.50 profit if I can show you how to make a lot more?

What if I'm so sure that you will make money my Lazy Man's Way that I'll make you a most unusual guarantee?

And here it is: I won't even cash your check or money order for 31 days *after* I've sent you my material.

That'll give you plenty of time to get it, look it over, try it out.

If you don't agree that it's worth at least a hundred times what you invested, send it back. Your *uncashed* check or money order will be put in the return mail.

The only reason I won't send it to you and bill you or send it C.O.D. is because both these methods involve more time and money.

And I'm already going to give you the biggest bargain of your life.

Because I'm going to tell you what it took me 11 years to perfect: How to make money the Lazy Man's Way.

O.K.—now I have to brag a little. I don't mind it. And it's necessary—to prove that sending me the 10 dollars . . . which I'll keep "in escrow" until you're satisfied . . . is the smartest thing you ever did.

I live in a home that's worth $250,000. I know it is, because I turned down an offer for that much. My mortgage is less than half that, and the only reason I haven't paid it off is because my Tax Accountant says I'd be an idiot.

My "office," about a mile and a half from my home, is right on the beach. My view is so breathtaking that people comment that they don't see how I get any work done. But I do enough. About 6 hours a day, 8 or 9 months a year.

The rest of the time we spend at our mountain "cabin." I paid $30,000 for it—cash.

I have 2 boats and a Cadillac. All paid for.

We have stocks, bonds, investments, cash in the bank. But the most important thing I have is priceless: time with my family.

And I'll show you just how I did it—the Lazy Man's Way—a secret that I've shared with just a few friends 'til now.

It doesn't require "education." I'm a high school graduate.

It doesn't require "capital." When I started out, I was so deep in debt that a lawyer friend advised bankruptcy as the only way out. He was wrong. We paid off our debts and, outside of the mortgage, don't owe a cent to any man.

It doesn't require "luck." I've had more than my share, but I'm not promising you that you'll make as much money as I have. And you may do better; I personally know one man who used these principles, worked hard, and made 11 million dollars in 8 years. But money isn't everything.

It doesn't require "talent." Just enough brains to know what to look for. And I'll tell you that.

It doesn't require "youth." One woman I worked with is over 70. She's travelled the world over, making all the money she needs, doing only what I taught her.

It doesn't require "experience." A widow in Chicago has been averaging $25,000 a

". . . I didn't have a job and I was worse than broke. I owed more than $50,000 and my only assets were my wife and 8 children. We were renting an old house in a decaying neighborhood, driving a 5-year old car that was falling apart, and had maybe a couple of hundred dollars in the bank.

Within one month, after using the principles of the Lazy Man's Way to Riches, things started to change — to put it mildly.

- *We worked out a plan we could afford to pay off our debts — and stopped our creditors from hounding us.*
- *We were driving a brand-new Thunderbird that a car dealer had given to us.*
- *Our bank account had multiplied tenfold.*
- *All within the first 30 days!*

And today . . .

- *I live in a home that's worth over $250,000.*
- *I own my "office." It's about a mile and a half from my home and is right on the beach.*
- *I own a lakefront "cabin" in Washington. (That's where we spend the whole summer — loafing, fishing, swimming and sailing.)*
- *I own two oceanfront condominiums. One is on a sunny beach in Mexico and one is snuggled right on the best beach of the best island in Hawaii.*
- *I have two boats and a Cadillac. All paid for.*
- *I have a net worth of over a Million Dollars. But I still don't have a job . . ."*

year for the past 5 years, using my methods.

What does it require? Belief. Enough to take a chance. Enough to absorb what I'll send you. Enough to put the principles into action. If you do just that—nothing more, nothing less—the results will be hard to believe. Remember—I guarantee it.

You don't have to give up your job. But you may soon be making so much money that you'll be able to. Once again—I guarantee it.

The wisest man I ever knew told me something I never forgot: "Most people are too busy earning a living to make any money."

Don't take as long as I did to find out he was right.

Here are some comments from other people. I'm sure that, like you, they didn't believe me either. Guess they figured that, since I wasn't going to deposit their check for 31 days, they had nothing to lose.

They were right. And here's what they gained.

$260,000 in eleven months

"Two years ago, I mailed you ten dollars in sheer desperation for a better life.

One year ago, just out of the blue sky, a man called and offered me a partnership . . . I grossed over $260,000 cash business in eleven months. You are a God sent miracle to me."

B. F., Pascagoula, Miss.

Made $16,901.92 first time out

"The third day I applied myself totally to what you had shown me. I made $16,901.92. That's great results for my first time out."

J. J. M., Watertown, N.Y.

'I'm a half-millionaire'

"Thanks to your method, I'm a half-millionaire . . . would you believe last year at this time I was a slave working for peanuts!"

G. C., Toronto, Canada

$7,000 in five days

"Last Monday I used what I learned on page 83 to make $7,000. It took me all week to do it, but that's not bad for five day's work."

M. D., Topeka, Kansas

Can't believe success

"I can't believe how successful I have become. . . . Three months ago, I was a telephone order taker for a fastener company in Chicago, Illinois. I was driving a beat up 1959 Rambler and had about

$600 in my savings account. Today, I am the outside salesman for the same fastener company. I'm driving a company car . . . I am sitting in my own office and have about $3,000 in my savings account."

G. M., Des Plaines, Ill.

I know you're skeptical. After all, what I'm saying is probably contrary to what you've heard from your friends, your family, your teachers and maybe everyone else you know. I can only ask you one question.

How many of them are millionaires?

So it's up to you.

A month from today, you can be nothing more than 30 days older — or you can be on your way to getting rich. You decide.

Sworn Statement
"On the basis of my professional relationship as his accountant, I certify that Mr. Karbo's net worth is more than one million dollars."
Stuart A. Cogan

Bank Reference
Home Bank
17010 Magnolia Avenue
Fountain Valley, California 92708

Joe Karbo
17105 South Pacific, Dept. 1000
Sunset Beach, California 90742

Joe, you may be full of beans, but what have I got to lose? Send me the Lazy Man's Way to Riches. But don't deposit my check or money order for 31 days after it's in the mail.

If I return your material — for any reason — within that time, return my uncashed check or money order to me. On that basis, here's my ten dollars.

Name _____

Address _____

City _____

State _____   Zip _____

1978 Joe Karbo

Figure 17.3   A good example of an ad that tells a story.

Screen." Then the first paragraph read as follows: "Yours absolutely free on a 30-day home trial and I won't collect even 1¢ from you until you've had a full month to enjoy and sell for only $20 my new TV projector kit that enlarges theater-size pictures from any television set." The third example is shown in Figure 17.4. The headline reads, "Hear the Tick of a Clock—a Pin Drop—A Kiss or Even a Sigh a Full ½ Block Away!"

Using a Quote

Using a quote is an excellent way of gaining your reader's interest. Duraclean, which provides dealerships under a franchise for cleaning furniture, carpets, and so forth, uses this technique very successfully. The headline reads, "I Wanted a Business Where I Could Work Part-Time, with a Small Investment, Something I Could Do Myself, a Quality Product in Great Demand, with Stability in Hard Times, with Good Profit Potential—I Found It All with Duraclean." Then the first paragraph is a quote: "This is by far the best deal I have ever had. I only regret I didn't find this 25 years ago." *Ms. Magazine* uses this technique in a headline that reads, "What Is *Ms. Magazine* and Why Is It Saying All These Terrible Things?" Then the lead-in begins with the quote, "I'm never too thin to feel fat." An ad that sells a course on vinyl repair starts out with a quote: "Repaired 63 chairs for a VA nursing home. The job paid $190, could have charged more. The nursing home previously paid an upholsterer $22,700 for repairing the same number of chairs." Note how effectively quotes can be used to make your copy interesting and to lead in to the rest of your advertisement or direct mail letter.

News

News can be used in two different ways to lead into your story. One way is simply a short statement that says something of news value. For example, a recent advertisement started with the simple statement, "The U.S. Mint stopped production of these commemorative coins after 1976." Or how about this one? "Break-ins are at an all-time high." Or this one: "Forty-six million small engines are in service today." The second type is an ad written entirely as if it were a news story. A good example of this is Ben Suarez's ad, "Ohio Man Discovers the Secret of How to Escape the American Rat Race," shown in Figure 17.5. Note how this ad leads off: "The secret to making a quick fortune in America has been reduced to a simple 7-step system by an entrepreneur from Canton, Ohio. It requires little or no money, a minimum of time, and no elaborate plant or equipment. In fact, you can do it in your home or anywhere." That ad was written in 1978. Figure 17.6 shows Suarez's latest ad using the same technique.

NOW! Amazing New 'Ampli-Fone' Pulls In, Magnifies, Clarifies All Sound Waves, Even A Whisper!

HEAR THE TICK OF A CLOCK— A PIN DROP— A KISS OR EVEN A SIGH A FULL ½ BLOCK AWAY!

PRICE SMASHING BREAKTHROUGH!
Not $49.95 $39.05 $29.95
Now Only $18⁸⁸

Just Like A Super-Powerful Antenna, Concealed Right Behind Your Ear!

AS SEEN ON TV

Magnifies Even The Faintest Sounds From 5 to 55 Times Louder!

AND CHECK THESE OTHER DELUXE FEATURES:
- On/Off switch at your fingertips
- 6 sound levels to choose from (up close to long distance)
- Weighs less than an ounce
- Fully adjustable for total comfort behind right or left ear
- Comes with extended lifetime power cell battery

FULL ONE YEAR MONEY BACK GUARANTEE

BUT SUPPLIES ARE SEVERELY LIMITED — AT THIS INCREDIBLE LOW PRICE WE ANTICIPATE A COMPLETE SELLOUT. TO MAKE SURE YOU DO NOT MISS OUT— ACT NOW!

NOW! HEAR HUSHED CONVERSATIONS — THE SOFTEST DOOR CHIMES — EVEN A BABY'S WHIMPER, up to 3 ROOMS OR EVEN 2 FLOORS AWAY!

It's the price breakthrough and technology breakthrough of the year! The incredible 'AMPLI-FONE'...science's micro-sonic personal sound amplifier that you've seen on TV — only NOW, INSTEAD OF $49.95, $39.95 or even $29.95 it's yours on a FULL NO-RISK TRIAL BASIS FOR ONLY $19.98, while limited supply still lasts!

SMALL AS A DIME— IT NESTLES OUT OF SIGHT RIGHT BEHIND YOUR EAR!

Based upon the same audio-technology used by the telephone company to increase volume reception for individuals and conference calls...the 'AMPLI-FONE' is now available for personal use to extend the level of your hearing range to as far as 1/4 MILE AWAY! Just think how this can dramatically change the quality of your daily life — transport you into a whole new world of sound you've never been able to enjoy until now.

For instance: NOW, at a football game you'll sit in the stands and hear the quarterback call the plays as clearly as if you were part of the backfield! NOW, you'll sit in the last row of a theater, the movies, a concert or lecture hall and hear every last word, every last note as distinctly as if you were on stage! NOW, enjoy TV, the radio, your Hi-Fi with the volume set on "low"

without annoying anyone else in the room. Yet the sounds, the words, the music you are listening to come in sharp, crisp, crystal clear!

Yes, NOW, thanks to 'AMPLI-FONE' even the poorest, weakest telephone connection...the faintest, faultiest, barely audible doorbells — even the most garbled announcements on department store public address systems, all come in LOUD, CLEAR, DISTINCT AS A CHURCHBELL! But by far the most dramatic proof of all...if you are an outdoorsman, NOW you'll track deer, rabbits, pheasant, etc. and actually hear them from hundreds of yards away before they hear you! The 'AMPLI-FONE' is absolutely awesome!

YES, JUST LIKE A TELESCOPE GIVES YOU SUPER HUMAN VISION THE 'AMPLI-FONE' GIVES YOU SUPER HUMAN HEARING!

In a nutshell — no matter where you are, no matter how clamorous the conditions — in a stadium, at the beach, in restaurants, why even on a roaring train or a plane with the engines firing away full blast...never again will you miss a word, a sound, a note or a single syllable, no matter how dim or muffled they may seem to others. Because with the 'AMPLI-FONE' you have SUPER HEARING ABILITY so keen, so sharp you can hear the TICK OF A CLOCK, A PIN DROP, A WHISPER, EVEN A SIGH OR A KISS FROM A FULL 1/2 BLOCK AWAY!

© 1994 Lipenwald, Inc.

Figure 17.4   An unusual and provocative headline for a good story ad.

NEWSPAPER REPRINT

Ohio Man Discovers The Secret of How to Escape The American Rat Race

7 Simple Rules Net This Working Man With No Money or Experience $145,000 in First Year

By John Whitehead,
Special Features Writer

(Canton, OH) The secret to making a quick fortune in America has been reduced to a simple 7 step system by an entrepreneur from Canton, Ohio. It requires little or no money, a minimum of time and no elaborate plant or equipment. In fact, you can do it in your home or anywhere.

There are hundreds of rags to riches stories each year in America. However, this one is very unique.

Most successful get rich ventures were spin-offs of something else, or somebody was in the right place at the right time. This venture was accomplished by a working man with no money or experience and was accomplished in a very short period of time.

The man who did it is Ben Swarez from Canton, Ohio, the Pro Football Hall of Fame city.

His neighbors here in Canton call it a movie script. One of the neighbors interviewed had this to say: *"It was unbelievable. One day he's driving around in a rusted out '68 Pontiac station wagon, living in an uncarpeted house that didn't even have a color T.V., and struggling to make ends meet like the rest of us. The next day he's driving in a brand new Lincoln Mark, a brand new Mercury station wagon, a $35,000 GMC motorhome, his house is fixed up like a palace, and he's traveling all over the country."*

So, how was all this accomplished. For that answer I went right to the horse's mouth, my main interview with the creator of the system, Ben Swarez.

QUESTION: OK, Ben, so how in the world did this all start?

ANSWER: I was typical of a good majority of Americans — working at a job for 10 years that I hated, worrying about layoffs, living from pay to pay with no money to do anything except buy the bare essentials. Work held little chance for advancement. Big companies are immoveable and impersonal. I found out quick that moving up had little to do with talent and hard work and more to do with politics, lodge membership, being a friend or relative of a high executive, or riding onto the coattails of an executive and hoping he ascends the organization. I wanted out but I saw no way to escape the proverbial rat race.

Then one day in April the last straw came. An invention of mine was shelved by my company because it had "shown up" the research division. My first thought was to get another job. But, then it hit me. You don't HAVE to work for someone else in this country. This is the land of free enterprise. At that point I said, "I don't know what I'm going to do, or how I'm going to do it, but I'm going into something for myself."

Says You Can Do It Anywhere. He Does It While Traveling In His Motor Home

"My system is geared to the working man who is in the same situation I was: living from pay to pay, no savings or assets, working an 8 hour a day job for a big company, no experience, no rich relatives, nothing."

OFF ON ANOTHER TRIP. "We never had the money for a vacation before, so we're making up for it by traveling off and on 4 months out of the year. We've been just about everywhere." Swarez does his system in his motor home while his wife, Nancy, drives and his two daughters, Sharon and Michele, play and sight-see. That's the family's pet shetland sheepdog on a favorite perch.

Swarez on the spacious wooded grounds of his second home which he uses as a retreat and a guest house.

Doing what he likes to do best on certain weekdays. "I especially like to loaf on Mondays because I hated that day so much when I worked for a big corporation."

QUESTION: Excellent point. Is this when you developed your system?

ANSWER: No, that came a little later — after some hard knocks trying to do things the orthodox way. I tried to start the standard types of businesses that require buying buildings, equipment, hiring people, etc. But, since I had no money I had to try to borrow to do this. I soon found out that banks don't lend you money for new businesses or buying established businesses for that matter. The only time banks lend you money is when you don't need it. The fact is that no one is going to

lend you money to start a business. I finally did manage to start a standard type business through renting and getting credit. To make a long story short, I ended up losing a lot of money I didn't have trying to do things this orthodox way.

Then I started to buy the "get rich books". I quickly found out that these are nothing but franchise schemes, selling jobs or stupid real estate deals that take you forever to make money.

Then another thing spurred me on. I read an article by the Social Security Administration.

(Over)

C-09

(continued)

Figure 17.5   An ad that looks like news.

It related, "out of every 100 persons reaching 65 years old 50 are flat broke, 30 are dead, 15 have a little money and only 5 are rich" I wasn't going to work 40 years and end up in a "home", flat broke.

QUESTION: So this is when you came up with the big system?

ANSWER: Yes, but there is a little more to it. I pondered and researched how to do it for months always running into stone walls. They say your subconscious does all your heavy creative work. It does. One night of all times when I was lifting weights in my basement the solution rolled out of my mind like a computer print out. It was the simplest, fastest and most direct way to make a lot of money. I quickly wrote it down and after analyzing it, the system boiled down to a few simple rules or steps.

You use these steps to assemble what I call a Net Profit Generator System or N.P.G.S. for short. That night I stayed up late and assembled N P.G.S -1.

To make a very long story short, the first N.P.G.S. failed miserably and I lost even more money. But, I could see that my N P.G.S. concept was sound. It just needed to be perfected. After going to the limit of my creditors and being $70,000 in debt, I came up with what I felt was a perfected system, N.P.G.S.-4. It was time to test it. If N.P.G.S.-4 failed, it was the end of the line.

QUESTION: That must have been a tense moment waiting for the results to come in?

ANSWER: It was real life drama at its highest intensity.

It was a muggy mid-August morning when I waited for the results to come in. I would know that day if it worked or not.

The phone rang with the results. I stood there with sweaty palms and my heart in my mouth. The news? N.P.G.S.-4 was a smashing success!

The first rollout paid off all my debts with money left over.

QUESTION: Incredible. When did you start making your first big money for yourself?

ANSWER: Very shortly afterward. I projected a way to do big rollouts without having to put up any money. My second rollout of N.P.G.S.-4 netted my first big payday. I made $80,000 clear!

QUESTION: I can't even imagine getting that much money all at once. What was it like?

ANSWER: It's almost impossible to verbalize. My wife and I just stared at the check for a long time. We had a two day celebration with a dinner and party. It's a fantastic experience to go into work and tell them you quit. I had a little fun doing it. The chance to say what you truly feel to people who have had you under their thumb for 10 years is truly a pleasant release of frustration.

The first thing I did was pay off all my bills. Then I paid off my house. I took the money to the savings and loan company who held the mortgage personally to see the looks on their faces. The teller did a double take. The manager came out and smiled insincerely and said "We don't get too many people paying off a $20,000 mortgage all at one time." Then we had a "burn the mortgage" party. Then I went to the showroom of the local Lincoln-Mercury dealer and laid down the cash for a brand new Mark. I never had a new car in my life. I never even had the experience of a new car even as a kid at home.

Then my wife and I went on a shopping spree for clothes. We had been making do with old clothes for so long they had become worn out. She always had to shop for clothes with very little money. I always joked with her that "If I gave you $5,000 to spend on clothes could

you do it in one day?" She used to say "I could do it in a couple hours." So that's what I did. I gave her $5,000 to go out and buy clothes. It ended up taking all day and she said she relished every minute.

We then took a long trip. In New York I bought her a large diamond at Tiffany's — another thing we always dreamed about.

But I'll tell you the money was not the most important benefit in this. What money really does is give you precious time. Time to be with your wife and children before they grow up before you know it — and time to do things you really want to do. Another priceless thing you gain is your self respect. No more crawling and kneeling because you're dependent. The words of Frank Sinatra's song "My Way" says it all.

QUESTION: This definitely could be a movie script. How did things go after that?

ANSWER: Excellent. The first year I assembled two more systems and made a total of $145,000.

QUESTION: You've been at it for 3½ years now. Were the succeeding years as good?

ANSWER: Better. Here are the results by year. The 1st year as mentioned I made $145,000; the 2nd year I made $205,000; and 3rd year $309,000. And already in the first half of this year I have made $200,000. I have audited financial statements from certified public accountants and income tax returns to verify this to any agency or investigator of any kind who wishes to challenge me on this.

QUESTION: That's quite a system. I understand you're now ready to tell everyone how you did it.

ANSWER: I have put it all into a book, but I may limit the number I will sell.

QUESTION: What can you tell me about the book?

ANSWER: It's called "7 Steps to Freedom, How to Escape the American Rat Race". It contains the complete step-by-step details on how to assemble an N.P.G.S. system which I finally reduced to just 7 simple steps. Here are some highlights of the system

• The system requires a minimum of time and money to start

• You don't need special experience or skills to do it.

• You don't need to buy or rent buildings, buy or rent equipment and you don't have to hire people

• You can do it anywhere in your house, while you travel or a favorite vacation spot or retreat

• With the system you can earn $10,000 to $500,000 in a matter of months and even within two days depending on which system you assemble.

• The money you make is all earned income which is subject to one of the lowest tax bites.

QUESTION: Did you say you can make big money within days?

ANSWER: No, that's an understatement. You can actually do it within hours in some cases You can compile a system in an afternoon one day and start having spendable money in your hands produced by the system the very next morning!

QUESTION: How much money do you average on a system?

ANSWER: I'd say the average is $200,000. That's the type I usually stick to. I'll tell you this, doing a system to make $10,000 or $20,000 is literally duck soup. I have these available all the time but don't even use them

QUESTION: You said you need no special talent or experience. Who all can do it?

ANSWER: You only need to follow directions. All you need is common sense, a sense of pride in your work and the ability to see a job through to completion. This system is also perfect for people who are confined at home, such as housewives.

QUESTION: O.K. So, why do you want to reveal your system to other people when it's obvious you're making loads of money with it?

ANSWER: There are several reasons. First, the old proverb is true. Everyone likes to brag when they accomplish something; and, I'm no different. Second, I am in the position now to completely retire. I have put all my money into a diversified portfolio of blue chip investments that no one can touch, including myself. So, I'm protected from losing my money myself or someone taking it away from me. These investments generate a comfortable guaranteed income for life for my family and me.

Also, I think I can keep everyone from knowing my secret by only making the book available on a limited, controlled basis. The book is not in book stores.

QUESTION: I shudder to ask, how much does a book cost?

ANSWER: If it was priced at what it's worth, few people could afford it. There's at least a million dollars' worth of knowledge in this book. I'm not exaggerating when I say I don't know of any other book in which a person stands to gain and benefit so much. But, I will make it a very reasonable price of $20.00. This book is being distributed for me under my control by the Publishing Corporation of America.

A most interesting interview and I would have to call this the book of the century. For those who want a copy of the book from this present press run, the following information is provided:

The book contains over 286 8½" x 11" pages containing detailed, illustrated instructions on how to set up a Net Profit Generator System (N.P.G.S.) complete with all necessary forms. It is written in clear, easy to understand language. Also included is a diary of how the system was developed with some very interesting behind the scenes tales. The amount of knowledge you pick up about human nature is staggering in this diary.

To order: 1) Get a blank piece of paper; 2) At the top of the paper, print the words "7 Steps to Freedom, How to Escape the American Rat Race", 3) Print your name and address; 4) Mail this along with $20.00 in cash, check or money order to Publishing Corporation of America; Dept. ; 4626 Cleveland Avenue N.; Canton, Ohio 44767.

Or, if you want us to start processing your order immediately, phone in your order as follows: 1) Dial this TOLL FREE number, 1-800-321-0888 (Ohio residents dial 1-800-362-0636) and ask for operator ; 2) Say the words "7 Steps to Freedom"; 3) Give your name and address; 4) Give the operator one of your following credit card numbers: Master Charge or Visa (also include your Interbank number). Or, if you don't want to use a credit card, tell the operator you want it mailed C.O.D. Operators are on duty right now and around the clock.

Direct any inquiries to (216) 494-4282. Please do not dial the toll free number for information. The operators are not permitted or qualified to answer questions.

This offer carries a full money-back guarantee.

C-09X

Figure 17.5 (Continued)

Figure 17.6   Benjamin Suarez's new ad.

Each of these methods of leading into your copy has its advantage for your particular product in your particular situation. Very frequently you may be able to try all four of these different types of lead-in and test them against one another to see how each does.

SHOWING BENEFITS AND ADVANTAGES

Now that we have established interest on the part of our prospective customer, we must immediately demonstrate the benefits and advantages of ordering. In doing so, you must tell the customer why he or she should buy. How do you do this? Refer to Maslow again and consider the motivations for human beings to do anything. State the advantages and benefits of your product or service in such a way as to satisfy these needs described by Maslow.

When you state these needs, state them in such a way that they are irresistible, in as strong terms as possible, while still being truthful and credible. Joe Karbo says that you must state the benefits and advantages of your product or service so strongly that the reader must conclude afterward that he or she would be a fool not to respond to your advertisement. In fact, in "The Lazy Man's Way to Riches" ad in Figure 17.3, Karbo actually says in the fourth paragraph, "What's more, I'm going to ask you to send me $10 for something that'll cost me no more than 50¢ and I'll try to make it so irresistible that you'd be a darn fool not to do it."

If you read further in Karbo's ad, you will see that he shows the benefits and advantages that appeal to human needs. Look at how Karbo describes his material goods—a home worth $250,000, an office a mile and a half from his home right on the beach, a cabin in the mountains, two boats and a Cadillac, stocks, bonds, investments—you could go right down Maslow's list to see what these appeal to, everything from safety and security needs to needs to belong, needs for love, esteem, recognition, status, and self-actualization. Further, note the other benefits, as stated by Joe Karbo: It does not require education, capital, luck, talent, youth, or experience. Joe practically guarantees your fortune and all this for how much? A mere $10. Isn't his ad irresistible, and wouldn't you feel like a fool not to risk $10 to achieve these benefits?

CREDIBILITY

Credibility is most important in making your copy effective and getting your potential customers to order because, regardless of what you say about the benefits or advantages of your product, if your potential customer does not believe what you say, he or she will not order your product or service. This is why, for many years, Joe Karbo did not state in his ads that he owned a Rolls-Royce, or that his homes had actually been valued at far more than the figures stated. Even though he did own a Rolls-Royce and more expensive homes, he knew these facts were less believable than that he owned a Cadillac (which Karbo did own) or a $250,000 house. Credibility also explains why Joe Sugerman takes such pains to explain the intricate details of his fabulous electronic products, along with providing good, clear photographs.

In my own use of a direct mail campaign for job finding and as recommended in my book, *The Executive's Guide to Finding a Superior Job,* I state that in a direct sales letter a paragraph must be included that states the specific area of study and name of the college or university that a job seeker attended. Why? Because anything else is merely unsupported claims. To give credibility, you must include a known quantity, a quantity that can be checked—in this case, noting your university or school by name.

USE OF TESTIMONIALS

But the listing of courses and names of universities will not work in an ad. What will work? Testimonials. And testimonials are crucial for giving the credibility necessary for your potential customer to order. Look at how the successful advertisements in this chapter have used testimonials. Why are testimonials so effective? Because they mean that someone else is complimenting you, rather than you tooting your own horn. If you are able to list the entire name—if you have the permission of the individual whose testimonial you have on file—that gives even more credibility because a person can actually check to verify that the testimonial is accurate.

Look at Karbo's ad again. At the end of the ad you'll find a box in which is contained a sworn statement: "On the basis of my professional relationship as his accountant, I certify that Mr. Karbo's net worth is more than $1 million. (signed) Stuart A. Cogan." This was one of the many innovations initiated by Joe Karbo. Like the testimonial, it is a powerful instrument of credibility. Since its first appearance, it has been copied by a lawyer, accountants, and others. Many ads contain not only the words "sworn statement" but also the actual imprint and signature seal of a notary public. These definitely add credibility.

Other means of achieving credibility are stating a bank, accountant, or attorney reference, or even showing the picture of a building your company owns. An imposing structure in itself will add credibility.

Clearly, every method of establishing credibility has not been exhausted; there are other ways which have yet to be thought of or become apparent that can assist greatly in accomplishing this most necessary of tasks in your advertisement. You are not limited to testimonials or statements by your accountant. Using your imagination, you can think of totally new ways to add credibility to your proposition.

ACTION

A face-to-face salesperson must ask for an order. This is a basic law of sales. And just as face-to-face salespeople do this, so must you, as a mail order salesperson selling through an advertisement, ask for the order. You do this by calling your customer to immediate action. In other words, you don't want your customer to wait and think it over for several days. You don't want him or her to cut out the coupon at the bottom of your advertisement and put it away for another day, or to wait until he or she is in the proper frame of mind. You want to compel your customer to order now, immediately.

Why is immediate action so necessary? Because mail order buying from advertisements in magazines or even ordering for information in a two-step offer is an impulse kind of purchase or action. Delay is fatal. Even with the best intent, if your potential customer clips the coupon with the intent of ordering, not now, but later, research has proven conclusively that in most instances he or she will not place this order. How do you accomplish this call to action? Here are three specific methods you can use to get your customer to order right now: limited time offer, limited quantity offer, or a special.

Limited time means that your offer is limited to a specific period. For example, if your ad appears in a magazine you might say, "Good for 30 days only." Or you can list a specific date after which the offer is no longer good. Limited quantity means that the quantity of whatever it is you are supplying is limited. This is a valid statement because it is always true. If you are able to state the precise limitations of your product, so much the better. A special means a special proposition, good for this ad only. For example, you may offer an additional premium to the first 100 customers who place an order. Or you may offer something free only to those who respond to this one ad.

The important thing is that the advertisement urges the potential respondent to act immediately. In Figure 17.3, Joe Karbo has done this subtly by saying, "A month from today you can be nothing more than 30 days older, or you can be on your way to getting rich. You decide."

THE COUPON

Most display or space advertisements have a coupon, and research has shown that a coupon works better and will outpull noncoupon ads in most instances. And this is true even of those coupons that are so small that it is almost impossible to write your name and address in the space provided. The exception is advertisements that appear to be news articles, such as Figure 17.5

SUMMARY

In this chapter, you've learned some very important things: Why the emphasis on copy is so important, how to structure your advertisement or direct mail letter, how to get attention with a headline, how to gain and maintain interest with your copy, how to show benefits and advantages, how to write outstanding copy, how to gain credibility in your advertisement or direct mail letter, how to get your customer to order now, as well as the differences between space advertising copywriting and direct mail copywriting.

Master the techniques of copywriting contained in this and the following chapter and your future in the direct mail order business will be assured.

18

How to Write Copy That Creates Sales

HOW TO WRITE OUTSTANDING COPY

Once you have attracted the attention of your reader, you want him or her to continue to read. So your copy must be not only structured, but also interesting and fun and easy to read. There are three basic principles that successful copywriters have found to work best.

1. Use short words, short sentences, and short paragraphs.
2. Write conversationally.
3. Keep your copy moving; don't let it bog down.

One book that is extremely valuable in helping you to become a successful copywriter is called *The Art of Readable Writing*, by Dr. Rudolf Flesch. In this stimulating guide, Dr. Flesch uses special graphs for calculating whether copy has human interest and reading ease. The human interest graph designed by Dr. Flesch is shown in Figure 18.1, while the reading ease graph is shown in Figure 18.2. The combination of these charts produces Dr. Flesch's readability formula. Here is how to use these graphs and compute the readability formula of any copy for an advertisement or a direct mail letter.

Step 1. Take samples from the advertisement, for example, every third or fourth paragraph. Each sample should start at the beginning of a paragraph. Let's analyze the advertisement, "Do You Make These Mistakes in English?" shown in Figure 10.1, for readability.

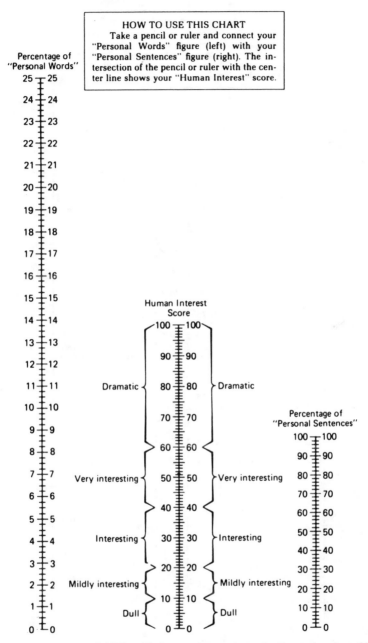

Figure 18.1 Dr. Rudolf Flesch's human interest graph. From the *Art of Readable Writing* (25th Anniversary Edition, 1974) by Rudolf Flesch. By permission of Harper and Row Publishers, Inc.

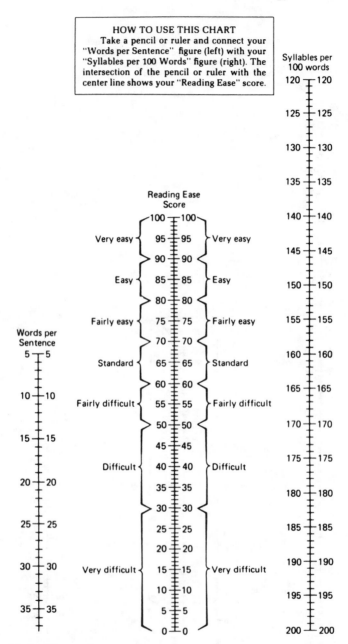

Figure 18.2 The reading ease graph developed by Dr. Rudolf Flesch. From the *Art of Readable Writing* (25th Anniversary Edition, 1974) by Rudolf Flesch. By permission of Harper and Row Publishers, Inc.

Step 2. Count the number of words in each sample up to 100 words. Count contractions and hyphenated words as one word. Count numbers and letters as words if written numerically or abbreviated (e.g., 1981 would count as one word, as would $5 or C.O.D.). Now, in "Do You Make These Mistakes in English?" there are 17 paragraphs, excluding the testimonials, headlines, and coupon. I will take as our sample the fourth, eighth, twelfth, and sixteenth paragraphs. The fourth paragraph contains 55 words, the eighth 101 words, the twelfth 41 words, and the sixteenth paragraph 32 words.

Step 3. Find the average sentence length for your sample. In other words, take all your samples, count the number of sentences, and divide by the number of words in those sentences. In doing so, follow the units of thought, not the punctuation: Sentences are marked at the end by periods, but sometimes the units of thought are marked by a colon or a semicolon. Count each separate unit of thought as a separate sentence. In the sample advertisement, I find four sentences in paragraph 4, eight in paragraph 8, two in paragraph 12, and one in paragraph 16, for a total of 15 sentences; there are 229 words, so the average sentence length is 15.26 words.

Step 4. Count the syllables in your samples, divide the total number of syllables by the total number of words, and multiply by 100. This will result in the total number of syllables per 100 words in the copy in the advertisement. In the four sample paragraphs there are 328 syllables. Dividing 328 by 229 and multiplying times 100 gives 143.23 syllables per 100 words. When you do this count, count the syllables as you pronounce the word, so that "$5" would be "5," one syllable, and "dollars," two more, or a total of three syllables. On the other hand, if you have a great number of figures in the samples that you are using, do not include the figures as part of your syllable count.

Step 5. Count the personal words in your sample. Personal words are all first-, second- and third-person pronouns except neuter pronouns such as *it, its,* and *itself,* and plurals such as *they, them, theirs, themselves,* if referring to things rather than people. Personal words also include words that can be assigned either to the masculine or the feminine gender, such as one's name or *father, brother, mother, sister, postman,* and so forth. Do not count those words that have a single word for either gender, such as *doctor, lawyer, teacher,* and so forth. Finally, you can also count as personal words those group words such as *people* and *folks.* In total, there are 27 personal words in all the samples combined. Twenty-seven divided by 229 and multiplied by 100 is 12.66 personal words per 100 words.

Step 6. Count the personal sentences in your samples. Personal sentences are spoken sentences marked by quotation marks; lead-in words such as "he said"; questions, requests, or directions aimed directly at the reader; explanations; exclamations; or grammatically incomplete sentences whose complete meanings must be inferred from the context in which they appear. If a particular sentence fits into more than one of these definitions, you should count it only once. As in steps 4 and 5, count the total number of personal sentences, divide by the total number of sentences, and multiple by 100 to find the number of personal sentences per 100 sentences. There are nine personal sentences in our samples. Nine divided by 15 sentences, times 100, is 60 personal sentences per 100 sentences.

Step 7. Now it is time to find your reading ease score, using Figure 18.2. To do this, take the average sentence length that we got in step 3, and the number of syllables per 100 words that we got in step 4. From step 3 we got 15.26 words per sentence, which we round off to 15, and in step 4, 143.23 syllables per 100 words, which we round off to 143. In Figure 18.2 we connect the words per sentence, which is the left-hand vertical column, with the syllables per 100 words on the right. In the center, under reading ease score, we read the score; ours is 71, which means that it is fairly easy to read, on a scale of from 0, very difficult, all the way up to 100, very easy.

Step 8. Now let's find our human interest score. Use the number of personal words per 100 words that we found in step 5, and the number of personal sentences per 100 sentences from step 6. In the same fashion as with the reading ease score, compute our human interest score. In step 5 we found 12.66, or 13, personal words per 100 words. In step 6 we found 60 personal sentences per 100 sentences, so we come up with a human interest score of 74, which is between *very interesting* and *dramatic*. Is it any wonder this ad ran for 40 years?

As an exercise, you might want to take a more modern ad and compute the readability score.

COMPUTER PROGRAMS THAT CAN HELP YOU WRITE COPY

There are computer programs available that can help you with your grammar and writing. Some even contain scales more sophisticated than reading ease and interest. With one, you can even come pretty close to imitating the style of a successful copywriter. Here are three programs I have found useful:

Corporate Voice, published by Scandinavian PC Systems, Inc., 51 Monroe St., Suite 1101, Rockville, MD 20850

Grammatik, published by Reference Software International, 330 Townsend St., Suite 123, San Francisco, CA 94107

Rightwriter, published by Que Software, 11711 North College Ave., Carmel, IN 46032

One additional tip in writing your copy and putting it into the skeleton or structure that we discussed earlier: Use lots of subheads for your paragraphs.

HOW DOES DIRECT MAIL COPYWRITING DIFFER FROM SPACE ADVERTISING COPYWRITING?

The basics of direct mail copywriting and space advertising copywriting are almost identical. The same structure should be followed, and the keys to success are the same. The biggest difference is that you have more space in which to sell and explain your proposition and your offer. There also may be some differences depending on whether you are selling to a customer or another business. Figure 18.3 is a letter to a consumer customer. Such letters can run to more than four pages. Figure 18.4 is a direct mail piece to an industrial customer. Usually the industrial customer has less time and will spend less time reading your letter. Therefore, an industrial customer letter should normally be from one to three pages long. Note that an industrial customer here means any customer who is not using your end product directly, but is using it in some way to assist him or her in selling to the final consumer. Figure 18.5 is a direct mail letter I wrote and used to help sell research at the university. This direct mail letter had better than a 30 percent response rate. Finally, look at Figure 18.6. This letter was used to sell a newsletter to professionals, yet the letter is six pages long. Professionals may be busy, but if the information is compelling, they will read it and act upon it. Note that in all four letters illustrated, the principles discussed above in copywriting apply.

YOUR COPYWRITING CHECKLIST

I have developed a special checklist that I use to check all of my copy. You can easily leave some important factor out of your copy, even after you have worked at it and polished it. I'm ashamed to admit that one beautiful piece of copy and layout I completed for a seminar left one important factor out: Where the seminar was being held. So there are some very good reasons for using a checklist. The one that follows is compiled from dozens of different sources. It enables me to check my copy to ensure that the headline is correct, that the offer is as I want it, that the copy context is as I want it, and that the copy quality is at its very highest. Use this checklist when you first begin to write your copy or construct your advertisements for direct

Figure 18.3   A direct mail piece to a consumer customer.

SOUNDS GALORE!

This CD has the best collection of high quality 16 bit sound effects you'll ever find. I absolutely guarantee it. There's over 2,300 sound effects that will captivate your imagination and turn your computer into a special effects juke box of animal noises, cartoon boings, farts, gongs and many other catagories of sounds that practically jump out of your PC! You decide when you want your computer to play the funny noises. It's a snap to personalize your PC with Wired for Sound Pro 3.0 CD.

230 VACATION PHOTO WALLPAPERS!

Do you ever think about that vacation you took last year and how beautiful it was? Well now you can bring those feelings back again with 230 vacation wallpapers. Imagine seeing the Effiel tower, natural scenes, animals, the Arizona desert, and city streets come alive on your desktop.

It's childs play to create your own multimedia enviroment with Wired for Sound Pro 3.0 CD's "Wallpaper Changer". All you have to do is search for the wallpapers you want, add one of 8 screen effects like a turning page, dissolve, or even a falling curtain. Save your preferences and presto you have wallpapers to enjoy.

5 HILARIOUS ANIMATED FACES

Now you can enjoy the animated characters of Jane, Joe, Bill Clinton, Ross Perot, and George Bush. These characters pop out, to keep you company for the lonely hours at your computer. No matter whether you are a democrat, republican, or independent, these politicians will keep you entertained while they yack. Even if you can't stand any of these guys, there's Jane the sultry flirt and Mr. Joe Antic. Both are funny beyond belief and will keep you rolling with laughter. Remember you won't find these faces on any other CD.

HOURS OF SYMPHONIC MUSIC

Listen to symphonic music right at your desk. No fiddling with tapes or CD's but hear the best music from the masters of Chopin, Beethoven and Mozart. You'll get 100 long play versions that are great for relaxation between work sessions at your computer or just use them in your own multimedia productions.

8 INTERNATIONAL LANGUAGES

Now take your desktop international. You can bring back all those high school language lessons with 8 foreign language talking clocks, calendars, and games. In fact you can change your computer so that all sounds are in the language you want. Only Wired for Sound Pro 3.0 CD has hundreds of language phrases in Italian, German, French, Chinese, Japanese, Russian, Spanish, and Swedish.

ACCENTS GALORE!

7 Accented Voices! Hey, make your talking clock sound like it's from the Bronx, the deep south or from England. Both male and female voices are included. There is even a sexy sultry voice.

150 MULTIMEDIA SCREEN SAVERS

These video clips are some of the most entertaining ever. You'll see comedy bloopers, animals, explosions, and time laps videos. They are great for use as screen savers or attach them to your favorite programs.

FUNNY BLOOPERS

You'll laugh like crazy at our bloopers! That's right, hear the outakes of all the impersonations, voices and video clips too juicy to talk about here. It's filled with laughs for everyone.

GREAT SOFTWARE!

Create your own multimedia presentations. That's right, you can create your own mini productions of video clips, music and photos to get your point across or just for fun. It's simple using the new multimedia juke box to put you in control of multimedia.

Browse thousands of "ROMarkable" material with CD-Browser! This powerful navigation tool helps you find the material you need to create your ultimate desktop. You'll find this indispensable as you breeze through 640 megabytes of great material!

Figure 18.3   (Continued)

New improved sound hook. We added some slick new features that let you chain sounds, photos, and even videos together with your favorite programs. For example, you can launch Excel with several sounds and even a video clip. You can play them randomly, or in succession.

HERE IS MY OFFER TO YOU!
Now that you've had the chance to read about Wired for Sound Pro 3.0 CD **let me make you an offer that'll knock your socks off**. In fact you'd better sit down! Here's the deal, **purchase Wired for Sound Pro 3.0 CD for just $39!** That's 640 megabytes of "ROMarkable" material for only $39. If you had to pay for all of these seperately you'd pay over $300. But you only pay $39. This is a heck of a deal.

I know you're saying, I don't own a CD-ROM drive. No problem, keep it until you purchase your CD-ROM drive. The way things are going in the industry, CD-ROM's are now the most requested upgrade for people like you in the know. When you eventually get your CD-ROM (maybe even this Christmas), you'll blast that puppy with 640 megabytes of "ROMarkable" material.

Remember you're the first to know about this offer! You must think I'm insane, but not really, because I want to keep our #1 CD-ROM software in the limelight. So run, don't walk, to your phone and dial **1-800-728-5767** *24hrs/day 7 days a week* to order this super deal. Or mail in the enclosed order form. You can expect delivery three (3) weeks after you order. So hurry, place your order before Christmas to receive prompt delivery of your product. With the new version of Wired for Sound Pro 3.0, and the free version of Wired for Sound Pro 3.0 CD, you can create your ultimate multimedia desktop.

Sincerly,

Ernest Priestly, President

P.S. Your satisfaction is guaranteed! I know you'll love this program. Just try Wired for Sound Pro 3.0 CD for 60 days and if you decide not to keep Wired for Sound Pro 3.0 CD for any reason, return it for a full no hassle refund. Happy holidays!

Figure 18.3   (Continued)

mail letters. After you are more experienced, you may find certain elements that are particularly useful in your work. If so, include them and eventually develop your own personalized checklist. Here is mine.

I. *Headline*
   A. Does the headline appeal to self-interest, offer exciting news, or arouse interest?
   B. Is the headline positive, rather than negative?
   C. Does the headline suggest that the reader can obtain something easily and quickly?
   D. Does the headline make use of the powerful words of mail order advertising?
   E. Does the headline stress the most important benefit of the product?
   F. Does the headline stop the reader and cause him or her to read further?
   G. Is the headline believable?
   H. Does the headline tie in with the copy?

J.W. MURDOCK
INDUSTRIAL PRODUCTS GUIDE
2403 Waukegan Rd. • Deerfield, Ill. 60015
(312) 948-8940

Now you can end messy,
time-consuming packaging problems
forever with super-adhesive,
wear and tear resistant
PVC sealing tape!

And here's a free Deluxe Tape Dispenser
to prove it! A $14⁹⁵ value —
FREE with your order!

Dear Friend,

Please take a look at the sample of PVC Sealing Tape that
came with this letter. It looks like an ordinary piece of
packaging tape, right? But now test it, pull on it . . .
try to remove it. You'll find it won't come off . . . now
just think how tightly it will hold your packages!

      PVC Sealing Tape uses a powerful new adhesive
      that gives it up to 90 lbs. tensile strength.
      It's tough. It's rugged. It holds up under
      weather, wear, tear, even impact. And what's
      more, PVC Tape won't peel, frazzle or get
      ragged with age--it holds and holds and even
      gets stronger the longer it's on!

With PVC Tape you can say goodbye to packaging problems
forever! That's why we hope you'll send in the Order Form
for this fast-acting, super-adhesive tape, and to persuade
you we'll send you a Free Deluxe Tape Dispenser--a $14.95
value--yours free with any size order of PVC Tape!

PVC Tape is pressure sensitive--it needs no messy glue that
gets on your clothes--you just place the Dispenser on the
carton you want to seal and smoothly glide it across the
surface. The Dispenser automatically gives just the right
pressure to seal your package. What's more, efficient,
fast-packaging PVC tape eliminates the need for costly

                             (over, please)

(continued)

Figure 18.4 A direct mail piece to an industrial customer.

```
                  packaging machines. With your Deluxe Dispenser you can seal
                  any size, any shape carton with a single easy motion--it
                  even cuts the tape for you.

                     It's safe, it's sure. PVC Tape meets all OSHA
                     standards for safety. There's no need to bother
                     with dangerous straps or staples. Plus, PVC
                     Tape can be used to give your packages a weather-
                     resistant, water-proof seal that discourages
                     pilfering and ensures that your package won't
                     accidentally open in transit. And it meets all
                     postal requirements, so you can use it on all
                     your outgoing mail.

                  If you send today for your PVC Tape (minimum order 12 rolls),
                  we'll rush you both the Tape and your Free Deluxe Dispenser.
                  Then, when you get them, try them out on the next big package
                  you have to ship. You'll be amazed how fast and accurately
                  the Dispenser works. And you'll see how PVC forms a strong
                  bond on any size, any odd-shaped, bulky package.

                  Please take advantage of this special offer, right away.
                  Send in the enclosed Form to order your super-adhesive PVC
                  Tape and get your free Deluxe Tape Dispenser as our gift.
                  Do it now!

                                       Cordially,

                                       Tom Brice

   TB:D1
                                       Tom Brice
                                       Vice President
```

Figure 18.4   (Continued)

II. *The Offer*
   A. Are all the elements of the offer present in the copy?
      1. Product
      2. Price
      3. Terms
      4. Guarantee
      5. Options
      6. Additional inducements to buy
      7. Dates
      8. Places

III. *Copy Content*
   A. Do you gain interest at once by use of a story, a startling or unusual statement, a quote, or news?
   B. Do you show benefits and advantages that appeal to emotional needs to such an extent that your offer is irresistible, and the reader would "have to be a fool not to order"?
   C. Do you establish credibility with your reader through the use of testimonials, statements by your accountant, or some other means?

CALIFORNIA STATE UNIVERSITY · LOS ANGELES

5151 STATE UNIVERSITY DRIVE LOS ANGELES, CALIFORNIA 90032

SCHOOL OF BUSINESS AND ECONOMICS
OFFICE OF THE DEAN (213) 224-3870

Dear

Quality of proposal not the main key to winning? Low price not of primary importance? These statements certainly didn't sound right, and I would have never believed them until I looked at the results of some preliminary research conducted on 51 small R & D contracts bid to the Government.

The focus on this research was on preproposal marketing and the number of contacts, type of contact, and quality of contact that project engineers make, or should make before the arrival of the RFP or before developing and submitting unsolicited proposals for small R & D contracts. The primary purpose of the research was to determine what influence preproposal marketing might have on winning these small contracts, valued at under $2 million each.

As you probably expected, it was definitely confirmed that preproposal market-ing did have a significant influence on winning or losing. Frankly, even though some proposals were not very good, and were even priced higher than competitive proposals, the number of contacts made with the customer influ-enced the results of the competition to an extraordinary degree. To be specific, for a total of 1,787 different contacts made on 51 contract bids, the average number of contacts for a win was 40.6 -- more than twice the average number of contacts (18.5) which resulted in a loss.

Fine, this was something we all more or less expected. However, we found out other things which were more surprising. For example, we learned that certain kinds of contacts with the customer are more important to winning than others. We found out when quality of contact is more important to winning than quantity of contacts. We looked at figures that told us whether the probability of winning increased with the number of contacts, and whether there is an optimal number of contacts for winning. We quantified how im-portant it is that you bring the customer to your facilities, and we dis-covered much, much more.

Can this information be of any practical value to you, a Government contractor? Let me answer by asking you some questions:

THE CALIFORNIA STATE UNIVERSITY AND COLLEGES

(continued)

Figure 18.5 A direct mail letter for university research.

-2-

1. You are on a fixed budget. Is it more important for winning to
   visit the customer at his facilities, or to meet him at a symposium?

2. A very competent engineer doesn't relate well to the customer, but
   no one else is available to meet with the customer. Do you cancel
   the meeting or hold it anyway?

3. Should you ever bid a contract without making contacts, and if so
   when?

4. Who is it more important for your customer to meet: The project
   engineer? The proposal manager? All engineers at the working
   level? Senior and top company management of the company? Marketing
   personnel?

5. What minimum number of preproposal contacts must you have in order
   to win?

6. What difference is there in preproposal marketing contacts between
   the various government agencies?

7. To what extent can a phone call substitute for face-to-face meetings?

8. What is the relative importance in contacts with the customer by
   engineering personnel, management personnel, and marketing personnel
   assigned to field representative duties?

9. To what extent can preproposal marketing compensate for the lack of
   quality in technical proposals and/or competitive pricing?

10. Does contact after receipt of an RFP hurt you or help you?

If the answers to these questions can be used by you, then the result of this
research is important to you and to the competitive position of your company
in the research and development field. Unfortunately, the study completed was
too small a sampling for conclusions upon which you should base decisions.
Further, it was also too small a sampling to allow for segmentation by different
Government agencies.

The Bureau of Business and Economic Research at California State University,
Los Angeles, however, is now embarking on a considerably larger research program
dedicated to investigation of preproposal marketing activities of small Government R & D projects. We are inviting a limited number of the leading companies
in industry to participate.

All industrial participants will receive progress reports and detailed technical
reports containing graphs, tables, and explicit conclusions from the research
which you can put to immediate use. The distribution of this information will
be limited to participating firms. In addition, segmentation of results for your

Figure 18.5   (Continued)

-3-

firm will be provided to you only. In this way, proprietary information of all participating firms will be fully protected.

Since participation in this program is a service to the community, all companies assisting in the funding of this research will receive a certificate of appreciation from the Bureau of Business and Economic Research at California State University Los Angeles.

I know you are busy. Therefore, if you are interested in receiving a copy of our proposal for the research, there is no need to write a formal letter -- just sign below and enclose your business card -- we'll see that you get a copy.

Sincerely,

William A. Cohen, Director
Bureau of Business & Economic Research

WC:ba

P.S. Because time is critical in coordinating the research of proposal activities for several firms simultaneously, and I know that this letter may find you traveling, I have taken the liberty of sending copies to your vice presidents of marketing and engineering/research and development. We will also respond to their requests for our proposal.

ATTN: William A. Cohen, Director
      Bureau of Business and Economic Research

Yes, I feel this research can be of importance to my firm. Please send a copy of your research proposal to the following address:

(Name) _____

(Address) _____

_____

_____

Figure 18.5 (Continued)

Discover in the next 3 minutes how a young practitioner
made the rapid ascent from a barely break-even psychologist
to a record-crushing superstar. And find out how you can
enjoy the *$1,100,000 All-Referral Practice* within 3 to 5
years from a cold start...or within 2 years for an existing
practice.

Just 24 months ago, a young, energetic psychologist out of school 4
years collected a worrisome $33,884 for the entire year (a mere $2,823 a
month.) But in the last 12 months he's made $564,155, over $1.1 million in
the last two years! And bought a gorgeous, new 4,500 square foot home. Two
brand-new, European sedans. And netted--actually took home--over $200,000
last year!

*"Image is very important to me. I'm conservative and most of my
practice depends upon referrals. So I couldn't do anything outlandish, nor
would I feel comfortable with that. But I found out I didn't have to. And
what I billed two years ago, I now produce in just over 3 weeks.*

*"People's perception of me has also radically changed from a run-of-
the-mill psychologist to a very successful, upper-income practitioner. You
might say I've become the 'hot' psychologist in town.*

*"And not only am I known all over town now, I'm well respected. And
that includes my direct competitors, although with them it's a little
difficult to tell the difference between respect and envy."*

Dear Colleague:

He was more than worried. After four years in practice, he had
a gross production he didn't want to tell even his best friend
about. Not that he wasn't trying--one public relations firm, a
practice management firm, The Welcome Wagon, public service columns
in the local newspaper, Yellow Pages plastic covers, sponsoring
local soccer teams, and on and on. Even a $4,800 newspaper
advertising fiasco.

NOTHING WORKED. That's what aggravated him. But what made him
anxious--*even frightened*--was far more serious. Production was
stuck. And his gross was about to plummet.

It was because there were more greedy, voracious competitors.
More HMOs. More PPOs. All trying to separate him from his existing
patients. And make sure he'd get no new ones.

And inevitably the FTC's Eyeglass II ruling would strike him.
That would mean corporate ownership of practices and corporate
power. Should he then go to work for Sears or General Motors when
they enter the profession, or R.J. Reynolds...or?

No wonder he was fearful, fearful of working too hard for his
money. Not that he was lazy by any means. But when he looked into
the future, he saw nothing but a constant struggle for a living.
Year after year with no hope for the $100,000 to $200,000 practice
of his dreams.

Turn here to discover more.............➡

Figure 18.6   Selling a newsletter to professionals.

Anyone facing this competition would worry about working too hard for too few dollars. What should he do?

We suggested he not worry. By joining THE PRACTICE BUILDER for $89, his practice grew--not slowly, but meteorically. Yet, in a totally manageable way.

In fact, in the past 2 years, his $2,823 became $47,013 a month--a total of $564,155 in the last year and $1.1 milllion in the last two! A ten-fold increase in 730 days.

What he did in 1 year he now does in 23 days! And he now feels energetic, as if practicing was worth it again. Plus his retirement's secure.

Would you like to know these $1,100,000 tactics and strategies? You can--since they're from THE PRACTICE BUILDER. Now for the first time, you can have a complete marketing service at your disposal--with $1,100,000 mental health marketing strategies and a $100,000-a-year personal advisor--for just $89.

IS THE PRACTICE BUILDER A NEW CONCEPT?

Definitely. Before THE PRACTICE BUILDER, therapists turned to magazines and run-of-the-mill newsletters for their marketing ideas. But two very unfortunate and costly situations affected your results.

First, these publications were not written by tried and proven marketers--not by shirt-sleeve experts with both a formal and "hard knocks" education in marketing--but by reporters. And they simply lacked the educational training to analyze any strategy. They could only report.

Because of this, you didn't know why a strategy worked or didn't, and whether you could use it in your marketplace and in your practice or not. Since no two practices are alike, you wondered how their strategy-of-the-month could fit all practices, especially yours?

And where exactly did this leave you? Perhaps in a situation similar to these psychologists who acted on faulty advice:

*** The New York PhD who lost $4,260 in a direct-mail fiasco.

*** The practitioner from Omaha who bought and sent a newsletter so poorly done that not one client commented on it--and it certainly didn't stem patients from hemorrhaging out of the practice as intended.

*** The California counselor who unwisely bought every Yellow Pages in sight. (His cost: $16,440. His loss: $11,400.)

Figure 18.6 (Continued)

<u>FOR $89, YOU NOW HAVE A PROFESSIONAL MARKETING THINK-TANK</u>

But THE PRACTICE BUILDER is different. Headed by MBAs in
Marketing from America's top Business Schools, The PRACTICE BUILDER
is the mental health professional's <u>only</u> Marketing Think-Tank in the
U.S. and Canada today. Here's what you'll find.

Our analysts take successful marketing strategies from big
business and translate them into **workable tactics** for
practitioners on **small budgets**. We test them in the field, work
out the bugs and send them to you 11 times a year in a confidential
12-page report.

Since these strategies are so carefully crafted and tested,
most often you can make FIVE TO TEN TIMES YOUR MONEY BACK from
promotion over the next <u>12 months</u>! If you're promoting now at all,
you can DOUBLE, TRIPLE, actually boost your present response by up
to NINE TIMES!

> **And these are the same strategies that produced
> over $500,000 a year and over $1.1 million in two
> years.** <u>They're exclusive</u>. And not found anywhere
> else...but that's not all.

<u>THE ALL-REFERRAL $1,100,000 PRACTICE CAN BE YOURS</u>

Our goal for you is not only $1,100,000 every two years, but
all from word-of-mouth. Yes, it is possible. Let me show you how.

All of us know word-of-mouth is the #1 source of new patients.
But did you know there are dozens of <u>sophisticated</u> strategies to
intentionally skyrocket those numbers? (Not common knowledge ones
like treating everyone nicely. But trackable, methodical, big-
number-producing strategies.) By using dozens of these, your base
grows quickly and inexpensively, and your word-of-mouth and gross
jump EXPONENTIALLY! And voila--$1,100,000 every two years from
word-of-mouth.

This is impossible to achieve in under six months unless the
practice is large already. But by using THE PRACTICE BUILDER'S
strategies, you can get there within 3 to 5 years from a cold
start...in as little as <u>2 years</u> with an existing practice.

<u>YOU GET YOUR OWN PERSONAL MARKETING CONSULTANT (FREE)</u>

We leave nothing to chance, not when it comes to your success.
So, from our Think-Tank, we assign to you your own personal PRACTICE
BUILDER Marketing Advisor.

Figure 18.6   (Continued)

Your PRACTICE BUILDER Advisor makes sure you:

1. Choose the optimal strategies just right for your practice.
He'll actually work with you to develop a straight-forward Marketing
Plan for you to follow, complete with an affordable budget. Doesn't
that solve your biggest problem of not knowing what to do?
(Consultants often charge $2,500 for this, but it's yours FREE with
your membership.)

2. Put everything into effect profitably. Since no two
practices are exactly alike, no two implementations are either.
Your PRACTICE BUILDER Advisor shows you the easiest, most cost-
effective ways...and points out the traps for the unsuspecting
marketer. (You'll discover your Advisor is also responsible for
protecting our good name from being associated with failure. So
you'll find him *conservative and cautious* in his approach.)

How else will you use your personal Advisor? With up to two
hours of personal consulting (eight times a year, 15 minutes per
session)--yours FREE--you'll explore every tactic to the $1,100,000+
practice:

**   Review your referrals from professionals and install a
sure-fire way to double any referral percentage, (perhaps
quadruple it if you haven't been pursuing them!)

**   **Analyze your existing Yellow Pages, business
cards, advertising or other promotion for FREE and
recommend how to boost your response by 2 to 9 times!**

**   Give you 24 different BASIC internal strategies which
cover everything from stimulating three times more patient
referrals to which of the hottest new services to add.

**   Turn your outdoor office sign into a patient-recruiter
rather than a simple announcement. (Did you know our
controlled test confirms that the right office sign can be your
#1 promotional return-on-investment?)

**   Direct you away from 53 "born losers" or gimmicks to
avoid in order to save your time and money and to make sure you
only spend time, money and energy on productive activities.

**   **Tell you about patient newsletters and why you
shouldn't be sending one! (What to do instead to make
your phone ring.)**

***** And tackle any question you have. Anytime. Just call
the **confidential number** I'll send you. **It's all for you.
And only about you**.

And remember, your Advisor has one more important respon-
sibility--to see that you have the highest quality, most professional image. *One that inspires prospects...and creates envy among
your peers.*

Figure 18.6 (Continued)

Unfortunately, today most therapists project an image either too commercial (like a retail tire store) or too bland so as to appear dowdy--creating the feeling you're 10 years behind and providing out-of-date service. THE PRACTICE BUILDER shows you how to create that most-respected of images... and your PRACTICE BUILDER Advisor makes sure everyone knows it. Is $89 too much for that?

DO YOU NEED THE PRACTICE BUILDER IF YOU ALREADY HAVE A MANAGEMENT FIRM, AD AGENCY OR MARKETING ADVISOR?

Without a doubt, YES! Here's why.

With the eruption of demand for marketing help, management firms, ad agencies and marketers from all fields became marketing experts--literally overnight. But the fact is that most management firms lack <u>any formal education</u> in marketing. And few of these "experts" have any <u>marketing experience</u>. Nor do they have the resources to do <u>controlled testing</u> to determine the most profitable promotions for mental health professionals.

That means they learn by trial and error--they try to learn with your dollars, but mostly, they just make <u>errors</u> while squandering your hard-earned budget.

So if you use a "Marketing Expert," then use THE PRACTICE BUILDER to protect yourself. With our strategies and advisor, you'll know if your "expert" is right or is going to cost you everything. Is $89 too much to protect your <u>hundreds or thousands</u> spent in promotion?

ISN'T THIS THE KIND OF PROVEN, IMMEDIATELY-USEFUL GUIDANCE YOU'VE BEEN LOOKING FOR?

Let me review for you--briefly--exactly what you'll receive when you become a member of THE PRACTICE BUILDER:

1. You'll receive THE PRACTICE BUILDER'S proven and tested strategies, 20-50 brand-new ideas mailed to you 11 times a year.

2. You'll receive FREE access to your own personal PRACTICE BUILDER Advisor, entitling you to eight in-depth telephone consultations a year including help with your complete Marketing Plan (worth $2,500!)

3. You'll get up to four Special Bonus Reports FREE--created especially for our new members--and full of <u>exclusive</u> strategies.

4. You'll most likely have a complete tax deduction as a business expense, thus reducing your cost even more.

Figure 18.6 (Continued)

5. **Most importantly, you'll receive those strategies,
already proven to create your $1,100,000 practice.**

6. Best of all, you get it all on a <u>TRIAL, NO-RISK</u> MONEY BACK
BASIS. Let me explain. **TRIAL**...You can review our exclusive
strategies your first month, cancel and get all your money back...
or...

NO RISK...You can personally profit from your second
month of THE PRACTICE BUILDER, our special bonus reports
and in-depth counsel with your personal marketing
advisor. <u>AND</u> if you have not already made more than your
membership cost, and in fact <u>SUBSTANTIAL PROFITS</u>, receive
a FULL refund even then.

Monthly you get 20-50 different strategies from the best
marketing minds in the business. Then you can have one of these
marketing stars personally fit these strategies to <u>your</u> practice.
All on a <u>TRIAL, NO-RISK</u> MONEY BACK BASIS. For just $89 for one
year--but I strongly urge you to choose the two year membership for
$149. Let me explain why.

Marketing takes time. It's not instantaneous. (Only hucksters
promise you that.) There are analytical, planning, action and
evaluation phases. And in your first year, we'll get you up and
charging ahead. But throughout the latter half and especially in
the second year, changes will be necessary. Your market, competition and you change and fine tuning is required. You'll need new
strategies and you'll need your Hotline Advisor to be on your phone.

Your two year membership gives you that continuity so crucial
to your long term success. And besides, it's smart to save 25% off
the regular price between the one and two year memberships.

So for your sake, don't delay. These prices are REDUCED. Only
during this short Membership Drive can you join THE PRACTICE BUILDER
for $89 for a one year membership...or $149 for the recommended two
year. **But to SAVE MONEY, you must order now.** Mail your order
today. There's nothing to lose.

And what can you gain? Perhaps a $1,172,906 practice in just
24 short months. So act right now.

Alan Bernstein

Alan L. Bernstein, MBA
President, THE PRACTICE BUILDER

P.S. For the <u>next two weeks only</u>, also get--FREE--four new Special
Bonus Reports. See the accompanying note for details. But
remember: You'll only receive them if you join within 2 weeks.

P.P.S. Mail your trial membership today...or for *fast* service,
charge it now toll-free: 1-800-333-3969, ext. 562. *(24 hours a day.)*

2755 Bristol, Suite 100 · Costa Mesa, California 92626-5909 · 1-800-333-3969 extension 562

Figure 18.6 (Continued)

   D. Do you demand immediate action on the part of your reader
      and give your reader reason to order *now* (limited quantities,
      time limit on offer, etc.)?

IV. *Copy Quality*
   A. Is the copy written in a conversational tone?
   B. Does your copy move right along?
   C. Do you use short words, short sentences, and short para-
      graphs?
   D. Do you use lots of subheads throughout your copy?
   E. Do you have a high Flesch reading ease score?
   F. Do you have a high Flesch human interest score?

SUMMARY

In this second chapter on copywriting, you learned to make your copy interesting and readable—two essential elements of copywriting that create
sales. You were also given a checklist covering the elements your copy
should include to ensure that you have presented all of the information
necessary in the most interesting way possible. The fact that I devoted two
full chapters to this subject should alert you to just how important good
copywriting is.

19

Preparing Art
and Graphics
at Low Cost

THE IMPORTANCE OF ARTWORK
IN MAIL ORDER SELLING

While it is true that copy is one of the primary factors in selling through direct mail or mail order, it is equally true that the proper artwork and graphics go hand in hand with good copy and can greatly enhance your chances of making the sale. Just as with copy, you don't have to do your own work: Anything and everything you need can be obtained from a variety of sources. On the other hand, if you are talented in preparing art or doing layout work or just want to do the thing yourself in order to keep your cost to a minimum, you can do so.

WHAT YOU WILL LEARN IN THIS CHAPTER

In this chapter, you will learn a number of money-making and money-saving ideas that will not only enable you to create or obtain quality artwork at low cost, but will also provide you with a number of options. Specifically, you will learn sources of free ideas for artwork and graphics, sources of low-cost artwork and photography, how to do a layout, typography, and illustrations, and finally, how to prepare what is known as camera-ready copy, which you give to your printer or publisher for reproduction.

SOURCES OF FREE IDEAS FOR YOUR ART

Even the most creative person in the world needs a place to begin for a source of new ideas. Here are four major sources of ideas that cost you absolutely nothing. It is not intended that you copy these things exactly. Rather, they are ideas from which you can begin and from which you can get concepts for illustration.

One of the primary sources of free ideas is work done by other mail order operators, which has been published in magazines or which you have received in direct mail pieces. Although mail order is growing every year, it is really a very old form of selling. Therefore, you have more than 100 years of artwork to look at, more than 100 years during which people who sell or once sold products either identical or very similar to yours have commissioned or done artwork on their own and had it published. Under the copyright law in effect when much of this material was published, the material is in the public domain if it's more than 56 years old, and you can actually copy it exactly as it is. More recent material is available to you every day in the form of advertisements you see in magazines or newspapers or your own mail. As with copy, I would recommend maintaining a file of good artwork—artwork you feel is appealing, that has proved to be successful, and that is applicable to the particular type of products you are selling. The idea is not to copy artwork, but to use the idea or concept as a starting point for your own.

Another source of free ideas is professionals in the field—printers, painters, designers, and so forth. All art professionals will have samples of artwork, different styles of type, of paper, and of just about everything you might think of to give you good ideas as to how to proceed and what type of graphics you might want for your ad. If you are considering having one of these professionals help you prepare your art for pay, you will definitely want to see their samples. During the process of gathering information, talking with them, and considering the possibilities, you will be exposed to many different ideas, which will help you refine your own concepts for your advertisement.

Government and corporate pamphlets, booklets, and other publications are a tremendous source of ideas you can incorporate into your advertisement. Large corporations spend thousands and thousands of dollars a year for artwork to illustrate their products in pamphlets, brochures, and annual reports. Frequently, you can get permission to use their artwork at no charge whatsoever. The U.S. government spends even more—millions of dollars, perhaps—to obtain high-quality artwork that is usually available to you, not only to help you generate ideas, but, in most cases, to use, free of charge. Anything published by the government is in the public domain, and you may use this material without having to secure permission. Government material has no copyright unless the material itself comes from a copyrighted source.

SOURCES OF LOW-COST ART

There are many different sources of art. Let's proceed from the most expensive to the most inexpensive. The most expensive way of getting high-quality art is maintaining your own staff. And should your mail order operation ever become the size of Neiman-Marcus, perhaps this expensive option is really the most economical, as it gives you the greatest amount of control. The art staffs of agencies or studios are relatively high-priced sources that can assist you in preparing your advertisements. However, you can expect to have top-of-the-line illustrations for your advertisements if you are dealing with experienced mail order people. Freelance artists typically work by the hour. They are usually less expensive than art studios or agency art staffs. An experienced freelance artist can be extremely economical while providing you with quality work and creative ideas. Printers specializing in the mail order business also frequently maintain an art staff and can provide you with a good job at a reasonable price. Because they're experienced in direct mail and mail order operations, you need not explain many of the peculiarities pertaining to mail order illustrations, such as why your layout must contain so much copy. They already know.

The art departments of colleges and universities represent a fantastic source of quality art, usually at very low cost. These are artists in the learning stage, but the learning stage does not necessarily mean a lowering of quality, and art students who need the money are frequently grateful for work you can give them. One prominent mail order dealer I know uses nothing but student art. In fact, he even holds competitions in which all entering art becomes his property and the winners receive cash prizes. This source of art for mail order advertisements has been much overlooked by many of the larger companies simply because they can afford to pay higher prices. But for quality art at relatively low cost, look into this source. It's good for you and for the art students as well.

Clip art is a type of syndicated art. It is done by artists, reproduced in great quantities, and sold to anyone who wants to use it. It is usually printed on heavy white stock and you merely clip it out with a pair of scissors and paste it in as necessary. Examples of clip art are shown in Figure 19.1. This is from a free sample clip book of line art provided by Volk, of Pleasantville, NJ 08232. Another prominent dealer of clip art is Dynamic Graphics, Inc., 6000 North Forest Park Road, Box 1901, Peoria, IL 61656-1901. Either of these companies will be happy to send you samples and price lists of their work. Clip art is usually furnished in booklets chock-full of hundreds of illustrations that you can cut out and use once you have purchased the booklet.

If you have a computer, many software programs are available that contain artwork which can be used. One such program is Desk Gallery published by Zedcor, Inc., 4500 E. Speedway Blvd., Suite 22, Tucson, AZ

Yes! We do cartoons and we do them exceptionally well - in many contemporary styles such as those you see here. All in simple black-and-white line, camera ready, easily and effectively reproduced. All this and more in the original "Clip Books" at an average cost of only $2.50 per week. Nearly 1,000 new illustrations each year. Four new books (a total of 40 pages) and four matching index folders every month.

Figure 19.1   Examples of clip art.

85712-5305. You should also check into the volumes of art on disks offered by The Artmaker Company, 1920 N. Claremont Blvd., #205-D, Claremont, CA 91711.

Outdated art—art on which the copyright has already expired and which is now in the public domain—is an incredibly good source of material for your advertisements. An example is shown in Figure 19.2. You can find old books of outdated art at your library. Or, you can buy an entire book of outdated art. Two good books you can clip for your use are *Attention Getters,* compiled by Robert Sietsema, and the *Complete Encyclopedia of Illustration* by J. G. Heck.

DEALING WITH ARTISTS

Before engaging an artist to work for you, you should meet with him or her and discuss the work he or she is doing now, as well as the work you want. You should see samples of work done for other clients. You should then tell the artist as much as possible about the artwork and advertising campaign you're planning to conduct. Sometimes it's very helpful, as well as time-saving, to work up rough sketches, using stick figures of your own concepts or ideas. From these figures, the artist can do a professional job while still following the general outline and broad principles you want to incorporate into your advertisement. The artwork shown in Figure 19.3 was created by an artist from my instructions in Figure 19.4. Be certain to get an estimate from the artist before you request work from him or her, and be absolutely certain that the artist is given a firm deadline.

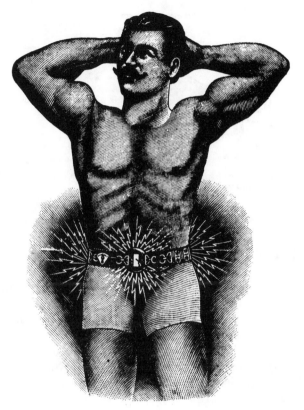

Figure 19.2 Example of outdated art in the public domain.

Figure 19.3 An original cartoon created by an artist from a rough sketch.

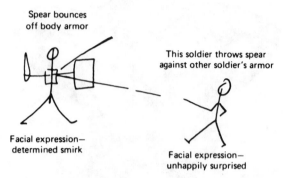

Figure 19.4   Rough sketch for cartoon in Figure 19.3.

SOURCES OF PHOTOGRAPHS

You can commission a photographer to make a special photograph of a product or situation for your advertisement. If you intend to show your product in the advertisement, this will be absolutely necessary unless you can obtain a glossy photograph from the manufacturer of the item itself. If special photography is necessary, do not attempt it yourself unless you are fully experienced in photography of this type. Also, when selecting a photographer, be certain that he or she is proficient in product photography and is not simply a portrait photographer. There is a tremendous difference, and you may not get satisfactory results if you attempt to get product photography through a commercial photographer who is experienced only with portraits. Again, asking is not enough; you should ask to see samples of the photographer's work. When I first started in mail order, I made this mistake myself. I spent $30 for a product photograph that was absolutely worthless. The photographer was experienced, but in portrait photography only. Don't make this mistake! It will cost you both time and money.

There are several other ways of getting photographs for your advertisements, some that will cost you a small amount and others that won't cost you a cent. Stock photographs are available from many sources throughout the country. These are photographs that have been collected and are kept on file. You merely look in a catalog and pick out the photograph you wish to use in your advertisement. You then buy a copy of the photograph from the owner. One major source of firms that have large files of stock photographs is the Yellow Pages of your telephone directory.

CD ROM

Today there are many sources of photographs on CD ROM. ROM stands for "Read Only Memory," so you can't imprint material on CD ROM disks. Of course you must have a computer with a CD ROM drive. If you do, many CD ROM disks are available.

Free Photographs

There are four basic sources of free photographs: Corporations and public relations firms, government agencies, trade organizations, and local newspapers. Be certain when you request the photograph that you get permission to use the photograph in your advertisement.

Usually any company will be more than happy to give you pictures of their product. Frequently they maintain photos of subjects somewhat removed from their product as well. To locate these companies, look up the subject by type of business in your local telephone book. If you want a photograph of a tractor in use, find a firm that manufactures tractors, or for a photograph of an airplane, write to a company that makes them. If you live in a small town and the company you want to write to is located elsewhere, call the local number and get the address of the main office. If there is no local number, you can use other directories, such as the Thomas Register of Manufacturers, or one of the directories published by Dun and Bradstreet, for locating these companies. Write a letter to the public relations office of the company you think may have the photograph you want, and don't forget to ask for permission to use the photograph in your ad.

Government Agencies

Just about every government agency has a photograph file, including the Department of Defense, the Department of Agriculture, and state and local government agencies. Just write a letter to the agency you think may have photographs of the subjects you want.

Trade Organizations

Trade organizations are manufacturers' organizations, professional associations, and so forth. You can also find a list of them in your telephone book under *Associations, Clubs,* or *Organizations.* Call or write those that are likely to have photographs of the subject you want. Here again, the photographs will probably be provided at little or no cost.

Local Newspapers

Local newspapers maintain a file of photographs, but there is likely to be some charge for each photograph provided.

One final word about photographs: If you are using a photographer, do not request more than one glossy copy of each photograph. If you require more than one glossy copy, it is easy to go to a duplicate photograph service, as described earlier, and have many, many copies made at a lower cost than the photographer's. You should be able to find a photograph duplicating service by consulting the Yellow Pages of your telephone book. However, if you are in an area where such a service is not available, I can recommend Duplicate Photo Laboratory, Inc., 1522 North Highland, Los Angeles, CA 90028.

LAYOUT

Layout refers to the arrangement that makes up your advertisement— whether it appears in print media or is a brochure or flier included with your direct mail package.

You always start your layout with a rough sketch that includes the headline, outlines of illustrations, and some rough ideas or room for the copy you are going to use in the advertisement. How you put these elements together is called composition.

THE SEVEN PRINCIPLES OF COMPOSITION

In general, there are seven principles to consider in laying out your advertisement: Unity, clarity, simplicity, rhythm, balance, proportion, and movement.

Unity

Unity refers to the fact that your entire advertisement should be laid out in such a fashion that it presents a unified whole, and that no single element seems to be outside the whole.

Clarity

Clarity means being clear, and the underlying message and point of your ad should come through very clearly without being confused by varying typeface sizes or too many different styles of typeface, or mixing photographs and line drawings indiscriminately, all of which will make your ad layout confusing to the reader.

Simplicity

When designing your layout, you should always remember "KIS," which means "keep it simple." Simplicity adds to the sharpness and distinctiveness of your layout. It means that your potential customer will grasp the message of your advertisement, whatever it is, without straining or having to look or read twice. To ensure simplicity after you complete the initial rough sketch of your layout, you should try to eliminate elements that do not add to the central message. The more elements, the more complex your ad will be. If the element adds something to the central message you're trying to get across, that's fine, but if not, the element will make your ad more complex at no benefit. Get rid of it.

Rhythm

Rhythm is typically obtained by two subcomponents—progression and repetition. A good example of progression and repetition is shown in Joe Karbo's "The Lazy Man's Way to Riches" and similar ads, which, paragraph after paragraph, give you strong reasons for placing an order for the product being offered. Each reason or "sales close" is separate, and yet each progresses logically until the call to action to order the item. This is rhythm raised to its highest state in advertising.

Balance

Balance conjures up the image of scales, one side balanced against the other. In art, it refers to the perception of the eye, not necessarily what the ruler itself measures, but where the eye or what the eye sees of the different elements you have brought together in your layout. A balance may be symmetrical, in which the layout seems to balance or weigh equally from side to side, or asymmetrical, in which one side of your advertisement has more material than the other side. Both types of balance can be correct, provided they are in the right proportions. Balance is very important for two reasons: First, a properly balanced ad will act as an attention getter and will assist your headline in performing this function; secondly, proper balance will assist in maintaining interest after the headline of your ad has been read.

Proportion

Proportion acts with balance to attract and maintain interest. It is concerned with how the different elements of your layout—headline, copy, illustrations—relate to one another and to the advertisement as a whole. There is a golden rule of proportion, which reads as follows: If you divide your composition into two parts, then the ratio of the smaller part to the larger part should be equal to the ratio of the larger part to the entire composition. This can be illustrated by drawing a line and dividing it such that if a smaller part of the line is .382 and the larger part of the line is

.618, the ratio of the smaller part to the larger is equal to the ratio of the larger part of the entire line as follows: .382 is to .618 as .618 is to 1. But forget the numbers. The eye must be the basic guide in determining how you break up your advertisement so that the proportions encourage the interest of your reader.

Movement

Movement is extremely important in mail order advertising. Movement across a layout may be in any direction. As a normal rule it's clockwise. In other words, a reader begins in the upper left-hand corner and ends at the lower right-hand corner. Anything in between the upper left-hand corner and the lower right that strikes the fancy of the reader may cause him or her to read. But your ultimate goal is to lead your potential customer all the way around in this direction. This is why in full-page advertisements, coupons are frequently found in the lower right-hand corner. Now, allowing for movement, there are two different theories of mail order advertisements and you should allow for both of them. The first one, the down-the-chute theory, is emphasized in many ads, including those by Ben Suarez. This theory says you begin to read the ad and progress all the way through it, never stopping so long as interest is maintained. Ben Suarez says you can tell whether your ad has proper movement by following the eyes of someone reading the ad. The eyes should continue down the page through the entire advertisement. But if he or she stops, there is some problem with either your layout or copy that has caused a snag. This theory is referred to as "down-the-chute" because once the reader begins reading, he or she goes all the way down and around until the reading is completed at the end of your advertisement. The other theory, which is also applicable in many cases in mail order, is that the reader does not go down a chute at all, but rather, once struck by your headline and beginning to read your ad, is attracted by various components or subparagraphs of the advertisement. Therefore, your potential customer may read a little here, read a little there, read a little somewhere else, as he or she progresses from upper left to lower right of the advertisement. To the best of my knowledge, extensive research has not been done on these theories. I believe both to be applicable, depending upon what the layout and copywriter of the advertisement intend. Both can and do work successfully. But you must consider from the beginning which you intend to follow and construct your ad appropriately. In either case, movement is important, and you must lead your reader to the final portion in the lower right part of your advertisement where the final close of the sale is made.

In accomplishing layout for mail order ads, remember that the ultimate purpose is not beauty, but rather to make the sale. Therefore, if your ad sells, it is a good advertisement. If it does not result in sales, it is not good, regardless of its appearance.

TYPOGRAPHY

Typography refers to the kind of type that is available for your ad. All kinds of typefaces are available in all sizes. In fact, there are over 1,000 different recognized type styles. Trying to cope with so many styles is made somewhat easier in that most styles can be classified as either serif or sans serif. Two exceptions are text and script. The basic difference between serif and sans serif type styles is that serif styles have little cross-strokes at the tops and bottoms of the letters and sans serif styles do not. Both are shown in Figure 19.5.

If you are doing your own typesetting, you have several different options to consider: Paste-up or rub-on type; VariTyper machine; a typewriter; cutouts, printed material, or clip art; desktop publishing; or typesetting. Typesetting your own material has been made much easier by the accessibility of personal computers. Many excellent layout and type programs are available.

Paste-Up or Rub-On Type

These are letters printed individually on paper or on clear acetate with an adhesive back. With one type you merely paste these letters on your layout sheet, and with the other you simply lay the sheet over and rub out the letter, which adheres to the sheet on which you are working.

VariTyper Machine

A VariTyper is a reasonably economical method that uses a special machine for composing your headlines or other type work. It offers a variety of different type sizes and styles, including italics, and is relatively easy to use.

Cutouts, Printed Material, or Clip Art

Material that has already been printed is also a source of material for your typography. Clip art generally refers to illustrations, but it also includes headlines and phrases. However, printed art, which you do not purchase but which has already been printed by someone else, is usable so long as

Executive Fitness
A Proven Way To

Figure 19.5   Examples of serif and sans serif type styles.

you do not use more than one or two words and thus get yourself in trouble with copyright law. Make sure that the printed material you use is clean. Generally a white background is best.

Desktop Publishing

Computers have revolutionized typesetting as they have everything else. Many word processing and graphic programs incorporate type fonts that are perfect for use in your advertisements. However, there is one requirement. You must have a printer that prints out high quality letters, such as a laser printer. But even if you don't own one, chances are you can rent one easily. If you have a CD ROM drive, there are literally thousands of fonts available at low cost.

Whatever method you use for reproducing the copy and headline in your layout, the type can be reduced or enlarged to any dimensions you desire in keeping with the overall layout and composition of your advertisement. One word of caution is appropriate here: Any enlargements of type will show up many errors that were concealed by small size. Therefore, extensive enlargement of typography produced by a typewriter should be very carefully tested before you commit yourself to an advertisement using this technique.

ILLUSTRATIONS

Illustrations consist of both drawings and photographs. In addition, illustrations for advertisements are broken down into two other groups. First are photographs and pencil drawings that have general shadings of tone, and second, line drawings that have no shadings. Illustrations that have general shading of tone are known as continuous tone or half-tone copy because they have no absolute separation into stark black and stark white. The difficulty with continuous tone or half-tone illustrations is that they contain various shades and tones of gray through black and white that can't be produced as you see them with only one ink color, no matter what method of printing is used. To get around this problem, an optical illustration is employed to enable use of only one ink color in the printer, but it is done in such a fashion that the photograph, pencil drawing, or whatever, appears to have many different tonal shades. This illusion is accomplished by breaking the image into hundreds and hundreds of small dots, done photographically through a special process. The original drawing or photograph is photographed again with a screen placed between the lens of the camera and its film. This screen, which looks much like the screen of a screen door, has extremely fine lines. It breaks the image photographed into an overall pattern of thousands of microscopic dots on the negative. These dots will vary in size according to the intensity of the tone in the photograph or illustration being reproduced. When the photograph is light, the dots are relatively small. When the photograph is darker, the dots become larger and may even join together on the negative. When this negative is reproduced through the printing process, the relative size of these dots creates an illusion of tones and shades. Figure 19.6 shows two ads, the bottom one illustrated with line copy, the top one illustrated with a photograph that has been reproduced. If you look very closely at the photograph or examine it with a magnifying glass, you will see that even though it appears to be tonal in quality, these tones come from the very small dots I just spoke about.

You can also reproduce continuous and half-tone illustrations that have been printed previously. Because these have already been through the screening process, it is not necessary to repeat it. However, if you reproduce a photograph or illustration that has already been printed, you lose some of the quality of the original.

As with type, the size of your illustration can vary, depending upon your desires and how it fits into the composition and layout you have designed. If you want to reduce or enlarge it, you can. Again, you must be very careful that in enlarging you do not expose errors that were not visible at its smaller size. Another important fact is that when you photographically enlarge or reduce an illustration, the enlargement or reduction occurs in all directions. Thus, an illustration that is reduced 50 percent in size will be only 25 percent the size of the original because each side has been reduced proportionally. This is shown in Figure 19.7, and it applies to your type and illustrations. However, it is easy to determine the proper reduction or enlargement of an illustration or copy by the diagonal line method. First, determine the dimensions of the illustration or piece of copy you intend to reduce or enlarge. Draw these dimensions on a separate piece of paper. Now, simply draw a line in the box outline of the illustration from left to right, as shown in Figure 19.8. Draw a horizontal line or a vertical line in the box illustration you have just drawn to the dimension to which your illustration must be either reduced or enlarged. For example, if the original size of your illustration was four by five inches and it is necessary that the five-inch side be reduced to three inches to fit into your layout, you can find the length that the other side of the illustration will appear by measuring three inches from point A in Figure 19.8, which gets you to point B. Draw a vertical line up from point B to point C. This is the length to which the other side of your illustration will be reduced. By using this method, you can see to what dimensions your illustrations must be reduced or enlarged without making an error that will cause you to have to repeat the attempt at arriving at the correct size.

Figure 19.6 The top ad is illustrated with a photograph, the bottom with a line drawing.

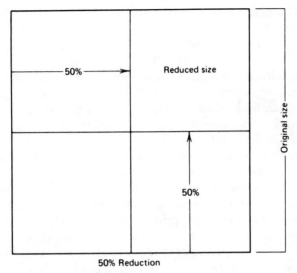

Figure 19.7 An illustration that is reduced 50 percent in size will be only 25 percent the size of the original.

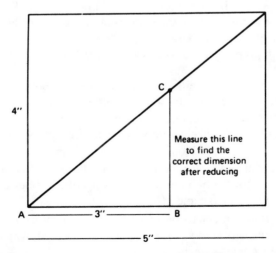

Figure 19.8 Reducing or enlarging an illustration.

PREPARING CAMERA-READY COPY

Camera-ready copy is the final artwork, including everything that goes into your advertisement—headline, illustration, and copy—exactly as you wish to see it printed. This paste-up, or mechanical, as it is called, is photographed, and the negative is used to make a master to create your advertisement. You can have someone prepare your camera-ready copy for you professionally, or if you have the necessary tools and want to do it yourself, I will show you how.

If you intend to create your own camera-ready copy, you should get the following tools together. First, non-reproducible blue pencils are necessary to make any comments to the photographer or printer that will not be reproduced in your advertisement. A drawing board—some flat board or table with a smooth surface—is required to do your work without a lot of trouble and many mistakes. India ink is a jet black, professional ink used by artists when preparing camera-ready copy. It is used to make corrections in copy that has been printed with minor mistakes so that a light area appears. Unwanted light areas are blackened with the India ink. Liquid whitener, also known as white opaque, is also used to correct errors, in this case by whiting the error out. Masking tape is necessary to hold the camera-ready copy page steady on the drawing board. Rubber cement is used to paste the type or artwork onto the paper. Rubber cement is very important, and it has major advantages over paste. First, it allows you to make corrections while you work, as the cement does not dry instantly, and excess cement creeping around the edge of what you are pasting is easily removed. Further, if you do make a mistake after the cement dries, you can easily separate the material you have pasted, make your correction, and repaste with a little additional rubber cement. Finally, you will need scissors for cutting, a pencil for drawing, and a ruler and triangles for getting proper dimensions.

The steps in preparation of your camera-ready copy are as follows.

1. Carefully proofread all copy. This is very important because once the master plate is made, some expense is required to rephotograph the artwork. Further, once your advertisement goes to press, any typographical or other errors will be very expensive for you to redo because they must be reprinted.

2. Make certain that all illustrations, headlines, and copy are the correct size. Do this before you start using your rubber cement. It will save you much time and effort.

3. Use rubber cement to paste on the illustrations, headlines, and so forth, on clean, heavy, white paper or cardboard, which is the background for your camera-ready copy.

4. Use your ruler and the triangles to ensure that positioning is absolutely accurate and precise.

After positioning and rubber cementing to the heavy cardboard or white paper, check each portion of the artwork to ensure that every line drawn is completely inked in. If it is not, use the India ink.

Now go over your artwork once again and remove any unwanted marking with the white opaque liquid. Be very careful; the white opaque runs easily. After completely finishing your camera-ready copy, protect it with either a protective sheet of plastic acetate or light plastic wrap. Remember that the plate made for your advertisement cannot be any clearer or better than the camera-ready copy from which it is started, so keep your camera-ready copy as clean as you can.

If you have a computer, all of this is much simpler. With the color laser printers available, even color can be a piece of cake. If you want to know more about preparing camera-ready artwork on a computer, contact your local computer store. It may cost you several thousand dollars for everything you need, but if you do a lot of advertising, it can be worth the expense and could actually save you money.

SUMMARY

In this chapter you've learned how to prepare or obtain your artwork and graphics at low cost. You now know free sources of ideas for your art, sources of low-cost art and photographs, how to accomplish your layout for your artwork, how to do your typography, what you must do to prepare your illustrations properly, and finally, how to prepare your own camera-ready copy. Use of these techniques can save you literally thousands of dollars while still enabling you to turn out really professional work.

20

Saving and
Making Money
with Your Printing

PRINTING IS ESSENTIAL TO YOUR MAIL ORDER BUSINESS

You will need printing for your stationery, your advertisements, brochures, sales letters, envelopes, and even invoice forms. The right printing is important to you because it represents your business just as a store and its atmosphere represent a retail business, or the appearance of a restaurant affects how the food tastes to customers. In the mail order business, your customers do not visit you at your place of business. Therefore, next to your products and the service you perform, the quality of the printing in your direct mail packages and other literature and stationery represents you and gives clues to your customer as to the quality of your business— whether it is a high-class or low-class business, whether you are trustworthy or untrustworthy, literate or illiterate. The right kind of printing actually makes money for you. At the same time, the right kind of printing at the right price can save you a lot of money. In this chapter we are going to talk about both stimulating sales and saving money through buying the correct printing for your business and your project.

WHO SHOULD YOU GO TO FOR YOUR PRINTING?

The price of any printing job that you might want—from a simple self-addressed return envelope to a complex multicolor brochure with many illustrations—will vary greatly from printer to printer, not because of any dishonesty on the part of printers or the printing trade, but because printers specialize in different types of printing operations. They have different equipment, they may specialize in different run sizes, the quality they offer may be different, the quantity suitable for their equipment may be different, and their experience and ability to buy paper and other materials differ. You should always get bids from at least five different printers for any extensive printing job. Do this until you begin doing business on a regular basis with one or more printers for certain different types of tasks. Some experienced mail order operators would advise always getting bids, even after you are established. However, once you develop a relationship with certain printers for certain types of printing, you will discover that other factors may become more important than price—reliability, for example, and the fact that if you are a regular customer you will probably get priority at difficult times when one press is down, paper is short, or your printer has other problems.

PRINTING METHODS

I'll tell you exactly how to go about getting these bids in a minute. First, let's look at the basic types of printing done in the mail order business in which you will probably be interested. Three different printing methods are most often used in mail order operations: Letterpress, offset lithography, and gravure.

Letterpress

Letterpress is the oldest printing process. Until fairly recently, it was the process most often used by operators in the mail order business. Even today letterpress is considered by many people to be the most versatile process, and it is still used for many newspapers, books, and magazines, as well as commercial work for mail order advertisers. With letterpress, the printing is accomplished by means of raised type, line, and dot surfaces for photographic plates, which are inked and then pressed onto the paper to make the printed copy. The type characters and other illustrations used for letterpress are always in reverse, so that when they print the image on the paper the image will be seen and read correctly. The elements of type are locked together to form words and the words locked together to form sentences. The versatility of a letterpress operation lies in the fact that parts of the printing surface can be changed without changing the entire page to be printed.

The advantages of letterpress printing are flexibility, in that you may change parts of the job easily; higher quality at much faster speeds than possible with other types of printing; a closer combination of colors than can otherwise be achieved; a wide range of accessory equipment available with the letterpress operation; and the additional operations possible on the same press, such as cutting and perforating, all done simultaneously at the time of printing.

The major disadvantage of letterpress is that it is expensive when compared with the available alternatives.

There are many different presses used for letterpress printing. We may classify these many different presses into three basic types: Platen, flatbed cylinder, and rotary.

Platen.   Platen is the original form of letterpress printing. The raised type surfaces and paper are carried on two opposing flat surfaces. The raised type surface plane is known as the bed. The flat surface that contains the paper is known as the platen. The raised type is inked with the platen press in an open position, then the bed and platen are brought together under pressure, as much as 600 pounds per square inch. The press is then brought to the open position and the printed paper removed. With a platen press, there is a general limitation as to the size of the printed matter, usually 14 by 22 inches. Operating speed is limited as well, usually to around 5,000 impressions an hour. For this reason, the platen press is generally used only for short runs, or for combination jobs where different cutting, perforating, or other special operations can be combined with the printing.

Flatbed Cylinder.   With the flatbed cylinder press a flat printing form of the raised letters or illustration is used. However, instead of being pressed against another surface in a plane-to-plane contact, the paper is on a cylinder form. As the cylinder turns, the paper is forced between the cylinder and the raised impression from the press. The cylinder itself applies the necessary pressure to print on the paper. The printing form containing the impression to be printed moves in a lateral fashion. After the impression is completed, it returns to its original position and the cylinder is raised, allowing the printed sheet to be released and the type form to be re-inked, and the process is then repeated. The speed of the flatbed cylinder is relatively slow, but many printing jobs for use in mail order can be produced on such a press, including brochures, catalogs, and other printed forms.

Rotary Press.   Rotary presses, unlike the flatbed press, require a curved printing surface. The rotary press is based on a cylinder-to-cylinder principle. The two cylinders turn in opposite directions at high speed, and as a result, this method of letterpress operation is the most efficient and fastest of the three types discussed. Rotaries are used typically for long runs such as newspapers, large circulation magazines, and very-high-volume direct mail. Newspapers can be produced through the rotary press method at the rate of 70,000 newspapers an hour. Because of the expense, a minimum run is usually 25,000 impressions. And the disadvantage here, because of the need for curved plates, which are more expensive, is cost. Another advantage is that many attachments are available to be put on the rotary press and allow folding, cutting, perforating, and so forth, at the same time the other high-speed operation takes place.

Offset Lithography

Whereas once letterpress was the most used printing process in mail order, the honor today goes to offset. Of the three major printing processes noted here, offset has had the greatest growth. It passed letterpress in dollar volume around 1965. Quality was once a problem with offset printing in comparison to letterpress, but not today. Today you can obtain quality equal to the letterpress operation, although quality does differ from printer to printer.

The offset process is based on photography. A special plate is made from a photograph of camera-ready copy and the offset image is transferred from the inked plate to a rubber blanket and then printed onto the paper. This printing from the blanket to the paper, or offsetting, is where the process gets its name. It is distinguished from other methods of printing such as letterpress or gravure in that both the printing and nonprinting areas of the plate are in the same plane: The printing surfaces are neither raised from nor indented into the plate. Another unique fact that makes the offset process possible is that the ink used has a grease base and will not mix with water, so raised impressions are not required for printing. The plate is used in such a way that those portions to be printed attract this greasy ink, whereas those portions not to be printed attract water, which is applied to the plate before the ink is applied. Because water and the greasy ink will not mix, the ink remains only on the area to be printed.

For mail order, there are two main methods of offset printing that you should know about and consider—sheet-fed offset and web offset. In sheet-fed offset, the sheets of paper to be printed are placed in the press one at a time. In web offset, a continuous roll of paper is used and the paper cut during or after printing operation, permitting extremely high speeds. The distinctions between the two methods in the past have been that sheet-fed offset has permitted better quality in printing and that the web press has had a cost advantage in large quantities while having restrictions on paper size that could be used. These two methods are very competitive for a number of operations once limited to one or the other, and both should be considered, depending upon the type of press your printer has and the particulars of your job.

The advantages of offset printing include cost savings over letterpress because of labor involved in typesetting and much cheaper plates. Also, the setup time for the press is generally much lower than that of letterpress, and you can obtain duplicate plates very inexpensively, compared to letterpress. Finally, it is easy to make reprints once you have an original using the offset method. For example, a book publisher who is publishing a new edition of a book need not reset type or make up new plates, but can make inexpensive offset plates from the original edition.

Gravure

The gravure method of printing is similar to letterpress in the sense that contact is made directly between the inked plate and the paper to be printed. However, gravure is the opposite to letterpress in that rather than a raised surface's being printed, a depressed surface is used for ink transference. The design to be printed is actually etched into the plate, forming small cavities that contain the ink. Like letterpress, the entire image is reversed. Gravure gives the highest quality reproductions of continuous tone art in all illustrations, including photographs. During the printing process, the etched plate is inked by ink roll or by a spray. But before it comes in contact with the paper to make the impression, excess ink is scraped from the surface by a sharp, flexible piece of metal or blade. Thus, only the ink remaining in the cavity on the plate is transferred to the paper to make the impression. Naturally, this process is expensive, so a typical run for the gravure process is long—250,000 and up.

COMPUTER GENERATED LETTERS

Although letterpress, offset, and gravure are the three basic processes of printing used in mail order, a newer printing process has been used to increase mail order sales at reduced cost. As was mentioned in previous chapters, whenever you can personalize anything in mail order, the product sells better. This is the story of computer letters, in which an individual can be addressed directly by name because it is printed by a computer. Each letter appears to be typed individually and you can bet that such a letter will pull far better than a letter that is not and that opens merely "Dear Friend," or even a form letter in which the name and address have simply been inserted. A computer letter sent to me is shown in Figure 20.1. You can locate people who do this type of printing in the classified sections of the magazines *Direct Marketing, Target Marketing,* and others. Here are two printers of computer letters you can write to, either for samples of their work or information about cost: Response Graphics, 1480 Renaissance Drive, Park Ridge, IL 60068, and Scan Forms, Inc., 181 Rittenhouse Circle, Bristol, PA 19007.

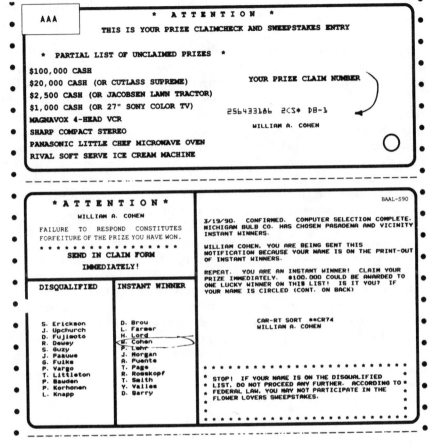

Figure 20.1 A computer-generated letter.

A number of different technological developments have led to personalization through nonimpact printing. Such printing is possible through the ink jet (the spraying of small dots of ink at high speed to form letters), lasers, and other processes. Along with a computer, these developments allow personalized messages to be printed using variable sizes of type, anywhere on the page, and oriented toward any direction. They permit a degree of creativity in personalization previously not economically feasible.

PREPARING A PRINTING PLAN AND FINDING A PRINTER

So much depends upon your printing that you should actually work up a formalized plan to ensure that the printing you need can be obtained when you need it and at the most cost-effective price. I have broken this process down into six steps.

Step 1. See a number of printers, at least five. I also recommend that you do this as soon as you have completed your overall project marketing plan. In this visit, you should tell the printer exactly what you want and ask for samples of similar material he or she has printed. Your specifications should include paper. You can see a number of different types of paper and decide on exactly what you want. Also explain the kind of illustrations you want, the quality of work you're looking for, the binding if this is important, the size and number of pages, the quality of the material, and the color or colors. Ask a bid for different quantity runs, but make sure your printer knows the quantity you are most likely to order. Finally, make sure that he or she understands when you need the material so that he or she knows whether other jobs may interfere with your project.

Be certain that you document exactly what it is you want and that you get prices and a time commitment in writing. Also, don't forget to ask how the price can be decreased. Is glossy paper really needed, considering how much you can save by not using it? You can save a lot of money by just asking the question. Finally, I would make sure that the printer you have contacted understands that he or she is in competition. If the quantity of material you're having printed is large enough, the printer may be willing to lower the price to beat out the competition. On the other hand, if this is an initial run for a small test, and you haven't done this before and do not have a regular printer, I would emphasize only that you would like to check this price against some others before making the final decision. Don't expect any major reductions in price because of competition for a limited job. Your job may just not be worth it. However, you can make sure that the printer understands that while you're just getting started now and need a small-quantity run, other runs are anticipated in larger quantities, and that once you have someone you are satisfied with you will probably tend to continue to work with that person for most of your printing.

In addition to considering printers locally, I would also consider printers who operate through mail order. Sometimes printing bought this way can save you a lot of money. On one offset job ordered through mail order, my local printer told me that he could not even purchase the paper for the amount the mail order offset printer was going to charge me. However, there is a trade-off. While you can frequently save money by dealing through the mail with certain firms, you lose a lot of control over the work. So, if you're going to deal through the mail in getting your printing, make certain that everything is exactly the way you want it before you order. It is very difficult to make changes in the original order by mail. Also, make certain that you order the printed material well ahead of time. Even then you may still have problems and need to make phone calls trying to get various details straightened out or to encourage the printer to get your work done faster. Remember, if you are dealing by mail, you will not be able to see your printer face-to-face and you may not be as persuasive on the telephone. If you're interested in low-cost mail order printing and you want to make a comparison, here are two such offset printers who do black and white work through the mail. Write for their catalogs and ask for additional information: Champion Printing Company, Box 14129, Cincinnati, OH 45250; and Dinner & Klein, 6th and Spokane St., P.O. Box 3814, Seattle, WA 98124.

Before making a commitment with one or another of the printers you have consulted, make certain you write down exactly what you want so that when you're comparing these printers, you are comparing apples with apples and not apples with oranges.

Step 2.   Get the actual bids in writing, including what is to be done and the prices from each printer. Again I caution you to make certain that you know exactly what each printer is going to supply so that you're making an accurate comparison among the five or more printers that you have solicited.

Step 3.   Make the comparison. Here you have to consider those factors that are most important to you in your unique situation. Is quality very important? Then you should very carefully consider the samples supplied by the individuals you have solicited. If quality is not so important, you must think about that too. You should also consider whether it is important to be geographically close to the printer, which gives you more control, or whether you are willing to give up some control for potential cost savings. And, of course, you should consider price. If it is not your first time and you have worked with some printers with whom you are happy, you might want to give a lot of consideration to reliability.

Step 4.   Prepare or have someone prepare your camera-ready copy if you are using offset. You should check it very carefully to make sure there are no errors. Keep in mind that from this step on, every single error will cost you additional money and it is best to catch errors before you submit the work to the printer. If you aren't using offset, you're giving the printer a detailed layout and manuscript. Do your job and make certain it is error free.

Step 5.   Take the camera-ready copy to your printer and he or she will supply you with proofs, which you can and should check over very carefully. This is your last chance to correct before going to press. It is more expensive to correct these initial proofs than it was to correct your camera-ready copy. However, it is still far cheaper than going to press and having something important left out or incorrect—typographical errors, error in address, address left off, and so forth. Have someone other than yourself check the proof before you tell the printer your work is ready for printing. If you aren't using offset, and with offset for an expensive run, you may get to check a single printed copy.

Step 6.   This is the final step, where you give your printer the okay to go ahead. It takes but a few minutes to read about this whole process, but please keep in mind that it takes a considerable time, and as one famous mail order man said about printers, the only thing consistent about them is that they are always late. So do not forget to allow yourself enough time when you start to complete the job on time.

This knowledge about the basics of printing is essential for your success. If you conduct your mail order business correctly with regard to the printing aspect, not only will you save money but your printing will make additional money for you.

SUMMARY

In this chapter we have discussed why printing costs are different from printer to printer and why it is important to get multiple bids for every major printing project. We've also discussed the three basic mail order printing methods—letterpress, offset lithography, and gravure—and the advantages and disadvantages of each method. Finally, we discussed a six-step printing plan you should follow every time you need to have printing done. Following this plan will ensure that your costs are minimized for the correct printing for your job.

Part V

Mail Order Measurement

21

Testing to Find Out Whether You'll Be Successful before You Invest Heavily

TESTING: WHY DO IT?

The quality of testing that is possible in mail order is a major advantage over any other type of business. Every successful mail order operator tests, so it's not just theory. It's a real part of mail order and vital to your success.

In earlier chapters, I introduced you to some methods of testing. In this chapter we're going to look at testing much more thoroughly. But first, let's consider some basic questions. Why test? Let us say that you are about to embark on a promotion for a new product. Your ads have been prepared. All the material for your direct mail packages has been developed and everything is ready to go. In the initial stages of the promotion you anticipate spending between $5,000 and $10,000. You have already researched the market thoroughly and picked a product. You know in your heart of hearts that this product cannot fail and your campaign will be a sure winner. Why not just jump in and spend your $5,000 to $10,000 and make the money as soon as possible?

Before I tell you what a test will do, let me say one thing that a test probably will not do: It will not make you money. If it does, that's all well and good, but that is not the objective. The purpose of the test is to save you from losing your $5,000 to $10,000 needlessly. The fact is that, despite preliminary research and good preparation, most new products fail in the marketplace. So how can you make money? The mail order operator makes money because of testing. Because even though the majority of his or her campaigns may be unsuccessful, he or she finds out that they're unsuccessful at the very beginning through testing. The successful mail order person spends maybe $500 or $1,000 on this test, and only if he or she is successful is the next step taken to spend the larger sums of money required. This means that even though an operator has loss after loss, when he or she finally does win, it's a big win. One success more than makes up for all the relatively small amounts of money spent on many tests for unsuccessful campaigns.

But that's not the only reason for testing. Even a successful product and offer can be tested for various features of the promotion, as we have talked about previously. Some copy may pull 500 percent or better than other copy for the same product. Surely it is worth a relatively small sum of money to find this out inasmuch as the return of this investment is so great both over the long run and in the immediate future.

We said that testing does cost money. Think of testing as buying intelligence or buying market research. It is far better to pay the small price to learn whether you can succeed with your proposition, or to learn which proposition is more profitable than another. The alternative is to jump in and make your mistakes, and possibly lose thousands of dollars in the process without any chance of recouping it. That makes mail order too much of a gamble. There is risk in mail order—after all, it is a business. But it is not gambling.

WHAT TO TEST

There are some major things that we test, including the following:

1. Profitability.
2. One ad against another (different copy, different graphics, or both, and positioning of ad).
3. One medium against another or one magazine against another.
4. Price.
5. The offer.
6. One list against another.
7. A direct mail package.
8. Elements of the direct mail package, including copy, graphics, the sales letter, the flier, self-addressed stamped envelope, wording of the guarantee, length of the period in which the money is refundable, and so forth.
9. Terms of payment.
10. Use of color.
11. Letterhead and stationery.

Testing for Profitability

Testing for profitability is perhaps the basic reason for testing. Some propositions are so inherently unprofitable that it is little use to try to modify your copy or the medium in which you're advertising to make them work. It just can't be done. It is better to know this up front so that, if necessary, you can drop a project that is unprofitable and move on to another, where the money is. Therefore, initial testing of any proposition we try in mail order is for the purpose of determining whether we can make a profit.

Testing One Ad against Another

In testing one ad against another, there are many things that we can test. I mentioned copy before. Sometimes just the copy change makes a tremendous difference. We can change the graphics, including the picture or illustration. Sometimes neither the copy nor the graphics by itself will make much difference: You must change both to get good results. The position of the ad in the magazine carrying it can be tremendously important. But to get special positioning in a magazine or newspaper frequently costs additional money. The question is whether this additional money is worth it. We must consider not only the number of responses received and the profitability for the first product sold, but more importantly, profitability over the entire period that the customer continues to buy from us.

Testing One Medium against Another
or One Magazine, Newspaper, Radio Station,
or Television Station against Another

Certain media in which we advertise will be more effective than others in producing orders and customers. We discover not only whether they are profitable, but also their relative effectiveness from testing. Why is this important? If we had all the money we could possibly use in every single promotional campaign, we could advertise and continue to advertise. As long as we were creating a profit, as long as it was profitable to continue advertising in every medium, we would do so. However, you will never have unlimited financial resources, no matter how big you get. Therefore, some newspapers or magazines will be more profitable than others. Also, certain types of advertising may be more effective than others—television may be better than radio or vice versa. We do these tests first, to find out whether the medium being tested is profitable at all. Once this testing is complete, we want to know the relative profitability of each. Only in this way will we know how to allocate our limited financial resources, not only between different advertising media for one project or product, but over several different projects simultaneously.

Testing Price

Earlier I discussed price and we looked at just how important price really is in its projection of image and its psychological impact on whether your customer will purchase. Also, I showed you an example with my own *Writer's Guide to Publication and Profit* of how lowering the price not only did not increase profits through greatly increased sales, but actually reduced sales. For certain products there is a selective ideal price perceived by your potential customers. Economists tell us that the demand curve generally slopes downward, as in Figure 21.1. As we reduce the price, more of whatever we are selling is bought by our customers. However, this simple downward-sloping demand curve is not the case for all products. Figure 21.2 shows a demand curve for a prestige product such as expensive jewelry. What this shows is that as price increases, the quantity demanded rises. It continues to rise until point x. Then as prices continue to increase, the quantity demanded declines.

Figure 21.3 shows a demand curve for a product for which there is no substitute. The price doesn't matter. The buyer will pay it because he must have the product. A medicine which could cure a fatal disease would be an example of such a product. Therefore, the quantity demanded is independent of the price.

For many mail order products, you must test to find out what the demand curve looks like. By testing various prices, we come up with the demand curve shown in Figure 21.4, which is that for my *Writer's Guide*

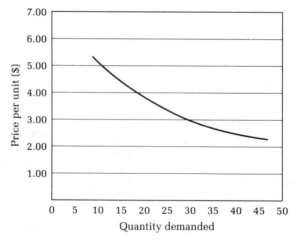

Figure 21.1 The normal downward-sloping demand curve. As price is reduced, quantity demanded increases. As price is raised, quantity demand decreases.

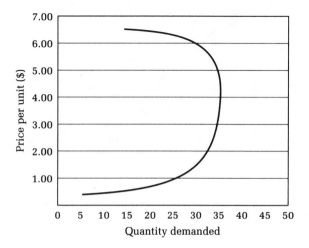

Figure 21.2 Demand curve for a prestige product.

to Publication and Profit. The shape of this curve is different, of course, depending upon your particular product and various other factors associated with your proposition. But it is important to know exactly what this demand curve is so that we can calculate the price we wish to charge for our item, keeping in mind that not only the first order, but also long-range profitability in the back-end part of the mail order business is important.

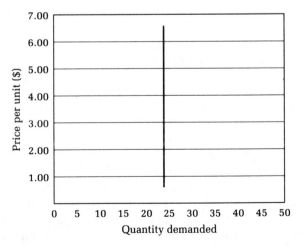

Figure 21.3 Demand curve for a product for which there is no substitute.

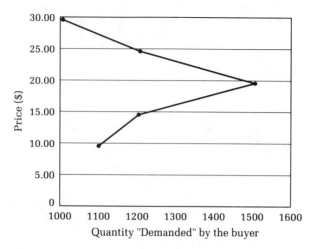

Figure 21.4 Demand curve for an actual product as a result of testing for the *Writer's Guide to Publication and Profit* showing selective demand at a certain price.

The Offer

I've mentioned it earlier in the book, but it doesn't hurt at all to say again that the offer can have a tremendous effect on purchase by your customer. Sometimes a simple change will have many times the profitability of the baseline offer with which you started. There are many ways of making a presentation to your customer, but one generally works best, and finding out which one this is can mean the difference in thousands and thousands of dollars every time you come up with a new product or service you offer through the mail.

Testing One List against Another

A single list can run to millions of names. Therefore, without having to mail to the entire list, you definitely want to know which list is better and more profitable than the others. Testing will supply this answer.

The Direct Mail Package

There are two theories about direct mail package testing. One says that every time you test you should test the entire package, including the copy, graphics, direct mail letter, return envelope, guarantee, and so forth, and that the direct mail package must be viewed as a single entity, not as separate elements, because the elements interact. According to this approach, you must test the entire direct mail package against another entirely different package to see which is best.

Elements of the Direct Mail Package

The alternative to testing the entire direct mail package is to test several of the important elements of this package—the sales letter, flier, publisher's letter and whether to include it, copy and graphics, how you word your guarantee and what kind of guarantee you give, whether you enclose a self-addressed, stamped envelope or only a self-addressed envelope, and the period for which the money is refundable. All of these elements will have a bearing on your orders and also on your profitability, so each element must be checked individually. For example, a short period for which the money is refundable—let's say, two weeks—may result in fewer orders than if you gave a full year or lifetime guarantee on an item. On the other hand, if the product for which you are conducting your promotional campaign is likely to have many, many returns after a certain period for one reason or another, maybe the shorter period for guarantee or money-back refund is best, even though it generates fewer orders. Along these lines, many mail order operators find that, regardless of their product, if they offer a very long or lifetime guarantee, they receive returns much later, even though their customers were clearly satisfied with their product initially.

What should you do—test the entire package, or each of the major elements? My advice is to tune your major elements first, and only after you have attained the maximum profitability should you begin testing the entire package against another package with different elements.

Terms of Payment

Terms of payment can have quite an effect on your customers' ordering of your product or service. If you offer to sell C.O.D. (cash on delivery), you will undoubtedly get many more orders than if you do not offer it. However, many of the people who order C.O.D. will choose not to pay the letter carrier and not to take delivery of the item. As a result, you pay the postage both ways and still don't make a sale. If you decide to offer C.O.D., you should test it. In the same way, many mail order operators allow time payments. If you do, you should recognize that, even under the best conditions and after many dunning letters to your customers who owe you money, you will probably receive full payment from only 60 percent of your customers. This is the reality of selling on credit, and you have to recognize it. However, you will certainly sell more if you do offer credit and a time payment plan. Now, if you are profitable, despite the drawbacks, and don't mind the paperwork, it's worthwhile for you to offer time payment.

On the other hand, if it is not profitable or you don't want the bother, don't offer it. In every case you must calculate for profitability, and these calculations must include the fact that you have other items to sell to your customer after the initial order.

Use of Color

Testing the use of color is important because color will increase the number of your orders in almost every case. However, use of multicolor brochures and of color in ads costs a lot of money. Is it worth the extra money to bring in these extra orders? You can find out by testing.

Letterheads and Stationery

You might think that letterheads and stationery have very little bearing on whether an individual will order from you, but this is not the case. The appearance of your outside envelope will even determine whether your customer opens it. Does the letterhead match the type of product that you're offering? You can lose credibility if your envelope appears to be from a lawyer or the U.S. government when you are selling a product that has no connection to either. You can tell the effect of your letterhead and stationery only by testing.

Basic Test Procedures and Decisions

Testing is never done haphazardly, and there are certain procedures and decisions that you must take into account as you enter into the process. When you start out, you must decide how confident you want to be in the results—how much risk you are prepared to assume in believing the results. If you want no risk whatsoever, then, of course, you must mail to the entire list of perhaps millions of names—not a very wise or practical approach. More realistically, a 95 percent confidence factor is usually acceptable. We will use the table shown in Figure 21.5 for doing the calculations associated with our testing. You must also decide how much error you are willing to accept as chance and what is unacceptable to you. If you are doing testing concerning direct mail, you must decide what your expected return will be before deciding on sample size. A different sample size is required, depending on your expected return. In fact, one basic procedure here that is hard for many beginners to understand is that sample size is dependent upon expected return, not on the total size of your list.

After these basic decisions are made, you will use the table shown in Figure 21.5 to pick the correct sample size, which is most important. There used to be an old rule in mail order: Check 10 percent of any list. Even today, many mail order or direct mail operators do very rough testing by simply testing lists by equal numbers, say 5,000 of one list, 5,000 of another list, and 5,000 of yet another. The problems with this approach are several. One obvious drawback is that the numbers you are testing may be larger than necessary. In that case, you are wasting money because you didn't have to test that many. On the other hand, this number may be too few names, in which case your results may be totally misleading. You may get good results with your test and then spend large amounts of money in mailing to what you thought was a successful list, only to lose a lot of money when you roll out and mail to the other names on the list. Or you could drop a list that would really pay off in general mailing if the test results on numbers too small to be truly representative of the rest of the list were poor.

After you have decided on the sample size, you mail to the sample size or, in the case of an ad campaign, you place your ads. When the results come in, you can use the table in Figure 21.5 to analyze your results. With this test, you're trying to answer two questions. First, you want to know if the results show a significant difference if you are testing one thing against another. In some cases, even though there is some difference in numbers of responses, the difference is not statistically significant. It could have happened by accident and have no real meaning. We'll talk about that in a minute. The second thing you want to know is how much error or deviation from the results you can possibly expect if you go ahead and mail to the remainder of the list—in other words, your confidence level, and the reason for your continuing to mail to the list.

USING THE TABLES FOR TESTING

Let's look at several different cases for each of the reasons you might use the tables. The first is determining sample size. Here, you want to know how many names you need to mail to in order to have a statistically representative sample of the list you are testing.

The first step is to decide on a confidence level. I have chosen the 95 percent confidence level table in Figure 21.5, which means that you can be 95 percent confident that the results you get are repeatable on subsequent similar samples. Some people in mail order use a 99 percent table. However, with a 99 percent table, you would need a much larger sample size than with a 95 percent confidence level table. Other mail order operators use a 90 percent table, meaning much greater risk, even though the sample size required is lower. I feel that a 95 percent confidence level is about the right one and I recommend that you use it.

The next step, if you are testing sample size for a list, is to calculate your expected return. Now, it is important that when you calculate your expected return or expected response it is not wishful thinking. Of course,

Percent Response	.02	.04	.06	.08	.10	.12	.14	.16	.18	.20	.30	.40	.50	.60	.70
							Limits of Error								
.1	95944.	23986.	10660.	5996.	3838.	2665.	1958.	1499.	1184.	959.	426.	240.	154.	107.	78.
.2	191696.	47924.	21300.	11981.	7668.	5325.	3912.	2995.	2367.	1917.	852.	479.	307.	213.	156.
.3	287256.	71814.	31917.	17953.	11490.	7979.	5862.	4488.	3546.	2873.	1277.	718.	460.	319.	234.
.4	382623.	95656.	42514.	23914.	15305.	10628.	7809.	5978.	4724.	3826.	1701.	957.	612.	425.	312.
.5	477799.	119450.	53089.	29862.	19112.	13272.	9751.	7466.	5899.	4778.	2124.	1194.	764.	531.	390.
.6	572783.	143196.	63643.	35799.	22911.	15911.	11689.	8950.	7071.	5728.	2546.	1432.	916.	636.	468.
.7	667574.	166894.	74175.	41723.	26703.	18544.	13624.	10431.	8242.	6676.	2967.	1669.	1068.	742.	545.
.8	762173.	190543.	84686.	47636.	30487.	21171.	15555.	11909.	9410.	7622.	3387.	1905.	1219.	847.	622.
.9	856581.	214145.	95176.	53536.	34263.	23794.	17481.	13384.	10575.	8566.	3807.	2141.	1371.	952.	699.
1.0	950796.	237699.	105644.	59425.	38032.	26411.	19404.	14856.	11738.	9508.	4226.	2377.	1521.	1056.	776.
1.1	1044819.	261205.	116091.	65301.	41793.	29023.	21323.	16325.	12899.	10448.	4644.	2612.	1672.	1161.	853.
1.2	1138650.	284663.	126517.	71166.	45546.	31629.	23238.	17791.	14057.	11387.	5061.	2847.	1822.	1265.	930.
1.3	1232289.	308072.	136921.	77018.	49292.	34230.	25149.	19255.	15213.	12323.	5477.	3081.	1972.	1369.	1006.
1.4	1325736.	331434.	147304.	82859.	53029.	36826.	27056.	20715.	16367.	13257.	5892.	3314.	2121.	1473.	1082.
1.5	1418991.	354748.	157666.	88687.	56760.	39416.	28959.	22172.	17518.	14190.	6307.	3547.	2270.	1577.	1158.
1.6	1512054.	378013.	168006.	94503.	60482.	42001.	30858.	23626.	18667.	15121.	6720.	3780.	2419.	1680.	1234.
1.7	1604924.	401231.	178325.	100308.	64197.	44581.	32754.	25077.	19814.	16049.	7133.	4012.	2568.	1783.	1310.
1.8	1697603.	424401.	188623.	106100.	67904.	47156.	34645.	26525.	20958.	16976.	7545.	4244.	2716.	1886.	1388.
1.9	1790090.	447522.	198899.	111881.	71604.	49725.	36532.	27970.	22100.	17901.	7956.	4475.	2864.	1989.	1461.
2.0	1882384.	470596.	209154.	117649.	75295.	52288.	38416.	29412.	23239.	18824.	8366.	4706.	3012.	2092.	1537.
2.1	1974486.	493622.	219887.	123405.	78979.	54847.	40296.	30851.	24376.	19745.	8775.	4936.	3159.	2194.	1612.
2.2	2066397.	516599.	229600.	129150.	82656.	57400.	42171.	32287.	25511.	20664.	9184.	5166.	3306.	2296.	1687.
2.3	2158115.	539529.	239791.	134882.	86325.	59948.	44043.	33721.	26643.	21581.	9592.	5395.	3453.	2398.	1762.
2.4	2249641.	562410.	249960.	140603.	89986.	62490.	45911.	35151.	27773.	22496.	9998.	5624.	3599.	2500.	1836.
2.5	2340975.	585244.	260108.	146311.	93639.	65027.	47775.	36578.	28901.	23410.	10404.	5852.	3746.	2601.	1911.
2.6	2432117.	608029.	270235.	152007.	97285.	67559.	49635.	38002.	30026.	24321.	10809.	6080.	3891.	2702.	1985.
2.7	2523067.	630767.	280341.	157692.	100923.	70085.	51491.	39423.	31149.	25231.	11214.	6303.	4037.	2803.	2060.
2.8	2623825.	653456.	290425.	163364.	104553.	72606.	53343.	40841.	32269.	26138.	11617.	6535.	4182.	2904.	2134.
2.9	2704390.	676098.	300488.	169024.	108176.	75122.	55192.	42256.	33388.	27044.	12020.	6761.	4327.	3005.	2208.

3.0	2794764.	698691.	310529.	174673.	111791.	77632.	57036.	43668.	34503.	27948.	12421.	6987.	4472.	3105.	2281.
3.1	2884946.	721236.	320550.	180309.	115398.	80137.	58876.	45077.	35617.	28849.	12822.	7212.	4616.	3205.	2355.
3.2	2974935.	743734.	330548.	185933.	118997.	82637.	60713.	46433.	36728.	29749.	13222.	7437.	4760.	3305.	2429.
3.3	3064732.	766183.	340526.	191546.	122589.	85131.	62546.	47886.	37836.	30647.	13621.	7662.	4904.	3405.	2502.
3.4	3154338.	788584.	350482.	197146.	126174.	87620.	64374.	49287.	38942.	31543.	14019.	7886.	5047.	3505.	2575.
3.5	3243751.	810938.	360417.	202734.	129750.	90104.	66199.	50684.	40046.	32438.	14417.	8109.	5190.	3604.	2648.
3.6	3332972.	833243.	370330.	208311.	133319.	92583.	68020.	52078.	41148.	33330.	14813.	8332.	5333.	3703.	2721.
3.7	3422001.	855500.	380222.	213875.	136880.	95056.	69837.	53469.	42247.	34220.	15209.	8555.	5475.	3802.	2793.
3.8	3510838.	877710.	390093.	219427.	140434.	97523.	71650.	54857.	43344.	35108.	15604.	8777.	5617.	3901.	2866.
3.9	3599483.	899871.	399943.	224968.	143979.	99986.	73459.	56242.	44438.	35995.	15998.	8999.	5759.	3999.	2938.
4.0	3687936.	921984.	409771.	230496.	147517.	102443.	75264.	57624.	45530.	36879.	16391.	9220.	5901.	4098.	3011.
4.1	3776197.	944049.	419577.	236012.	151048.	104894.	77065.	59003.	46620.	37762.	16783.	9440.	6042.	4196.	3083.
4.2	3864265.	966046.	429363.	241517.	154571.	107341.	78863.	60379.	47707.	38643.	17175.	9661.	6183.	4294.	3155.
4.3	3952142.	988036.	439127.	247009.	158086.	109782.	80656.	61752.	48792.	39521.	17565.	9880.	6323.	4391.	3226.
4.4	4039827.	1009957.	448870.	252489.	161593.	112217.	82445.	63122.	49874.	40398.	17955.	10100.	6464.	4489.	3298.
4.5	4127319.	1031830.	458591.	257957.	165093.	114648.	84231.	64489.	50955.	41273.	18344.	10318.	6604.	4586.	3369.
4.6	4214619.	1053655.	468291.	263414.	168585.	117073.	86013.	65853.	52032.	42146.	18732.	10537.	6743.	4683.	3441.
4.7	4301728.	1075432.	477970.	268858.	172069.	119492.	87790.	67214.	53108.	43017.	19119.	10754.	6883.	4780.	3512.
4.8	4388644.	1097161.	487627.	274290.	175546.	121907.	89564.	68573.	54181.	43886.	19505.	10972.	7022.	4876.	3583.
4.9	4475368.	1118842.	497263.	279710.	179015.	124316.	91334.	69928.	55251.	44754.	19891.	11188.	7161.	4973.	3658.
5.0	4561900.	1140475.	506878.	285119.	182476.	126719.	93100.	71280.	56320.	45619.	20275.	11405.	7299.	5069.	3724.
5.1	4648240.	1162060.	516471.	290515.	185930.	129118.	94862.	72629.	57386.	46482.	20659.	11621.	7437.	5165.	3794.
5.2	4734388.	1183597.	526043.	295899.	189376.	131511.	96620.	73975.	58449.	47344.	21042.	11836.	7575.	5260.	3865.
5.3	4820344.	1205086.	535594.	301271.	192314.	133898.	98374.	75318.	59510.	48203.	21424.	12051.	7713.	5356.	3935.
5.4	4906107.	1226527.	545123.	306632.	196244.	136281.	100125.	76658.	60569.	49061.	21805.	12265.	7850.	5451.	4005.
5.5	4916679.	1247920.	554631.	311980.	199667.	138658.	101871.	77995.	61626.	49917.	22185.	12479.	7987.	5546.	4075.
5.6	5077059.	1269265.	564118.	317316.	203082.	141029.	103613.	79329.	62680.	50771.	22565.	12693.	8123.	5641.	4145.
5.7	5162246.	1290562.	573583.	322640.	206490.	143396.	105352.	80660.	63731.	51622.	22943.	12906.	8260.	5736.	4214.
5.8	5247241.	1311810.	583027.	327953.	209890.	145757.	107087.	81988.	64781.	52472.	23321.	13118.	8396.	5830.	4283.
5.9	5332045.	1333011.	592449.	333253.	213282.	148112.	108817.	83313.	65828.	53320.	23698.	13330.	8531.	5924.	4353.
6.0	5416656.	1354164.	601851.	338541.	216666.	150463.	110544.	84635.	66872.	54167.	24074.	13542.	8667.	6019.	4422.

Figure 21.5 Test sample table for mailing response levels and a 95 percent confidence level.

429

you should always "wish" big. You could wish that every single recipient of your direct mail package would respond. Then you would get a 100 percent response. But, of course, that's totally unrealistic. Some people have very profitable businesses at less than a 1 percent response. If you don't have prior records to go on, start with assuming a 1 percent response. Or you could calculate the response you need to break even and add a minimum profit and use that. Let's assume in our example that we expect to get a 1 percent return.

Our next step is to decide by how much we can miss our expected return and still have an acceptable lower response limit. For example, we assumed that we would get a 1 percent return. How low can we get and still be okay? Some people would say breakeven. Some people would say something else. In this case, let's assume that we can live with a .2 percent difference. A .8 percent return will still be all right—we will still make money. Okay. We now refer to Figure 21.5. First, look at the response column all the way to the left and read down until you see the figure 1.0, which stands for 1 percent response. Go horizontally to the right and look under the .20 limits of error column. This means the .2 percent difference we decided we could live with in this particular situation. Read right across from the 1 percent response at the left, and under .20, we read the figure 9,508. This is the minimum sample size we should use, rounded off to 9,500 or 10,000.

HOW TO ANALYZE THE RESULTS

Let's assume that we mailed 10,000 packages each to two different lists. In one list we got a 1 percent response. In the second we got a 1.5 percent response. Now, if we look at these percentages by themselves, we would say the second list is better. But is it? Is this difference statistically significant? This is an important question because, if it is not statistically significant, we should treat the lists equally. One may really not be better than the other, even though from the percentage of responses received, one list appears to be better. To find this out we again enter with a 1 percent response. Move horizontally to the right until you find the number nearest 10,000. In this case we find the number we had before, 9,508. Then read up to .20. This means that if the difference is within .20, the number is not statistically significant. In this case the number is 1.0 to 1 percent we got on one list, minus 1.5 percent we got on the other, or a .5 percent difference. Because .5 percent is greater than the .2 percent we just calculated, this number is statistically significant and list 2 is greater than list 1. However, if the two lists had been 1 percent and 1.2 percent, respectively, there would have been no actual difference in quality between the two lists. They would have been considered the same in responsiveness and we would have treated them the same in our future operations . . . unless subsequent retestings proved the difference to be significant.

Now let's see how we test for permissible error in future mailings. Let's say that we mailed 30,000 pieces and got a 3 percent response. We enter our table again with 3 percent and read right across to the number closest to 30,000. This is 27,948. Again we read right up to .20. This means that the results we actually received were 3 percent, plus or minus .2 percent. Furthermore, in returns you can expect in the future from this mailing, the percentage can vary from 2.8, which is 3.0 minus .2 percent, to 3.2 percent, which is 3.0 plus .2 percent.

HOW TO TEST ADS

Testing ads requires somewhat special techniques because of certain inherent problems. It doesn't make much sense to test one ad in one issue and a different ad in a different issue of the same magazine. Why not? In the first place, one issue may attract buyers or pull better than others. Perhaps one issue contains an exposé and is therefore read by more potential customers. If you advertise in different issues, the position of the ad in the magazine may well be different unless a special position is purchased. Some national, local, or even international event that occurs at the time of publication of one issue can affect results. When a really hot news item, such as the tremendous changes in Eastern Europe and Russia, takes place, certain magazines will be much more closely read and bought at much higher levels than is the norm. At certain times the event itself may affect mail order purchase, such as when President Kennedy was assassinated. Products identified with President Kennedy were purchased at much higher levels than normally even though most mail order offers in the mail at that time suffered grievously. Also, in certain issues of the magazine, competition may be evident or not, or may be more severe than in others. For all these reasons, it seems that the obvious approach to testing different ads in different issues of the same magazine isn't a very good solution. What is a good solution, then?

Well, one way to do this type of test is to use different geographical areas of distribution of the same magazine, so that in the same month you can have a different ad in each geographical area. However, there are some problems here as well. Circulation levels are different in different geographical areas of the country. Also, certain types of offers may not pull the same in different areas of the country, depending upon the climate, attitude of the people, and many other factors. You may be able to sell a heavy wool coat through a direct mail ad along the eastern seaboard in the middle of the winter. In California or Florida or Hawaii, it would be highly unlikely.

A better solution is a so-called split run. A split run means that you run two different ads in a single issue of the magazine, but every other magazine leaving the production plant has one ad, while the other issue has the other ad. These two different ads are keyed differently so that you can measure the results easily. Also, in every geographical area, both ads appear in equal numbers. Now, there are some drawbacks with this approach too. You can expect to pay additional costs for a split run. And, not all magazines offer the split-run feature. If you want to advertise with a split run, you should see the appropriate volume of SRDS or the rate card. Either will tell you whether the split run is available and the cost. Then you can make your decision.

Telescopic testing is a variation of the split run. With the use of telescopic testing, you can test many more than two ads at the same time. In fact, the name comes from actually telescoping a year's work into a single test. Let's say that you have ads A, B, C, and D, and you want to test them simultaneously. In one geographical region of the magazine you test A versus B. In the second region you test A versus C. In the third, A versus D, and so forth. Regardless of the results achieved with ad A, we assign it a numerical weighting of 100. We then compare the results of each other ad against ad A and assign every other ad proportional numerical values. Then we rank the ads accordingly. Let's see how this works out. Let us say in region 1 ad A pulled 3,000 inquiries and ad B got 2,000. In region 2, ad A pulled 3,200 and ad C, 5,000. In region 3, ad A pulled 500 inquiries and ad D, 1,000. From looking at these raw data, all we can see is that in region 1 ad A was better than ad B; in region 2 ad C was better than ad A; and in region 3 ad D was better than ad A. But which of these ads is best and how do they rank? Well, we let the results of ad A equal 100. To calculate B, we divide B's returns by A's and multiply times 100, so the results for ad B are 67. In the same way, C equals 156 and D, 200. Therefore, the best ad is ad D, the second best ad is ad C, the third, ad A, and the worst, ad B. Of course, telescopic testing also costs more and a split-run capability is necessary.

Another technique that is effective and doesn't cost quite as much as split runs or telescopic testing is called crisscross testing. If you are testing two different ads, do the crisscross by testing two different magazines or newspapers. The first month you test one ad in, say, *Hunting and Fishing* magazine and the second ad in *Outdoor Life*. Then, the second month, you crisscross: The second ad goes in *Hunting and Fishing* and the first ad in *Outdoor Life*. You then compare the results to see which ad is better.

Another technique along the same lines is to alternate your ads in the same magazine every other month. This technique takes a long time to work, up to six months or more. And remembering what I said earlier about the competition coming in and copying a successful campaign, you certainly wouldn't want to expose yourself by testing in this fashion right at the start. However, at some point after you are established in the marketplace, it can be a fully acceptable way of testing two good ads against one another.

What do the results mean when you're testing one ad against the other, or one ad in three different magazines? Let's say you're running one ad in three different magazines. In one month, magazine A brings you 500 orders, magazine B brings 300 orders, and magazine C results in 100 orders. In their raw form, these figures mean very little. However, when combined with the cost of advertising, they will tell you not only whether you are profitable, but also what your profitability is. If advertisement A costs $3,000, you are paying $6 per order. If advertisement B costs $1,500, this ad cost you $5 per order. And if advertisement C costs you $300, it costs $3 per order. If the combined cost of fulfillment, overhead, advertising, and so forth was $4, then you lost $2 per order in advertising in magazine A, you made $1 advertising in B, and you made $2 per order in advertising in C. Okay. So we eliminate magazine A because you are losing money. However, in magazine B, even though you made only $1 per order you made $300 because there were 300 orders. In magazine C, even though we made $2 per order, we made only $200 total. Therefore, profitability was greater in magazine C, but magazine B was more profitable. Of course, as always, we must consider back-end profits and profitability to get the true picture. If we consider everything together, perhaps even magazine A is worth advertising in.

DIRECT MAIL TESTING

You must be extremely careful in testing direct mail lists in that you must be sure that you have a fair sample in terms of sample size. It has been the practice for some time to request an Nth name list, as described in an earlier chapter. However, even the Nth name is not completely statistically correct because Nth names are not random names. Many mail order experts today are recommending geographical selections as being more correct statistically and netting better results for the test versus the results received later when the full list is used. A geographical name split can be done fairly easily using several zip code numbers. A method that provides a more representative selection of names can be worked out with your list broker, manager, or compiler. Frequently you can arrive at a better sampling methodology than the Nth name selection, and today random name selection is available.

You should also test your largest good list first. If one list has a total of 500,000 names and another has only 20,000, it's far better to start testing the larger list first, because if it is successful, it allows you a much better population base to mail to than would the smaller list. However, you should use the largest "good" list. "Goodness" is a measure of quality, and you must remember that the most recent mail order buyers' names are much better than those whose purchases were made at an earlier date. It has been calculated that lists lose their effectiveness at the rate of as high as 20 percent a year; thus even a few months can make big differences in results.

YOU CAN TEST MORE THAN ONE THING AT A TIME

For many years, some mail order experts were fond of saying that you could test only one thing at a time. In fact, by the use of what is called *matrix testing*, you can test several different items at the same time. The advantage is not only that you receive the results much more quickly, but also that you can save a lot of money. Here's how. First, as shown earlier, you must arrive at the correct sample size necessary considering your confidence level, acceptable error limits, and expected response. Let's assume a sample size of 10,000. You want to test two different copy appeals, which means 10,000 names against 10,000 names, for a total of 20,000. Further, if you wanted to test two different headlines against each other, you would need an additional 10,000 names against 10,000 names. If you wanted to check copy 1 against copy 2, and headline 1 against headline 2, in a sample of 10,000, you would need an additional 10,000, plus 10,000, plus 10,000, or 40,000 names. An example of matrix testing is shown in Figure 21.6. You can still have 20,000 names per test as required, but instead of a 40,000 total, your total required sample mailing is to only 20,000 names. How is this done? Simply set up your mailing in four equal segments of 5,000 each. One segment receives copy 1 and headline 1; 5,000 receive copy 1 and headline 2; 5,000 receive copy 2 and headline 1; and 5,000 receive copy 2 and headline 2. Naturally, you can also use the same technique to test three things at once, as long as your matrix has the same number of boxes on each side.

There is one small problem with this technique. Look at Figure 21.7 which shows the results you might get from a matrix test, testing two headlines and two different copies. Now the question is, do you choose the best combination of headline and copy, or the best of each and then combine? If you get results like those shown when using matrix testing, you must exercise some judgment as to whether the most important factor is the interaction between the copy and the headline, in which case you would choose a combination, or whether the headline or copy by itself is most important, in which case you would choose the best of each and then combine.

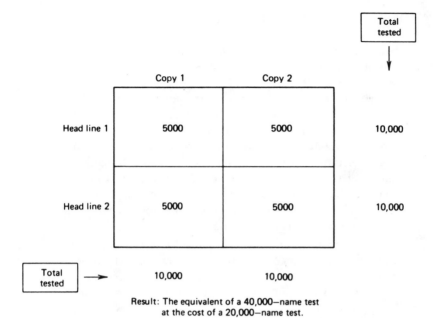

Figure 21.6   An example of matrix testing.

	Copy 1	Copy 2	
Headline 1	95 orders	120 orders	215
Headline 2	125 orders	73 orders	198
	210	193	

Figure 21.7   A problem with matrix testing.

CAUTIONARY NOTES IN TESTING

There are some important cautions you should observe when you do your testing in mail order.

1. Sometimes observed differences are not real, and if retested, they will disappear. This is especially noticeable if the percentage differences are not very large. For example, Dick Hodgson reports in his book, *Direct Mail and Mail Order Handbook,* that a number of leading direct mail advertisers have sent identical mailing pieces to different large lists and observed differences as large as 10 to 25 percent. The solution to this problem is that if you do not observe great differences in testing two or more items, be sure to retest at least once to confirm your initial results.

2. Don't jump the gun when your results start coming in, but wait until the full results of your test are known. On the other hand, use the projection techniques discussed earlier to project the remainder of the results after a reasonable period of time—say, 30 days.

3. Don't make unwarranted assumptions in your test. For example, when I sold the *Writer's Guide to Publication and Profit,* at one point my classified ad tested the use of "free details" versus "free instructions." "Free instructions" pulled considerably more inquiries than "free details." However, remember that I was selling this on a two-step basis. And despite the fact that "free instructions" drew more inquiries, "free details" brought in more *orders.* Why was this so? I believe it was because "instructions" encouraged the respondent to believe he or she was getting a great deal more than a sales package, and so the credibility of my promotion suffered. The result was fewer orders.

4. Don't test insignificant things such as the type of stamp, small differences in envelope size, print size, and the like. Test the big things we talked about earlier in this chapter. However, I want to point out here that some factors that appear to be insignificant on the surface may, in fact, be very important. One such item is the signature. For a typical sales letter, it has been found that a signature printed in blue pulls much better than one printed in black, even though the cursive is obviously printed, not handwritten. A handwritten signature pulls better than a printed signature, regardless of color. But you must calculate the cost of hand signing your mailing.

5. Don't forget to calculate the sample size necessary to make your test valid. It is foolish to think that you are saving money by testing a sample so small that your results will not be applicable to a larger population. The difference in sample size does make a significant

difference. Also remember that it is not the number you mail to, but the number of returns you receive that is important for your test. Therefore, your sample mailing size must always be calculated on your expected returns.

6. Finally, to have a valid test for direct mail, you must mail all your test pieces at the same time, as even a day can make a tremendous difference in the results and therefore invalidate your test. In the same way, if you do magazine or newspaper tests, or tests with other media, you must use some technique to overcome the fact that one identical ad in two different magazines of the same month or two different ads in the same magazine in two different months cannot be compared accurately. You must find some way to ensure that the majority of the conditions you can control are identical, such as crisscross testing, alternating ads in different months, or split run.

SUMMARY

In this chapter, we've discussed the basics of testing. Your ability to test successfully will be one of the great determinants as to whether you will succeed or fail with your mail order promotions. Our discussion centered not only on what testing is, but also on why it is necessary. We talked about what to test and what not to test, as well as the steps of testing and how to use the table provided to obtain a proper sample, to determine the importance of differences you note in the results of your test, and the variance that might normally occur even though your results are accurate.

While it is not true that every mailing or advertisement you ever do should be a test, it is true that you should keep accurate records for every promotional activity you do in mail order. By carefully comparing these and monitoring changes that may occur, you will be able to judge how your product is doing as it proceeds through its life cycle, what your competition is doing, and how changes in the marketplace affect your promotion.

Do not be afraid to refer to this chapter again and again as you begin your mail order business, start placing advertisements, start on your direct mail campaigns, and observe measurable results. The information in this chapter will help you achieve your greatest goals in mail order.

22

Cost and Profit Calculations Made Easy

Many of us don't care very much for mathematics. You may think math is dull when compared with the fun of writing copy or preparing graphics, or the excitement of locating new products, or the truly incredible thrill of opening envelopes stuffed with checks and dollars. Or you may just be turned off by math because you feel it is complicated and difficult to understand. Whatever your reason, let me assure you that math is essential for operating a mail order business profitably and an important part of your mail order business plan. You don't need to be a mastermind to master it. I'm going to show you how in this chapter. Once you get your financial calculations together, you will know where you are headed and what you must do, and you will be able to devise ways of doing it to achieve your profit goals and objectives. If you don't do these calculations you will be constantly adrift and unable to control your business. With these calculations, you will know:

- Whether your project is financially successful or not.
- How much improvement is needed to make your project profitable.
- Where the best opportunities for improving your project are.

If you want to make it big in mail order—if you really want to succeed—please don't skip this important chapter.

THE BREAKEVEN ANALYSIS

The breakeven analysis is an excellent technique for determining the ultimate success of your mail order project even before you start it. The breakeven analysis will tell you:

- How many units you must sell to start making money.
- How much profit you will make at any given level of sales.
- How changing your price will affect profitability.
- How expense reductions of different types will affect profitability.

To do a breakeven analysis, you must first separate the costs associated with a project into two kinds—fixed and variable costs.

Fixed costs are those expenses associated with a project that you would have to pay whether you sold one unit or 10,000 units, or for that matter, sold none at all. For example, if you rented a garage to be used in your business, and the owner charged you $1,200 to rent this garage for a period of one year, this would be a fixed cost for that year. It would stay the same whether you sold any product or not. Or, maybe you are going to develop your own proprietary mail order product for this project. Let's say that you estimate it will cost $2,000 to develop this product. This development cost would also be considered a fixed cost because the $2,000 does not vary with the number of units you will eventually sell—it is the same whether you sell 100 units or 100,000. Because many fixed costs, such as space rental, are tied to a time period (in this case, $1,200 a year for the garage), you need to estimate the time you are talking about to come up with the total fixed cost. The fixed cost for two years for the garage would be $1,200 times 2, or $2,400, assuming you could rent the garage for that period.

Variable costs vary directly with the number of units sold. For example, if the manufacturer of the product charges you $1.80 per unit, that $1.80 is a variable cost. In the same way, if postage for mailing your product to the customer is 50 cents, that 50 cents is a variable cost. If you sell 10 units, postage costs will be $5. If you sell 100 units, your total variable costs for postage will be 50 cents times 100, or $50.

For some costs it is more difficult to decide whether the cost should be considered a fixed or variable cost, and frequently there is no "right" answer—it is your decision as president and manager of your own company. The general guideline is this: If you can see a relationship between cost and number of units sold, consider the cost variable; if you can find no relationship, consider it a fixed cost.

The total cost of any project always equals the total fixed costs plus total variable costs. For example, let's say that you are going to sell red widgets by mail. You looked at this red widget project and decided that your fixed costs included the following: utilities, $100 a month; office supplies, $50 a month; depreciation on part of your home for an office, office furniture, and telephone, $200 a year; developing the item, $1,000; and patenting it another $2,500. We will say that you estimate that you will be selling the product for three years. Let's say that you have also identified the following variable costs:

Cost to produce	$1.00
Cost of postage and packaging	0.50

Finally, you have decided that you are going to sell this item only through space advertising. Based on prior experience, you estimate that it will cost you $3 in advertising per red widget sold. Here is the way our costs stack up:

Fixed Costs

Utility expense at $100/month, 36 months	$3,600
Telephone at $200/year, 3 years	600
Product development	1,000
Patenting expense	2,500
Total fixed cost	$7,700

Variable Costs

Cost	$1.00 per unit
Cost of postage of packaging	0.50 per unit
Cost of advertising	3.00 per unit
Total variable cost	$4.50 per unit

Now, how in the world can we add them together to arrive at our grand total of costs for red widgets unless we know how many units we are going to sell? The answer is, we can't—but this is how the whole concept of breakeven comes together.

To calculate breakeven we start with profit. What is profit? Profit is the number of units sold multiplied times the price at which we are selling them. We then subtract the number of units sold multiplied times the total variable cost minus the total fixed cost. Or, if you like equations, here is what it looks like. Where P = profit, p = price, U = number of units sold, V = variable cost, and F = fixed cost,

$$P = (U \times p) - (U \times V) - F$$

or we can simplify this equation so that we have

$$P = [U \times (p - V)] - F$$

Now let's try our profit formula out. If we sell 1,000 units and our selling price is $10 per unit, what is our profit? Well, we already know that fixed costs are $7,700 and that variable costs are $4.50 per unit, so we come out with

$$P = [1,000 \times (\$10 - \$4.50)] - \$7,700$$
$$= \$5,500 - \$7,700$$
$$= -\$2,200$$

Whoops! That's a minus number. That means that instead of making a profit, we lost money—$2,200, to be exact. Well now, how many red widgets do we need to sell to make money? That is, how many units do we need to sell just to break even, the point at which we won't make any money, but we don't lose any either?

Let's go back to our profit formula. At breakeven, profit is equal to zero, because there is no profit. So, we know what profit equals. What we don't know is U, the number of units we need to sell to break even. Okay,

$$P = [U \times (p - V)] - F, \text{ and } P = 0$$

That means $[U \times (p - V)] - F = 0$, and now

$$U = \frac{F}{p - V}$$

Now, we know that $F = \$7,700$, $P = \$10$, and $V = \$4.50$. Therefore,

$$U = \frac{\$7,700}{\$10 - \$4.50} = 1,400$$

So, if we don't change price or reduce our expenses in any way, we need to sell 1,400 red widgets before we start making any money. So remember:

$$P = [U \times (p - V)] - F$$

and

$$U = \frac{F}{p - V}$$

These two formulas can tell you a lot about your project before you even start.

There is a way of calculating all of this graphically without using the formulas. A *breakeven chart* has a major advantage over the breakeven and profit formulas: It shows pictorially the relationship of fixed variable and total expenses to sales at all volumes of sales. That means that you can calculate profits at any level of sales without using an equation. Here is how to construct a breakeven chart.

Step 1.   Get some graph paper and label the horizontal line on the bottom *Units Sold*. Label the vertical line at the left of the graph *Dollars (Sales and Expenses)*. Divide each line into equal parts of dollars and units and label it appropriately.

Step 2.   Analyze all of your costs for the project and decide whether each is fixed or variable. Decide on the period of sales for your project. Total up your fixed and variable costs.

Step 3.   Draw a horizontal line to intersect the proper point on the vertical line to represent fixed costs, as at A in Figure 22.1.

Step 4.   Calculate the dollar value of sales for any unit number. For example, if we sell 2,000 units, how much is this in sales dollars? For red widgets, total sales volume could be 2,000 × $10, or $20,000. Plot this point at 2,000 units and $20,000 on the chart as point a. Put one end of a ruler at the 0 point in the lower left corner of the chart and the other end at the point you just plotted. This is the total sales line B in Figure 22.1.

Step 5.   Calculate the dollar value for variable cost for any unit number. For example, for red widgets, variable cost is $4.50 per unit. At, say, 2,000 units, total variable cost is 2,000 × $4.50, or $9,000. Add $9,000 to the fixed cost (in this case, $7,700) to come up with $16,700. Plot this on the chart (b in Figure 22.1). Lay one end of the ruler at the point where the fixed cost line B intersects the vertical

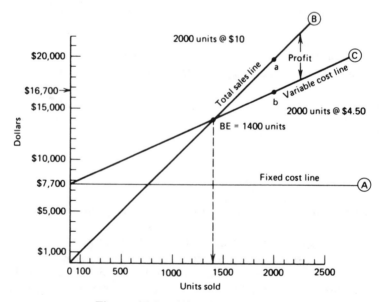

Figure 22.1   A breakeven chart.

dollar scale and the other at the point you just plotted. Draw a line to form the variable cost line C in Figure 22.1.

Now your breakeven chart is complete. The point at which the total sales line and variable cost line intersect is the breakeven point, which you read on the horizontal unit scale at the bottom of the chart. In Figure 22.1, breakeven is 1,400 units, as we calculated before using our formula.

To calculate profit for any number of units you want, simply subtract the dollar value read at opposite the proper point on the variable cost line C from the dollar value read opposite the proper point on the total sales line B. For example, to calculate the profit if you sell 2,000 red widgets, read right up from 2,000 units on the unit scale to point b on the variable cost line. Read straight across from point b to $16,700 on the vertical dollar scale. Now read straight up from 2,000 units on the unit scale to point a on the total sales line. Read straight across from point a to $20,000 on the vertical dollar scale: $20,000 minus $16,700 equals $3,300 if you sell 2,000 units. Do the same thing for any number of units to calculate profit.

Use breakeven analysis any time you want to calculate profit or how many units you must sell before you begin to make money.

COST AND PROFIT CALCULATIONS
WITH INQUIRY FOLLOW-UP

We now know how to apply breakeven analysis to a straightforward mail order or direct mail proposition in which the costs are pretty much up front—we place the classified or display (space) advertisement or send out our advertisement in a direct mail piece to the customer. The customer orders, and that's it. Now we're going to complicate our cost and profit calculation a little by using a slightly different method of mail order operation—the inquiry/follow-up, or two-step promotion, that we discussed in Chapter 8.

The complication is that we don't ask for the money right away. Instead, we invite our potential customer to write to us for additional information, and it is with the additional information that we make the sale. The inquiry/followup can be initiated with a classified ad, a display ad, or a direct mail piece. It is generally an essential method when trying to sell a high-priced item. When I sold a set of booklets called the *Writer's Guide to Publication and Profit,* the first step was a small classified ad reading "Write for profit. Free details." To all those who wrote, I sent a complete sales package that described my proposition in more detail—and about 15 percent of those inquiring ordered. How you do cost calculations for this type of offer is what we are going to talk about now.

Let's look at my breakeven calculation for the sale of my writer's booklet through the two-step operation. In one magazine, one classified advertisement for free details of my full proposition cost $45. The in-the-mail cost of my four brochures was $2 and my selling price was $19.95. The in-the-mail cost of sales literature sent to inquiries received as a result of my classified advertisement was 50¢ per package. Now our breakeven equation is

$$BE = \frac{\text{Fixed costs}}{\text{Selling price} - \text{Variable costs}}$$

If we want to calculate the number of inquiries we need to break even for this project, disregarding overhead costs such as salary, the $45 is a fixed cost because it does not vary with the number of sets of booklets we sell. It remains the same whether we sell one set or 1,000. The in-the-mail cost of $2 for the brochures would be a variable cost, because, if we sell one set the cost is $2, but if we sell 1,000, this cost is $2,000.

Now comes the problem. Clearly the 50¢ per sales literature package is a variable cost, but how do we calculate it for each set of brochures sold? We lack one very important bit of information. We do not know the conversion rate—that is, we want to know what percentage of inquiries we are able to convert to paying customers. What we need to do here is assume various conversion rates and calculate a breakeven point for each. Let's take conversion rates of 5, 10, 15, and 20 percent. If we convert 5 percent of our inquiries to customers, that means we get five customers ($100 \times .05$) for every 100 inquiries, or one customer out of every 20 sales literature packages sent. Therefore, the cost in packages for one sale is $20 \times .50$, or = $10. For a conversion rate of 10 percent, cost is $5; for 15 percent, $3.33; for 20 percent, $2.50.

We add this variable cost to the variable cost of $2 for the in-the-mail cost of the booklets. This gives us the following:

Conversion rate	5%	10%	15%	20%
Total variable cost	$12.00	$7.00	$5.33	$4.50

We can now calculate the number of units sold needed to break even for each potential conversion rate.

If we can convert 5 percent of the inquiries into customers,

$$BE = \frac{\$45.00}{\$19.95 - \$12.00} = 5.7, \text{ or } 6 \text{ sales}$$

For 10 percent conversion,

$$BE = \frac{\$45.00}{\$19.95 - \$7.00} = 3.5, \text{ or } 4 \text{ sales}$$

For 15 percent conversion,

$$BE = \frac{\$45.00}{\$19.95 - \$5.33} = 3.1, \text{ or } 4 \text{ sales}$$

For 20 percent conversion,

$$BE = \frac{\$45.00}{\$19.95 - \$4.50} = 2.9, \text{ or } 3 \text{ sales}$$

To compute profit with the two-step type of mail order sale you must assume a certain conversion rate. If you want to calculate profit at 60 inquiries for your ad at a conversion rate of 10 percent, your number of sales would be 60 × .10, or 6. Your fixed cost would still be $45. Your variable cost would be 6 times $2 for the set of booklets plus 60 × .50 for the sales literature. That's a total of $42 variable cost. Because of the two-step operation and the complication of the number of inquiries versus number of sales, it is easier to state our original profit equation this way:

Profit = Gross revenue − Variable costs − Fixed costs
Gross revenue = 6 × $19.95 = $119.70
Profit, therefore, = $119.70 − $42.00 − $45.00, or $32.70

Now what about calculating the number of inquiries we must convert to break even once we know the total number of inquiries? Let's say that at the end of the first month we have 26 inquiries and we project these returns to be a total of 52 inquiries (we'll learn how to project returns this way in a later chapter). Okay, with 52 inquiries, the cost for the sales literature will be 52 × .50, or $26. In this way, we'll treat the number of inquiries as a fixed cost, not a variable cost, since once the mailing to the inquiries has been made, it will remain the same whether we sell one set of booklets or 1,000. Our equation is:

$$BE = \frac{\$45 + \$26}{\$19.95 - \$2} = 3.95, \text{ or } 4 \text{ sales}$$

$$\frac{4 \text{ sales}}{52 \text{ inquiries}} = \text{a conversion rate of 7.7\% for breakeven}$$

BACK-END PROFITS

The name may not be very elegant, but the back-end profit concept is the key to big money and success in mail order. The concept is simple: Rather than concentrating on making your money on the initial proposition to a prospective customer, you use this initial proposition mainly to get the customer to order. If you make money, that's great. But even if you don't break even, you now have the name of an individual who has demonstrated an interest in your products or service in the best possible way—by actually placing an order. You can now make huge profits by selling similar or related items to your customers without the cost of obtaining their names. Now comes the big question: As you aren't making your money with the first order, how do you know whether your magazine advertisement, direct mail piece, or two-step sale is profitable or not?

Let's assume the following as facts for a minute. For each unit of product we sell on our first deal, we will sustain a loss of $1. However, in fulfilling this first customer order, we enclose a bounce-back offer that advertises a similar product with the order. Let's say that 4 percent of our customers reorder on the bounce-back, which has a selling price of $50 and a variable cost of $20.00 per unit. Now, if the first order came from a magazine advertisement costing $5,000, what we would like to know is how many orders we must get from the advertisement to break even. Here's how we figure it out. Our breakeven equation is

$$BE = \frac{\text{Fixed costs}}{\text{Selling price} - \text{Variable costs}}$$

In this case, the only fixed cost is the $5,000 for the magazine advertisement. Variable costs include the $1 we lose on each first order plus 40 percent of the $2 per unit cost of the bounce-back. Similarly, we use 40 percent of the $5 per unit selling price on the bounce-back. Now our breakeven equation looks like this:

$$BE = \frac{5,000}{(.40)(50.00) - (.40)(20.00) - 1.00}$$

$$= \frac{5,000}{20.00 - 8.00 - 1.00}$$

$$= \frac{5000}{11.00} = 454.6 \text{ units}$$

Now let's say that, to each customer who orders on the first bounce-back, you send a second bounce-back, and that 20 percent order. Will this affect the breakeven on your ad? Most certainly! If the selling price of $50.00 and the in-the-mail variable cost of $20.00 remain the same, we have one additional selling price of .20 ($50.00) and one additional variable cost of .20 ($20.00). Now breakeven for the advertisement is:

$BE =$

$$\frac{5,000}{(.40)(50.00) + (.20)(50.00) - (.40)(20.00) - (.20)(20.00) - 1.00}$$

$$= \frac{5,000}{17} = 291.1 \text{ units}$$

Once you know how many of your customers reorder on each offer, the average amount of reorder, and your average cost, you can easily calculate your breakeven number of orders or inquiries for each advertisement in this same way. Later I will show you how to estimate your response from any advertisement. Using response estimates and this equation, you will know at once whether an ad is going to be profitable—and whether to continue to use the ad or to drop it.

HOW TO TELL WHETHER YOU ARE WINNING OR LOSING

There is a basic question that will help you analyze your results to show whether you are winning or losing in your mail order business. This equation is return on investment, frequently referred to as ROI.

"It takes money to make money" is an old saying that emphasizes the fact that any business requires an investment, whether the investment is your own money or money borrowed from someone else. If you have invested your money in the bank, you are earning interest, or profit, on your investment. For example, if you have $5,000 in your bank account and it is paying 7 percent interest per annum, your annual ROI is 7 percent. You can calculate ROI for any investment you have by the simple equation

$$ROI = \frac{\text{Net profit}}{\text{Total investment}}$$

ROI is the most popular measurement of business success in use today. Not only businesspeople, but also bankers, accountants, investors, and all types of financial analysts calculate ROI for individual companies or divisions of companies to determine how they are doing. Based on their analyses, firms receive loans or do not, are bought and sold, or even expanded or liquidated. ROI is used in big firms and small, and you can use it too as an indication of whether your profits are what they should be.

What ROI can you expect from your mail order business? Bob Stone says a 15 percent ROI is not unusual, and, in fact, for large companies a 15 percent ROI is not bad. But your operation, with a much lower overhead, should do even better. Let's look at the ROI equation again.

$$ROI = \frac{Net\ profit}{Total\ investment}$$

Net profit is fairly straightforward. The figure that goes here is the net profit we realize for the year after taxes. The total investment figure is a bit more complicated. Some mail order beginners tend to leave out all investments that don't consist of cold, hard cash. This is wrong. Total investment includes any negotiable commodity. It could be money, but it might also be an automobile, or part of an automobile, the labor that goes into your business—both yours and that of others—or costs associated with the use of part of your home as an office. Whether or not you pay yourself a salary, or use your personal car on company business but don't charge your company, investments are being made in your business operation. If you don't calculate them in computing your ROI, they haven't gone away: The result will be a less-than-accurate ROI. So be certain to calculate all your expenses as part of your total investment, and if some of these expenses don't have an established value because you haven't started paying yourself a salary from your business yet, you should still figure an hourly rate for your labor and include it as part of total investment. You will see the importance of this is in a minute. To help ensure that you don't forget expenses as a part of your total investment, I have included a list of potential mail order expenses at the end of this chapter.

Let us say that net profit for the year was $5,000, for a total investment of $25,000. Remember, this $25,000 must include everything, including an hourly or daily rate tacked onto the hours of time we invested in the business, even if we didn't take out a salary. ROI will equal 5,000/25,000, or 20 percent. That's not bad, but can it be better? It can if we can increase the profit of $5,000 without increasing the total investment, or if we can reduce the total investment without decreasing the net profit. So we analyze both, and here's why it's important that such things as your labor be documented as part of total investment. Maybe we can increase ROI by reducing your labor. Maybe you're paying yourself $10 an hour for such things as stuffing envelopes, when you can pay some kid to do the same thing after school at less than half your labor rate. The net savings will increase your ROI, and that illustrates one of the main reasons for your calculating ROI—you should always analyze it to see if you can do better by more efficient selling or a more efficient investment.

SHOULD YOU DO IT OR NOT? A MATHEMATICAL GUIDE TO INVESTMENT DECISIONS

At some time in your career as a mail order businessperson, you will come face-to-face with an opportunity that, if taken, will require a major business investment. Many of your business decisions will be made on the basis of an educated guess. You make the decision based on your judgment, your experience, and what you have learned from other sources, such as this book. However, a really big investment should not be made without consideration of a major quantitative factor that we haven't talked about up to now. This factor is the time value of money. It refers to the fact that there are alternative choices for the use of the money required for your investment, and that this fact must be taken into consideration when making any major investment decision.

Let's look at an example. Let's say that you are considering an investment of $10,000 for a new sorting machine. The terms of payment are $5,000 down and $2,500 a year for two years. The machine will last 10 years, and after that you can sell it for scrap for $500. Why buy the machine? Well, because if you don't have the machine, you are paying to have your mailings sorted by hand, which is costing you $1,300 a year. So if we didn't consider the time value of money, our calculations would look like this:

Costs		Savings
$5,000	down payment	$1,300 per year
$5,000	at $2,500 per year	for 10 years
−$ 500	salvage value after 10 years	= $13,000
$9,500		

$13,000 − $9,500 = $3,500

This calculation says we should definitely buy the machine. But wait. We said there was a time value to money. This means we could do something else with the money. Maybe we could put it in the bank and get 7 percent interest per year, compounded yearly. This is the adjustment we must make for our basic calculations. These calculations are capital budgeting, and they can be of considerable importance if the investment we are considering is large enough.

Let's look at our example again and at Figures 22.2 and 22.3. Figure 22.2 gives the present value of $1 received at the end of any number of years, up to 50. Figure 22.3 shows the present value of $1 received annually at the end of each year for any number of years we care to choose, up to 50. In both figures, the horizontal line across the top of the page represents different interest percentages, from 1 to 50 percent at various intervals.

Now our basic task to make a comparison, considering the fact that there are alternative uses for our money that will pay us interest, is to bring all calculations to the present.

Let's look at costs first. The $5,000 down payment is already in the present, so there is nothing to do here. Next we have $2,500 to be paid for

n/r	1%	2%	3%	4%	5%	6%	7%	8%	9%	10%	11%	12%	13%	14%	15%
1	.9901	.9804	.9709	.9615	.9524	.9434	.9346	.9259	.9174	.9091	.9009	.8929	.8850	.8772	.8696
2	.9803	.9612	.9426	.9246	.9070	.8900	.8734	.8573	.8417	.8264	.8116	.7972	.7831	.7695	.7561
3	.9706	.9423	.9151	.8890	.8638	.8396	.8163	.7938	.7722	.7513	.7312	.7118	.6931	.6750	.6575
4	.9610	.9238	.8885	.8548	.8227	.7921	.7629	.7350	.7084	.6830	.6587	.6355	.6133	.5921	.5718
5	.9515	.9057	.8626	.8219	.7835	.7473	.7130	.6806	.6499	.6209	.5935	.5674	.5428	.5194	.4972
6	.9420	.8880	.8375	.7903	.7462	.7050	.6663	.6302	.5963	.5645	.5346	.5066	.4803	.4556	.4323
7	.9327	.8706	.8131	.7599	.7107	.6651	.6627	.5835	.5470	.5132	.4817	.4523	.4251	.3996	.3759
8	.9235	.8535	.7894	.7307	.6768	.6274	.5820	.5403	.5019	.4665	.4339	.4039	.3762	.3506	.3269
9	.9143	.8368	.7664	.7026	.6446	.5919	.5439	.5002	.4604	.4241	.3909	.3606	.3329	.3075	.2843
10	.9053	.8203	.7441	.6756	.6139	.5584	.5083	.4632	.4224	.3855	.3522	.3220	.2946	.2697	.2472
11	.8963	.8043	.7224	.6496	.5847	.5268	.4751	.4289	.3875	.3505	.3173	.2875	.2607	.2366	.2149
12	.8874	.7885	.7014	.6246	.5568	.4970	.4440	.3971	.3555	.3186	.2858	.2567	.2307	.2076	.1869
13	.8787	.7730	.6810	.6006	.5303	.4688	.4150	.3677	.3262	.2897	.2575	.2292	.2042	.1821	.1625
14	.8700	.7579	.6611	.5775	.5051	.4423	.3878	.3405	.2992	.2633	.2320	.2046	.1807	.1597	.1413
15	.8613	.7430	.6419	.5553	.4810	.4173	.3624	.3152	.2745	.2394	.2090	.1827	.1599	.1401	.1229
16	.8528	.7284	.6232	.5339	.4581	.3936	.3387	.2919	.2519	.2176	.1883	.1631	.1415	.1229	.1069
17	.8444	.7142	.6050	.5134	.4363	.3714	.3166	.2703	.2311	.1978	.1696	.1456	.1252	.1078	.0929
18	.8360	.7002	.5874	.4936	.4155	.3503	.2959	.2502	.2120	.1799	.1528	.1300	.1108	.0946	.0808
19	.8277	.6864	.5703	.4746	.3957	.3305	.2765	.2317	.1945	.1635	.1377	.1161	.0981	.0829	.0703
20	.8195	.6730	.5537	.4564	.3769	.3118	.2584	.2145	.1784	.1486	.1240	.1037	.0868	.0728	.0611
21	.8114	.6598	.5375	.4388	.3589	.2942	.2415	.1987	.1637	.1351	.1117	.0926	.0768	.0638	.0531
22	.8034	.6468	.5219	.4220	.3418	.2775	.2257	.1839	.1502	.1228	.1007	.0826	.0680	.0560	.0462
23	.7954	.6342	.5067	.4057	.3256	.2618	.2109	.1703	.1378	.1117	.0907	.0738	.0601	.0491	.0402
24	.7876	.6217	.4919	.3901	.3101	.2470	.1971	.1577	.1264	.1015	.0817	.0659	.0532	.0431	.0349
25	.7798	.6095	.4776	.3751	.2953	.2330	.1842	.1460	.1160	.0923	.0736	.0588	.0471	.0378	.0304
26	.7720	.5976	.4637	.3607	.2812	.2198	.1722	.1352	.1064	.0839	.0663	.0525	.0417	.0331	.0264
27	.7644	.5859	.4502	.3468	.2678	.2074	.1609	.1252	.0976	.0763	.0597	.0469	.0369	.0291	.0230
28	.7568	.5744	.4371	.3335	.2551	.1956	.1504	.1159	.0895	.0693	.0538	.0419	.0326	.0255	.0200
29	.7493	.5631	.4243	.3207	.2429	.1846	.1406	.1073	.0822	.0630	.0485	.0374	.0289	.0224	.0174
30	.7419	.5521	.4120	.3083	.2314	.1741	.1314	.0994	.0754	.0573	.0437	.0334	.0256	.0196	.0151
35	.7059	.5000	.3554	.2534	.1813	.1301	.0937	.0676	.0490	.0356	.0259	.0189	.0139	.0102	.0075
40	.6717	.4529	.3066	.2083	.1420	.0972	.0668	.0460	.0318	.0221	.0154	.0107	.0075	.0053	.0037
45	.6391	.410	.2644	.1713	.1112	.0727	.0476	.0313	.0207	.0137	.0091	.0061	.0041	.0027	.0019
50	.6080	.3715	.2281	.1407	.0872	.0543	.0339	.0213	.0134	.0085	.0054	.0035	.0022	.0014	.0009

n/r	16%	18%	20%	22%	24%	26%	28%	30%	32%	34%	36%	38%	40%	45%	50%
1	.8621	.8475	.8333	.8197	.8065	.7937	.7813	.7692	.7576	.7463	.7353	.7246	.7143	.6897	.6667
2	.7432	.7182	.6944	.6719	.6504	.6299	.6104	.5917	.5739	.5569	.5407	.5251	.5102	.4756	.4444
3	.6407	.6086	.5787	.5507	.5245	.4999	.4768	.4552	.4348	.4155	.3975	.3805	.3644	.3280	.2963
4	.5523	.5158	.4823	.4514	.4230	.3968	.3725	.3501	.3294	.3102	.2923	.2757	.2603	.2262	.1975
5	.4761	.4371	.4019	.3700	.3411	.3149	.2910	.2693	.2495	.2315	.2149	.1998	.1859	.1560	.1317
6	.4104	.3704	.3349	.3033	.2751	.2499	.2274	.2072	.1890	.1727	.1580	.1448	.1328	.1076	.0878
7	.3538	.3139	.2791	.2486	.2218	.1983	.1776	.1594	.1432	.1289	.1162	.1049	.0949	.0742	.0585
8	.3050	.2660	.2326	.2038	.1789	.1574	.1388	.1226	.1085	.0962	.0854	.0760	.0678	.0512	.0390
9	.2630	.2255	.1938	.1670	.1443	.1249	.1084	.0943	.0822	.0718	.0628	.0551	.0484	.0353	.0260
10	.2267	.1911	.1615	.1369	.1164	.0992	.0847	.0725	.0623	.0536	.0462	.0399	.0346	.0243	.0173
11	.1954	.1619	.1346	.1122	.0938	.0787	.0662	.0558	.0472	.0400	.0340	.0289	.0247	.0168	.0116
12	.1685	.1372	.1122	.0920	.0757	.0625	.0517	.0429	.0357	.0298	.0250	.0210	.0176	.0116	.0077
13	.1452	.1163	.0935	.0754	.0610	.0496	.0404	.0330	.0271	.0223	.0184	.0152	.0126	.0080	.0051
14	.1252	.0985	.0779	.0618	.0492	.0393	.0316	.0253	.0205	.0166	.0135	.0110	.0090	.0055	.0034
15	.1079	.0835	.0649	.0507	.0397	.0312	.0247	.0195	.0155	.0124	.0099	.0080	.0064	.0038	.0023
16	.0930	.0708	.0541	.0415	.0320	.0248	.0193	.0150	.0118	.0093	.0073	.0058	.0046	.0026	.0015
17	.0802	.0600	.0451	.0340	.0258	.0197	.0150	.0116	.0089	.0069	.0054	.0042	.0033	.0018	.0010
18	.0691	.0508	.0376	.0279	.0208	.0156	.0118	.0089	.0068	.0052	.0039	.0030	.0023	.0012	.0007
19	.0596	.0431	.0313	.0229	.0168	.0124	.0092	.0068	.0051	.0038	.0029	.0022	.0017	.0009	.0005
20	.0514	.0365	.0261	.0187	.0135	.0098	.0072	.0053	.0039	.0029	.0021	.0016	.0012	.0006	.0003
21	.0443	.0309	.0217	.0154	.0109	.0078	.0056	.0040	.0029	.0021	.0016	.0012	.0009	.0004	.0002
22	.0382	.0262	.0181	.0126	.0088	.0062	.0044	.0031	.0022	.0016	.0012	.0008	.0006	.0003	.0001
23	.0329	.0222	.0151	.0103	.0071	.0049	.0034	.0024	.0017	.0012	.0008	.0006	.0004	.0002	.0001
24	.0284	.0188	.0126	.0085	.0057	.0039	.0027	.0018	.0013	.0009	.0006	.0004	.0003	.0001	.0001
25	.0245	.0160	.0105	.0069	.0046	.0031	.0021	.0014	.0010	.0007	.0005	.0003	.0002	.0001	.0000
26	.0211	.0135	.0087	.0057	.0037	.0025	.0016	.0011	.0007	.0005	.0003	.0002	.0002	.0001	
27	.0182	.0115	.0073	.0047	.0030	.0019	.0013	.0008	.0006	.0004	.0002	.0002	.0001	.0000	
28	.0157	.0097	.0061	.0038	.0024	.0015	.0010	.0006	.0004	.0003	.0002	.0001	.0001		
29	.0135	.0082	.0051	.0031	.0020	.0012	.0008	.0005	.0003	.0002	.0001	.0001	.0001		
30	.0116	.0070	.0042	.0026	.0016	.0010	.0006	.0004	.0002	.0002	.0001	.0001	.0000		
35	.0055	.0030	.0017	.0009	.0005	.0003	.0002	.0001	.0001	.0000					
40	.0026	.0013	.0007	.0004	.0002	.0001	.0001	.0000							
45	.0013	.0006	.0003	.0001	.0001	.0000									
50	.0006	.0003	.0001	.0000											

Figure 22.2 Present value of \$1 received at end of n number of years.

n/r	1%	2%	3%	4%	5%	6%	7%	8%	9%	10%	11%	12%	13%	14%	15%
1	.9901	.9804	.9709	.9615	.9524	.9434	.9346	.9259	.9174	.9091	.9009	.8929	.8850	.8772	.8696
2	1.9704	1.9416	1.9135	1.8861	1.8594	1.8334	1.8080	1.7833	1.7591	1.7355	1.7125	1.6901	1.6681	1.6467	1.6257
3	2.9410	2.8839	2.8286	2.7751	2.7232	2.6730	2.6243	2.5771	2.5313	2.4869	2.4437	2.4018	2.3612	2.3216	2.2832
4	3.9020	3.8077	3.7171	3.6299	3.5459	3.4651	3.3872	3.3121	3.2397	3.1699	3.1024	3.0373	2.9745	2.9137	2.8550
5	4.8534	4.7135	4.5797	4.4518	4.3295	4.2124	4.1002	3.9927	3.8897	3.7908	3.6959	3.6048	3.5172	3.4331	3.3522
6	5.7955	5.6014	5.4172	5.2421	5.0757	4.9173	4.7665	4.6229	4.4859	4.3553	4.2305	4.1114	3.9975	3.8887	3.7845
7	6.7282	6.4720	6.2303	6.0020	5.7864	5.5824	5.3893	5.2064	5.0330	4.8684	4.7122	4.5638	4.4226	4.2883	4.1604
8	7.6517	7.3255	7.0197	6.7327	6.4632	6.2098	5.9713	5.7466	5.5348	5.3349	5.1461	4.9676	4.7988	4.6389	4.4873
9	8.5660	8.1622	7.7861	7.4353	7.1078	6.8017	6.5152	6.2469	5.9952	5.7590	5.5370	5.3282	5.1317	4.9464	4.7716
10	9.4713	8.9826	8.5302	8.1109	7.7217	7.3601	7.0236	6.7101	6.4177	6.1446	5.8892	5.6502	5.4262	5.2161	5.0188
11	10.3676	9.7868	9.2526	8.7605	8.3064	7.8869	7.4987	7.1390	6.8051	6.4951	6.2065	5.9377	5.6869	5.4527	5.2337
12	11.2551	10.5753	9.9540	9.3851	8.8632	8.3838	7.9427	7.5361	7.1607	6.8137	6.4924	6.1944	5.9176	5.6603	5.4206
13	12.1337	11.3484	10.6350	9.9856	9.3936	8.8527	8.3577	7.9038	7.4869	7.1034	6.7499	6.4235	6.1218	5.8424	5.5831
14	13.0037	12.1062	11.2961	10.5631	9.8986	9.2950	8.7455	8.2442	7.7862	7.3667	6.9819	6.6282	6.3025	6.0021	5.7245
15	13.8650	12.8493	11.9379	11.1184	10.3797	9.7122	9.1079	8.5595	8.0607	7.6061	7.1909	6.8109	6.4624	6.1422	5.8474
16	14.7179	13.5777	12.5611	11.6523	10.8378	10.1059	9.4466	8.8514	8.3126	7.8237	7.3792	6.9740	6.6039	6.2651	5.9542
17	15.5622	14.2919	13.1661	12.1657	11.2741	10.4773	9.7632	9.1216	8.5436	8.0216	7.5488	7.1196	6.7291	6.3729	6.0472
18	16.3983	14.9920	13.7535	12.6593	11.6896	10.8276	10.0591	9.3719	8.7556	8.2014	7.7016	7.2497	6.8399	6.4674	6.1280
19	17.2260	15.6785	14.3238	13.1339	12.0853	11.1581	10.3356	9.6036	8.9501	8.3649	7.8393	7.3658	6.9380	6.5504	6.1982
20	18.0455	16.3514	14.8775	13.5903	12.4622	11.4699	10.5940	9.8181	9.1285	8.5136	7.9633	7.4694	7.0248	6.6231	6.2593
21	18.8570	17.0112	15.4150	14.0292	12.8211	11.7641	10.8355	10.0168	9.2922	8.6487	8.0751	7.5620	7.1015	6.6870	6.3125
22	19.6604	17.6580	15.9369	14.4511	13.1630	12.0416	11.0612	10.2007	9.4424	8.7715	8.1757	7.6446	7.1695	6.7429	6.3587
23	20.4558	18.2922	16.4436	14.8568	13.4886	12.3034	11.2722	10.3711	9.5802	8.8832	8.2664	7.7184	7.2297	6.7921	6.3988
24	21.2434	18.9139	16.9355	15.2470	13.7986	12.5504	11.4693	10.5288	9.7066	8.9847	8.3481	7.7843	7.2829	6.8351	6.4338
25	22.0232	19.5235	17.4131	15.6221	14.0939	12.7834	11.6536	10.6748	9.8226	9.0770	8.4217	7.8431	7.3300	6.8729	6.4641
26	22.7952	20.1210	17.8768	15.9828	14.3752	13.0032	11.8258	10.8100	9.9290	9.1609	8.4881	7.8957	7.3717	6.9061	6.4906
27	23.5596	20.7069	18.3270	16.3296	14.6430	13.2105	11.9867	10.9352	10.0266	9.2372	8.5478	7.9426	7.4086	6.9352	6.5135
28	24.3164	21.2813	18.7641	16.6631	14.8981	13.4062	12.1371	11.0511	10.1161	9.3066	8.6016	7.9844	7.4412	6.9607	6.5335
29	25.0658	21.8444	19.1884	16.9837	15.1411	13.5907	12.2777	11.1584	10.1983	9.3696	8.6501	8.0218	7.4701	6.9830	6.5509
30	25.8077	22.3965	19.6004	17.2920	15.3724	13.7648	12.4090	11.2578	10.2737	9.4269	8.6938	8.0552	7.4957	7.0027	6.5660
31	26.5423	22.9377	20.0004	17.5885	15.5928	13.9291	12.5318	11.3498	10.3428	9.4790	8.7331	8.0850	7.5183	7.0199	6.5791
32	27.2696	23.4683	20.3888	17.8735	15.8027	14.0840	12.6466	11.4350	10.4062	9.5264	8.7686	8.1116	7.5383	7.0350	6.5905
33	27.9897	23.9886	20.7658	18.1476	16.0025	14.2302	12.7538	11.5139	10.4644	9.5694	8.8005	8.1354	7.5560	7.0482	6.6005
34	28.7027	24.4986	21.1318	18.4112	16.1929	14.3681	12.8540	11.5869	10.5178	9.6086	8.8293	8.1566	7.5717	7.0599	6.6091
35	29.4086	24.9986	21.4872	18.6646	16.3742	14.4982	12.9477	11.6546	10.5668	9.6442	8.8552	8.1755	7.5856	7.0700	6.6166
40	32.8347	27.3555	23.1148	19.7928	17.1591	15.0463	13.3317	11.9246	10.7574	9.7791	8.9511	8.2438	7.6344	7.1050	6.6418
45	36.0945	29.4902	24.5187	20.7200	17.7741	15.4558	13.6055	12.1084	10.8812	9.8628	9.0079	8.2825	7.6609	7.1232	6.6543
50	39.1961	31.4236	25.7298	21.4822	18.2559	15.7619	13.8007	12.2335	10.9617	9.9148	9.0417	8.3045	7.6752	7.1327	6.6605

n/r	16%	18%	20%	22%	24%	26%	28%	30%	32%	34%	36%	38%	40%	45%	50%
1	.8621	.8475	.8333	.8197	.8065	.7937	.7813	.7692	.7576	.7463	.7353	.7246	.7143	.6897	.6667
2	1.6052	1.5656	1.5278	1.4915	1.4568	1.4235	1.3916	1.3609	1.3315	1.3032	1.2760	1.2497	1.2245	1.1653	1.1111
3	2.2459	2.1743	2.1065	2.0422	1.9813	1.9234	1.8684	1.8161	1.7663	1.7188	1.6735	1.6302	1.5889	1.4933	1.4074
4	2.7982	2.6901	2.5887	2.4936	2.4043	2.3202	2.2410	2.1662	2.0957	2.0290	1.9658	1.9060	1.8492	1.7195	1.6049
5	3.2743	3.1272	2.9906	2.8636	2.7454	2.6351	2.5320	2.4356	2.3452	2.2604	2.1807	2.1058	2.0352	1.8755	1.7366
6	3.6847	3.4976	3.3255	3.1669	3.0205	2.8850	2.7594	2.6427	2.5342	2.4331	2.3388	2.2506	2.1680	1.9831	1.8244
7	4.0386	3.8115	3.6046	3.4155	3.2423	3.0833	2.9370	2.8021	2.6775	2.5620	2.4550	2.3555	2.2628	2.0573	1.8829
8	4.3436	4.0776	3.8372	3.6193	3.4212	3.2407	3.0758	2.9247	2.7860	2.6582	2.5404	2.4315	2.3306	2.1085	1.9220
9	4.6065	4.3030	4.0310	3.7863	3.5655	3.3657	3.1842	3.0190	2.8681	2.7300	2.6033	2.4866	2.3790	2.1438	1.9480
10	4.8332	4.4941	4.1925	3.9232	3.6819	3.4648	3.2689	3.0915	2.9304	2.7836	2.6495	2.5265	2.4136	2.1681	1.9053
11	5.0286	4.6560	4.3271	4.0354	3.7757	3.5435	3.3351	3.1473	2.9776	2.8236	2.6834	2.5555	2.4383	2.1849	1.9769
12	5.1971	4.7932	4.4392	4.1274	3.8514	3.6059	3.3868	3.1903	3.0133	2.8534	2.7084	2.5764	2.4559	2.1965	1.9845
13	5.3423	4.9095	4.5327	4.2028	3.9124	3.6555	3.4272	3.2233	3.0404	2.8757	2.7268	2.5916	2.4685	2.2045	1.9897
14	5.4675	5.0081	4.6106	4.2646	3.9616	3.6949	3.4587	3.2487	3.0609	2.8923	2.7403	2.6026	2.4775	2.2100	1.9931
15	5.5755	5.0916	4.6755	4.3152	4.0013	3.7261	3.4834	3.2682	3.0764	2.9047	2.7502	2.6106	2.4839	2.2138	1.9954
16	5.6685	5.1624	4.7296	4.3567	4.0333	3.7509	3.5026	3.2832	3.0882	2.9140	2.7575	2.6164	2.4885	2.2164	1.9970
17	5.7487	5.2223	4.7746	4.3908	4.0591	3.7705	3.5177	3.2948	3.0971	2.9209	2.7629	2.6206	2.4918	2.2182	1.9980
18	5.8178	5.2732	4.8122	4.4187	4.0799	3.7861	3.5294	3.3037	3.1039	2.9260	2.7668	2.6236	2.4941	2.2195	1.9986
19	5.8775	5.3162	4.8435	4.4415	4.0967	3.7985	3.5386	3.3105	3.1090	2.9299	2.7697	2.6258	2.4958	2.2203	1.9991
20	5.9288	5.3527	4.8696	4.4603	4.1103	3.8083	3.5458	3.3158	3.1129	2.9327	2.7718	2.6274	2.4970	2.2209	1.9994
21	5.9731	5.3837	4.8913	4.4756	4.1212	3.8161	3.5514	3.3198	3.1158	2.9349	2.7734	2.6285	2.4979	2.2213	1.9996
22	6.0113	5.4099	4.9094	4.4882	4.1300	3.8223	3.5558	3.3230	3.1180	2.9365	2.7746	2.6294	2.4985	2.2216	1.9997
23	6.0442	5.4321	4.9245	4.4985	4.1371	3.8273	3.5592	3.3253	3.1197	2.9377	2.7754	2.6300	2.4989	2.2218	1.9998
24	6.0726	5.4509	4.9371	4.5070	4.1428	3.8312	3.5619	3.3272	3.1210	2.9386	2.7760	2.6304	2.4992	2.2219	1.9999
25	6.0971	5.4669	4.9476	4.5139	4.1474	3.8342	3.5640	3.3286	3.1220	2.9392	2.7765	2.6307	2.4994	2.2220	1.9999
26	6.1182	5.4804	4.9563	4.5196	4.1511	3.8367	3.5656	3.3297	3.1227	2.9397	2.7768	2.6310	2.4996	2.2221	1.9999
27	6.1364	5.4919	4.9636	4.5243	4.1542	3.8387	3.5669	3.3305	3.1233	2.9401	2.7771	2.6311	2.4997	2.2221	2.0000
28	6.1520	5.5016	4.9697	4.5281	4.1566	3.8402	3.5679	3.3312	3.1237	2.9404	2.7773	2.6313	2.4998	2.2222	2.0000
29	6.1656	5.5098	4.9747	4.5312	4.1585	3.8414	3.5687	3.3316	3.1240	2.9406	2.7774	2.6313	2.4999	2.2222	2.0000
30	6.1772	5.5168	4.9789	4.5338	4.1601	3.8424	3.5693	3.3321	3.1242	2.9407	2.7775	2.6314	2.4999	2.2222	2.0000
31	6.1872	5.5227	4.9824	4.5359	4.1614	3.8432	3.5697	3.3324	3.1244	2.9408	2.7776	2.6315	2.4999	2.2222	2.0000
32	6.1959	5.5277	4.9854	4.5376	4.1624	3.8438	3.5701	3.3326	3.1246	2.9409	2.7776	2.6315	2.4999	2.2222	2.0000
33	6.2034	5.5320	4.9878	4.5390	4.1632	3.8443	3.5704	3.3328	3.1247	2.9410	2.7777	2.6315	2.5000	2.2222	2.0000
34	6.2098	5.5356	4.9898	4.5402	4.1639	3.8447	3.5706	3.3329	3.1248	2.9410	2.7777	2.6315	2.5000	2.2222	2.0000
35	6.2153	5.5386	4.9915	4.5411	4.1644	3.8450	3.5708	3.3330	3.1248	2.9411	2.7777	2.6215	2.5000	2.2222	2.0000
40	6.2335	5.5482	4.9966	4.5439	4.1659	3.8458	3.5712	3.3332	3.1250	2.9412	2.7778	2.6316	2.5000	2.2222	2.0000
45	6.2421	5.5523	4.9986	4.5449	4.1664	3.8460	3.5714	3.3333	3.1250	2.9412	2.7778	2.6316	2.5000	2.2222	2.0000
50	6.2463	5.5541	4.9995	4.5452	4.1666	3.8461	3.5714	3.3333	3.1250	2.9412	2.7778	2.6316	2.5000	2.2222	2.0000

Figure 22.3   Present value of $1 received annually at end of year for *n* years.

Cost and Profit Calculations Made Easy

the next two years. Look at Figure 22.2 for the end of year 1 under the 7 percent column and we see .9346. Under year 2 and 7 percent, we see .8734. Further, there is a salvage value for our machine of $500 after 10 years. Looking at year 10 and 7 percent, we copy down the number .5083. Now we add our costs up as follows:

Costs

Down payment	$5,000.00
$2,500 at end of year 1 = ($2,500)(.9346)	+2,336.50
$2,500 at end of year 2 = ($2,500)(.8734)	+2,183.50
$500 salvage value after 10 years = ($500)(.5083)	− 254.15
	$9,265.85

For our savings of $1,300 per year for 10 years, we use Figure 22.3. At year 10 and 7 percent, we read 7.0236.

Savings

Labor savings = ($1,300)(7.0236) $9,130.68

Note the difference. Because $9,130.68 in savings is less than our costs of $9,265.85, even considering the salvage value, we should not buy the machine after all. In this example, the difference changed from a savings of $3,500 in buying the machine to a loss of $135.17. Larger investments or different percentages of interest considered would show even greater differences. For example, instead of putting your money in the bank at 7 percent interest, what if you put it into advertising and your ROI is 15 percent? Instead of the 7 percent column, you would use the one that reads 15 percent. You might want to do this using 15 percent as an exercise, just to make sure you understand how to do it. If you do, you will find that your costs less salvage are $8,940.65, while your savings of $1,300 per year brought to the present are only $6,524.44. This means that you would really be losing $2,416.21 ($8,940.65 − $6,524.44) if you made this investment. So keep this capital budgeting concept in mind before you make any major investment and use Figures 22.2 and 22.3 to help you make the right decision.

MAIL ORDER BUSINESS EXPENSES

Here is a list of expenses common to many mail order businesses. Use it in your business planning before you start and also to help you include all of your investments when calculating your ROI.

Product Costs

1. Amount paid to supplier for product.
2. Manufacturing costs if you make product yourself.
3. Printing costs if product is a course, manual, or book.
4. Packaging costs.
5. Shipping costs for raw materials or the product to be shipped to you from supplier.
6. Postage cost to your customers.
7. Allowance for damage or return by customer (I usually start with a 5 percent figure here until I can calculate my costs for this product from actual experience).
8. Allowance for bad checks (I usually start by assuming I'll have about 5 percent in bad checks and then correct my figures based on actual experience).
9. Storage costs.

Typical Overhead Expenses

1. Automobile.
2. Insurance.
3. Licenses.
4. Office rent.
5. Office supplies, including stationery.
6. Professional services (accountant, attorney, etc.).
7. Salaries.
8. Taxes.
9. Telephone.
10. Utilities, including gas, water, and electricity.

Advertising Expenses

1. Advertising agency.
2. Addressing and stuffing envelopes.
3. Copyrighting.
4. Mailing list rental.
5. Media advertising.
6. Photography and artwork.
7. Postage.
8. Printing.
9. Typesetting.

You may not have all of these expenses. You may not want to use the services of an advertising agency. In fact, earlier in the book I showed you how to save 15 percent on all of your advertising by setting up your own in-house advertising agency. But these lists include many expenses you might overlook, and you should consider them before proceeding.

SUMMARY

In this chapter we've gone into some very important calculations that can affect the profitability and success or failure of your business. These included:

Breakeven both for your business and on a project basis

Calculating breakeven graphically

Breakeven for the two-step offer

The profitability formula

Calculating number of replies to break even on an ad, considering back-end profits

The ROI concept and how to calculate ROI

How to do capital budgeting when making major investment decisions

All of these concepts and calculations are important. Come back to this chapter and refer to it whenever you need to make profit or cost calculations in your business.

23

Developing a Mail Order Marketing Plan

A marketing plan can be extremely important in your mail order business for any new product, project, or business. Yet many mail order operators neglect the marketing plan, or, at best, formulate a half-baked one that does not consider all the various aspects that are important for success. Some indication of how important marketing plans are is the fact that if you were to have someone else create the marketing plan that I am going to show you how to develop in this chapter, it would cost you somewhere between $500 and $25,000. In fact, one firm with which we are familiar does nothing but develop marketing plans for small companies. It does them by mail and receives large sums of money for every plan it develops for its clients.

A marketing plan is very important because it does some very important things for you. Many say that my description of a marketing plan sounds very much like a business plan. They are right. A good marketing plan and a good business plan are essentially identical. Here's what a good marketing plan will do for you:

1. It acts as a road map.
2. It assists you with management control.
3. It helps you in briefing new employees and other personnel.
4. It helps you obtain financing.
5. It helps to stimulate thinking and make better use of resources.
6. It aids in assignment of responsibilities, tasks, and timing.
7. It gives an awareness of problems, opportunities, and threats.

ROAD MAP

A marketing plan acts as a road map in getting you from where you are now to where you want to be: successful, profitable, and making lots of money from the product you are thinking of introducing. Now, if you were traveling from your home to somewhere you had never been before, it could be very difficult for you to find the place if you didn't consult a road map. This is exactly what the marketing plan does for you. Regardless of how long you have been in business, you have never been to exactly this place, where you want to go with the new product. The marketing plan acts as your road map and guide, and it takes you step by step until you finally reach your goal.

MANAGEMENT CONTROL

Along with being a road map, the marketing plan acts as a tool that allows you, as a manager, to control your progress. It is a fact that nothing will go exactly as planned. However, the fact that you have a complete plan laid out and documented will allow you to see the exact difference between what is happening and what you have planned and intended to happen to reach your goal. But more than that, the marketing plan will assist you in returning to the proper course to reach the goal you have decided upon.

BRIEFING NEW EMPLOYEES AND OTHER PERSONNEL

As a small businessperson, you may work alone, with a small number of other people, or with many other people. At some point in your progress toward your ultimate goal of success with this mail order product, you will want to brief someone else about what you are doing and those tasks you wish him or her to do or become involved with. If you have everything documented in a marketing plan, this is a relatively easy task. You can brief suppliers, new employees, or even a spouse as to not only where you are going, but how you plan to get there and how you want them to help.

OBTAINING FINANCING

As I mentioned earlier, you may need financing at some point in the growth and development of your mail order company. If so, a full business plan will assist you in getting it, whether it be from the Small Business Administration, a bank, or a venture capitalist. A marketing plan is the heart of a good business plan. You can use your marketing plan as your business plan to help you in acquiring the capital that you will need.

STIMULATE THINKING AND MAKE BETTER
USE OF RESOURCES

Strategy in marketing depends on utilizing and building on one's strengths and making one's weaknesses irrelevant to attain a sustained differential advantage at the decisive point in your campaign so as to lead to success. As one develops a marketing plan, thinking is stimulated, and as the plan unfolds, it is changed and modified as new ideas are generated. As a result, the strategy and the tactics necessary to reach the objectives and goals of the marketing plan are continually improved.

ASSIGNMENT OF RESPONSIBILITIES, TASKS, AND TIMING

Any marketing plan is only as good as those who must implement it. Therefore, it is absolutely crucial that the responsibilities of everyone be indicated and that tasks be thoroughly understood by all individuals who have roles to play in implementation. Further, these actions must be scheduled so that the overall plan is executed in a coordinated fashion to maximize the impact of the strategy while taking full recognition of what you can't control in the marketplace. There is an old adage that "if everyone is responsible for accomplishing any task, then no one is responsible," and it is very likely that the task will not be accomplished or at least not be accomplished with the proper timing and coordination. The marketing plan assures that every task has an assigned individual who is responsible and that the timing and scheduling is coordinated to maximize the effectiveness of what is done.

AWARENESS OF PROBLEMS, OPPORTUNITIES, AND THREATS

The very construction of a marketing plan requires an investigation into the situation so that problems, opportunities, and threats are precisely identified. So the more you plan, as the plan develops, the more you will understand the nature of these problems, opportunities, and threats and what can be done about them. In no case should problems, opportunities, or threats be ignored, but rather the marketing plan must be constructed and, if necessary, modified during its development so as to take advantage of the opportunities, solve the problems, and, if possible, avoid or overcome the threats.

Some time ago, Roy Abrams spoke to a group of professional mail order people who were taking New York University's Extension Course in Direct Marketing. Roy Abrams had held senior positions in a variety of large direct mail and mail order companies, including such positions as senior vice president of the Longines Symphonette, director of merchandising at American Express, and vice president of merchandising at Columbia House. Here's what he said about the marketing plan: "Whether in a small company or a large company, the marketing plan is important because in today's business environment, every profitable dollar must be squeezed out of every market and every medium. The road to doing this is to develop a full marketing plan."

THE MARKETING PLAN'S STRUCTURE

Now let's take a look at the structure of a marketing plan. What are the secrets that would require you to spend $500, $5,000, or more if you were to pay someone else to develop your plan? Look at Figure 23.1. This is a complete outline of a full marketing plan for a mail order direct mail business. If you complete every one of the sections, you will have gone a long way toward ensuring your success with the new product or product line you are introducing.

The Executive Summary

The executive summary is an overall view of your project and its potential, including what you want to do, how much money and what other resources are needed for the project, and specific financial measurements such as return on investment that might be anticipated. The executive summary is extremely important and should not be overlooked. As the title implies, it is an overview or summary or abstract of the entire plan intended for a decision-making audience. As the executives review your marketing plan, they will frequently skip around to parts of the plan that are of more interest to them. In fact, few marketing plans will be read word for word in their entirety by top executives in your company. Rather, certain sections will be read in detail and other sections only scanned. However, almost every executive will read the executive summary.

It is therefore important that in this summary you capture the essence of your plan in a few short, terse paragraphs so that you can describe the thrust of what the plan purports to do, the objectives and goals that are the intent of the plan, and a bird's-eye view of the strategy that will be used to accomplish these objectives and goals. This summary shouldn't exceed two or three pages at the maximum. It may only be a couple of paragraphs long.

A few minutes' reading of your executive summary should allow the reader to understand what it is you want to do, how much it will cost, and what the chances of success are. Most important, he or she will understand the competitive differential advantage inherent in your marketing plan that will cause it to succeed.

EXECUTIVE SUMMARY

(Overview of entire plan, including a description of the product or service, the differential advantage, the required investment, and anticipated sales and profits).

Table of Contents

I. Introduction. (What is the product and why will you be successful with it at this time?)

II. Situation Analysis

1. The Situational Environ
   A. Demand and demand trends. (What is the forecast demand for the product? Is it growing or declining? Who is the decision maker, the purchase agent? How, when, where, what, and why do they buy?)
   B. Social and cultural factors.
   C. Demographics.
   D. Economic and business conditions for this product at this time in the geographical area selected.
   E. State of technology for this class of product. Is it high-tech state of the art? Are newer products succeeding older ones frequently (very short life cycle)? In short, how is technology affecting this product or service?
   F. Politics. Is politics (current or otherwise) in any way affecting the situation for marketing this product?
   G. Laws and regulations. (What laws or regulations are applicable here?)

2. The Neutral Environ
   A. Financial environs. (How does the availability or nonavailability of funds affect the situation?)
   B. Government environs. (Will legislative action or anything else currently going on in state, federal, or local government be likely to affect marketing of this product or service?)
   C. Media environs. (What's happening in the media? Does current publicity favor or disfavor this project?)
   D. Special interest environs. (Aside from direct competitors, are any influential groups likely to affect your plans?)

3. The Competitor Environ
   A. Describe your main competitors and their products, plans, experience, know-how, financial, human and capital resources, suppliers, and strategy. (Do they enjoy any favor or disfavor with the customer? If so, why? What marketing channels do competitors use? What are your competitors' strengths and weaknesses?)

(continued)

Figure 23.1 Marketing plan outline.

    4. The Company Environ

        A. Describe your product, experience, know-how, financial, human and capital resources, suppliers, etc. (Do you enjoy any favor or disfavor with the customer? If so, why? What are your strengths and weaknesses?)

III. The Target Market

    1. Describe your target market segment in detail using demographics, psychographics, geographics, life style, or whatever segmentation is appropriate. (Why is this your target market and not some other segment?)

IV. Problems, Opportunities, and Threats

    1. State or restate each opportunity and indicate why it is in fact an opportunity. State or restate every problem and indicate what you intend to do about each problem.

V. Marketing Objectives and Goals

    1. Precisely state marketing objectives in terms of sales volume, market share, return on investment, or other objectives for your marketing plan.

VI. Marketing Strategy

    1. Consider alternatives for overall strategy. Further describe your strategy as to whether you are using product differentiation, market segmentation, or positioning, etc., and how you are employing these strategies. Note what your main competitors are likely to do when you implement this strategy and what you will do to take advantage of the opportunities created and avoid the threats.

VII. Marketing Tactics

    1. State how you will implement the marketing strategy(ies) chosen in terms of product, price, promotion, distribution, and other tactical or environmental variables.

VIII. Control, Implementation, and Financial Plans

    1. Calculate break-even and accomplish a break-even chart for your project. Compute sales projections on a monthly basis for a three-year period. Compute cash flows on a monthly basis for a three-year period. Indicate start-up costs and monthly budget for this period.

IX. Summary

    1. Summarize advantages, costs, and profits, and clearly state the differential advantage that your plan for this product or service offers over the competition and why the plan will succeed.

X. Appendices

    1. Include all supporting information that you consider relevant.

Figure 23.1 (Continued)

Table of Contents

You may wonder about the discussion of something so mundane and simplistic as a table of contents in a discussion as important and sometimes as complicated as that of marketing planning. Yet, the table of contents is extremely important as a part of the marketing plan. As noted previously, most executives will not read the entire plan in detail except for the executive summary and certain areas that may be of particular interest to them.

For example, an investor with a financial background will be very interested in the financial part of your marketing plan and what different elements of the plan will cost to implement and when these monies will be needed. An experienced mail order investor will want to know all about your product right away. These executives may even skip items that you think are crucial. Therefore, it is not sufficient that every subject area critical to the project be covered in your plan. In addition, because of other readers who may be interested in your plan or may be required to take some action as a part of it, you must make it as easy as possible to find any topic of interest quickly. The table of contents is used for this purpose. If you do not use a table of contents, other executives and individuals involved in the implementation of your marketing plan will probably make some attempt at locating the information they want. But if they cannot find it, they may assume that it is not there. This is not only a question of wasted time but of a negative impact on those whose support in adoption or implementation may be crucial to success. Therefore, inclusion of a table of contents is mandatory.

Introduction

The introduction is the explanation of the details of your project. Unlike the executive summary, it is not an overview of the project. Its purpose is to give the background of the project and to describe your product or service so that any reader will understand exactly what it is you are proposing. The introduction can be a fairly large section. After reading it the evaluator should understand what the product or service is and what you propose to do with it.

Situation Analysis

The situation analysis is a detailed description of the environment or the company and the product, product line, or service at the time the plan will be initiated and implemented. It should include a detailed discussion of the environment you face, including your company, your competition, and other important elements. It must describe market characteristics, including the segments of the overall market in which you're interested, growth trends, specific customer identification, buyer attitudes and habits, geographical location of the market segments, industry pricing, size of the various market segments in dollars and units, technological trends, distribution factors and issues, and other important characteristics.

Demand.   Under *Demand*, you should note how strong the need is for this new product and also what need the product is satisfying. Remember that products satisfy psychological needs, as conceptualized by Maslow, and are not necessarily purchased for the obvious use of the product. I once bought a brass case for carrying my business cards from an ad I saw in the *Wall Street Journal*. The manufacturer engraved my initials on the side of the case at no extra charge. Did I buy the case only to carry my business cards, or does my need for status fit in here somewhere? You should also note, under *Demand*, the extent of this need. This means both how strong the need is that will be fulfilled by your product, and also whether it will be satisfied again and again by repeated purchases of your product or a follow-up product, and whether the demand is a short-lived fad or a long-term need that will enable your product to have a long life cycle.

Legal Restrictions.   Legal restrictions do not always exist. But when they do, it is important to consider them, especially if you are dealing with a product related to drugs or one controlled by a federal regulatory agency. If you have such a product, be certain to contact the agency, find out about possible license requirements and restrictions, and write these restrictions into your plan.

Competition.   Regardless of the product you offer, you will always have competition, even if the competition does not offer exactly the same product or service, but sells a product that fills the same need. Look at the ordinary bicycle. If you sell bicycles, your competition may be not only other bicycle manufacturers or sellers or distributors, but also, because it is in part a recreational vehicle, firms that provide other forms of recreation. In the same way, when hand-held calculators came out in the early 1970s, priced at approximately $200 and with relatively limited functions, their competition was not only other manufacturers of these new electronic calculating devices, but also the manufacturers of the traditional slide rules, which were then selling for as much as $100. Even though the products were not identical, for some people they filled the same need.

When you consider your competition, you should also consider the fact that your competition will not remain static. If you introduce a new product into the marketplace that competes with a product that is already there, you can bet that if you are successful, you will not be ignored. Your competition will then initiate some other strategy to try to overcome your success. If you introduce a successful new product that competes against a similar product already in the marketplace, you might expect your competition to do something with the price, to change the offer, or perhaps to change its advertising in some way. So when you formulate the portion of your marketing plan having to do with competition, think ahead, just as a chess or checkers player must plan ahead. Think about what your competition is going to do next, and what you might have to do in response.

Unique Advantages You Have.   Your firm is not the same as my firm or any other mail order firm in existence. You, as an individual, and therefore your firm, as well, have certain unique advantages. These may be knowledge of a certain industry, a price break you are able to offer because you are obtaining the product more cheaply than your competition can or because you are producing the product yourself, engineering knowledge, certain financial knowledge, certain unique connections. These advantages may be any of a thousand different things, and they will add greatly to your chances of success with your product. It is important to write these advantages down in your marketing plan to make certain that you do not overlook them and that you exploit them to the maximum. Spend some time thinking about this particular part of the marketing plan because many advantages you may take for granted are, in fact, not enjoyed by anyone else in your marketplace. If you ignore these advantages, it will be as if they did not exist. But if you use them, you may have something that your competition does not have and is unable to get.

Target Market.   Usually, the larger your market potential target is, the better. But there are several strategies you might follow, and it may be advantageous to offer your product only to a certain segment of the total potential market. This is called market segmentation, and it offers you a major advantage. You can concentrate all your resources against this specific segment and be stronger against it than your competition can be if it spreads its advertisements through publications read by every single potential customer who may be even remotely interested in your proposition. I once wrote a book called *The Executive's Guide to Finding a Superior Job,* which was published by AMACOM, a division of the American Management Association. This book was segmented in two ways. First, it is a book on job finding and is therefore not of interest to everyone, but only to people who are looking for a job. Second, because I used the word *executive* in the title, I segmented my market again to concentrate only on the target market of people who considered themselves to be in decision-making roles. Now, you may think that this segmentation could have an adverse effect since it reduced the total growth size of the market to which I was appealing. However, *The Executive's Guide to Finding a Superior Job* was a tremendous success with this segmentation strategy primarily because AMACOM's target market consists primarily of corporate executives. Within three years, the book went into four printings and later came out in a second edition. So consider the target market to which you are offering your product and describe it fully in your marketing plan. The selection of a target market in itself can help your product to be successful.

An updated version of this is now published by my company, Global Associates Publishing Company, 1556 N. Sierra Madre Villa, Pasadena, CA 91107 under the title *Get a Great Job Fast* for a broader segment of the job-finding target market.

Problems, Opportunities, and Threats

Problems and opportunities are different sides of the same coin. Very frequently when you note a problem, you will also see that within this problem lies an opportunity for success. Listerine mouthwash has a rather harsh taste—in the words of the competition, "mediciney." However, Listerine has managed to make this "problem" into an "opportunity" because the company realized that many people feel that if mouthwash does have a harsh taste, it may be harsher on germs, whereas a mouthwash that tastes sweet or, in the words in one advertisement, "like soda pop," may not be killing germs as well. List every problem, as well as the opportunity the problem may present. In every case it is insufficient simply to state the problem or the opportunity or threat; rather it is important to state also alternative courses of action for overcoming the problems, taking advantage of the opportunities, and avoiding the threats.

Marketing Objectives and Goals

Objectives and goals must be clearly spelled out and identified. A marketing objective might be to become the leading supplier of a certain product. Underneath this objective, certain goals are established. One goal might be attainment of a 30 percent market share within the next three years. Goals could pertain to volume of sales, return on investment, or measurable aims. Remember that you can't get "there" until you know where "there" is. Thus, the importance of objectives and goals. Also, be careful that objectives or goals are not mutually exclusive. For example, attaining a certain market share may require sacrifice of some profit.

Marketing Strategies

Strategies are the actions that you must take to reach your goals and objectives and will be discussed in more detail in forthcoming chapters in this book. A marketing strategy may mean *mass marketing*, that is, trying to sell the same product to everyone; a strategy of *market segmentation,* where you attempt to sell your product and concentrate your resources only on certain segments of the marketplace; a strategy of *product differentiation,* where your product is differentiated from those of your competitors; a strategy of *positioning,* where your product is positioned in the minds of its potential buyers relative to other products offered; a strategy of *internationalization,* where your product is differentiated depending upon the different country in which it is marketed; or one of *globalization,* where the same product is marketed identically in the same manner in every single country. In any case, strategies must be specified and described in detail along with the differential advantages that adoption will enable.

Marketing Tactics

Tactics are the specifics of how we carry out our strategy. Thus, a strategy of product differentiation may require differentiation by product tactics in which we change the packaging; pricing tactics where the price is altered or modified; promotion tactics where a previously ignored difference is emphasized and promoted; or distribution tactics where a faster means of getting the product to the consumer or buyer is used to differentiate our product from that of our competitors.

Product Tactics. Product tactics are obviously very important. There are three basic things you can do with any product: introduce it, drop it, or change it. Each of these possibilities has an important impact on profitability, and you might consider each for inclusion in your marketing plan. However, we are going to focus here on your product introduction. I suppose this is as good a spot as any to point out that estimates of new product failure run as high as 90 percent: That means that 9 out of every 10 new products introduced into the marketplace fail. They fail for a variety of reasons, including lack of knowledge by the introducer, failure to develop a marketing plan, and failure to do many of the things found in this chapter and elsewhere in this book. The bottom line is that many new products fail even with the best intent and wishes of those who introduce them.

Now, because most new products fail, you may wonder why you should bother to introduce a new product at all. Why can't you find one product or a couple of products that are successful, stay with them, and make your money with them in the future? In some cases this is possible. But in most cases, it is not, because of what is called the product life cycle, shown in Figure 23.2.

According to this concept, every product goes through a number of stages, which may be named differently, but which all mean essentially the

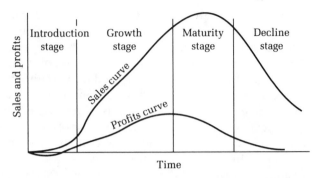

Figure 23.2   The product life cycle.

same thing. First, a product goes through an introduction and growth stage. Then it becomes mature and the market becomes saturated. Finally, the product goes into decline. In Figure 23.2, you will see two curves. One shows profit margins. You can see that, as the product progresses from introduction into growth and maturity, the profit margins increase. But then, sometime in the maturity stage, profit margins begin to decline. The sales volume curve, however, does not follow the profit margin curve exactly. The sales volume continues to rise, even as profit margins begin to go down. This happens because, even though sales are increasing, competition is entering the market and the product is becoming obsolete. There may be considerable price competition as the market becomes saturated with the product. What this means is that if you want your firm to continue to be profitable, you must continue to introduce new products. You cannot be satisfied with one profitable "winner."

Another useful product tactic you can employ has to do with product differentiation. Using this product strategy, while you continue to satisfy the needs of your customers with a product similar to that offered by your competitors, you differentiate your product from theirs by its unique advantages. These advantages may be almost anything. They may have to do with the fact that your product is personalized with the buyer's name, initials, or picture and your competitor's product is not personalized. Or they may have to do with the performance of your product, your product's quality, or reliability. Whatever advantages you choose to promote, differentiating your product from that of your competition can work very effectively to increase your sales and profits.

Another product tactic you can adopt for an older product is product extension. In other words, you already have—and have had for some time—a product in the marketplace, and it has begun to go into the saturation and decline stage of the product life cycle. The product extension tactic can breathe new life into it as if it were a new product in the introduction stage.

To employ a product extension tactic, you must find some way of extending its life. One way is to find a completely new use for the product, which can mean an entirely different market. An example is Arm and Hammer baking soda. For years people used baking soda for baking only (that's what it was made for, wasn't it?), but some years ago Arm and Hammer got a fantastic idea for extending the product life cycle. The company advertised the use of baking soda to absorb odors in refrigerators. Did this extend the life of this product? You bet it did. A good example of product extension in mail order products was that done by *Moneysworth,* a successful newsletter in newspaper format published by Ralph Ginzburg. Ginzburg had a column called "The Steal of the Month." And the "steal" was usually a book published by one of the larger publishers, which Ginzburg had obtained at closeout prices because the product was in the decline stage of its life cycle. Ginzburg described the book in his column as if it were new, listing advantages that appealed to the totally new market represented by *Moneysworth.* Further, he offered these books at a tremendous discount. You can bet that Ginzburg sold lots of books through this product extension tactic. As a result, this successful formula was copied by many others.

Price Tactics. Development of a price tactic should never be overlooked in mail order, and naturally, it too goes into your marketing plan. Basically, you can price high or low or you can meet the competition's price. Pricing tactics have to be considered carefully because the price that you select has an important effect on the image of the product or service that you are offering. This image helps to determine your market and whether your product will be successful. High price is frequently called a price-skimming tactic. It is very effective because if you are first to the marketplace with your new product, you can charge high because you have no competition. As competition enters the marketplace at a lower price, you reduce your price to meet your competition and use the increased financial resources you have to expand your advertising and maintain your share of the marketplace. Or, in some cases, you can actually raise your price, positioning your product as "top of the line" over your competitor's product.

A low price is basically a penetration tactic and is usually effective when your competition is already established in the marketplace and your product isn't very different from your competitor's product. To get in and take part of your competition's business away, you must give your potential customers a reason to buy from you. One reason is low price. However, there are some problems with low price, and one of them is that if your competition has followed a skimming tactic, it now has the financial resources to turn around and do to you what I said you could do to it if you were first in the marketplace.

A "meet the competition" price is simply going in at the same price as your competition with a similar or identical product or service. If you do this you must follow a product differentiation strategy or offer something unique. Otherwise, why should customers turn from the competition and buy from you? There is no reason to when either the customer is already buying successfully from your competition, or your competition has already established a name in the marketplace. I believe this to be one of the main reasons that Joe Karbo's competitors generally have not been successful with a very similar product. Joe had already established himself in the marketplace, and at the same or a similar price, a potential customer would rather buy from the original.

I have said this to you before, and I will say it again now: *Testing is the heart of mail order.* This is especially true of price, regardless of what basic strategy you have decided to use. I introduced a price of $19.95 for a set of four books on how to write for publication. At $19.95, the product was reasonably successful. Thinking to increase the number of sales, I tested other prices, $14.95 and lower. To my amazement, I discovered that as I reduced the price, the number of sales actually went down! Wouldn't you have thought that I would sell more books at a lower price? I quickly returned to my successful $19.95 price. Sales went up again. You know what I did next. I increased the price to $24.95. But sales went down and the higher price didn't make up for these lost sales.

In analyzing these tests, I decided that the reason for the phenomenon was the fact that there were many courses in writing for publication selling for $50 or more, but none between $19.95 and $50. On the other hand, below my price of $19.95, the next competitor's price was $10 for a short booklet. I believe that at $19.95 my books were perceived as a bargain, compared with the $50 to $200 courses. However, at $14.95 or less, my product was compared with the booklet offered at $10 and it was considered a very expensive $10 item. Why wasn't $24.95 the right price? Good question! I never did figure that one out. That's another reason why testing is so important.

Promotional Tactics.   Promotional tactics include three of the four essentials for mail order discussed earlier: The product, the offer, the medium, and the creative package. Remember that the offer has to do with how you present your deal to the prospective customer. Two for $1, one for $1 and one free, one for 99¢ and the second for 1¢—all are the same deal presented in a different way. In this section you should list the different offers that you anticipate trying, along with the different prices you are going to test according to the price strategy you decided on earlier.

Magazines, television, and radio are all examples of advertising media. Which magazines, television channels, or radio stations to choose comprises the second part of medium selection. The order of selection is also part of our tactics. See Chapter 10 for more details on how to pyramid our advertising logically, greatly enhancing our chances of success.

The third part of our promotional tactics has to do with creativity, which includes the graphics and the copy we are going to use to advertise our mail order or direct mail product. At the time of developing the marketing plan, we may or may not have the graphics and copy already prepared. However, we should at least indicate the general style of graphics and copy that will be used, or, if it is a direct mail package, exactly what the elements of that direct mail package will be.

Distribution Tactics.   You may think that distribution tactics are unnecessary. We're going to distribute through mail order, aren't we? However, there are many possibilities here.

If we manufacture the product ourselves, we may send the product right from our own home. If we have bought the product wholesale, in quantity, we could do the same thing. If someone else makes the product, we could have them drop-ship for us, which means we send them the name of the customer along with the wholesale price we have agreed upon, and the manufacturer sends the product to the customer. Or maybe we don't want to sell direct to the final customer, but want to wholesale or drop-ship ourselves. Or we could sell through agents. Or we could sell through some combination of these methods. All can work to make you rich. There is no one best distribution tactic. Many mail order operators sell direct, drop-ship, and wholesale to customers all over the world; Joe Sugarman sells his electronic products direct; Joe Cossman sold millions of ant farms, imitation shrunken heads, Potato Spud Guns, and a host of other unusual products both direct to customers and by wholesaling through "middlemen." Whatever your method of distribution tactics, this is the time to think it through and document it in your marketing plan.

Control, Implementation, and Financial Plans

Section VIII of the marketing plan concerns control and implementation and your financial planning. In Figure 23.3, you will see actual forms you may use for your own marketing plan for this section. Basically, what we are doing in this section is noting every single action and task we must accomplish to introduce our new product into the marketplace and make it profitable, and what each action and task will cost, along with what we anticipate it will bring in sales. We may also include a breakeven analysis in this section, as illustrated in Chapter 22, and use some of the techniques described to calculate breakeven or profitability for a particular magazine advertisement or series of advertisements.

PROJECTED INCOME STATEMENT

Months after Starting Business

	1	2	3	4	5	6	7	8	9	10	11	12
Total net sales												
Cost of sales												
Gross profit												
Expenses (controllable)												
Salaries												
Payroll taxes												
Advertising												
Automobile												
Dues and subscriptions												
Enterainment												
Legal and accounting												
Office supplies												
Telephone												
Utilities												
Miscellaneous												
Total												
Expenses (fixed)												
Depreciation												
Insurance												
Rent												
Taxes and licenses												
Loan payments												
Total												
NET PROFIT (OR LOSS) (before taxes)												

Figure 23.3   Financial forms for your marketing plan.

Strategy Implementation Time Schedule.   Section VIII should include a *Strategy implementation time schedule.* An outline is shown in Figure 23.4. The strategy implementation time schedule is extremely important, enabling you to know when you are supposed to do what. Writing down every action and task you must do as a part of your plan will help you remember everything essential and will also act as a reminder as to when to do it. Figure 23.4 is an example only. Use the same general outline for your plan, and write down exactly which action the plan will require, month by month.

Simply initiating the plan and hoping for the best is insufficient to ensure success. As a matter of fact, due to a changing environment, such a procedure is almost certain to result in failure. Therefore, it is important to specify a means of evaluation and control even before the plan is implemented and as a part of the plan itself. For example, what will be done if

CASH FLOW PROJECTIONS

Months after Starting Business

	Start-up or prior to loan	1	2	3	4	5	6	7	8	9	10	11	12	TOTAL
Cash (beginning of month)														
Cash on hand														
Cash in bank														
Cash in investments														
Total cash														
Income (during month)														
Cash sales														
Credit sales payments														
Investment income														
Loans														
Other cash income														
Total Income														
TOTAL CASH AND INCOME														
Expenses (during month)														
Inventory or new material														
Wages (including owner's)														
Taxes														
Equipment expense														
Overhead														
Selling expense														
Transportation														
Loan repayment														
Other cash expenses														
TOTAL EXPENSES														
CASH FLOW EXCESS (end of month)														
CASH FLOW CUMULATIVE (monthly)														

Figure 23.3   (Continued)

BALANCE SHEET
(Project at Start-up and After One Year)

	YEAR 1	YEAR 2
Current assets		
Cash	$	$
Accounts receivable		
Inventory		
Fixed assets		
Real estate		
Fixtures and equipment		
Vehicles		
Other assets		
License		
Good will		
TOTAL ASSETS	$	$
Current liabilities		
Notes payable (due within 1 year)	$	$
Accounts payable		
Accrued expenses		
Taxes owed		
Long-term liabilities		
Notes payable (due after 1 year)		
Other		
TOTAL LIABILITIES	$	$
NET WORTH (ASSETS minus LIABILITIES)	$	$

TOTAL LIABILITIES plus NET WORTH should equal ASSETS

Figure 23.3   (Continued)

sales are not at the level anticipated or forecast? Will the plan be dropped? Will the plan be modified? How will it be modified? What if certain parts are profitable and others not? Or certain geographical areas profitable and others not? What will we do about new competitors entering the market or a change in an old competitor's strategy? How will these facts alter the plan and, indeed, how will these results be known and the effects of these facts be determined? Failing to anticipate an evaluation and control means is like pointing an automobile at a destination, closing your eyes, pushing the gas pedal, and crossing your fingers. The chances of arriving safely at your destination, even if it is only a short distance, are slim. Feedback is needed to measure the changes in the environment as you proceed. Then, action must be taken to allow for these changes and keep your vehicle on course to your destination. In the same fashion, changes in the environs must be anticipated and means of measuring these changes as well as variances in anticipated results and means of measuring these variances must be developed and specified in the marketing plan.

Weeks After Project Initiation

TASK	1	2	3	4	5	6	7	8	9	10	11	12	13	14	15	16	17	18	19	20	21	22	23	24	25	26	27
Prepare classified copy	↑																										
Place first ad		↑																									
Order product for test		↑																									
Prepare and order follow-on material			↑																								
Product inventory received					↑																						
Follow-on material received					↑																						
First ad appears								↑																			
Send follow-on material																											↑
Profitability forecast											↑																
Additional ads placed													↑														
Additional product inventory ordered													↑														
Additional follow-on material ordered													↑														
Product inventory received															↑												
Follow-on material received															↑												
Additional ads appear																					↑						
Send follow-on material																											↑

Figure 23.4 Strategy implementation time schedule.

Summary Section

The summary section tells your reader what you already told him, but in just a few paragraphs. It is a restatement of what you said in your executive summary. Use different words to tie everything together and "sell" your product to the reader one more time.

SUMMARY

The marketing plan is very important for your success in this business. With it, you will enhance your chances of succeeding because

1. You will have a road map to tell you exactly where to go and when you should be at each point along the road.
2. You will be able to check constantly to see how you are progressing against what you have planned to do. If there are problems, you can then take the necessary action to solve them and still proceed toward your goal.
3. When you must brief and talk to other people regarding what you are doing in your mail order business, you will be able to use your marketing plan or parts of it. In this way it will be clear in their minds how the part they play fits into your overall picture. This plan can help you get the money you need to start.

A Personal Postscript
from the Author

As I reviewed the material in this 4th edition of the book, I thought about the hundreds of different topics and techniques we've discussed. I believe that I have told you every single thing that you need to be a success in mail order. I say this based not only on my own personal experience, but also on the experience of hundreds of others who have taken my courses and attended my seminars: I have heard from my students all over the country who have followed my instructions, and I know that these instructions work and lead to success. However, to be successful in mail order, just reading this book is insufficient. You must act. You must actually start a business to reap any benefit from the information I have given you. Further, even though the information is correct and will lead to success, you will find additional secrets in mail order, secrets you cannot get from anywhere but your own experience. This means the final chapter of this book is really your own and is not contained between these covers. For it is your own adventure in mail order and the secrets and success you will gain from it. You may not become an overnight mail order millionaire, but if you start your business and lay it out according to the instructions that I have given you, whether you are part- or full-time, you can make a good profit. And you will find all sorts of other rewards. Some will be financial. Others will relate to the personal satisfaction that you are making a significant contribution to the joy and betterment of other people who are your customers. The greater service that you render to others, the greater your own rewards, financial and otherwise, will be. To this end, I wish you the tremendous good fortune and success that can be yours.

Appendix A
The Direct Marketing
Association's Guidelines for
Ethical Business Practices

DIRECT
MARKETING
ASSOCIATION
GUIDELINES
for...

Ethical

Business

Practices

dma

2

*T*he Direct Marketing Association's Guidelines for Ethical Business Practices are intended to provide individuals and organizations involved in direct mail and direct marketing with principles of conduct that are generally accepted nationally and internationally. These Guidelines reflect DMA's long-standing policy of high levels of ethics and the responsibility of the Association and direct marketers to the consumer and the community— a relationship that must be based on fair and ethical principles.

*W*hat distinguishes the Guidelines, which are self-regulatory in nature, is that all are urged to support them in spirit and not to treat their provisions as obstacles to be circumvented by legal ingenuity. The Guidelines are intended to be honored in the light of their aims and principles.

*T*hese Guidelines are also part of the DMA's general philosophy that self-regulatory measures are preferable to governmental mandates whenever possible. Self-regulatory actions are more readily adaptable to changing techniques, economic and social conditions, and they encourage widespread use of sound business practices.

*B*ecause it is believed that dishonest, misleading, immoral, salacious or offensive communications make enemies for all advertising/marketing including direct response marketing, observance of these Guidelines by all concerned is recommended.

Table of Contents

The Terms of the Offer [4]

Honesty
Article #1
All offers should be clear, honest and complete so that the consumer may know the exact nature of what is being offered, the price, the terms of payment (including all extra charges), and the commitment involved in the placing of an order. Before publication of an offer, direct marketers should be prepared to substantiate any claims or offers made. Advertisements or specific claims which are untrue, misleading, deceptive, fraudulent or unjustly disparaging of competitors should not be used.

Clarity
Article #2
A simple statement of all the essential points of the offer should be clearly displayed in the promotional material. When an offer illustrates goods which are not included or cost extra, these facts should be made clear.

Print Size
Article #3
Print which by its small size, placement or other visual characteristics is likely to substantially affect the legibility of the offer, or exceptions to it should not be used.

Actual Conditions
Article #4
All descriptions and promises should be in accordance with actual conditions, situations and circumstances existing at the time of the promotion. Claims regarding any limitations (such as time or quantity) should be legitimate.

Disparagement
Article #5
Disparagement of any person or group on grounds of race, color, religion, national origin, sex, marital status or age is unacceptable.

5

Standards
Article #6
Solicitations should not contain vulgar, immoral, profane, or offensive matter nor promote the sale of pornographic material or other matter not acceptable for advertising on moral grounds.

Advertising to Children
Article #7
Offers suitable for adults only should not be made to children.

Photographs and Art Work
Article #8
Photographs, illustrations, artwork, and the situations they represent, should be accurate portrayals and current reproductions of the product, service, or other subject in all particulars.

Sponsor and Intent
Article #9
All direct marketing contacts should disclose the name of the sponsor and each purpose of the contact. No one should make offers or solicitations in the guise of research or a survey when the real intent is to sell products or services or to raise funds.

Identity of Seller
Article #10
Every offer and shipment should sufficiently identify the full name and street address of the direct marketer so that the consumer may contact the individual or company by mail or phone.

Solicitation in the Guise of an Invoice
Article #11
Offers that are likely to be mistaken for bills or invoices should not be used.

Postage and Handling Charges
Article #12
Postage or shipping charges and handling charges, if any, should reflect as accurately as practicable actual costs incurred.

Special Offers

6

Use of the Word "Free" and other Similar Representations
Article #13

A product or service which is offered without cost or obligation to the recipient may be unqualifiedly described as "free".

If a product or service is offered as "free", for a nominal cost or at a greatly reduced price and the offer requires the recipient to purchase some other product or service, all terms and conditions should be clearly and conspicuously disclosed and in close conjunction with the use of the term "free" or other similar phrase.

When the term "free" or other similar representations are made (for example, 2-for-1, half price or 1-cent offers), the product or service required to be purchased should not be increased in price or decreased in quality or quantity.

Negative Option Selling
Article #14

All direct marketers should comply with the FTC regulation governing Negative Option Plans. Some of the major requirements of this regulation are listed below:

Offers which require the consumer to return a notice sent by the seller before each periodic shipment to avoid receiving merchandise should contain all important conditions of the plan including:

a. A full description of the obligation to purchase a minimum number of items and all the charges involved and,

b. the procedures by which the consumer receives the announcements of selections and a statement of their frequency; how the consumer rejects unwanted items and how to cancel after completing the obligation.

7
Negative Option Selling (Continued)

The consumer should be given advance notice of the periodic selection so that the consumer may have a minimum of ten days to exercise a timely choice.

Because of the nature of this kind of offer, special attention should be given to the clarity, completeness and prominent placement of the terms in the initial offering.

Sweepstakes
Article #15
All direct marketers should abide by the DMA Guidelines for Self-Regulation of Sweepstakes Promotions. Articles #16 through #18 (below) contain the basic precepts of these Guidelines.

Clear and Conspicuous Disclosure of Rules
Article #16
All terms and conditions of the sweepstakes, including entry procedures, the number and types of prizes, the closing dates, eligibility requirements, and the fact that no purchase is required should be disclosed in a clear and conspicuous manner in the promotion.

Devices, check boxes, reply envelopes and the like used for entering the sweepstakes only should be as conspicuous as those utilized for ordering the product or service and entering the sweepstakes.

Prizes
Article #17
All prizes advertised should be awarded. Winners should be selected in a manner that ensures fair application of the laws of chance.

Chances of Winning
Article #18
No sweepstakes promotion, or any of its parts, should state or imply that a recipient has won a prize or overstate the chances of winning.

Price Comparisons [8]
Article #19
Price comparisons may be made in two ways:
a. between one's price and a former, future or suggested price or
b. between one's price and the price of a competitor's comparable product.

In all price comparisons, the compared price against which the comparison is made must be fair and accurate.

In each case of comparison to a former, suggested or competitor's comparable product price, substantial sales should have been made at that price in the recent past.

For comparisons with a future price, there should be a reasonable expectation that the future price will be charged in the foreseeable future.

Guarantees
Article #20
If a product or service is offered with a "guarantee" or a "warranty", the terms and conditions should either be set forth in full in the promotion, or the promotion should state how the consumer may obtain a copy. The guarantee should clearly state the name and address of the guarantor and the duration of the guarantee.

Any requests for repair, replacement or refund under the terms of a "guarantee" or "warranty" should be honored promptly. In an unqualified offer of refund, repair or replacement, the customer's preference shall prevail.

Special Claims

Use of Test or Survey Data
Article #21
All test or survey data referred to in advertising should be competent and reliable as to source and methodology, and should support the specific claim for which it is cited. Advertising claims should not distort the test or survey results nor take them out of context.

Testimonials and Endorsements[9]
Article #22
Testimonials and endorsements should be used only if they are:
  a. Authorized by the person quoted,
  b. Genuine and related to the experience of the person giving them and
  c. Not taken out of context so as to distort the endorser's opinion or experience with the product.

The Product _____

Product Safety
Article #23
Products should be safe in normal use and be free of defects likely to cause injury. To that end, they should meet or exceed current, recognized health and safety norms and be adequately tested, where applicable. Information provided with the product should include proper directions for use and full instructions covering assembly and safety warnings, whenever necessary.

Product Distribution Safety
Article #24
Products should be distributed only in a manner that will provide reasonable safeguards against possibilities of injury.

Product Availability
Article #25
Direct marketers should only offer merchandise when it is on hand or when there is a reasonable expectation of its receipt.

Direct marketers should not engage in dry testing unless the special nature of that offer is disclosed in the promotion.

Fulfillment [10]

Unordered Merchandise
Article #26
Merchandise should not be shipped without having first received a customer's permission. The exceptions are samples or gifts clearly marked as such, and merchandise mailed by a charitable organization soliciting contributions, as long as all items are sent with a clear and conspicuous statement informing the recipient of an unqualified right to treat the product as a gift and to do with it as the recipient sees fit, at no cost or obligation to the recipient.

Shipments
Article #27
Direct marketers are reminded that they should abide by the FTC regulation regarding the prompt shipment of prepaid merchandise, the Mail Order Merchandise (30 Day) Rule.

Beyond this regulation, direct marketers are urged to ship all orders as soon as possible.

Credit and Debt Collection

Equal Credit Opportunity
Article #28
A creditor should not discriminate on the basis of race, color, religion, national origin, sex, marital status or age. If the individual is rejected for credit, the creditor should be prepared to give reasons why.

Debt Collection
Article #29
Unfair, misleading, deceptive or abusive methods should not be used for collecting money. The direct marketer should take reasonable steps to assure that those collecting on the direct marketer's behalf comply with this guideline.

Use of ¹¹ Mailing Lists _____

List Rental Practices
Article #30
Every list owner who sells, exchanges, or rents lists should see to it that each individual on the list is informed of those practices, and should offer an option to have the individual's name deleted when rentals or purchases are made.

The list owner should remove names from its lists when requested directly by the individual, and by use of the DMA Mail Preference Service name removal list.

List brokers and managers should take reasonable steps to assure that list owners and compilers follow these list practices.

Personal Information
Article #31
All list owners, brokers, managers, compilers, and users should be protective of the consumer's right to privacy and sensitive to the information collected on lists and subsequently considered for transfer, rental, sale, or exchange.

Information such as, but not limited to, medical financial, insurance or court data, and data that may be considered to be personal and intimate in nature by all reasonable standards, should not be included on lists that are made available for transfer, rental, sale or exchange when there is a reasonable expectation by the consumer that the information would be kept confidential.

Mailing lists should not be transferred or used except for marketing purposes.

Any advertising or promotion for lists being offered for transfer, rental, sale or exchange

12

should reflect a sensitivity for the individual on those lists. Promotional methods and language that tend to portray or characterize those individuals in a disparaging way should be avoided.

List Usage Agreements
Article #32
List owners, brokers, compilers and users should make every attempt to establish the exact nature of the list's intended usage prior to the sale or rental of the list. Owners, brokers and compilers should not permit the sale or rental of their lists for an offer that is in violation of any of the Ethical Guidelines of DMA. Promotions should be directed to those segments of the public most likely to be interested in their causes or to have a use for their products or services.

List Abuse
Article #33
No list or list data should be used in violation of the lawful rights of the list owner nor of the agreement between the parties; any such misuse should be brought to the attention of the lawful owner.

Telephone Marketing

(See Articles #9 and #27)
Reasonable Hours
Article #34
All telephone contacts should be made during reasonable hours.

Disclosure and Tactics
Article #35
All telephone solicitations should disclose to the buyer during the conversation the cost of the merchandise, all terms, conditions and the

13
payment plan and whether there will be postage and handling charges. At no time should "high pressure" tactics be utilized.

Use of Automatic Electronic Equipment
Article #36
No telephone marketer should solicit sales using automatic electronic dialing equipment unless the telephone immediately disconnects when the called person hangs up.

Taping of Conversations
Article #37
Taping of telephone conversations should not be conducted without all-party consent or the use of a beeping device.

Telephone Name Removal/ Restricted Contacts
Article #38
Telephone marketers should remove the name of any contact from their telephone lists when requested to do so.

Telephone marketers should not call telephone subscribers who have unlisted or unpublished telephone numbers unless a prior relationship exists.

Fund Raising

(See Article #26)
Commission Prohibition/ Authenticity of Organization
Article #39
Fund raisers should make no percentage or commission arrangements whereby any person

14
or firm assisting or participating in a fund raising activity is paid a fee proportionate to the
funds raised, nor should they solicit for non-
functioning organizations.

Laws, Codes, and Regulations
Article #40

Direct marketers should operate in accordance
with the Better Business Bureau's Code of
Advertising and be cognizant of and adhere
to laws and regulations of the United States
Postal Service, the Federal Trade Commission, the Federal Reserve Board, and other
applicable Federal, state and local laws governing advertising, marketing practices, and
the transaction of business by mail, telephone, and the print and broadcast media.

*   *   *

DMA Ethics Department

¹⁵

In its continuing efforts to improve the public confidence in direct mail and direct marketing, DMA sponsors several activities in its Ethics Department.

Ethical Guidelines are maintained, updated periodically and distributed to the field.

A Committee on Ethical Business Practices monitors the mails and direct offerings to the consumer and investigates complaints brought to its attention.

An Ethics Policy Committee initiates programs and projects directed toward improved ethical activity in the direct marketing area.

MOAL (Mail Order Action Line) handles consumer mail order complaints, MPS (Mail Preference Service) offers mail flow reduction to consumers, and TPS (Telephone Preference Service) offers to reduce the number of national commercial telemarketing calls consumers receive.

All ethics activities are directed by a full-time Director of Ethical Practices.

For additional information or to report questionable practices contact:

Director, Ethics and Consumer Affairs
Direct Marketing Association, Inc.
1101 17th St. N.W., Suite 900
Washington, D.C. 20036

Members of DMA proudly display this symbol and slogan:

"Look for this symbol when you buy direct."

Appendix B
A Potpourri of
Mail Order Ideas
and Techniques

Mail order has to be a highly innovative business to succeed. Almost every day new opportunities are born and presented to the prospective mail order entrepreneur. This appendix illustrates some unusual ideas and techniques you can use to build big profits in your mail order business.

ALERTING YOUR CUSTOMERS OF UPCOMING
IMPORTANT MAIL WITH A POSTCARD

One technique that can greatly increase your response over what you might normally get is to alert your customers of upcoming important mail with a postcard. An example is shown in Figure B.1, a *Readers' Digest* postcard announcing an upcoming sweepstakes. The advantage of this system is that the card is more likely to be read than the contents of an envelope that must be ripped open. If your customer can be presold with the postcard, he or she will be looking for the envelope containing your material when it comes. The bottom line is that your response will be increased. Of course, the cost is greater. You must discover through testing whether the additional profits are worth the additional expense or not.

I received a postcard, and then a letter, and finally a full package—all to offer me information about a 900 telephone service. That mailing was pretty creative, so let's take a look at it. First came the postcard in

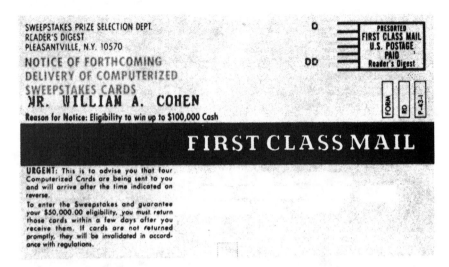

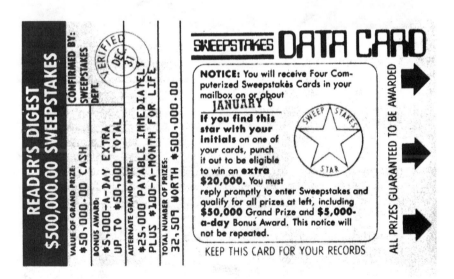

Figure B.1   The Reader's Digest sweepstakes alert card: personalized front and back.

Figure B.2. (Have you ever heard of Weedo, Kentucky?) Two days later, I received the letter in Figure B.3. The envelope bore the same seal as the letter. Several days later, I received a large envelope. The envelope read "28,000,000 reasons not to go to Weedo, Kentucky." Inside was a letter from Pacific Bell (Figure B.4) plus a brochure describing the 900 service

Weedo, Kentucky – Bigger than Jessup

Weedo, Kentucky is a great place to visit, but none of your customers live there. So if, like a lot of smart companies, you're thinking of boosting your bottom line with a 900 service, why pay for places that won't pay you back?

Your business is in California. So are your customers. And a 900 number is the most profitable way to keep in touch with them. Unfortunately, with today's services, you're forced to pay for national coverage you don't need. As they say in Weedo: "You shouldn't have to buy the whole cow, just to get the filet."

So why doesn't somebody offer a 900 service devoted exclusively to the California market?

Jumbo Card

Mr. William A. Cohen
Global Associates

Figure B.2   Postcard from Weedo, Kentucky: front and back.

Dear William Cohen,

    I am writing you on behalf of my town, Weedo, of which I am the mayor and have been since Pa died. And I've been working on a plan to modernize our fair city which I call "The Emmett T. Wiggins Modernization Plan." I want to make Weedo the pearl of southwestern Kentucky and much better than Jessup, no matter what that Hank Jessup says.

    Anyway, that's why I was strutting like a bandy rooster when some California businesses, like yours, started offering some of them lucrative pay-per-call 900 programs here. But, if you don't mind my saying so, you're going about this thing all wrong. Now you and I both know a 900 number is the hot trend in business. It suits your customer service needs and gives you great new promotion opportunities -- basically, it's just a real fine way to bring your goods to market and boost your bottom line.

    But you got to offer programs we're going to be interested in. Nobody in Weedo wants to transfer funds to a bank in Fresno or hear about a sweepstakes in Frisco. So I figured maybe you just didn't know what we'd like.

<u>Stuff Weedonians would like</u>

1. Hog hotline
2. Worm and nightcrawler updates
3. Quilting tips
4. Talk with a guy who knew Elvis
5. Cooking with crawdad

    I mean if you have a 900 program that's only going to appeal to folks in California, why are you paying for national coverage? If you're going to do that, you should just offer your program in California and save yourself a passel of money. But I guess they don't have a 900 service just for California. Or do they?

                             Busily modernizing,

                             Emmett T. Wiggins
                             Mayor

P.S. I didn't mention that, contrary to what the Census says, we have 72 people, not 65. And (here's the clincher) 20 of them have phones. Enough said.

Mayor Emmett T. Wiggins, R.F.D. 4, Weedo, Kentucky 42088

Figure B.3   Letter from "the mayor" of Weedo, Kentucky.

2600 Camino Ramon, Room 4W250
San Ramon, CA 94583

PACIFIC ✪ BELL.

A Pacific Telesis Company

Dear William Cohen:

The role of telecommunications in advertising and promotions is rapidly expanding. In fact, the advent of pay-per-call phone services means a whole new way to reach your market. Along with a whole new way to do business.

The problem?

With today's services, you have to pay a lot of money, for a lot of coverage you don't need. Californians are your target audience -- all 28 million of them. But you're stuck footing the bill for Weedo. And Wysalia. And Worm Hollow.

No longer. Now there's Pacific Bell California 900, the first service devoted entirely to the California market. In the glut of mass advertising, California 900 fulfills your need to efficiently reach your customers. And in a business of near misses, it means quick and quantifiable hits.

In other words, we give you the exact market coverage you need, at a price you can afford.

Set up a statewide product promotion virtually overnight. Add a 900 number to your print campaigns for self-liquidating advertising. Create a telephone-based contest that will keep your customers coming back for more. Or install a 24-hour service line that won't drain your bottom line. No matter what your product or service, California 900 can work for you.

And at Pacific Bell, we don't just provide the technology, we work in concert with you on your 900 program. We take care of all the billing. We help you design your promotions. We even offer our own voice response service, Pacific Bell California Call Management. We make it simple. And we make it work.

See how with our free California 900 video and information kit. Just mail the enclosed reply card or call the California 900 Development Team toll free at 811-1900, Ext. 187. Outside the toll free area, call collect at 1-415-823-1900, Ext. 187.

Sincerely,

Susan Higbee
Executive Director Sales/Service

P. S. The California 900 videotape offers an entertaining glimpse into the future of pay-per-call services, and how they are changing the way Californians live and work. Call for your free copy. Toll free: 811-1900, Ext. 187. Outside of the toll free area, call collect: 1-415-823-1900, Ext. 187.

Figure B.4   The letter from Pacific Bell.

and the response card in Figure B.5. However, even this wasn't the end. A package came. The outside read "Afraid of losing your shirt on 900 service to Weedo?" Inside was more information on the 900 service . . . and a t-shirt. Emblazoned on it was the caption "My old 900 service went to Weedo, Kentucky and all I got was this lousy t-shirt."

Note how a nonexistent town was used to capture my interest, prepare me for information about the offering, and tie the whole thing together. Sure the campaign was expensive. But in this case, it was worth the investment because of the payout if the prospect signed up. You can bet the response rate was high.

SELLING YOUR PRODUCT WITH POSTCARDS

It is also possible that you can sell products by postcard. Now, you don't have much room to sell on a postcard, so you must use the space you have very cleverly. Certain products and services that require long descriptions cannot be sold this way. But some lend themselves to this type of promotion, and, as is shown in Figure B.6, it can be done very effectively and inexpensively. In the promotion in the figure, the company, S.C. Patents, has indicated that there have been 14 patents issued after mine that the U.S. Patent Office has classified as being identical to my patent. Naturally, most inventors will want to know whether their patents dominate those issued after theirs. Why? Because if so, they could collect a royalty. So the company offers to send a copy of each later patent classified with my patent at a cost of $35, plus $1 for each patent copy. This simple copy on this inexpensive postcard brings a very high rate of response. Another example of this technique is shown in Figure B.7, which advertises a business opportunity.

YOU MAY HAVE A PRODUCT YOU CAN DROP-SHIP TO OTHER DEALERS, OR DROP-SHIP FOR THEM

You may have a product you can sell not only directly to your ultimate customer, but also at a discount to other mail order dealers, and allow them to sell—actually, compete—with you. This isn't as farfetched an idea as it may sound and it allows for greatly increased distribution. One company that does this is Wilshire Book Company. Figure B.8 is a letter Melvin Powers has sent out showing the discount for his books and describing circulars advertising his many book titles through which other mail order dealers can sell his products. As I advised earlier, it is not wise to sell products under these conditions unless you have a catalog or you have other products in your product line that you control. Someone then offers your

500

Appendix B

CALIFORNIA, HERE I COME.
WITH CALIFORNIA 900
AND A FREE VIDEO FROM PACIFIC BELL.

Pacific Bell wants to make sure you don't wind up in Weedo, Kentucky. That's why we developed *California 900.* It's the one 900 service exclusively dedicated to the 28 million consumers of the California market.

And we'd like to show you just how it works, with our free video, *"California 900: Applications for the Information Age."* This VHS-format tape illustrates how consumers are taking advantage of the convenience and timeliness of pay-per-call services. And how companies like yours are cashing in on the information economy.

Plus, we'll send you our *California 900*

information kit, with all the details on setting up your own targeted 900 service. So if your company's interested in realizing new profits and improving customer service, just drop this card in the mail. Or give us a call.

Call toll free at 811-1900, Ext. 187, or collect at 1-415-823-1900, Ext. 187.

☐ **Please send me my complimentary video and information kit.**

Name

Company

Address

City   State   Zip

☐ **Please have a Pacific Bell Account Executive contact me.**

(   )   AM   PM
Phone   Best time to call

A PACIFIC TELESIS COMPANY   **PACIFIC ✪ BELL.**
© 1989 Pacific Bell   Information Services

Figure B.5   Response card on the Weedo campaign.

||.|¹·¹·¹¹||||¹¹¹·¹·¹¹¹·¹¹·¹|¹·¹¹¹·¹·¹|¹·¹¹·¹·¹·|.|.¹·¹||

Pacific Bell Response Center
(Room 4W200)
P.O. Box 5145
San Ramon, CA 94583-9910

POSTAGE WILL BE PAID BY ADDRESSEE

BUSINESS REPLY MAIL
FIRST CLASS   PERMIT NO. 1654   SAN FRANCISCO, CA

NO POSTAGE
NECESSARY
IF MAILED
IN THE
UNITED STATES

Wish you weren't here?

A PACIFIC TELESIS COMPANY / / **▮▮▮▮▮**━━━━━━━━━━━ **PACIFIC✪BELL**.
Information Services

Figure B.5   (Continued) Reverse side of Weedo campaign response card.

DATA BASE EXPANSION NOTICE

An expanded computer search of your Patent No. 3803639
shows that there are ____14____ patent(s), issued after your patent, that the
U.S. Patent Office has classified identically with your patent (same class and
subclass).

You will undoubtedly want to know:
1. Whether your patent dominates the later issued patent(s); and
2. Any state of the art advances shown by the later patent(s).

We will send you a copy of each later patent identically classified with
your patent at a cost of $35.00 plus $1.00 for each patent copy if you will
return this card with your remittance of $ ____49.00____ to:

SC Patents, Inc.
P.O. Box 2327
2001 Jeff Davis Hwy. (Suite 1012)
Arlington, VA 22202

We automatically refund $1.00
for each later patent that is
your own. Full refund if all
later patents are your own

703-979-7232

SCP-34

Figure B.6   Patent update service sold by postcard.

Dear Homebased Entrepreneur,

Earn $4,000.00 per month part-time with a
computer and still retain the security of your
present position.

You do not need to own, or know how to
run a computer - we will provide free training.

Free cassettes and literature explain details.
Call Toll Free: 1-800-343-8014, ext. 1734.

Computer Business Services   CBSI Plaza   Sheridan, IN 46069

Figure B.7   A postcard advertising a business opportunity.

Melvin Powers

Wilshire Book Company

12015 Sherman Road, No. Hollywood, California 91605

(213) 875-1711
(213) 983-1105

YOU CAN MAKE MONEY SELLING QUALITY PAPERBACK BOOKS BY MAIL
I HAVE FOR 25 YEARS AND I'M WILLING TO SHARE MY SECRETS

Yes, you can do just that by using our book circulars. We'll sell you
these circulars at reasonable prices and ship them postpaid. Examine
the titles--books for every reading taste.

YOU GET A WHOPPING 50% OFF THE PRICES SHOWN IN THE CIRCULARS

Enclose these inserts with your direct mail solicitations, with your
orders and with all your outgoing mail. Then sit back and watch the
orders pour in.

ORDERS DROP-SHIPPED SAME DAY RECEIVED

As the orders come in, send us your addressed labels, your remittance,
and indicate on the back of each label the names of the books to be
shipped. We'll process your order the same day we receive it. Or we're
willing to sell you the books and you do your own shipping. In either
case, our discount is 50%. Send us the postage you receive.

SAVE MONEY WITH UNIMPRINTED CIRCULARS -- INCREDIBLY LOW COST

Set the wheels in motion. Order these circulars, including your
remittance. Circulars will be sent immediately. Simply stamp your
name and address in the blank space.

HOW TO WRITE A HIT SONG MAILER	$10 per 1,000 postpaid
HOW TO WRITE A HIT SONG MAILER	$1 per 100 postpaid
JOIN THE WINNERS' CIRCLE MAILER	$10 per 1,000 postpaid
JOIN THE WINNERS' CIRCLE MAILER	$1 per 100 postpaid
MAGIC MAILER - selling 23 books	$10 per 1,000 postpaid
MAGIC MAILER - selling 23 books	$1 per 100 postpaid
SELF-IMPROVEMENT MAILER - selling 333 books	$30 per 1,000 postpaid
SELF-IMPROVEMENT MAILER - selling 333 books	$3 per 100 postpaid

ACT TODAY FOR TOMORROW'S PROFITS

This could be one of the best investments you'll ever make. I'm pleased
to discuss your individual mail order needs and I welcome the opportunity
to meet you if you are in the Los Angeles area. This is my 25th year
servicing mail order companies. I'm as close as your telephone and I'm
available for consultation. I will answer your letters promptly.

WILSHIRE BOOK COMPANY

Melvin Powers

Melvin Powers, President

Figure B.8   Wilshire Book Company circular selling to other mail order dealers.

products as an adjunct to his or her product line. Other than that, the dealers offering your products can't make a profit because of the smaller size of the market and an insufficient markup. However, if the dealer is already selling by mail, it does make sense to sell a product such as Melvin's, and it will make sense also for other dealers to sell many of your products. You do this by promoting your product to them. Many will be delighted to include your product in their product line, and both of you will profit.

SELL YOUR PRODUCT AT LOW COST BY SHARING THE COST WITH OTHER ADVERTISERS

Another great new idea is cooperative mailing, which means that a direct mail advertisement going to a prospective customer contains not only promotional materials from you, but also those from other mail order dealers. The advantages of this system are several. First, you share the cost of using the mailing list. Second, you share the tremendous cost of postage. Third, you probably reduce your printing costs. Figures B.9, B.10, and B.11 are examples from a package of postcards in which one side is the advertisement and the other side is a self-addressed, stamped indicia, enabling the potential customer to fill the card out and send it to the dealer. These cards either are bound together or come in booklet form so that one customer may see 50, 100, or more cards all at one time, all from different advertisers. Your potential customers, who have been selected because of certain factors they have in common and a probable interest in your product, go through the

Figure B.9   Example of a product sold in a deck of postcards.

JVC LICENSED AND APPROVED
DUPLICATED VHS TAPES — THE BEST THERE IS

	The Finest Broadcast Quality Custom Duplicated VHS Tapes		Super VHS Quality Custom Loaded SVHS Bulk Tapes	
	Stock #	Price	Stock #	Price
ALL TAPES 100% GUARANTEED	T-010	1.25	SVHS T-010	2.50
	T-015	1.35	SVHS T-015	2.95
- All A Grade	T-030	1.65	SVHS T-030	3.15
- All Broadcast Quality	T-045	1.90	SVHS T-045	3.38
- All 100%	T-060	2.20	SVHS T-060	3.51
Guaranteed	T-090	2.85	SVSS T-090	3.88
- JVC Licensed	T-120	3.45	SVHS T-120	4.20
	MINIMUM ORDER 50 PCS.			MINIMUM ORDER 50 PCS.

FREE CATALOG

CALL TOLL-FREE:
1-800-881-6191 (FL) Tapes
1-800-899-5059 (MN) Unlimited

Figure B.10   Example of a product sold in a deck of postcards.

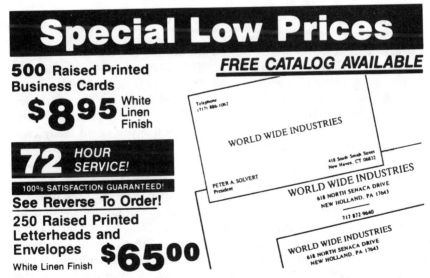

Special Low Prices

500 Raised Printed Business Cards

$8⁹⁵ White Linen Finish

FREE CATALOG AVAILABLE

72 HOUR SERVICE!

100% SATISFACTION GUARANTEED!

See Reverse To Order!

250 Raised Printed Letterheads and Envelopes $65⁰⁰

White Linen Finish

Telephone (717) 886-1067

WORLD WIDE INDUSTRIES

418 South Smith Street New Haven, CT 06832

PETER A. SOLVERT President

WORLD WIDE INDUSTRIES

618 NORTH SENACA DRIVE NEW HOLLAND, PA 17643

717 872 9640

WORLD WIDE INDUSTRIES

618 NORTH SENACA DRIVE NEW HOLLAND, PA 17643

Figure B.11   Example of a product sold in a deck of postcards.

entire list and fill out response cards to those advertisements they find interesting. There are many different kinds of mailings of this type, and to
recommend specific advertisers, let me again remind you of SRDS. Look
in the *Direct Response* section of their business publications volume and
check for cooperative mailings. As with magazines or newspapers, one factor of the cost is going to be the circulation. Picking the right cooperative
mailing is just as easy. If you have a product that appeals to doctors, look
for a cooperative mailing that goes to doctors.

PEOPLE MAY READ YOUR LETTER
IF YOU TELL THEM NOT TO

Here's an innovative way to get your customers to read your follow-up letters. Look at Figure B.12. This is a follow-up letter for a Mellinger promotion. Note that more than half the front page of the letter has been
X'ed out, and above it is printed in block letters, "Don't bother to read
this letter. Just let me lend you a copy of the *Complete Mellinger Guide to
Mail Order Money-Making.*" And yes, sure enough, many potential customers will read every single word, and then turn over the second page,
which isn't crossed out at all, and read that too. This type of promotion
uses a psychological principle of great power. So, make a big X that draws
attention to the copy over it, and then tell your customer not to read. He
or she will probably disregard your instructions.

DO THE UNUSUAL AND THINK CREATIVELY

In mail order, creativity and doing the unusual pay off. I'm going to show
you several good examples here of what I'm talking about.

The first example is in Figure B.13. It appears to be a ripped-off portion of a newspaper, and in the upper left-hand corner are the words, apparently written in ink, "Hi, I thought of you while I read this book.
There are some incredible ideas in it a person like you could really capi-
talize on." And then there's an initial—"J." Well, the only article that
you can read in the "ripped newspaper" is a review, entitled, "Ideas and
Products That Are Making a Bundle," of a book, *Hottest New Business
Ideas,* by Chase Revel. This really isn't a newspaper. In fact, the paper itself is of higher quality than you might have thought. One of the individuals who developed this promotion device with Chase Revel said that one
of the problems was to make the ragged edges of the die so that it would
appear to be ripped from a newspaper. You can bet that an unusual promotion like this makes money. By the way, if you look at the reverse side

Don't bother to read this letter.

Just let me LEND you a copy of

the complete Mellinger Guide

to Mail Order Money Making.

Dear Friend:

Since you're paying no attention to my first suggestion, maybe I can get you to act on the second one.

I'm not going to give my Guide to you. I'm not going to sell it to you. I'm not going to cut the price to induce you to buy it.

You take a full week to read it. But it won't take that long because some people who started reading it were so impressed with the profits they could make that they finished it in one night. It's that good!

You'll be fascinated with the ease in starting a money-making business in spare time at home. You will see how I give you access to new mail-order products--how they can be drop shipped (which means no investment in merchandise)--where to advertise--even how to get FREE ADS in magazines.

Also, the very exclusive feature of your membership in Mail Order Exchange is explained--how it gives you 14 actual samples of products that sell by mail--how its monthly Trade Bulletins provide names and addresses of suppliers with the products that they offer, new postal regulations to keep you abreast of changes and stories about successful M.O.E. Members.

The Guide and my full year's consultation service are based upon my better than 30 years first hand experience in over $20 Million, mail order sales. Could you ask for more competent advice?

The idea for "Guide Borrowing" is the result of reports of many M.O.E. members who loaned their Guides to friends. They too wanted Guides for their own use. And, speaking of friends, after you look over everything that I send you, talk it over with your family or business advisors. Get

(please read other side)

(continued)

Figure B.12 A unique way to get your letter read: Tell the customer not to read it!

- 2 -

the benefit of their opinions. Then you can make your decision. If you
decide to keep the Guide and enter the profitable mail order business, you
can depend upon my full support to make you a big success.

If you decide that my plan is not for you, return the Guide within
seven days after you receive it--just as you would return anything else
that you would borrow and the loan of the Guide won't cost you a cent!

Let me repeat that I don't want you to buy my Guide. I don't want you
to send me a $10.00 deposit. I just want you to borrow my Guide for a week
on this liberal proposition. Send me a deposit of only $5. I'll trust you
for the entire worth of the Guide if you will trust me.

Michael Braverman and I had this mutual trust and here is what this
22 year old man reported after he had my Guide less than six months:

    His product was a desk lighter that sold for $5.88.
    Acting upon our advice, he received much free adver-
    tising. First month's sales $3,117.00 and 400 cash
    customers. For the following 12 months he expected
    his earnings to be $30,000.00.

Please do not think that I promise that you will make $30,000 during
the first year. All I promise now is to send you the complete Guide postpaid upon receipt of your deposit. And, if you don't see greater money
making possibilities in mail order than what you are doing, fire the Guide
back--our check for your deposit will go in the next mail to you.

So, use the enclosed "Guide Borrowing Request". Fill it in and mail
it to me with your deposit in the enclosed postage paid envelope. Do it
while this offer is open and give yourself a look into the inner plans of
a business that is making fortunes for many others.

Sincerely,

BLM   :C2   President

Figure B.12   (Continued)

in Figure B.13, you will see the extent to which the illusion has been carried. Even "daily stock prices" are listed!

Figure B.14 is from another outstanding promotion, created by Eric
Weinstein, president of Revelco, Inc., a list broker and manager. You will
see that this promotion appears to be on lined notebook paper, and it's
typed in a very strange fashion. You will see hundreds of mistakes in these
two short paragraphs. And the bottom line is this—the writer says, "Please
pardon all the mistakes, but I've just put up a brand new list and it's so hot
I figured you'd rather get the jump on it and hear about it quickly than
wait for a printer to get out a fancy promotion. This list is so hot it's burning out the tape drives in our computer. It's a dynamic business buyers' list
and here are the particulars. All are paid-up, credit-approved buyers of

...cluding ...rgy, educati... ...ment. Howe often employs a comparative ap-proach in discussing issues such as foreign trad... ...omic organization, and allocation of ...rces (drawing comparisons with such w...ely divergent examples as the United States and ...angladesh to illustrate his points), and h...... the many paradoxes of China's economy, such as the fact that American ex-

...rt of Chin... equivalents, the official text (translated) o... Tse-tung's now famous tract "On the Ten Ma-jor Relationships," and, most valuable of all, a discussion entitled "How to find out about and keep up with economic developments in China." What could be more sensible?

Ideas and products that are making a bundle

HOTTEST NEW BUSINESS IDEAS, by Chase Revel. BaronBrook Publishing Company, $9.95.

BY MICHAEL JOHNSON

Imagine a roach ranch whose owner grows roa-ches for chicken feed; a company that pays 50 cents a pound for vacuum cleaner dust and can't get enough; another records latest best-seller books on tape cassettes for people who don't have time to read, and has so much business that deliveries are a month behind; a new plastic ice that makes hot-weather ice skating possible any-where without expensive refrigeration; a powder developed from kidney beans that reduces calorie intake by 80 percent when sprinkled on any food; and an expensive mechanism that allows you to start your car from your bedroom for a cold-weather warm-up. That's just a few of 258 re-freshing ideas in the most fascinating business book I've reviewed in years.

Entitled "Hottest New Business Ideas," it was written by the nation's foremost authority on small business, Chase R. Revel. Revel's back-ground is almost as interesting as the book. A millionaire several times over from 18 small busi-nesses he created, Revel publishes the only maga-zine devoted to small business, *Entrepreneur.* He recently signed a contract to write a syndicated column in 150 major newspapers.

Revel used the giant research department of his magazine to collect the information on these unusual ideas and products from around the world. The book is written in a breezy, no-non-sense, easy-to-read style. Each page brings forth more amazement that the previous. Some of the ideas sound crazy and many people started their business on a whim and with little cash. Numer-ous ones operate out of their homes, and already a few are millionaires from their ideas.

The factor I found most thought-provoking is that most of the ideas in the book seemed like they would work in almost any city.

For example, a "No-Alcohol Bar" for non-drinkers; fence rental for building contractors to prevent pilferage from new building sites; a video taping service for real estate brokers so buyers don't have to drive around wasting the sales-man's time; a new but simple machine that makes an authentic charcoal sketch of anyone in only 2½ minutes; records that sing to your child using his *own* name; a midwestern lady that takes craft supplies to nursing and convalescent homes and nets $600 a week from her route; a Florida man with a display of stuffed sharks like the one in JAWS which he opens at fairs and malls and takes in $500 to $1,000 a day; and a pilot who buys hand-made sailboats in Taiwan to ship them back to the U.S. to sell at four to five times what he paid.

Also included for those of us who have ideas for products is a name and address source of 200 Japanese manufacturers who will create or dupli-cate practically any product at way below U.S. wholesale prices.

I mentioned only the ideas that intrigued me. You'll probably find many others out of the 258 that will stimulate you. Unfortunately, the pub-lisher specializes in technical books and doesn't have a bookstore distribution system. However, you can order "Hottest New Business Ideas" by Chase Revel, $9.95 postpaid direct from the pub-lisher: BaronBrook Publishing Company, 631 Wilshire Boulevard, Dept. 2021, Santa Monica, California 90401.

By the way, the author is slated to appear soon on the Mike Douglas and Dinah Shore TV shows with this unusual book.

(left column, partially obscured) ...ector is A flirtation begins ...ts. There are promises support. The conspiracy odd ... of chafing under ...e and ... macho. The ... extinguish Trujillo o... ...ine his regime will ... of the Goat is... Invent the ...ation ho... ...waf...ng general ...tary Pupo Roman... n the pl.t. (It is ...ough, however, to ...ually murdere... ...ough he is related to ...jillo family). ...old Caribbean hand ... ...n Ciudad T... ...after the nation ...d able t... ...erve it ...ence ...tails the conspira... ...mentum for the ... to stop it, hough the K... administration ...onin... The CIA contrib...on: ...e ...f. He reconstr...t... ...nning ac-hed under the ey... the SIM (secret ...e r... ...ray with the h... ...armed ...his driver, the ...... period of and the ...ligious ...tribution of ...s... and entirely v... ...s are caught... ...mili... ...d friends ...uelly in SIM... ...any die. One old served his... ...flesh for d...... ...the assass...s go...do...shooting ...the ...ers ...red later at a ...party ...lo play... of the ...gossip ...Many of the people inv...ed in the were related to the Trujillo... ...lood or ...riage or long association; thus ...iederich's ...researched story has about it the air of a ...ieval family upheaval. There are hints, too, ...Trujillo may have seen it all coming, ...gh he died firing his revolver. He had been ...ll. Had it all become too much? ...the whole the killing of Trujillo is a blend ...ivete and gallantry, costly in blood, yet an ...nditure that somehow started the whole ...us Trujillo edifice crumbling. ...iederich doesn't harp on the mischievous ...lity of the CIA's involvement—encouraging ...assassination then backing out—but no ...d. the implications are there.   G.C.

(continued)

Figure B.13   The Chase Revel "newspaper," front view.

personal sales and management programs, etc., of all kinds of formats, print, cassette, film and videotape. All are discretionary check signers of medium and large companies. A recency of ten months or less! Most are phone derived (70% with the balance direct mail). 80 percent are multiple buyers. It's called the Applied Concepts Business Buyers' List and the average unit of purchase is $350. That's a lot of money. This list is fresh, red hot, and certain to become a proven money-maker for any quality offer. Try a test soon. Sincerely, Eric Weinstein. P.S. The quantity is 25,000 and the price is $55 per. How about some business?"

Did I say earlier that a good response may be 3, 4, 5, or even less than 1 percent? Well, Eric Weinstein got an incredible 21.6 percent response with this letter. Along with the order, many people told Eric, "Why don't you hire a secretary, for crying out loud?" That's creativity.

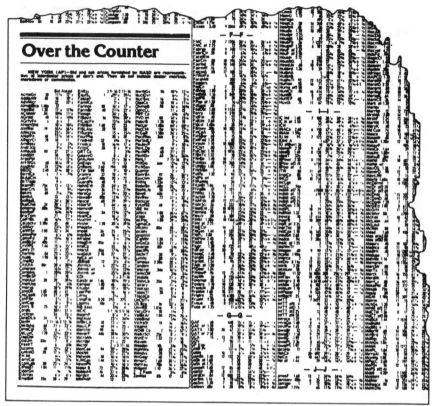

Figure B.13   (Continued) Back of Chase Revel "newspaper."

If you've flown on an airplane, you know what I have shown in Figure B.15. Yes, this is a sanitary bag, also known as a barf bag, used in case you get motion sickness while flying. But my gosh! What is that on the side of it? "Super film developing offer, only $1.79." Can you imagine that? Here we have an advertisement on the side of a barf bag! Remember that people must have flown for 50 years in airplanes without ever seeing anything on the side of a barf bag, and here we have a full-page advertisement. This kind of creativity is what pays off. Think of the unusual that hasn't been done before. It will make you money.

DO YOU WANT TO ATTEND EVERY MAJOR MAIL ORDER CONFERENCE IN THE COUNTRY?

It would probably be physically impossible to attend every major mail order conference across the country, even if you could afford it. And believe me, the cost would not be small. In addition to paying the conference fees,

July 31

Mr. John Jones
631 Wilshire Bld.
Santa Monica, CA   90401

Dear Mr. Jones:

Please pardon alll of the mistakes—but i8ve just put up a ~~NEW~~ BRAND NEW list and it"s
~~so hot it figured you'd rather getthe jump on it & hear about it quickly than wait for a~~
printer to gte out a fancy ʏpromotion.

~~This list is so hot its burning out the tape drives in our computer. It8s a dynamite busness~~
buyers list and heres the parti caulars—allare PAID UP CREDIT APPROVED BUYERS
~~OF PERSSONEL, SALES DAN MANAGEMENT PROGRAMS, ETC. AND ALL KINDS~~
OF FORMATES—print, cassette, film an video tape—ALL ARE DISCRETIONARY
CHECK SINERS OF MEDIUM AND LARGE ⊠ COMPANIES. A recency of !0 omnths or
~~less'!. Mostly phone derived (70% with the balance direct mail). 80% are MULTIPLE~~
BUYERS. Its called ~~in~~/the APPLIED CONCEPTS Business Buyers List and the average
~~unit of purchase is $350. Thats a lot of money—this list is fresh~~ ~~hot~~ red hot, and certain
to become a proven money-maker for any quality offer.

                        try a test soon.

Sincerely,

Eric Weinstein
~~P.s. The quantity/ is 25M & the price is 55 per—how about~~
                some business?

Figure B.14   Eric Weinstein's "mistake"-filled letter. The recipients took notice!

which are $200 or $300 or more, you would have to travel back and forth across the entire country and pay the air fares and hotel bills. Fortunately, it's not necessary, for there's a company that makes tapes of every single major mail order conference—Hoke Communications, 224 Seventh Street, Garden City, NY 11535. Hoke Communications publishes a catalog called *Ideas in Sound,* which contains hundreds of different tapes made of every single conference, course of instruction, and almost anyone who has stood before a microphone to say something about direct mail or mail order. This catalog is available to you by writing to Hoke Communications.

CAN YOU USE A PRIVATE MAIL MONITOR SERVICE?

In the course of your business you may find a use for a private mail monitor service, which can do several things for you. First, it can tell you if your mail is being delivered. Second, it can tell you how long it takes for your mail to be delivered so that you can decide when is the optimum time for mailing. And third, it can tell you if your list is being protected against

Figure B.15 An advertisement on the back of a sanitary bag.

unauthorized use. Remember that if you rent a list, you are renting it for one-time use only, and someone else has the authority to use your list depending on the number of times he or she is paying for it. What does a service like this cost? Well, here's one company that will monitor your mail in 50 cities for $200 a year—U.S. Monitor Service, 86 Maple Avenue, New York City, NY 10956-5036. Write and ask for additional information if you're interested.

HAND-ADDRESSED ENVELOPES

Personalization is certainly the key in mail order and in direct mail, and one way you can obtain it is to have your addressing done by hand. Naturally, it is more expensive, and perhaps you have to hire students to keep your costs down. But today when labels, computer letters, and so forth are the norm, a handwritten envelope stands out and it will probably stand a good chance of being opened.

Because of the large amount of direct mail I get, I don't always open the printed ones, but if I see something handwritten, I will definitely open it and read what is inside. Recently I received such a handwritten envelope. The envelope was marked "Personal." I opened it to find an apparently typewritten sheet, signed "Anonymous." Actually, rather than typewritten, it was offset typewriting. What was it selling? A system for winning at the stock market. I didn't order the system, but I certainly read the letter, and I bet with the right list it would bring a good response.

INCREASE YOUR SURVEY RESPONSE BY GIVING MONEY AWAY

It is said that you can't give money away but that isn't totally true, and *Advertising Age* and a few other companies have proved it in a rather strange fashion. Figure B.16 is a survey sent to the subscribers of *Advertising Age*. Attached to it, although not shown, was a brand new, crisp $1 bill. You will see this referred to in the P.S. in the letter, which says, "The enclosed one dollar bill is a small token of our appreciation for your cooperation." Can you imagine the psychological impact of this? No one likes to spend time filling out a survey form. On the other hand, what do you do when you get $1 in the mail? Do you send it back? Do you keep it, do nothing, and feel guilty? Or do you complete the survey? Well, tests have proven that a much greater majority of people complete the survey than ordinarily would and it's well worth that crisp dollar enclosed, whether the reader completes the survey or just puts the money in his or her pocket. So you *can* make money by giving money away.

SELL THROUGH OTHER LARGE MAIL ORDER HOUSES

Here's a variation of selling to other dealers. What you do is sell to other large mail order houses that use catalogs, and they sell your product through their catalogs. Where do you get the names and addresses of these firms? Every mail order firm that carries your type of product is a possible candidate to sell your product. How do you approach these companies? Well, you usually won't have to send them the product. What you must send them is a glossy photograph of the product, along with a complete description, price information, and the availability of delivery, as well as drop-shipping information, if applicable. Naturally, you should make your

Advertising Age

The International Newspaper of Marketing • 740 Rush St., Chicago, Ill. 60611 • (312) 649-5200 Telex: 254248 Cable: CRAINCOM

Dear Subscriber:

My Editors and I try hard to give you an interesting
and useful publication; but to do even better in the 1980's,
we need reactions directly from people like you. So, we
decided to conduct this special survey of our readers to
learn more about their information interests.

Since you are a part of a small and scientifically
selected sample, your response is vital to the success of
this project. I promise that your answers will be held in
confidence; they will be tabulated in with those of others
in the sample to develop a representative picture of our
subscriber's interests.

Please complete the attached questionnaire and return
it to us in the postage-paid reply envelope; you'll find that
it takes but a few minutes. The sole purpose of the number
on the back of the return envelope is to avoid sending a
second questionnaire to people who complete and return the
first one. If, however, you prefer not to be identified
even for this limited purpose, just cut off the number.

The Editors and I personally will be very grateful for
your help.

Best wishes,

Louis F. DeMarco
Publisher

P.S.   The enclosed $1 bill is a small token of our apprecia-
tion for your cooperation.

A PUBLICATION OF CRAIN COMMUNICATIONS INC

Figure B.16   *Advertising Age* letter with survey. A $1 bill was enclosed.

product sound interesting and salable. Remember, catalog space is valuable! By using this methodology, you can really multiply the effectiveness of your campaign and your ability to reach greater numbers in your market. You will have to allow at least a 50 percent discount to these firms, even higher in large quantity, but the number of units you can sell this way makes it all worth it. This is the one method that Joe Cossman used to sell millions of units of every single product he offered. It's a great way to make a fortune.

You can get addresses of mail order companies with catalogs from the sources I gave to you in Chapter 15.

FREE MAIL ORDER HELP FROM THE U.S. POSTAL SERVICE

Yes, the U.S. Postal Service is eager to help you build your mail order business. And why not? The more business you do, the more the Postal Service does. Write and ask them for these free booklets:

Third Class Mail Preparation. This is a 55-page manual that tells you all about bulk business mail and how to get the most out of it, including third-class bulk mail preparation requirements, the procedures for obtaining a permit, and the requirements for payment of the annual bulk mailing fee.

A Guide to Business Mail Preparation. Here's a book that will tell you how to prepare your mailings for processing on the latest high-speed automated mail sorting equipment. This can not only save you time, but also money. When they sent my copy, they included a clear plastic automation gauge that lets you check your envelopes for correct positioning bar codes and facing identification marks. You'll learn more about these when you read the booklet.

Postal Addressing Standards. This booklet tells you the standard abbreviations used by the Postal Service and other important facts about postal addressing. It can save you money because if you use the wrong abbreviation, your mailings can get lost or misdirected. In addition, some abbreviations are needed due to overly long addresses.

5 Creative Solutions For Your Business Needs. In this booklet, Uncle Sam's Postal Service gives you a collection of cost-effective techniques for managing your mail. These include ways to speed up your orders and receivables, Postal Services discounts, keeping track of your customers and minimizing undeliverable mail, and ways to improve your address files.

If you want these or other booklets published from time to time by the U.S. Postal Service, write them at the following address: U.S. Postal Service, Marketing Department, 475 L'Enfant Plaza, SW, Washington, DC 20260-6300.

SOME SPECIALS ON COLOR PRINTING

If you want full color printing on glossy stock, U.S. Press, P.O. Box 640, Valdosta, GA 31603-0640 (their toll-free number is (800)227-7377)

offers 5,000 6 × 4¼-inch postcards for $435, 5,000 8½ × 11-inch cata-
log sheets for $545 or 5,000 11 × 17-inch brochures for $1,605. Or you
might be interested in 50,000 copies of your own full size, full color,
eight-page catalog. If so, you can get them from Econocolor™, 7405 Industrial Road, Florence, KY 41042-9975. Their toll-free number is
(800)877-7405.

You can also obtain color printing catalogs from Rapidcolor, 705 East
Union St., West Chester, PA 19382, (800)872-7436 and Color Now!, 115
West 190th St., Gardena, CA 90248, (800)257-4968.

Or maybe you can use a full color glossy minicatalog about the size of a
postcard? These little catalogs can be used as inserts in card pacs, included
with statements or shipments as "bounce backs," mailed solo in an envelope, inserted in magazines or other catalogs. You can have either 16 or 32
pages. And the price is right—as low as a few cents each in very high quantities. Write for information from Web Specialties, Inc., 401 S. Milwaukee
Ave., Wheeling, IL 60090.

PROMOTE BOOKS BY TELEPHONE

If you are a book publisher or author, you can promote your book 24-hours
a day using a service offered by The 24-Hour Talking Book Directory,
14241 Ventura Blvd., #201, Sherman Oaks, CA 91423, (818)788-2040.
An interested prospect dials in on a toll-free 800 line and hears you speak
about your book for up to five minutes. It's easy to record the message, as
it can be done from any location using a touchtone telephone. Anyone can
access your message free of charge, 24-hours a day, from any touchtone
telephone in the country. It's great for tie-ins with press releases, advertisements in print, radio, or TV. If you want to try it out right now, see
Figure B.17 for a selection of books and dial (800)266-5779 to try it out.

REACH MILLIONS OF PROSPECTS WORLDWIDE
BY COMPUTER AT LOW COST

I said that computers had revolutionized mail order, but the best news is
that the revolution is still going on. You may have heard of the Internet.
It is a worldwide network that can tie together all computers with a device called a modem. You want a modem which runs at the speed of
14,400 baud for use on the Internet. Such a modem can be obtained for
about $100. The modem attaches to your computer and works over your
telephone line. Now you are in a position to communicate with other
computer users that have access to the network. As this is written, there
are 45,000 networks tied into the Internet. That represents 30 million

ATTENTION PUBLISHERS, PUBLICISTS, AUTHORS

Welcome to the 24-Hour Talking Book Directory! We're dedicated to promoting new and backlisted titles 24 hours a day, on our nationwide bookline. By listing your titles on our directory, you can reach the following markets:

DR. RUTH - Box 1134

- **Trade** — regular listings in Publishers Weekly (see below).
- **Consumers** — our consumer directories are free to the public. They're distributed to bookstores, libraries, schools, and many other locations across the country..
- **30 Minute TV Show** — Each week, an author from the Directory will be interviewed on America Talks™ to be broadcast in the Los Angeles Market.
- **Tie-Ins** — press releases, print advertisements, radio, and TV can all be tied in to your authors' recordings by simply providing our 800 number plus your author's four-digit box code.

CONVENIENT   From their own locations, authors have up to five minutes to introduce their titles using any touchtone telephone.

FREE ACCESS   Anyone can access the system FREE OF CHARGE 24 hours a day from any touchtone telephone in the country.

Janice Tracht author of
Re-Nurturing
Box 2532

The Talking Book Directory is a 24-hour nationwide bookline available to you at ONE LOW MONTHLY PRICE.

WHERE'S THE ONLY PLACE YOU CAN HEAR AUTHORS TALKING ABOUT THEIR BOOKS 24-HOURS A DAY?

The 24-Hour Talking Book Directory

To Listen, Call 1-800-BOOKS-PW

Press 6 for the Directory, then enter the box # for the title you would like to hear.

Box #	ISBN	Title	Author/Reader*	Publisher	Pub Date	Price
1100	**	A message from the Editor-in-Chief of *Publishers Weekly*	**	**	**	**
2400	0-553-56607-5	Dead Man's Island	Carolyn Hart*	Bantam Books	6/94	$4.99P
2410	0-9627403-5-7	Low-Fat Living for Real People	Linda Levy* & Francine Grabowski	Lake Isle Press	10/94	$12.95P
1104	0-06-016848-X	Men Are From Mars, Women Are From Venus	John Gray, Ph.D.*	Harper Collins	5/92	$23.00H
1108	0-201-63288-8	Motherless Daughters	Hope Edelman*	Addison-Wesley	5/94	$23.00H
1123	1-880032-42-2	Creating Affluence	Deepak Chopra, M.D.*	New World Library	10/93	$12.95H
1134	0-8264-0625-4	Dr. Ruth's Encyclopedia of Sex	Ruth Westheimer, Ph.D.*	Continuum	6/94	$29.50H
1145	0-399-22760-1	Fat Chance	Lesléa Newman*	G.P. Putnam's Sons	10/94	$14.95H
1146	0-8129-1983-1	The Cancer Recovery Eating Plan	Daniel Nixon, M.D.*	Times Books	10/94	$25.00H
1147	0-8129-2141-0	The Limits of Medicine	Edward Golub, Ph.D.*	Times Books	10/94	$23.00H
1148	0-9632698-3-6	Cancel April 15	Frank Champagne*	Veda Vangarde Publishing	3/93	$10.95P
1155	0-9640530-0-4	At the Expense of Victory	Ed DeMello*	Kenobi Productions	11/94	$18.95P
1200	0-9641239-9-1	The Original LOVERS' QUESTIONAIRE Book	Lorilyn Bailey*	Lormax Communications	11/94	$9.95P
2300	1-881374-72-6	The Dark Chronicles	Cynthia Soroka*	Flash Blasters Inc.	2/95	$5.99P
2500	1-56790-113-1	Men: The Handbook	Mindi Rudan*	Cool Hand Communications	12/94	$12.95P
2415	0-9640354-6-4	How to Dump Your Wife	Lee Covington*	Fender Publishing	8/94	$25.00H
2600	0-9623611-0-0	No Regrets	Alexandra Swann*	Cygnet Press	10/89	$16.95P
1080	1-881052-54-0	Customers As Partners	Chip R. Bell*	Berrett/Koehler Publishers	10/94	$24.95H
2620	0-9641416-0-4	Journey Through Illness and Beyond	Brenda S. Lukeman*	Steppingstones Press	1/95	$9.95P
2532	0-938179-39-X	Re-Nurturing	Janice Tracht*	Mills & Sanderson, Publishers	12/94	$12.95P
3500	0-380-77416-X	Selling is a Woman's Game	Nicki Joy* w/Susan Kane-Benson	Avon Books	1/95	$10.00P
2420	0-7178-0706-1	Siqueiros: His Life and Works	Phillip Stein	International Publishers Co.	11/94	$29.95P
2125	0-9643072-1-9	On Becoming Human	Arthur Niehoff*	Hominid Press	5/95	$14.95P
1129	0-9624142-3-9	America's Biggest Cover-Up	Neenyah Ostrom*	That New Magazine	10/93	$14.95H
2200	0-9641457-0-7	Route 66: A Guide Book	Bob Moore*	Innovative Publishing Group	9/94	$17.95P
1995	0-399-22605-2	After a Suicide	Susan Kuklin*	G.P. Putnam's Sons	9/94	$15.95H
3210	0-9640963-4-X	Gospel of Goddess	William Bond & Pamela Suffield*	Artemis Creations	8/94	$18.95P

To start today, please submit review copies to:

The 24-Hour Talking Book Directory

14241 Ventura Boulevard #201, Sherman Oaks, CA 91423

Or call (818) 788-2040 for information and an application form.

Figure B.17   The 24-Hour Talking Book Dictionary.

people! It is estimated that by the year 2000, 100 million people will be using the Internet. Further, your ability to get to this market fast, with color and multimedia advertisements is almost unlimited . . . and no more time and space limitations to your ads!

If you want to get into this new means of mail order marketing, I recommend you get a copy of the book *Marketing on the Internet* by Jill H. Ellsworth and Matthew V. Ellsworth, published by John Wiley & Sons, Inc. and available at your local bookstore for $24.95.

HOW YOUR CUSTOMER CAN GET YOUR CATALOG 24-HOURS A DAY INSTANTLY

Technology is truly amazing. Now someone has come up with a way of combining a fax machine and your computer. The result is, at any time, day or night, your customer can dial in with his fax machine and get your catalog and other sales information. You can continue to sleep peacefully and best of all, you don't pay a penny. The system is called Fax-On-Demand, or FOD. With it, you save money on printing, postage, stuffing envelopes, etc., and you get your information to your customer instantly. All your customer does is to call in on his or her fax machine and press the right buttons to let your machine know what information to request. There are a number of different systems available costing from several hundred to several thousand dollars. Some will even take orders for you!

If you want more information on different machines and you have a fax machine, use its handset. For information on:

RoboFax-EZ call FaxQuest (800)925-7626 or (415)563-0155 or Hello Direct (408)972-1061

FaxlinkPRO call Voicelink (708)866-0404, Ext. 5

Phoneoffice call Edens Technology (309)862-1804

Faxess call ComArt International (800)FAX-DEMO, Doc 455

FactsLine call Ibex (800)289-9998 or Valley Infosystems (800)769-9147

FaxBack™ call FaxBack, Inc. (800)329-2225 or (503)645-7511

Special Request call Spectrafax (800)833-1329

Novafax call Novacore Technologies (508)371-2424

FaxFacts call Copia (708)924-3030

Command Fax call Nuntius Corporation (314)947-1710 or (314)776-7076

FMS1000 call Ricoh (800)241-RFMS

FlashFAX call Brooktrout Technology (800)333-5274

For more information, Dan Poynter, author and president of Para Publishing has prepared a special study on this system. Use the handset of your fax machine and call (805)968-8947. Request document 311. You can also get his document 101, which is a complete list of documents you can get from him by fax.

If you want a free booklet, "How To Turn Your FAX Machine into a Marketing Powerhouse!" call or write USWest Enhanced Services at 1999 Broadway, 10th Floor, Denver, CO 80202-9532, (800)945-9494.

WANT TO MARKET THROUGH THE *YELLOW PAGES?*

The *Yellow Pages* can represent a new medium for mail order entrepreneurs. Annual U.S. *Yellow Pages* billings are in excess of $9 billion and mail order marketers are taking advantage of specialized directories, new color options, audiotext, "the talking yellow pages," and use of coupons in their ads to increase business. To find out all about these opportunities, write

Figure B.18   The Merchant CD-ROM catalog.

the Yellow Pages Publishers Association, 340 East Big Beaver Road, 5th Fl., Troy, MI 48083. Request their booklets, *Yellow Pages and the Media Mix* and *Target Marketing Through the Yellow Pages.*

GET YOUR CATALOG ON A CD ROM

Magellan Interactive Media has included a number of complete catalogs such as L.L. Bean, PC Flowers, Hello Direct, and others all on one CD. It's called The Merchant CD-ROM Catalog Shopping. Last holiday season they did a mailing of a free sample CD ROM to prospects. You can see it in Figure B.18. Customers pay a small amount to subscribe to the CD ROM catalog. If you want to learn more about this opportunity you can contact them at (800)561-3114 or write The Merchant, 1850 Union St., Suite 1281, San Francisco, CA 94123-9863.

SUMMARY

In this chapter I've given you a number of different and innovative techniques, special methods, and money-making ideas that you can incorporate into your mail order operation. Remember that mail order rewards the creative and innovative operator with success. If you can think of a new twist or a new idea from one of the concepts I have shown you, or from one of the idea kits or catalogs you receive from someone else, it can make you a fortune. But don't forget—as with everything else in mail order, you must test to make sure that your idea is profitable before you sink large sums of money in it.

Appendix C
Mail Order Associations and
Direct Marketing Clubs*

Arizona

PHOENIX DIRECT MARKETING CLUB
c/o Market Builders
831 N. Alvaro Circle
Mesa, AZ 85205-5458
(602)641-1901

California

DIRECT MKTG. CLUB OF SOUTHERN CALIF.
2401 Pacific Coast Hwy. #102
Hermosa Beach, CA 90254
(310)374-7499

SAN DIEGO DIRECT MARKETING CLUB
Western Graphics
7614 Lemon Avenue
Lemon Grove, CA 91945
(619)466-4157

---

* Because many clubs have new officers installed annually, addresses may not be current.
However, the old addressee may be able to supply the club's new address and phone number.

NORTHERN CALIFORNIA CATALOG CLUB
Boudin Bakery
c/o 132 Hawthorne Street
San Francisco, CA 94101
(415)882-1826

DIRECT MARKETING ASSOCIATION OF ORANGE COUNTY
c/o American Homeowners
5942 Edinger Avenue Ste. 113
Huntington Beach, CA 92649-1763
(714)939-1785

Connecticut

DIRECT MARKETING ASSOCIATION OF CONNECTICUT
Newton Manufacturing Co.
176-2 Lincoln Street
Waterbury, CT 06710-1548
(203)757-4404

District of Columbia

DIRECT MARKETING ASSOCIATION OF WASHINGTON
c/o American Chemical Society
1155 16th Street NW
Washington, DC 20006
(202)872-4393

WOMEN'S DIRECT RESPONSE GROUP OF WASHINGTON
c/o 7923 Richfield Road
Springfield, VA 22153
(703)451-7531

Florida

FLORIDA DIRECT MARKETING ASSOCIATION
c/o Dunhill Intn'l. List Co.
1951 Northwest 19th Street
Boca Raton, FL 33431-7344
(305)974-7800

(Miami-Fort Lauderdale area)
FLORIDA D.M. ASSOCIATION
8851 N.W. 10th Place
Plantation, FL 33322-5007
(305)472-6374

(Tampa-St. Petersburg-Sarasota area)
FLORIDA D.M. ASSOCIATION
c/o Instant Wed, Inc.
3235 San Bernardino Street
Clearwater, FL 34619
(813)724-1624

Southwest Chapter
FLORIDA DIRECT MARKETING ASSN.
3521 Tassel Flower Court
Bonita Springs, FL 33923
(813)495-8918

Georgia

DIRECT MARKETING SPECIAL INTEREST GROUP OF THE
ATLANTA CHAPTER OF THE AMERICAN MKTG. ASSOC.
c/o King & More!, Inc.
90 West Wieuca Road, Suite 210
Atlanta, GA 30342
(404)252-0841

Hawaii

DIRECT RESPONSE ADVERTISING &
MARKETING ASSN. OF HAWAII
c/o Val Pak Hawaii
1833 Kalakaua Avenue, Ste. 1010
Honolulu, HI 96815-1528
(808)944-2000

Illinois

CHICAGO ASSOCIATION OF DIRECT MARKETING
c/o First Card
2500 Westfield Drive E-3
Elgin, IL 60123
(708)931-2881

WOMEN'S DIRECT RESPONSE GROUP OF CHICAGO
2100 Lincoln Park West, #10B-S
Chicago, IL 60614
(312)549-1289

Indiana

DIRECT MARKETING ASSOCIATION OF INDIANAPOLIS
c/o Southam Bus. Communications
7355 N. Woodland Drive
Indianapolis, IN 46206
(317)297-5500

Kentucky

LOUISVILLE DIRECT MARKETING ASSN.
c/o Halbleib/Beggs, Inc.
637 West Main Street
Louisville, KY 40202
(502)585-3403

Maryland

MARYLAND DIRECT MARKETING ASSN.
c/o Integrated Marketing Svces.
3018 Courtside Road
Mitchellville, MD 20721
(301)249-0981

DIRECT MARKETING ASSOCIATION OF BALTIMORE
c/o Doner Direct
400 East Pratt Street
Baltimore, MD 21202
(410)385-9347

Massachusetts

NEW ENGLAND DIRECT MARKETING ASSOCIATION
c/o Brookshore Lithographers, Inc.
214 Prospect Street
Brockton, MA 02401
(508)586-6157

Michigan

DIRECT MARKETING ASSOCIATION OF DETROIT
General Motors Corporation
NASO-Marketing Services
465 W. Milwaukee Room 809
Detroit, MI 48202
(313)974-7474

Minnesota

MIDWEST DIRECT MARKETING ASSN.
c/o DB Direct, Inc.
700 South 7th Street
Delano, MN 55328-0069
(612)972-3338

Missouri

DIRECT MKTG. ASSN. OF ST. LOUIS
c/o ICS Diversified
St. Louis, MO 63146
(314)997-6767

KANSAS CITY DIRECT MARKETING ASSN.
Marketing Communications Inc.
10605 West 84th Terrace
Lenexa, KS 66214
(913)492-1575

Nebraska

MID-AMERICA DIRECT MARKETING ASSN.
Total Mailing Services
8833 J. Street
Omaha, NE 68127
(402)339-7685

New York

DIRECT MARKETING CLUB OF NEW YORK
Direct Marketing Magazine
224 7th Street
Garden City, NY 11530
(516)746-6700

DIRECT MARKETING CREATIVE GUILD
c/o Westerhoff Direct Marketing
101 Fifth Avenue
New York, NY 10003
(212)645-0344

DIRECT MKTG. IDEA EXCHANGE, INC.
c/o New York Times
229 West 43rd Street
New York, NY 10036
(212)556-4158

HUDSON VALLEY DIRECT MKTG. CLUB
c/o Marvel Associates
199 Sound Beach Avenue
Old Greenwich, CT 06870
(203)637-4777

MAIL ADVERTISING SERVICE ASSOCIATION OF NY
c/o Jim Prendergast & Assoc.
220 E. 42nd Street (402)
New York, NY 10017
(212)687-8805

LONG ISLAND DIRECT MARKETING ASSOCIATION
Direct Marketing Magazine
224 Seventh Street
Garden City, NY 11530
(516)868-1732

UPSTATE NEW YORK DIRECT MARKETING ASSOCIATION
Sigma Marketing Group, Inc.
1850 S. Winton Road
Rochester, NY 14618
(716)473-7300

WOMEN'S DIRECT RESPONSE GROUP
c/o The Coolidge Company, Inc.
25 West 43rd Street
New York, NY 10036
(212)642-0350

FULFILLMENT MANAGEMENT ASSOC. INC. (NEW YORK)
Communications Data Svces., Inc.
230 Park Avenue, Suite 606
New York, NY 10169
(212)661-1410

Ohio

CINCINNATI DIRECT MARKETING CLUB
Hensley Segal
11590 Century Blvd.
Cincinnati, OH 45246
(513)671-3811

DAYTON DIRECT MARKETING CLUB
Fension Envelope Co.
5045 N. Main St., Suite 340
Dayton, OH 45415-3637
(513)279-0885

MID-OHIO DIRECT MARKETING ASSOCIATION
Highlights for Children
2300 West 5th Avenue
P.O. Box 269
Columbus, OH 43216-0269
(614)486-0631

NORTHEAST OHIO DIRECT MARKETING ASSOCIATION
Datascope, Inc.
13401 S. Woodland Road #6
Cleveland, OH 44120
(216)295-1516

Oklahoma

DIRECT MARKETING ASSOCIATION OF TULSA
c/o O'Neil & Associates
951 West Main, Suite 200
Jenkes, OK 74037
(918)298-0045

Oregon

OREGON DIRECT MARKETING ASSOCIATION
Lynx Communications
2901 Carriage Way
West Linn, OR 97068
(503)239-8338

Pennsylvania

PHILADELPHIA DIRECT MARKETING ASSOCIATION
Allen Envelope
1001 Cassatt Road
Berwyn, PA 19312

Tennessee

NASHVILLE ASSOCIATION OF DIRECT MKTG.
c/o The Sunday School Board
127 Ninth Avenue North
Nashville, TN 37234
(615)251-2518

Texas

HOUSTON DIRECT MARKETING ASSOCIATION
R.L. Polk List Services
#2 Northpoint Drive, Suite 860
Houston, TX 77060
(713)222-8871

DIRECT MARKETING ASSOCIATION OF NORTH TEXAS
c/o Foreman/Stephenson & Assoc.
2100 West Grapevine Hwy., Suite 1080
Grapevine, TX 76051
(214)650-9625

Vermont

VERMONT/NEW HAMPSHIRE DIRECT MARKETING GROUP
c/o Duncan Direct Associates
16 Elm Street
Peterborough, NH 03458
(603)924-3121

Washington

SEATTLE DIRECT MARKETING ASSOCIATION
The Mailhandlers Inc.
520 S. Front Street
Seattle, WA 98108
(206)763-9060

SPOKANE DIRECT MAIL MARKETING ASSN.
c/o Opportunity Distribution
P.O. Box 14335
Spokane, WA 99214
(509)922-5129

Wisconsin

WISCONSIN DIRECT MARKETING ASSOCIATION
A.B. Data Ltd.
8050 N. Port Washington Road
Milwaukee, WI 53217
(414)352-4404

National

ASSOCIATION OF DIRECT MARKETING AGENCIES
342 Madison Avenue
New York, NY 10173
(212)687-2100

BUSINESS PROFESSIONAL ADVERTISING ASSOCIATION
205 East 42nd Street
New York, NY 10017
(212)661-0222

DIRECT MARKETING CREDIT ASSOCIATION
c/o Grolier Enterprises
Sherman Turnpike
Danbury, CT 06816
(203)797-3500, ext. 3642

DIRECT MARKETING IDEA EXCHANGE
475 Park Avenue South, Room 3500
New York, NY 10016
(212)924-1200

ENVELOPE MANUFACTURERS ASSOCIATION
1 Rockefeller Plaza
New York, NY 10020
(212)255-5885

FULFILLMENT MANAGEMENT ASSOCIATION
25 West 43rd Street
New York, NY 10036
(212)262-8800

INTERNATIONAL MAIL ADVERTISING ASSOCIATIONS
7315 Wisconsin Ave., 818 E.
Washington, DC 20014
(301)654-7030

MARKETING COMMUNICATIONS EXECUTIVES
2130 Delancy Place
Philadelphia, PA 19103
(215)732-9340

PARCEL SHIPPERS ASSOCIATION
1211 Connecticut Avenue, NW
Washington, DC 20036
(202)296-3690

U.S. ELECTRONIC MAIL ASSOCIATION
Harvard Square, Box 43
Cambridge, MA 02138
(617)742-2500

Canada

CANADIAN DIRECT MARKETING ASSN.
1 Concorde Gate, Suite 607
Don Mills, Ontario, Canada M3C 3N6
(416)391-2362

Appendix D
Some Mail Order Advertising Agencies

A&B Advertising
4700 Stamp Road
Temple Hills, MD 20748

Lucien Cohen Advertising Design
1201 Broadway
New York, NY 10001

Chapman Direct Advertising
230 Park Ave. S
New York, NY 10003

Dependable Direct, Inc.
245 Plainfield Ave.
Floral Park, NY 11011

Dickinson Direct Mail
120 Campanelli Dr.
Braintree, MA 02184

Franklin & Joseph
237 Mamaroneck Ave.
White Plains, NY 10605

Gurley Direct Marketing
278 Franklin Road
Brentwood, TN 37027

Hal Langerman
25 Norristown Rd.
Blue Bell, PA 19422

Harris Marketing Services
1620 Arlington Blvd.
Arlington, VA 22209

Kauftheil/Rothschild
220 W. 19th St.
New York, NY 10011

John Klein & Associates
20700 Miles Ave.
Cleveland, OH 44128

Bob Levy Advertising
11 W. 30th St.
New York, NY 10001

Marc Direct
Four Station Sq.
Pittsburgh, PA 15219

MultiSales
2495 Roxburgh Dr.
Roswell, GA 30076

Saugatuck Marketing Group
18 Kings Highway, N
Westport, CT 06880

SRH Direct Marketing
1 Memorial Dr.
St. Louis, MO 63102

Trend Direct, Inc.
300 Park Avenue South
New York, NY 10010

The Marketing Workshop
16490 Harbor Blvd.
Fountain Valley, CA 92705

Appendix E
Some Sources of Mailing Lists

Action Markets
1710 Hwy. 35
Ocean, NJ 07712

American Consumer Lists
5711 South 86th Circle
P.O. Box 27347
Omaha, NE 68127

American List Counsel
88 Orchard RD CN-5219
Princeton, NJ 08543

Ed Burnett Consultants, Inc.
100 Paragon Dr.
Montvale, NJ 07645

ChiltonDirect Marketing
1 Chilton Way
Radnor, PA 19089

Compilers Plus, Inc.
466 Main St.
New Rochelle, NY 10801

Direct Media
200 Pemberwick Rd.
Greenwich, CT 06830

Dunhill International
1951 NW 19th St.
Boca Raton, FL 33431-7344

Edith Roman
253 W. 35th St., 16th Fl.
New York, NY 10001

Hugo Dunhill Mailing Lists
630 Third Avenue
New York, NY 10017-6772

Infomat
1815 W. 213th St.
Torrance, CA 90501

Information Marketing Services
8130 Boone Blvd., Suite 310
Vienna, VA 22182

The Kleid Co.
530 Fifth Ave.
New York, NY 10036-5198

List Services Corporation
6 Trowbridge Dr.
P.O. Box 516
Bethel, CT 06801-0516

PCS Mailing List
39 Cross St.
Peabody, MA 01960

Research Projects Corporation
4 S. Pomperaug Ave.
Woodbury, CT 06798

Response Media Products
2323 Perimeter Park Dr.
Atlanta, GA 30341

RMI Direct Marketing
4 Skyline Dr.
Hawthrone, NY 10532

Zeller List Corporation
15 E. 26th St.
New York, NY 10010

Appendix F
Mail Order Magazines and Newsletters

Catalog Age
Six River Bend Center
911 Hope St.
P.O. Box 4949
Stamford, CT 06907-0949

Catalog Newsletter
11 W. 42nd St.
New York, NY 10036

Classified Communication
P.O. Box 4242
Prescott, AZ 86302-4242

Direct Magazine
Six River Bend Center
911 Hope St.
P.O. Box 4949
Stamford, CT 06907-0949

Direct Marketing
224 Seventh St.
Garden City, NY 11530-5771

Direct Response Newsletter
Creative Direct Marketing Group
1815 W. 213th St., Suite 210
Torrance, CA 90501

Direct Response Specialist
4036 Mermoor Court
Palm Harbor, FL 34685

DM News
19 W. 21st St.
New York, NY 10010-6805

The Gary Halbert Letter
423 Front St., 2nd Fl.
Key West, FL 33040

Mail Order Briefings
Teague Publishing Group
P.O. Box 14689
Dayton, OH 45413

Mail Order Digest
2807 Polk St., NE
Minneapolis, MN 55418

Mail Profits Magazine
P.O. Box 4785
Lincoln, NE 68504

Mailing List Tidbits
4205 Menlo Dr.
Baltimore, MD 21215

Mail: The Journal of
Communication Distribution
One Milstone Rd.,
Gold Key Box 2425
Milford, PA 18337-9607

Passport, The United States
Postal Service
P.O. Box 23793
Washington, DC 20026-3793

Target Marketing
401 N. Broad St.
Philadelphia, PA 19108-1074

Telemarketing
One Technology Plaza
Norwalk, CT 06854-1924

TeleProfessional
209 W. Fifth St., Suite N
Waterloo, IA 50701-5420

Who's Mailing What
P.O. Box 8180
Stamford, CT 06905

Also check with the mail order associations and direct marketing clubs
listed in Appendix C—many publishing their own newsletters.

Appendix G
A Business Guide to the Federal Trade Commission's Mail Order Rule

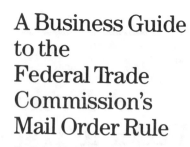

A Business Guide to the Federal Trade Commission's Mail Order Rule

The Federal Trade Commission prepared this business guide to the FTC Mail Order Rule for your use as a mail order seller. It should answer questions you may have about the Rule's requirements and reduce customer problems in this area.

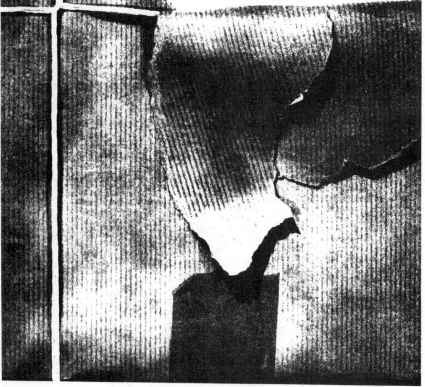

1 Introduction

What is the Mail Order Rule

The Mail Order Rule was issued by the Federal Trade Commission (FTC) to correct growing problems with late or undelivered mail order merchandise. Under this Rule, you have a duty to ship merchandise on time. You also must follow procedures that the Rule requires if you cannot ship ordered merchandise on time.

When there is a shipping delay, the Rule requires that you notify your customers of the delay and provide them with an option either to agree to the delay or to cancel the order and receive a prompt refund. For each additional delay, your customers must be notified that they must send you a signed consent to a further delay or a refund will be given.

Why Was the Rule Issued

The Rule was issued after federal, state, and local consumer protection authorities received thousands of consumer complaints about mail order problems. The major complaints were: failure to deliver merchandise, late delivery of merchandise, failure to make prompt refunds, and failure to answer customer inquiries about delayed or lost orders. For example:

- One consumer wrote about Christmas decorations she ordered in early October that were finally shipped the day before Christmas. This consumer wrote twice to the company about her order, the second time requesting a refund. Both inquiries were ignored.
- Another consumer complained about a company that failed to send a stereo component he ordered with payment in July. By late October, the only communication he received from the company was his canceled check.

Title 16—Commercial Practices
CHAPTER I—FEDERAL TRADE COMMISSION
PART 435—MAIL ORDER MERCHANDISE
Promulgation of Trade Regulation Rule

THE FEDERAL TRADE COMMISSION, pursuant to the Federal Trade Commission Act, as amended, 15 U.S.C. 41, et seq., and the provisions of Subpart B, Part I of the Commission's Procedures and Rules of Practice, 16 CFR 1.11, et seq., has conducted a proceeding for the promulgation of a Trade Regulation Rule concerning Undelivered Mail Order Merchandise and Services. Notice of this proceeding, including a proposed Rule, was published in the FEDERAL REGISTER on September 28, 1971 (36 FR 19092 (1971)). Interested parties were thereafter afforded opportunity to participate in the proceeding through the submission of written data, views and arguments, and to appear and express their views orally and to suggest amendments, revisions, and additions to the proposed Rule.

The FTC received 3,200 similar consumer complaints prior to beginning its rulemaking process. In addition, the President's Office of Consumer Affairs (OCA) received over 1,000 complaints concerning mail order practices, 60% of which concerned non-delivery. OCA complaint statistics for mail order were second only to complaints about autos and auto services.

The rulemaking record contains more than 10,000 pages of complaints regarding mail order sales. State and local agencies urged the Commission to take action to correct these problems. Industry members provided valuable input as to the feasibility and practicality of a mail order rule.

On October 22, 1975, the FTC promulgated the Mail Order Rule, and it went into effect on February 2, 1976.

Why You Should Comply with the Rule

When you comply with the Rule, you are being responsive to your customers. This is beneficial to you and to your customers because it promotes a positive industry image. Compliance creates consumer trust in buying by mail and fosters repeat mail order business. Of course if you ship on time, the requirements of the Rule pertaining to "option notices" do not apply.

Although most members of the mail order industry adhere to the Rule's requirements, there are some who do not. The FTC's Bureau of Consumer Protection monitors consumer complaints to ensure that businesses comply with the Rule. The FTC also provides compliance information, such as this manual, and assistance to all industry members.

AFTER IT HAD CONSIDERED THE SUGGESTIONS, CRITICISMS, objections, and other pertinent information in the Record, the Commission on March 8, 1974, published a revised proposed rule in a notice in the FEDERAL REGISTER (39 FR 9201 (1974)) extending an opportunity to interested parties to submit data, views or arguments regarding the revised proposed Rule. A period of over 90 days was allowed for the submission of written comments on the revised proposal. Written comments of the Direct Mail/Marketing Association (DM/MA) were admitted into the Record at a subsequent date and the public was given 30 days to submit written views and comments related to the DM/MA submission (39 FR 40515 (1974)).

The Commission has now considered all matters of fact, law, policy and discretion, including the data, views and arguments presented on the Record by interested parties in response to the Notices, as prescribed by law, and has determined that the adoption of the Trade Regulation Rule set forth herein and its Statement of Basis and Purpose[1] is in the public interest.

Accordingly, the Commission hereby amends Subchapter D, Trade Regulation Rules, Chapter I of 16 CFR by adding a new Part 435 as follows:

Sec.
435.1   The Rule.
435.2   Definitions.

AUTHORITY: The provisions of this Part 435 issued under 38 Stat. 717, as amended, 15 U.S.C. 41, et seq.

---

[1] Statement of Basis and Purpose filed as part of the original document.

2 How to Comply with the Rule

This section of the manual provides **THE TEXT OF THE RULE, WITH EXPLANATIONS OPPOSITE** of how to comply with the Rule.

§ 435.1   The Rule.

IN CONNECTION WITH MAIL ORDER SALES in commerce, as "commerce" is defined in the Federal Trade Commission Act, it constitutes an unfair method of competition, and an unfair or deceptive act and practice for a seller:

(a)(1) To solicit any order for the sale of merchandise to be ordered by the buyer through the mails unless, at the time of the solicitation, the seller has a reasonable basis to expect that he will be able to ship any ordered merchandise to the buyer: (i) within that time clearly and conspicuously stated in any such solicitation, or (ii) if no time is clearly and conspicuously stated, within thirty (30) days after receipt of a properly completed order from the buyer.

(2) To provide any buyer with any revised shipping date, as provided in paragraph (b), unless, at the time any such revised shipping date is provided, the seller has a reasonable basis for making such representation regarding a definite revised shipping date.

(3) To inform any buyer that he is unable to make any representation regarding the length of any delay unless (i) the seller has a reasonable basis for so informing the buyer and (ii) the seller informs the buyer of the reason or reasons for the delay.

(b)(1) Where a seller is unable to ship merchandise within the applicable time set forth in paragraph (a)(1), above, to fail to offer to the buyer, clearly and conspicuously and without prior demand, an option either to consent to a delay in shipping or to cancel his order and receive a prompt refund. Said offer shall be made within a reasonable time after the seller first becomes aware of his inability to ship within the applicable time set forth in paragraph (a)(1), but in no event later than said applicable time.

What to Know When You Make an Offer

When you offer to sell merchandise by mail, the Rule requires you to have a "reasonable basis" for expecting to ship within the time stated in your solicitation.

For example, if you know before advertising your products that your suppliers are on strike and are likely to remain on strike for several months, you do not have a "reasonable basis" for expecting to ship within a month.

The shipping date, when provided in your offer, must be clearly and conspicuously stated:

ADVERTISEMENT
Cardigan Sweaters
S, M, L — Beige or Blue
$29.95 plus tax
Allow 5 weeks for shipment.

If you do not provide a shipping date, you must ship the merchandise within 30 days of receiving a "properly completed" order. An order is properly completed when you receive payment accompanied by all information you need to fill the order. Payment may be made by cash, money order, check, or credit card, according to your company policy. If a credit card is used for a purchase, the order is properly completed when you charge your customer's account.

When you cannot ship on time, you must provide your customer with an "option" notice. The notice must provide an option to cancel the order and receive a prompt refund, or to agree to a delay in shipping. And, as with the original date, you must have a reasonable basis for setting that shipping date.

You must also have a reasonable basis for telling your customers that you do not know when you can ship merchandise. In that case, you must provide the specific reasons for the shipping problem. For example, you could state that a fire destroyed the warehouse holding the goods and you are unable to provide a revised shipping date because you

do not know how long it will take to replace
the merchandise.

When You Should
Send a First Notice

If a shipment is delayed, the Rule requires that
you give your customers an option:

- to consent to a delay; or
- to cancel the order and receive a prompt
  refund.

People in the trade often refer to the notice as
a "delay" notice. More accurately, it should be
called an "option" notice. You violate the Rule
if you only provide a notice of delay without
also providing an option to cancel the order.

Remember, you must send the notice after
you first become aware that there will be a
shipping delay. The notice must be sent:

- before the promised shipping date; or
- within 30 days after you receive the order
  (if no date was provided in your
  solicitation).

(b)(i) ANY OFFER TO THE BUYER of such an option shall fully inform the buyer regarding his right to cancel the order and to obtain a
prompt refund and shall provide a definite revised shipping date, but
where the seller lacks a reasonable basis for providing a definite
revised shipping date the notice shall inform the buyer that the seller
is unable to make any representation regarding the length of the
delay.

What a First
Notice Must Say

If you provide a revised shipping date of 30
days or less, you must have a reasonable basis
for making the change. The notice must
inform your customers that non-response is
considered consent to be a delay of 30 days or
less.

If you are unable to provide a revised shipping
date, your notice must state that you cannot
determine when the merchandise will be
shipped. It must also state that the order will
be automatically canceled unless:

- you ship the merchandise within 30 days of
  the original shipping date and you have not
  received your customer's cancellation
  before shipment; or

(ii) WHERE THE SELLER HAS PROVIDED a definite revised shipping
date which is thirty (30) days or less later than the applicable time set
forth in paragraph (a)(1), the offer of said option shall expressly
inform the buyer that, unless the seller receives, prior to shipment
and prior to the expiration of the definite revised shipping date, a
response from the buyer rejecting the delay and canceling the order,
the buyer will be deemed to have consented to a delayed shipment on
or before the definite revised shipping date.

(iii) Where the seller has provided a definite revised shipping date
which is more than thirty (30) days later than the applicable time set
forth in paragraph (a)(1) or where the seller is unable to provide a
definite revised shipping date and therefore informs the buyer that
he is unable to make any representation regarding the length of the
delay, the offer of said option shall also expressly inform the buyer
that his order will automatically be deemed to have been canceled
unless (A) the seller has shipped the merchandise within thirty (30)
days of the applicable time set forth in paragraph (a)(1), and has

received no cancellation prior to shipment, or (B) the seller has received from the buyer within thirty (30) days of said applicable time, a response specifically consenting to said shipping delay. Where the seller informs the buyer that he is unable to make any representation regarding the length of the delay, the buyer shall be expressly informed that, should he consent to an indefinite delay, he will have a continuing right to cancel his order at any time after the applicable time set forth in paragraph (a)(1) by so notifying the seller prior to actual shipment.

(iv) Nothing in this paragraph shall prohibit a seller who furnishes a definite revised shipping date pursuant to paragraph (b)(1)(i), from requesting, simultaneously with or at any time subsequent to the offer of an option pursuant to paragraph (b)(1), the buyer's express consent to a further unanticipated delay beyond the definite revised shipping date in the form of a response from the buyer specifically consenting to said further delay. *Provided, however,* that where the seller solicits consent to an unanticipated indefinite delay the solicitation shall expressly inform the buyer that, should he so consent to an indefinite delay, he shall have a continuing right to cancel his order at any time after the definite revised shipping date by so notifying the seller prior to actual shipment.

(b)(2) Where a seller is unable to ship merchandise on or before the definite revised shipping date provided under paragraph (b)(1)(i) and consented to by the buyer pursuant to paragraph (b)(1)(ii) or (iii), to fail to offer to the buyer, clearly and conspicuously and without prior demand, a renewed option either to consent to a further delay or to cancel the order and to receive a prompt refund. Said offer shall be made within a reasonable time after the seller first becomes aware of his inability to ship before the said definite revised date, but in no event later than the expiration of the definite revised shipping date. Provided, however, that where the seller previously has obtained the buyer's express consent to an unanticipated delay until a specific date beyond the definite revised shipping date, pursuant to paragraph (b)(1)(iv) or to a further delay until a specific date beyond the definite revised shipping date pursuant to this paragraph (b)(2), that date to which the buyer has expressly consented shall supersede the definite revised shipping date for purposes of this paragraph (b)(2).

(i) ANY OFFER TO THE BUYER of said renewed option shall provide the buyer with a new definite revised shipping date, but where the seller lacks a reasonable basis for providing a new definite revised shipping date, the notice shall inform the buyer that the seller is unable to make any representation regarding the length of the further delay.

(ii) The offer of a renewed option shall expressly inform the buyer that, unless the seller receives, prior to the expiration of the old definite revised shipping date or any date superseding the old definite revised shipping date, notification from the buyer specifically consenting to the further delay, the buyer will be deemed to have rejected any further delay, and to have canceled the order if the seller is in fact unable to ship prior to the expiration of the old definite revised shipping date or any date superseding the old definite revised shipping date.

- you receive within 30 days of the original date your customer's consent to the delay.

Your notice must provide this information if the definite revised shipping date is more than 30 days after the original date.

When you are unable to provide a revised shipping date, you must inform your customers of their continuing right to cancel the order by notifying you prior to actual shipment.

What Later Notices Must Say

If you are unable to ship the merchandise on or before your revised shipping date, you must notify your customers again. This is called a "renewed option" notice. This notice must inform your customers of their right to consent to a further delay, or to cancel the order and receive a prompt refund.

The renewed option notice must inform customers that if they do not agree in writing to this delay, their order will be canceled. Unless you receive your customer's express written consent to the second delay before the first delay period ends, you must cancel the order and provide a full refund.

Keep in mind that you do not have to offer a "renewed option" to customers who consent to an indefinite delay in response to the first option notice. But any customer who agrees to an indefinite delay has the continuing right to cancel the order at any time before the merchandise is shipped.

How You Should Send Notices

You should send any option notice by first class mail, and your notice should provide a written means for your customers to respond. A prepaid business mail reply or prepaid postage card meets this requirement.

The notice is most advantageous for you if at some point you have to prove that you complied with the Rule. If the FTC takes action against a company, the firm must be able to show that any other form of notice it used was equal to or better than the written form described in the Rule. For example, an "800" telephone number for customers' use in canceling orders is an adequate substitute, if you can prove that the system met the Rule's requirements. This would include being able to show that the 800 number could readily and consistently be used to cancel an order because you provided adequate and competent staff to take cancellations. You should keep records of all cancellations.

When You *May* Cancel an Order

In some cases you can have an option to cancel an order or to send out another notice. You may make this decision when you are unable to ship merchandise on time or within the delay period to which your customer agreed. But if you decide to cancel the order,

Provided, however, that where the seller offers the buyer the option to consent to an indefinite delay the offer shall expressly inform the buyer that, should he so consent to an indefinite delay, he shall have a continuing right to cancel his order at any time after the old definite revised shipping date or any date superseding the old definite revised shipping date.

(iii) This paragraph (b)(2) shall not apply to any situation where a seller, pursuant to the provisions of paragraph (b)(1)(iv), has previously obtained consent from the buyer to an indefinite extension beyond the first revised shipping date.

[i]t constitutes an unfair method of competition, and an unfair or deceptive act and practice for a seller:...

(b)(3) WHEREVER A BUYER HAS THE RIGHT to exercise any option under this part or to cancel an order by so notifying the seller prior to shipment, to fail to furnish the buyer with adequate means, at the seller's expense, to exercise such option or to notify the seller regarding cancellation. In any action brought by the Federal Trade Commission alleging a violation of this part, the failure of a respondent-seller:

(i) To provide any offer, notice or option required by this part in writing and by first class mail will create a rebuttable presumption that the respondent-seller failed to offer a clear and conspicuous offer, notice or option;

(ii) To provide the buyer with the means in writing (by business reply mail or with postage prepaid by the seller) to exercise any option or to notify the seller regarding a decision to cancel, will create a rebuttable presumption that the respondent-seller did not provide the buyer with adequate means pursuant to this subparagraph (3).

NOTHING IN PARAGRAPH (B)of this part shall prevent a seller, where he is unable to make shipment within the time set forth in paragraph (a)(1) or within a delay period consented to by the buyer, from deciding to consider the order canceled and providing the buyer with notice of said decision within a reasonable time after he becomes aware of said inability to ship, together with a prompt refund.

[i]t constitutes an unfair method of competition, and an unfair or deceptive act and practice for a seller:...

(c) To FAIL TO DEEM AN ORDER CANCELED and to make a prompt refund to the buyer whenever:

(1) The seller receives, prior to the time of shipment, notification from the buyer canceling the order pursuant to any option, renewed option or continuing option under this part;

(2) The seller has, pursuant to paragraph (b)(1)(iii), provided the buyer with a definite revised shipping date which is more than thirty (30) days later than the applicable time set forth in paragraph (a)(1) or has notified the buyer that he is unable to make any representation regarding the length of the delay and the seller (i) has not shipped the merchandise within thirty (30) days of the applicable time set forth in paragraph (a)(1), and (ii) has not received the buyer's express consent to said shipping delay within said thirty (30) days;

(3) The seller is unable to ship within the applicable time set forth in paragraph (b)(2), and has not received, within the said applicable time, the buyer's consent to any further delay;

(4) The seller has notified the buyer of his inability to make shipment and has indicated his decision not to ship the merchandise;

(5) The seller fails to offer the option prescribed in paragraph (b)(1) and has not shipped the merchandise within the applicable time set forth in paragraph (a)(1).

you must inform your customer of this decision and provide a prompt refund.

Whether you cancel or send another notice, you must inform your customer about it within a reasonable time after you know you cannot ship the merchandise.

When You *Must* Cancel an Order

You must cancel an order and provide a prompt refund:

- when your customer does not agree to a delay and exercises the option to cancel an order before it has been shipped;
- when you notify your customer of your inability to ship the merchandise and of your decision to cancel the order;
- when you are unable to ship merchandise before the revised shipping date and you have not received your customer's consent to a further delay;
- when the delay is indefinite and you have not shipped the merchandise or received your customer's consent to an indefinite delay;
- when the definite revised shipping date in the first option notice is more than 30 days after the original shipping date, and you have not shipped the merchandise, nor received your customer's consent to the delay within 30 days of the original shipping date; or
- when you cannot ship on time and do not notify your customers of their options.

All refunds must be sent to the buyer by first class mail. If the buyer paid by cash, check, or money order, you must refund payment within seven (7) days after the order is canceled. For credit card sales, you must make refunds within one billing cycle after the order is canceled. Under no circumstances are you to substitute credit vouchers or script for a refund.

Why You Should Keep Records

If for some reason your company has problems in shipping on time, your customers may begin to file complaints with you, and with local, state, or federal law enforcement agencies. Because the Federal Trade Commission has enforcement jurisdiction under the Mail Order Rule, many complaints are forwarded to the FTC from other agencies.

When the FTC takes action against a company and alleges that it violated the Rule, the company must have records or other documentary proof that will show the steps it took to comply. Systems and procedures for complying with the Rule are carefully reviewed. Lack of such proof creates a rebuttable presumption that the company failed to comply. This means that the seller must be able to show that it used reasonable systems and procedures to comply with the Rule. Consequently, it is in your best interest to establish an accurate, up-to-date record-keeping system.

(a)(4) IN ANY ACTION BROUGHT BY THE FEDERAL TRADE COMMISSION, alleging a violation of this part, the failure of a respondent-seller to have records or other documentary proof establishing his use of systems and procedures which assure the shipment of merchandise in the ordinary course of business within any applicable time set forth in this part will create a rebuttable presumption that the seller lacked a reasonable basis for any expectation of shipment within said applicable time.

(d) In any action brought by the Federal Trade Commission, alleging a violation of this part, the failure of a respondent-seller to have records or other documentary proof establishing his use of systems and procedures which assure compliance, in the ordinary course of business, with any requirement of paragraphs (b) or (c) of this part will create a rebuttable presumption that the seller failed to comply with said requirements.

What the Rule Does Not Cover

The following mail order sales are exempt from the Rule:

- magazine subscriptions (and similar serial deliveries), except for the first shipment;
- sales of seeds and growing plants;
- orders made on a collect-on-delivery basis (C.O.D.);
- transactions covered by the FTC's Negative Option Rule (such as book and record clubs);
- mail order photo-finishing; or
- orders made by telephone and charged to a credit card account.

NOTE 1: This part shall not apply to subscriptions, such as magazine sales, ordered for serial delivery, after the initial shipment is made in compliance with this part.

NOTE 2: This part shall not apply to orders of seeds and growing plants.

NOTE 3: This part shall not apply to orders made on a collect-on-delivery (C.O.D.) basis.

NOTE 4: This part shall not apply to transactions governed by the Federal Trade Commission's Trade Regulation Rule entitled "Use of Negative Option Plans by Sellers in Commerce," 16 CFR 425.

NOTE 5: By taking action in this area, the Federal Trade Commission does not intend to preempt action in the same area, which is not inconsistent with this part, by any State, municipal, or other local government. This part does not annul or diminish any rights or remedies provided to consumers by any State law, municipal ordinance, or other local regulation, insofar as those rights or remedies are equal to or greater than those provided by this part. In addition, this part does not supersede those provisions of any State law, municipal ordinance, or other local regulation which impose obligations or liabilities upon sellers, when sellers subject to this part are not in compliance therewith. This part does supersede those provisions of any State law, municipal ordinance, or other local regulation which are inconsistent with this part to the extent that those provisions do not provide a buyer with rights which are equal to or greater than those rights granted a buyer by this part. This part also supersedes those provisions of any State law, municipal ordinance, or other local regulation requiring that a buyer be notified of a right which is the same as a right provided by this part but requiring that a buyer be given notice of this right in a language, form, or manner which is different in any way from that required by this part.

In those instances where any State law, municipal ordinance, or other local regulation contains provisions, some but not all of which are partially or completely superseded by this part, the provisions or portions of those provisions which have not been superseded retain their full force and effect.

NOTE 6: If any provision of this part or its application to any person, partnership, corporation, act or practice is held invalid, the remainder of this part or the application of the provision to any other person, partnership, corporation, act or practice shall not be affected thereby.

NOTE 7: Section 435.1(a)(1) of this part governs all solicitations where the time of solicitation is more than 100 days after promulgation of this part. The remainder of this part governs all transactions where receipt of a properly completed order occurs more than 100 days after promulgation of this part.

Where to Go for Help

For more information, contact:
- the Federal Trade Commission, Enforcement Division, B.C.P., Washington, D.C. 20580,
- the Direct Marketing Association, 1730 K Street, N.W., Washington, D.C. 20006;
- your local United States Postal Service; and
- your local consumer protection office.

State and local governments also may have requirements with which you must comply. You should consult each agency for information about laws that affect your operations.

Definitions

§ 435.2 Definitions.

For purposes of this part:

(a) "Shipment" shall mean the act by which the merchandise is physically placed in the possession of the carrier.

(b) "Receipt of a properly completed order" shall mean:

(1) Where there is a credit sale and the buyer has not previously tendered partial payment, the time at which the seller charges the buyer's account;

(2) Where the buyer tenders full or partial payment in the proper amount in the form of cash, check or money order, the time at which the seller has received both said payment and an order from the buyer containing all the information needed by the seller to process and ship the order.

Provided, however, that where the seller receives notice that the check or money order tendered by the buyer has been dishonored or that the buyer does not qualify for a credit sale, "receipt of a properly completed order" shall mean the time at which (i) the seller receives notice that a check or money order for the proper amount tendered by the buyer has been honored, (ii) the buyer tenders cash in the proper amount or (iii) the seller receives notice that the buyer qualifies for a credit sale.

(c) "Refund" shall mean:

(1) Where the buyer tendered full payment for the unshipped merchandise in the form of cash, check, or money order, a return of the amount tendered in the form of cash, check, or money order;

(2) Where there is a credit sale:

(i) And the seller is a creditor, a copy of a credit memorandum or the like or an account statement reflecting the removal or absence of any remaining charge incurred as a result of the sale from the buyer's account;

(ii) And a third party is the creditor, a copy of an appropriate credit memorandum or the like to the third party creditor which will remove the charge from the buyer's account or a statement from the seller acknowledging the cancellation of the order and representing that he has not taken any action regarding the order which will result in a charge to the buyer's account with the third party;

(iii) And the buyer tendered partial payment for the unshipped merchandise in the form of cash, check, or money order, a return of the amount tendered in the form of cash, check, or money order.

(d) "Prompt refund" shall mean:

(1) Where a refund is made pursuant to Definition (c) (1) or (2) (iii), a refund sent to the buyer by first class mail within seven (7) working days of the date on which the buyer's right to refund vests under the provisions of this part;

(2) Where a refund is made pursuant to Definition (c) (2) (i) or (ii), a refund sent to the buyer by first class mail within one (1) billing cycle from the date on which the buyer's right to refund vests under the provisions of this part.

(e) The "time of solicitation" of an order shall mean that time when the seller has:

(1) Mailed or otherwise disseminated the solicitation to a prospective purchaser;

(2) Made arrangements for an advertisement containing the solicitation to appear in a newspaper, magazine, or the like, or on radio or television, which cannot be changed or canceled without incurring substantial expense; or

(3) Made arrangements for the printing of a catalog, brochure or the like which cannot be changed without incurring substantial expense, in which the solicitation in question forms an insubstantial part.

Effective: February 2, 1976.

Promulgated October 22, 1975, by the Federal Trade Commission.

CHARLES A. TOBIN,
Secretary

[FH Doc. 75-28203 Filed 70-21-75; 3:45 am]

3 Questions and Answers About the Rule

The FTC receives questions from mail order sellers who want to know how to comply with the Rule. The following questions are those that are asked most frequently.

What to Do When You Start a Mail Order Business

Q: What advice do you give someone who is planning to start a mail order business?

A: The FTC suggests that you do the following:
  - Learn the requirements of the Mail Order Rule.
  - Familiarize yourself with state laws in areas where you plan to do business. For example, some states, such as Wisconsin, have additional mail order requirements that should be followed.
  - Ask experienced mail order sellers for practical hints to help you avoid the pitfalls in mail order business.

Q: How important is it to set up a customer service procedure?

A: An efficient customer service procedure is beneficial to you and your customers. Customers often complain that they have been treated badly by the companies they have contacted. But the number of complaints should drop significantly if your customer service personnel communicate responsively with your customers when they have problems.

Q: Our company has read the Mail Order Rule, but we still have questions about what we can and cannot do. Who should we contact?

A: It depends on whether you need a formal or an informal response.
  - You should feel free to write the FTC Enforcement Division to ask questions about the Rule and how your operations are affected. Staff advice is not binding on the Commission, but this advice can be helpful.
  - You may obtain a binding advisory opinion from the Commission if you send a specific, written inquiry about the legality of certain conduct. Advisory opinions apply only to proposed conduct, not to conduct that is in practice. The opinions are usually restricted to questions that are not clearly answered by the terms of the Rule. Ask the FTC staff about the procedure for obtaining an advisory opinion.

When You Must Ship an Order

Q: *We advertise a shipment date of six weeks. What happens if there is a workers' strike or some other unanticipated event and shipment is delayed? Have we violated the Rule?*

A: If you calculated the shipping date correctly in the first place, you have complied with the Rule. But if you discover that a delay cannot be avoided, you must notify your customers and provide the option notice. If you fail to do this, you have unilaterally changed the sales contract and have violated the Rule.

Q: *We advertise several products but do not indicate a shipping date in our ads. When must we ship?*

A: If your solicitation does not state when you plan to ship the merchandise, the Rule requires that you ship it within 30 days after you receive a properly completed order (that is, when you have received payment and sufficient information to fill the order).

Q: *How can we protect our company accounts from customers who bounce checks or do not qualify for credit?*

A: Be prompt in depositing checks and checking your customers' credit-worthiness. Remember, the order is properly completed, triggering the 30-day period, when you receive payment and all information needed to process the order. For example, if the buyer does not send enough cash to cover the cost of an order, the order is not properly completed. You may wait for the check to clear before mailing, as long as you ship within the 30-day period.

Q: *What about a credit sale?*

A: When you receive a properly completed order with a charge account number, the clock starts when you charge your customer's account.

Q: *If a customer orders an item which is not in stock when the order is received, can we substitute an item of similar or better quality without the customer's consent?*

A: No. The FTC has established that you must obtain your customer's authorization to substitute merchandise different from that ordered.

What Items Are Covered

Q: *Are mail order sales between businesses covered by the Rule?*

A: Yes. Mail order transactions between businesses are covered. This would include specialty items, such as calendars, pens, and ashtrays which bear advertising messages and are not sold to the general public.

Q: *Does the Rule cover orders placed by telephone?*

A: The Rule covers those situations in which you solicit orders by telephone and require your customers to mail the order accompanied by payment. If the mail is used to finalize the sale, the Rule applies. If mail is not used, the Rule does not apply.

Q: *Does the Rule cover orders placed over the telephone involving credit card payment?*

A: No. The Rule does not cover charges to a credit card account when the order is placed over the telephone.

What Rule Applies to Unordered Merchandise

Q: *Is it legal to send unordered merchandise through the U.S. Mail?*

A: No. The unordered merchandise statute provides that only two kinds of merchandise can be sent legally through the U.S. Mail without a consumer's prior consent:
- free samples that are clearly and conspicuously marked as such; and
- merchandise mailed by a charitable organization asking for contributions.

Consumers may consider unordered merchandise sent through the U.S. Mail as a free gift. They are not obligated to return it or to pay for it. Also, it is illegal for a company to send any bill or dunning communication seeking payment or return of unordered merchandise.

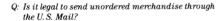

Why Record-Keeping is Important

Q: *Does the Rule require us to keep records?*

A: No. The Mail Order Rule does not impose record-keeping requirements on mail order sellers. But if you are ever involved in an action with the FTC, you must have records that prove you complied with the Rule. Therefore, it is advisable to establish a record-keeping method that best suits your situation and demonstrates compliance with the Rule.

Q: *How long do we have to keep customer complaint letters?*

A: The Rule does not specifically indicate whether or how long you must keep complaint letters. Complaint letters, when adequately answered, may be used as proof that you complied with the Rule if you are ever questioned. It is probably advisable to keep such correspondence and other records for a period of three to five years.

When the FTC Takes Action

Q: *What actually happens when the FTC receives a complaint against a company?*

A: The staff checks to see whether the company has been advised of the Rule's requirements. If not, then a copy of the Rule with an explanation letter is usually sent to the firm. The FTC evaluates consumer complaints to see whether a pattern of violations is developing. The FTC then contacts the company to determine whether further action is necessary.

Q: *Under what circumstances will the Commission sue a mail order firm for violating the Rule?*

A: If a company is violating the Rule, it runs the risk of being sued. The Commission evaluates many criteria to determine whether an action is in the public interest.

Q: *What are the penalties for violating the Rule?*

A: The FTC Act provides that a person, partnership, or corporation may be liable for civil penalties of up to $10,000 per violation. In addition, the FTC can sue for consumer redress.

Q: *What can industry members expect from the FTC in the future?*

A: Because the industry is steadily growing, an increased enforcement presence can be expected. This may mean actions for civil penalties against firms who fail to comply with the Rule. At the same time, the FTC is part of a government-wide effort to encourage industry members to effectively regulate themselves. The FTC is working to assist businesses as they undertake voluntary compliance with the Rule. This manual is part of that effort.

4 Sample Notices

Sample Option Notice
[Rule Section 435.1(b)(1)(ii)]

When you are unable to ship on time and wish to provide a **revised shipping date which is 30 days or less** after the original date, use a form such as this to notify your customers. This form must be sent out by first class mail within a reasonable time after you become aware that there will be a shipping delay. It must be sent before the promised date, or if no date was promised, within 30 days after you receive a properly completed order.

Dear Customer:

Thank you for your order. We are sorry to inform you that there will be a delay in shipping the merchandise you ordered. We shall make shipment by the revised shipping date of (   ). It is quite possible we could ship earlier.

You have the right to consent to this delay or to cancel your order and receive a prompt refund. Please return this letter in the enclosed postpaid envelope with your instructions indicated by checking the appropriate block below.

Unless we hear from you prior to shipment or prior to *the revised shipping date*, it will be assumed that you have consented to a delayed shipment on or before the definite revised shipping date stated above.

Sincerely yours,

Name & Title of Signer
Company Name
Address

Enclosure: Envelope

☐ Yes, I will accept a further delay in shipment of my order for this item until _____
(Insert date which is 30 days or less.)

☐ I cannot wait. Please cancel my order for this item and promptly refund my money. _____
Please Sign Here

Sample Renewed Option Notice

[Rule Section 435.1(b)(2)(i)-(ii)]

When you are unable to ship merchandise on or before the promised definite revised shipping date, and wish to provide **a new definite revised shipping date,** use a form such as this to notify your customers.

Dear Customer:

We are sorry to inform you that there will be a further delay in shipping the merchandise you ordered. We shall make shipment by *(new definite revised shipping date)*. It is quite possible we could ship earlier.

You have the right to consent to a further delay or to cancel your order and receive a prompt refund. Please return this letter in the enclosed postpaid envelope with your instructions indicated by checking the appropriate block below.

Unless we hear from you prior to the old shipping date to which you previously agreed, it will be assumed that you have rejected any further shipping delay and your order will be canceled and a prompt refund made.

Sincerely yours,

Name & Title of Signer
Company Name
Address

Enclosure: Envelope

☐ Yes, I will accept a delay in shipment of my order for this item until

_____
(Insert date which is 30 days or less.)

☐ I cannot wait. Please cancel my order for this item and promptly refund my money.

_____
Please Sign Here

Index